Lecture Notes in Computer Science 12382

More information about this subseries at http://www.springer.com/series/7409

Guojun Wang · Bing Chen ·
Wei Li · Roberto Di Pietro ·
Xuefeng Yan · Hao Han (Eds.)

Security, Privacy, and Anonymity in Computation, Communication, and Storage

13th International Conference, SpaCCS 2020
Nanjing, China, December 18–20, 2020
Proceedings

 Springer

Editors
Guojun Wang
Guangzhou University
Guangzhou, China

Wei Li
Computer Science
Georgia State University
Atlanta, GA, USA

Xuefeng Yan
Nanjing University of Aeronautics
and Astronautics
Nanjing, China

Bing Chen
Aeronautics and Astronautics
Nanjing University
Nanjing, China

Roberto Di Pietro
College of Science and Engineering
Qatar Foundation Education City
Doha, Qatar

Hao Han
Nanjing University of Aeronautics
and Astronautics
Nanjing, China

ISSN 0302-9743   ISSN 1611-3349   (electronic)
Lecture Notes in Computer Science
ISBN 978-3-030-68850-9   ISBN 978-3-030-68851-6   (eBook)
https://doi.org/10.1007/978-3-030-68851-6

LNCS Sublibrary: SL3 – Information Systems and Applications, incl. Internet/Web, and HCI

This Springer imprint is published by the registered company Springer Nature Switzerland AG
The registered company address is: Gewerbestrasse 11, 6330 Cham, Switzerland

Preface

The 13th International Conference on Security, Privacy and Anonymity in Computation, Communication and Storage (SpaCCS 2020) was held in Nanjing, China on December 18–20, 2020, hosted by Nanjing University of Aeronautics and Astronautics and co-organized by Key Lab of Information System Requirement, Jiangsu Computer Society, and the Collaborative Innovation Center of Novel Software Technology and Industrialization.

The previous SpaCCS conferences were held in Atlanta, USA (2019), Melbourne, Australia (2018), Guangzhou, China (2017), Zhangjiajie, China (2016), Helsinki, Finland (2015), Beijing, China (2014), Melbourne, Australia (2013), Liverpool, UK (2012), and Changsha, China (2011). The conference aims to bring together world-class researchers and practitioners to share their research achievements, emerging ideas, and trends in these highly challenging research fields.

This year, the conference received 88 submissions from many different countries. All submissions were reviewed by at least three experts with relevant subject matter expertise. Based on the recommendations of the reviewers and subsequent discussions of the program committee members, 30 papers were selected for oral presentation at the conference and inclusion in this Springer LNCS volume (i.e., an acceptance rate of 34.1%). In addition to the technical presentations, the program included a number of keynote speeches by world-renowned researchers. We would like to thank the keynote speakers for their time and willingness to share their expertise with the conference attendees.

SpaCCS 2020 was only possible because of the support and dedication of a large number of individuals and organizations worldwide. A long list of people volunteered their time and energy to put together the conference and deserve special thanks. First and foremost, we would like to offer our gratitude to the Steering Committee Chairs, Prof. Guojun Wang from Guangzhou University, China and Prof. Gregorio Martínez Pérez from University of Murcia, Spain, for guiding the entire process of the conference. We are also deeply grateful to all the Program Committee members for their time and efforts in reading, commenting, debating, and finally selecting the papers.

We would like to offer our gratitude to the General Chairs, Prof. Zhiqiu Huang, Prof. Zhipeng Cai, Prof. Xuefeng Yan, and Prof. Aniello Castiglione, for their tremendous support and advice in ensuring the success of the conference. Thanks also go to: Program Chairs, Guojun Wang, Bing Chen, Wei Li, and Roberto Di Pietro; Workshop Chair, Ryan Ko; Local Organizing Committee Chairs, Hao Han and Kun Zhu; Publicity Chairs, Xin Li, Alberto Huertas Celdrán, Shuhong Chen, Marco Guazzone, Yan Huang, and Weizhi Meng; and Conference Secretariat, Liming Fang.

It is worth noting that SpaCCS 2020 was held jointly with the 11th International Workshop on Trust, Security and Privacy for Big Data (TrustData 2020), the 10th International Symposium on Trust, Security and Privacy for Emerging Applications (TSP 2020), the 9th International Symposium on Security and Privacy on the Internet of Things (SPIoT 2020), the 6th International Symposium on Sensor-Cloud Systems (SCS 2020), the 2nd International Workshop on Communication, Computing, Informatics and Security (CCIS 2020), the 1st Workshop on Intelligence and Security in Next Generation Networks (ISNGN 2020), and the 1st International Symposium on Emerging Information Security and Applications (EISA 2020).

Finally, we thank you for contributing to and participating in the SpaCCS 2020 conference and hope you found the conference a stimulating and exciting forum! Hopefully, you also enjoyed the beautiful city of Nanjing, China!

December 2020

Guojun Wang
Bing Chen
Wei Li
Roberto Di Pietro
Xuefeng Yan
Hao Han

SpaCCS 2020 Organizing and Program Committees

General Chairs

Zhiqiu Huang	Nanjing University of Aeronautics and Astronautics, China
Zhipeng Cai	Georgia State University, USA
Xuefeng Yan	Nanjing University of Aeronautics and Astronautics, China
Aniello Castiglione	University of Naples Parthenope, Italy

Program Chairs

Guojun Wang	Guangzhou University, China
Bing Chen	Nanjing University of Aeronautics and Astronautics, China
Wei Li	Georgia State University, USA
Roberto Di Pietro	Hamad Bin Khalifa University, Qatar

Program Vice Chairs

Fengyuan Xu	Nanjing University, China
Lu Zhou	Nanjing University of Aeronautics and Astronautics, China
Shouling Ji	Zhejiang University, China
Willy Susilo	University of Wollongong, Australia
Frank Jiang	Deakin University, Australia
Debiao He	Wuhan University, China

Program Committee

Abdessamad Imine	University of Lorraine, France
Abdul Ali	Universiti Kuala Lumpur, Malaysia
Aleksandra Mileva	Goce Delčev University of Štip, Macedonia
Alessandra De Benedictis	University of Naples Federico II, Italy
Andrea Saracino	Istituto di Informatica e Telematica CNR, Italy
Ankit Chaudhary	Northwest Missouri State University, USA
Antonio Ruiz-Martínez	University of Murcia, Spain
Anupam Chattopadhyay	Nanyang Technological University, Singapore
Arcangelo Castiglione	University of Salerno, Italy
Ashok Das	International Institute of Information Technology, Hyderabad, India
Avishek Adhikari	University of Calcutta, India

Biju Issac	Northumbria University, UK
Bo Sheng	University of Massachusetts Boston, USA
Bohan Li	Nanjing University of Aeronautics and Astronautics, China
Carlo Blundo	University of Salerno, Italy
Cataldo Basile	Politecnico di Torino, Italy
Celestine Iwendi	Bangor College China, China
Chiu C. Tan	Temple University, USA
Christian Esposito	University of Naples Federico II, Italy
Dimitrios Karras	Sterea Hellas Institute of Technology, Greece
Ed Novak	Franklin and Marshall College, USA
Félix García	University of Murcia, Spain
Fengyuan Xu	Nanjing University, China
Flora Amato	University of Naples Federico II, Italy
George Karakostas	McMaster University, Canada
Hovhannes Harutyunyan	Concordia University, Canada
Ilaria Matteucci	Istituto di Informatica e Telematica CNR, Italy
Jinyue Xia	IBM Research Institute, USA
Jorge Bernal Bernabé	University of Murcia, Spain
Jose Morales	Carnegie Mellon University, USA
Juan Muñoz Gea	Universidad Politécnica de Cartagena, Spain
Junggab Son	Kennesaw State University, USA
Kalman Graffi	Heinrich Heine University Düsseldorf, Germany
Larbi Boubchir	University of Paris 8, France
Leandros Maglaras	De Montfort University, UK
Liming Fang	Nanjing University of Aeronautics and Astronautics, China
Marco Guazzone	University of Piemonte Orientale, Italy
Massimo Ficco	University of Campania Luigi Vanvitelli, Italy
Meng Han	Kennesaw State University, USA
Mingwu Zhang	Hubei University of Technology, China
Nataša Živić	University of Siegen, Germany
Nicola Zannone	Eindhoven University of Technology, The Netherlands
Nicolas Sklavos	University of Patras, Greece
Nikos Komninos	City, University of London, UK
Oscar Esparza	Universitat Politècnica de Catalunya, Spain
Pascal Lorenz	University of Upper Alsace, France
Patrick Siarry	Université Paris-Est Créteil, France
Pavel Loskot	Swansea University, UK
Pin-Yu Chen	IBM T. J. Watson Research Center, USA
Ping Yang	State University of New York at Binghamton, USA
Quoc-Tuan Vien	Middlesex University, UK
Yongjun Ren	Nanjing University of Information Science and Technology, China
Roberto Di Pietro	Hamad Bin Khalifa University, Qatar
Roberto Nardone	University of Naples Federico II, Italy

Selena He	Kennesaw State University, USA
Sherali Zeadally	University of Kentucky, USA
Sudip Chakraborty	Valdosta State University, USA
Traian Truta	Northern Kentucky University, USA
Tung Nguyen	Intelligent Automation, Inc, USA
Ugo Fiore	University of Naples Federico II, Italy
Wissam Mallouli	Montimage, France
Xuan Guo	University of North Texas, USA
Yan Huang	Kennesaw State University, USA
Yifan Zhang	Binghamton University, USA
Youwen Zhu	Nanjing University of Aeronautics and Astronautics, China
Yu Bai	California State University, Fullerton, USA
Yubao Wu	Georgia State University, USA
Yushu Zhang	Nanjing University of Aeronautics and Astronautics, China
Zaheer Khan	University of the West of England, UK
Zhiwei Wang	Nanjing University of Posts and Telecommunication, China
Zhe Liu	Nanjing University of Aeronautics and Astronautics, China
Zhengrui Qin	Northwest Missouri State University, USA

Workshop Chair

Ryan Ko	University of Queensland, Australia

Local Organizing Committee Chairs

Hao Han	Nanjing University of Aeronautics and Astronautics, China
Kun Zhu	Nanjing University of Aeronautics and Astronautics, China

Publicity Chairs

Xin Li	Nanjing University of Aeronautics and Astronautics, China
Alberto Huertas Celdrán	Waterford Institute of Technology, Ireland
Shuhong Chen	Guangzhou University, China
Marco Guazzone	University of Piemonte Orientale, Italy
Yan Huang	Kennesaw State University, USA
Weizhi Meng	Technical University of Denmark, Denmark

Publication Chairs

Tao Peng	Guangzhou University, China
Xiaofei Xing	Guangzhou University, China

Registration Chair

Chunpeng Ge	Nanjing University of Aeronautics and Astronautics, China

Conference Secretariat

Liming Fang	Nanjing University of Aeronautics and Astronautics, China

Web Chair

Ran Wang	Nanjing University of Aeronautics and Astronautics, China

Steering Committee

Guojun Wang (Chair)	Guangzhou University, China
Gregorio Martínez Pérez (Chair)	University of Murcia, Spain
Jinjun Chen	Swinburne University of Technology, Australia
Weijia Jia	Beijing Normal University - Hong Kong Baptist University United International College, China
Ryan Ko	Queensland University, Australia
Constantinos Kolias	University of Idaho, USA
Jianbin Li	North China Electric Power University, China
Jie Li	Shanghai Jiao Tong University, China
Yang Xiang	Swinburne University of Technology, Australia
Zheng Yan	Aalto University, Finland/Xidian University, China
Wanlei Zhou	University of Technology Sydney, Australia
Mário Freire	University of Beira Interior, Portugal
Minyi Guo	Shanghai Jiao Tong University, China
Wei Jie	University of West London, UK
Georgios Kambourakis	University of the Aegean, Greece
Jianhua Ma	Hosei University, Japan
Félix Gómez Mármol	University of Murcia, Spain
Geyong Min	University of Exeter, UK
Peter Mueller	IBM Zurich Research Laboratory, Switzerland
Indrakshi Ray	Colorado State University, USA
Kouichi Sakurai	Kyushu University, Japan
Juan E. Tapiador	University Carlos III of Madrid, Spain

Sabu M. Thampi	Indian Institute of Information Technology and Management, India
Jie Wu	Temple University, USA
Yang Xiang	Swinburne University of Technology, Australia
Laurence T. Yang	St. Francis Xavier University, Canada

Sponsors

Contents

Privacy-Preserving and Scalable Data Access Control Based on Self-sovereign Identity Management in Large-Scale Cloud Storage

Min Xiao$^{(\boxtimes)}$, Zhongyue Ma, and Tao Li

College of Computer Science and Technology, Chongqing
University of Posts and Telecommunications, Chongqing 400065, China
xiaomin@cqupt.edu.cn

Abstract. Ciphertext-Policy Attribute-based Encryption (CP-ABE) can realize
fine-grain access control by data encryption in an untrusted environment and thus
has become the promising data security protection mechanism for outsourced
cloud storage. Although CP-ABE scheme with single attribute authority (AA)
has been extended to multi-AA and threshold multi-AA schemes to deal with
single-point bottleneck on both security and performance in large-scale cloud
storage, management of identity attributes still depends on a trusted center, which
leaves the scalability of user attribute revocation unresolved in large-scale cloud
or cross-cloud access. To solve the above problem, the proposed scheme combines
blockchain based self-sovereign identity management (BbSSIM) technology and
threshold CP-ABE to achieve access control based on the self-sovereign identity,
which removes the trusted intermediaries in a decentralized and trustless environment. Besides good scalability, the attribute revocation, key generation and data
access process all keep the user anonymous and thus the user's privacy is well
protected.

Keywords: Cloud storage · Blockchain · Self-sovereign identity management ·
Access control

1 Introduction

Cloud storage is an important service of cloud computing, which allows data owners to
outsource their data in the cloud that provides a flexible and convenient way for users to
access data from anywhere on any device. Because the cloud storage service separates
the role of data owners from service provider, and data owner does not interact with
the user directly to provide data access service, the data access becomes a challenging
for cloud storage system. The existing methods [1] usually delegate data access control
to a trusted server, which is responsible for defining and implementing access policies.
However, the cloud server cannot be fully trusted by data owner, because the cloud
server may grant data access rights to unauthorized users for more profit. Therefore,
the traditional server-based data access control methods are no longer suitable for cloud
storage system. To solve the problem of data access control in large-scale cloud storage
system, which the data user is responsible for defining and executing access policies.

© Springer Nature Switzerland AG 2021
G. Wang et al. (Eds.): SpaCCS 2020, LNCS 12382, pp. 1–18, 2021.
https://doi.org/10.1007/978-3-030-68851-6_1

2 Related Work

Ciphertext-Policy Attribute-based Encryption (CP-ABE) is considered to be one of the most suitable methods for data access control in cloud storage systems, because it gives data owner more direct control on access policies and does not require the data owner to distribute key. In CP-ABE scheme, there is an authority that is responsible for attribute management and key distribution. The data owner defines the access policies and encrypts data according to the policies. Each user will be issued a secret key reflecting its attributes. A user can decrypt the data only when its attributes satisfy the access polices. However, the original ABE schemes rely on an authority to distribute keys for users, which has the single of failure and scalability problems. Some multi-authority CP-ABE schemes have been proposed for data encryption, they cannot be directly to data access control for multi-authority cloud storage systems, So, it is difficult to apply to large-scale or distributed systems. In order to overcome CP-ABE scheme with single attribute authority (AA) has been extended to multi-AA and threshold multi-AA schemes to deal with single-point bottleneck on both security and performance in large-scale cloud storage.

Blockchain is one of the technology innovations for sharing data across organization through a peer-to-peer network. It can remove the intermediaries and allow users manage their own identities without relying on third-party certificate authority. The internet applications were built without a way to know who and what you are connecting to. This limits what we can do with it and exposes us to growing dangers. Kim [2] proposed The Laws of Identity, which prevent the loss of trust and give users a deep sense of safety, privacy and certainty about who they are relating to in cyberspace. The blockchain-based identity is also called the self-sovereign identity (SSI), which transfers access control rights and management of identities form traditional identity providers to the control of identity owners. The distributed nature of the blockchain allows the user's identity to be verified as an attribute statement. Self-sovereign identity is realized by Decentralized Identifier (DID), and DID is an open standard being developed by W3C.

Many scholars propose some solutions for digital identities, AI-Bassam [3] introduces a decentralized PKI system, which utilizes the transparency of the blockchain and has fine-grained attribute management for the web-of-trust. In his work, he defines several identity related smart contracts such as adding attributes, signing attributes and revoking signatures. Fromknecht et al. [4] proposes a new, decentralized alternative PKI, based on Bitcoin. Each entity maintains a public ledger of domains and their associated public keys. They also define a set of key operations like registering, updating, verifying and revoking. However, this solution may disclose users' privacy. Axon [5] analyzes the privacy requirements of different PKI use cases, which participating entities' cations cannot be tracked by their use of public keys. Therefore, he proposes a blockchain-based PKI privacy-awareness. Augot et al. [6] presents an identity management scheme built into Bitcoin, allowing users to directly manage their own identities. More importantly, they make use of a zero-knowledge proof to ensure anonymity of identity.

In addition, several products and criteria are proposed, such as Uport, Shocard, Sovrin, W3C Decentralized Identifiers (DID). Uport[1] proposes a decentralized application to solve the digital identity problem, built on Ethereum. Uport identities can take many forms: individuals, devices or institutions, and be cryptographically linked to off-ledger data stores. It mainly uses smart contract to design digital identity model, and ensures reliability and usability of identities through a set of operations such as key revocation and identities recovery. ShoCard[2] provides the ability for organization to authenticate a user, exchange auditable authorization and exchange attestation of a user's credentials. The ShoCard identity management platform has integrated mobile Apps and servers, different users can independently retrieve blockchain records directly and use them for verification. Sovrin provides a new paradigm to manage digital identities from the distributed ledger to devices. It adds the identity layer for every entity on the Internet and operates as a global public utility designed to provide permanent, private, and trustworthy identities. Sovrin is a permissioned blockchain in a P2P network, which nodes are divided into validator nodes and observer nodes to ensure performance and scalability. More importantly, it implements privacy-aware by design on a global scale, selective disclosure of personal data using zero-knowledge proof cryptography. To provide economic incentives for credentials issuers, owners and verifiers, the Sovrin[3] token is designed for privacy-preserving value exchange. To sum up, the blockchain-based identity management system is viewed as the self-sovereign identity (SSI), which eliminate identity provider through establishing the blockchain identity on SSI platform.

In this paper, we study the problems of attribute management, key distribution and attribute revocation in large-scale cloud storage systems and proposes a privacy-preserving and scalable data access control scheme based on self-sovereign identity management.

2.1 Our Motivation

CP-ABE is proposed to realize fine-grain access control in an untrusted environment and thus has become a promising data security protection mechanism for outsourced cloud storage. In CP-ABE, attributes are used to describe a data user's credentials, data owner encrypts data under his/her own designated access policy, and only if a data user's attributes satisfy the access policy embedding in ciphertext, the data user can decrypt the ciphertext correctly. In the outsourced cloud storage setting, the access control mechanism based on CP-ABE has the following advantages.

1. Data can be kept confidential even in an untrusted environment.
2. Data owner controls who can access his/her data by embedding his/her own designated access policy to ciphertext.
3. Access policy is enforced by the cryptography and thus there is no need to rely on any online trusted server to mediate access control.

---

[1] Uport: Open Identity System for The Decentralized Web, https://www.uport.me, last accessed 2020/5/12.

[2] Shocard: Secure Enterprise Identity Authentication, https://shocard.com, last accessed 2020/5/12.

[3] Sovrin-Identity for All, https://sovrin.org, last accessed 2020/5/12.

4. Only one copy of ciphertext is generated for each file, but it can be decrypted by multiple users without sharing key.
5. A user only holds one secret key, but he can access multiple ciphertexts owned by different data owners, thus it is possible to achieve cross-domain data access.

Figure 1 shows a classical access control model based on CP-ABE, where there are five types of entities: multiple cloud servers (CSs) or cloud service providers (CSPs), massive data owners and data users, one or more attribute authorities (AAs) and potential trusted authority TA. The AAs configure the CP-ABE environment and distribute attribute private keys to the data users. The data owner encrypts sensitive data with CP-ABE and outsources it to the CS, then the data user sends access requests to the CS and the CS returns the requested ciphertexts (sometimes the pre-decrypted token) as a response. Only if the user's attributes satisfy the access policy embedded in ciphertext, can the data user correctly decrypt the ciphertext. The potential TA is a root of trust in the system and responsible for management and authentication of all entities' identity and attributes. Although CP-ABE scheme with single AA has been extended to multi-AA scheme and threshold multi-authority CP-ABE to deal with single-point bottleneck on both security and performance, the trust assumption for TA leaves the bottleneck problem unresolved when applying ABE in large-scale or distributed cloud storage. Especially, the user attribute revocation [7] has always not been solved well. The existing schemes present two kinds of techniques: key update mechanism [8] and attribute revocation list (ARL) [9] mechanism. The former is to update the keys of all unrevoked users by AA or a trusted third party.

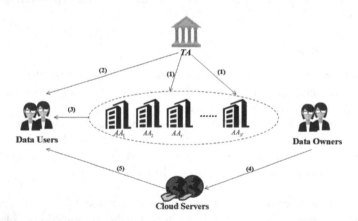

(1) *AAs* register to *TA* to gain(*aid*,*aid.cert*);   (2)*Users* register to *TA* to gain (*uid*,*uid.cert*);
(3) *Users* gain his attribute *SK* from *N* AAs;   (4) *Owners* upload (*CT*) to the cloud server
(5)*Users* download(*CT*) from the cloud server

Fig. 1. Classical access control model based on CP-ABE.

To solve the above problem, we combine blockchain based identity management technology and threshold CP-ABE to achieve access control based on the self-sovereign identity, which removes the intermediaries and allows users to manage their own identity attributes without relying on trusted third parties in decentralized and trustless environments. Therefore, the proposed scheme eliminates the bottleneck in classical CP-ABE and has good scalability. Furthermore, the attribute revocation, key generation and data access process all keep the user anonymous and the user's privacy is well protected in such an open environment without trusted center.

2.2 Our Contributions

The main contributions of this work can be summarized as follows:

1. To the best of our knowledge, we are the first to design CP-ABE scheme without trusted identity authority assumption to deal with the scalability problem for data access control in large-scale cloud storage.
2. By combining blockchain based self-sovereign identity management with ARL mechanism, the maintenance responsibility for revocation list is transferred from a trusted third party to the peers in peer-to-peer network, and thus effective and instant user attribute revocation without relying on any trusted third party can be achieved. Furthermore, ARL is only relevant to attribute issuers, not attribute owners, thus, user attribute revocation process keeps attribute owner anonymous. As far as we know, it is the first time that the anonymous and instant user attribute revocations are implemented simultaneously.
3. In attribute certificate, the signatures of the issuer are used to achieve anonymous key generation and data access, that is, who owns the given attributes is kept secret from all key generation nodes and who is accessing a file set is kept secret from the cloud server.
4. We formally analyze and prove under general group model that the proposed scheme is secure and privacy-preserving in an open environment without trusted center.

3 System Model and Security Model

3.1 System Model

Referring to existing blockchain based self-sovereign identity solutions,, we define three roles for the implementation of self-sovereign identity: identity credential owner, identity credential issuer and identity credential verifier. In the proposed data access control system, there are four entities (without TA) data owner, data user, cloud server and AA. All entities register to the BbSSIM platform as nodes and can act as one or multiple roles. Figure 2 shows the system model of the scheme.

Identity Credential Owner. Each subject in the blockchain can be identity credential owner. The identity credential is a set of identity information, including globally unique and cryptographically verifiable identifier (VerID) and many identity attributes. Every VerID is created by blockchain technology and has an associated blockchain public-private key pairand VerID document stored on blockchain. The key pair is used for the purpose of authentication or secure communication. The VerID document contain the blockchain public key for the VerID, other materials that the identity owner wishes to

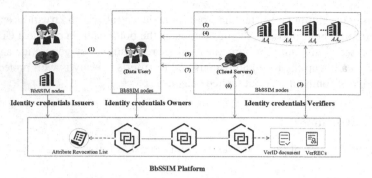

(1) Issues verifiable attribute credentials (VerACs) ;   (2) Anonymously requests attribute secret keys;
(3)Looks up attribute issuer' s PK on the blockchain and verifies the issuer' s signatures on the VerAC and attribute revocation;
(4) Selected verifier nodes jointly generate attribute secret keys shares;   (5) Anonymously requests data access;
(6)Looks up attribute issuer' s PK on the blockchain and verifies the issuer' s signatures on the VerAC and attribute revocation;
(7)Pre-decrypts the ciphertexts and return the results;

Fig. 2. System model of access control based on self-sovereign identity.

disclose (such as credentials, the service endpoints for interaction) and some necessary links. The identity owner signs his/her own VerID document with blockchain private key to ensure the integrity of the document and prove his/her ownership of the document.

Identity Credential Issuer. Any subject with a VerID can work as an issuer that digitally issues and signs verifiable attribute credentials (VerACs) for other subjects. A VerAC is a cryptographically non-repudiable set of statements with a locally unique VerIA number on the issuer side and can be verified by issuer's blockchain public key, which is stored in issuer's VerID document and can be indexed by the issuer's VerID. In addition, there is a link in the issuer's VerID document pointing to an attribute revocation list (ARL), which publishes all revoked VerACs that he/she issued in the past. The ARL is stored on the blockchain and each revocation statement can be indexed by issuer's VerID and VerIA number.

Identity Credential Verifier. The verifier verifies the VerACs when a user submits her/his VerACs for key generation or data access authorization. The verification process has two sub steps: verify signature on the VerAC and look up the ARL to confirm whether the VerAC has been revoked.

Each node sends verifiable reputation evaluation credentials (VerRECs) to other nodes. The cryptographic nature of blockchain can protect the integrity and reliability of the reputation evaluation. VerRECs serves as the incentive for both good behavior and block publication instead of digital conis, therefore no miners are needed. In our access control system, each blockchain node maintains a distributed ledger of VerRECs, which achieves consistent with the consensus algorithms. Proof-of-Reputation (POR) consensus algorithm [10] is used in this system to select AAs (identity credentials verifiers).

4   The Proposed Scheme

In this section, we detailed describe the proposed scheme, which mainly consists of five phases: **System Setup, Data Outsourcing Storage, Anonymous Key Generation, Anonymous Data Access, Anonymous Attribute Revocation**. The system parameters of proposed scheme are show in Table 1.

Table 1. Our proposed system parameters

Parameter	Meaning
BbSSIM	Blockchain based self-sovereign identity management
VerID	Verifiable Identifier
VerAC	Verifiable attribute credential
CS/CSP	Cloud server/cloud service provider
VerREL	Verifiable evaluation links
VerREC	Verifiable reputation evaluation certification
VerARCs	Verifiable attribute revocation credentials
ARL	Attribute revocation list
VerIA_Number	The number of the attribute credential
POR	Proof-of-Reputation

4.1   System Setup

4.1.1   The BbSSIM Setup

Data owners, data users, attribute authorities and cloud servers, are registered to the BbSSIM and makes the following configuration.

1. Creates a globally unique and verifiable identifier (VerID), blockchain public-private key (PK_{VerID}, SK_{VerID}) and associated VerID document, which consists the VerID, blockchain public key PK_{VerID}, registered cloud server addresses CS_{VerID}, verifiable evaluation links $VerREL_{VerID}$ and the identity owner's signature on the above content with SK_{VerID}, thus VerID document can be denoted as following tuple:

$$\left\{ \begin{array}{c} VerID, PK_{VerID}, CS_{VerID}, VerREL_{VerID} \\ Sign_{owner}[VerID \parallel PK_{VerID} \parallel CS_{VerID} \parallel VerREL_{VerID}] \end{array} \right\} \tag{1}$$

where $CS_{VerID} = [CS_{ad_1}, \ldots, CS_{ad_m}]$ points to the cloud servers that an entity wants to access.

2. Receives/Issues verifiable reputation evaluation certification (VerREC) from/to other nodes. A VerREC refers to a proof evaluating the behavior of a node in the blockchain network and each node can send VerRECs for other nodes by signing the reputation values with its blockchain private key. At the same time, each node stores the

received VerREC in his/her verifiable reputation evaluation list (VerREL). A VerREC is defined as follows:

$$\left\{ \begin{array}{c} VerID, reputation\_value, Time, VerID_{issuer} \\ Sign_{issuer}[H[Evaluated_{VerID} \parallel reputation\_value \parallel Time]] \end{array} \right\} \qquad (2)$$

3. Receives/issues verifiable attribute credential (VerAC) from/to other nodes and a VerAC is defined as:

$$\left\{ \begin{array}{c} VerID_{owner}, Attribute, Time, VerID_{issuer}, VerIA\_Number \\ Sign_{issuer}[H[VerID_{issuer} \parallel VerIA\_Number \parallel Attribute]] \\ Sign_{issuer}[H[VerID_{issuer} \parallel VerIA\_Number \parallel Attribute \parallel H(VerID_{owner})]] \end{array} \right\} \qquad (3)$$

where $VerID_{owner}$ is attribute owner's VerID, attribute refers to a specific attribute (such as teacher), $VerIA\_Number$ refers to the number of the attribute credentials and is unique on the credential issuer side, $VerID_{issuer}$ is the certificate issuer's VerID, two signatures are created by the certificate issuer with blockchain private key SK_{VerID} and the known hash function. The double signatures are used to prove ownership of attribute under the premise of protecting the privacy of users.

4. Issues verifiable attribute revocation credentials VerARCs to the attribute revocation list (ARL) and a VerARC is defined as:

$$\left\{ \begin{array}{c} VerID_{issuer}, VerIA\_Number, Time \\ Sign_{issuer}[H[VerID_{issuer} \parallel VerIA\_Number \parallel Time]] \end{array} \right\} \qquad (4)$$

Note that, the attribute revocation is performed anonymously because VerARC doesn't reveal the attribute owner's identity information. ARL is public and maintained by all blockchain nodes and is retrieved based on the issuer's identifier $VerID_{issuer}$ and the number of the attribute credential $VerIA\_Number$.

4.1.2 Cryptography System Setup

1. **Attribute Authority Generation**. In the blockchain, each node's reputation level can be evaluated based on all its VerRECs. N nodes are selected as the attribute authorities by utilizing the Proof-of-Reputation (POR) consensus algorithm.

2. **Attribute Authorities Initiate the Cryptography System**. During this period, two bilinear groups G and G_T with the prime p-order and a generator g of G are chosen according to the security parameter λ. A bilinear map $e : G \times G \rightarrow G_T$, and two cryptographic hash functions $H : \{0, 1\}^* \rightarrow G$ and $H_1 : \{0, 1\}^* \rightarrow Z_p^*$ are defined respectively. The universe of the attribute is denoted by a set $S = \{1, \ldots, z\}$ and the threshold by t. Attribute authorities are denote as $VVerID_1, \ldots, VVerID_N$, and jointly implement threshold CP-ABE scheme to generate their own attribute secret keys shares and the related attribute public key by the following steps.

(a) For each attribute x, AA_m with $VVerID_m$ selects two random numbers $\alpha_{m,x}, \beta_{m,x} \in Z_p$, $m \in [1, N]$ as its secret key share. In this way, the secret key of the attribute x is implicitly expressed: $\alpha_x = \sum_{m=1}^{N} \alpha_{m,x}$ and $\beta_x = \sum_{m=1}^{N} \beta_{m,x}$. The attribute secret key (α_x, β_x) shouldn't be gained by any AA_m alone, each AA_m randomly selects two $t - 1$ degree polynomials over Z_p^*.

$$f_m(z) = a_{m,0} + \cdots + a_{m,t-1}z^{t-1}, \; l_m(z) = b_{m,0} + \cdots + b_{m,t-1}z^{t-1} \qquad (5)$$

$a_{m,0}, \ldots, a_{m,t-1} \in Z_p, b_{m,0}, \ldots, b_{m,t-1} \in Z_p$, which satisfy the formula $\alpha_{m,x} = f_m(0) = a_{m,0}, \beta_{m,x} = l_m(0) = b_{m,0}$. After that, AA_m computes and broadcasts $A_{m,k} = e(g,g)^{a_{m,k}}, B_{m,k} = g^{b_{m,k}}, k \in [0, t-1]$ and calculates the sub-share $s_{m,j} = f_m(H_1(VVerID_j)), o_{m,j} = l_m(H_1(VVerID_j))$ for other AA_j and sends $s_{j,m}, o_{j,m}$ to $AA_{j,j\in[1,\ldots,m-1,m+1,\ldots,N]}$. Meanwhile, AA_m calculates $s_{m,m} = f_m(H_1(VVerID_m))$, $o_{m,m} = l_m(H_1(VVerID_m))$ for itself.

(b) After receiving the sub-shares $s_{j,m}, o_{j,m}$ from $AA_j, j \in [1, \ldots, m-1, m+1, \ldots, N]$, each AA_m verifies whether the equation $e(g,g)^{s_{j,m}} = \prod_{k=0}^{t-1} A_{j,k}^{H_1(VVerID_m)^k}$ and $g^{o_{j,m}} = \prod_{k=0}^{t-1} B_{j,k}^{H_1(VVerID_m)^k}$ are valid or not. If they are valid, AA_j is considered to be honest. Otherwise, AA_m broadcasts that an error has been found. Next, AA_j must resend the sub-share $s_{j,m}, o_{j,m}$ until it passes the verification.

(c) According to the above phases, each AA_m has broadcasted values $\{A_{m,0} = e(g,g)^{\alpha_{m,x}}, B_{m,0} = g^{\beta_{m,x}}\}, m \in [1, N]$ which can be verified publicly. Therefore, the attribute x public key can be computed as: $e(g,g)^{\alpha_x} = e(g,g)^{\sum_{m=1}^{N} \alpha_{m,x}} = \prod_{m=1}^{N} A_{m,0}, g^{\beta_x} = g^{\sum_{m=1}^{N} \beta_{m,x}} = \prod_{m=1}^{N} B_{m,0}, APK_x = (e(g,g)^{\alpha_x}, g^{\beta_x})$.

After the above three sections, adds parameters APK_x to $params$. The public parameters of the cryptography system are $params: \{p, g, e, G, G_T, H, H_1, APK_x\}$.

4.2 Data Outsourcing Storage

The data owner encrypts sensitive data with CP-ABE and outsources it to the cloud server. The data encryption algorithm is as follows.

Algorithm 1. Data Encryption.

Input: this algorithm takes as inputs the message m, public parameters $params$, a set of attribute public key $\{APK_x\}_{x \in R_\tau}$ and access structure matrix $\tau = (M, \rho)$, where M is a $l*n$ matrix and the function ρ maps each row i of M to each attribute x, and R_τ denotes the set of attributes in the access structure.

Output: CT

1. randomly selects a vector $\vec{v} = (s, v_2, \ldots, v_n)^\neg \in Z_p^n$.

2. computes $\lambda_i = M_i \cdot \vec{v}$, where M_i is the row i of M.

3. chooses a random vector $\vec{w} \in Z_p^n$ with 0 as its first entry and computes $\omega_i = M_i \cdot \vec{w}$.

4. randomly selects $r_1, \ldots, r_n \in Z_p$ and calculates the ciphertext CT using the attribute public keys form $params$, where

$$\left\{ \begin{array}{l} \tau, C_0 = m \cdot e(g,g)^s, C_{1,i} = e(g,g)^{\lambda_i} \cdot e(g,g)^{\alpha_{\rho(i)} r_i}, \\ C_{2,i} = g^{r_i}, C_{3,i} = g^{\beta_{\rho(i)} r_i} \cdot g^{\omega_i}, \forall \rho(i) \in R_\tau \end{array} \right\}$$

4.3 Anonymous Key Generation

When a data user wants to access some encrypted data in cloud, he/she needs to obtain data access key by submitting necessary attribute credentials to AAs. In order to protect the identity privacy of the user, the anonymous key generation request (AKGR) takes the form of $\left(PK_{temp} \| H(VerID_{owner}) \| VerAC_1 \| \ldots \| VerAC_u\right)$, where PK_{temp} is a temporary public key that the user generates locally for secure transmission of the attribute secret key shares from AAs. In AKGR, the $H(VerID_{owner})$ is used to protect the identity privacy of the data user. The data user encrypts respectively the AKGR with the blockchain public key PK_{AA_m} of each AA_m and sends the ciphertext to the corresponding AA_m. After receiving the request, the AA_m performs the following Algorithm 2.

Algorithm 2. Anonymous Key Generation.

Input: public parameter *params*, anonymous key generation request AKGR:
$\left(PK_{temp} \| H(VerID_{owner}) \| VerAC_1 \| \ldots \| VerAC_u\right)$

Output: the attribute secret key share ciphertext.

---

1. decrypts the request with his/her own blockchain private key.

2. for $x = 1$ to u :

   (a) verifies the signature:

$Sign_{VerID_{owner}} \left[H(Attribute_x \| VerIA_x\_Number \| VerID_{issuer} \| H(VerID_{owner})) \right]$ in $VerAC_x$. If failed, terminate the procedure.

   (b) looks up the ARL by the tuple $(VerID_{issuer}^{(x)}, VerIA_x\_Number)$ as index to check whether the attribute x of the user has been revoked. If revoked, terminate the produces.

3. for $x = 1$ to u :

generates the following attribute secret key share:

$$K_{x,VerID_{owner},m} = g^{Ask_{m,\alpha_x}} \cdot H(VerID_{owner})^{Ask_{m,\beta_x}}$$

4. encrypts the attribute secret key shares $\{K_{x,VerID_{owner},m}, x = 1,\ldots,u\}$ with the temporary public key PK_{temp} in AKGR and sends the ciphertext back to the data user.

The data user decrypts the received ciphertexts from multiple AAs, if there are more than t attribute secret key shares $K_{x,VerID_{owner},m}$. The data user performs the Lagrange Interpolating algorithm and obtains the complete attribute secret key:

$$\{K_{x,VerID_{owner}} = g^{\alpha_x} \cdot H(VerID_{owner})^{\beta_x}, x = 1, \ldots, u\}$$

$$
\begin{aligned}
K_{x,VerID_{owner}} &= \prod_{m=1}^{t} K_{x,VerID_{owner},m}^{\Delta_{m,S}(0)} \\
&= \prod_{m=1}^{t} \left(g^{Ask_{m,\alpha_x}} \cdot H(VerID_{owner})^{Ask_{m,\beta_x}} \right)^{\Delta_{m,S}(0)} \\
&= g^{\sum_{m=1}^{t} Ask_{m,\alpha_x} \Delta_{m,S}(0)} \cdot H(VerID_{owner})^{\sum_{m=1}^{t} Ask_{m,\beta_x} \Delta_{m,S}(0)} \\
&= g^{\alpha_x} \cdot H(VerID_{owner})^{\beta_x}
\end{aligned}
\tag{6}
$$

4.4 Anonymous Data Access

4.4.1 Cloud Server Pre-decryption

When a data user wants to access sensitive data from the cloud server, he/she submits an anonymous data access request (ADAR) as follows to the cloud server: $\left(H(VerID_{owner})^{1/t} \parallel Cert(x), x = 1, \ldots, u \parallel FL \right)$, where $Cert(x)$ denotes as:

$$
\left\{
\begin{array}{c}
K_{x,VerID_{owner}}^{1/t}, Attribtue_x, VerIA_x\_Number, VerID_{issuer}^{(x)} \\
Sign_{VerID_{issuer}} \left[H\left(Attribtue_x \parallel VerIA_x\_Number \parallel VerID_{issuer}^{(x)} \right) \right]
\end{array}
\right\}
\tag{7}
$$

where t is a random number $t \in Z_p^*$, $VerID_{issuer}^{(x)}$ is issuer's VerID of the attribute x, $VerIA_x\_Number$ refers to the certification number of the attribute x, and the signature $Sign_{VerID_{issuer}} \left[H\left(Attribtue_x \parallel VerIA_x\_Number \parallel VerID_{issuer}^{(x)} \right) \right]$ is a component in verification $VerAC(x)$ of attribute x, FL is the list of files that the data wants to access.

The user of data encrypts ADAR with the blockchain public key of the cloud server and sends the ciphertext to the cloud server. Cloud server decrypts the received ciphertext of the access request and implements the following Algorithm 3. The user's attribute set $I \subset \{1, \ldots, l\}$, say denote as $I = \{i : \rho \in R_\tau\}$, meets the access policy in the file ciphertext.

Algorithm 3. Anonymous Data Access.

Input: public parameter *params*, anonymous data access request ADAR.

Output: the pre-decryption result.

---

1. for $x = 1$ to u :

(a) verifies the signature:

$Sign_{VerID_{issuer}}[H(Attribute_x||VerIA_x\_Number||VerID^{(x)}_{issuer})]$ in $Cert(x)$. If failed, terminate the procedure.

(b) looks up the ARL by the tuple $(VerID^{(x)}_{issuer}, VerIA_x\_Number)$ as index to check whether the attribute x of the user has been revoked. If revoked, terminate the produces.

2. searches files in FL and tests whether the attribute set in ADAR meets the access policies in file ciphertext.

3. for a file matched successfully, pre-decrypts the file ciphertexts by the following calculation:

$$\frac{e(H(VerID_{owner})^{1/t}, C_{3,i})}{e(K_{\rho(i), VerID_{owner}}^{1/t}, C_{2,i})} = \frac{e(H(VerID_{owner})^{1/t}, g^{\omega_i})}{e(g^{\alpha_{\rho(i)}/t}, g^{r_i})}$$

and sends the pre-decryption result to the user.

$$\left\{ C_0 = m \cdot e(g,g)^s, C_{1,i} = e(g,g)^{\lambda_i} \cdot e(g,g)^{\alpha_{\rho(i)} r_i}, \frac{e(H(VerID_{owner})^{1/t}, g^{\omega_i})}{e(g^{\alpha_{\rho(i)}/t}, g^{r_i})} \right\}$$

4.4.2 User Decryption

When a data user receives the pre-decryption from the cloud server, he/she decrypts the result to obtain the final plaintext by the following calculation. If $\{\lambda_i\}$, $i \in I$ are valid shares of encryption factor s according to M, user chooses constant $\{d_i \in Z_p\}$, $i \in I$ that can be constructed $s = \sum_{i \in I} d_i \lambda_i$. In addition, it also can be $\sum_{i \in I} d_i M_i = (1, \ldots, 0)$.

$$A = \left\{ \frac{e(H(VerID_{owner})^{1/t}, g^{\omega_i})}{e(g^{\alpha_{\rho(i)}/t}, g^{r_i})} \right\}^t = \frac{e(H(VerID_{owner}), g^{\omega_i})}{e(g^{\alpha_{\rho(i)}}, g^{r_i})} \tag{8}$$

when the user receives the pre-decryption and partial ciphertext from the cloud server, he utilizes A to decrypt the ciphertext and get the message m.

$$m = \frac{C_0}{\prod_{i \in I} (C_{1,i} \cdot A)^{d_i}} = \frac{C_0}{\prod_{i \in I} (C_{1,i} \cdot \frac{e(H(VerID_{owner}), g^{\omega_i})}{e(g^{\alpha_{\rho(i)}}, g^{r_i})})^{d_i}} \tag{9}$$

4.5 Anonymous Attribute Revocation

When the user's identity attribute changes, the related issuer constructs a verifiable attribute revocation certification: $VerARC = \{VerID_{issuer} \parallel VerIA\_Number \parallel Time\}$ and synchronizes it to ARL maintained by all nodes. The ARL doesn't contain the user's identity attribute information and thus can protect the user's identity privacy.

5 Security Analysis

5.1 Security Analysis

Anonymity. In our scheme, anonymity is mainly reflected in three process of anonymous attribute secret key generation, anonymous data access and anonymous attribute revocation.

Anonymous Attribute Secret Key Generation. The anonymity of attribute secret key generation is reflected in the fact that the data user generates a pair of temporary keys (PK_{temp}, SK_{temp}) to ensure the security during secret key generation process. In addition, only the hash value of the data user's identifier $H(VerID_{user})$, PK_{temp} and VerAC are included in the constructed key generation request. The attribute authority uses the verifiable identifier $(VerID_{issuer})$ of the VerAC issuer and the number of the attribute credentials $(VerIA\_Number)$ as the index of the ARL to verify whether the attribute of the data user in the key request has been revoked. Signature of key generation request:

$$Sign_{VerID_{owner}}[H(Attribute_x \parallel VerIA_x\_Number \parallel VerID_{issuer} \parallel H(VerID_{owner}))],$$

where includes the hash of the VerID of data user $H(VerID_{owner})$ to ensure the binding relationship between the data user and attribute issued by identity attribute issuer.

Anonymous Data Access. When the data user requests the cloud server provider to access data, the data access request only contains the converted the hash value of the data user's identifier $H(VerID_{user})^{1/t}$ and attribute certification $Cert$. The ARL mechanism is used to verify whether data user's attribute has been revoked by using the verifiable identifier $(VerID_{issuer})$ of the VerAC issuer and the number of the attribute credentials $(VerIA\_Number)$ as index. At the same time, the cloud server provider performs predecryption operation that uses $H(VerID_{owner})^{1/t}$ and the converted attribute secret key $K_{x,VerID_{user}}^{1/t}$. In this way, the identity privacy of data users is protected and the efficiency of the system is improved.

Anonymous Attribute Revocation. Li et al. [11] propose a verifiable threshold multiple authority access control scheme, in which all AAs jointly manage a system attribute set. They utilize a secret sharing approach to generate a shared master key among multiple authorities, where all AAs collaborate with each other to generate the key. In this scheme, user's secret keys can be generated by contacting a threshold number of AAs. However, this scheme does not address the revocation problem. In our scheme, we propose a revocable threshold multiple authority CP-ABE scheme with the management of joint attribute sets to advance the above system. When the user's identity changes, the identity certificate issuer can construct an anonymous attribute revocation statement to revoke the previously issued identity attribute. The statement only contains $VerID_{issuer}$ and verifiable identity attribute number $VerIA\_Number$, and the attribute revoked time. The ARL records the $VerID_{issuer}$ and verifiable identity attribute number $VerIA\_Number$. The attribute authority and cloud server provider use the identity attribute $VerID_{issuer}$ and $VerIA\_Number$ as the index of the ARL to verify whether the identity attribute of the data user has been revoked. In the process, the identity information of the attribute owner (data user) is not included, and anonymous attribute revocation is achieved and user privacy is protected. At the same time, the statement is synchronized to the distributed ledger maintained by all nodes.

Privacy. In our solution, data access, key generation, and attribute revocation are anonymous. Through the anonymous mechanism, users will not use their real identity information to other nodes when interacting with data. Disclosing user identity information to attribute authority may cause connection problems, which may damage the user's privacy, especially in the case of communication between parties. In our solution, the user's interaction operation only uses the hashed verifiable identity($H(VerID_{user})$) and verifiable attribute certificate number, so that the user's identity information will not be leaked, the user's identity privacy can be well protected accordingly. At the same time, because these operations are anonymous, the user's identity traceability is a problem to be solved.

Collusion Attack. When some malicious users collude with each other, they may share their attribute secret keys to gain more privilege. The attribute secret key is associated with the user's unique verifiable identifier (VerID), users cannot collude together to gain illegal access by combining their attribute secret key share. In addition, our scheme can resist the collusion attack even some AAs are corrupted by the adversary. In the attribute secret key generation, we utilize DKG generates attribute $x's$ secret key ($\alpha_x = \sum_{m=1}^{N} \alpha_{m,x}, \beta_x = \sum_{m=1}^{N} \beta_{m,x}$) and makes public attribute $x's$ public key ($e(g,g)^{\alpha_x}, g^{\beta_x}$). At the end of the protocol each AA has attribute secret key sub-secret ($\alpha_{m,x}, \beta_{m,x}$), called a share of ($\alpha_x, \beta_x$). The protocol is secure with threshold (t, n) if in the presence of an adversary who corrupts at most t AAs, the protocol generates the desired attribute secret key sub-shares and does not reveal any information about (α_x, β_x), except for what is implied by the public attribute $x's$ public key ($e(g,g)^{\alpha_x}, g^{\beta_x}$).

6   Performance Analysis

In this section, we use the elliptic curve "SS512" in our program to construct bilinear pairs. We develop operations of each phase with the help of library gmp-5.1.3, pbc-0.5.14 and openssl-1.0.2 on the ubuntu 16.04 with an Intel Core i5-8300H CPU at 2.3 GHz and 8G RAM.

6.1 Encryption and the Local Decryption of User

Since the verification of VerACs, the generation of transactions and the delivery of messages mainly rely on the BbSSIM platform environment, we only consider the efficiency simulation of data outsourced storage and the local decryption of user. In order to facilitate the analysis of the experimental results, it is assumed that there are five attribute authorities. In order to ensure the accuracy and credibility of the experiment, all the simulation results are the mean of ten trials.

Since the recent work is very little related to our solution, we have selected the threshold multi-authority access control system (TMACS) in [11] as our comparison solution, which mainly compares the time overhead of the system during encryption and decryption. In order to compare the time cost of data outsourced storage of the data owner in this scheme and in TMACS scheme, let T_m represents the power operation on the group G, T_e denotes the bilinear operation on the group G and n is the number of attributes in the access policy, where $T_m < T_e$. The time complexity of TMACS scheme in the process of data $O(3nT_m + (2n+1)T_e)$ outsourced storage is $O((3n+1)T_m + T_e)$, while the time complexity of this scheme is. In comparison, the time complexity of this solution is higher in data outsourcing storage, and the overhead is larger with the increase of the number of attributes. However, there are multiple different organizations in the system, our solution has better scalability and security. From Fig. 3, it can be found that the data owner encrypts the data under the same access policy, and the time overhead of our scheme is relatively high. However, in the process of the local decryption of user, the data users directly download the data ciphertext from the cloud server. In our solution, the main computing cost is delegated to the cloud server provider, which sends the pre-decryption result to the user, and the user decrypts it locally. As shown in Fig. 4, the time required for the data user to decrypt is reduced compared to the TMACS scheme. The cloud server provider uses the converted attribute secret key and verifiable identity for pre-decryption, which greatly reduces the local computing burden of users.

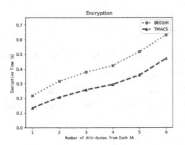   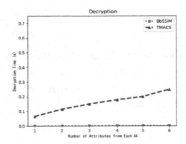

Fig. 3. Data Encryption.   **Fig. 4.** The Local Decryption of Data User.

6.2 Attribute Secret Key Generation

In this scheme, the Pedersen's DKG protocol is used to solve the single-point failure problem in the attribute secret key generation of data user. The system contains at least t trusted attribute authorities, and jointly generates attribute secret key sub-shares for users. Data user interacts with any t AAs, user locally generate his/her attribute secret key. In the initialization phase, the attribute authority is set to 9, and the threshold value is set to 5. As can be seen from Fig. 5, in the process of attribute secret key generation, the delay of the attribute secret key sub-shares transfer process is not considered. As the threshold value t increases, which share the time of attribute secret key sub-shares and restore attribute secret key will increase.

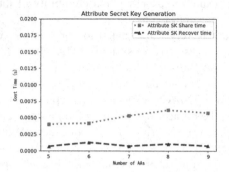

Fig. 5. Attribute Secret Key Generation.

6.3 Security Against Compromising AAs

In this section, we consider the security analysis the attack that the adversary compromises AAs. As long as there are more than t trusted AAs, our system can work properly. Therefore, the adversary has to compromise more than t AAs to assign attribute secret key sub-shares for him/her. The parameter γ indicates the probability that an illegal adversary gets the partial attribute secret key sub-shares, the probability of BbSSIM security is:

$$\sum_{m=0}^{t-1} C_N^m \gamma^m (1 - \gamma)^{N-m} \tag{10}$$

As shown in Fig. 6, when the attribute authority is set to 5, 10, 15, 20, the security of the system increases with the increase of t. For example, the system can be secure with probability close to 1, when we set the value of t only equal to 7 rather than a larger value in a system with 15 AAs, even the adversary broke the system with a probability of 0.3.

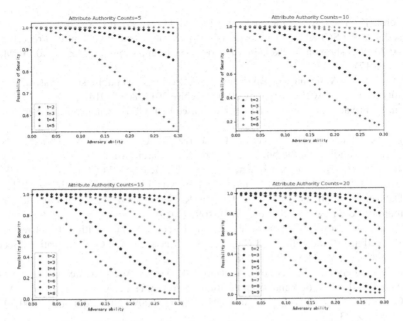

Fig. 6. Probability of Security Against Compromising AAs.

7 Conclusion

In this paper, we analysis blockchain-based identity management, namely uPort, ShoCard, Sovrin and DID, revealing drawbacks to meet the needs of traditional access control scheme based on CP-ABE. To overcome the limitation and weaknesses of identity attributes: persistence, request and verification, we propose BbSSIM that aims to provide a trusted identity by protecting users' identity. The proposed system follows a DID standard that enables users manage and control their identity attribute claims. The use of blockchain, along with smart contracts enabled the secure and trustworthy management of identities. By combining blockchain-based identity management and threshold multiple authority CP-ABE, we address the single-point failure and do not affect the overall of the network. We introduce ARL mechanism on top of BbSSIM, which supports dynamically change data users' privileges without disclosing any sensitive information. To sum up, the proposed scheme can not only securely outsource expensive computations to cloud server provider but also administrate a wide range of attributes and efficiently control user access privileges. In addition, some communication and computation are needed among the AAs to exchange attribute secret key shares and reconstruct the attribute secret key. For future work, we will utilize a new framework to eliminate communication costs and explore the application of blockchain-based identity management.

References

1. Sohr, K., Drouineaud, M., Ahn, G.-J.: Analyzing and managing role-based access control policies. IEEE Trans. Knowl. Data Eng. **20**(7), 924–939 (2008)

2. Cameron, K.: The Laws of Identity, vol. 12, pp. 8–11. Microsoft Corp (2005)
3. Mustafa, A.-B.: SCPKI: a smart contract-based PKI and identity system. In: Proceedings of the ACM Workshop on Blockchain, Cryptocurrencies and Contracts, pp. 35–40. ACM, Abu Dhabi (2017)
4. Fromknecht, C., Velicanu, D., Yakoubov, S.: A decentralized public key infrastructure with identity retention. IACR Cryptology ePrint Archive 2014, 803 (2014)
5. Axon, L.: Privacy-awareness in Blockchain-based PKI. CDT Technical Paper Series 21, 15 (2015)
6. Augot, D., Chabanne, H., Chenevier, T., George, W., Lambert, L.: A user-centric system for verified identities on the bitcoin blockchain. In: Garcia-Alfaro, J., Navarro-Arribas, G., Hartenstein, H., Herrera-Joancomartí, J. (eds.) ESORICS/DPM/CBT -2017. LNCS, vol. 10436, pp. 390–407. Springer, Cham (2017). https://doi.org/10.1007/978-3-319-67816-0_22
7. Al-Dahhan, R.R., Shi, Q., Lee, G.M., Kifayat, K.: Survey on revocation in ciphertext-policy attribute-based encryption. Sensors 19(7), 1695 (2019)
8. Boldyreva, A., Goyal, V., Kumar, V.: Identity-based encryption with efficient revocation. In: Proceedings of the 15th ACM Conference on Computer and Communications Security, pp. 417–426. ACM, Alexandria (2008)
9. Ibraimi, L., Petkovic, M., Nikova, S., Hartel, P., Jonker, W.: Mediated ciphertext-policy attribute-based encryption and its application. In: Youm, H.Y., Yung, M. (eds.) WISA 2009. LNCS, vol. 5932, pp. 309–323. Springer, Heidelberg (2009). https://doi.org/10.1007/978-3-642-10838-9_23
10. Gai, F., Wang, B., Deng, W., Peng, W.: Proof of reputation: a reputation-based consensus protocol for peer-to-peer network. In: Pei, J., Manolopoulos, Y., Sadiq, S., Li, J. (eds.) DASFAA 2018. LNCS, vol. 10828, pp. 666–681. Springer, Cham (2018). https://doi.org/10.1007/978-3-319-91458-9_41
11. Li, W., Xue, K., Xue, Y., Hong, J.: TMACS: a robust and verifiable threshold multi-authority access control system in public cloud storage. IEEE Trans. Parallel Distrib. Syst. 27(5), 1484–1496 (2015)

Attention Mechanism Based Adversarial Attack Against Deep Reinforcement Learning

Jinyin Chen[1,2(✉)] [ID], Xueke Wang[2] [ID], Yan Zhang[2], Haibin Zheng[2], and Shouling Ji[3]

[1] Institute of Cyberspace Security, Zhejiang University of Technology, Hangzhou 310023, China
chenjinyin@zjut.edu.cn
[2] The College of Information Engineering, Zhejiang University of Technology, Hangzhou 310023, China
{2111903100,2111903240}@zjut.edu.cn, haibinzheng320@gmail.com
[3] The College of Computer Science and Technology, Zhejiang University, Hangzhou 310058, China
sji@zju.edu.cn

Abstract. Deep reinforcement learning (DRL) aims to maximize long-term future rewards to achieve specific goals by learning polices based on deep learning models. However, existing research has found that machine learning models are vulnerable to maliciously craft adversarial examples, so does the DRL since it uses deep model to learn policies. Usually gradient information is adopted to generate adversarial perturbation on the clean observation states to fail DRL. In order to develop a novel attack method for further defect detection of DRL, we propose a novel attention mechanism based adversarial attack. Instead of gradient information, we make full use of hidden features extracted in the DRL by attention operations to generate more effective adversarial examples. Both channel attention and pixel attention are applied to extract feature to modify the clean state to an adversarial one. Deep Q-Learing Network (DQN), one of the state-of-the-art DRL models, is utilized as the target model to train Flappybird game environment to guarantee continuous running and high success rate. Comprehensive attack experiments are carried out on DQN to testify the attack performance in aspects of reward and loss convergence.

Keywords: Deep reinforcement learning · DQN · White-box attack · Attention mechanism · Feature transformation

1 Introduction

Reinforcement learning(RL) [1], a branch of machine learning, is usually a process of continuous decision. Deep reinforcement learning (DRL) makes full use

© Springer Nature Switzerland AG 2021
G. Wang et al. (Eds.): SpaCCS 2020, LNCS 12382, pp. 19–43, 2021.
https://doi.org/10.1007/978-3-030-68851-6_2

of neural network as the parameter structure to optimize the RL algorithm by combining the ability of decision-making and deep learning perception. Convolutional neural network has natural advantages for image processing, so the policy of DRL is optimized through neural network training. In recent years, DRL has led to rapid development in many fields, with important achievements obtained in fields such as game player, autonomous driving, robot control, traffic control, financial transactions and cyber security [2], etc.

However, neural network and deep learning models are vulnerable to adversarial attacks caused by creating malicious examples, which increases the hidden trouble for RL. Zegedy et al. [3] found that deep neural networks are highly vulnerable to attack in the field of image classification firstly. The explanation for the vulnerabilities of neural networks is also given by Goodfellow et al. [4], who proposed that the main reason that neural networks are susceptible to adversarial perturbations lies in the nature of their linear behavior in high-dimensional space. Therefore, it will be a meaningful research on how to construct a safe RL system.

The weakness of RL is also easy to be exploited by attackers. The existing attack methods can be divided into white-box attacks and black-box attacks.

White-box attack was proposed earlier by Goodfellow [4], who first use gradient-based attack on neural networks. Tretschk et al. [5] used the counter transform network to generate perturbations to attack the RL environment. Then Huang et al. [6] applied FGSM attack method to Atari2600 games. The white-box attack methods for RL also include start point-based adversarial attack (SPA) [7] on Q-learning and white-box based adversarial (WBA) [8] attack on Deep Q-Learing(DQN). One of the efficient attack methods is common dominant adversarial examples generation method(CDG) [9] and snooping threat models [10] attack model launch destructive attacks on the environment of DQN and PPO by observing the reward of the agent's action. There is also a white-box attack method guided by the value function [11] similar to the strategic time attack idea of Lin et al. [12], which uses the model based on value function to evaluate the value of the current state to decide when to attack. Besides, poisoning attack [7] is applied to the multi-agent game environment on the MuJoCo platform.

On the other hand, black-box attack methods on RL are also proposed, such as policy induction attack(PIA) [13], strategic time attack and puzzle attack proposed by Lin et al. [14], and transferable black-box attack method proposed by Zhao et al. [15], which reduces accumulated rewards. Existing attack methods on the RL agents assume that the opponent can access the learning parameters of the target agent or the environment where the agent interacts, and then launch destructive attacks on the DRL environment by observing the behavioral reward signal of the agent. In this paper, we propose a new attack method based on the above research of RL security. Our novel attack approach emplys the attention mechanism. Attention mechanism is a data processing method in machine learning, which is widely used in various types of machine learning tasks such as natural language processing, image recognition and speech recognition. It can help enhance semantic recognition, natural language translation and so on. However, the field of deep reinforcement learning which has attracted much attention recently has not yet utilized this method. Therefore, we intend to explore the influence of attention mechanism in the field of reinforcement learning safety. Furthermore, we pay attention to the deep features of the deep reinforcement learning model and use different interpolation strategies of image processing before channel and pixel attention. The different interpolation strategies include bicubic interpolation, Bilinear interpolation nearest neighbor method and area interpolation. Bicubic interpolation usually produces the best and most accurate interpolation patterns. Bilinear interpolation is faster, but less accurate. Other interpolation techniques are usually not accurate enough, which will break the original focus area of depth model features. Therefore, this paper proposes a novel reinforcement learning attack method using the attention mechanism, and combining image interpolation method.

The main contributions of this paper can be summarized as follows:

1) The attacker can obtain complete model information and extract disturbed pixel information from the feature information easily of the deep convolutional layer by using the attention mechanism, which strengthens the attack effect;
2) In this paper, different interpolation strategies are integrated into DRL feature transformation and feature pixel reconstruction is carried out;
3) In the experiment, we use DQN in the Flappybird [16] game environment to train RL agent. Besides, the reward value during the game's attack is reduced after attacking.

Moreover, the perturbation size imperceptible to human eyes is used to achieve the purpose of confusing the agent preferably. The attack method proposed in this paper can be very destructive under a small perturbation amplitude.

2   Related Network

In this section, we introduce the principle of RL, as well as attacks and defense methods in the field of RL security.

2.1   Deep Reinforcement Learning (DRL)

The main idea of the RL is based on the interactive learning of agents and environments. The traditional supervised learning in machine learning aims at learning a good model by giving some label data sets, with the purpose of making good decisions for the unknown data. But sometimes, we don't know what the label is, which means that you don't know what the good outcome is at the beginning. Instead of giving the label, RL returns a reward value that determines what the result of the action has taken in the current state is ("good" or "bad"), which is a mathematical Markov Decision Process (MDP) essentially. The learning process of RL is dynamic, which needs continuous interaction. Compared with supervision learning and unsupervision learning, RL involves more data objects, including action a, environment s, state transition probability p and return function R. Since the external environment provides little information, RL agents must learn from its own experience. The RL agent interacts with the environment in a "trial and error" way to learn, which obtains rewards to guide behavior. The goal is to maximize the Long-term reward for the agent while the reward value is used to evaluate the quality of the actions, rather than directly guide the agent how to take the correct action. RL is essentially a Markov decision process used to model the decision problem of reinforcement learning.

However, DRL combines the strengths of deep learning and RL as an end-to-end system of perception and control. Deep learning has strong perception ability, but lacks certain decision-making ability. RL has the ability to make decisions but no way to solve the perception problem. DRL solves the above defects.

2.2   Attack on DRL

DRL has the advantages of deep learning and RL, also inherits the defects of both. Deep learning [17] has long been proved to be vulnerable to malicious perturbation by attackers [18]. Furthermore, the network model is highly vulnerable.

Huang et al. [6] first found that neural network policy is susceptible to adversarial attack in DRL. The form of attack they adopted is to add tiny perturbations to the input state of DQN [19,20] to cause wrong actions of the agent, which is called FGSM attack method proposed by Goodfellow et al. [4]. Using this method, Huang et al. for the first time verified that the agents trained by DRL models based on the algorithms of DQN, TRPO [5,11] are vulnerable to the attack of adversarial perturbations. Moreover, they found that the transferability of cross-dataset proposed by Szegedy et al. [3] in 2013 was also suitable for RL. Currently one of the most intensive research application environments of DRL is the game environment. Lin et al. [14] put forward a black-box attack method based on Atari2600 game environments, which was strategic time attack. Lin et al. also proposed a confuse attack. The experiment used the adversarial example generation algorithm proposed by Carlini and Wagner [21], which aimed to start from the state at a certain moment to add perturbation to the agent, so that the agent could reach the expected state after n steps. Subsequently, Kos et al. [22] proposed an attack method guided by value function, whose main idea was to use the value function module to choose whether to attack the value of the current state. Behzdan and Munir [13] proposed PIA, which generated a perturbation at each time step to affect the next state. This attack method used imitation learning to speed up the establishment of the equivalent model and provided a new scheme for attacking the DRL model under the black-box setting.

RL is also widely applied in path planning. For instance, Liu et al. [23] proposed the RL path planning attack method of base-value iterative network.

Xiang et al. [24] proposed a counter attack method based on starting point attack named SPA, which trained RL based on q-learning algorithm and aimed to establish a probability output model of path points based on the original model. Bai et al. [8] proposed WBA method based on the SPA attack method trained by DQN, which does not only require the angle analysis of the points on the planning path, but also limited by the scenarios. A new gradients based attack method [25] for A3C algorithm in the path planning scenario of atrai game was proposed by Chen et al. [9]. Chen also tried to find the dominant gradient perturbation zone, and added baffle to the optimized path trained by the agent to fool the agent. Although this attack can maximize the loss function of agents in a short time and have a certain impact on their performance, agents can still recover after long-term training.

In addition to the path planning problem, RL attack methods are also applied to other fields. Tretschk et al. [26] integrated the new counter attack technique of counter transform network into the strategic network structure. In this way, through a series of attacks, the target policy network can optimize the adversarial reward instead of the original reward during training. A new black-box attack method based on the FGSM proposed by Huang et al. [6] was proposed by Behzdan and Munir [13], who used the multi-robot game in MuJoCo as RL training environment and the games trained by Bansal et al. [7] as assessment environment. Russo et al. [27] proposed an attack method based on optimization in RL. Matthew Inkawhich et al. [10] proposed SRA attack model. In addition, Zhao et al. [15] used DQN to train the seq2seq model, and directly transferred the adversarial examples in the trained model to A2C. In this paper, we further explore and propose a new attack method based on attention mechanism.

2.3   Defense of DRL

In recent works, more defense methods has been proposed and applied in deep learning and RL security domain to improve robustness. The existing defense methods in deep learning can be divided into three categories.

The first category is to modify the input of the model for defense, the second is to modify the objective function, and the last is to change the structure of the model. Gu et al. [28] proposed an algorithm called counter robust A3C. In this algorithm, the adversarial agent trains and learns in a noisy environment to make A3C model more robust to adversarial perturbation, thus making it more adaptive to that environment. Lin et al. [12] proposed a defense method belonging to the first category of defense based on state prediction module plus pixel compression transformation, which realized the detection and defense of adversarial examples based on Atari2600 game environment. Besides, Marc Fischer et al. [29] proposed a network architecture called robust student-DQN(RS-DQN), which allowed online robust training in parallel with Q networks while maintaining competitive performance. RS-DQN method combined with antagonistic training and robust training to resist attacks during training and testing.

In terms of changing model parameters defense methods, Vahid Behanzadan and Arslan Munir [30] proved that adding noise to DQN model parameters and retraining the original model can resist attacks. In addition, Havens et al. [31] proposed an novel algorithm to detect the existence of attacks by observing the advantages of sub-policies using a hierarchical framework. Based on this framework, Lee et al. [32] further explored the feasibility of using it as a defense framework and implemented defense on DRL.

In terms of the application of RL path planning, Michael Everett et al. [33] proposed an additional authentication defense to resist the impact of adversarial perturbations on agent behavior.

3   Preliminaries

In this section, we introduced the basic model of RL, the principle of attention mechanism and the feature transformation method of RL neural network, which are used throughout the paper.

3.1   The Basic Model of RL

MDP is the theoretical framework of RL, the next state is only related to current state, rather than the previous state. MDP is described by the tuples of (S, A, P, R, γ). Where $S = \{s_1, s_2, s_3, \ldots, s_t\}$ is the state set, $A = \{a_1, a_2, a_3, \ldots, a_t\}$ is the action set, P is the state transition probability, R is the reward function, λ is the discount factor used to calculate the long-term cumulative return. The state transition matrix of markov decision process is $P_{ss'}^a = P[S_{t+1} = s'|S_t = s, A_t = a]$. The goal of RL is to find the optimal policy under the given markov decision-making process. The policy represented by π refers to the mapping of state set to action set, which means that the output distribution of actions in a given state s represented as $\pi(a|s) = p[A_t = a|S_t = s]$. When the agent adopts the policy, the cumulative return obeys an arbitrary distribution. The expected value of the cumulative return of the state is the state-value function, defined as:

$$v_\pi(s) = E_\pi \left[\left(\sum_{k=0}^{\infty} \gamma^k \right) R_{t+k+1} | S_t \right] \tag{1}$$

Cumulative return is $G_t = R_{t+1} + \gamma R_{t+2} + \cdots = \sum_{k=0}^{\infty} \gamma^k R_{t+k+1}$ used to measure the value of the state s_i. However, the cumulative return is a random variable, rather than a determined value, so it cannot be described. But its expectation is a definite value, and it can be defined as a function of state values, which can be expressed as:

$$q_\pi(s, a) = E_\pi \left[\sum_{k=0}^{\infty} \gamma^k R_{t+k+1} | S_t = s, A_t = a \right] \tag{2}$$

The expected value of the state-value function and the state-behavior value function are calculated by the Bellman equation. It can be obtained from the definition of the state value function $v(s) = E[G_t|S_t = s] = E[R_{t+1} + \gamma v(S_{t+1})|S_t = s]$. The state-action value function also can be obtained as $q_\pi(s,a) = E_\pi[R_{t+1} + \gamma q(S_{t+1}, A_{t+1})|S_t = s, A_t = a]$. The optimal state value function and the optimal state-behavior value function of the Bellman optimization equation are as follows:

$$v^*(s) = \max_a R_s^a + \gamma \sum_{s' \in S} P_{ss'}^a v^*(s') \tag{3}$$

If the optimal state-action value function is known, the optimal policy can be determined by directly maximizing.

3.2 Attention Mechanism

Attention model is widely used in natural language processing, image recognition, speech recognition and other areas of deep learning tasks. It is one of the core technologies of deep learning technology that deserves the more attention and deep understanding. The attention mechanism stems from the study of human vision. In cognitive science, because of the bottlenecks of information processing, humans selectively focus on one important part of all information and ignore other visible information, which is often referred to as attentional mechanism. Attention mechanism is the attention to input weight allocation. It was first used in encoder-decoder, where the attention mechanism obtained the input variable of the next layer by weighting average the hidden state of all time steps of the encoder. Attention mechanism was first proposed by Bahdanau et al. [34], which is mainly used as a translation model to solve the problem of translation kernel alignment (seq2seq+attention is adopted in this paper). In this paper, we extract the deep feature of the model to reconstruct the feature using the deep feature map and fuse with the input state to obtain the attention feature $W_{s'}$, then extract the pixel features $W_{s''}$ from $W_{s'}$. Thereby confusing the agent.

3.3 DRL Feature Transformation

We extracted the deep feature map of DRL and carried out feature transformation. The feature transformation of DRL combined with bicubic interpolation of image. We also use different interpolation methods for comparison. Compared with the nearest neighbor interpolation, bilinear interpolation and area interpolation, the calculation process of the double cubic interpolation is more complicated. Bicubic interpolation is the most common interpolation method in two-dimensional space, which is used to obtain the value of the function f at points (x, y) by weighted average of the last 16 sampling points in the rectangular grid. Moreover, we need to interpolate cubic functions using two polynomials, one in each direction. The bicubic interpolation method based on bicubic basis function has the following basic functions:

$$W(x) = \begin{cases} (c+2)|x|^3 - (c+2)|x|^2 + 1, & |x| \leq 1 \\ c|x|^3 - 5c|x|^2 + 8c|x| - 4c, & 1 < |x| < 2 \\ 0, & otherwise \end{cases} \tag{4}$$

where, c is the hyperparameter, x is the position of the pixel point, and $W(.)$ is the weight value function of the corresponding pixel point. For the interpolated pixel points (x, y) (x and y can be floating point numbers), take the 4×4 neighborhood points (x_n, y_m), $n, m = 0, 1, 2, 3$. Interpolation is performed according to the following formula:

$$g(x, y) = \sum_{n=0}^{3} \sum_{m=0}^{3} g(x_n, y_m) W(x - x_n) W(y - y_m) \tag{5}$$

where, x and y are the position of the row and column of the corresponding pixel matrix, $g(.)$ is the pixel value function of corresponding points, $W(.)$ is the weight value function of corresponding pixel points. We combine the deep feature of DRL with the pixel transform method to obtain the reconstruction feature of the deep feature map.

4   Adversarial Attack Based on Attention Mechanism

In our work, we use attention-based attack method as a white-box attack against trained model policy π_θ, model structure and parameters are available to attackers. First of all, we give a general block diagram of the attack, as shown in Fig. 1 below. In any threat model, we assume that the adversary can intercept and manipulate the incoming game frames. In our threat model, the adversary can spy on rewards and action signals. Start by initializing a state from the reinforcement learning environment. The attacker gets deep features of the current state and the agent recognizes the current state, thus generating the antagonistic state. Then, in step 6, The trained agent observes an antagonistic state and gives an evil action. Finally, in step 8, the environment gives out minimal feedback rewards.

4.1   General Introduction to Attack

Vulnerability Analysis of RL: The learning process of RL agent itself is a process of constant learning. Even a small perturbation is likely to break the equilibrium state that is about to be established. As we all know, neural network, as the core technology of deep learning, has been proved to be extremely vulnerable to disturb in this regard, many scholars in different fields have voiced and proposed many defense methods. DRL not only makes use of deep learning but also utilizes its own policy learning, which makes it more vulnerable to

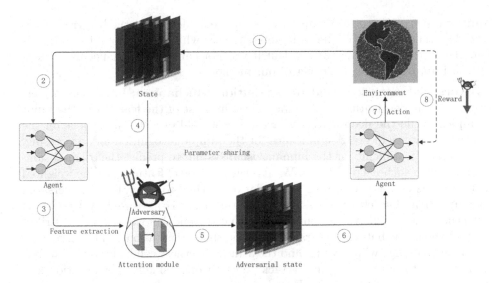

Fig. 1. Framework of attention threat model for DRL

attackers. Moreover, standard reinforcement learning evaluation methods have not been clearly proposed. The current main evaluation standard is to observe the reward value and visualize the training effect, but the calculation standard of the reward value also change with the environment and training methods. Besidese, the award value in the process of training is in the stage of dynamic calculation, which is bounded to have a problem of fitting or underfitting. In a word, RL is still very fragile. In this paper, we propose a new attack method that can break the balance state of the trained DQN during testing. At the same time, long-term cumulative reward value is still used to be the metric to evaluate the effectiveness of the attack method. We use several of the previously proposed attack methods to compare with our proposed and compare the reward value under the same perturbation size to understand the successful effect of the method we proposed.

Object of Attack: In this paper, we attack the trained model based on DQN algorithm. Off-policy is applied in Q-Learning which is also extended in DQN. The biggest difference is that DQN model no longer generates a complete Q-Table at initialization time compared with reinforcement learning based on conventional Q-Learning algorithm. The Q-Value of state is generated by neural network by inputing the characteristic features of current state. Then, we choose an action based on Q-Value. However, the existence of neural network makes DRL more susceptible to perturbation. We will attack the trained DQN during testing. In order to understand whether our attack method still has limitations, we use several attack methods previously proposed to make a comparison. We compare the size of the reward value under the same perturbation size, as well as observe the loss of forecast Q value and target of Q value. Because we attack during testing, the corresponding loss after the attack is not the bigger the better. On the contrary, we hope it gets smaller, which means our loss value is smaller in the case of the attack. But it was not carried out by specific actions, which improves the attack effect of our method.

Adversarial Attack Based on Attention Mechanism: In the neural network, the hidden features of the model retain most of the features of the input samples, while the deep features have a larger field of vision and focus on the features that are of great significance for the sample recognition and processing. However, it is difficult for the human visual system to predict the original samples through such deep features. We use the deep pixel feature and the weighted attention as well as the bicubic interpolation method to generate the adversarial perturbation. The effectiveness of the perturbation is measured by the attack effectness and the perturbation intensity that depends on the size and distribution of the perturbation. Generally speaking, the perturbation will be larger, the distribution range will be wider and the attack effectness will be better. However, it is better to obtain the same attack effect through smaller perturbation and the narrow distribution range. Based on above, we apply a new attack method in RL which is the adversarial attack method based on attention mechanism. As shown in Fig. 2, the general framework of the attack method based on attention mechanism is given. We choose the output of the second convolution layer of the neural network model based on DQN as the object of attention, which can be seen from the Fig. 2. Then, we extract the output feature value of this layer and carry out the attention conversion of weight and pixel. At the same time, we also carry out feature reconstruction and size transformation. Finally, the perturbation value is obtained and added to the clean state to generate the adversarial example.

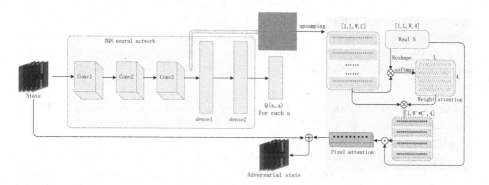

Fig. 2. Framework of the attention mechanism method

4.2 Attack Method Description

In the experiment, we extract the deep feature of the model to reconstruct the feature using the deep feature map and fused with the input state to confuse the agent. The first step of our attack method is to extract the features of deep neural network. During testing, the size of the state is $[L, W, C]$. The input of DQN algorithm to the model is four consecutive frames, so the input size to the model is $[L, W, C, D]$. Where, W is the number of pixels in the vertical direction of the state, L is the number of pixels in the horizontal direction of the state, C is the number of pixel channels, and D is the number of iterative states. We extract the deep feature image g with the size of $[1, L_1, W_1, C_1]$. Moreover, it is necessary to use double cubic interpolation to ample the feature graph to get the reconstructed feature image with the size of $[1, L, W, C]$. Next, we need to distribute the weights. First of all, we need to extract the original state S^{re} with the size of $[L, W, C, 4]$. Then turning the measure to the size of $[L, 4, B]$ by reshaping, where $B = W * C$. Next we change the figure size $[1, L, W, C]$ for reconstructing features q_s. Through the reshaping conversion, we gain the reconstructed feature gragh g_s, whose size is $[1, C, B_s]$, Then calculate the weight of channel attention. The calculation formula as follows:

$$W_{rle} = sorftmax\left(tanh\left(s^{re} \otimes g_s\right)\right) \tag{6}$$

where, $softmax(.)$ is activation function. We also need to reshape the feature of W_{rle} to gain the new size of $[1, 1, L, 4]$. What's more, it is necessary to obtain the weight of reconstructed channel spatial attention.

$$W_{rle}^{re} = W_{rle} \otimes g_m \tag{7}$$

where, W_{rle} is the weight of channel spatial attention, g_m is the feature graph after the transformation of original state space and then, further extract the deep features. First of all, it is necessary to change the size of $W_{rle}^{r}e = W_{rle}$ into $[1, B, 4]$. At the same time, the original state transition size needs to reshape into $[L, B_s, 4]$. After converting above two, activated by the function $tanh(.)$ and then get the final attentional feature:

$$W_{rle} = sorftmax(tanh\left(vec\right)) \quad where \quad vec = \frac{\sum_{i=1}^{n} Z_i}{n} \tag{8}$$

$$x = W_{rlc}^{re^*} \otimes S^{re} \tag{9}$$

where, Z_i is the average value of the second dimensional elements of x. Finally, adjust the size of W_{att} into $[1, L, W, 1]$ to get the mapping feature W_{adv}, which is the perturbation we will use. During testing, the perturbation is obtained dynamically. Running every frame of image to get a deep perturbation $\rho = W_{adv}$ based on attention, which is added to the input state to get the adversarial state:

$$s_{adv}^t = s_{re}^t + \rho^t \tag{10}$$

where, s_{adv}^t is the perturbation state at time t, s_{re}^t is the original state at time t, ρ^t is the perturbation used to generate the perturbation state at time t.

5   Experimental Evaluation

In this section, we give the experimental results of baseline methods and the attack method we proposed. At the same time, we analyze the data and curve of the experiment results.

5.1   Experimental Description

Experimental Environment: Flappybird [16] game environment based on DQN [19,20] deep reinforcement learning.

The Perturbation Limits: The usual methods of perturbation calculation include L_0 norm, L_2 norm and L_∞ norm, where norm is used to calculate the number of changes in pixel points. L_∞ norm is used to calculate the pixel, with the most perturbation. L_∞ norm is similar to euclidean distance, and the root mean square of the sum of squares of absolute values about disturbed pixel points is calculated.

Baseline Attack Method: FGSM [4], MI-FGSM [35], PGD [36].

We use gradient-based adversarial attack methods as comparative experiments. During the test, we use cross entropy between the predicted Q value and the target Q value as the loss function. Then add the gradient value of the loss function to the input state as the perturbation.

5.2   Experimental Results

The experimental environment is Flappybird game environment based on DQN algorithm. We proposed an attacking method based on attentional mechanism, named RLAT, whose core is to use deep features of neural network to generate perturbation pixel matrix for attack. The image interpolation method uses the bicubic interpolation method before channel and pixel attention in RLAT. As a comparison we use different interpolation strategies. Which include bilinear interpolation, nearest neighbor method and area interpolation. Different names are given to attack methods according to different interpolation strategies including RLAT-BI, RLAT-NN, RLAT-AI.

As a visual comparison, we present three screenshots of the game's environment in different situations. As shown in Fig. 3 below, we can see three states under different attack methods, including the state without disturbing, under RLAT method and under baseline attack methods. Figure 3(a) shows the path of the undisturbed agent. Figure 3(b) uses the attentional mechanism to attack. Under the same size of perturbation, the actions of the agent deviate greatly from the reality. As shown in Fig. 3(c), the movement direction of the attacked bird with baseline. Obviously, the bird still knows the upward movement, so the reward value is definitely higher than our attack method.

The development of computer vision provides a guarantee that RL model can achieve the desired results. And the computer's observation of the environment greatly benefits from the development of neural network. Besides, the RL model

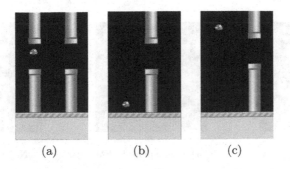

(a)   (b)   (c)

Fig. 3. Agent action visualization diagram.

based on DQN algorithm makes good use of the convolutional neural network. Each layer of convolution is related to different information about the input state. The attention of the visual neural network is useful because it helps us understand whether the network is viewing the appropriate part of the image, or whether the network is misleading. In the experiment, we paid more attention to the convolution of the last layer to obtain its gradient. Then find the average value of the gradient of the feature map. Finally we take out the activation value of the last convolutional layer. Meanwhile, we multiplied them by the average of the characteristic gradient. This process can be understood as the multiply of the importance of each channel by the convolution activation value, instead of performing weighted operations. Finally, we generated a heat map based on the obtained values, and then merged it with the original image. As shown in Fig. 4, it is the state gradient distribution map generated corresponding to various attack methods. The first four maps correspond to four different attack methods, while figure Fig. 4(a) shows the state that has not been attacked. Figure 5 is the superposition of the corresponding states in Fig. 5 and heat maps in Fig. 4. It can be seen from Fig. 5 that the neural network can focus on the aggregation part of the image, which is all around the bird besides, the main part is still the position of the bird and the part of the pipelines.

The perturbation in the experiment is calculated using l_2 norm. FGSM, MI-FGSM and PGD are used in the comparative experiment. Instead of comparing the experimental results with the results under minimum perturbation, the perturbation norm of l_2 is limited to (1.15 ± 0.1). The comparison experiments of several attack methods are given below, which are executed under the same perturbation size. In the experiment, we compare the experimental results under large perturbations, where the selection of perturbation size is also very destructive. As shown in Fig. 6, the box plots of reward values corresponding to different attack methods are given. In Fig. 6(a)–(e), the abscissa corresponds to the number of game rounds (every 50 rounds is used as the abscissa value), and the ordinate corresponds to the reward value of each round. Where, Fig. 6(b)–(e) show the reward values corresponding the different methods when the perturbation size of every attack method is (1.15 ± 0.1). Figure 6(a) is the box graph of

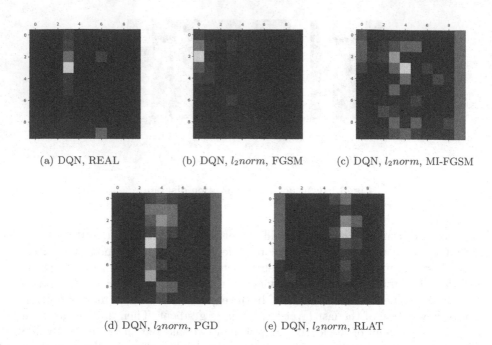

(a) DQN, REAL   (b) DQN, $l_2 norm$, FGSM   (c) DQN, $l_2 norm$, MI-FGSM

(d) DQN, $l_2 norm$, PGD   (e) DQN, $l_2 norm$, RLAT

Fig. 4. Hot map of pixel gradient distribution. The first four figures respectively correspond to different attack methods. The perturbation size is limited to the same range ($l_2(\rho) = 1.15 \pm 0.1$), which are the visual results at the end of the game after the attack. The last diagram is the undisturbed heat map.

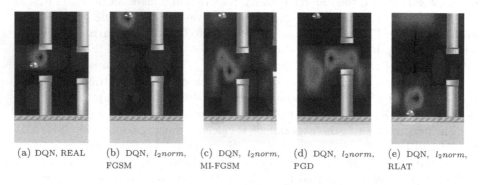

(a) DQN, REAL   (b) DQN, $l_2 norm$,   (c) DQN, $l_2 norm$,   (d) DQN, $l_2 norm$,   (e) DQN, $l_2 norm$,
                   FGSM   MI-FGSM   PGD   RLAT

Fig. 5. Visualization results after merging heat map with original image. The first four figures correspond to four different attack methods respectively, and the perturbation size is limited to the same range ($l_2(\rho) = 1.15 \pm 0.1$), which is the visualization result when the game end. The last figure is the heat map without perturbations. The figure is the superposition of the heat map corresponding states in Fig. 5.

the reward values when there is no attack. It is obvious from the figures that we can see the upper and lower bounds of the reward value, as well as some abnormal reward values. At the same time, we also give the results of several attack meth-

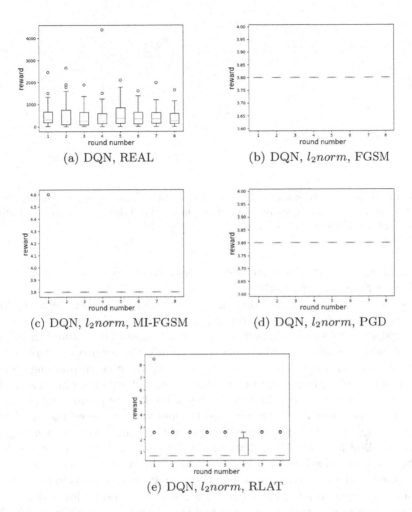

Fig. 6. Under different attack methods, the perturbation size is limited to the same size ($l_2(\rho) = 1.15$). The reward value subheading is marked with the perturbation size and the RL algorithm–DQN. The ordinate of the orange line in the figure is the median value of the corresponding data set, which is used to measure the mean value of the data set. (Color figure online)

ods in a coordinate graph, which can be well compared, shown in Fig. 7(b) and Fig. 7(d). Figure 7(a) shows the box graph of the reward value without attack. The abscissa of Fig. 6 corresponds to various attack methods. When there is no attack, we use the label "REAL" to represent it. We know that the smaller the reward value is, the worse the game effect is, and the more failures there are. From Fig. 6 and Fig. 7, we can see that the reward value obtained under RLAT attack method is smaller than other attack methods, and the upper limit of the reward value is also smaller than the corresponding reward value of other attack

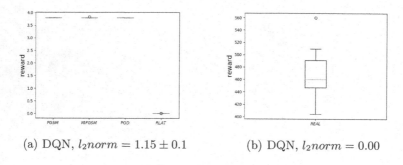

(a) DQN, $l_2norm = 1.15 \pm 0.1$ (b) DQN, $l_2norm = 0.00$

Fig. 7. Under different attack methods, different perturbations correspond to the mean value of the reward box. The data of every attack method is 8 sets of data corresponding to the average data of every 50 rounds.

methods. Therefore, our attack method is more advantageous than other attack methods under the large perturbation.

Since the attack is executed during testing, the loss gradient used by the attacker is different from the loss during model training. Therefore, we don't need to update the model parameters, only need to use the trained model to get the predicted Q value. At the same time, we use the reward value policy of the current state to obtain the maximum target Q value corresponding to the next state, and the gradient used by the gradient-based attacking method is the input gradient value corresponding to the loss of predicted Q value and target Q value. In the experiment, we also recorded the loss value between the predicted and target Q value at the end of each round of the game. As shown in Fig. 8, the corresponding loss value box diagram for different attack methods is given. In Fig. 8(a)–(e), the abscissa corresponds to the number of game runs (every 50 rounds is used as the abscissa value), and the ordinate corresponds to the reward values of each round. Where, Fig. 8(b)–(e) is the corresponding loss value when the perturbation size of each attack method is (1.15 ± 0.1), and Fig. 8(a) is the box graph of the loss values when there is no attack. From the figures, we can clearly see the upper and the lower bounds of the loss value, as well as some abnormal loss values. At the same time, we also give the results of several attack methods in a coordinate graph, which is convenient to compare shown in Fig. 9. The abscissa corresponds to various attack methods. When there is no attack, we use the label "REAL" to represent it. As can be seen from Fig. 8 and Fig. 9, compared with other attack methods, the value loss corresponding to the RLAT attack method is smaller. After that game environment is attacked, both observer and agent are difficult to know whether the environment is malicious interfered with. The FGSM attack method is more advantageous among the other attack methods. So, it can be concluded that the attack methods of RLAT and FGSM have a better ability to confuse agents. What's more, our attacking method is better than FGSM. The place where is the large loss large is just the action

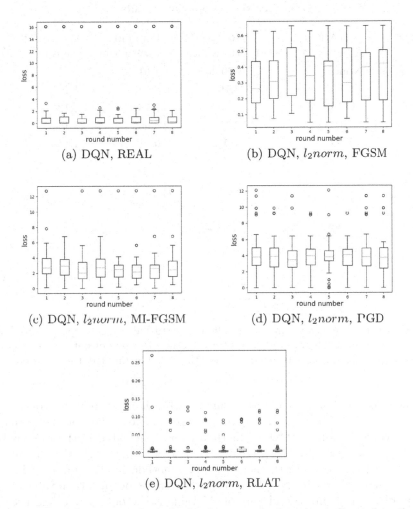

(a) DQN, REAL

(b) DQN, l_2norm, FGSM

(c) DQN, l_2norm, MI-FGSM

(d) DQN, l_2norm, PGD

(e) DQN, l_2norm, RLAT

Fig. 8. Under different attack methods, the perturbation size is limited to the same size ($l_2(\rho) = 1.15$). The subheading is marked with the perturbation size and the reinforcement learning algorithm–DQN. The ordinate of the orange line in the figure is the median value of the corresponding data set, which is used to measure the mean value of the data set. (Color figure online)

before the bird crosses the barrier, which will not have a great impact on the failure of the game. The reward value of the state crossing the barrier is very small, while the reward value of the attacked state is relatively large. Therefore, our attack method is easier to confuse agents than other attack methods under large perturbation.

According to the above experiments, we have organized and analyzed the data during the experiment. The summaries of experimental results are shown in Table 1 below. In the table, the first column is the corresponding game sce-

Table 1. Experimental data results

Game	TestAttack $l_2\left(\left(\rho\right)\right) = 1.15 \pm 0.1$	Reward (400 turns mean)	Loss (400 turns mean)	$l_2\left(\left(\rho\right)\right)$ (all steps mean)
Flappybird	None	470.20	1.61	–
	FGSM	3.79	0.34	1.151
	MI-FGSM	3.80	2.73	1.127
	PGD	3.79	3.96	1.150
	RLAT	1.052	0.013	1.150

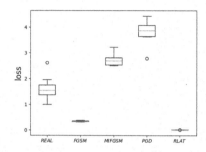

Fig. 9. Under different attack methods, different perturbations correspond to the box plot of the mean loss. The data of each attack method is 8 sets of data corresponding to the average data of every 50 rounds. Where the REAL counterpart is not attacked.

nario, the second column is the corresponding attacking methods and non-attack scenarios, and the third column is the average reward value obtained according to the corresponding attacking methods. Loss calculated in the table is the cross entropy loss between the predicted Q value and the target Q value in the experiment. RLAT refers to the new attacking method for RL proposed in this paper. The fifth column in the table corresponds to the perturbation value of our attack method, and the second part of the table is the defense method used in the experiment extension and the corresponding cross-entropy loss of the reward value.

At the same time, we also conducted a lot of experiments under different sizes of perturbation for our attacking methods. As shown in the Fig. 10 below, which is the reward value curve box figure under our attacking methods, whose vertical coordinate is the average reward value for each round and constant coordinate is the number of game rounds (take the abscissa value once every 50 rounds). If the agent hits barriers while running, the game can be counted as one round. It can be clearly seen from the Fig. 11 on the fluctuation of reward value that the larger the perturbation, the smaller the fluctuation. At the same time, we also give the results of RLAT attack method corresponding to different perturbation values on a coordinate graph, which are beneficial for comparison to find the effect of disturbance sizes on the game. In order to compare the influence of different interpolation methods on the experimental results, RLAT-BI, RLAT-

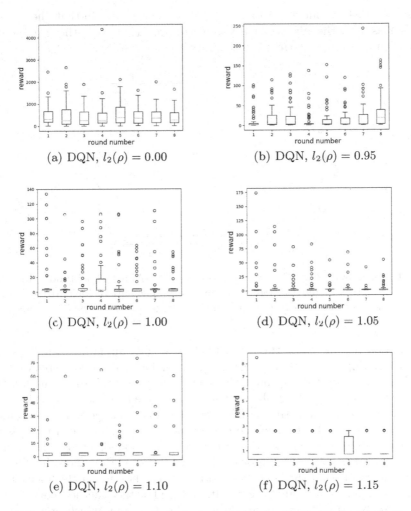

Fig. 10. Under the RLAT attack method, the reward value is obtained by using different perturbation sizes. The subheading is marked with the perturbation size and the RL algorithm -DQN. The box chart contains the maximum, minimum, median, upper quartile, lower quartile, and abnormal values of a set of data. The abnormal values are marked by dots. The ordinate of the orange line in the figure is the median value of the corresponding data set, which is used to measure the mean value of the data set. At the same time, the figure also shows the degree of dispersion of data in each group. (Color figure online)

NN and RLAT-AI attack methods are also added as comparison in Fig. 11, which used different interpolation strategies. It can be seen from the experimental results that the cumulative reward is smaller after the attack using the other interpolation methods. It also suggests that attacks are more destructive. In Fig. 11, the abscissa corresponds to the perturbation value, which is 0.00 when there is no attack. From Fig. 10 and Fig. 11, we can conclude that the reward value decreases as the disturbance value increase. Therefore, the greater the perturbation, the stronger the attack ability.

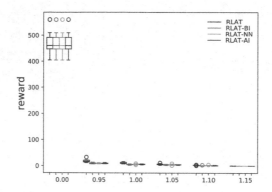

Fig. 11. Under RLAT, RLAT-BI, RLAT-NN and RLAT-AI attack methods, the mean value of the reward box under different perturbations. The data of each attack method contains eight sets of data corresponding to the average data of every 50 rounds.

In addition to comparing the reward values, we also summarize the loss values shown in Fig. 12, which is the box graph of loss values corresponding to different perturbation values under the same attack method. In the figure, the abscissa corresponds to the number of runs of the game (every 50 rounds is taken as the abscissa value), and the ordinate corresponds to the loss of each round. Figure 12(a) is a box diagram of the corresponding loss value when there is no attack, where we can clearly see the upper and lower bounds of loss values, and some abnormal loss values. It can be clearly seen from the Fig. 12 on the fluctuation of reward value that the larger the perturbation, the smaller the fluctuation. At the same time, we also give the results of RLAT attack method corresponding to different perturbation values on a coordinate graph, which are benefical for comparison to find the effect of disturbance sizes on the game. In order to compare the influence of different interpolation methods on the experimental results, RLAT-BI, RLAT-NN and RLAT-AI attack methods are also added as comparison in Fig. 13, which used different interpolation strategies. It can be seen from the experimental results that the cumulative loss is larger after the attack using the other interpolation methods. It also suggests that attacks are less hidden. The abscissa corresponds to the perturbation value, which is represented by the label "REAL" when there is no attack. From Fig. 12 and Fig. 13, we can see that the larger the perturbation value, the smaller the loss value, and the smaller the fluctuation of the loss value. It is concluded that RLAT attack method has better hidden. After comprehensive consideration, using the bicubic interpolation method to resize image and the attention mechanism to enhance the attack of RL learning scenes are more hidden and more effective. Therefore, it can be concluded from the loss value that the stronger the attack, the more

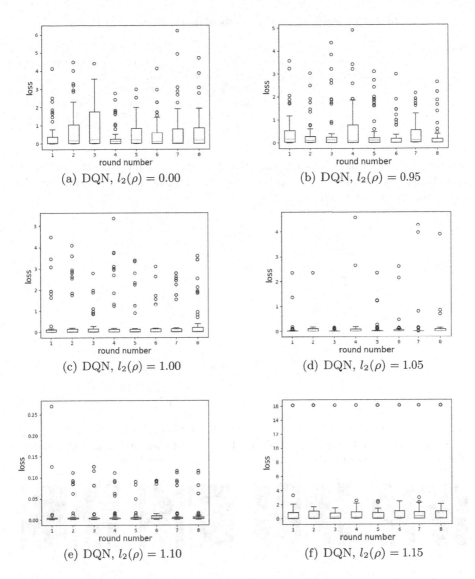

Fig. 12. Box graph under the same attack method with different values of perturbation. The subheading is marked with the perturbation size and the RL algorithm-DQN. The ordinate of the orange line in the figure is the median value of the corresponding data set, which is used to measure the mean value of the data set. (Color figure online)

likely the agent will make wrong actions and the more difficult it is to detect perturbations.

We summarize the reward value and loss value shown in Table 2 under RLAT, RLAT-BI, RLAT-NN and RLAT-AI attack methods, which record the corresponding perturbation value, reward and loss value under corresponding attack-

Table 2. Corresponding data results of different attack methods.

Attack methods		$l_2(\rho)$						$l_2(\rho)$					
		0.00	0.95	1.00	1.05	1.10	1.15	0.00	0.95	1.00	1.05	1.10	1.15
RLAT	Reward	470.20	19.12	11.24	6.59	3.10	1.025	Loss 1.61	0.64	0.45	0.42	0.012	0.013
RLAT-BI			9.90	5.43	4.32	1.72	0.70		1.07	0.65	0.44	0.16	0.002
RLAT-NN			9.26	6.33	4.18	2.48	0.70		1.07	0.64	0.52	0.41	0.002
RLAT-AI			9.99	6.24	4.57	1.84	0.70		0.97	0.69	0.49	0.10	0.002

ing method. It can also be seen from the data in the table that the larger the perturbation, the smaller the reward value, the smaller the prediction deviation of Q value and the stronger the attack.

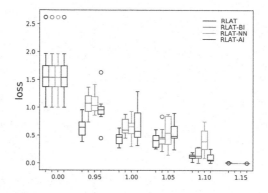

Fig. 13. Box graph of the mean loss under RLAT, RLAT-BI, RLAT-NN and RLAT-AI attack methods of different perturbations. The data of each attack method contains eight sets of data corresponding to the average data of every 50 rounds.

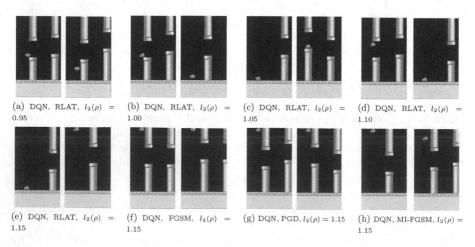

(a) DQN, RLAT, $l_2(\rho) =$ 0.95

(b) DQN, RLAT, $l_2(\rho) =$ 1.00

(c) DQN, RLAT, $l_2(\rho) =$ 1.05

(d) DQN, RLAT, $l_2(\rho) =$ 1.10

(e) DQN, RLAT, $l_2(\rho) =$ 1.15

(f) DQN, FGSM, $l_2(\rho) =$ 1.15

(g) DQN, PGD, $l_2(\rho) = 1.15$

(h) DQN, MI-FGSM, $l_2(\rho) =$ 1.15

Fig. 14. Visualization results under the different attack methods, and the figure shows several frames of the game about to fail after the attack.

5.3 Experimental Visualization Results

In the experiment, we also recorded the visual result diagram of the game operation interface shown in Fig. 14(a)–(e), which correspond to different perturbation sizes, under our attack method. Figure 14(e)–(h) show the visualization results under different attack methods, in which the perturbation range of these attack methods are same. The visual images are taken from the states where the game is about to fail, and only part of the frames are given instead of the complete video effect.

6 Conclusion

Through the above experimental analysis, we study the influence of deep features of DRL neural network model on observation of DRL environment. According to the characteristics of adversarial attack, we propose a new attack method, which no longer requires to carry out back propagation to obtain the gradient information of the target model, but only needs to extract deep features and perform feature transformation to finally obtain the perturbation so as to effectively confuse the agent. Similarly, we make the reward value obtained of each action of the agent smaller and increase the frequency of game failures by adding perturbation to the environment state of DRL, which is essentially to change the policy of the agent. The new attack method used in this experiment belongs to the white-box attack method, which needs to know various parameters of the model and DRL environment information.

In the future, the research on RL will continue to focus on improving its performance. And the research fields in RL including not only its attack and defense, algorithm improvement and optimization, training efficiency improvement, but also in the interpretability of RL model, security boundary analysis. It needs further integration into the practical application.

Acknowledgment. This research was supported by the National Natural Science Foundation of China under Grant No. 62072406, the Natural Science Foundation of Zhejiang Provincial under Grant No. LY19F020025, the Major Special Funding for "Science and Technology Innovation 2025" in Ningbo under Grant No. 2018B10063.

References

1. Sutton, R.S., Barto, A.G.: Reinforcement Learning: An Introduction. MIT Press, Cambridge (2018)
2. Peters, M., Goltz, J., Wiedenmann, S., Mundt, T.: Using machine learning to find anomalies in field bus network traffic. In: Wang, G., Feng, J., Bhuiyan, M.Z.A., Lu, R. (eds.) SpaCCS 2019. LNCS, vol. 11611, pp. 336–353. Springer, Cham (2019). https://doi.org/10.1007/978-3-030-24907-6_26
3. Szegedy, C., et al.: Intriguing properties of neural networks. arXiv preprint arXiv:1312.6199 (2013)

4. Goodfellow, I.J., Shlens, J., Szegedy, C.: Explaining and harnessing adversarial examples. arXiv preprint arXiv:1412.6572 (2014)
5. Mnih, V., et al.: Asynchronous methods for deep reinforcement learning. In: International Conference on Machine Learning, pp. 1928–1937 (2016)
6. Huang, S., Papernot, N., Goodfellow, I., Duan, Y., Abbeel, P.: Adversarial attacks on neural network policies. arXiv preprint arXiv:1702.02284 (2017)
7. Bansal, T., Pachocki, J., Sidor, S., Sutskever, I., Mordatch, I.: Emergent complexity via multi-agent competition. arXiv preprint arXiv:1710.03748 (2017)
8. Bai, X., Niu, W., Liu, J., Gao, X., Xiang, Y., Liu, J.: Adversarial examples construction towards white-box Q table variation in DQN pathfinding training. In: 2018 IEEE Third International Conference on Data Science in Cyberspace (DSC), pp. 781–787. IEEE (2018)
9. Chen, T., et al.: Gradient band-based adversarial training for generalized attack immunity of A3C path finding. arXiv preprint arXiv:1807.06752 (2018)
10. Inkawhich, M., Chen, Y., Li, H.: Snooping attacks on deep reinforcement learning. arXiv preprint arXiv:1905.11832 (2019)
11. Schulman, J., Levine, S., Abbeel, P., Jordan, M., Moritz, P.: Trust region policy optimization. In: International Conference on Machine Learning, pp. 1889–1897 (2015)
12. Lin, Y.-C., Liu, M.-Y., Sun, M., Huang, J.-B.: Detecting adversarial attacks on neural network policies with visual foresight. arXiv preprint arXiv:1710.00814 (2017)
13. Behzadan, V., Munir, A.: Vulnerability of deep reinforcement learning to policy induction attacks. In: Perner, P. (ed.) MLDM 2017. LNCS (LNAI), vol. 10358, pp. 262–275. Springer, Cham (2017). https://doi.org/10.1007/978-3-319-62416-7_19
14. Liu, J., et al.: A method to effectively detect vulnerabilities on path planning of VIN. In: Qing, S., Mitchell, C., Chen, L., Liu, D. (eds.) ICICS 2017. LNCS, vol. 10631, pp. 374–384. Springer, Cham (2018). https://doi.org/10.1007/978-3-319-89500-0_33
15. Zhao, Y., Shumailov, I., Cui, H., Gao, X., Mullins, R., Anderson, R.: Blackbox attacks on reinforcement learning agents using approximated temporal information. arXiv preprint arXiv:1909.02918 (2019)
16. Ebeling-Rump, M., Kao, M., Hervieux-Moore, Z.: Applying q-learning to flappy bird. Department of Mathematics and Statistics, Queens University (2016)
17. Ma, K., Jiang, R., Dong, M., Jia, Y., Li, A.: Neural network based web log analysis for web intrusion detection. In: Wang, G., Atiquzzaman, M., Yan, Z., Choo, K.-K.R. (eds.) SpaCCS 2017. LNCS, vol. 10658, pp. 194–204. Springer, Cham (2017). https://doi.org/10.1007/978-3-319-72395-2_19
18. Yan, X., Cui, B., Li, J.: Malicious domain name recognition based on deep neural networks. In: Wang, G., Chen, J., Yang, L.T. (eds.) SpaCCS 2018. LNCS, vol. 11342, pp. 497–505. Springer, Cham (2018). https://doi.org/10.1007/978-3-030-05345-1_43
19. Mnih, V., et al.: Playing atari with deep reinforcement learning. arXiv preprint arXiv:1312.5602 (2013)
20. Mnih, V., et al.: Human-level control through deep reinforcement learning. Nature 518(7540), 529–533 (2015)
21. Carlini, N., Wagner, D.: Towards evaluating the robustness of neural networks. In: 2017 IEEE Symposium on Security and Privacy (SP), pp. 39–57. IEEE (2017)
22. Kos, J., Song, D.: Delving into adversarial attacks on deep policies. arXiv preprint arXiv:1705.06452 (2017)

23. Lin, Y.-C., Hong, Z.-W., Liao, Y.-H., Shih, M.-L., Liu, M.-Y., Sun, M.: Tactics of adversarial attack on deep reinforcement learning agents. arXiv preprint arXiv:1703.06748 (2017)

24. Xiang, Y., Niu, W., Liu, J., Chen, T., Han, Z.: A PCA-based model to predict adversarial examples on q-learning of path finding. In: 2018 IEEE Third International Conference on Data Science in Cyberspace (DSC), pp. 773–780. IEEE (2018)

25. Chatterjee, P., Yalchin, A., Shelton, J., Roy, K., Yuan, X., Edoh, K.D.: Presentation attack detection using wavelet transform and deep residual neural net. In: Wang, G., Feng, J., Bhuiyan, M.Z.A., Lu, R. (eds.) SpaCCS 2019. LNCS, vol. 11637, pp. 86–94. Springer, Cham (2019). https://doi.org/10.1007/978-3-030-24900-7_7

26. Tretschk, E., Oh, S.J., Fritz, M.: Sequential attacks on agents for long-term adversarial goals. arXiv preprint arXiv:1805.12487 (2018)

27. Russo, A., Proutiere, A.: Optimal attacks on reinforcement learning policies. arXiv preprint arXiv:1907.13548 (2019)

28. Gu, Z., Jia, Z., Choset, H.: Adversary A3C for robust reinforcement learning. arXiv preprint arXiv:1912.00330 (2019)

29. Fischer, M., Mirman, M., Vechev, M.: Online robustness training for deep reinforcement learning. arXiv preprint arXiv:1911.00887 (2019)

30. Behzadan, V., Munir, A.: Mitigation of policy manipulation attacks on deep q-networks with parameter-space noise. In: Gallina, B., Skavhaug, A., Schoitsch, E., Bitsch, F. (eds.) SAFECOMP 2018. LNCS, vol. 11094, pp. 406–417. Springer, Cham (2018). https://doi.org/10.1007/978-3-319-99229-7_34

31. Havens, A., Jiang, Z., Sarkar, S.: Online robust policy learning in the presence of unknown adversaries. In: Advances in Neural Information Processing Systems, pp. 9916–9926 (2018)

32. Lee, X.Y., Havens, A., Chowdhary, G., Sarkar, S.: Learning to cope with adversarial attacks. arXiv preprint arXiv:1906.12061 (2019)

33. Lütjens, B., Everett, M., How, J.P.: Certified adversarial robustness for deep reinforcement learning. arXiv preprint arXiv:1910.12908 (2019)

34. Bahdanau, D., Cho, K., Bengio, Y.: Neural machine translation by jointly learning to align and translate. arXiv preprint arXiv:1409.0473 (2014)

35. Dong, Y., et al.: Boosting adversarial attacks with momentum. In: Proceedings of the IEEE Conference on Computer Vision and Pattern Recognition, pp. 9185–9193 (2018)

36. Madry, A., Makelov, A., Schmidt, L., Tsipras, D., Vladu, A.: Towards deep learning models resistant to adversarial attacks. arXiv preprint arXiv:1706.06083 (2017)

Attribute-Based Searchable Encryption Scheme with Fuzzy Keywords

Xinyu Song, Zhan Zhou, Weijie Duan, Zhongyi Liu, and Chungen Xu[✉]

School of Science, Nanjing University of Science and Technology,
Nanjing 210094, China
853223876@qq.com, zhouzhan58@126.com, 1092523436@qq.com,
ZhongyiLiu950217@outlook.com, xuchung@njust.edu.cn

Abstract. With the rapid development of cloud computing technology, users prefer cloud servers to store data. Scholars have proposed many searchable encryption schemes to ensure the confidentiality and search ability of the data. Based on the existing scheme, this paper proposes a new attribute-based searchable encryption scheme with fuzzy keywords. The primary purpose of this scheme is to achieve user access control and fuzzy keyword search. In this scheme, a tree-shaped access structure is used to implement the user's access control, and only the user whose attributes meet the requirements can perform search operations. Fuzzy multi-keyword search can be achieved by using a collision-free hash function and a secure KNN encryption method. Through security analysis, this scheme satisfies the confidentiality of index and search trapdoors. There is also no relevance in search trapdoors, and this scheme achieves CPA security.

Keywords: Searchable encryption · Attribute-based encryption · Fuzzy keywords · Multiple keywords

1 Introduction

With the rapid development of cloud computing technology in recent years, thanks to the flexibility and speed of cloud servers, more and more users tend to store data in cloud servers. Cloud servers not only reduce storage space and management overhead on local servers, but also achieve data sharing at the same time. To solve the security problems of the cloud server, the data must be encrypted before uploaded to the cloud server, but this also brings specific difficulties to the retrieval of cloud services.

In 2000, Song et al. [1] proposed a ciphertext searchable encryption scheme. In this scheme, data is stored in a cloud server in the form of the ciphertext, and only legitimate users have retrieval capabilities. In 2005, Sahai et al. [2] proposed an attribute-based encryption scheme to generalize user identity information to attributes related to the user's identity. Subsequently, according to the different

© Springer Nature Switzerland AG 2021
G. Wang et al. (Eds.): SpaCCS 2020, LNCS 12382, pp. 44–61, 2021.
https://doi.org/10.1007/978-3-030-68851-6_3

manifestations and application scenarios of the ciphertext and the key, attribute-based encryption of key strategy (KP-ABE) [3] and attribute-based encryption of ciphertext strategy (CP-ABE) [4] were proposed.

In addition to implementing access control for users, how to expand the query method of single keyword exact matching in the basic scheme to meet wider query needs is also an important research direction of searchable encryption. In 2004, GolleP [5] proposed a keyword retrieval scheme to realize the retrieval of multiple keywords. Li et al. [6] proposed a fuzzy keyword retrieval scheme in 2010. Ref. [20, 21] also proposed different fuzzy keyword search methods later in 2013, respectively implementing a single sortable fuzzy keyword search and verifiable fuzzy keyword search scheme.

In 2014, Li Shuang et al. [10] proposed an attribute-based searchable encryption scheme, which combines searchable technology and attribute-based encryption technology, breaking the previous "one-to-one" communication method. In the same year, Ref. [15] proposed a searchable encryption scheme that achieves the access control to users and the retrieval of multiple keywords. Ref. [24] proposed a multi-server multi-keyword searchable encryption scheme, which uses multiple servers to store data and conducts multi-keyword searches. This scheme only stores data messages in the form of the ciphertext to the cloud servers, but it cannot search for all messages. This scheme only supports searching for multiple precise keywords. In 2019, Ref. [26] proposed an authorized searchable encryption scheme under a multi-authority setting, which allowed the authorization process to be performed only once on policies from multiple permissions. Ref. [25] proposed a practical multi-client dynamic searchable encryption system, which provided fine-grained access control through attributes based on encryption and the number theory technique.

Although the schemes above provide us with ways to achieve the access control and the keyword retrieval, there are still some problems that have not been solved. In the traditional attribute-based encryption scheme, most of them are single-keyword or multi-precision keyword retrieval with low fault-tolerance. Once data users make mistakes in keywords, they cannot get the correct results. The best way to solve this problem is to implement a fuzzy keyword encryption scheme. However, most of the existing schemes fail to combine the attributes and the fuzzy keyword retrieval well. How to design a scheme to achieve fuzzy keyword retrieval while achieving access control is very important.

In this paper, we propose an attribute-based fuzzy multi-keyword searchable encryption scheme based on existing research, using an access tree to achieve user access control and wildcards to construct fuzzy sets of modular keywords. We also use hash functions and the KNN encryption method to realize a fuzzy multi-keyword search. In our scheme, the data owner encrypts the message and customizes the access structure, generates a secure index and uploads it to the cloud server. When data users need a specific data file, they need to upload search credentials and search trapdoors to a specific server. Only when the data user's attributes meet the access structure can the search server implement search, and finally the storage server returns the relevant ciphertext. The ciphertext is decrypted by the data user.

The remaining of this paper is as follows. In Sect. 2, we roughly introduce the existing research results and their shortcomings. We propose the scheme formalization and security model in Sect. 3. Section 4 gives the preliminary knowledge. In Sect. 5, we present the corresponding algorithm in detail. Then we conducted the security analysis in Sect. 6. Section 7 gives a performance analysis of our scheme. Finally, a summarization of the scheme is given.

2   Related Works

In this section, we will briefly review the existing achievements on searchable encryption, attribute-based encryption, and fuzzy multi-keyword queries.

2.1   Searchable Encryption

In 2000, the one-to-one searchable encryption mechanism was first proposed by Song et al. [1]. They encrypted the plaintext files separately. By scanning the entire encrypt file and comparing it with the ciphertext, the keywords are confirmed and the number of occurrences is counted, but this scheme requires a lot of computing resources. Goh [7] proposed an index-based searchable encryption scheme. This scheme stores the keywords of a single file in the file index and implements search with the help of Bloom filter operations. The many-to-one searchable encryption scheme was proposed by Boneh et al. [8] in 2004 They gave the constitution of searchable encryption based on public keys and the proof of its security. Subsequently, searchable encryption based on connection keywords [5,9] and other schemes were proposed. Searchable encryption technology has been greatly developed.

2.2   Attribute-Based Encryption

Attribute-based encryption is developed from Fuzzy Identity-based Encryption (Fuzzy-IBE). In Ref. [2], Sahai and Waters first proposed attribute-based (ABE) encryption, which nested attributes of users in ciphertext or keys to achieving access control to users. Still, this scheme can only support the threshold strategy. In order to express a more flexible access control strategy, scholars proposed two types of ABE mechanisms: key strategy attribute encryption (KP-ABE) [3] and ciphertext strategy attribute encryption (CP-ABE) [4]. After that, BALU et al. [11] and HUR et al. [12] proposed a hidden strategy based on a tree structure. LAI et al. [22] and WANG et al. [23] proposed a strategy hiding scheme based on linear secret sharing structure.

In 2014, Li Shuang et al. [10] proposed an attribute-based searchable encryption scheme that used access trees to control access of users and achieve fine-grained and secure sharing of keyword ciphertext, but the scheme cannot give support to the user automatically generating search credentials. In Ref. [28], a novel fuzzy ABAC model (FABAC) was proposed that introduced the fuzzy mechanism into decision-making process to attain better tradeoff between security and usability. Ref. [13] proposed a multi-server searchable ciphertext policy attribute-based encryption scheme based on authorization. Using multiple attribute authorization agencies to solve the problem of user key leakage, but this scheme only supports "and" and "or" access strategies and only supports a single precise keyword search.

2.3   Fuzzy Multi-keyword Query

After the searchable encryption method was first proposed by Song et al. [1], Park et al. [5,9] proposed a searchable encryption based on connection keywords. Cao and Wang et al. [14] proposed a multi-keyword searchable encryption scheme. This scheme constructs vectors for indexes and keywords during searching and realizes multi-keyword searching through vector operations. In Ref. [15], the author introduced attribute-based encryption technology into the multi-keyword search and authorized users through attribute certificates. But this scheme only supports the retrieval of precise keywords.

Li et al. [6] first proposed a fuzzy single-keyword retrieval scheme based on wildcards in 2010. However, if multiple keyword searches were to be performed, the algorithm required multiple rounds. Ref. [16] proposed a fuzzy query method (MFS) that supports multiple keywords, but the use of Bloom filter results in low accuracy. In Ref. [17], the author proposed an improved fuzzy multi-keyword query method, which used collision-free hash function to construct multiple keywords in the same fixed-length vector and used the safe KNN technology to achieve fuzzy multi-keyword query. However, this scheme only gives a search model of keywords, and can not achieve user access control. Ref. [27] proposed a verifiable encryption scheme supporting fuzzy Search. Through principle of matrix operations, it realizes the fuzzy retrieval over encrypted data, and enables the user to verify the correctness of the retrieval results efficiently.

3   Scheme Formalization and Security Model

This paper proposes an attribute-based searchable encryption scheme with fuzzy keywords. As shown in Fig. 1, this scheme includes the following six parties: Multi-attribute Authorization Center, Data Owner, Data User, Verification Server, Search Server, and Storage Server. These parties can be described as follows:

- Multi-attribute Authorization Center: We suppose that it is trusted. It is responsible for generating the system master key and public parameters, managing system attributes, and distributing private keys for Data User.
- Data Owner: Encrypt the message and upload the customized access structure to Storage Server to help Data User generate some private keys. Generate an encrypted index of keywords and upload it to Search Server.

- Data User: Generate search credentials and trapdoor information based on the private key and public parameters of the system. Decrypt the ciphertext returned by Storage Server to get the plaintext.
- Verification Server: Verify the attributes of Data User based on the search credentials. Only when the attributes satisfy the access structure, Search Server will perform the search based on the trapdoor information.
- Search Server: When the attributes of Verification Server are verified, Search Server will perform a file search based on the trapdoor information.
- Storage Server: Store the ciphertext and return the corresponding ciphertext to Data User according to the search results of Search Server.

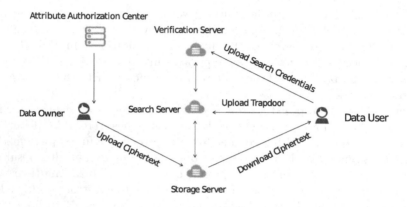

Fig. 1. System architecture

3.1   Concepts of the Scheme Formalization

The multi-server attribute-based fuzzy keyword encryption scheme proposed in this paper includes the following basic algorithms: System Setup, Key Generation, Encrypt, Trapdoor Generation, Test, Search, Decrypt.

- **Setup**$(\lambda, U) \to (msk, params)$: Executed by the attribute authority, take the system security parameters λ and global attribute set U as input to obtain the system master key msk and the public parameter $params$.
- **KeyGen**$(msk, params, L) \to (SK, SK_1, PK_1)$: Verification Server and Search Server generate its public key PK_1 and private key SK_1. Data User and Multi-Attribute Authorization Center jointly generate the user's private key SK.
- **Encrypt**$(m, W, w, params) \to (C_0, C_1, \{C_{i,j,1}, C_{i,j,2}\}, \gamma, I)$: Data Owner selects the message m to be encrypted and chooses the access strategy W to customize the access tree γ. Data Owner also selects keywords w to generate an encrypted index I and uploads it to the server.

- **TokenGen**$(PK_1, SK, \widetilde{w}) \rightarrow (TK, Q)$: Data User generates search credentials TK based on his/her private key SK and the server's public key PK_1. Trapdoor Q is generated based on his/her own private key SK, and the fuzzy keyword set $\widetilde{w}$ to be queried.
- **Test**$(TK, C_0, \gamma) \rightarrow b$: Verification Server performs attribute verification based on the search credentials obtained from Data User.
- **Search**$(Q, I) \rightarrow M$: When the verification of the user's attribute is passed, Search Server searches the ciphertext according to the trapdoor information Q and the encrypted index I. Storage Server sends the corresponding ciphertext M to Data User according to the search results.
- **Decrypt**$(M, SK) \rightarrow m$: Data User decrypts the ciphertext M according to the private key SK to obtain the message m.

3.2 Security Model

If an attacker's advantage $Adv_{Ad(k)}$ in the security game is negligible, then the scheme is called CPA security. The following is the construction process of choosing the plaintext security model in the security game plan. Let the attacker be Ad and the challenger be C. The specific game process is as follows:

(1) Initial: Attacker Ad sends the challenge structure W^* to Challenger C.
(2) Setup: C runs the Setup algorithm to obtain the public parameters of the scheme $params = \{Y, e, g, G_1, G_2, T_{i,j}\}$ and sends it to Ad.
(3) Phase 1: Ad can make multiple inquiries in any polynomial time.
  Private key query: Ad asks C about the private key of the selected attribute set Att. C runs Key Generation algorithm and sends the private attribute key $SK^* = \left\{ d_1^*, d_0, \left\{ d_{i,j,1}^*, d_{i,j,2}^* \right\}_{i \in (1,n), j \in (1,n_i)} \right\}$ to Ad.
  Search credential query: C runs Trapdoor Generation algorithm to output search credential $TK^* = \left\{ T_1, T_2^*, T_3, T_4^*, \left\{ d_{i,j,1}'^*, d_{i,j,2}'^* \right\}_{i \in (1,n), j \in (1,n_i)} \right\}$ and send it to Ad.
(4) Challenge: Ad submits two equal-length messages m_0 and m_1 to C. C encrypts the message m_ζ, $\zeta \in \{0,1\}$, and sends the challenged ciphertext C_0^* and M^* to attacker Ad.
(5) Phase 2: The attacker repeats the operations of the inquiry phase 1.
(6) Guess: Ad outputs a pair of guesses of ζ. If $\zeta = \zeta'$, then Ad successfully obtains a valid ciphertext of any message, and the advantage of successful guessing is defined as $Adv_{Ad} = \left| Pr\left[\zeta = \zeta' \right] - \frac{1}{2} \right| = \epsilon$.

3.3 Goals of the Scheme

The designed attribute-based fuzzy multi-keyword scheme should achieve the following secure and functional goals:

(1) Data and query privacy: The privacy of the data stored in the data storage must be guaranteed; that is, the cloud server cannot learn any underlying information except the encrypted data and the query itself.

(2) User access control: Only users who meet the attribute requirements can perform ciphertext retrieval.

(3) Fuzzy multi-keyword search: Users are allowed to have a certain fault tolerance rate when performing a multi-keyword search.

4   Preliminaries

4.1   Explanation of Main Symbols

Definitions of symbols are shown in Table 1.

Table 1. Explanation of symbols

Symbol	Explanation
$U = \{att_1, att_2, \ldots, att_n\}$	Global attribute collection
msk	System master key
$params$	System public parameters
Pk_1	Server public key
Sk_1	Server private key
$L = \{l_1, l_2, \ldots, l_n\}$	User's attribute set
SK	User's private key
m	Plaintext
W	Access strategy
$w = \{w_1, w_2, \ldots, w_{n'}\}$	Keyword set
$I = (I_a, I_b)$	Encrypted index
TK	Search credential
$\widetilde{w} = \{\widetilde{w}_1, \widetilde{w}_2, \ldots, \widetilde{w}_{n'}\}$	Query keyword set
$Q = (Q_a, Q_b)$	Trapdoor information

4.2   Bilinear Map

Let G_1 and G_2 be two multiplicative cyclic groups with the prime order P, and set the generator of group G_1 to be g. There exists a bilinear map e: $G_1 \times G_1 \to G_2$ that satisfies the following properties [18]:

(1) Bilinearity: for all $x, y \in G_1$, $a, b \in Z_P$, there is $e\left(x^a, y^b\right) = e\left(x^b, y^a\right) = e\left(x, y\right)^{ab}$.

(2) Non-degeneracy: there is $e\left(g, g\right) \neq 1$, where 1 is the unit of G_2.

(3) Computability: for all $x, y \in G_1$, there is an effective polynomial time algorithm for calculating $e\left(x, y\right) \in G_2$.

4.3 Difficult Problems in Cryptography

The security of this scheme is based on the difficult problems of cryptography, and then we define these problems.

(1) BDH problem [19]: Definite $e\colon G_1 \times G_1 \to G_2$ to be a bilinear pair. With a given quadruple (g, g^a, g^b, g^c) where $a, b, c \in Z_P$ are unknown, calculate $e(g,g)^{abc} \in G_2$.

(2) DBDH problem: Definite $e\colon G_1 \times G_2 \to G_T$ to be a bilinear pair. Select the generator $P \in G_1, Q \in G_2$ and randomly choose $a, b, c \in Z_P^*$, $A = P^a$, $B = P^b$, $C = Q^c$, $Z = e(P,Q)^d$. Determine whether d is equal to abc.

4.4 Fuzzy Set Construction

In this scheme, we use wildcards to construct fuzzy sets of keywords. Wildcards $*$ are used to indicate all editing operations at each position of the keyword, including replacement, insertion, and deletion. Then the fuzzy keyword set corresponding to the keyword w can be expressed as $S_{w,d} = \{S'_{w,0}, S'_{w,1}, \dots, S'_{w,r}, \dots, S'_{w,\Lambda}\}$.

4.5 Access Tree Construction

In this paper, an access tree is used to implement user access control [10]. Each non-leaf node in the tree represents a threshold described by child nodes and thresholds. The threshold of node x is denoted by k_x and the number of child nodes is recorded as num_x, satisfying $1 \leqslant k_x \leqslant num_x$. In particular, the "or" gate is represented when $k_x = 1$, and the "and" gate is represented when $k_x = num_x$. Leaf nodes are related to attributes and the threshold is equal to 1.

Let the root node of the access tree be r, and the hidden secret be β. The access tree numbers the child nodes of each node; that is, the child nodes are numbered from l to num. We use the recursive algorithm to establish the access tree starting from the root node, and we randomly select a polynomial q_x for each node x from top to bottom. Then the order d_x and threshold k_x satisfy the relation $d_x = k_x - 1$. For the root node, we have $q_r(0) = \beta$. The remaining d_r points are randomly selected. The other node x set value $q_x(0) = q_{parent(x)}(index(x))$ down from the root node, where $parent(x)$ represents the parent node of x and $index(x)$ represents the number of the child node, and the remaining d_x points are randomly selected.

After the above operations, all polynomials are determined. For each leaf node x, it is related to the attribute. So far, with the above algorithm, we can generate an access tree for user access control.

4.6 Secure KNN Encryption Method

In 2009, Wong W K et al. [29] proposed the Secure KNN computing method for encrypted data. In this paper, we use this method to build security index. I is the vector to be encrypted and Q is the query vector. Let $S' \in \{0,1\}^d$ be a bit string of length d and randomly select $d \times d$ invertible matrix M_1 and M_2. For loop variable k from 1 to d, if $S'[k] = 1$, then $I[k]$ is randomly decomposed into $I_a[k]$ and $I_b[k]$. If $S'[k] = 0$, then $I[k] = I_a[k] = I_b[k]$.

According to the above rules, I will be divided into two vectors I_a and I_b. The final encrypted index is $I' = (I'_a, I'_b)$. Which satisfies $I'_a = M_1^T I_a$ and $I'_b = M_2^T I_b$. Use the same method on Q and we have $Q' = (Q'_a, Q'_b)$, satisfying $Q'_a = M_1^{-1} Q_a$ and $Q'_b = M_2^{-1} Q_b$. We can find that

$$
\begin{aligned}
{I'_a}^T \cdot Q'_a + {I'_b}^T \cdot Q'_b &= \left(M_1^T I_a\right)^T \cdot \left(M_1^{-1} Q_a\right) + \left(M_2^T I_b\right)^T \cdot \left(M_2^{-1} Q_b\right) \\
&= I_a^T \cdot Q_a + I_b^T Q_b = I^T Q
\end{aligned}
\tag{1}
$$

The dot product of encrypted index and query index is equivalent to the dot product of original vector and query vector. However, due to the original vector and the invertible matrix conducting multiplication operation and getting a new vector, it will hide the real vector.

5   Attribute-Based Searchable Encryption Scheme with Fuzzy Keywords

In this section, we will give the specific algorithm of this scheme.

(1) System Setup: The algorithm is first executed by N attribute authority centers AA_i. The security parameters λ is taken as input. Selects the group G_1 and G_2 of the order P. The generator of the bilinear map G_1 is denoted by g. Each AA_i selects $\alpha_k \in Z_P$ ($k \in \{1, 2, \ldots, N\}$) randomly and then calculates $Y_k = e(g,g)^{\alpha_k}$ and sends it to all other attribute authorities. Let

$$
Y = \prod_{k=1}^{N} Y_k = e(g,g)^{\sum_{k=1}^{N} \alpha_k}
\tag{2}
$$

AA_i selects $t_{i,j} \in Z_P^*$ ($i \in (1,n), j \in (1, n_i)$) for $att_1, att_2, \cdots, att_n$ randomly and calculate $T_{i,j} = g^{t_{i,j}}$. Data owner randomly chooses $r \in Z_P^*$. After $d_1 = g^r$ is calculated and it is sent to the user.

Then the system master key msk which is kept by the multi-attribute authority and the public system parameters $params$ are output.

$$
\begin{aligned}
msk &= \{\alpha_k, r\} \\
params &= \{Y, e, g, G_1, G_2, T_{i,j}\}
\end{aligned}
\tag{3}
$$

(2) Key Generation: The key generation is divided into two steps.
Step1: The Verification Server and the Search Server separately select random $a, b \in Z_P^*$ as their private keys. The public key is:

$$
PK_1 = g^{ab}
\tag{4}
$$

The private key is output as followed.

$$SK_1 = ab \tag{5}$$

Step2: Let $L = \{l_1, l_2, \ldots l_n\}$ be the attribute set of user, the authority center AA_i selects random $\lambda_i \in Z_P^*$. Make calculations of $d_{i,j,1} = g^{r + \lambda_i t_{i,j}}$, $d_{i,j,2} = g^{\lambda_i}$ ($i \in (1, n)$, $j \in (1, n_i)$), $d_0^k = g^{\alpha_k}$, and the authority center sends the attribute private key component to the data user. After calculating $d_0 = \prod_{k=1}^{N} d_0^k = g^{\sum_{k=1}^{N} \alpha_k}$, the user's private key is:

$$SK = \left\{ d_1, d_0, \{d_{i,j,1}, d_{i,j,2}\}_{i \in (1,n), j \in (1, n_i)} \right\} \tag{6}$$

(3) Encrypt: The encryption algorithm is divided into three steps: ciphertext encryption, access tree generation and query keyword index encryption.

Step1: Data Owner selects message $m \in G_1$ and random $\beta \in Z_P^*$. Calculate:

$$C_0 = g^\beta, \ C_1 = mY^\beta \tag{7}$$

Step2: Data Owner chooses the access strategy W. The root node of the access tree is r and the secret is β. The recursive algorithm is used to generate the access tree γ. For leaf nodes $i \in attr(x)$, we have

$$C_{i,j,1} = g^{q_x(0)}, \ C_{i,j,2} = T_{i,j}^{q_x(0)}, i \in (1, n), j \in (1, n_i) \tag{8}$$

Step3: Data Owner randomly selects invertible matrixs $M_{1_{d \times d}}$ and $M_{2_{d \times d}}$. $S' \in \{0, 1\}^d$ is a bit string of length d. $P = \{P_1, \ldots, P_L\}$ represents a set of L prime numbers. The set of L random characters is denoted by $S = \{S_1, \ldots, S_L\}$ and k_f is a character string with a length of K bit.

Data Owner chooses keyword set $w = \{w_1, \ldots, w_{n'}\}$. We assume that $|w[j]|$ indicates the length of the jth keyword, $w[j](l)$ represents the lth letter of the jth keyword, and the maximum length of the keyword is denoted by L. W is padded by $S = \{S_1, \ldots, S_L\}$ to make the length of the keyword to be L, so as to hide the length of each keyword. Construct a d-dimensional vector p for w and initialize each element to 1. For $1 \leqslant l \leqslant L$, calculate:

$$position_l = \begin{cases} H(j, w[j](l)) & l \in [1, |w[j]|] \\ H(j, S[l - |w[j]|]) & l \in [|w[j]|, L] \end{cases} \tag{9}$$

In this equation, $|w[j]|$ refers to the length of the keywords without padding characters and $position_l$ represents the $position_l$-th position of the d-dimensional vector p. H is a collision-free hash function. Output the value of $position_l$ position of p: $p[position_l] = p[position_l] \times P_l$.

For loop variable k from 1 to d, if $S'[k] = 1$, then $p[k]$ is randomly decomposed into $p_a[k]$ and $p_b[k]$, satisfying $p[k] = p_a[k] + p_b[k]$. When $S'[k] = 0$, then $p[k] = p_a[k] = p_b[k]$. According to the above rules, it will divide p into two vectors, p_a and p_b. The final encrypted index is $I = (I_a, I_b)$, satisfying $I_a = M_1^T p_a$, $I_b = M_2^T p_b$.

Finally, the data owner uploads the ciphertext, access structure and encrypted index to the server.

(4) Trapdoor Generation: There are two sections of this algorithm.

1) Data User input PK_1 and SK, select $\mu \in Z_P^*$ randomly. Let $T_1 = g^{ab\mu}, T_2 = g^{\lambda_i\mu}, T_3 = T_{i,j}^{\mu} = g^{t_{i,j}\mu}, T_4 = d_0^{\mu}, d\prime_{i,j,1} = g^{(r+\lambda_i t_{i,j})\mu}, d\prime_{i,j,2} = g^{\lambda_i r\mu}$. Then the search credential is

$$TK = \left\{ T_1, T_2, T_3, T_4, \{d\prime_{i,j,1}, d\prime_{i,j,2}\}_{i\in(1,n), j\in(1,n_i)} \right\} \tag{10}$$

2) Data User sends search request to Data Owner and then Data Owner sends $sk = \{M_1, M_2, S\prime, S, P, k_f\}$ to the user. User chooses keyword set $\widetilde{w} = \{\widetilde{w}_1, \ldots, \widetilde{w}_{n'}\}$ to query. Fill $\widetilde{w}$ with $S = \{S_1, \ldots, S_L\}$ to make the length of the keyword queried to be L, thereby hiding the length of each keyword. The Data Owner constructs a d-dimensional vector $\widetilde{p}$ for $\widetilde{w}_i$, in which each element is initialized to 1. For $1 \leqslant l \leqslant L$, if $\widetilde{w}[l] \neq *$, calculate:

$$position_l = \begin{cases} H(j, \widetilde{w}[j](l)) & l \in [1, |\widetilde{w}[j]|] \\ H(j, S[l - |\widetilde{w}[j]|]) & l \in [|\widetilde{w}[j]|, L] \end{cases} \tag{11}$$

Here $|\widetilde{w}[j]|$ refers to the length of the queried keyword without the filler character, $position_l$ represents the $position_l$-th bit of the d-dimensional vector $\widetilde{p}$. H is a collision-free hash function. The value is $\widetilde{p}[position_l] = \widetilde{p}[position_l] \times \frac{1}{P_l}$. If $\widetilde{w}[l] = *$, then $position_{l1} = F_{k_f}(\prime a \prime), \ldots, position_{l26} = F_{k_f}(\prime z \prime)$, where $position_{l1}$ represents the $position_l th$ bit of the d-dimensional vector $\widetilde{p}$, and F_{k_f} is a pseudo-random function. Then calculate $\widetilde{p}[position_{lk}] = \widetilde{p}[position_{lk}] \times \frac{1}{P_l}$ with k from 1 loop to 26.

Select the prime number v randomly and we have $q = v\widetilde{p}$. For the loop variable k from 1 to d, if $S\prime[k] = 0$, then $q[k]$ is randomly divided into $q_a[k]$ and $q_b[k]$, satisfying $q[k] = q_a[k] + q_b[k]$. If $S\prime[k] = 1$, then $q[k] = q_a[k] = q_b[k]$. Divide q into two vectors q_a and q_b. According to the above rules, the final trapdoor is:

$$Q = (Q_a, Q_b), \quad Q_a = M_1^{-1}q_a, Q_b = M_2^{-1}q_b. \tag{12}$$

(5) Test: The Verification Server verifies whether the attributes of the Data User meet the requirements of the access tree based on the search credentials and the access tree.

Define a recursive algorithm $DecryptNode(x)$. When x is a leaf node and its attribute is i, then there is

$$DecryptNode(x) = \begin{cases} \dfrac{e\left(C_{i,j,1}, d'_{i,j,1}\right)}{e\left(C_{i,j,2}, d'_{i,j,2}\right)} & i \in U \\ \bot & i \notin U \end{cases} \tag{13}$$

When x is not a leaf node, for all child nodes z, if there is a node set S_x of the arbitrary size k_x and all the nodes are child nodes of x. Let $i = index(x)$, $S\prime_x = \{index(z) | z \in S_x\}$. k_x is the threshold of the node and we have

$$DecryptNode\,(x) = \prod_{z \in S_x} DecryptNode\,(z)^{\Delta_{i,S'_x}(0)}$$

$$= \prod_{z \in S_x} \left(e\,(g,g)^{\mu q_z(0)} \right)^{\Delta_{i,S'_x}(0)}$$

$$= \prod_{z \in S_x} \left(e\,(g,g)^{\mu q_{parent(z)}(index(z))} \right)^{\Delta_{i,S'_x}(0)}$$

$$= \prod_{z \in S_x} e\,(g,g)^{\mu q_x(i)^{\Delta_{i,S'_x}(0)}} = e\,(g,g)^{\mu q_x(0)} \qquad (14)$$

$\Delta_{i,S'_x}(0)$ is the Lagrange coefficient. Otherwise outputs $\perp$ by the recursive function.

In summary, the complete definition of function $DecryptNode\,(x)$ has been obtained, and $DecryptNode\,(r) = e\,(g,g)^{\mu\beta}$ can be calculated if and only if the attributes satisfy the access tree. Let

$$E = \frac{e\,(C_0, T_2)\,e\,(T_1, T_3)}{e\,(T_2, T_3^{ab})} \qquad (15)$$

Determine whether E is equal to $DecryptNode\,(r)$. If it is equal to $DecryptNode\,(r)$, then return value $b = 1$, otherwise $b = 0$.

(6) Search: When the Verification Server returns the value $b = 1$, the search server performs a ciphertext search based on the trapdoor of the user. Calculate the dot product of the trapdoor $Q = (Q_a, Q_b)$ and the encrypted index $I = (I_a, I_b)$.

$$I_a Q_a + I_b Q_b = \left(M_1^T p_a \right) \cdot \left(M_1^{-1} q_a \right) + \left(M_2^T p_b \right) \cdot \left(M_2^{-1} q_b \right)$$

$$= p_a^T \cdot q_a + p_b^T \cdot q_b = vp\tilde{p} \qquad (16)$$

When the dot product is an integer, the storage server calculates $M' = \frac{e(C_0, d'_{i,j,2})C_1}{e(C_0, T_4)}$ and returns the ciphertext C_0 and M' to the user.

(7) Decrypt: When the user gets the ciphertext C_0 and M', we have the message $m = \frac{M'(C_0, T_{i,j})}{e(C_0, d_{i,j,1})}$.

6 Security Analysis

6.1 The Correctness and Security of Indexing and Searching Trapdoors

Confidentiality of Indexing and Searching Trapdoors: In this scheme, Data Owner randomly selects a set $S = \{S_1, \ldots, S_L\}$ containing L random characters and transmits it to Data User through a secure channel. The keyword sets w and $\tilde{w}$ are filled with these characters to hide the true length of each keyword, and Data Owner uses a pseudo-random function to make the constructed keyword vector random. At the same time, the secure index $I = (I_a, I_b)$ is obtained by constructing the original index p_a and p_b and multiplying the invertible matrix. Similar to the file keyword index, the query keyword index hides the original vector $\widetilde{p}$ through multiplying the invertible matrix, and we have a new vector $Q = (Q_a, Q_b)$. In the case where Search Server and Storage Server do not know the user's private key, when the dimension of the invertible matrix is large, it is difficult for an attacker to obtain the plaintext effectively. So that the scheme can be computationally safe.

Search for the Irrelevance of Trapdoors: The trapdoor unlinkability in this scheme is the same as the WMFS advanced scheme in Ref. [17], which is limited by the length of the paper and will not be described here.

6.2   Ciphertext Indistinguishability

The security proof of this scheme is based on the DBDH problem (Decisional Bilinear Diffie-Hellman). If the advantage of the attacker Ad is negligible, it indicates that the scheme is to satisfy CPA security.

Proof: Use proof by contradiction. Assuming that attacker Ad's advantage $Adv_{Ad} = \epsilon$ is not negligible in polynomial time, the attacker wins. Use the following games to illustrate further:

(1) Initial: Attacker Ad sends the challenged structure W^* to challenger C.
(2) Setup: Challenger C chooses the group G_1, G_2 with the order P and the generator g. Take the safety parameter λ as input. The challenger C runs Setup to obtain the system's public parameter $params = \{Y, e, g, G_1, G_2, T_{i,j}\}$ and sends it to attacker Ad. C randomly chooses s, t and sets the server's public and private key to be $(SK_1, PK_1) \rightarrow (st, g^{st})$.
(3) Phase 1: Attacker Ad can interrogate multiple times in any polynomial time. Ad applies for the private key from challenger C for its attribute set $L^* = (l_1^*, l_2^*, \ldots, l_n^*)$, where l_i^* does not satisfy the access structure W^*. C enters the public parameter $params$ of the system to execute Key Generation and output attribute private key:

$$SK^* = \left\{ d_1^*, d_0, \left\{ d_{i,j,1}^*, d_{i,j,2}^* \right\}_{i \in (1,n), j \in (1, n_i)} \right\} \tag{17}$$

$$d_0 = \prod_{k=1}^{N} d_0^k = g^{\sum_{k=1}^{N} \alpha_k}, \ d_{i,j,1}^* = g^{a + bt_{i,j}},$$

$$d_{i,j,2}^* = g^b \left(1 \in (1, n), j \in (1, n_i) \right), \ d_1^* = g^a$$

Challenger C sends SK^* to Ad.
(4) Ad applies to C for a search certificate. C randomly chooses $\mu \in Z_P^*$ and calculates

$$T_1 = g^{st\mu}, \ T_2^* = g^{b\mu}, \ T_3 = T_{i,j}^\mu = g^{t_{i,j}\mu}, \ T_4^* = d_0^\mu,$$

$$dr_{i,j,1}^* = g^{(a + bt_{i,j})\mu}, \ dr_{i,j,2}^* = g^{ab\mu} \tag{18}$$

Search credential $TK^* = \left\{ T_1, T_2^*, T_3, T_4^*, \left\{ d'^*_{i,j,1}, d'^*_{i,j,2} \right\}_{i \in (1,n), j \in (1,n_i)} \right\}$ is output and sent to Ad.

(5) Challenge: Ad randomly sends two equal-length messages m_0 and m_1 to C. C randomly selects $\zeta \in (0,1)$ to encrypt message m_ζ. Set $\beta = c$ and perform Encrypt. Calculate:

$$C_0^* = g^c, \ C_1^* = m_\zeta Y^c, \ M^* = \frac{e\left(C_0^*, d'^*_{i,j,2}\right) C_1^*}{e\left(C_0^*, T_4^*\right)} \tag{19}$$

Define $T = \frac{M^*}{m_\zeta}$, and send C_0^* and M^* to attacker Ad.

(6) Guess: Attacker Ad outputs a conjecture on $\zeta \prime \in \{0,1\}$. If $\zeta = \zeta \prime$, the attacker guesses correctly and challenger C outputs $b = 1$, indicating $T = (g,g)^{abc}$. Otherwise, challenger C outputs $b = 0$, which means that T is a random value of G_2.

The probability of a challenger solving the difficult problem is as follows:

When the output is $b = 1$, $T = (g,g)^{abc}$, that is, attacker Ad gets a valid ciphertext about m_ζ. By definition, Ad has a non-negligible advantage ε, so

$$Pr\left[\zeta = \zeta \prime | b = 1\right] = \frac{1}{2} + \varepsilon \tag{20}$$

When the output is 0, $T \in G_2$. T is a random value of G_2, so the attacker cannot obtain a valid ciphertext about m_ζ. The probability at this time is

$$Pr\left[\zeta = \zeta \prime | b = 0\right] = \frac{1}{2} \tag{21}$$

To sum up, the advantage of being able to correctly guess $\zeta = \zeta \prime$ in the above game is

$$Adv_B = |Pr\left[\zeta = \zeta \prime\right] - \frac{1}{2}| = |\frac{1}{2}\left(\frac{1}{2} + \varepsilon\right) + \frac{1}{2} \times \frac{1}{2} - \frac{1}{2}| = \frac{\varepsilon}{2} \tag{22}$$

Based on the above security definition and security countermeasures, in any polynomial time, the advantage of Ad in the game is negligible, so this scheme is CPA secure.

7 Performance Analysis

In this section, we analyze the efficiency of our scheme and conduct the experiment to evaluate its practice.

7.1 Efficiency Analysis

First, we give some necessary definitions of symbols in the Table 2.

The calculation cost of each algorithm is shown in the Table 3.

Table 2. Definition of symbols

Symbol	Explanation
H	The hash computation cost
P	A bilinear pairing operation cost
E	The cost of an exponentiation operation on pairing
F	The pseudorandom function cost
n	The number of attributes
$n\prime$	The number of keywords
s	The number of wildcard
L	The length of keywords
M	The cost of scalar multiplication on elliptic curve
m	The number of attribute authorization center AA_i

Table 3. Performance analysis of the scheme

	Key Generation	Encrypt	Trapdoor Generation	Test	Decrypt
Our scheme	$(1 + 2n + N)E + (N + n)M$	1. $2E$	1. $(2n + 4)E$	$3P + E + 3M$	$3P + 4M$
		2. $2nE$	2. $(n\prime l - s)H + 26sF + 2d^2$		
		3. $n'LH + 2d^2$			

7.2 Experiment Evaluation

In order to better evaluate our program, we will show the results of our experiments in this section. All the experiments are on a Windows 10 Dell laptop (Intel Core (TM) i5-8250U CPU @ 1.60 GHz, 4 GB memory).

First of all, our scheme is relatively simple for encryption and decryption. It has less computational overhead and higher encryption and decryption operating efficiency. Secondly, the generation of the encrypted index is related to the number of keywords and the number of letters it contains. When the length of the security index is fixed, the number of keywords and the letters will be larger, and the time cost of the algorithm will be greater. The time cost of the query trapdoor generation is similar to that of the security index generation. However, due to the existence of wildcards, it is necessary to traverse 'a' to 'Z' through the calculation of pseudo-random functions, so the actual time cost is higher than the security index generation. The difference lies in the number of wildcards. Therefore, we only give the test results of key generation and query index generation here. We choose SM3 as the hash function which was issued by the Chinese State Password Administration on December 17, 2010 and its relevant standard is "GM/T 0004-2012 SM3 cipher hash algorithm". The time mentioned below refers to the average system time. The detailed experimental results are as follows:

Figure 2a shows the time cost of the key generation. We test with the number of attributes from 1 to 30. The results show that the time of the key generation increases with the number of AA_i and the number of attributes. When n is less than 8 and N is less than 30, our algorithm can be completed in 1 s.

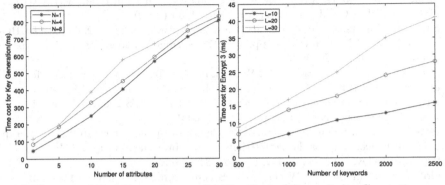

(a) The cost of Key Generation   (b) The Cost of Query Index Generation

Fig. 2. Experimental results

Figure 2b shows the time cost of query index generation. We test with $L = 10, 20, 30$ and the number of keywords from 500 to 2500. The results show that the cost of key generation increases with the increase in the number of keywords. When L is less than 30 and the number of keywords is less than 2500, our algorithm can be completed in 40 ms with high efficiency.

In this scheme, encryption and decryption are relatively simple and index generation is efficient. However, due to the large time cost of exponential operation and bilinear operation, this scheme still has some shortcomings to be improved.

8   Conclusion

This paper proposes an attribute-based fuzzy multi-keyword searchable encryption scheme. Data Owner encrypts the message and customizes the access structure. Only when the attributes of the user meet the access structure, the search server can conduct a search algorithm, thereby realizing user access control. A collision-free hash function and a secure KNN encryption method are used to generate a secure index and upload it to the cloud server. Data users upload search trapdoors to the search server, implementing a fuzzy multi-keyword search. Finally, the relevant ciphertext returned by the storage server is decrypted by the user. This scheme in this paper satisfies the confidentiality and correctness of index and search trapdoors and also meets the non-relevance of search trapdoors. Through security analysis, the scheme also achieves CPA security.

Acknowledgments. This work was funded by the National Undergraduate Training Program for Innovation and Entrepreneurship (Item number: 201910288084Z), National Natural Science Foundation of China (No: 62072240) and The National Key Research and Development Program of China (No. 2020YFB1804604).

References

1. Song, D.X., Wagner, D., Perrig, A.: Practical techniques for searches on encrypted data. In: Proceedings of the 2000 IEEE Symposium on Security and Privacy (S&P 2000), Berkeley, CA, USA, 14–17 May, pp. 44–55 (2000)
2. Sahai, A., Waters, B.: Fuzzy identity-based encryption. In: Cramer, R. (ed.) EURO-CRYPT 2005. LNCS, vol. 3494, pp. 457–473. Springer, Heidelberg (2005). https://doi.org/10.1007/11426639_27
3. Goyal, V., Pandey, O., Sahai, A., Waters, B.: Attribute-based encryption for fine-grained access control of encrypted data. In: Proceedings of the 13th ACM Conference on Computer and Communications Security (CCS 2006), Alexandria, VA, USA, 30 October–3 November, pp. 89–98 (2006)
4. Bethencourt, J., Sahai, A., Waters, B.: Ciphertext-policy attribute-based encryption. In: Proceedings of the 2007 IEEE Symposium on Security and Privacy (SP 2007), Berkeley, CA, 20–23 May, pp. 321–334 (2007)
5. Golle, P., Staddon, J., Waters, B.: Secure conjunctive keyword search over encrypted data. In: Jakobsson, M., Yung, M., Zhou, J. (eds.) ACNS 2004. LNCS, vol. 3089, pp. 31–45. Springer, Heidelberg (2004). https://doi.org/10.1007/978-3-540-24852-1_3
6. Li, J., Wang, Q., Wang, C., Cao, N., Ren, K., Lou, W.: Fuzzy keyword search over encrypted data in cloud computing. In: Proceedings of the 2010 International Conference on Computer Communications(INFOCOM 2010), San Diego, CA, USA, 14–19 March, pp. 1–5 (2010)
7. Goh, E.-J.: Secure indexes. Cryptology ePrint Archive: Report 2003/216, 16 March 2004. http://eprint.iacr.org/2003/216
8. Waters, B.R., Balfanz, D., Durfee, G., Smetters, D.K.: Building an encrypted and searchable audit log. In: Proceedings of the 11th Annual Network and Distributed System Security Symposium (NDSS 2004), San Diego, California, USA, 5 February, pp. 9–12 (2004)
9. Park, D.J., Kim, K., Lee, P.J.: Public key encryption with conjunctive field keyword search. In: Lim, C.H., Yung, M. (eds.) WISA 2004. LNCS, vol. 3325, pp. 73–86. Springer, Heidelberg (2005). https://doi.org/10.1007/978-3-540-31815-6_7
10. Shuang, L., Maozhi, X.: Attribute-based public encryption with keyword search. Chin. J. Comput. 37(5), 1017–1024 (2014)
11. Balu, A., Kuppusamy, K.: Privacy preserving ciphertext policy attribute based encryption. In: Meghanathan, N., Boumerdassi, S., Chaki, N., Nagamalai, D. (eds.) CNSA 2010. CCIS, vol. 89, pp. 402–409. Springer, Heidelberg (2010). https://doi.org/10.1007/978-3-642-14478-3_40
12. Hur, J.: Attribute-based secure data sharing with hidden policies in smart grid. IEEE Trans. Parallel Distrib. Syst. 24(11), 2171–2180 (2013)
13. Yulei, Z., Wenjing, L., Xiangzhen, L., Yongjie, Z., Caifen, W.: Searchable multi-server CP-ABE scheme based on authorization. J. Electron. Inf. Technol. 41(8), 1808–1814 (2019)
14. Cao, N., Wang, C., Li, M., Ren, K., Lou, W.: Privacy-preserving multi-keyword ranked search over encrypted cloud data. IEEE Trans. Parallel Distrib. Syst. 25(1), 829–837 (2011)
15. Khader, D.: Attribute based search in encrypted data: ABSE. In: Proceedings of the 2014 ACM Workshop on Information Sharing & Collaborative Security (WISCS 2014), Scottsdale, Arizona, USA, 3–7 November, pp. 31–40 (2014)

16. Wang, B., Yu, S., Lou, W., Thomas Hou, Y.: Privacy-preserving multi-keyword fuzzy search over encrypted data in the cloud. In: Proceedings of the 2014 IEEE Conference on Computer Communications (IEEE INFOCOM 2014), Toronto, ON, Canada, 27 April–2 May, pp. 2112–2120 (2014)

17. Pei, S.: Research on efficient and secure fuzzy search over encrypted data in cloud computing. Hunan University MA thesis, Hunan (2018)

18. Zhang, F., Safavi-Naini, R., Susilo, W.: An efficient signature scheme from bilinear pairings and its applications. In: Bao, F., Deng, R., Zhou, J. (eds.) PKC 2004. LNCS, vol. 2947, pp. 277–290. Springer, Heidelberg (2004). https://doi.org/10.1007/978-3-540-24632-9_20

19. Boyen, X., Waters, B.: Anonymous hierarchical identity-based encryption (without random oracles). In: Dwork, C. (ed.) CRYPTO 2006. LNCS, vol. 4117, pp. 290–307. Springer, Heidelberg (2006). https://doi.org/10.1007/11818175_17

20. Zhou, W., Liu, L., Jing, H., Zhang, C., Yao, S., Wang, S.: K-gram based fuzzy keyword search over encrypted cloud computing. J. Softw. Eng. Appl. 06(01), 29–32 (2013)

21. Wang, J., et al.: Efficient verifiable fuzzy keyword search over encrypted data in cloud computing. Comput. Sci. Inf. Syst. 10(2), 667–684 (2013)

22. Junzuo, L., Robert, D., Yingjiu, L.: Expressive CP-ABE with partially hidden access structures. In: Proceedings of the 7th ACM Symposium on Information, Computer and Communications Security (ASIACCS 2012), Seoul, Korea, 2–4 May, pp. 18–19 (2012)

23. Le, W., Zherong, Y., Rongjing, L., Xiang, W.: A CP-ABE privacy preserving method for wearable devices. Netinfo Secur. 18(6), 77–84 (2018)

24. Haiping, H., Jianpeng, D., Hua, D., Ruchuan, W.: Multi-sever multi-keyword searchable encryption scheme based on cloud storage. J. Electron. Inform. Technol. 39(2), 389–396 (2017)

25. Xu, L., Xu, C., Liu, J.K., Zuo, C., Zhang, P.: Building a dynamic searchable encrypted medical database for multi-client. Inf. Sci. 527, 394–405 (2019)

26. Xu, L., Sun, S., Yuan, X., Liu, J., Zuo, C., Xu, C.: Enabling authorized encrypted search for multi-authority medical database. IEEE Trans. Emerg. Top. Comput. PP(99), 1 (2019)

27. Huang, R., Li, Z., Wu, G.: A verifiable encryption scheme supporting fuzzy search. In: Wang, G., Feng, J., Bhuiyan, M.Z.A., Lu, R. (eds.) SpaCCS 2019. LNCS, vol. 11611, pp. 397–411. Springer, Cham (2019). https://doi.org/10.1007/978-3-030-24907-6_30

28. Xu, Y., Gao, W., Zeng, Q., Wang, G., Ren, J., Zhang, Y.: FABAC: a flexible fuzzy attribute-based access control mechanism. In: Wang, G., Atiquzzaman, M., Yan, Z., Choo, K.-K.R. (eds.) SpaCCS 2017. LNCS, vol. 10656, pp. 332–343. Springer, Cham (2017). https://doi.org/10.1007/978-3-319-72389-1_27

29. Wong, W.K., et al.: Secure kNN computation on encrypted databases. In: Proceedings of the 2009 ACM SIGMOD International Conference on Management of Data (SIGMOD 2009), Providence, Rhode, Island, USA, 29 June–2 July, pp. 139–152 (2009)

Improving Deep Neural Network Robustness with Siamese Empowered Adversarial Training

Yu Zhu, Zongfei Li$^{(\boxtimes)}$, Fengyuan Xu, and Sheng Zhong

National Key Lab for Novel Software Technology, Nanjing University,
Nanjing 210093, China
nju15261401932@126.com

Abstract. Deep neural networks (DNNs) have been widely used in many critical application domains. However, the security of DNNs are threatened by adversarial examples, and the problem has not been fully solved. In this work, observing the deficiency of existing adversarial training methods, we propose a new adversarial training method with a specially-crafted contrastive loss and the siamese training architecture. Our method fully leverages the distance relationships between the benign examples and adversarial examples. We conduct extensive experiments to evaluate our proposed design. The results show that the DNN models trained by our methods are more robust to adversarial examples compared to those been trained with other SOTA methods.

Keywords: Neural network · Adversarial training · Siamese architecture

1 Introduction

Due to its impressive performance, Deep neural networks (DNNs) have been widely used in many application domains, such as computer vision [8,18], natural language processing [4,21], signal processing, binary analysis [5,19], and so on. However, under the prosperity, adversarial example [23], a slightly perturbated version of the normal input, which can fool DNNs without attracting human attention, brings a significant security challenge to the application of DNNs in critical tasks.

Lots of works [7,11,13,15] have been proposed for improving the robustness of DNNs to adversarial examples. Among all the proposed defensive methods, adversarial training is widely used and shown to be the cutting-edge approach [12]. The main idea of adversarial training is to dynamically generate adversarial examples after each training iteration and inject them into the next mini-batch training data with the right label. And models trained with adversarial training can have better classification boundaries.

© Springer Nature Switzerland AG 2021
G. Wang et al. (Eds.): SpaCCS 2020, LNCS 12382, pp. 62–75, 2021.
https://doi.org/10.1007/978-3-030-68851-6_4

Although adversarial training achieves good results, they are still not good enough to solve this security problem [10]. And we observe that existing adversarial training based methods failed to fully leverage the distance relationships between adversarial and benign examples during model training. Specifically, traditional adversarial training only tries to make the network to learn the distribution of adversarial examples but does not actively make the classification boundary tighter. I.e., it neglects to reduce the distances between the adversarial examples and the samples of the same data category (the adversarial example have the same data category of the sample where it comes from), and to enlarge the distances between the adversarial examples and the samples of different categories. In this paper, we call the two types of distance as **intra-class distance** and **inter-class distance**, respectively. And the distance can be evaluated by calculating the Euclidean distance between the intermediate features, such as the output of the layer before the softmax layer.

There are already two existing works that consider leveraging the distance information for better model robustness, but none of them fully explores the distance information. [10] shows an adversarial training method introducing a special loss in triplet form to represent the distance information. In particular, the intra-class distance is evaluated by only computing the distances between the adversarial examples and their corresponding clean samples. [12] also proposes a similar loss, while the intra-class distance is evaluated by calculating the distances between the adversarial examples and randomly chosen clean samples from the same data category. These designs are either not considering all the cases or are not flexible in evaluating the intra-class distance.

Observing the inefficiency of the existing defensive methods, we propose a new adversarial training architecture using siamese network structure [1] and contrastive loss [3]. To be specific, apart from the traditional adversarial training loss, we design a new contrastive loss aiming at reducing the above-mentioned intra-class distance and enlarging the inter-class distance to achieve better model robustness to adversarial examples. The intra-class distance is evaluated by combining the design concept of [10] and [12], and we make it more flexible by balancing the two design choices. And the inter-class distance is directly computed by following the above-mentioned definition. When performing training, a mini-batch of data and the corresponding adversarial examples are fed into the two branches of the siamese network, separately. Guided by the combined loss, our adversarial training design achieves the best model robustness in most cases compared with other designs, which is shown by extensive experiments.

Main Contributions. First, we propose a siamese adversarial training architecture by designing a special loss that comprehensively leverages the distance relationships between adversarial and benign examples. Second, we evaluate our design with extensive experiments and empirically show that the models trained with our method are more robust to adversarial examples compared with other SOTA adversarial training methods.

2 Background and Related Works

2.1 Adversarial Attacks

Given a trained network f, an input data x, and its corresponding label y, if there is a $\hat{x}$ (a perturbed version of x) that mislead the network f while keeping the L_p distance between $\hat{x}$ and x less than a given threshold T, we call $\hat{x}$ an adversarial example of f. There are many methods for generating adversarial examples. They can be roughly divided into two types, one-step attack and iterative attack, based on whether or not they are iteratively optimized.

There are many famous attacks, such as Fast Gradient Sign Method (FGSM) [7] and Carlini and Wagner's method (CW) [2]. FGSM is a simple but effective adversarial example generating method. It perturbs the benign input along the direction of the gradient of the loss w.r.t. the input. The adversarial example can be calculated by

$$\hat{x} = x + \epsilon \cdot sign(\nabla_x l(x, y)),$$

where ϵ limits the perturbation scale, $sign()$ is sign function, and $\nabla_x l(\cdot)$ is the gradient of loss. CW formulizes the problem of generating adversarial examples as an optimization problem. The goal of this problem is to find the minimum perturbation to fool the classifier f. Multiple loss functions have been proposed in [2] to make this problem easier to optimize.

Iterative attacks, including Basic Iterative Method (BIM) [9], Projected Gradient Descent (PGD) [11], and Momentum Iterative Method (MIM) [6], also show impressive attack abilities. BIM is an iterative version of FGSM using the result of the current step as the input of the next step. PGD is a powerful variant of BIM. Different from BIM, the computing of PGD methods start from a random point. MIM is another attack based on BIM integrated with the momentum technique. At each iteration, it updates the gradient by accumulating the momentum along with the gradient direction.

2.2 Defenses to Adversarial Examples

Many methods for defending adversarial examples have been proposed. We mainly introduce adversarial training based defensive methods because they are the state-of-the-art defensive methods [12] and will be the basis of the method of this paper.

Adversarial training [7] is one of the most influential approaches in defending adversarial examples. At each training iteration, adversarial examples are generated based on the model at the current state. The generated adversarial examples will be labeled with correct labels and used as part of the training data of the next iteration. [7] first introduced the concept of adversarial training, and the adversarial examples in the training process were generated by using the FGSM attack. [11] demonstrated that using more powerful attacks to generate adversarial examples in training could achieve better model robustness. And the PGD attack was recommended in their study.

Combining the concept of deep metric learning and adversarial training for better model robustness is also studied by some works. [10] and [12] propose adversarial training architectures with triplet loss. The loss function can be abstracted as: $L = L_{at} + L_{triplet} + R$, where L_{at} is the ordinary adversarial training loss, $L_{triplet}$ is the loss component for decreasing and increasing the intra-class and inter-class distance mentioned in Sect. 1 respectively, and R represents the regularization term. In [10], the $L_{triplet}$ can be expressed in the form of:

$$\sum_i^k \max(\|f(x_i^{adv}) - f(x_i)\| - \|f(x_i^{adv}) - f(x_i^n)\| + \alpha, 0),$$

where samples x_i and x_i^n are from different data categories and x_i^{adv} is the adversarial version of benign input x_i. The $L_{triplet}$ of [12] is in a similar form:

$$\sum_i^k \max(\|f(x_i^{adv}) - f(x_i^p)\| - \|f(x_i^{adv}) - f(x_i^n)\| + \alpha, 0),$$

where x_i^p is benign sample from the same data category of x_i. And the case that exchanging x_i^{adv} with x_i^p is also considered. The first method only uses $\|f(x_i^{adv}) - f(x_i)\|$ to evaluate the intra-class distance (see Sect. 1) and neglects the case $\|f(x_i^{adv}) - f(x_i^p)\|$ when x_i and x_i^p are not identical. And the second method does not emphasis the importance distance relationship between x_i and x_i^{adv}. Considering the deficiency of two methods, we are going to design an adversarial training method trying to fully leverage the distance relationship aiming at provide better model robustness.

3   Methodology

In this section, we will introduce the ordinary Siamese Network and contrastive loss in Sect. 3.1. Then we present our Siamese adversarial training in Sect. 3.2.

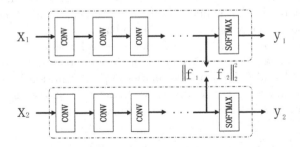

Fig. 1. Ordinary Siamese Network

3.1   Siamese Network and Contrastive Loss

As shown in Fig. 1, the Siamese architecture consists of two identical neural networks with shared parameters. At each step, it gets pairs of samples, and samples in one pair can be in different data categories. Distance between the pair inputs will be calculated, which will be used as a part of network loss. When the contrastive loss is combined with Siamese architecture, the loss can be formalized as follows:

$$l_{con}(x_1, x_2, t) =\ t||f(x_1) - f(x_2)|| +$$
$$(1 - t)\{max(0, m - ||f(x_1) - f(x_2)||)\} \tag{1}$$

x_1 and x_2 are two inputs. t indicates whether or not x_1 and x_2 are from the same data category. If the two inputs are of the same data category, then t will be 1, otherwise t is 0. f is usually a DNN model without the softmax layer, which outputs the intermediate feature representation. This loss can guide the DNN in reducing the Euclidean distance between the features from inputs with the same data category. And for features from different data categories, the loss will enlarge the distance until it reaches m.

3.2   Siamese Adversarial Training

Traditional adversarial training mixes adversarial examples into training mini-batch. The loss function can be formalized as:

$$L_{at}(X, \hat{X}, Y) = \frac{\alpha}{n} \sum_{i=0}^{n} l(x_i, y_i) + \frac{\beta}{n} \sum_{i=0}^{n} l(\hat{x}_i, y_i) \tag{2}$$

At each training iteration, X is the training mini-batch, and $x_i \in X$. $\hat{X}$ is the set of adversarial examples ($\hat{x}_i \in \hat{X}$). Each $\hat{x}_i$ is generated by leveraging adversarial attack methods (like FGSM, PGD) base on the benign input x_i. y_i is the data label. $l(x_i, y_i)$ is the classification loss guiding the network to correctly classify benign examples, and $l(\hat{x}_i, y_i)$ oversees the network to learn the distribution of adversarial examples to achieve better robustness. α and β are the hyper-parameters to balance the two items. n is the batch size.

As we can see, the loss function of traditional adversarial training does not consider the distance relationships between the adversarial examples and the benign samples. We add the distance relationship information by using siamese training architecture with contrastive loss. Equation 3 shows the basic idea of our loss function.

$$L_{sat}(X, \hat{X}, Y, \hat{Y}, T) = \frac{\alpha}{n} \sum_{i=0}^{n} l(x_i, y_i)\ +$$
$$\frac{\beta}{n} \sum_{i=0}^{n} l(\hat{x}_i, \hat{y}_i) + \frac{\gamma}{n} \sum_{i=0}^{n} l_{con}(x_i, \hat{x}_i^r, t_i). \tag{3}$$

$\hat{Y}$ represents the labels of $\hat{X}$. α, β, and γ are hyper-parameters to balance the three parts, n is the batch size, $l(\cdot)$ is the cross-entropy loss function evaluating the classification correctness, and $l_{con}(\cdot)$ is the contrastive loss function (Eq. 1). The first two items in the right of the Eq. 3 represent the ordinary adversarial training loss, and the third item $\frac{\gamma}{n}\sum_{i=0}^{n} l_{con}(x_i, \hat{x}_i^r, t_i)$ is the item for representing the distance relationships. $\hat{x}_i$ is the adversarial example. There are three possible relationships between $\hat{x}_i^r$ and x_i. R1) $\hat{x}_i^r$ can be the adversarial version of x_i. R2) $\hat{x}_i^r$ is not the adversarial version of x_i, but they are of the same data category. R3) $\hat{x}_i^r$ and x_i are of different data categories. We incorporate the design of controlling the ratio of pairs of three relationships in the siamese training architecture. The details are shown in Algorithm 1.

At each training iteration, our algorithm first chooses one branch of the siamese architecture and generates a batch of adversarial examples from the current training mini-batch, just as the original adversarial training does. Instead of simply concatenating $\hat{X}$ with X as a new mini-batch, we use them as the inputs of the two branches of the siamese architecture, separately. To fully take advantage of the distance relationship information, we rearrange the order of the items in $\hat{X}$. For a batch of adversarial examples $\hat{X} = (\hat{x}_1, \hat{x}_2, \ldots, \hat{x}_n)$, we first split them into two parts $\hat{X}_1 = (\hat{x}_1, \hat{x}_2, \ldots, \hat{x}_k)$ and $\hat{X}_2 = (\hat{x}_{k+1}, \hat{x}_{k+2}, \ldots, \hat{x}_n)$. Then we shuffle $\hat{X}_2$ and concatenate it back to $\hat{X}_1$. We call the partial-shuffled adversarial examples as the new $\hat{X}$. We update each $\hat{y}_i$ in $\hat{Y}$ with the correct label. Then we use Y and $\hat{Y}$ to generate the contrastive loss tags $T = (t_1, t_2, \ldots, t_n)$ following the rule: if $y_i = \hat{y}_i$, then $t_i = 1$, else $t_i = 0$.

Note that data partition ratio $\lambda - \frac{k}{n}$ controls the ratio of relationship types of the $<x_i, \hat{x}_i^r,>$ pairs. And our design emphasizes the distance relationship R1 and R3 while taking R2 into consideration, which is a practical method to solve the deficiency of existing works.

Algorithm 1. Siamese Adversarial Training

Input: Training set: D, Batch size: n, Data partition ratio λ;
Output: DNN model parameters θ;
 1: Initialize θ, Calculate $k = \lfloor n \times \lambda \rfloor$;
 2: **for** epoch $= 1 \ldots N$ **do**
 3:     **for** mini-batch $X = (x_1, \ldots, x_n) \subset D$ **do**
 4:         Generate adversarial examples $\hat{X} = (\hat{x}_1, \ldots, \hat{x}_n)$ from X under current model parameters θ ;
 5:         Split $\hat{X}$ into $\hat{X}_1 = (\hat{x}_1, \ldots, \hat{x}_k)$ and $\hat{X}_2 = (\hat{x}_{k+1}, \ldots, \hat{x}_n)$;
 6:         Shuffle $\hat{X}_2$;
 7:         Update $\hat{X}$ with $\hat{X} = \{\hat{X}_1, \hat{X}_2\}$;
 8:         Update the labels $\hat{Y}$;
 9:         Calculate contrastive loss tags $T = (t_1, t_2, \ldots, t_n)$ using Y and $\hat{Y}$;
10:         Update θ with stochastic gradient descent using Equation 3;
11:     **end for**
12: **end for**

---

4   Evaluation

In this section, we compare our method to original adversarial training on different datasets. First, we describe our datasets, networks, and hyperparameters in Sect. 4.1, then we present and analyze various experiments in the following subsections.

4.1   Settings

In this work, we evaluate the performance of our method on Cifar10, Cifar100, and SVHN datasets. For each dataset, we use L_∞ to bound the distance between adversarial examples and clean data. We trained models with our algorithm using adversarial examples generated by FGSM and PGD attacks, which are named as **SAT-FGSM** and **SAT-PGD**. To have a comprehensive comparison, we also trained baseline models. **NT** refers to naive trained models without any protections, while **AT-FGSM** and **AT-PGD** refer to traditional adversarial trained models with malicious samples generated by FGSM or PGD, respectively.

All the following experiments were conducted with Pytorch framework [16] on a Nvidia Titan Xp GPU, and all the adversarial examples we used were generated by Foolbox [17], a python toolbox to create adversarial examples. If not specified, we choose ResNet18 network and set $\lambda = 0.5, \alpha = 0.5, \beta = 0.5, \gamma = 1.0$ as default. We will further evaluate different networks and partition ratios in subsequent parts.

4.2   Performance Under White-Box Attacks

As we mentioned before, all these models were trained with at most one kind of L_∞ bounded attacks, which is FGSM or PGD, so it is straightforward to evaluate their performance under L_∞ bounded attacks first. We consider the white-box scenario in which adversary has full knowledge of our trained models, including network architecture and parameters, and use four L_∞ bounded attacks (FGSM, PGD, BIM, and MIM) to evaluate these models. In addition to this, we also evaluate the model performance under L_2 or L_0 bounded attacks, which is CW(L_2), BIM(L_2) and JSMA(L_0).

For the L_∞ bounded attacks, we set $L_\infty = 8/255$ and applied 7 iterations for PGD, BIM and MIM. For L_2 bounded attacks, we applied 10 iterations for CW and 7 iterations for BIM(L_2), and for L_0 bounded attack JSMA, we set $L_0 = 0.02$ and ran 1000 iterations. Because of the low speed of JSMA, we randomly selected 1,000 test images for each dataset under this attack. The model accuracy is shown in Table 1.

In the experiments of Cifar10, we can observe that the standard model cannot resist white-box attacks, even for the weakest attack FGSM, the accuracy is only 37%, and it is less than 5% for other attacks. The AT-FGSM method boosts the model accuracy significantly compared to the standard model. It achieves 74.7% accuracy under the FGSM attack, however, it fails to recognize PGD attacks. The AT-PGD method further improves the model robustness on iterative attacks

Table 1. Accuracy under different attacks on Cifar10, Cifar100 and SVHN.

Method	Benign	FGSM	PGD	BIM(∞)	MIM	CW	BIM(L_2)	JSMA
Cifar10								
NT	**0.931**	0.371	0.000	0.032	0.044	0.009	0.006	0.000
AT-FGSM	0.929	0.747	0.046	0.246	0.261	0.080	0.123	0.064
AT-PGD	0.864	0.525	0.432	0.669	0.673	0.395	0.527	0.289
SAT-FGSM	0.927	**0.796**	0.475	0.534	0.547	**0.485**	0.489	**0.368**
SAT-PGD	0.851	0.568	**0.495**	**0.689**	**0.690**	0.465	**0.554**	0.362
Cifar100								
NT	0.703	0.133	0.001	0.009	0.007	0.005	0.005	0.012
AT-FGSM	**0.709**	**0.459**	0.011	0.056	0.047	0.019	0.023	0.172
AT-PGD	0.592	0.257	0.211	0.391	0.393	0.201	0.260	0.196
SAT-FGSM	0.678	0.449	0.088	0.223	0.210	0.085	0.107	0.224
SAT-PGD	0.611	0.290	**0.254**	**0.426**	**0.428**	**0.223**	**0.282**	**0.226**
SVHN								
NT	0.961	0.587	0.024	0.265	0.282	0.014	0.074	0.067
AT-FGSM	0.960	0.674	0.018	0.224	0.223	0.007	0.066	0.061
AT-PGD	0.952	0.751	0.422	0.617	0.610	0.286	0.466	0.346
SAT-FGSM	**0.968**	0.847	0.600	0.713	**0.747**	0.523	0.674	0.498
SAT-PGD	0.961	**0.883**	**0.881**	**0.804**	0.732	**0.641**	**0.683**	**0.543**

with the accuracy increased by around 40% while on the single-step attack, FGSM, the accuracy decreased by 22.2%. Compare to AT-PGD, our SAT-FGSM approach achieves better results on FGSM and PGD, increased by 27.1% and 4.3%, respectively. Although our SAT-FGSM method has worse accuracy on BIM and MIM, it raises lower bound on adversarial attacks. It's worth noting that training with FGSM is much faster than the PGD-based training method, so we believe in some cases the SAT-FGSM method would be very advantageous. The accuracy of the SAT-PGD method improved by 1.7% to 8.0% compares to AT-PGD.

We conducted similar experiments on Cifar100, which is more complicated than Cifar10. When the models trained with FGSM attacks, we can observe that our SAT-based method gets slightly decreased result in FGSM attack while achieves better performance on iterative attacks. When the models trained with PGD attacks, the SAT-based method performs better than AT with the accuracy increased around 3%. Unfortunately, the SAT-FGSM method fails to boost the lower bound on this dataset.

Different from Cifar10 and Cifar100, the SAT-FGSM method on SVHN achieves better performance than AT-PGD under all kinds of evaluated white-box attacks, which means we can use less time and resource to train. If we don't care about time or resources, we can train our models with PGD, and it would bring us 12.2% to 45.9% improvements.

After comparing SAT-based methods to AT-based methods, we can conclude that training models with siamese architecture and contrastive loss could bring us considerable benefits.

4.3 Performance Under Black-Box Attacks

Previous experiments have demonstrated that combining contrastive loss into adversarial training algorithms can boost models' robustness on white-box attacks. We evaluate the performance under black-box attacks in this section. We use two black-box adversarial attacks: **Single Pixel Attack** [20] and **Transfer Attack** [14]. For the single pixel attack, we perturb only one pixel and set it to the min or max value for each image. We traverse through the pixels until we find an adversarial sample. For transfer attacks, the pre-trained NT models are used as shadow models to generate malicious examples based on FGSM, PGD, and CW attacks. Then the malicious data are sent to each model to calculate their adversarial accuracy. The results are illustrated in Table 2.

As we can see, our approach does the best under the single pixel attack on all three datasets. For transfer attacks, except for FGSM-based one, our method obtains the best outcome in the vast majority cases. Because of the half best results are achieved by SAT-FGSM, we believe that the FGSM-based siamese adversarial training algorithm has an advantage in defending against black-box attacks.

Table 2. Accuracy under Black-Box Attacks, Single Pixel Attack and Transfer Attacks based on FGSM, PGD and CW, on Cifar10, Cifar100 and SVHN.

	Method	One pixel	Transfer attacks		
			FGSM	PGD	CW
Cifar10	AT-FGSM	0.732	0.749	0.827	0.908
	AT-PGD	0.723	**0.847**	0.855	0.863
	SAT-FGSM	**0.743**	0.799	**0.873**	**0.928**
	SAT-PGD	0.730	0.834	0.842	0.859
Cifar100	AT-FGSM	0.438	0.420	0.470	**0.668**
	AT-PGD	0.420	**0.571**	0.579	0.598
	SAT-FGSM	**0.538**	0.534	**0.600**	0.658
	SAT-PGD	0.447	0.541	0.548	0.571
SVHN	AT-FGSM	0.853	0.700	0.583	0.843
	AT-PGD	0.805	**0.867**	0.885	0.923
	SAT-FGSM	**0.875**	0.765	0.740	0.870
	SAT-PGD	0.826	0.863	**0.911**	**0.925**

4.4 Generalization to More Powerful PGD Attack

To further evaluate the robustness of our proposed method, we gradually increase the strength of the PGD attack and observe the performance of these pre-trained models on Cifar10 and SVHN. Our experiments were split into two parts. First, we fixed the perturbation bound, which was equals to 8/255, then we generated adversarial examples with different iterations ranging from 2 to 40. We test these models' accuracy. In the second experiment, we used constant iterations, 7, and different perturbation bound, 2/255 to 18/255.

The results are presented in Fig. 2, with the increase of iterations or perturbation bound, the AT-FGSM drops the fastest and soon approaches zero, which means standard FGSM-based adversarial training would make only a slight boost on adversarial robustness. We can also find that the SAT-PGD method has the best performance in all circumstances, showing a strong generalization. When we compare SAT-FGSM to AT-PGD, we can see that the dropping rate of SAT-FGSM is lower than AT-PGD with small iteration while higher with large iteration. We think the reason is that FGSM is a one-step attack, models trained with it would likely prefer small-iteration attacks. Nevertheless, our SAT-FGSM outperforms AT-PGD with a clear margin on SVHN and has a comparable performance with AT-PGD on Cifar10.

4.5 Effect of Different Data Partition Ratio

We set $\lambda = 0.5$ in previous experiments to make sure the number of similar pairs and different pairs nearly equal. In this subsection, we further investigate the influence of different data partition ratios. We trained models with different $\lambda = 0, 0.25, 0.5, 0.75, 1.0$ on Cifar10 and SVHN and presented the results in Table 3.

As we can see, under white-box attacks, our models achieve best performance when λ equals to 0.25 on Cifar10 while λ equals 0 or 0.5 on SVHN. Under black-box attacks, we could get the best accuracy when λ equals to 0 on both datasets. We could also observe that the accuracy decrease along with the increase of λ from 0 to 1 on most cases.

4.6 Effect of Different Network Architectures

Because of all the previous experiments were conducted using ResNet18, we carried experiments on Cifar10 with InceptionV3 [22] and ResNet50 [8] to demonstrate the proposed method is effective on different neural networks. All the models were trained with FGSM or PGD attacks, L_∞ is set to 8/255. FGSM, PGD, and CW(L_2) were used to evaluate the performance and the results were summarized in Table 4.

The SAT-FGSM achieves the best performance on InceptionV3 and increases the robustness by 4.2% to 25.5%. However, it cannot defend PGD and CW on ResNet50, instead, the SAT-PGD boosts the robustness ranging from 3.0% to 5.8%.

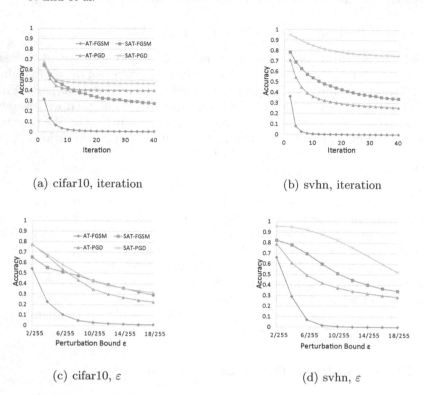

(a) cifar10, iteration

(b) svhn, iteration

(c) cifar10, ε

(d) svhn, ε

Fig. 2. Different Iterations and Perturbation Bound of PGD Attack. The plots show the accuracy under PGD attacks with iterations ranging from 2 to 40 in (a) and (b) while perturbation bound ranging from 2/255 to 18/255 in (c) and (d). The dataset in (a) and (c) is Cifar10, otherwise SVHN. The legends in (b) and (d) are the same as that in (a) or (c).

Table 3. Accuracy under both white and black attacks with different λ ranging from 0 to 1.0 on Cifar10, ResNet18.

	λ	Benign	White-box attack		Black-box attack	
			FGSM	CW	Single pixel	FGSM
Cifar10	0.00	**0.868**	0.566	0.462	**0.757**	**0.854**
	0.25	0.855	**0.570**	**0.469**	0.738	0.840
	0.50	0.851	0.568	0.465	0.730	0.834
	0.75	0.841	0.566	0.461	0.717	0.830
	1.00	0.836	0.565	0.457	0.738	0.821
SVHN	0.00	0.951	0.882	**0.695**	**0.803**	**0.867**
	0.25	0.942	0.789	0.564	0.800	0.866
	0.50	**0.961**	**0.883**	0.641	0.826	0.863
	0.75	0.931	0.876	0.538	0.738	0.864
	1.00	0.934	0.720	0.392	0.766	0.860

Table 4. Model performance on different network architectures on Cifar10.

Network	Method	Clean	FGSM	PGD	CW(L_2)
InceptionV3	NT	0.922	0.335	0.000	0.005
	AT-FGSM	0.940	0.589	0.075	0.078
	AT-PGD	0.868	0.549	0.450	0.422
	SAT-FGSM	**0.942**	**0.844**	**0.492**	**0.509**
	SAT-PGD	0.835	0.548	0.481	0.461
ResNet50	NT	**0.913**	0.392	0.000	0.007
	AT-FGSM	0.909	0.430	0.001	0.000
	AT-PGD	0.839	0.499	0.418	0.389
	SAT-FGSM	0.899	**0.638**	0.110	0.058
	SAT-PGD	0.814	0.537	**0.476**	**0.419**

4.7 Effect of Different Distance Functions

As we mentioned before, we chose the euclidean distance to calculate the distance of features of pairs in the contrastive loss. In this part, we evaluate the effect of different distance functions, which are the exponential distance and the cosine distance. We trained ResNet18 on Cifar10 dataset using PGD examples and presented the classification accuracy in Table 5. Under FGSM, PGD and CW attacks, models trained with the exponential distance could achieve comparable performance against the euclidean distance, while the cosine distance is less effective. However, the euclidean distance achieves the worst accuracy under JSMA.

Table 5. Classification robustness by using different distance functions in the contrastive loss. Models were trained with PGD examples on Cifar10, ResNet18.

Distance	Clean	FGSM	PGD	CW(L_2)	JSMA
Euclidean	0.851	**0.568**	**0.495**	**0.465**	0.362
Exponential	0.849	0.564	0.476	0.451	**0.423**
Cosine	**0.858**	0.539	0.430	0.425	0.399

4.8 Comparison with Triplet Adversarial Training

In this subsection, we compare our methods with triplet-based adversarial training (**TAT**). [10], **TAT1**, proposed to train models with a variety of attacks except PGD, while [12], **TAT2**, only trained models with PGD attack. To achieve a fair comparison, we trained models with both FGSM and PGD and evaluated their performance under different attacks. We used ResNet18 in this part and trained models on Cifar10. The results were shown in Table 6. As we can see, in all circumstances, our SAT-based methods achieved the best performance.

Table 6. Comparison with triplet-based adversarial training on Cifar10, ResNet18.

Method	Benign	FGSM	PGD	CW	MIM
TAT1-FGSM	0.885	0.761	0.227	0.168	0.299
TAT2-FGSM	0.855	0.511	0.413	0.391	0.665
TAT1-PGD	0.862	0.526	0.439	0.414	0.670
TAT2-PGD	0.830	0.509	0.445	0.397	0.664
SAT-FGSM	**0.927**	**0.796**	0.475	**0.485**	0.547
SAT-PGD	0.851	0.568	**0.495**	0.465	**0.690**

5   Conclusion

In this paper, we propose a new adversarial training method based on siamese architecture. With the apposite data partition mechanism, our method could significantly boost the model robustness on adversarial attacks.

References

1. Bromley, J., Guyon, I., LeCun, Y., Säckinger, E., Shah, R.: Signature verification using a "Siamese" time delay neural network. In: Advances in Neural Information Processing Systems (NeurIPS), pp. 737–744 (1994)
2. Carlini, N., Wagner, D.: Towards evaluating the robustness of neural networks. In: 2017 IEEE Symposium on Security and Privacy (SP), pp. 39–57 (2017)
3. Chopra, S., Hadsell, R., LeCun, Y.: Learning a similarity metric discriminatively, with application to face verification. In: 2005 IEEE Computer Society Conference on Computer Vision and Pattern Recognition (CVPR), pp. 539–546 (2005)
4. Collobert, R., Weston, J.: A unified architecture for natural language processing: deep neural networks with multitask learning. In: Proceedings of the 25th International Conference on Machine Learning (ICML), pp. 160–167 (2008)
5. Dahl, G.E., Stokes, J.W., Deng, L., Yu, D.: Large-scale malware classification using random projections and neural networks. In: 2013 IEEE International Conference on Acoustics, Speech and Signal Processing (ICASSP), pp. 3422–3426 (2013)
6. Dong, Y., et al.: Boosting adversarial attacks with momentum. In: Proceedings of the IEEE Conference on Computer Vision and Pattern Recognition (CVPR), pp. 9185–9193 (2018)
7. Goodfellow, I.J., Shlens, J., Szegedy, C.: Explaining and harnessing adversarial examples. arXiv preprint arXiv:1412.6572 (2014)
8. He, K., Zhang, X., Ren, S., Sun, J.: Deep residual learning for image recognition. In: Proceedings of the IEEE Conference on Computer Vision and Pattern Recognition (CVPR), pp. 770–778 (2016)

9. Kurakin, A., Goodfellow, I., Bengio, S.: Adversarial machine learning at scale. arXiv preprint arXiv:1611.01236 (2016)
10. Li, P., Yi, J., Zhou, B., Zhang, L.: Improving the robustness of deep neural networks via adversarial training with triplet loss. In: Proceedings of the 28th International Joint Conference on Artificial Intelligence (IJCAI), pp. 2909–2915 (2019)
11. Madry, A., Makelov, A., Schmidt, L., Tsipras, D., Vladu, A.: Towards deep learning models resistant to adversarial attacks. arXiv preprint arXiv:1706.06083 (2017)
12. Mao, C., Zhong, Z., Yang, J., Vondrick, C., Ray, B.: Metric learning for adversarial robustness. In: Advances in Neural Information Processing Systems (NeurIPS), pp. 478–489 (2019)
13. Meng, D., Chen, H.: Magnet: a two-pronged defense against adversarial examples. In: Proceedings of the 2017 ACM SIGSAC Conference on Computer and Communications Security (CCS), pp. 135–147 (2017)
14. Papernot, N., McDaniel, P., Goodfellow, I.: Transferability in machine learning: from phenomena to black-box attacks using adversarial samples. arXiv preprint arXiv:1605.07277 (2016)
15. Papernot, N., McDaniel, P., Wu, X., Jha, S., Swami, A.: Distillation as a defense to adversarial perturbations against deep neural networks. In: 2016 IEEE Symposium on Security and Privacy (SP), pp. 582–597 (2016)
16. Paszke, A., et al.: Pytorch: an imperative style, high-performance deep learning library. In: Advances in Neural Information Processing Systems (NeurIPS), pp. 8024–8035 (2019)
17. Rauber, J., Brendel, W., Bethge, M.: Foolbox: a python toolbox to benchmark the robustness of machine learning models. arXiv preprint arXiv:1707.04131 (2017)
18. Ronneberger, O., Fischer, P., Brox, T.: U-net: convolutional networks for biomedical image segmentation. In: Navab, N., Hornegger, J., Wells, W.M., Frangi, A.F. (eds.) MICCAI 2015. LNCS, vol. 9351, pp. 234–241. Springer, Cham (2015). https://doi.org/10.1007/978-3-319-24574-4_28
19. Saxe, J., Berlin, K.: Deep neural network based malware detection using two dimensional binary program features. In: 2015 10th International Conference on Malicious and Unwanted Software (MALWARE), pp. 11–20 (2015)
20. Su, J., Vargas, D.V., Sakurai, K.: One pixel attack for fooling deep neural networks. IEEE Trans. Evol. Comput. **23**, 828–841 (2019)
21. Sutskever, I., Vinyals, O., Le, Q.V.: Sequence to sequence learning with neural networks. In: Advances in Neural Information Processing Systems (NeurIPS), pp. 3104–3112 (2014)
22. Szegedy, C., Vanhoucke, V., Ioffe, S., Shlens, J., Wojna, Z.: Rethinking the inception architecture for computer vision. In: Proceedings of the IEEE Conference on Computer Vision and Pattern Recognition (CVPR), pp. 2818–2826 (2016)
23. Szegedy, C., et al.: Intriguing properties of neural networks. arXiv preprint arXiv:1312.6199 (2013)

Predicting Advanced Persistent Threats for IoT Systems Based on Federated Learning

Zitong Li, Xiang Cheng, Jiale Zhang, and Bing Chen[✉]

College of Computer Science and Technology, Nanjing University of Aeronautics
and Astronautics, Nanjing 21106, China
{lizitong,xcheng_1988,jlzhang,cb_china}@nuaa.edu.cn

Abstract. With the Internet of Things (IoT) experiencing an accelerating evolution, the IoT devices are widely implemented both in the industrial system and daily life. The IoT system has characteristics of lack of update, longer lifetimes, and delayed patching, making it suffer from diverse attacks especially the Advanced Persistent Threats (APTs). Various detection technologies that emerged, however, are far from satisfied the need for effective security defense for IoT systems against APT campaigns. Therefore, we propose an APT Prediction Method based on Federated Learning (APTPMFL) deployed on the edge computing infrastructure to predict the probability of subsequent APT attacks that occur in IoT scenarios. It is the first approach to apply a federated learning mechanism for aggregating suspicious activities in the IoT systems to train the APT prediction model without correlation rules. We present an edge computing-based framework to train and deploy the model which can alleviate the computing and communication overhead of the typical IoT systems. The sophisticated evolution processes of APT can be modeled by federated learning meanwhile the private data will not leakage to other organizations. Our evaluation results show that APTPMFL is capable of predicting subsequent APT behaviors in the IoT system accurately and efficiently.

Keywords: APT · Federated learning · Attack prediction · IoT · Edge computing

1 Introduction

With the continuous development of information technology, the production and operation activities of all walks of life gradually depend on its unique convenience and efficiency [14]. Take full advantage of the various high-efficiency information systems (especially the IoT system), the restrictions of region and time of service and business are broken. However, the widely used Internet of things technology also faces huge information security risks and hidden dangers [16]. It is mainly caused by the characteristics of the IoT system: lack of update, longer lifetimes, delayed patching, and consequences of compromise [1].

Advanced Persistent Threats (APTs) are a type of most menace multiple-step attacks that are launched by skilled and nation-sponsored cyber criminals [13]. APT actors persistently penetrate the targeted organization utilizing a wide spectrum of technics and

© Springer Nature Switzerland AG 2021
G. Wang et al. (Eds.): SpaCCS 2020, LNCS 12382, pp. 76–89, 2021.
https://doi.org/10.1007/978-3-030-68851-6_5

zero-day vulnerabilities until they achieve their goals of data exfiltration or sabotage networks [15]. Ascribe to its permeability, concealment, and pertinence, the APT could bring severe threats to the IoT systems. To defend these increasingly complex and potential security threats, researchers and organizations have put forward various detection technologies, such as intrusion detection technology [17], malicious code detection technology, vulnerability detection technology, etc. The APT attacks usually adopt the way of step-by-step penetration and long-term latency to achieve the final purpose of exfiltrating confidential data. It is far from satisfying the need for effective security defense for the Internet of things system to merely detect APT attack behaviors [2]. Therefore, it is urgent to propose an effective and robust method to predict the probability of subsequent APT attacks occurs based on the recognized APT attacks and corresponding subsequent activities (like system logs) in the IoT system.

Throughout the existing related researches, predicting the APT attacks in the IoT scenarios mainly faces the following challenges: (1) **Unbalanced and scarce dataset.** Because of multi-steps and various advanced technics conducted by attackers, it is challenging for a single organization to capture data that covers complete APT stages and sufficient attack patterns. Besides, different organizations will suffer from different APT attacks, which leads to the imbalance of APT data. Moreover, IoT devices generate little logs and communication traffic, thus a lack of sufficient data to enable each organization to train an effective model independently. (2) **Isolated data island**. Data generated by a single organization are not sufficient to describe the complex APT process. Consequently, integrating data from several organizations to train a model is a promising way to defend against APT. Nevertheless, they are reluctant to disclose their data on account of data privacy. Accordingly, the emergence of the isolated data island makes it strenuous to aggregate isolated data. (3) **Limited resources of IoT devices**. Since IoT devices are function-specific, their storage capacity and computing power are limited. It is not feasible to process and analyze data on IoT devices directly.

To tackle the challenges illustrated above, we propose an APT Prediction Method based on Federated Learning (APTPMFL) to predict the probability of subsequent APT attack phase occurs in IoT scenarios. When an APT attack at a certain stage is detected in the enterprise, suspicious logs are analyzed continuously to predict the probability of the APT process evolve from the current stage to the next stage. The contributions we make are shown as follows:

(1) It is the first approach to apply the federated learning mechanism for aggregating suspicious activities in the IoT systems. Benefiting from machine learning, we can get a trained APT prediction model without correlation rules.
(2) We present an edge computing-based framework to train and deploy the prediction model in typical IoT systems. The *Edge Servers* can not only share the computing overhead for the IoT devices but also alleviate the communication overhead between IoT devices and *Security Service Cloud*.
(3) The *Edge Servers* collect the system logs and alerts from its managed IoT devices, training the prediction model locally and only upload the parameter updates to the *Security Service Cloud*. In this way, we can not only train a model to describe the evolutionary process of APT but also guarantee the privacy data will not leakage to other organizations.

The rest of the paper organizes as follows. Section 2 summarizes the related works of attack prediction in cyber security. Section 3 provides an overview of the federated learning-based APT prediction architecture for IoT Systems. This architecture contains a description of the proposed APTPMFL and the edge computing framework for deploying the APT prediction method. Section 4 presents the design details of the APTPMFL, which consists of the federated learning approach and the APT attack prediction. Section 5 shows a view of our experiments and analysis. Section 6 presents some conclusions.

2 Related Work

At present, the hot topic of attack prediction is related to the four topics as following: Attack/Intrusion prediction, Attack projection, Attack intention recognition, and Network security situation forecasting [2]. The task of attack intention recognition and attack projection are tied to intrusion detection. The core task of them is to predict an adversary's next step moving and his ultimate goal. The attack/intrusion prediction is much more general as it only focuses on predicting malicious activity occurs. The network security situation forecasting is essentially a generic use concept related to cyber situation awareness. The outcome is a forecast of the number of malicious activities and vulnerabilities fluctuation in the network.

For solving the challenge of attack activities prediction, Polatidis et al. [3] presented that the recommender system can be applied to defense the cyber threat effectively and practically by making predictions about the ensuing attack behaviors in attack graphs. The Bayesian classier was developed by Okutan et al. [4] that utilized to predict the attack probability in a given day by processing signals extracted from social media and overall events. Huang et al. [5] focused on Industrial cyber-physical systems (ICPSs) security and proposed a novel risk assessment approach which in virtue of a Bayesian network to model the propagation of malicious activities and predict the probability of IoT devices being attacked. Okutan et al. [6] designed an innovative, automatic attack prediction system called CAPTURE which comprehensively uses generated signals to train a Bayesian classifier which is used to forecast the cyber threat. Dowling et al. [7] implemented dynamic and adaptive honeypots to capture malicious dataset which used to analyze attack types and model temporal attack patterns. A novel attack prediction method based on information exchange and data mining is presented in [8], which defines rules to describe the general malicious patterns by extracting information from numerous alerts. The literature [11] designed a Bayesian game framework based on game theory to analyze multiple APT attack stages and deceptive strategies. Behaviors of APT actors can be predicted by the perfect Bayesian Nash equilibrium (PBNE) to make a defensive strategy. A targeted complex attack network model entitled TCAN is developed in literature [12]. The model predicts the optimum attack path by means of constructing a dynamic attack graph and monitor state change.

Most of the previous prediction methods for APT attacks are to define correlation rules by analyzing the historical data, then conduct further analysis by reasoning. This approach is effective in the prediction of known attack patterns. But for APT attacks that ever-changing and commonly use zero-day vulnerabilities, accurately predicting the behavior of adversaries is still extremely challenging. A system based on machine learning named MLAPT is suggested in [9]. The proposed system developed eight modules to detect various technics of APT and the machine-learning-based prediction framework takes associated alerts as input to calculate the probability of alerts to evolve a full APT scenario. A data-snapshot-based malware prediction approach is described in [10]. Using recurrent neural networks, this approach can predict an executable whether malicious or not in the early stage of software execution.

3 APT Prediction for IoT System

3.1 System Architecture

As shown in Fig. 1, the system proposed in this paper has capable of analyzing log data generated by IoT devices in real-time and accurately predicting the evolution of APT attacks. In the beginning, a model containing multiple APT attack patterns is trained in the edge computing infrastructure in a distributed learning manner. After that, a well-trained model will be applied to the participating organizations to protect their IoT systems against APT attacks. It is worth noting that the purpose of our system is not to detect APT attacks but to predict the probability of the evolution of the APT campaign to the next stage after detecting a certain stage of APT attacks. Our system is deployed on *Edge Servers* and *Security Service Cloud* in the IoT edge computing environment.

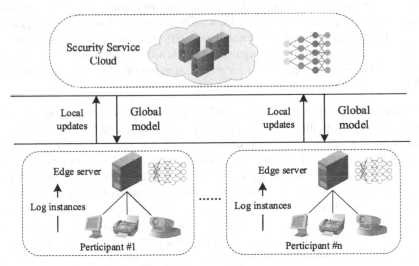

Fig. 1. System architecture.

Edge Server. The *Edge servers* are physically close to the systems that are generating the data, hence the data created by IoT devices can be efficiently collected and processed. On the one hand, the role of the *Edge Servers* are participants in federated learning to train a prediction model. Federated learning is a distributed machine learning approach with efficient communication and privacy protection. The *Edge Servers* collect log data in the organization to train a model locally and update the model parameters to the *Security Service Cloud*. Participants can learn various APT attack patterns without exchanging dataset. On the other hand, The *Edge Servers* monitor IoT devices and perform APT attack prediction through the trained model.

Security Service Cloud. Each *Edge Server*, which from different organizations, updates the model parameters to the *Security Service Cloud* after training the model locally, and then the *Security Service Cloud* is responsible for aggregating the parameters from *Edge Servers* into a global model and distributing the aggregated model to each *Edge Server*. Therefore, data privacy is preserved and transmission efficiency is improved due to all participants only need to interact with the *Security Service Cloud* for model parameters without having to exchange their data. Different *Edge Servers* belong to different organizations, and *Security Service Cloud* maintains a repository of APT attack patterns for participants. Meanwhile, the challenge of imbalanced APT data can also be alleviated thanks to the distributed learning model.

3.2 Threat Model and Assumptions

Threat Model. In most cases, the following attack phases can be abstracted from APT attack scenarios in the IoT environment. Initially, an APT performer gains access to the system illegitimately through the point of entry. Next, the attacker establishes a connection with the C&C server and communicates to obtain the attack instruction. After that, the attacker discovers and collects assets within the organization for privilege escalation and lateral movement. Eventually, the adversary will destroy infrastructures or exfiltrate confidential data of the organization to achieve its ultimate goal. During this process, the APT actor will persistent for an extended period of time and use numerous technics.

Assumption. Since our system is deployed in an edge computing environment of the IoT network, we first assume that the *Security Service Cloud* and *Edge Servers* will not be compromised. Once they are compromised, the training and application of the model will not be accomplished. Besides, we assume that the model will not be poisoned by attackers during the model training process, i.e. every participant in federated learning is benign and trusted. At last, we assume the integrity of the data collection framework which records operations of the system completely and data will not be tampered by attackers. The assumptions are only intended to facilitate the evaluation of our method. However, the model security and data privacy mechanisms should be further considered to defend against attacks and we leave them to our future works.

4   APTPMFL Design

4.1   Federated Learning Approach

The ICP-GRU model proposed in this paper is deployed on each *Edge Server* involved in federated learning. The employ of CNN and GRU can fully extract the feature information of the target dataset along with the correlation between data. The training process of

ICP-GRU is shown in Fig. 2. The first step is to standardize and normalize the original data. Since the attributes of some features are character types, such as *pname, q_domain*, and *referer*, all the symbolic features are needed to convert into numerical types before inputting the dataset into the neural network. At the same time, the value of each feature dimension is inconsistent, and the range of values is also highly different. Some data with high values on high-magnitude features have a large weight, thus ignoring some hidden information on low-level data. After that, the target data is input into the ICP-GRU for model training. At last, the trained model can be used to predict the following actions of APT attacks.

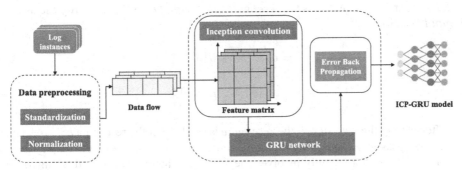

Fig. 2. ICP-GUR training process.

Inception Convolution. As CNN achieved excellent performance in image processing, it is also constantly being applied to other fields. However, traditional CNN only focuses on extracting local features and neglects the aggregation of multiple local features. To address the problem, Google proposed a convolutional neural network architecture in the GoogLeNet network called Inception. The Inception module aggregates $1 * 1, 3 * 3$, $5 * 5$ convolution kernels, and max-pooling into one layer. Multiple convolution kernels extract information of different scales of log instances, and the fusion can obtain a better representation. We adopt the Inception module to perform convolution operation to extract features from multiple scales of the log instances and make the network powerful.

After data preprocessing, the dataset arranged according to timestamp is fed into the Inception convolution module in the form of data flow for training. The data flow is split into fixed-size vectors and each vector contains n pieces of data. After processing each vector, an $n * m$ feature matrix can be formed where m represents the number of features of each data. The inception convolution module will extract the features of the dataset through convolution kernels of $1 * 1, 2 * 2$, and $3 * 3$ and max-pooling of $2 * 2$, and the same convolution should be utilized to match the width and height of the output matrix. Nevertheless, the Inception module is resource-consuming when performing the convolution operation. Therefore, the $1 * 1$ convolution is inserted before $2 * 2$ and $3 * 3$ convolution and after max-pooling to reduce the feature dimension and speed up the calculation.

GRU Networks. Gated Recurrent Unit (GRU) is a type of RNN and similar to LSTM, which is proposed to address the problems of long-term memory and gradient in back-propagation. The reason why GRU is adopted in our system is that it not only achieves the effect equivalent to LSTM but also saves more computing resources, which can greatly improve training efficiency.

Similar to RNN, the hidden state h^{t-1} passed by the previous node and the current input x^t constitute the inputs of GRU. Combining x^t and h^{t-1}, GRU will get the output of the current node as y^t and the hidden state h^t passed to the next node. Initially, two gates are obtained by the previous state h^{t-1} and the current node input x^t. As shown in formula (1) and (2), r indicates the *reset gate*, z is the *update gate*, and σ represents the *Sigmoid* function.

$$r = \sigma\left(W^r x^t + U^r h^{t-1}\right) \tag{1}$$

$$z = \sigma\left(W^z x^t + U^z h^{t-1}\right) \tag{2}$$

After getting the gate signal, the *reset gate* is used to get the reset data $h^{t-1} \odot r$ i.e., $h^{t-1'}$. Then pass $h^{t-1'}$ and x^t into the *tanh* activation function so that the output range is $(-1, 1)$. The h' here mainly involves the currently entered data x^t and adding h' to the current hidden state in a targeted manner is equivalent to memorizing the state at the current moment. The formula is:

$$h' = \tanh\left(W^h x^t + U^h\left(h^{t-1} \odot r\right)\right) \tag{3}$$

Finally, GRU carried out two operations both forgetting and memorizing at the same time. With the *update gate* obtained earlier which the value range is $(0, 1)$, $(1 - z) \odot h^{t-1}$ defines how much the previous memory is forgotten, and $z \odot h'$ defines how much of the h' containing the current node information to keep around. The closer the update gate is to 1, the more memory is reserved, and the closer the update gate is to 0, the more memory is forgotten. The formula for updating is:

$$h^t = (1 - z) \odot h^{t-1} + z \odot h' \tag{4}$$

Multi-scale features hidden in the data flow can be extracted after the ICP model processing plenty of log instances. The data is subsequently input into the GRU network in serialized form to learn the temporal features by selectively learning and forgetting. The model parameters are continuously updated through the gradient backpropagation, and a powerful APT attack prediction model will be obtained in the wake of multiple rounds of iterations.

Federated Learning Process. The system proposed in the paper is applied to the IoT edge computing environment. As shown in Fig. 3, the federated learning process consists of the following steps: 1) Each enterprise's *Edge Server*, as a participant in federated learning, requests an ICP-GRU model from the *Security Service Cloud*. 2) The *Security Service Cloud* posts an initialized model to each *Edge Server* once the participants' requests are received. 3) Each *Edge Server* inputs locally collected data into the model for training. Participants process their dataset independently and do not interact with each other. 4) Each participant updates the local model parameters instead of their data to the *Security Service Cloud* when the model training is done. 5) The *Security Service Cloud* aggregates them into a global model after receiving local updated models. 6) The *Security Service Cloud* will deliver the aggregated global model to each *Edge Server* again. After multiple rounds of re-training, the global model aggregated by the *Security Service Cloud* learned APT attack patterns recorded by several enterprises. Eventually, the *Security Service Cloud* delivers the global model to each participant which is employed to predict the process of APT attackers in the enterprise.

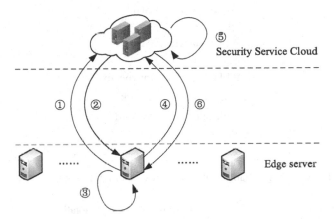

Fig. 3. Federated learning process.

4.2 APT Attack Prediction

APT attackers penetrate the target system for an extended period of time and launch attacks slowly making defenders have to monitor the system behavior incessantly, which brings great challenges to process data efficiently and detect attacks accurately. However, this low-and-slow attack is a double-edged sword. The long span of time between the APT attack phases which leaves enough time for defenders to predict the attacker's next move. When an APT attack at a certain stage is detected in the enterprise and alerts are triggered, suspicious logs are analyzed continuously to predict the attacker's behavior so that the necessary defensive measures are taken before the APT attackers achieve their purpose.

Log Instance. Log instances transformed from log data of IoT devices infected by APT attacks are used for model training and APT attack prediction. The detection system will generate a series of alerts when a certain APT attack step is detected in the IoT systems. We set 7 features for the alert class to further analyze the alert information namely, *Alert_Type*, *Src_Ip*, *Dest_Ip*, *Src_Port*, *Dest_Port*, and *Victim_HostIp*.

Each alert instance is stored in a seven-tuple, $A(I(alert)_m) = (a_1, a_2, a_3, a_4, a_5, a_6, a_7)$. Although attacks trigger alerts, there are still plentiful related unaggressive malicious behaviors that have not been detected which could be a stepping stone for the attacker to perform the next attack.

Table 1. Log types from different recorders.

Type	Logs	Recorders
1	Object access logs	Audit
2	Process create logs	Audit
3	WFP connect logs	Audit
4	HTTP logs	Internet explorer
5	DNS logs	Tshark
6	Authentication logs	Syslogd

Table 2. Log instance features extracted from different log types.

Type	Logs	Features	Annotation
1	Log3	h_ip	Host IP address
2	Log3	d_ip	Destination IP address
3	Log3	h_port	Host port number
4	Log3	d_port	Destination port number
5	Log3	type	Request/response
6	Log5	q_domain	DNS queried domain name
7	Log5	r_ip	DNS resolved IP address
8	Log2	ppid	Base-16 parent process ID
9	Log1 Log2 Log3	pid	Base-16 process ID
10	Log1 Log2 Log3 Log6	pname	Process
11	Log1	objname	Object name
12	Log4	res_code	Response code
13	Log4	referer	Refer of requested URI
14	Log1-Log6	timestamp	Event timestamp

Consequently, alert attributes values will be analyzed to locate threatened IoT devices after alerts are triggered. The log data generated by targeted IoT devices, which will be processed into log instance, are collected by the *Edge Servers* ceaselessly. The type of log hinges on data providers and the operating system installed in IoT devices. On the assumption that all log data derive from Windows Embedded Compact (Windows CE) IoT devices. Various types of log provided by different application programs or record facilities are shown in Table 1. Log data are supposed to transform into a uniform format for the purpose of processing data effectively. As shown in Table 2, 14 features are selected from the log data to constitute the log instance. Due to different log data sources and not all features are contained in each log instance, the types of log instances are also given in Table 2. Each log instance can be described as a 14-tuple: $A\big(I(log)_m\big) = (a_1, a_2 \ldots a_{13}, a_{14})$. If the log instance has only part of the features, the other missing values are set to zero.

Detail of APT Prediction. For the sake of APT prediction, we abstract 4 APT stages under the IoT environment, i.e., *Point of entry*, *C&C communication*, *Asset/Data discovery*, and *Data exfiltration*. Log instances defined above are divided into benign and suspicious by *Log Instance Community Detection* algorithm proposed in our previous work [13], and only suspicious instances can be utilized to train the model.

If a certain APT stage is detected at time T_1 and corresponding alerts are triggered, log instances of threatened devices are recorded start at $T_1 - \tau$. In the training phase, suppose that the APT stage i and $i + 1$ are detected at the time of T_1 and T_2 respectively. All suspicious log instances within the time window $[T_1 - \tau, T_2]$ are feed to the network to train the model, and the ground truth label is T_2. It means that when the IoT devices suffer from these suspicious activities, the APT process will evolve from stage i to stage $i + 1$ with a high probability. In the testing phase, the suspicious log instances are feed into the well-trained model in realtime, and the output of the model is a number in the range of $(0, 1)$ which indicates the probability of the system will suffer the next APT attack stage. Once the output value surpasses the *prediction threshold* λ, the organization is in danger of the next APT attack stage with high confidence.

5 Experimental Evaluation of APTPMFL

Unfortunately, the appropriate system log dataset and attack alert dataset associated with typical APT attacks are not acquirable. However, our previous work [13] has accomplished the construction of the APT scenario and log instance correlation. Therefore, we adopt the labeled log instances and recognized APT scenarios generated in our previous work as simulated data to evaluate the performance of APTPMFL. To make the laboratory environment reflect the characteristics of the real IoT system as similar as possible, we link four identical hosts (a Red Hat Linux operating system running on a host with an Intel Core i7-8550u 2.53 GHz CPU, 16 GB RAM) to deploy an edge computing network based on federated learning. The laboratory environment is shown in Fig. 4. The first host works as the *Security Service Cloud*, and the other three hosts work as the *Edge Servers*. The reason for deploying the identical computing resource on the three hosts is that we respectively set eight virtual machines in the victim *Edge Servers* as virtual IoT devices. Half of the *Edge Servers'* computing resource is shared by the virtual IoT devices. It means an *Edge Server* owns 8 GB RAM, and each virtual IoT device occupies 1 GB RAM. This resource allocation scheme is very consistent with the real IoT system. The APTPMFL is proposed to meet the challenge of resource limitation of the IoT devices. Even though we do not implement the real IoT operation-flow, each virtual IoT device just has 1 GB RAM resource and without any updated patches can competently simulate and testify the efficiency of our method in the IoT system.

To accomplish the federate learning training process of APTPMFL, we allocate the labeled log instances to each virtual machine (works as the IoT devices) and allocate the recognized APT scenarios to the *Edge Servers*. Then, the virtual machines will transmit part of the logs to the *Edge Servers* for training the ICP-GRU models and keep the other logs for testifying the prediction performance. Each module of APTPMFL works on the corresponding locations based on the proposed edge computing-based framework. Finally, we verify the performance of our method based on some evaluation indicators.

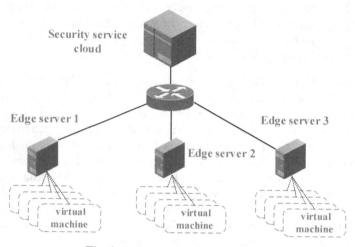

Fig. 4. Laboratory environment setup.

The essence of proposing the APTPMFL is to predict the probability of subsequent APT attacks occurs in IoT scenarios. We implemented the algorithm and federated learning framework on the laboratory *Edge Servers* and *Security Service Cloud*. For the sake of verifying whether the proposed method can effectively predict the probability of subsequent APT attacks occurs in the laboratory environment, we select the F1 score and the False Positive Rate *(FPR)* to evaluate the performance of APTPMFL. The leading reason for adopting the F1 score instead of the common indicators $Recall = TP/(FN + TP)$ and $Precision = TP/(TP + FP)$ is that the two indicators above are mutually exclusive in some cases, needing a harmonic mean to balance respective defects. The parameters *TP, FN,* and *FP* respectively count the number of true-positive prediction probability, the number of false-negative prediction probability, and the number of false-positive prediction probability. Thereby, the formal description of the F_1-score is shown in formula 5. This *FPR* focuses on representing the proportion of false alert of the organization is in danger of the next APT attack stage. The formal description of *FPR* is shown in formula 6.

$$F_1 = \frac{2Recall \cdot Precision}{Recall + Precision} \tag{5}$$

$$FPR = \frac{FP}{FP + TN} \tag{6}$$

We will evaluate the prediction performance of the APTPMFL by analyzing the results of the *FPR* and F_1-scores. The *prediction threshold* λ can influence the prediction result as less next step APT attack alerts will generate with its value higher. We have evaluated the prediction performance of APTPMFL on the 7 typical APT attack scenarios, such as Op-Clandestine Fox, Hacking Team, APT on Taiwan, Tibetan and HK, Op-Tropic Trooper, Russian Campaign, and Attack on Aerospace. The corresponding system logs are reconstructed by one of our previous work [13].

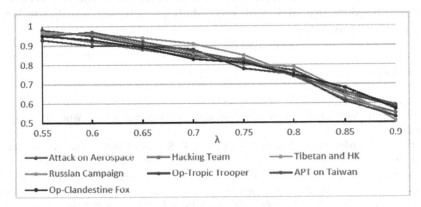

Fig. 5. The F_1 various with threshold λ fluctuation.

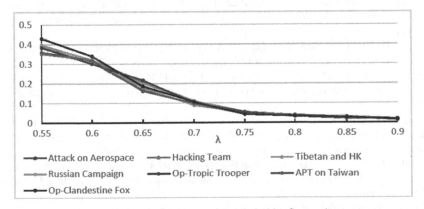

Fig. 6. The *FPR* various with threshold λ fluctuation.

The performances of APTPMFL predicting the 7 typical APT attacks are shown in Fig. 5 and Fig. 6. It is easy to get the result that both the *FPR* and F_1 will reduce with the value of *prediction threshold* λ increases. It is due to the lower λ will make more log instances are detected as activities of the APT attack stage and the benign log instances will have a higher possibility to be incorrectly detected. We work hard for getting a proper threshold to make our method achieve preferable prediction performance on the 7 typical APT attack scenarios. Fortunately, when the value of the prediction threshold λ is 0.75, the F_1-scores are not too low (At around 80%) as well as the *FPR* can drop to an acceptable level (not exceed 5%).

6   Conclusion

We present APTPMFL, a federated learning-based APT prediction method deployed on the edge computing environment. A model containing multiple APT attack patterns is trained in a distributed learning manner and the well-trained model will be implemented to predict the probability of subsequent APT attacks occurs in IoT scenarios. As a result, the experiments show that APTPMFL successfully predicts APT activities with high accuracy and low false rates.

References

1. Palani, K., Holt, E., Smith, S.: Invisible and forgotten: zero-day blooms in the IoT. In: IEEE International Conference on Pervasive Computing and Communication Workshops, pp. 1–6 (2016)
2. Husák, M., Komárková, J., Bou-Harb, E., Čeleda, P.: Survey of attack projection, prediction, and forecasting in cyber security. IEEE Commun. Surv. Tutor. **21**, 640–660 (2019)
3. Polatidis, N., Pimenidis, E., Pavlidis, M., Mouratidis, H.: Recommender systems meeting security: from product recommendation to cyber-attack prediction. In: Boracchi, G., Iliadis, L., Jayne, C., Likas, A. (eds.) EANN 2017. CCIS, vol. 744, pp. 508–519. Springer, Cham (2017). https://doi.org/10.1007/978-3-319-65172-9_43
4. Okutan, A., Yang S.J., McConky, K.: Predicting cyber attacks with Bayesian networks using unconventional signals. In: Conference on Cyber & Information Security Research, pp. 1–13 (2017)
5. Huang, K., Zhou, C., Tian, Y.C., Qin, Y.: Assessing the physical impact of cyberattacks on industrial cyber-physical systems. IEEE Trans. Industr. Electron. **65**(10), 8153–8162 (2018)
6. Okutan, A., Werner, G., McConky, K., Yang, S.J.: POSTER: cyber attack prediction of threats from unconventional resources (CAPTURE). In: ACM SIGSAC Conference, pp. 2563–2565 (2017)
7. Dowling, S., Schukat, M., Melvin, H.: Using analysis of temporal variances within a honeypot dataset to better predict attack type probability. In: International Conference for Internet Technology and Secured Transactions (ICITST), pp. 349–354 (2017)
8. Husák, M., Kašpar, J.: Towards predicting cyber attacks using information exchange and data mining. In: International Wireless Communications Mobile Computing Conference (IWCMC), pp. 536–541 (2018)
9. Ghafir, I., Hammoudeh, M., Prenosil, V., et al.: Detection of advanced persistent threat using machine-learning correlation analysis. Future Gener. Comput. Syst. **89**, 349–359 (2018)
10. Rhode, M., Burnap, P., Jones, K.: Early-stage malware prediction using recurrent neural networks. Comput. Secur. **77**, 578–594 (2018)

11. Huang, L., Zhu, Q.: Adaptive strategic cyber defense for advanced persistent threats in critical infrastructure networks. Perform. Eval. Rev. **46**(2), 52–56 (2018)
12. Niu, W., Zhang, X.S., Yang, G.W., et al.: Modeling attack process of advanced persistent threat using network evolution. IEICE Trans. Inf. Syst. **E100-D**(10), 2275–2286 (2017)
13. Cheng, X., Zhang, J., Chen, B.: Cyber situation comprehension for IoT systems based on APT alerts and logs correlation. Sensors **19**(18), 4045 (2019)
14. Belhadj-Aissa, N., Guerroumi, M.: A new classification process for network anomaly detection based on negative selection mechanism. In: Wang, G., Ray, I., Alcaraz Calero, J.M., Thampi, S.M. (eds.) SpaCCS 2016. LNCS, vol. 10067, pp. 238–248. Springer, Cham (2016). https://doi.org/10.1007/978-3-319-49145-5_24
15. Alshamrani, A., Myneni, S., Chowdhary, A., et al.: A survey on advanced persistent threats: techniques, solutions, challenges, and research opportunities. IEEE Commun. Surv. Tutor. **21**(2), 1851–1877 (2019)
16. Mall, P., Bhuiyan, M.Z.A., Amin, R.: A lightweight secure communication protocol for IoT devices using physically unclonable function. In: Wang, G., Feng, J., Bhuiyan, M.Z.A., Lu, R. (eds.) SpaCCS 2019. LNCS, vol. 11611, pp. 26–35. Springer, Cham (2019). https://doi.org/10.1007/978-3-030-24907-6_3
17. Ara, L., Luo, X.: A data-driven network intrusion detection model based on host clustering and integrated learning: a case study on botnet detection. In: Wang, G., Feng, J., Bhuiyan, M.Z.A., Lu, R. (eds.) SpaCCS 2019. LNCS, vol. 11611, pp. 102–116. Springer, Cham (2019). https://doi.org/10.1007/978-3-030-24907-6_9

DFspliter: Data Flow Oriented Program Partitioning Against Data Stitching Attacks

Chenyu Zhao[1,2]([envelope]) and Hao Han[1,2]([envelope])

[1] College of Computer Science and Technology,
Nanjing University of Aeronautics and Astronautics, Nanjing 211106, China
{cyzhao,hhan}@nuaa.edu.cn
[2] Collaborative Innovation Center of Novel Software Technology
and Industrialization, Nanjing 211106, China

Abstract. Sensitive data disclosure caused by attacks is always a serious problem in the field of information security. It has been one of the focuses of researchers' attention in recent years. As defense solutions against control-flow hijacking attacks widely deployed, an attack method targeting non-control data named data stitching attack was developed. It can mount significant damage on applications but difficult to be detected or defended since it does not change control flow of the victimized program. For the purpose of protecting programs from data stitching attack, we propose DFspliter, an automated program partitioning method focusing on data flows. It can protect any C program by dividing the monolithic program into several blocks. Each block runs in a exclusive process. If attacks cause data leakage in a block, only the data in this block might be stolen, while the data in other blocks will not be affected. We implement our method in the form of an LLVM plug-in, so that software developers can automatically complete the process with only a few compilation commands. Finally, an example modeled after the real-world vulnerability is used to show the effectiveness of our method.

Keywords: Program partitioning · Data stitching attack · Complier plug-in · Data flow

1 Introduction

Today, it is not uncommon for applications to be attacked. The flaws in the program itself and the bugs accidentally left will become weaknesses and bring opportunities for attackers. In order to solve this problem, researchers have proposed different solutions. Program partition is one of them. One of the examples is that modern applications such as Google Chrome follows the multi-process model and divide the program into different processes. So errors in one process will not directly affect other processes. Thanks to this, more than 600 security vulnerabilities was detected in the code of Chrome in 2014, but the damage

G. Wang et al. (Eds.): SpaCCS 2020, LNCS 12382, pp. 90–103, 2021.
https://doi.org/10.1007/978-3-030-68851-6_6

caused by these vulnerabilities is very limited [11]. However, manual program partition will increase the difficulty of development and maintenance, and thus increase the cost. This is not affordable for some development teams.

Among the current attack methods on applications, there is a method called data stitching attack [4]. It is proposed under the background that it is more and more difficult to implement an attack on the control flow. Data stitching attack can stitch together different data flows which are not related in the original program. After making these data flows relevant, the attacker can use the original output in the program to obtain some sensitive data that should not be output without modifying the control flow. Current data protection methods are mostly focusing on control flow, so the defense effect against such attacks is not satisfactory.

With the goal of defending against data splicing attacks, we propose an automated program partitioning method called DFspliter. Developers do not need to consider security when writing code. They only need to do is adding a few commands when compiling. Our method will divide the program into several program blocks, and different program blocks run in different process spaces. Our partitioning method will prioritize safety, and followed by efficiency. Once a program block is attacked, only the data in the attacked block may be tampered with or stolen. The data in other blocks will not be affected. Because the low data coupling between different program blocks, it will be difficult for the attacker to calculate data that has not been leaked based on part of the leaked data.

Main contributions of this paper are as follows:

- DFspliter will focus on the transfer of data between instructions on the basis of the program dependency graph, and analyze this data flow. We divide the data flows with strong correlation into the same block as much as possible, and divide the data streams with weak correlation into different blocks as much as possible.
- We partition the program on the function level. Considering the additional communication overhead caused by passing parameters and other reasons after partitioning, our method will try to reduce the communication overhead by merging some program blocks while having no significant negative impact on security.
- We plan to implement the proposed method in the form of LLVM Pass. Processes communicate through pipes with well-defined interfaces, and the original semantics of the program does not change before and after segmentation.
- Our method will minimize the artificial component, users do not need to rewrite a lot of code, only need to use LLVM to load the required Pass to automatically complete the segmentation. However, considering the complexity of pointers and environmental variables, some manual work may be required.

The rest of this paper is organized as follows. Section 2 is related works. Section 3 is the design of our method, which introduces the program partitioning method proposed in this paper in two parts. Section 4 is the implementation, which introduces the preliminary implementation of our method based on LLVM. Section 5 is the system verification, which shows the effect of applying a prototype of our method to a sample program. Section 6 is conclusion.

2   Related Work

Recently, researches on program segmentation can be divided into two directions. One direction is privilege splitting. Privileges are generally expressed as system calls used by the program. These methods restrict the system calls that can be used by each program block after segmentation, reducing the privilege obtained by the attacker after a successful attack. The other direction is protecting sensitive data, such as user passwords, user privacy, private keys, etc. The common method of protecting sensitive data is separating the part that containing sensitive data from the original program, with targeted protection through various methods such as encryption and verification.

Some methods require a lot of manual operation. These tools provide runtime analysis results of the program and interfaces required for manual segmentation. The developer understands the privileges required by each part of the source code according to the runtime analysis results of the program. Then use specifically implemented interface in operating systems to achieve segmentation, such as Wedge [1]. These methods save the workload of analysis for the developer, but the remaining workload is still considerable. In addition, Wedge also needs to add special primitives in the operating system to support program partitioning. Although it is relatively easy to implement in the open source operating systems such as Linux, there will be difficulties in implementation in systems such as Windows. Modifying the program by developer will also request the ability of programming, which may affect the efficiency of the modified program.

When automation level increased, program partitioning tools require developers to use comments to mark the required privileges in the source code, or manually distinguish the privileges obtained from automatic analysis. The main purpose of Trellis [10] is to provide different privilege for different users. Privtrans [2] and ProgramCutter [14] are intended to limit the set of system calls that the program can use to avoid giving the attacker excessive privileges when the program is attacked. All these three tools mentioned above can automatically work based on the specific comments or the manual classification of privileges written by the developer. These tools also include process isolation or monitoring. Among them, Trellis needs to add special system calls to the operating system, and perform operations such as lifting privilege through the system call, and monitoring program and its system call. Privtrans and ProgramCutter need to modify a series of function calls that cross boundaries, replacing each ordinary function call with IPC (Inter Process Communication) or RPC (Remote Procedure Call). But this process cannot be completed automatically, especially for those complex data structures defined by developers. They still need to manually write interfaces, and tools can simplify this part of the work.

Some tools are almost completely automatic. These tools, such as Trapp [12, 13], can automatically identify different privileges according to the calling situation of library functions, and perform the partitioning highly automatically based on a small number of preset parameters. The effect of automatic partitioning may not be as good as those with manual intervention. Trapp uses IPC to communicate, and its performance overhead is generally not obvious in the test program. But if the split location is just in a high-frequency function call, it may bring significant performance overhead. The main problem of automatic privilege splitting is the difficulty to take into account the implied privilege requirements in operating environments and configuration files, which may cause errors in the modified program. To solve this problem, it is inevitable to add manual interference.

Program partitioning technology in the direction of protecting sensitive data generally relies on developers' manual work. These methods generally needs programmers to marking the location where sensitive data is generated or where sensitive data has died. The tool can analyze and rewrite the program according to the annotations in the source code and the program dependency graph. Then protect the designated sensitive data in a targeted manner. In addition, some methods such as MPI [9] require developers to explain the main data structure. Then the program is divided accordingly to fit the high-level design of the program, and separate different data more naturally. Some solutions, such as Glamdring [5] and SeCage [8], use hardware-provided features such as Intel SGX to rewrite programs. They have excellent defense capabilities against attacks, but these methods are obviously hardware-related, so it may be difficult to migrate to different hardware architectures.

Solutions that only rewrite the program itself, such as Program-mandering [7] and PtrSplit [6], use complex methods to deal with complex parameters, especially the structure of C/C++ that contains pointers and allocates memory through `malloc`. Improper handling may cause overly complex IPC or RPC and affect the performance of the partitioned program. But the performance problem is expected to be solved through more diversified indicators. And the effectiveness of partitioning can be improved at the same time. Some methods such as PtrSplit and Program-mandering only divide the program into two program blocks and protect one of them. This may cause the protected part to be too large in some cases, which may result in a decrease in security or operating efficiency. However, these methods are expected to be extended to multiple partitions to make up for this defect.

3   System Design

Our method splits applications into multiple blocks at function level by inferring weakly correlated data flows represented by sequences of instructions that operate on the same data in Program Dependence Graph (PDG) [3]. Each block will run in a separate process and function calls between blocks are achieved by well-defined interfaces. Through separation, the compromise of one block does not directly lead to the compromise of other blocks. Many modern applications such as Chrome browser are designed in this distributed style to increase security, but there is no automated methods to partition legacy programs based on the separate set of data flows inferred from those programs.

The outline of our system is shown in Fig. 1. It takes the source code of a monolithic C program as input. Firstly, it establishes PDG based on the source program. Then it detects data flows based on PDG and calculates the partitioning scheme. Finally, it modifies the input code to implement segmentation. It is difficult to conduct a pure automated system including code analysis and code modification, we just implemented a prototype to establishing PDG and calculating partition scheme.

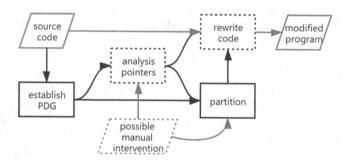

Fig. 1. System outline.

3.1   Motivation Example

First, we use a running example as follows as an example to explain data stitching attack. It is modeled after a web server. Firstly, it loads a private key from a file to establish HTTP connection. After receiving a connection from client, it reads the message received and sanitizes it by calling checkInput. Then, the program calls getFile to read the content of the file and send it to the client.

Before loading the content of the file, the program uses strcat to get the full path. If the string reqFile has enough length to cause overflow at strcat, the second pointer reqFile will be changed. As long as the attacker chooses a message with appropriate length, the second pointer can point to the address where private key privKey stored. Then the private key will be sent to the client as a part of output. The data flow of the private key and the data flow of the input file name has no intersection. They have no dependence on each other and have no shared memory. But the attacker can force the reqFile point to the private key by causing overflow with out changing the control flow.

```
void getFile(char *reqFile, char *output){
    char fullPath[BUFSIZE] = "/path/to/root/", output[
        BUFSIZE];
    strcat(fullPath, reqFile);//stack buffer overflow
    result = retrieve(fullPath);
    sprintf(output,"%s:%s",reqFile,result);
}
int server(){
    char *userInput, *privKey, *result, output[BUFSIZE];
    privKey = loadPrivKey("/path/to/privKey");
    GetConnection(privKey, ...);//HTTPS connection using
        privKey
    userInput = read_socket();
    if (checkInput(userInput)) {//user input OK, parse
        request
        getFile(getFileName(userInput),output);
        sendOut(output);
    }
}
```

To defend against this attack, a feasible method divides the program into two parts running in different processes. The function server is executed in one part and the function getFile is executed in the other. Only the process that runs server has the private key stored in it memory, so the attacker can not get it in the other process and the security is enhanced.

However, the source code of real-world programs usually not available for attackers. So what will be attacked are binary programs. And the attack is hard to predict from source code alone. In this situation, we aim to provide protection for all data flows rather than one or two of them. We analyze the program to get sequences of instructions that operate on the same data in succession with limited modification times. Then we partition the source program into several blocks running in different processes and minimize the sequences of instructions between blocks. After that, if one of those blocks is attacked, only the data used in the victimized block may be stolen and data in other blocks which is the majority is not affected.

3.2   Design of PDG

In the method proposed in this paper, most of the analysis and processing steps need to be based on the PDG. Therefore, establishing the program dependency graph according to the input code is the first step of the entire processing flow.

The program dependency graph was first proposed in 1984. It is a directed graph that intuitively describes the data dependency and control dependency in the program. It is the basis of many program analysis methods and code optimization methods. Each point of PDG corresponds to a statement of high-level language or an instruction in assembly language. The edge of PDG represents the dependency between instructions or statements, which can be divided into control dependency and data dependency. Among them, data dependency can be divided into two cases: def-use dependency and read after write dependency.

If the execution of instruction I1 is determined by another instruction I2, I1 control depends on I2. If the first executed instruction I1 and the later executed instruction I2 exchange execution sequence, the result may change, then I2 data depends on I1.

According to the basic definition of PDG, we build nodes corresponding to all instructions, global variables, and parameters of functions and calls in the program.

Control dependent edges and data dependent edges are built within the function. The control dependent edge is from the jump instruction node to each instruction node in all the basic blocks controlled by it to decide whether to execute. For the def-use dependency, if an operand of one instruction is the result of another instruction, an edge will be built from the instruction node that provides the result to the instruction node that uses the result. For the read-after-write dependency, if two instructions operate on the same part of memory, an edge will be built from the instruction node that writes the memory to the instruction node that reads the memory.

On the basis of the definition of PDG, in order to pertinently handle function calls, two nodes in different but related functions are divided into the following 4 cases. These dependent edges need to be built separately.

- If a function is called, build an edge from the actual parameter node to the formal parameter node.
- If a function has a return value, build an edge from the return value in the called function to the return value in the caller function.
- If an instruction reads a global variable, build an edge from the global variable to the instruction.
- If an instruction writes a global variable, build an edge from the instruction to the global variable.

After the dependency of call and return is processed as above, the return value in the caller function will not be directly connected to the actual parameters.

3.3   Partitioning Method

The data that can be obtained by data stitching attack must be in the memory when the program runs to the location of the vulnerability. Therefore, we divide the program into multiple blocks. Different blocks contain different sets of functions and runs in different processes. This can reduce the data that may be leaked when under attack, thereby improves the security of the program. In order to defend data splicing attacks better, we should make each piece of data to appear in as few program blocks as possible after partitioning. In addition, the data that has been modified multiple times is generally weakly associated with the original data, and they can be regarded as different data. We define instruction flow as follows to represent data flow with limited modifications:

Definition 1. *A set of a chosen instruction and instructions that may operate on the same data before or after the execution of the chosen instruction with modification times on the path less or equal than K.*

For convenience, we call an instruction flow by the name of the chosen instruction. In the definition, K is an adjustable parameter, which is used to indicate how many times a piece of data has been modified can be regarded as completely different data. The smaller the K, the stricter the requirement. The larger the K, the more ambiguous the requirement. In the current prototype system, we set K to 5.

In programs, searching for the instruction flow for each instruction as the chosen instruction may cause greater time penalty and lots of repeated calculations. Considering that the granularity of our partitioning is at the function level, the partitioning process mainly focuses on the instruction flow between each pair of functions, rather than processing every instruction. Accordingly, the instruction flow between functions can be defined as follows:

Definition 2. *The instruction flow set $ds(f_A, f_B)$ from function f_A to function f_B is a set of instruction flows that take one of the instructions of f_A that store parameters, set arguments of call instructions, and set return values as the chosen instruction and contain at least one instruction in f_B.*

For example, in the program shown in Sect. 3.1, $ds(\texttt{server}, \texttt{getFile})$ has the instruction flows starting from `userInput` and `output` in `server`.

We then calculate the optimal partitioning based on the relevance between blocks, the complexity of each block, and the time penalty.

Relevance. The instruction flow in the program generally has different degrees of importance. Among them, the widely used but basically unchanged data may be more important because it may play a controlling role or be a parameter of multiple calculation processes. For each instruction flow x, the number of instructions in it is defined as its influence range $ir(x)$, which is used to describe the importance of the instruction flow. Then the relevance $R(f_A, f_B)$ of function f_A and f_B can be defined as follows:

$$R(f_A, f_B) = \max_{i \subset ds(f_A, f_B)} ir(i) + \max_{j \in ds(f_B, f_A)} ir(j) \tag{1}$$

In our example shown in Sect. 3.1, $R(\texttt{server}, \texttt{getFile})$ is eaual to $ir(\texttt{userInput})$ because $ir(\texttt{userInput})$ is larger than $ir(\texttt{output})$ and `getFile` has no return value.

Complexity. Even if the program is divided into multiple processes for execution, the program blocks that are directly attacked may still leak the data it contains. Therefore, it is necessary to control the size of each block to prevent it from leaking too much data or contains too many weaknesses when it is attacked. We define the complexity of a program block b as $C(b)$. To achieve a higher automation level, we do not request programmer to provide annotation information. That means we do not have clearly indicating where the program has a bug or where data leakage may occur. So complexity may be the total number of lines in source code, the number of instructions and other indicators that make sense.

Time Penalty. After the source program rewritten into a multi-process program, some function calls will be rewritten as inter-process communication (IPC), and data required for program execution such as parameters and return values should be passed between processes, which will cause additional time penalty. For any function f_A, define the time penalty $T(f_A)$ as the time required to call the function through IPC. Then define the set of functions called through IPC as G. In our method, an IPC contributes 100 times time penalty than a byte transmitted between processes. These values are based on our test of IPC performance under the Linux system.

Priority should be given to security during partitioning, so relevance is the most important indicator. Complexity and time penalty are secondary indicators. Define $B(f_A)$ as the block where function f_A is located. Then during the partitioning, the following expression needs to be minimized:

$$k_1 * \sum_{B(i)!=B(j)} R(i,j) + k_2 * \max_k C(k) + k_3 * \sum_{l \in G} T(l) \tag{2}$$

Among them, k_1, k_2, and k_3 are adjustable parameters, which we will determine in future work, or leave them as user-set parameters. In our example, there is only two functions, so $R(\texttt{server}, \texttt{getFile})$ is the largest. Then, the two functions will be divided into two blocks. And the sensitive data in `server` will be separated from the vulnerable `getFile`.

4 Implementation

We implement the major part of our method in the form of LLVM pass under the framework of the open source project LLVM. This section will introduce the realization of our method described in Sect. 3 in two parts.

LLVM is a collection of modular, reusable compiler and tool chain technology. It has a special intermediate language called LLVM IR. The front end of LLVM is responsible for translating high-level languages into LLVM IR. The most common front end is the compiler Clang. There are various passes in the middle, and each pass is a specific function that can be applied to LLVM IR. The back end is responsible for assembling LLVM IR into machine code that can run on target machine. We implement our method as a series of passes with a total of 2578 lines of code.

4.1 Implementation of PDG

We establish PDG based on LLVM IR and implements it in the form of an LLVM pass. There is no strict sequence requirement for the establishment of PDG, which basically conforms to the description in Sect. 3.2.

In the process of creating nodes, we build nodes for instructions and global variables respectively. For call instructions in LLVM IR, We build special call nodes and connect them with corresponding parameter trees.

When analyzing control dependence, we use the post dominator tree built in LLVM. When analyzing read-after-write dependence, we use alias analysis built in LLVM to improve accuracy. When analyzing the def-use dependence, thanks to the static single assignment (SSA) feature of LLVM that each variable assigned as the result of an instruction can be assigned only once, where does an operand comes from can be determined easily.

To handle inter-procedural dependence, we build parameter trees [6] instead of a single node for every formal parameters, actual parameters, and return values. The parameter trees include detailed information about structures, arrays and pointers based on the type of parameters. Edges are built with nodes on parameter trees to represent inter-procedural dependence and read-after-write dependence.

Some call instructions in the program may call functions through function pointers. In this situation, LLVM IR cannot determine the called function. The analysis of function pointers is a complicated task, and we are not focusing on it now. If this happens, our method will try to match the possible called functions by type, and build a corresponding dependent edge for each function that meets the conditions.

4.2 Implementation of Partitioning

In our implementation, the function nodes in PDG are colored to represent the partitioning scheme. Each color represents a block of the modified program. We implemented this in the form of an LLVM Pass.

First, we process the corresponding points in the PDG of the formal parameters, actual parameters, and return values in the function. According to the definition of the instruction flow, the forward tracking or reverse slicing is performed with these points as the chosen point to obtain the functions that instruction flows can reach and instruction flows' influence range. It should be noted that forward tracking and reverse slicing are only performed along the data dependent edges, and do not involve control dependent edges. These are also limited by the number of data modification K. After that, each pair of functions is processed and the relevance between them is calculated.

What we have implemented is a simple prototype system, without considering the complexity of program blocks and time penalty. So only security is considered when coloring, that is, the relevance between functions.

At the beginning of the partitioning process, all functions are located in separate program blocks. For a program with n functions, the algorithm continues to merge the program blocks according to the relevance between the functions until the number of program blocks does not exceed $\log_2 n + 1$. For each step of merging, each pair of program blocks is scanned, and the sum of the relevance between the functions located in it is calculated. Then in each step of merge, the algorithm selects a pair of program blocks with the largest sum of relevance and merge them into one block.

5   Evaluation

5.1   Validation of DFspliter

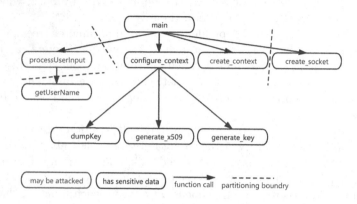

Fig. 2. Partitioning result of ssl_server.

We use a C program named `ssl_server` as a test program (Fig. 2). Part of the program is shown as follows. It is a vulnerable server program based on open SSL and has a corresponding attack program `ssl_client` with it. `ssl_server` generates a pointer `ctx` in the `main` function by calling the `create_context` function, which has a wide range of influence. After that, a private key `pkey` for encrypted communication is generated by calling `configure_context` in the function `main` and stored in the memory pointed to by `ctx`. After everything is ready, the main function cyclically receive messages from the client, and processes and responds through the `processUserInput` function. There are vulnerabilities in the `processUserInput` function that can be exploited by data stitching attack. When the message length is appropriate, the private key may be sent back to the client as a message.

```
void configure_context(SSL_CTX *ctx){
    /* Generate private key pkey */
    SSL_CTX_use_PrivateKey(ctx, pkey);
}
char buf[1024];
char* processUserInput(char *input, int size){
    char *yourName, greeting[16] = "Welcome ";
    yourName = getUserName(input);
    strcat(greeting, yourName);
    sprintf(buf, "%s: %s", yourName, greeting);
    return buf;
}
int main(int argc, char **argv){
    /* Prepare for connection */
```

```
ctx = create_context();
configure_context(ctx);
sock = create_socket(4433);
while(1) {
    /* Accept a request and start connection */
    bytes = SSL_read(ssl, buf, sizeof(buf));
    char *output = processUserInput(buf, bytes);
    SSL_write(ssl, output, strlen(output));
    /* End connection */
}
/* Clean up */
}
```

We use the prototype described in Sect. 4 to strengthen `ssl_server`, and rewrite the source program into a multi-process program according to the partitioning result. The program is partitioned into 4 blocks that run in different processes and communicate with each other through named pipes. First 3 blocks contains `create_context`, `processUserInput` and `getUserName` respectively. The function containing the sensitive data `pkey`, including the main function, is located in the fourth block. Since there is no `pkey` stored in the process where the vulnerable `processUserInput` is located, the private key can no longer be obtained through data stitching attacks, and the security of the program is improved.

5.2 Performance Overhead

We use another C program to test the communication overhead after partitioning. Part of this program is shown as follows. This program has a function named `refuse`, which is called by `main` when the input is illegal. What the function `refuse` does is opening a file, writing a constant string into the file and closing the file. To test the overhead, we change the type and the number of parameters of `refuse` and rewrite the program into a 2-process program which divides the two functions into different processes. We always provide an illegal input and let `main` calls `refuse` 1000 times. The results are shown in Table 1.

```
void refuse(int y){//Parameter may be changed
    f=fopen("/* File name */","w");
    fprintf(f,"do not support argument y=%d !\n",y);
    fclose(f);
    return;
}
int main(int argc,char** argv){
    int x,y,z;
    scanf("%d%d",&x,&y);
    for(int i=0;i<1000;++i)
        if(y>=0){/* Do something */}
        else refuse(y);
    return 0;
}
```

Table 1. Communication Overhead of different parameters

Parameters type in C	Number of parameters	Time spent before partitioning (ms)	Time spent after partitioning (ms)	Communication Overhead (%)
int	1	60.95	68.75	12.79
int*	1	58.31	69.91	19.89
int[1000]	1	58.45	87.80	50.21
int	10	56.90	80.10	40.77

Communication overhead is slightly lower than that of reading and writing files. Inter-process calls have a basic time consumption, so are parameter transmissions. The increase in the number of bytes transferred will also bring additional time cost, but not as much as the number of parameters. Generally, most of the running time is spent on logic of programs rather than calling a function 1000 times, so the communication overhead is acceptable. Our approach also tries to avoid transmissions of parameters with large number of bytes.

6   Conclusion

We designed and partially implemented a program partitioning method called DFspliter based on LLVM. Any C language program with single block can be automatically divided into a program consist with multiple program blocks during the compilation process. Each block will execute in a different process and communicates with others through well-defined interfaces. Because different processes have different memory spaces and different data stored in them, potentially sensitive data can be protected. When one block is attacked, it will not affect the security of data in other blocks. Aiming at the characteristics of data stitching attacks, our method uses data flow as the main basis for partitioning procedures, and improves the pertinence of segmentation by splitting different data flow with lower correlation into different program blocks. In order to get better partitioning result, we used a special algorithm to perform coloring operations based on the analysis of data flow. Finally, the input program can be changed into a multi-process program and the security is increased.

Acknowledgements. We sincerely thank reviewers for their insightful feedback. This work was supported in part by NSFC Award #61972200.

References

1. Bittau, A., Marchenko, P., Handley, M., Karp, B.: Wedge: splitting applications into reduced-privilege compartments. In: 5th USENIX Symposium on Networked Systems Design and Implementation, pp. 309–322 (2008)
2. Brumley, D., Song, D.: Privtrans: automatically partitioning programs for privilege separation. In: 13th USENIX Security Symposium, pp. 57–72 (2004)
3. Ferrante, J., Ottenstein, K.J., Warren, J.D.: The program dependence graph and its use in optimization. ACM Trans. Program. Lang. Syst. (TOPLAS) 9(3), 319–349 (1987)
4. Hu, H., Chua, Z.L., Adrian, S., Saxena, P., Liang, Z.: Automatic generation of data-oriented exploits. In: 24th USENIX Security Symposium, pp. 177–192 (2015)
5. Lind, J., et al.: Glamdring: automatic application partitioning for Intel SGX. In: 2017 USENIX Annual Technical Conference, pp. 285–298 (2017)
6. Liu, S., Tan, G., Jaeger, T.: PtrSplit: supporting general pointers in automatic program partitioning. In: Proceedings of the 2017 ACM SIGSAC Conference on Computer and Communications Security, pp. 2359–2371 (2017)
7. Liu, S., et al.: Program-mandering: quantitative privilege separation. In: Proceedings of the 2019 ACM SIGSAC Conference on Computer and Communications Security, pp. 1023–1040 (2019)
8. Liu, Y., Zhou, T., Chen, K., Chen, H., Xia, Y.: Thwarting memory disclosure with efficient hypervisor-enforced intra-domain isolation. In: Proceedings of the 22nd ACM SIGSAC Conference on Computer and Communications Security, pp. 1607–1619 (2015)
9. Ma, S., Zhai, J., Wang, F., Lee, K.H., Zhang, X., Xu, D.: MPI: multiple perspective attack investigation with semantic aware execution partitioning. In: 26th USENIX Security Symposium, pp. 1111–1128 (2017)
10. Mambretti, A., et al.: Trellis: Privilege separation for multi-user applications made easy. In: International Symposium on Research in Attacks, Intrusions, and Defenses, pp. 437–456 (2016)
11. Rogowski, R., Morton, M., Li, F., Monrose, F., Snow, K.Z., Polychronakis, M.: Revisiting browser security in the modern era: New data-only attacks and defenses. In: 2017 IEEE European Symposium on Security and Privacy (EuroS&P), pp. 366–381 (2017)
12. Trapp, M., Rossberg, M., Schaefer, G.: Program partitioning based on static call graph analysis for privilege separation. In: 2015 IEEE Symposium on Computers and Communication (ISCC), pp. 613–618 (2015)
13. Trapp, M., Rossberg, M., Schaefer, G.: Automatic source code decomposition for privilege separation. In: 2016 24th International Conference on Software, Telecommunications and Computer Networks (SoftCOM), pp. 1–6 (2016)
14. Wu, Y., Sun, J., Liu, Y., Dong, J.S.: Automatically partition software into least privilege components using dynamic data dependency analysis. In: 2013 28th IEEE/ACM International Conference on Automated Software Engineering (ASE), pp. 323–333 (2013)

Revisiting Attacks and Defenses in Connected and Autonomous Vehicles

Ziyan Fang[1,2]($\boxtimes$), Weijun Zhang[1,2], Zongfei Li[3], Huaao Tang[3], Hao Han[1,2]($\boxtimes$), and Fengyuan Xu[3]

[1] College of Computer Sciences and Technology,
Nanjing University of Aeronautics and Astronautics, Nanjing 211106, China
`542897592@qq.com, 807301949@qq.com, hhan@nuaa.edu.cn`
[2] Collaborative Innovation Center of Novel Software Technology
and Industrialization, Nanjing 210093, China
[3] State Key Laboratory for Novel Technology, Nanjing University,
Nanjing 210046, China

Abstract. With the development of the automotive industry, the security of connected and autonomous vehicles (CAVs) has become a hot research field in recent years. However, previous studies mainly focus on the threats and defending mechanisms from the networking perspective, while newly emerging attacks are targeting the core component – AI of CAVs. Therefore, the defense methods against these attacks are urgently needed. In this paper, we revisit emerging attacks and their technical countermeasures for CAVs in a layered inventory, including in-vehicle systems, V2X, and self-driving. We believe that this survey provides insights on defending adversary attacks on CAVs and will shed light on the future research in this area.

Keywords: Connected and autonomous vehicles · V2X · In-vehicle network · Vehicle security · Autonomous vehicle algorithms

1 Introduction

The automotive industry is undergoing massive digital transformation towards connected and autonomous vehicles (CAVs). Compared with traditional cars, CAVs have great potential to achieve extended driving automation with strengthened environment awareness improved by vehicle connectivity. The Association of Automotive Engineers (SAE) definitions for levels of automation divide vehicles into 6 levels. However, only cars in L4 and L5 are considered autonomous vehicles. The L4 has fully automated driving feature in specific environments, while L5 can do all the driving in all circumstances.

Their self-driving capability is achieved through three layers: perception, cognition and execution as shown in Fig. 1. The perception layer is used to capture vehicle's internal and surrounding status via in-vehicle sensors and environmental sensors. With assistant of V2X communication, the cognition layer recognizes

© Springer Nature Switzerland AG 2021
G. Wang et al. (Eds.): SpaCCS 2020, LNCS 12382, pp. 104–117, 2021.
https://doi.org/10.1007/978-3-030-68851-6_7

vehicle's motion states and external threats based on the perception layer, and then determines the trajectory of the vehicle through deep learning algorithms. Finally, the execution layer controls the vehicle by issuing commands to Electronic Control Units (ECUs) and actuators through in-vehicle networks (e.g., CAN bus, FlexRay, MOST).

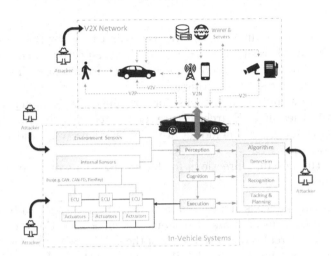

Fig. 1. The structure of connected and autonomous vehicles

Modern cars are quite insecure and vulnerable from an information system perspective. Although some security mechanisms have been adopted by automotive suppliers after a 2014 Jeep Cherokee was hacked by Miller and Valasek [26], new vulnerabilities continue to rise every year. A large number of studies show that the attack surface of CAVs is broad. A set of features in in-vehicle systems, V2X communication, autonomous algorithms might allow misuse of or a breach into CAVs, resulting in much more profound and widespread effects. Therefore, it is important of protecting future CAVs from hackers and cyberattacks.

In literature, there are many survey papers about automotive security. For example, work [3] study vulnerabilities and defenses in Controller Area Network (CAN) bus with more focus on authentication. Work [44] summarize the V2X technology and its protocol vulnerabilities, as well as corresponding defense measures. Work [43] discusses the security issues of connected vehicles from three categories, and introduces the trend of network attacks and the protection requirements that should be developed for networked services. Work [34] provides an overview of the security issues in AV but with emphasis on attacking sensors and iris recognition systems. However, those surveys are not specific to CAVs and mainly focus on the networking aspect rather than the system and algorithm perspective.

In this paper, we review potential attacks and their technical countermeasures for CAVs in a layered inventory: in-vehicle systems, V2X and autonomous algorithms corresponding to execution, cognition and perception layers, respectively. We summarize the attack threats in each layer. Compared with the threats in traditional vehicles, attackers not only attack ECU and CAN networks, they also attack environmental sensors and autonomous vehicle algorithms in CAVs. Later in this survey, we provide insights on corresponding defense approaches to address those attack threats. In summary, the contributions of this paper include:

- To our best understanding, this survey is the first to study the attack surface and defensive mechanisms for CAVs from the perspective of the system and algorithms, while previous study mostly is network-oriented. This will shed light on the future research in this area.
- We explore new potential attacks for emerging CAVs along with existing vulnerabilities in E/E architecture, and categorize the various security approaches from 3 layers, including in-vehicle systems, V2X and autonomous driving algorithms.
- We discuss the possible directions for future research works on security and privacy issues in CAVs.

The rest of this paper is structured as follows: Sect. 2 specifically introduces the architecture of connected and autonomous vehicles. Section 3 describes the attacks that may be realized at each layer of the CAVs. Section 4 introduces the corresponding defense methods in detail for possible attacks. Section 5 describes the possible directions for future research works on security and privacy issues in CAVs, followed by the summary of the paper. Section 6 summarizes this survey.

2 Background

CAVs include not only autonomous driving but also the connection between the vehicle and the surrounding environment. In this section, we briefly present the main components of CAVs, which are typical targets of modern vehicle attacks discussed in next section.

2.1 In-Vehicle Networks

The in-vehicle network of CAVs connects sensors, Electronic Control Units (ECUs) and actuators of the car with a point-to-point connection into a complex network structure. They together are the guarantee for the normal and security vehicle driving, and are the critical components of the vehicle. The failure of any one may cause the abnormal driving of the vehicle, and even a traffic accident in a serious situation.

Sensors in CAVs can be divided into two categories: internal sensors and external sensors. The former, arranged inside a car, is used to check the function of the vehicle. For example, the oxygen sensor monitors the content of exhaust gases for the proportion of oxygen. Sensors in the latter category provide the car visuals of its surroundings and help it detect the speed and distance of nearby objects, as well as their three-dimensional shape. Three primary external vehicle sensors are camera, radar and LiDAR.

Electronic Control Units (ECUs) are used to enable computer-based control of a vehicle. Based on the information sent by vehicle sensors, ECUs determine the running states and control the vehicle to work together. A modern car may have up to 70 ECUs - and each of them is assigned a specific function (e.g., engine control). Typically, ECUs are grouped into several subnetworks according to their functions. For example, the ECUs in charge of steering and braking are grouped together.

Bus networks, like the nervous system of the human body, interconnect ECUs and enable the information sensed by one part to be shared with other parts of the vehicle. The autopilot system in CAVs use such networks to transmit control commands. Example bus networks include Controller Area Network (CAN), CAN-FD, FlexRay, and automotive Ethernet. Among them, CAN is the standard for in-vehicle communications today in fact. The detail of CAN can be found in many good surveys such as [19].

2.2 Vehicle-to-X Communication (V2X)

V2X which stands for vehicle-to-everything technology enables cars to communicate with their surroundings and makes driving safer and more efficient. V2X covers Vehicle to vehicle (V2V), Vehicle to infrastructure (V2I), Vehicle to Network(V2N), Vehicle to Pedestrian (V2P) and others. Working together, they provide a guarantee for the security driving of vehicles. In CAVs, V2X offers an additional means to sense environment conditions other than typical sensors, e.g., retrieving traffic information and other vehicle's location for route planning.

Currently, there are two main types of communication technologies used for V2X: Dedicated Short Range Communication (DSRC) and Long Term Evolution for V2X (LTE-V2X). The DSRC system consists of a series of IEEE and SAE standards. DSRC uses IEEE 802.11p protocol which is also called Wireless Access in the Vehicular Environment (WAVE), at the physical layer and media access control (MAC) layer, while its network architecture and security protocols are defined in IEEE 1609 WAVE.

2.3 Autonomous Algorithms

Autonomous driving requires the car to be like human to recognize something that appears in surrounding environment and to forecast the changes that are possible to these surroundings. A deep neural network with various autonomous algorithms is equivalent to a human brain. Based on their tasks, those algorithms can be broadly grouped into three categories as follows:

- **The detection of an object:** Object detection based on deep learning is often used in the detection of traffic signs/lights and other vehicles in the proximity. Based on the data provided by environmental sensors attached to the vehicle, object detection algorithms can pinpoint the location of traffic signs/lights and other vehicles. Together with other autonomous algorithms, the autopilot system will make a decision whether the car needs to slow down or stop. The state-of-the-art learning-based object detection algorithms include Faster R-CNN, etc.

- **The recognition of an object:** Object detection is typically coupled with the task of object recognition which is used to identify the class of objects, e.g., whether an object is a traffic sign, vehicle, or pedestrian. Common recognition algorithms are alexnet and senet.
- **The tracking of an object and trajectory planning:** Trajectory planning is based on path planning and obstacle avoidance planning. At present, it is mainly based on reinforcement learning and time series algorithms to achieve high standards of unmanned driving technology. In particular, reinforcement learning is widely used in automatic driving trajectory decision-making.

3   Attack Surface for CAVs

In this section, we revisit the attack surfaces of CAVs and identify three key components: in-vehicle systems, V2X communication, and autonomous algorithms. We separate them primarily into two categories: *remote* and *internal* as shown in Fig. 2.

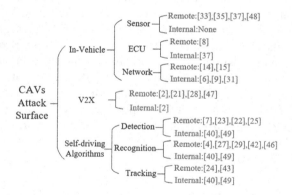

Fig. 2. Example of potential attacks by various research groups

3.1   Attacks Against In-Vehicle Systems

In-vehicle systems consist of three major components: sensors, ECUs and bus networks. Each of them may be compromised with both remote and internal attacks. Remote includes primarily any form of wireless communications interface. Internal includes both physical access such as the USB or OBD-II port, and internal elements of the in-vehicle system interconnected on the network or the network itself.

Network: The CAN network is an important attack surface. Due to the broadcast nature of CAN as well as a lack of encryption, an attacker with access to internal network can monitor and reverse engineer the network architecture, collect personally sensitive information, or perform DoS attacks. Access to the network can be obtained through a physical interface or through a variety of wireless attack vectors.

The attacks on wireless interfaces are almost remote attacks. Work [14] analyzed relay attacks on Passive Keyless Entry and Start (PKES) systems used in modern cars. Work [15] proposed that by recovering the cryptographic algorithms and keys from ECUs, an adversary can gain unauthorized access to a vehicle. There are many internal attacks on CAN. For example, the attackers can eavesdrop CAN data by installing interceptors on the CAN network [6]. The eavesdropping attack is the starting point for many attacks, such as spoofing attacks, Dos attacks [6,31] and replay attacks. Work [9] discussed two kinds of spoofing attacks, which are masquerade attack and fabrication attack.

ECU: Compromising an ECU can also provide access to other shared secrets (such as cryptographic keys) which allow an attack to extend to other components on the vehicle.

One of the remote attacks is proposed by work [8] named battery drain attack due to the ECU wake-up mechanism. On the other hand, an attacker can physically internal attack the ECU through voltages, currents, and other physical means, such as overcurrent attacks [37]. This attack makes the microprocessor fail or burn out by exceeding the maximum rating of the microprocessor.

Sensor [33,37]: Sensors can be manipulated directly to achieve a particular effect. By modifying the physical property detected by a sensor, tampering with the sensor hardware, or through electromagnetic attacks, the input for which an ECU will make a decision can be modified directly.

Attacks on sensors are mostly remote attacks, such as jamming attacks [47] and spoofing attacks [47]. Noise can change sensor data to provide malicious input to components using the data. The tire pressure sensor in the TPMS (Tire Pressure Monitoring System) can be used for observation and tracking purposes and as an activation trigger for other attacks [35].

3.2   Attacks Against V2X Communication

Vehicles across different manufacturers share DSRC as a common attack surface since they communicate with each other on the same V2X system. Separate from the remote code execution risk, false data provided through a V2X system can cause disruptions in traffic flow and pose a risk to personal safety through physical effects. In addition, any vulnerability may have the potential to spread to other vehicles or infrastructure quickly.

Most of the attacks on V2X are remote attacks which are carried out through the **V2X communication protocols** such as IEEE 802.11p. These attacks include [28]:1) *Black hole attack*: The compromised node will not relay the data packet to adjacent nodes, and the data packet will be intercepted and discarded by the attacker [2]. 2) *Flooding attack*: By flooding the MAC, the attacker will send countless data packets to make the victim node unusable. 3) *Jamming attack*: By using a jammer to identify the data packet and launch attack, the attacker can broadcast signals to destroy the data or block the channel, etc. [21]. 4) *Sybil attack*: The attacking station will send false V2X messages, which will simulate fake sites on the road and prevent other sites from sending real messages.

Vehicle ransomware [46] is also a remote attack but it is based on **terminal nodes**, such as mobile phones and the vehicle-mounted security vulnerabilities. Attackers can indirectly infect botnets to vehicles through smartphones, navigation, etc. and through vulnerabilities such as the Bluetooth buffer overflow vulnerability of in-vehicle infotainment units to lock the key parts of the vehicle.

Eavesdropping attacks [2] can be internal attacks or remote attacks. In the internal attack, attackers can collect information anywhere without permission, such as the data management system. In the remote attack, attackers can eavesdrop on vehicle information due to the plaintext transmission.

3.3 Adversarial Attacks Against Autonomous Algorithms

If autonomous algorithms are attacked, the autopilot system may make an adverse decision, resulting in devastating consequences. Similar to Sect. 2.3, we divide algorithm-related attacks into three tasks.

Attacks on Object Detection Algorithms [7,23,39,48]**:** They are mostly based on three techniques: *feature extraction region, iterative optimization,* and *Generative Adversarial Network (GAN).* Since target detection algorithms need to extract the region of interest, attackers corrupt the extracted region by interference. DPATH attack [25] is to make the region where the adversarial patches exists as the only valid region of interest, while potential proposal region are ignored. BPATH attack [22] generates and refines the adversarial background patches in the overall loss optimization iterations.

Attacks on Object Recognition Algorithms [4,27,41,45]**:** Three categories as shown below. Because there are few cases of classification algorithm, however they are the most classical in the field of deep learning vision, simply mention it as a category.

– *Fast Gradient Sign based Adversarial attacks:* Iterative Targeted Fast Gradient Sign Method which is based on FGSM algorithm applies the target FGSM multiple times for a more powerful example of confrontation.
– *Optimization based Approach:* In this way, the adversary samples are obtained by solving optimization problems. By replacing the class variables in the antidisturbance with target class with the lowest recognition probability, the least likely class iterative methods are obtained.

– *Universal Adversarial Perturbation:* Universal advanced perturbations computed by Moosavi-Dezfooli et al. [29]. can generate any image attack disturbance, which is also almost invisible to human beings.

Attacks on the Trajectory Algorithms [42,48]: Trajectory algorithms are mainly attacked by *strategical time attack* and *enhancing attack* [24]. Strategically time attack is a traditional and conventional learning method. Enhancing attack's goal is to induce the agent to go to a specified state makes the performance of agent worse.

4 Survey of Technical Defense

This section will provide an overview of existing defensive approaches in response to the attack model presented in Sect. 3.

4.1 Defensive Approaches for In-Vehicle Systems

Authentication-Based Countermeasures: The lack of authenticity within automotive networks is a prime cause of the failure of today's automotive security. We admit that cryptography and key management is a requirement for any system that attempts to implement authentication. However, implementation of any form of cryptography on the car's resource constrained ECUs performing real-time control may not be practicable. Therefore, securing the external gateways and communications paths to the CAN bus may prove more valuable and workable than securing the individual nodes through cryptography.

One method of adding authentication between CAN nodes is through the use of Message Authentication Codes (MACs). For example, work [18] proposed the IA-CAN (Identity-Anonymized CAN) protocol. This scheme randomizes the CAN ID on a frame-by-frame basis to provide sender authentication and prevent attackers from injecting fake messages. In work [12], Parrot system was proposed to defend against the spoofing attack. The ECU equipped with Parrot System can identify spoofing messages on the bus that impersonate one of its own IDs.

In addition, there are other authentication-based defense methods. Work [30] have summarized some defenses and evaluated them through custom security testing standards. Therefore, in these paper we will not repeat them.

Fingerprint-Based Countermeasures: Fingerprint-based access control prevents attackers from accessing certain resources by verifying them as unauthorized nodes. Certain physical characteristics/uniqueness such as the voltage, the signal rising and falling edge characteristics and the clock frequency are utilized to recognize legitimate ECUs, so this type of approaches can prevent spoofing attacks. For example, work [10] firstly proposed the voltage profile of the ECU as its specific fingerprint to identify the attacker ECU by measuring and using the voltage on the vehicle network and implemented the corresponding detection tool called Viden. Work [20] improved Viden by only measuring the dominant voltage of the ECU as a signaling feature, and using high and low signals rather than differential signals which would make it more error-prone in identifying attacker ECUs.

To prevent bus-off attacks (i.e., a type of denial-of-service attacks), work [11] proposed VoltageIDS, an intrusion detection system based on voltage characteristics. VoltageIDS uses electrical characteristics which is the time when the status of the signal changes from 0 to 1 and 1 to 0 as the fingerprint characteristics of the CAN message.

Furthermore, the defensive approaches for in-vehicle systems are not limited to ECU-based "fingerprints". Work [36] developed a motion-based IDS (MIDS). This method determines whether the data is normal or has been tampered based on the fingerprint characteristics of the vehicle's behavior correlation at a certain time, such as wheel speed, vehicle speed, etc.

IDS-Based Countermeasures: The intrusion detection method in the automotive domain depends on how the detection mechanism is utilized within the system. The anomaly-based IDS is the most common and promising approach used in the automotive IDS compared to the signature- and statistical-based technique. As mentioned above, Work [9] proposed the clock-based intrusion detection system (CIDS). It exploited the timing interval of CAN traffic and the frequency of CAN packet sequences in identifying anomalies within the CAN bus network.

The signature-based approach detects an attack by utilizing a set of identified signatures, malicious events, or rules stored in the database module of IDS. For example work [40] extracted the attack signatures obtained from standard ECU specifications using finite-state automate (FSA) in detecting an anomalous sequence of CAN packets via the in-vehicle network.

Other Defensive Approaches: There are other defense methods and are not based on the three categories above. Work [35] provided some defense guidance against TPMS attacks which is encrypting TPS packets and placement of additional password checksums, such as message authentication codes, before CRC checksums. Besides, Mehmet Bozdal, et al. [6] have been made a survey on the other defensive approaches and we will not repeat in this paper.

4.2   V2X Security Defense

V2X attacks are mostly remote attacks, so this section will focus on security defense methods against them.

Remote attacks are usually completed through protocol vulnerabilities. Many researchers have found methods to against them. The model proposed in work [1] uses advanced encryption standards to achieve user privacy. Using the randomness of channels in a vehicle network to share keys solves the key distribution problem of advanced encryption standards. Work [5] proposed a secure and intelligent routing protocol where they use double encryption on packets and use the authentication scheme to measure the trust of nodes. However, this method increases processing time and adds network overhead. Work [49] proposed a new method to create passwords based on one-time authentication asymmetric group key protocols Mixed zones to protect against malicious eavesdropping. Security information is encrypted using group keys to improve vehicle privacy.

In particular, for the Sybil attack, work [16] used directional antennas to identify the source of the message. If a malicious vehicle broadcasts a large number of messages, it will be discovered by other vehicles.

4.3 Defensive Measures for Autonomous Algorithms

Countermeasures for Object Detection and Recognition: To improve the performance of the machine learning models against adversarial attacks, existing solutions developed in other domains may not be directly used for autonomous driving. For example, the detection of adversarial attacks may not be useful. However, there exist suitable solutions to help the CAVs defend against adversarial attacks in literature.

These approaches include but not limited to: 1) *data augmentation*, using image processing methods to help augment the quantity and diversity of the training set; 2) input transformation, using image processing methods to disturb or even remove the adversarial perturbations; 3) *adversarial training* [17]; and 4) *defensive distillation* [32];

Input transformation through image processing methods(e.g. JPEG compression) is considered to be the potential defensive measure. Work [50] discussed that input transformation may not be useful if the adversarial samples are generated with various transformations and random noise.

Adversarial training was discussed in work [38,50]. The idea of adversarial is producing adversarial samples during the training process and injecting them to the training set. Work [50] discussed that adversarial training can be bypassed through transferability or generating new adversarial samples against the improved models. Besides adversarial training, defensive distillation was also evaluated in work [13].

Countermeasures for Object Tracking and Trajectory Algorithms: To defend attacks on object tracking and trajectory, since object tracking and trajectory is now mainly based on reinforcement learning and time series algorithm, common defensive measures against adversarial attacks might be useful, such as adversarial training, defensive distillation, and data augmentation.

Objective function plays a pivotal role in reinforcement learning algorithm, and changing the objective function might also help to defend attacks on the object tracking and trajectory such as adding stability term and adding regularization term. By measuring the difference of the output produced from different input of versions of perturbations, the purpose of adding stability term is to help DNN generate similar output against natural perturbations. The idea of adding regularization term to defend is adding the norm of adversarial perturbations to the objective function, thus attenuating the effect of adversarial perturbations.

5   Discussion

The security issues of CAVs are still considered to be open research areas, and many issues need to be resolved. This section will discuss some of these issues. As CAVs are becoming more popular, people are now getting concerned if it is necessary to regulate their use. For example, in 2018 in Arizona (USA) the first case of an autonomous car killing a pedestrian has been registered. In this case, who should be considered to be at fault? The problem is related to whether the driver in the car controls the vehicle at the moment of the accident. Is the car manufacturer at fault, or should the attackers who hacked self-driving take the responsibility. Identifying or fingerprinting drivers is one of proposed approaches to answer these questions. There have been many studies on combining vehicle network data with machine learning in recent years, collecting vehicle data to learn the driver's behavioral characteristics, as each driver's unique "fingerprint", and successfully identifying the driver during driving. However, there is no solution to determine whether is automatic driving or human driving. We believe that each driver's style of driving the vehicle, is different, including the AI driver. In this way, by collecting enough in-vehicle data, it is possible to determine whether the car was driven autonomously or artificially when a car accident occurs. Yet it needs further investigation.

In addition, certain vehicle attacks currently do not have effective solutions, such as the battery exhaustion attack against the ECU wake-up mechanism, the interference attacks faced by environmental sensors, and fast gradient sign based adversarial attacks on sensors that process images, etc. Some of them are mentioned above. These attacks have received a lot of in-depth research, but few countermeasures are available. Therefore, the CAVs security is still long way to go.

6   Conclusion

In this survey, we systematically discuss attacks and defense methods for connected and autonomous vehicles, as well as security of CAVs algorithms. In order to better present the most current research in this area, we divide CAVs into three layers: in-vehicle network, V2X, and autonomous vehicle algorithms. Besides, we divide the attacks on each layer into two categories: remote attacks and internal attacks, and list examples of each type of attack in the form of a table. Then we synthesize and summarize existing defenses to determine their effectiveness against these identified attacks. Finally, we provide further discussion on the security of CAVs. This survey provides a good foundation for researchers interested in the connected and autonomous vehicles and provide a systematic overview of the security issues for them.

Acknowledgement. We sincerely thank reviewers for their insightful feedback. This work was supported in part by NSFC Award #61972200.

References

1. Abdelgader, A.M., Shu, F.: Exploiting the physical layer security for providing a simple user privacy security system for vehicular networks. In: International Conference on Communication, Control, Computing and Electronics Engineering (ICCCCEE), pp. 1–6. IEEE (2017)
2. Alnasser, A., Sun, H., Jiang, J.: Cyber security challenges and solutions for V2X communications: a survey. Comput. Netw. **151**, 52–67 (2019)
3. Avatefipour, O., Malik, H.: State-of-the-art survey on in-vehicle network communication (CAN-Bus) security and vulnerabilities. arXiv preprint arXiv:1802.01725 (2018)
4. Baluja, S., Fischer, I.: Adversarial transformation networks: learning to generate adversarial examples. arXiv preprint arXiv:1703.09387 (2017)
5. Bhoi, S.K., Khilar, P.M.: SIR: a secure and intelligent routing protocol for vehicular ad hoc network. IET Netw. **4**(3), 185–194 (2014)
6. Bozdal, M., Samie, M., Jennions, I.: A survey on can bus protocol: attacks, challenges, and potential solutions. In: International Conference on Computing, Electronics & Communications Engineering (ICCECE), pp. 201–205. IEEE (2018)
7. Chen, S.-T., Cornelius, C., Martin, J., Chau, D.H.P.: ShapeShifter: robust physical adversarial attack on faster R-CNN object detector. In: Berlingerio, M., Bonchi, F., Gärtner, T., Hurley, N., Ifrim, G. (eds.) ECML PKDD 2018. LNCS (LNAI), vol. 11051, pp. 52–68. Springer, Cham (2019). https://doi.org/10.1007/978-3-030-10925-7_4
8. Cho, K.T., Kim, Y., Shin, K.G.: Who killed my parked car? arXiv preprint arXiv:1801.07741 (2018)
9. Cho, K.T., Shin, K.G.: Fingerprinting electronic control units for vehicle intrusion detection. In: USENIX Security Symposium (USENIX Security), pp. 911–927 (2016)
10. Cho, K.T., Shin, K.G.: Viden: attacker identification on in-vehicle networks. In: ACM SIGSAC Conference on Computer and Communications Security (CCS), pp. 1109–1123 (2017)
11. Choi, W., Joo, K., Jo, H.J., Park, M.C., Lee, D.H.: VoltageIDS: low-level communication characteristics for automotive intrusion detection system. IEEE Trans. Inf. Forensics Secur. (IEEE T INF FOREN SEC) **13**(8), 2114–2129 (2018)
12. Dagan, T., Wool, A.: Parrot, a software-only anti-spoofing defense system for the CAN bus. In: Embedded Security in Cars Europe (ESCAR), p. 34 (2016)
13. Deng, Y., Zheng, X., Zhang, T., Chen, C., Lou, G., Kim, M.: An analysis of adversarial attacks and defenses on autonomous driving models. arXiv Signal Processing (2020)
14. Francillon, A., Danev, B., Capkun, S.: Relay attacks on passive keyless entry and start systems in modern cars. In: Proceedings of the Network and Distributed System Security Symposium (NDSS) (2011)
15. Garcia, F.D., Oswald, D., Kasper, T., Pavlidès, P.: Lock it and still lose it -on the (in)security of automotive remote keyless entry systems. In: USENIX Security Symposium (USENIX Security) (2016)

16. Golle, P., Greene, D., Staddon, J.: Detecting and dorrecting malicious data in VANETs. In: ACM International Workshop on Vehicular Ad Hoc Networks (VANET), pp. 29–37 (2004)
17. Goodfellow, I.J., Shlens, J., Szegedy, C.: Explaining and harnessing adversarial examples. In: International Conference on Machine Learning (ICML) (2015)
18. Han, K., Weimerskirch, A., Shin, K.G.: A practical solution to achieve real-time performance in the automotive network by randomizing frame identifier. In: Embedded Security in Cars Europe (ESCAR), pp. 13–29 (2015)
19. Ishak, M.K., Leong, C.C., Sirajudin, E.A.: Embedded ethernet and controller area network (CAN) in real time control communication system. In: Zawawi, M.A.M., Teoh, S.S., Abdullah, N.B., Mohd Sazali, M.I.S. (eds.) 10th International Conference on Robotics, Vision, Signal Processing and Power Applications. LNEE, vol. 547, pp. 133–139. Springer, Singapore (2019). https://doi.org/10.1007/978-981-13-6447-1_17
20. Kneib, M., Huth, C.: Scission: signal characteristic-based sender identification and intrusion detection in automotive networks. In: ACM SIGSAC Conference on Computer and Communications Security (CCS), pp. 787–800 (2018)
21. Laurendeau, C., Barbeau, M.: Threats to security in DSRC/WAVE. In: Kunz, T., Ravi, S.S. (eds.) ADHOC-NOW 2006. LNCS, vol. 4104, pp. 266–279. Springer, Heidelberg (2006). https://doi.org/10.1007/11814764_22
22. Li, Y., Bian, X., Lyu, S.: Attacking object detectors via imperceptible patches on background. Computing Research Repository (CoRR) (2018)
23. Li, Y., Tian, D., Bian, X., Lyu, S., et al.: Robust adversarial perturbation on deep proposal-based models. arXiv preprint arXiv:1809.05962 (2018)
24. Lin, Y.C., Hong, Z.W., Liao, Y.H., Shih, M.L., Liu, M.Y., Sun, M.: Tactics of adversarial attack on deep reinforcement learning agents. arXiv preprint arXiv:1703.06748 (2017)
25. Liu, X., Yang, H., Song, L., Li, H., Chen, Y.: DPatch: attacking object detectors with adversarial patches. Computing Research Repository (CoRR) (2018)
26. Miller, C., Valasek, C.: Remote exploitation of an unaltered passenger vehicle. Black Hat USA **2015**, 91 (2015)
27. Milton, M.A.A.: Evaluation of momentum diverse input iterative fast gradient sign method (M-DI2-FGSM) based attack method on MCS 2018 adversarial attacks on black box face recognition system. arXiv preprint arXiv:1806.08970 (2018)
28. Mokhtar, B., Azab, M.: Survey on security issues in vehicular ad hoc networks. Alex. Eng. J. (AEJ) **54**(4), 1115–1126 (2015)
29. Moosavi-Dezfooli, S.M., Fawzi, A., Fawzi, O., Frossard, P.: Universal adversarial perturbations. In: IEEE Conference on Computer Vision and Pattern Recognition (CVPR), pp. 1765–1773 (2017)
30. Nowdehi, N., Lautenbach, A., Olovsson, T.: In-vehicle CAN message authentication: an evaluation based on industrial criteria. In: IEEE Vehicular Technology Conference (VTC-Fall), pp. 1–7. IEEE (2017)
31. Palanca, A., Evenchick, E., Maggi, F., Zanero, S.: A stealth, selective, link-layer denial-of-service attack against automotive networks. In: Polychronakis, M., Meier, M. (eds.) DIMVA 2017. LNCS, vol. 10327, pp. 185–206. Springer, Cham (2017). https://doi.org/10.1007/978-3-319-60876-1_9
32. Papernot, N., McDaniel, P., Wu, X., Jha, S., Swami, A.: Distillation as a defense to adversarial perturbations against deep neural networks. In: IEEE Symposium on Security and Privacy (S&P), pp. 582–597. IEEE (2016)
33. Petit, J., Stottelaar, B., Feiri, M., Kargl, F.: Remote attacks on automated vehicles sensors: experiments on camera and lidar. Black Hat Eur. **11**, 2015 (2015)

34. Raiyn, J.: Data and cyber security in autonomous vehicle networks. Transp. Telecommun. J. **19**(4), 325–334 (2018)
35. Rouf, I., Miller, R.D., Mustafa, H.A., Taylor, T., Seskar, I.: Security and privacy vulnerabilities of in-car wireless networks: a tire pressure monitoring system case study. In: USENIX Security Symposium (USENIX Security) (2010)
36. Sagong, S.U., Poovendran, R., Bushnell, L.: Inter-message correlation for intrusion detection in controller area networks. Technical report, Washington University (2019)
37. Sagong, S.U., Ying, X., Poovendran, R., Bushnell, L.: Exploring attack surfaces of voltage-based intrusion detection systems in controller area networks. In: Embedded Security in Cars Europe (ESCAR) (2018)
38. Sitawarin, C., Bhagoji, A.N., Mosenia, A., Chiang, M., Mittal, P.: DARTS: deceiving autonomous cars with toxic signs. arXiv Cryptography and Security (2018)
39. Stewart, J.: Self-driving cars use crazy amounts of power, and it's becoming a problem. wired.com, Transportation (2018)
40. Studnia, I., Alata, E., Nicomette, V., Kaâniche, M., Laarouchi, Y.: A language-based intrusion detection approach for automotive embedded networks. Int. J. Embed. Syst. (IJES) **10**(1), 1–12 (2018)
41. Su, J., Vargas, D.V., Sakurai, K.: One pixel attack for fooling deep neural networks. IEEE Trans. Evolu. Comput. (TEVC) **23**(5), 828–841 (2019)
42. Sun, J., et al.: Stealthy and efficient adversarial attacks against deep reinforcement learning. arXiv preprint arXiv:2005.07099 (2020)
43. Takahashi, J.: An overview of cyber security for connected vehicles. IEICE Trans. Inf. Syst. **101**(11), 2561–2575 (2018)
44. Wang, J., Shao, Y., Ge, Y., Yu, R.: A survey of vehicle to everything (V2X) testing. Sensors **19**(2), 334 (2019)
45. Wiyatno, R., Xu, A.: Maximal Jacobian-based saliency map attack. arXiv preprint arXiv:1808.07945 (2018)
46. Wolf, M., Lambert, R., Enderle, T., Schmidt, A.: Wanna drive? Feasible attack paths and effective protection against ransomware in modern vehicles. In: Embedded Security in Cars Europe (ESCAR) (2017)
47. Yan, C., Xu, W., Liu, J.: Can you trust autonomous vehicles: contactless attacks against sensors of self-driving vehicle. DEFCON **24**(8), 109 (2016)
48. Zang, S., Ding, M., Smith, D., Tyler, P., Rakotoarivelo, T., Kaafar, M.A.: The impact of adverse weather conditions on autonomous vehicles: how rain, snow, fog, and hail affect the performance of a self-driving car. IEEE Veh. Technol. Mag. **14**(2), 103–111 (2019)
49. Zhang, L.: OTIBAAGKA: a new security tool for cryptographic mix-zone establishment in vehicular ad hoc networks. IEEE Trans. Inf. Forensics Secur. **12**(12), 2998–3010 (2017)
50. Zhao, Y., Zhu, H., Liang, R., Shen, Q., Zhang, S., Chen, K.: Seeing isn't believing: towards more robust adversarial attack against real world object detectors. In: ACM SIGSAC Conference on Computer and Communications Security (CCS), pp. 1989–2004 (2019)

An Improved Cryptanalysis Algorithm for Chebyshev Map-Based Discrete Logarithm Problem

Wei Peng$^{(\boxtimes)}$ (ID), Shang Song (ID), and Wenzheng Liu (ID)

College of Computer, National University of Defense Technology,
Changsha 410073, Hunan, China
wpeng@nudt.edu.cn, songsh83@163.com, 910972029@qq.com

Abstract. Chebyshev map is a chaotic map frequently used in design of cryptography schemes and cryptosystems based on the hardness of the Chebyshev map-based discrete logarithm (CMDL) problem. The properties of Chebyshev map have great impact on the security of these cryptosystems. It has been known that the polynomial sequences generated by Chebyshev map defined on finite fields exhibit strong periodical features which may be utilized for cryptanalysis. This paper presents the periodical properties of Chebyshev polynomial sequences. Based on the properties, an improved cryptanalysis algorithm is proposed for the CMDL problem. It turns out that a chebyshev map-based cryptosystem using Chebyshev prime number as its modulus will have better security, where the Chebyshev prime number is defined as the prime number p satisfying that $(p+1)/2$ or $(p-1)/2$ is also a prime number. In support of cryptanalysis, fast algorithms to calculate the value of a Chebyshev polynomial and find the minimal period of a Chebyshev polynomial sequence are proposed, too. An example is given to show the process of cryptanalysis. Computational results have shown that only a small fraction of prime numbers are valid Chebyshev prime numbers.

Keywords: Cryptanalysis · Chebyshev map · Discrete logarithm problem · Chebyshev prime number · Algorithm

1 Introduction

Chaotic maps have been used to design cryptographic algorithms and cryptosystems for many years. Among them, the Chebyshev map defined on finite fields is one frequently used. The Chebyshev map has the semi-group property which makes it appealing for designing cryptosystems. The Chebyshev map is not only used in encryption [1], but also widely used in key agreement protocols [2–5], authentication [6] or authenticated key exchange schemes [7–10], digital signature and signcryption schemes [11]. Public-key cryptosystems [12–14] and identity-based encryption schemes [15] can be constructed with it, too. Thus, the security of the Chebyshev map is very important for these schemes or systems.

© Springer Nature Switzerland AG 2021
G. Wang et al. (Eds.): SpaCCS 2020, LNCS 12382, pp. 118–130, 2021.
https://doi.org/10.1007/978-3-030-68851-6_8

Modern cryptosystems are always based on one or some hard problems in the computational sense. The cryptosystems using Chebyshev map as their core function are usually based on the hardness of the Chebyshev map-based discrete logarithm (CMDL) problem and the Chebyshev map-based Diffie-Hellman (CMDH) problem. It has been known that the Chebyshev sequences generated by the Chebyshev map on finite fields have strong periodical properties. It is argued that these properties can be utilized for effective Cryptanalysis on the CMDL or CMDH problem. Liao et al. [16] and Li et al. [17] have studied the periodical properties of Chebyshev polynomial sequences respectively and suggested cryptanalysis using these properties. However, how to design a cryptanalysis algorithm using these periodical properties is still a challenging task.

In this paper, we present the periodical properties of Chebyshev polynomial sequences at first. Based on the properties, an improved cryptanalysis algorithm is proposed for the chebyshev map-based discrete logarithm problem. To support the cryptanalysis, an algorithm to find the minimal period of a Chebyshev polynomial sequence is proposed. A fast algorithm to calculate the value of a Chebyshev polynomial is proposed, too, which has the same time complexity but is simpler than the modified characteristic polynomial algorithm [18]. Then, a method to select the proper parameters for a chebyshev map-based cryptosystem is suggested. For such a cryptosystem with a prime number p as its modulus parameter, any Chebyshev polynomial sequence will have an ordinary period $p + 1$ or $p - 1$. Thus, the modulus parameter must be chosen carefully to resist cryptanalysis. Such a prime number p is called Chebyshev prime number if $p + 1$ or $p - 1$ can only be divided by 2 and another prime number.

We give an example to show how to find a solution to the CMDL problem using the proposed cryptanalysis algorithm. The computational results of the distribution of Chebyshev prime numbers are also presented. It turns out that only a small fraction of prime numbers are valid Chebyshev prime numbers, e.g., only 7% prime numbers less than 10^9 are Chebyshev prime numbers.

2   Related Work

There have been a lot of work which use chaotic systems to design cryptographic algorithms [1–15,19]. Among them, the Chebyshev chaotic map is frequently used. It is used in color image encryption as a symmetric encryption method [1]. It is the cornerstone of some public-key encryption systems [13]. It is utilized to design key agreement protocols [2–5], authentication schemes [6–9], identity-based encryption and digital signature schemes [15], signcryption schemes [11], and so on. Li et al. have proposed several algorithms to calculate the value of Chebyshev polynomial [18]. Among them, the modified characteristic polynomial algorithm is recommended which has the time complexity of $O(lb(n))$ where $lb(n)$ is the number of bits of n as a binary string.

The properties of Chebyshev maps have been investigated in the research of security of Chebyshev map-based cryptosystems. For Chebyshev map-based cryptosystems work on real numbers in $[-1, 1]$, an attack is proposed to recover the corresponding plaintext from a given ciphertext [20]. For Chebyshev map-based cryptosystems defined on finite fields, Kocarev et al. pointed out that the problem of finding the index of a Chebyshev polynomial can be reduced to the discrete logarithm problem [12]. The periodical properties of Chebyshev map over the finite field Z_p have been studied deeply in the work done by Liao and Li, repectively [16,17]. Liao et al. analyzed the security issues of public-key schemes based on Chebyshev polynomials from a practical viewpoint. They have also proved that the security of encryption algorithm based on Chebyshev polynomials is stronger than computational Diffie-Hellman (CDH) problem, but weaker than the discrete logarithm problem [16]. By converting the Chebyshev discrete logarithm problem into a general discrete logarithm problem (GDLP) on a group G, Li et al. proposed a baby-step giant-step algorithm to the problem [17]. With the periodical properties, a Chebyshev map-based cryptosystem is not secure if the modulus parameter p is not selected properly so that there are many Chebyshev polynomial sequences with small periods. However, they did not describe how to utilize the periodical properties to design a cryptanalysis algorithm in detail. The periodical properties of Chebyshev polynomials modulo a prime power have been discovered, too [21]. These properties are used for analysis of the security of the corresponding cryptosystems [22].

Based on the periodical property of Chebyshev polynomial sequences, an attack scheme with Chebyshev sequence membership testing is proposed using the quadratic relationship between two consecutive Chebyshev polynomials [23]. It may not be very effective considering the large search space with large parameter values from a practical aspect.

3   Preliminaries

3.1   Chebyshev Chaotic Maps

Definition 1 (Chebyshev map). The original Chebyshev map is defined as $T_n(x) : [-1, 1] \rightarrow [-1, 1]$, where n is an integer and x is a real number. Formally, it is defined as

$$T_n(x) = cos(n \cdot arccos(x)), x \in [-1, 1], n \in Z \tag{1}$$

or defined recursively as

$$T_n(x) = 2xT_{n-1}(x) - T_{n-2}(x) \tag{2}$$

with $T_0(x) = 1$ and $T_1(x) = x$.

The Chebyshev map is a chaotic map due to its recursive characteristic.

Proposition 1 (Chaotic property). The Chebyshev map $T_n(x) : [-1, 1] \rightarrow [-1, 1]$, $n > 1$, is a chaotic map with invariant density $f * (x) = \frac{1}{\pi\sqrt{1-x^2}}$ and positive Lyapunov exponent $\lambda = \ln(n)$.

Definition 2 (Extended Chebyshev map). The extended Chebyshev map is defined on interval $(-\infty, +\infty)$, which is

$$T_n(x) = 2xT_{n-1}(x) - T_{n-2}(x) \ (mod \ p), \ x \in (-\infty, +\infty) \tag{3}$$

where p is a large prime number. It has been proved that both the Chebyshev Map and the extended map have the semi-group property.

Proposition 2 (Semi-group property). For $n, m \in N$, the extended Chebyshev map satisfies

$$T_n(T_m(x)) = T_m(T_n(x)) = T_{nm}(x) \ (mod \ p) \tag{4}$$

where p is large prime number and $x \in (-\infty, +\infty)$.

Although the extended Chebyshev map is defined on interval $(-\infty, +\infty)$, it is often discussed on the finite field Z_p. This paper only concerns the extended Chebyshev map over finite field Z_p, so we will use Chebyshev map to refer to it in the following text. It has many useful properties in Z_p. For example, the multiplication of $T_n(x)$ and $T_m(x)$ has the following property.

Proposition 3 [23]. Given the extended Chebyshev map $T_m(x)$ and $T_m(x)$, $x \in Z_p$, $m, n \in Z_p^*$, $n \geq m$, p is a large prime number, we have

$$2T_n(x)T_m(x) = T_{n+m}(x) + T_{n-m}(x) \ (mod \ p) \tag{5}$$

Alternatively, the extended Chebyshev map can be represented with the following expression:

$$T_n(x) = \frac{1}{2}[(x + \sqrt{x^2 - 1})^n + (x - \sqrt{x^2 - 1})^n] \ (mod \ p) \tag{6}$$

Chaotic map-based cryptography is established on the related computational hard problems of chaotic maps, especially the Chebyshev map-based discrete logarithm problem and the Chebyshev map-based Diffie-Hellman problem.

Definition 3 (Chebyshev Map-based Discrete Logarithm (CMDL) problem). The CMDL problem is defined as: given x and y, it is computationally infeasible to find r such that $T_r(x) = y \ mod \ p$, where p is a large prime number. For any adversary $\mathcal{A}$, its advantage probability to solve the CMDL problem is

$$Adv_{\mathcal{A}}^{CMDL}(t) = Pr[\mathcal{A}(x,y) = r : r \in Z_p^*, y = T_r(x)(mod \ p)]. \tag{7}$$

3.2 Periodical Properties of Chebyshev Map on Finite Fields

The Chebyshev map $T_n(x)$ over Z_p is also called as a Chebyshev polynomial. For convenience, we call n as the index of the Chebyshev polynomial $T_n(x)$ in the following text. A Chebyshev polynomial sequence is a sequence of Chebyshev map values on finite field Z_p. It is a periodical sequence determined by its generator x and p. In Chebyshev map-based cryptosystems, most operations are done on Chebyshev polynomial sequences. Hence the properties of Chebyshev polynomial sequences have significant influence on the security of these cryptosystems, especially the periodical properties.

Denote the minimal period of a Chebyshev polynomial sequence with generator x by $T_{min}(x)$. Every Chebyshev polynomial sequence has an ordinary period $T_{or}(x)$ which is only dependent on p.

Proposition 4 [17]. Given x and p, a Chebyshev polynomial sequence has an ordinary period $T_{or}(x) = p-1$ if and only if $\sqrt{x^2-1}$ is in Z_p; when $T_{min}(x) > 2$, $T_{or}(x) = p+1$ if and only if $\sqrt{x^2-1}$ is not in Z_p. Besides, its minimal period $T_{min}(x)$ is a factor of its ordinary period, i.e., $T_{min}(x)|T_{or}(x)$.

Proposition 5 [17]. The elements of a Chebyshev polynomial sequence distribute evenly symmetrically in a period. Let d be a period of the sequence, then there is $T_{nd+i}(x) = T_{(n+1)d-i}(x)$, where n is any integer and i is an integer satisfying $0 \le i < d$.

Proposition 6 [17]. If there are two integers a, b satisfying $T_a(x) = T_b(x)$ (mod p), then $a = \pm b$ (mod $T_{min}(x)$).

The order of an element x in group Z_p, denoted by $ord(x)$, is defined as the least positive number such that $x^{ord(x)} = 1$. If we view the Chebyshev polynomial $T_n(x)$ as a multiplication x^n in group Z_p, then the order of x is actually the minimal period of a Chebyshev polynomial sequence with the generator x and p, i.e., $ord(x) = T_{min}(x)$. Based on the lemmas in [16], the period of a Chebyshev polynomial sequence using $T_n(x)$ as its generator, $ord(T_n(x))$, is related to both n and the order $ord(x)$.

Proposition 7 [16]. $ord(T_n(x)) = \frac{ord(x)}{(n,ord(x))}$, where $(n, ord(x))$ denotes the greatest common divider of n and $ord(x)$.

Proposition 8 [16]. For every integer $T|p-1$ or $T|p+1$, there are K x's in Z_p for which the period of Chebyshev polynomial sequences with the generator x and p is T, where

$$K = \begin{cases} 1, & T = 1 \text{ or } 2 \\ \frac{\varphi(T)}{2}, & T > 2 \end{cases} \tag{8}$$

$\varphi(\cdot)$ is the Euler's totient function. When T goes over all factors of $p-1$ and $p+1$, there are p different x's.

4 An Improved Cryptoanalysis Scheme for Chebyshev Discrete Logarithm Problem

Based on the periodical properties of Chebyshev polynomial sequences, we propose an improved cryptanalysis scheme for Chebyshev map-based discrete logarithm (CMDL) problem. That is, given x, p and $y = T_n(x)$ (mod p), we try to find the minimal feasible value of n. Since the elements of a Chebyshev polynomial sequence distribute evenly symmetrically in a period, there must be $0 \le n \le ord(x)/2$.

4.1   Cryptanalysis Algorithm for CMDL Problem

Every Chebyshev polynomial sequence has an ordinary period $p - 1$ or $p + 1$, and the minimal period of a sequence is a factor of the ordinary period according to Proposition 4. As p is a prime number, the ordinary period must be an even number. The minimal periods of Chebyshev polynomial sequences take all factors of the ordinary period according to Proposition 8. So, there must be Chebyshev polynomial sequences with the minimal period of 2, $(p - 1)/2$ and $(p + 1)/2$. If the generator x and p are not selected properly, the cryptosystems based on Chebyshev map will be weak to be attacked (Fig. 1).

Algorithm 1: Improved cryptanalysis algorithm for CMDL

Input: a prime number p, and $x \in Z_p$;
  $y \in Z_p$ where $y = T_n(x) \ (mod \ p)$, $y \neq 1$ and $y \neq x$;
Output: the minimal feasible value of n

Step 1 Compute $ord(x)$ and $ord(y)$ which are the minimal periods of Chebyshev polynomial sequences with generator x and y, respectively;
Step 2 Let $k = ord(x)/ord(y)$. If $k > 1$, then let $x_1 = T_k(x)$ and $ord(x_1) = ord(y)$, or else let $x_1 = x$ and $ord(x_1) = ord(x)$;
Step 3 Find the minimal feasible value of h satisfying $y = T_h(x_1) \ (mod \ p)$ and $0 < h \leq ord(x_1)/2$. That is, let $h = ChebyAnalyzeSub(x_1, ord(x_1), y)$;
Step 4 return $n = k * h$.

Fig. 1. Improved cryptanalysis algorithm for CMDL problem

The main idea of the cryptanalysis scheme is to utilize the periodical properties of Chebyshev polynomial sequences to improve the performance of existing cryptanalysis algorithms. Based on Proposition 7, we can find the greatest common divider of n and $ord(x)$ if we can obtain the minimal periods of Chebyshev polynomial sequences with generator x and $T_n(x)$, respectively. That will help to reduce the search space of the Chebyshev discrete logarithm problem and improve the performance of cryptanalysis. The proposed scheme is illustrated by the Algorithm 1.

At first, the algorithm computes the minimal periods of the Chebyshev polynomial sequences with the generator x and y, respectively. Then the greastest common divider of n and $ord(x)$ is obtained based on the Proposition 7. The problem is reduced to find the index of y in a sequence with the minimal period $ord(y)$. As $ord(y)$ is only a factor of $ord(x)$, the search space is reduced.

The algorithm uses a subprocedure $ChebyAnalyzeSub()$ to find the minimal feasible value of h satisfying $y = T_h(x_1) \ (mod \ p)$ and $0 < h \leq ord(x_1)/2$. The subprocedure is shown in Fig. 2.

In the subprocedure, the search space can be reduced further if the minimal period $ord(x_1)$ is not a prime number. By dividing $ord(x_1)$ into a prime number p_1 and a number q, the problem is reduced to search in a sequence with q as its period. The search space is reduced recursively in Step 5. It ensures that the

Procedure: ChebyAnalyzeSub($x_1, ord(x_1), y$)
Input: $x_1 \in Z_p$ and $ord(x_1)$, $y \in Z_p$ where $y = T_h(x_1)$ $(mod\ p)$, $y \neq 1$;
Output: the minimal feasible value of h
Step 1 If $y = x_1$, then $h = 1$, return h;
Step 2 Or else, if $ord(x_1)$ is a prime number, then use an existing method to find the minimal feasible solution h, i.e., the baby-step giant-step algorithm [17];
Step 3 Or else, let $ord(x_1) = p_1 * q$ where p_1 is a prime number and $p_1 > 1$;
Step 4 Let $x_2 = T_{p_1}(x_1)$, $ord(x_2) = q$ and $y_2 = T_{p_1}(y)$;
Step 5 Calling $ChebyAnalyzeSub(x_2, ord(x_2), y_2)$ to get h_2 such that $y_2 = T_{h_2}(x_2)$ $(mod\ p)$;
Step 6 Let $h = k_2 * q \pm h_2$ and find the minimal integer k_2 satisfying $y = T_h(x_1)$ $(mod\ p)$ and $0 < h \leq ord(x_1)/2$.

Fig. 2. Cryptanalysis subprocedure for CMDL problem

Algorithm 2: Choose parameters for Chebyshev map
Step 1 Select a large prime number p;
Step 2 Let $r = (p + 1)/2$. If r is not a prime number, then go to Step 1;
Step 3 Select a random number x such that $1 < x < p$ and $ord(x) = p + 1$.

Fig. 3. Choose parameters for Chebyshev polynomials

search space is always constrainted to a Chebyshev polynomial sequence with a prime period.

To resist the above cryptanalysis algorithm, parameters of a cryptosystem based on Chebyshev polynomials must be chosen carefully. Specifically, the generator x and p should be chosen to satisfying that $ord(x)$ has least prime factors. The main steps to chosen x and p is illustrated in Fig. 3.

Some operations in the cryptanalysis algorithm have great impact on the algorithm performance, such as computing the value of a Chebyshev polynomial, computing the minimal period of a Chebyshev polynomial sequence, finding a prime factor of a period value. All prime factors of $ord(x)$ can be found in advance using an existing integer factorization method, while any factors of $ord(T_n(x))$ are factors of $ord(x)$ based on Proposition 7. To compute the value of a Chebyshev polynomial and the minimal period of a Chebyshev polynomial sequence, two algorithms are proposed in the next section.

4.2   Auxiliary Algorithms

For any Chebyshev polynomial sequence, its minimal period is always a factor of its ordinary period which is $p - 1$ or $p + 1$. Therefore, we can find its minimal period in the factors of its ordinary period. The algorithm to compute the minimal period of a Chebyshev polynomial sequence is shown in Fig. 4.

Algorithm 3: Compute minimal period of sequence
Input: a prime number p, and $x \in Z_p$;
Output: the minimal period $ord(x)$.

Step 1 Compute the ordinary period:
    if $T_{p-1}(x) = 1$, then let $ord(x) = p - 1$, or else let $ord(x) = p + 1$;
Step 2 Assume $ord(x) = p_1^{e_1} p_2^{e_2} \cdots p_k^{e_k}$, where p_i is a prime number and e_i is a positive integer, $1 \le i \le k$. Let i from 1 to k do the following steps:
    Step 2.1 Let $m = ord(x)/p_i$, compute $T_m(x)$ and $T_{m+1}(x)$;
    Step 2.2 If $T_m(x) = 1$ and $T_{m+1}(x) = x$, then let $ord(x) = m$, or else let $i = i + 1$.

Fig. 4. Compute the minimal period of a Chebyshev sequence

Computing the value of a Chebyshev polynomial $T_n(x)$ is a basic operation in above algorithms, given the value of n, x and p. A fast algorithm is required when n is a large number.

Assume n is a $(m + 1)$-bit binary string, i.e., $n = b_m b_{m-1} \cdots b_1 b_0$, where $b_i \in \{0, 1\}$, $0 \le i < m$ and $b_m = 1$. n can also be represented by a polynomial:

$$n = b_m \cdot 2^m + b_{m-1} \cdot 2^{m-1} + \cdots + b_1 \cdot 2 + b_0 \tag{9}$$

Define $w[m] = b_m$ and $w[i] = 2w[i + 1] + b_i$, $0 \le i < m$, then we have $n = w[0]$. Define $A_i = T_{w[i]}(x)$ and $B_i = T_{w[i]+1}(x)$, $0 \le i < m$.

For $0 \le i < m - 1$, when $b_i = 0$,

$$\begin{aligned}
A_i &= T_{w[i]}(x) = T_{2w[i+1]}(x) = T_2(T_{w[i+1]}(x)) \\
&= 2\left[T_{w[i+1]}(x)\right]^2 - 1 = 2A_{i+1}^2 - 1 \ (mod \ p) \\
B_i &= T_{w[i]+1}(x) = T_{2w[i+1]+1}(x) \\
&= 2T_{w[i+1]}(x)T_{w[i+1]+1}(x) - T_1(x) \\
&= 2A_{i+1}B_{i+1} - x \ (mod \ p)
\end{aligned} \tag{10}$$

When $b_i = 1$,

$$\begin{aligned}
A_i &= T_{w[i]}(x) = T_{2w[i+1]+1}(x) \\
&= 2T_{w[i+1]}(x)T_{w[i+1]+1}(x) - T_1(x) \\
&= 2A_{i+1}B_{i+1} - x \ (mod \ p) \\
B_i &= T_{w[i]+1}(x) = T_{2w[i+1]+2}(x) = T_2(T_{w[i+1]+1}(x)) \\
&= 2\left[T_{w[i+1]+1}(x)\right]^2 - 1 = 2B_{i+1}^2 - 1 \ (mod \ p)
\end{aligned} \tag{11}$$

Since $b_m = 1$, when $b_{m-1} = 0$,

$$\begin{aligned}
A_{m-1} &= T_{w[m-1]}(x) = T_2(x) \ (mod \ p) \\
B_{m-1} &= T_{w[m-1]+1}(x) = T_3(x) \ (mod \ p)
\end{aligned} \tag{12}$$

when $b_{m-1} = 1$,

$$\begin{aligned}
A_{m-1} &= T_{w[m-1]}(x) = T_3(x) \ (mod \ p) \\
B_{m-1} &= T_{w[m-1]+1}(x) = T_4(x) \ (mod \ p)
\end{aligned} \tag{13}$$

Based on the equations (10)–(13), we propose a fast algorithm to calculate the value of a Chebyshev polynomial $T_n(x)$, as shown in Fig. 5. Obviously, the complexity of computing the value of a Chebyshev polynomial $T_n(x)$ is $O(m)$ where m is the length of binary string n. Although the time complexity of the algorithm is the same as that of the modified characteristic polynomial algorithm [18], it is simpler as the latter requires more multiplication operations.

5   Computational Results

5.1   An Example

Here we present an example to show how to find a solution to the Chebyshev map-based discrete logarithm (CMDL) problem using the proposed method. Suppose $p=3640471$. The generator x is randomly selected using the algorithm proposed in [17] such that $ord(x) = p + 1$, i.e., $x = 320274$. Given $y = 2039998$, we try to find n such that $T_n(x) = y$.

Algorithm 4: Compute value of Chebyshev polynomial
Input: a prime number p, $x \in Z_p$ and n $(n > 1)$;
Output: the value of Chebyshev polynomial $T_n(x)$.

Step 1 Assume $n = b_m b_{m-1} \cdots b_1 b_0$, where $b_i \in \{0,1\}$, $0 \le i < m$ and $b_m = 1$.
   If $b_{m-1} = 0$, then let $A_{m-1} = T_2(x)$ $(mod\ p)$ and $B_{m-1} = T_3(x)$ $(mod\ p)$,
   or else let $A_{m-1} = T_3(x)$ $(mod\ p)$ and $B_{m-1} = T_4(x)$ $(mod\ p)$.
Step 2 Let k be the lowest index satisfying $b_k = 1$ and $b_i = 0$, $0 \le i < k$.
   If $k = m$, then let $k = m - 1$. For i from $m - 2$ to k do the following steps:
   Step 2.1 If $b_i = 0$, then let $A_i = 2A_{i+1}^2 - 1$ $(mod\ p)$ and
   $B_i = 2A_{i+1}B_{i+1} - x$ $(mod\ p)$;
   Step 2.2 Or else let $A_i = 2A_{i+1}B_{i+1} - x$ $(mod\ p)$ and $B_i = 2B_{i+1}^2 - 1$ $(mod\ p)$;
Step 3 For i from $k - 1$ to 0 do the following steps: $A_i = 2A_{i+1}^2 - 1$ $(mod\ p)$;
Step 4 Return $T_n(x) = A_0$.

Fig. 5. Compute the value of a Chebyshev polynomial

According to Algorithm 1, at first, we calculate $ord(x)$ and $ord(y)$ which are the periods of Chebyshev polynomial sequences with generator x and y, respectively. As $p + 1 = 2^3 \times 11 \times 41 \times 1009$ and $p - 1 = 2 \times 3 \times 5 \times 121349$, it is easy to obtain $ord(x) = 3640472$ and $ord(y) = 1820236$ using the Algorithm 3. Then we get the greatest common divider $k = (n, ord(x)) = ord(x)/ord(y) = 2$. Let $x_1 = T_k(x) = T_2(x) = 3048359$ and $ord(x_1) = ord(y) = 1820236$.

In step 3 of Algorithm 1, we call the procedure *ChebyAnalyzeSub()* to find the minimal value of h such that $y = T_h(x_1)$ $(mod\ p)$. In the procedure, as $ord(x_1) = 2^2 \times 11 \times 41 \times 1009$, we let $p_1 = 2$ and $q = 910118$. Then we have $x_2 = T_{p_1}(x_1) = 2121777$, $ord(x_2) = 910118$ and $y_2 = T_{p_1}(y) = 316004$. The procedure *ChebyAnalyzeSub()* is called recursively in Step 5 of the procedure with new parameters $(x_2, ord(x_2), y_2)$. The procedure returns the minimal value of h_2 such that $T_{h_2}(x_2) = y_2$. The process to find the value of h_2 is shown in Fig. 6. At last we get $h_2 = 4487$. At Step 6 of the procedure, a propriate value of k_2 is found such that $h = k_2 * q \pm h_2$ and $y = T_h(x_1)$. Here we have $h = 4487$. At last step of the algorithm 1, we obtain the final value of n which is $k * h = 2 \times 4487 = 8974$.

Since the ordinary period of any Chebyshev polynomial sequence is always an even number, the procedure *ChebyAnalyzeSub()* will be called recursively at least once if n is also an even number. In this case, considering the elements of a Chebyshev polynomial sequence always distribute evenly symmetrically in a period, the actual search space of the CMDL problem will be only $O(ord(x)/4)$.

5.2   Distribution of Chebyshev Prime Number

If a Chebyshev map-based cryptosystem is strong to resist cryptanalysis, not only its generator x but also the large prime number p must be chosen carefully. A random prime number p can not guarantee the strength of the cryptosystem if its ordinary period $p + 1$ and $p - 1$ can be decomposed into some small prime numbers. Here we study experimentally the distribution of the prime numbers which are suitable for the cryptosystems.

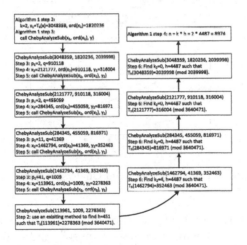

Fig. 6. An example of running the algorithm

Definition 4 (Chebyshev prime number). For a prime number p, it is called Chebyshev prime number if $(p + 1)/2$ or $(p - 1)/2$ is also a prime number.

A Chebyshev polynomial sequence using a Chebyshev prime number as its parameter will have at least one ordinary period which can only be divided into 2 and another prime number. The number and ratios of prime numbers are presented in Table 1 and Fig. 7, respectively. The ratio of prime numbers is defined as the ratio of prime numbers in the range from 2 to n. The ratio 1 of Chebyshev prime numbers is the ratio of Chebyshev prime numbers in the range from 2 to n. The ratio 2 of Chebyshev prime numbers is the ratio of Chebyshev prime numbers and the prime numbers in the same range.

Table 1. Number of prime numbers in range 2 to n

n	Prime numbers	Chebyshev prime numbers
10^3	168	45
10^4	1229	223
10^5	9592	1341
10^6	78498	8623
10^7	664579	61395
10^8	5761455	459120
10^9	50847534	3550286

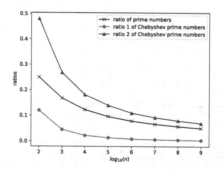

Fig. 7. Ratios of prime numbers and Chebyshev prime numbers

From Table 1, it turns out that there are only 5% prime numbers and 0.355% Chebyshev prime numbers which are less than 10^9, and only about 7% prime numbers are valid Chebyshev prime numbers in the same range. So when a Chebyshev map-based cryptosystem is implemented, its parameters x and p must be chosen carefully to ensure its security.

6   Conclusion

This paper presents the periodical properties of the Chebyshev map over finite fields. Based on these properties, an improved cryptanalysis algorithm is proposed for the Chebyshev map-based discrete logarithm problem. Other auxiliary algorithms are also proposed, including an algorithm to find the minimal period of a Chebyshev polynomial sequence and a fast algorithm to calculate the value of a Chebyshev polynomial. We use an example to illustrate the cryptanalysis process using the proposed algorithm. The modulus parameter p of Chebyshev map must be a large prime number so that the ordinary period $p+1$ or $p-1$ can only be divided into 2 and another prime number. Computing results have shown that only a small fraction of prime numbers are Chebyshev prime numbers.

Acknowledgments. This work was supported by the project from National Natural Science Foundation of China under grant no. 661702541.

References

1. Deng, S., Huang, G., Chen, Z., Xiao, X.: Self-adaptive image encryption algorithm based on chaotic map. J. Comput. Appl. **31**(6), 1502–1504 (2011)
2. Tseng, H.-R., Jan, R.-H., Yang, W.: A chaotic maps-based key agreement protocol that preserves user anonymity. In: IEEE ICC, pp. 850–855 (2009)
3. Li, C.-T., Lee, C.-C., Weng, C.-Y.: A secure chaotic maps and smart cards based password authentication and key agreement scheme with user anonymity for tele-care medicine information systems. J. Med. Syst. **38**, 77 (2014)
4. Shu, J.: An efficient three-party password-based key agreement protocol using extended chaotic maps. Chin. Phys. B **24**(6), 060509 (2015)
5. Jangirala, S., Das, A.K., Wazid, M., Kumar, N.: Anonymous lightweight chaotic map-based authenticated key agreement protocol for industrial internet of things. IEEE Trans. Dependable Secure Comput. **17**, 1133–1146 (2018)
6. Hao, X., Wang, J., Yang, Q., et al.: A chaotic map-based authentication scheme for telecare medicine information systems. J. Med. Syst. **37**, 9919 (2013)
7. Chain, K., Chang, K.-H., Kuo, W.-C., Yang, J.-F.: Enhancement authentication protocol using zero-knowledge proofs and chaotic maps. Int. J. Commun. Syst. **30**(1), e2945 (2017)
8. Roy, S., Chatterjee, S., Das, A.K., et al.: Chaotic map-based anonymous user authentication scheme with user biometrics and fuzzy extractor for crowdsourcing internet of things. IEEE Internet Things J. **5**(4), 2884–2895 (2018)
9. Chatterjee, S., Roy, S., Das, A.K., et al.: Secure biometric-based authentication scheme using Chebyshev chaotic map for multi-server environment. IEEE Trans. Dependable Secure Comput. **15**(5), 824–839 (2018)
10. Liu, W., Wang, X., Peng, W.: Secure remote multi-factor authentication scheme based on chaotic map zero-knowledge proof for crowdsourcing internet of things. IEEE Access **8**(1), 8754–8767 (2020)
11. Hue, T.T.K., Hoang, T.M., Braeken, A.: Lightweight signcryption scheme based on discrete Chebyshev maps. In: 12th International Conference for Internet Technology and Secured Transactions (ICITST-2017) (2017)
12. Kocarev, L., Makraduli, J., Amato, P.: Public-key encryption based on Chebyshev polynomials. Circ. Syst. Signal Process. **24**(5), 497–517 (2005)
13. Lima, J.B., Panario, D., de Souza, R.M.C.: Public-key encryption based on Chebyshev polynomials over GF(q). Inf. Process. Lett. **111**, 51–56 (2010)
14. Lawnik, M., Kapczyński, A.: Application of modified Chebyshev polynomials in asymmetric cryptography. Comput. Sci. **20**(3), 289–303 (2019)

15. Islam, S.H.: Identity-based encryption and digital signature schemes using extended chaotic maps (2014)
16. Liao, X., Chen, F., Wong, K.-W.: On the security of public-key algorithms based on Chebyshev polynomials over the finite field Z_N. IEEE Trans. Comput. **59**(10), 1392–1401 (2010)
17. Li, Z., Cui, Y., Jin, Y., Xu, H.: Parameter selection in public key cryptosystem based on Chebyshev polynomials over finite field. J. Commun. **6**(5), 400–408 (2011)
18. Li, Z., Cui, Y., Xu, H.: Fast algorithms of public key cryptosystem based on Chebyshev polynomials over finite field. J. China Univ. Posts Telecommun. **18**(2), 86–93 (2011)
19. Fu C., Zhang G.-Y., Gao B.-L., Sun J., Wang X.: A new color image encryption scheme based on chaotic hénon Map and lü System. In: SpaCCS 2017 (2017)
20. Bergamo, P., D'Arco, P., De Santis, A., Kocarev, L.: Security of public key cryptosystems based on Chebyshev polynomials. IEEE Trans. Circ. Syst. I **52**(7), 1382–1393 (2005)
21. Yoshioka, D.: Properties of Chebyshev polynomials modulo p^k. IEEE Trans. Circ. Syst.-II: Exp. Briefs **65**(3), 386–390 (2018)
22. Yoshioka, D.: Security of public-key cryptosystems based on Chebyshev polynomials over $\mathcal{Z}/p^k\mathcal{Z}$. IEEE Trans. Circ. Syst.-II: Exp. Briefs **67**(10), 2204–2208 (2020)
23. Farash, M.S., Attari, M.A.: Cryptanalysis and improvement of a chaotic map-based key agreement protocol using Chebyshev sequence membership testing. Nonlinear Dyn. **76**, 1203–1213 (2014)

Reinforcement-Learning Based Network Intrusion Detection with Human Interaction in the Loop

Ze Liu[✉]

Department of Computer Science and Engineering, Nanjing University of Science and Technology, Nanjing 210094, China
steve7@njust.edu.cn

Abstract. With the rapid explosion of Internet traffic volume and the continuous evolution of cyber-attack technology, existing network intrusion detection mechanisms are confronted with growing threats of more sophisticated attack traffic. Continuous recognition and modeling of new attack patterns on-the-fly are desired with human-aided automated learning. Numerous learning-based intrusion detection methods have been put forward in recent years, but the traditional data-training-testing-iterating based machine learning procedure really lacks involvement of human intelligence and instant feedbacks when being applied in the ambiguous and volatile network intrusion traffic. This paper proposes a novel approach for learning-based intrusion detection based on interactive reinforcement learning with human experience and interaction in the loop. We first transform the process of intrusion detection into a general Markov Decision Process. Then the interactive human input as manually labeling the observed network traffic occasionally is introduced into the modeling interactions to accelerate the model convergence. We customize a hybrid structure of the Q-network for such interactive network intrusion detection with Long Short-Term Memory incorporated into deep reinforcement learning. Experimental results on the NSL-KDD dataset show that the proposed modeling and detection solution achieves significantly higher precision and recall rates compared with previous learning-based detection mechanisms, with continuous model optimization by human intelligent interactions.

Keywords: Intrusion detection · Cyber security · Deep reinforcement learning · Long short-term memory

1 Introduction

Nowadays, traffic classification and analysis technology based on machine learning have demonstrated its effectiveness and adaptability. By precepting network traffic distributions for the security situation, and by recognizing anomalous traffic patterns for attack detection, learning-based network traffic engineering achieves many successes to enhance network emergency response efficiency, detect malicious network behaviors,

© Springer Nature Switzerland AG 2021
G. Wang et al. (Eds.): SpaCCS 2020, LNCS 12382, pp. 131–144, 2021.
https://doi.org/10.1007/978-3-030-68851-6_9

and maintain network space security. With heterogeneous Internet applications and their variant functionalities, the complexity and diversity of network traffic challenges the existing data classification and analysis techniques. In network intrusion detection practice, machine learning algorithms are confronted with many obstacles, such as sparse samples of anomalies, lack of labeled data, a complex correlation between different monitoring indicators. All these may lead to slow convergence, poor robustness and unstable performance in model learning.

In recent years, Reinforcement Learning (RL), as an important branch of machine learning, has been widely applied and achieved remarkable results in many application fields such as gaming, robot control, and recommendation system when combined with deep learning. But combining RL with IDS is insufficiently studied due to the difficulty of designing the learning adjustment and feedback functions in the network traffic anomaly detection scenario. Obviously, IDS human administrators are of great experience and authoritative weight when differentiating benign and malicious network traffic. It would achieve the best detection accuracy if we could always have such a manual detector sitting in front of traffic monitor evaluating and labeling every going through traffic observation and summarizing for models, although such manual procedure will definitely suffer from poor automation and low throughput. We propose to introduce human intelligence as interaction into the learning loop to automatically model the internal characteristics of network traffic. RL procedure is combined with the infrequent but dominant interactions from human supervisors, which accelerate the convergence speed and realize fast and accurate attack identification in the model. The principal innovations and contributions of this combination are as follows:

- The method of reinforcement learning is adopted to train network intrusion detectors, which improves the adaptability of the model and realizes real-time detection.
- The reward function in reinforcement learning is integrated with a human trainer's feedback, which is used to accelerate the convergence process of the model.
- Using prioritized experience replay to solve the problem of extremely unbalanced samples in intrusion detection, which has a better effect than over-sampling and under-sampling.
- Taking Long Short-Term Memory (LSTM) neural network as the principal structure of the Q-network, which can better process temporal features and achieve higher accuracy.

The rest paper elaborates with more details. Section 2 presents a literature review of the related research area. Section 3 describes the proposed intrusion detection method with human interaction interleaved. Section 4 presents experiment and results, compares the proposed with other techniques, to evaluate its advantage. Section 5 concludes with summarized insights and further discussion.

2 Related Work

Over the last few years, the existing research has put forward several intrusion detection methods. In general, these methods can be divided into misuse detection algorithms and anomaly detection algorithms. This section will clarify and discuss the distinction bewteen the technology and theory of different intrusion detection algorithms.

The basic rationale of misuse detection is to extract features of known intrusion behaviors and attempts, collect common patterns and write them into the rule base, and then match the detected network behaviors with the patterns of the database. Based on the Libcap technic, Snort is an extensively used typical misuse detection system [1], which is a relatively mature light-weight Intrusion Detection System (IDS) with the characteristics of small volume, flexible operation and highly capable system. Kalnoor et al. [2] propose deploying the IDS in wireless sensor network using pattern matching technique. Lee et al. [3] present an efficient and flexible pattern-matching algorithm for inspecting packet payloads using a head-body finite automaton. Le Dang et al. [4] note an algorithm for multiple-pattern exact matching, which reduces character comparisons and memory space based on graph transition structure and searches technique with dynamic linked list.

Anomaly detection is to establish a normal behavior model, so that the status that traffic behaviors depart from the normal behaviors are considered abnormal. Pajouh et al. [5] propose a novel two-tier classification models based on machine learning approaches Naive Bayes, certainty factor voting version of KNN classifiers and also Linear Discriminant Analysis for dimension reduction. Flanagan et al. [6] propose an evolution module of the Micro-Clustering Outlier Detection machine learning algorithm, which is designed to implement the time series method, using distance-based outlier detection and cluster density analysis. Garg et al. [7] suggest a hybrid anomaly detection scheme called as Ensemble-based Classification Model to detect anomalies. Ara et al. [8] develop a host clustering algorithm to group the hosts into clusters and unique hosts. Callegari et al. [9] investigate an anomaly detection system that detects traffic anomalies by estimating the joint entropy of different traffic descriptors.

With the advancement of artificial intelligence, traditional algorithms cannot sustain the application of IDS. Javaid et al. [10] adopt self-taught learning, a deep learning technique based on sparse auto-encoder and soft-max regression, to develop an IDS model. Yin et al. [11] explore how to set an IDS based on deep learning, and they propose a deep learning approach for intrusion detection using recurrent neural networks. Shone et al. [12] propose Non-Symmetric Deep Auto-encoder for unsupervised feature learning. Manavi et al. [13] apply Gated Recurrent Unit (GRU) to investigate the behavior patterns of requests that enter the distributed network, through which attacks are detected and a prompt alarm is sent to administrators. Lopez-Martin et al. [14] evaluate the performance of several deep reinforcement learning algorithms on labeled intrusion detection datasets.

Overall, based on the foregoing discussion, the traditional data mining algorithm is the focal point of intrusion detection technology research. The artificial intelligence algorithm represented by neural networks is brought into attention. However, as the network environment is getting increasingly complicated, and intrusion behavior frequently varieties, many methods cannot quickly adapt to the rapidly changing environment. Thus, it is pivotal to develop a more applicable algorithm in the field of intrusion detection.

3 Detection Mechanism

This paper presents a new design of intrusion detection based on network traffic. As a direct adaptive optimal control method [错误!未找到引用源。], reinforcement learning is adopted to train network intrusion detectors. On the basis of constructing intrusion detection as a Markov Decision Process (MDP), this paper further adopts the Double Deep Q-Network (DDQN) algorithm [15] with an interactive feedback method to detect the undesirable intrusions.

3.1 Building MDP

For modeling the intrusion detection problem, we adopt the Markov Decision Process formalism. The specific definitions of MDP are as follows:

State Space. S represents the state space, that is, all states that an agent can traverse. $s_t \in S, t = 0, 1, 2, \ldots, T$, which represents the traffic data of the network environment at time t.

Action Space. A refers to action space, namely, all actions that can be taken by an agent. $a_t \in A, t = 0, 1, 2, \ldots, T$, represents the action selected by the agent in the state s_t, which equivalent to the classification result.

Reward. $R : S \times A \to R$, R is the reward function that associates a real value to every state-action pair, which can be recorded as $r(s, a)$. The reward value can be a binary form of positive and negative, or a continuous value.

Value Function. Since the reward value is only referred to the evaluation of the current state-action pair, it is impossible to measure and compare the merits and demerits of different strategies. Thus, the value function is introduced to represent the expected cumulative reward of strategy π under the current state. The value function is divided into state-value function and action-value function, which are defined as follows.

$$V_\gamma^\pi(s) = E_\pi \left[\sum_{t=0}^{\infty} \gamma^t r_{t+1} | s_0 = s \right] \tag{1}$$

$$Q_\gamma^\pi(s, a) = E \left[\sum_{t=0}^{\infty} \gamma^t r_{t+1} | s_0 = s, a_0 = a \right] \tag{2}$$

Strategy. The strategy π is the mapping s to a, that is $a = \pi(s)$, the internal model of the agent to be continuously updated. In MDP, the goal is to find the optimal policy π^*, which maximizes the expected rewards when the agent selects actions in each state. In the application field of intrusion detection, π^* is equivalent to the distribution of real attack types.

3.2 Interactive Feedback

Generally, autonomous learning is feasible for an agent using reinforcement learning; nevertheless, a prominent strategy is to use an external trainer to provide guidance in specific states, which can accelerate the convergence process. Furthermore, there exist various modalities of interaction between an agent and an external trainer, such as imitation, demonstration, and feedback. By incorporating the guidance of a human trainer, this paper aims to build an intrusion detection model based on the interactive feedback method.

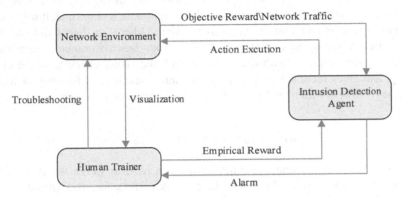

Fig. 1. Interactive reinforcement learning

As shown in Fig. 1, the model principally is composed of three parts: the network environment, human trainer, and intrusion detection agent. The interaction is a two-way process, primarily between the human trainer and the agent through a visual interface. Specifically, the agent transmits abnormal information to the human trainer in real time; meanwhile, the human trainer gives feedback to the agent after prompt verification and accurate judgment. The state vector and feedback value will be stored in the experience replay pool of the agent as historical records for the iterative model updating. Briefly, the human trainer has a policy π^* which is targeted to teach the agent. The human trainer communicates this policy by giving feedback as the agent acts in the environment. The goal of the agent is to learn the target policy π^* from the corresponding feedback.

Network Environment. During each time step, the network environment transmits the network traffic to the intrusion detection agent as the state vector and visually displays it to the human trainer. Meanwhile, the environment returns reward value based on the variation of network performance indicators, such as response time, throughput and concurrency. It is considered as an objective reward, noted as $r^E(s, a)$. As for converting the variation of network performance indicators to reward, this can be investigated as future innovations.

Human Trainer. By monitoring the real-time traffic information of the visual interface, the human trainer can evaluate the conditions of the agent's performed actions, then gives feedback to encourage it to perform particular actions in specific states to obtain better performance. This type of reward is regarded as an empirical reward, refers to $r^H(s, a)$. In the intrusion detection scenario, abnormal traffic contains more information relative to normal traffic, so that the interaction occurs only when the agent alarms or the system fails. If the agent raises a false alarm or a missing alarm, the human trainer tends to give a negative feedback signal; if the attack is correctly identified, positive feedback will be given.

Intrusion Detection Agent. After receiving the state vector, the agent implements data preprocessing and feature extraction, and then inputs it into the Q-network for detection. The agent chooses the action with the maximum Q-value as the detection result at the current time step. If the agent estimates that the current state is abnormal, it will raise an alarm to expect the human administrators to intervene. Otherwise, there will be no future action. Normally, the agent will receive $r^E(s, a)$ from the environment. Occasionally, the human trainer interacts with the agent through the visual interface in the current time step, and gives feedback $r^H(s, a)$. Consequently, the reward function of MDP is reformed as below, in which the feedback of the human trainer is directly used for reward shaping.

$$r(s, a) = \alpha \cdot r^H(s, a) + (1 - \alpha) \cdot r^E(s, a) \tag{3}$$

In Eq. 3, α is a predefined parameter, which is used to weigh the two kinds of feedback. For example, the volatility of the network performance indicator principally locates in $[0, 0.1]$, while the feedback of human can be any continues value. So that the weighting factor is served to assign different weights level to the objective reward and empirical reward. Both feedback signals will be applied to update the model.

3.3 Details of DDQN Algorithm

The following section details the process of prioritized experience replay based DDQN algorithm. Figure 2 demonstrates the framework of the proposed method.

Initialization. In the initial stage, according to the ε-greedy strategy, ε is initialized to weigh exploration and exploitation. To avoid the fluctuation resulted by a single Q-network, two neural networks with the same parameters are initialized. The current network is denoted as Q and the target network as Q'. θ and θ' represents the parameters of the two networks respectively. In addition, a fixed size experience replay pool needs to be initialized. The experience replay pool is designed to ensure the independence of samples in training. In intrusion detection, owing to the sparse positive samples, it is far more important for the agent to learn from the attack samples. In this case, the priority of the sample can be further defined according to the prioritized experience replay [17]. Generally, TD error is used to represent the priority, and Eq. 4 is the calculation formula of TD error.

$$\delta_t = r_{t+1} + \gamma \max_a Q(s_{t+1}, a_{t+1}|\theta) - Q(s_t, a_t|\theta) \tag{4}$$

Data Preprocessing. At each time step, the agent will receive the current state in the network environment and need to preprocess the raw data. Preprocessing includes missing value filling and normalization. The feature extraction of network traffic mainly concentrates on connection, content, host and temporal characteristics. Finally, the state vector s_t for intrusion detection is generated by feature selection.

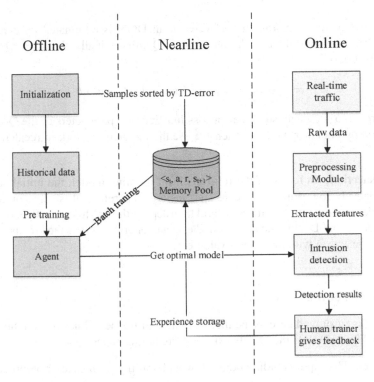

Fig. 2. The framework of the intrusion detection method based on reinforcement learning

Experience Storage. The agent explores state space by selecting random actions or select the best actions based on the current strategy. Then the agent executes an action, that is, to make a judgment whether the observed traffic data is normal behavior or attack behavior. The human trainer gives empirical reward to the agent after receiving the alarm information. Meanwhile, the agent receives the state of the next time step and stores $\langle s_t, a_t, r_t, s_{t+1} \rangle$ in the experience replay pool. To ensure that every sample can be used at least once, the priority is set to $p_t = \max_{i<t} p_i$ when an experience is stored for the first time.

Model Update. According to the priority, batch samples are collected to update the Q-network and recalculate the priority of the samples. Prioritized experience replay alters the distribution of the state space, so the deviation is incorporated in the update. It is necessary to set the importance-sampling weights to correct the deviation. Afterward, the loss function is defined in Eq. 5.

$$\frac{1}{m} \sum_{i=1}^{m} w_t (y_t - Q(s_t, a_t|\theta))^2 \tag{5}$$

The problem of overestimation of Q-value in DQN is eliminated by decoupling the action selection and the calculation of target Q-value. Finally, the target Q-value is obtained by Eq. 6.

$$y_t = r_t + \gamma Q'(s_{t+1}, \arg \max_a Q(s_{t+1}, a|\theta)|\theta') \tag{6}$$

According to the mean square error loss function, the parameters of the Q-network are updated by backpropagation. Then we use the updated network to recalculate TD error.

Online Detection. In terms of the reinforcement learning model, the initial accuracy will be relatively low if using the cold start method. Therefore, it is common to adopt historical labeled data for pre-training, and then deploy the pre-trained model online for real-time detection. During the detection, the agent generally adopts the greedy strategy, that select the action with the best Q-value each time.

3.4   Structure of the Q-Network

LSTM [18] is employed here as the main structure of the neural network in the DDQN algorithm. Figure 3 plots the Q-network structure in this paper.

Input Layer. The input is bidirectional flow with multi-attributes after preprocessing.

LSTM Layer. The retention degree of the memory unit of the LSTM node for the input information value is achieved by a gate to determine which information is remembered or discarded. The input value of the current layer is the output of the previous hidden layer. The values of all gates are affected by the current input and the output of the previous hidden layer.

DNN Layer. Essentially, Deep Neural Network (DNN) is a multi-layer perceptron with hidden layers. In the model proposed in this paper, the output of the LSTM network layer is the input of the DNN network layer. DNN sets a fully connected hidden layer to fit the value function in the DDQN algorithm.

Output Layer. The number of nodes in the output layer depends on the functional requirements of the intrusion detector. The output of each node corresponds to the expected cumulative reward value for selecting the action. Finally, the agent will select the action according to the maximum value.

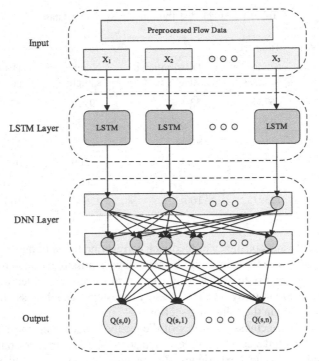

Fig. 3. The architecture of the Q-network

4 Experiments and Evaluation

4.1 Experimental Environment

The experiment was performed on a desktop with 16 GB of RAM, Intel Core CPU i7-7700 CPU 3.6 GHZ, and graphics card Nvidia GeForce GTX 1080. The experiments are conducted using the Python programming language for the reinforcement learning algorithm, and the TensorFlow library to implement the neural network.

4.2 Dataset

To verify the effectiveness of the proposed method, this paper conducts a set of experiments using the NSL-KDD dataset [19], which is the most typical dataset and the benchmark for modern-day internet traffic. Within the dataset exists four different classes of attacks: Denial of Service (DoS), Probe, User to Root(U2R), and Remote to Local (R2L). In Table 1, the distribution of different attacks in the train set and test set is tabulated.

4.3 Simulation of Human Interaction

In this experiment, the human trainer, as an independent subject, is modeled with multi-attribute parameters, including the probability of feedback (P), the constancy of feedback (C), the correctness of feedback (O), and the rewards of feedback (R).

Table 1. Attack distribution in NSL-KDD dataset

Attack category	Train set		Test set	
	Number of samples	Distribution of attacks in %	Number of samples	Distribution of attacks in %
Normal	67343	53	9711	43
Dos	45927	37	7458	33
Probe	11656	9.11	2421	11
U2R	52	0.04	200	0.9
R2L	995	0.85	2654	12.1
Total	125973	100	22544	100

The probability and constancy of feedback correspond to the frequency and duration steps of interaction. The frequency will be set as low as possible; otherwise, with a high rate of interaction, reinforcement learning will turn to supervised learning. Thus, the values of P and C are initially set as 0.01 and 1 timesteps. The discussion of parameter selection is presented in the following section.

Moreover, the correctness or quality of the feedback should be considered to determine whether the guidance is valid, given that the human trainer could also make mistakes. Based on practical experience, this analysis set the error frequency to 0.001.

Additionally, the human trainer's feedback rewards are set as below. The ultimate goal of the reinforcement learning agent is to maximize long-term cumulative rewards so that the agent can identify attacks accurately. By setting different reward functions, the human trainer can enable agents to achieve diversified goals. This means that if the human trainer intends to reduce the omissive judgment rate, the reward values of TP and FN are supposed to be larger. Generally, the omissive judgment rate is more serious than false-positive rate (Table 2).

Table 2. Setting of feedback rewards

Result	TP	TN	FP	FN
Reward	5	1	−1	−5

4.4 Results Analysis

The core point of this method is that the intrusion detection agent can continuously accumulate experience through interaction with the human trainer. Figure 4 presents that during the training process, the detection accuracy improves as the cumulative reward increase. Finally, the agent on the train set achieves the accuracy of 99%.

Meanwhile, compared the method in this paper with that of the forerunner, including Auto-Encoder (AE) [20], Sparse Auto-Encoder (SAE) [21], None-Symmetric Deep

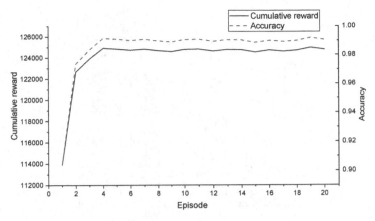

Fig. 4. Model accuracy and reward on the train set

Auto-Encoder (NDAE) [12], Self-Taught Learning (STL) [10], Recurrent Neural Network (RNN) [11] and Gated Recurrent Unit (GRU) [13]. It is noteworthy that all metrics are calculated by the weighted average. As shown in Table 3, the proposed method outperformed other regular used classifiers with accuracy and F1 score both reached 0.98 on the test dataset.

Table 3. Classifier performance results of different algorithm

Algorithm	Precision	Recall	F1 score	Accuracy
STL	0.8379	0.6950	0.7576	0.7880
AE	0.8222	0.7974	0.7647	0.7974
SAE	0.8460	0.9280	0.8870	0.8720
NDAE	0.9999	0.8542	0.8737	0.8542
RNN	0.9088	0.9054	0.8893	0.9054
GRU	0.9270	0.9317	0.9232	0.9317
Proposed	**0.9735**	**0.9871**	**0.9830**	**0.9871**

In addition to LSTM, the Q-value function can be approximated by other neural networks. In this paper, other neural networks for sequence modeling are selected for the comparative analysis, including Deep Neural Networks (DNN), Gated Recurrent Unit (GRU), and Temporal Convolutional Networks (TCN). Figure 5 demonstrates the experimental results of intrusion detection using different neural network structures in the reinforcement learning algorithm DDQN. The effectiveness of DNN and TCN is relatively poor. Although TCN achieves 95% precision, the recall rate is 10% lower than LSTM. Due to the similar structure of GRU and LSTM, the results of GRU are closer to LSTM to some extent.

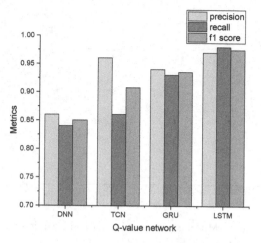

Fig. 5. Comparison of different neural networks

Finally, we compare the experimental results of different interaction parameter combinations. Particularly, we choose the weighting factor and probability of feedback to evaluate the performance of their different combinations. Candidates for weighting factor are [0.25, 0.5, 0.75, 1]. Correspondingly, interaction frequency is set as [0, 0.01, 0.1, 1]. In the experiment, the greater the weighting factor, the greater the proportion of empirical reward. Moreover, as mentioned in Sect. 3.2, the human trainer gives feedback only when the agent alarms or the system fails. The normal network traffic given no feedback, owing to it is redundant and time-consuming. Consequently, the human trainer only needs to mark around 600 experiences when interaction frequency is 0.01, which is quite small relative to the amount of the whole dataset.

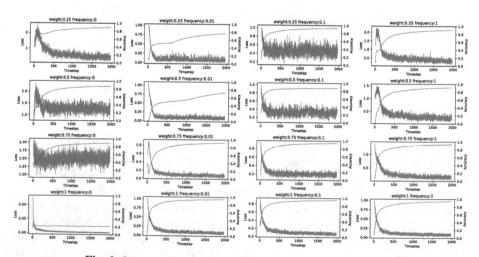

Fig. 6. Losses and accuracy of different parameter combinations

As shown in Fig. 6, when the interaction frequency is 0, the agent converges after 500 timesteps by using only the objective reward to update. When weight and frequency are set to 1 and 0 respectively, the agent has no feedback from any source. Thus, all samples in the experience buffer have no valid information, which leads to quite low accuracy. With the enhancement of weight and frequency, the convergence speed is faster, and higher accuracy can be achieved. Basically, the agent can converge within 250 timesteps after adding the empirical reward. Considering the practical labor and time costs, this paper tends to select a combination of lower interaction frequency and higher weighting factor, so that the agent can converge promptly at low-cost.

5 Conclusion

This paper primarily explores and discusses the application of interactive reinforcement learning in intrusion detection. The intrusion detection process in cyberspace security is constructed as a Markov Decision Process. Simultaneously, the human trainer's feedback to the intrusion detection agent is regarded as an external reward, so as to acquire the reinforcement learning algorithm. In this context, the agent is capable of gradually improving the ability of intrusion detection during the interaction with a human trainer. In the practical operation of the proposed model, LSTM is considered as the neural network structure of the DDQN algorithm to approximate the Q-value function. In the experiment based on the NSL-KDD dataset, this paper further compares and discusses the results of different machine learning methods and neural network structures. The model proposed achieves a larger-than 97% precision with significant privilege over others.

References

1. Roesch, M.: Snort: lightweight intrusion detection for networks. In: Large Installation System Administration Conference (LISA), vol. 99, no. 1, pp. 229–238 (1999)
2. Kalnoor, G., Agarkhed, J.: Pattern matching intrusion detection technique for Wireless sensor networks. In: 2016 2nd International Conference on Advances in Electrical, Electronics, Information, Communication and Bio-Informatics (AEEICB), pp. 724–728. IEEE (2016)
3. Lee, C.L., Yang, T.H.: A flexible pattern-matching algorithm for network intrusion detection systems using multi-core processors. Algorithms 10(2), 58 (2017)
4. Le Dang, N., Le, D.N., Le, V.T.: A new multiple-pattern matching algorithm for the network intrusion detection system. Int. J. Eng. Technol. Sci. 8(2), 94–100 (2012)
5. Pajouh, H.H., Dastghaibyfard, G.H., Hashemi, S.: Two-tier network anomaly detection model: a machine learning approach. J. Intell. Inf. Syst. 48(1), 61–74 (2017)
6. Flanagan, K., Fallon, E., Connolly, P., et al.: Network anomaly detection in time series using distance based outlier detection with cluster density analysis. In: 2017 Internet Technologies and Applications (ITA), pp. 116–121. IEEE (2017)
7. Garg, S., Singh, A., Batra, S., et al.: EnClass: ensemble-based classification model for network anomaly detection in massive datasets. In: 2017 IEEE Global Communications Conference (GLOBECOM), pp. 1–7. IEEE (2017)
8. Ara, L., Luo, X.: A data-driven network intrusion detection model based on host clustering and integrated learning: a case study on botnet detection. In: Wang, G., Feng, J., Bhuiyan, M.Z.A., Lu, R. (eds.) SpaCCS 2019. LNCS, vol. 11611, pp. 102–116. Springer, Cham (2019). https://doi.org/10.1007/978-3-030-24907-6_9

9. Callegari, C., Pagano, M.: A novel bivariate entropy-based network anomaly detection system. In: Wang, G., Atiquzzaman, M., Yan, Z., Choo, K.-K.R. (eds.) SpaCCS 2017. LNCS, vol. 10658, pp. 168–179. Springer, Cham (2017). https://doi.org/10.1007/978-3-319-72395-2_17

10. Javaid, A., Niyaz, Q., Sun, W., et al.: A deep learning approach for network intrusion detection system. In: Proceedings of the 9th EAI International Conference on Bio-inspired Information and Communications Technologies (formerly BIONETICS), pp. 21–26 (2016)

11. Yin, C., Zhu, Y., Fei, J., et al.: A deep learning approach for intrusion detection using recurrent neural networks. IEEE Access 5, 21954–21961 (2017)

12. Shone, N., Ngoc, T.N., Phai, V.D., et al.: A deep learning approach to network intrusion detection[J]. IEEE Trans. Emerg. Top. Comput. Intell. 2(1), 41–50 (2018)

13. Manavi, M., Zhang, Y.: A new intrusion detection system based on gated recurrent unit (GRU) and genetic algorithm. In: Wang, G., Feng, J., Bhuiyan, M.Z.A., Lu, R. (eds.) SpaCCS 2019. LNCS, vol. 11611, pp. 368–383. Springer, Cham (2019). https://doi.org/10.1007/978-3-030-24907-6_28

14. Lopez-Martin, M., Carro, B., Sanchez-Esguevillas, A.: Application of deep reinforcement learning to intrusion detection for supervised problems. Expert Syst. Appl. 141, 112963 (2019)

15. Sutton, R.S., Barto, A.G., Williams, R.J.: Reinforcement learning is direct adaptive optimal control. IEEE Control Syst. Mag. 12(2), 19–22 (1992)

16. Van Hasselt, H., Guez, A., Silver, D.: Deep Reinforcement learning with double Q-learning. In: 30th Association-for-the-Advancement-of-Artificial-Intelligence (AAAI) Conference on Artificial Intelligence, pp. 2094–2100 (2016)

17. Schaul, T., Quan, J., Antonoglou, I., et al.: Prioritized experience replay. In: Proceedings of the 4th International Conference on Learning Representations (ICLR), pp. 322–355 (2016)

18. Hochreiter, S., Schmidhuber, J.: Long short-term memory. Neural Comput. 9(8), 1735–1780 (1997)

19. Tavallaee, M., Bagheri, E., Lu, W., et al.: A detailed analysis of the KDD CUP 99 data set. In: 2009 IEEE Symposium on Computational Intelligence for Security and Defense Applications (CISDA), pp. 1–6. IEEE (2009)

20. Zhang, C., Ruan, F., Yin, L., et al.: A deep learning approach for network intrusion detection based on NSL-KDD dataset. In: 2019 IEEE 13th International Conference on Anti-counterfeiting, Security, and Identification (ASID), pp. 41–45. IEEE (2019)

21. Gurung, S., Ghose, M.K., Subedi, A.: Deep learning approach on network intrusion detection system using NSL-KDD dataset. Int. J. Comput. Netw. Inf. Secur. (IJCNIS) 11(3), 8–14 (2019)

Research on Security of Access Control for Cloud Computing Environment

Zhengdong Cui[1(✉)] and Feng Xu[1,2(✉)]

[1] Nanjing University of Aeronautics and Astronautics, Nanjing 211106, China
cuizhengdong@nuaa.edu.cn, nuaaos@163.com
[2] Collaborative Innovation Center of Novel Software Technology and Industrialization,
Nanjing 211106, China

Abstract. Cloud computing is considered as one of the most dominant paradigms in the Information Technology industry these days. It offers new cost effective services. With the rapid development of cloud computing, cloud security issues are becoming increasingly prominent and urgently need to be dealt with. Access control, as an important measure for traditional information and system protection, can effectively prevent illegal users from accessing protected objects, limit users' permission, and protect information resources from illegal use and access. This paper mainly discusses the improvement of the existing access control model in the cloud computing environment, the cloud data security protection technology, the introduction of risk perception and trust mechanism to implement access control to dynamically detect user identity and authorization technology for the vulnerabilities in the cloud system. We also point out some future research directions in cloud computing.

Keywords: Cloud computing · Access control · Data security · Risk perception and trust mechanism

1 Introduction

Cloud computing is a business model based on virtualization, network, and distributed technology. It has the characteristics of dynamic expansion, resource sharing, virtualization, on-demand deployment, and cost-effective. Cloud computing greatly improves the efficiency of information sharing and the utilization of computing and storage resources, and is widely used in the industry. However, with the rapid development and widespread use of cloud computing, the security issues of cloud computing has increasingly become a common concern [1, 2].

At present, cloud computing security mainly contains three categories [3], namely cloud virtualization security, cloud data security and cloud application security. Cloud virtualization security mainly involves the illegal invasion of virtual machines, data centers and cloud infrastructure; cloud data security mainly protects the confidentiality, integrity and searchability of cloud storage data; cloud application security mainly includes outsourced computing, network and terminal equipment security.

© Springer Nature Switzerland AG 2021
G. Wang et al. (Eds.): SpaCCS 2020, LNCS 12382, pp. 145–158, 2021.
https://doi.org/10.1007/978-3-030-68851-6_10

For cloud data security, in order to protect data security and content privacy, the data of the cloud server is usually encrypted and then decrypted by the user. In this process, the proxy re-encryption algorithm and attribute encryption algorithm are used to solve the problem of identity difference between data owners and users; access control technology is used to manage the authorized access range of resources; searchable encryption technology is used to achieve ciphertext retrieval and verify the integrity of the data through integrity audits and ownership certificate at last.

Cloud computing cannot effectively protect information resources due to the following characteristics: (1) The dynamic nature of cloud resources makes cloud computing complex. (2) The entities in the cloud are in different security domains and there is a lack of trust between entities. (3) The conventional access control model lacks sufficient flexibility and scalability in management. (4) Diversity and heterogeneity of cloud service technology. (5) Conflicts between different access control strategies and access control interfaces. (6) Resource sharing among untrusted tenants, multi-tenancy and virtualization technology. Therefore, it is necessary to design security mechanisms and architectures to protect confidentiality, integrity and availability of the data [4, 5].

This paper first introduces the current security threats faced by cloud computing and the reasons why traditional access control technologies are no longer applicable to cloud computing. Section 2 describes the basic principles of traditional access control technology. Section 3 introduces some access control models and technologies that are currently researched which aim to solve the problems in the cloud environment. Section 4 compares and analyzes the advantages and disadvantages of the access control models proposed in the cloud environment. Finally, the future research trends are prospected.

2 Basic Principles of Access Control Model

2.1 Traditional Access Control Technology

The purpose of access control is to restrict the access of the access subject to the access object and make the information resources accessible within the scope of laws [6]. The access control model basically contains three components: subject, object and access control strategy. The subject is an active entity that sends the access request and applies for getting access. The object is a passive entity which receive access from other entities, which is the recipient of the access. The access control strategy is a set of access rules from the subject to the object.

Due to the differences in military and commercial security policy requirements, two unique strategies have been developed, which produce two different access control models, namely Discretionary access control (DAC) and Mandatory access control (MAC). The subject of DAC manages the object and decides whether to grant the object access right or part of the access right to other subjects autonomously. While MAC focuses on protecting the confidentiality of the system, following two basic rules: "No reading upward" and "No writing downward" to achieve mandatory access control, preventing information with a high security level from flowing into objects with a low security level, the representative model is the Bell-LaPadula (BLP) model [7].

In order to solve the problem of inflexibility in the binding of subjects and specific entities in traditional access control and realize flexible authorization of subjects, Sandhu ct al. proposed the RBAC model [8, 9]. As shown in Fig. 1, the upper part of the RABC model consists of four basic elements, namely, user (U), role (R), session (S) and Permission (P). The lower part of the model is the RBAC management model. RBAC associates permissions with roles and then assigns users to the roles, then the users get permissions through the roles.

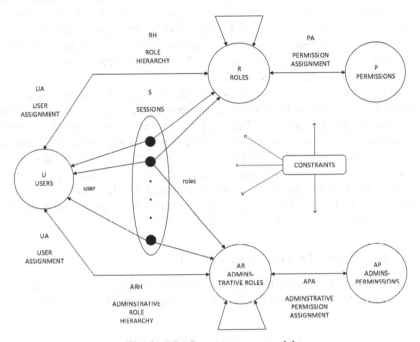

Fig. 1. RBAC management model

In reality, RBAC also has some problems [10], such as lack of information sensitivity classification and delegation mechanism, unable to support access in a distributed environment. To these problems, the researchers proposed some extended models based on RBAC, such as task-based access control model, attribute-based access control model, etc., which will be described in Section III.

2.2 Access Control Model Language

In the development and application of access control models and technologies, a variety of access control languages have been proposed to effectively describe the process of user access and rights management, and a close combination of access control theory and engineering practice has been achieved [11]. There are currently three main common access control language:

Security assertion markup language (SAML) [12] is a XML-based standard for exchanging authentication and authorization data between different security domains. The SAML standard defines identity providers and service providers to conduct the following work: 1) Authentication declaration, indicating whether the user has been authenticated, usually used for single sign-on; 2) Attribute declaration, indicating the attributes of the subjects; 3) Authorization declaration, indicating the authorities of the resources.

Services provision markup language (SPML) [13] is an XML-based standard that is mainly used to create user account service requests and process service requests related to user account service management. Its main purposes are as following: One is to automate IT configuration tasks and make it easier to encapsulate the security and audit requirements of the configuration system through standardized configuration work; the second is to achieve interoperability between different configuration systems, which can be achieved through the open standard SPM interface.

Extensible access control markup language (XACML) [14] is a XML-based policy language and access control decision request/response language. The protocol supports parameterized policy description and can enforce effective access control on Web services. The protocol primarily defines a standard format for representing authorization rules and policies, as well as a standard method for evaluating rules and policies to make authorization decisions. XACML provides the function of handling complex policy collection rules, supplementing the shortcomings of SAML which is very suitable for access control in large cloud computing platforms and plays an important role in achieving joint access control across multiple trust domains.

2.3 Technical Means of Access Control Model

Regarding data security issues in the cloud environment, the current academic researches on access control technology mainly include three aspects, as shown in Table 1:

Table 1. Access control technology

Name	Example	Function
Access control model	TRBAC, ABAC,RBAC	Statically assigned permissions
Encryption algorithm	ABE	Protect stored data and interact with host and object
Risk perception and trust mechanism	MTBAC, Risk perception and trust mechanism	Dynamically determine access rights

There are many researches on the access control model in the cloud computing environment, which mainly concentrate on improving and expanding the model in the new cloud computing environment so that the model can better serve the cloud computing. The research about access control based on the encryption mechanism is mainly focused on ABE cryptosystem-based cloud computing access control. The ABE cryptosystem-based access control is usually used for data access to cloud storage. The risk perception and trust mechanisms are usually combined with the access control model to achieve dynamic authorization of the access control model.

3   Access Control Model and Technology in Cloud Computing Environment

With the development of network technology and cloud computing technology, access control as the core content of cloud computing security has become a research hotspot. The current researches on cloud computing access control mainly focus on the following three aspects: improving the original access control model, using the ABE cryptosystem to protect cloud data security, and combining risk assessment and trust mechanisms to dynamically detect user qualifications and authorizations.

3.1   Improvement of Traditional Access Control Model

The access control model is a method to describe the security system according to a specific access strategy and establish a security model. Users (tenants) can obtain permissions through the access control model and then access the data in the cloud, so the access control model is versatile to statically assign user permissions. The access control models in cloud computing are based on the traditional access control model, and improvements are made on the traditional access control model to make it more suitable for cloud computing environments.

Task-Based Cloud Access Control. In 1997, Thomas et al. adopted a task-oriented view and proposed a task-based access control model (TBAC) [15]. From the perspective of a task, a security model and a security mechanism are established and a dynamic real-time management is provided during the task processing period. Document [16] combines tasks with RBAC and proposes the T-RBAC model. In the T-RABC model, the workflow is decomposed into interdependent tasks, and then the tasks are assigned to roles. The roles are obtained by executing task nodes. The cloud server authorized by the principal owner acts as a trusted intermediary to pass the access request during the authorization process. The cloud server is used to share some of the authorization work and reduce the burden on users. Figure 2 is the T-RBAC access control model.

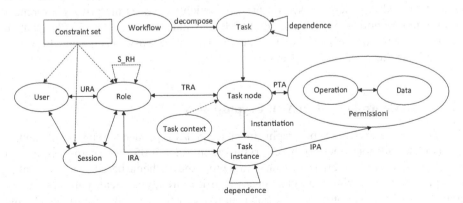

Fig. 2. TRABC model

Huang et al. first classify roles on the server side of the cloud computing environment, and assign different access roles according to the different access objects; then they classify the permissions differently in the task assignment phase, which can further solve the problem of low efficiency and frequent access during the process of the subject's access to the object [17]. Senam et al. [18] combined the task and role access control model to establish a four-layer control model that includes users, roles, tasks, and permissions. The divided atomic tasks are assigned to users, and authorization is completed when the tasks are active. After the tasks are completed, the permissions are withdrawn to achieve dynamic access control.

Attribute-Based Cloud Computing Access Control. The attribute-based access control model (ABAC) aims to solve the problem of granular access control and dynamic expansion of large-scale users in current complex information systems. The model relies on a set of attributes associated with the requester or the resource to be accessed in order to make access decisions [19]. There are many ways to define or use attributes in this model. The attributes can be the user's work start date, the user's location, the user's role, or all and these attributes may or may not be related [20]. After defining the attributes used in the system, each attribute is considered as a discrete value, and the policy decision point compares the values of all attributes with a set of values to decide whether to grant or deny access. These types of models are also called policy-based access control (PBAC) or claim-based access control (CBAC). Ei et al. summarized the cloud environment into three attributes [21], including users of cloud resources, cloud resources and specific access environments, and access control of attributes in the cloud is performed through RBAC. Al-Amri S [22] proposed an ABAC intelligent model based on knowledge agent for IaaS and access control logic-general logic formal logic (ACL-DL). The model infers access decisions based on formal logic, supporting context-aware mechanisms and duty-separated mechanisms. Bouchami et al. [23] proposed an access control model based on ABAC. They emphasized that the ABAC model is flexible because it takes into account other attributes such as user behavior, context vulnerability and resource attributes. Their work focuses on how to define the risk level between collaborative environments and solves dynamic problems. M. ED-DAIBOUNI [24] and others proposed an ABAC model based on privacy, which integrates the privacy awareness module into the policy information point (PIP) and adds a "privacy level" (PL) element to indicate the privacy level of the resource. Each resource is associated with a PL value, thus ensuring the principle of privacy.

3.2   Access Control Based on ABE Cryptosystem

The research on the ABE cryptographic mechanism has expanded the concept of identity based on the traditional identity-based cryptosystem since 2005, and regards identity as a collection of attributes. Sahai and Waters first proposed a scheme based on fuzzy identity encryption [25], applying biological characteristics directly as identity information to identity-based encryption schemes, Sahai introduced the concept of attributes in the paper. In 2006, Goyal et al. proposed attribute-based encryption schemes based on fuzzy identity-based encryption schemes. Encryption scheme ABE [26], then derived two ABE algorithms related to the policy tree, namely, key strategy ABE (key-policy attribute-based encryption, KP-ABE) and ciphertext strategy ABE (cipher-policy attribute-based encryption, CP-ABE for short).

In the KP-ABE scheme, the access structure used to describe the access control strategy is combined with the user's private key, and the attribute set is associated with the resource to be accessed. The access control strategy in this way is set by the data recipient, and the user can set the message to be received. User has a higher degree of freedom. The data owner can only use attributes to describe the data and cannot set the corresponding access control strategy, so the control of the data is weak. The CP-ABE scheme is the opposite of KP-ABE. At this time, the access control strategy is set by the data owner, and the data owner has a higher degree of freedom. The CP-ABE mechanism is more suitable for access control services. In the cloud computing environment, the CP-ABE mechanism is also widely used.

The ABE cryptosystem in a cloud computing environment includes four elements: data provider, trusted third-party authorization center, cloud storage server, and user. The model is shown in Fig. 3:

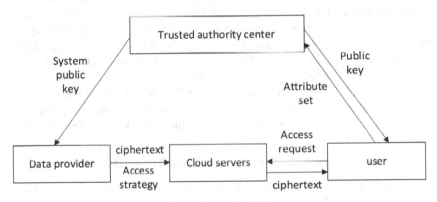

Fig. 3. ABE model

First, the trusted authorization center generates the master key and public parameters, and passes the system public key to the data provider; after receiving the system public key, the data provider encrypts the file with the policy tree and system public key, encrypts the ciphertext and strategy The tree is uploaded to the cloud server; then, when a new user joins the system, upload his own attribute set to the trusted authorization center, and submit a private key application request, the trusted authorization center calculates the attribute set and master key submitted by the user The private key is generated and passed to the user. Finally, the user downloads the data of interest. If the attribute set meets the policy tree structure of the ciphertext data, the ciphertext can be decrypted; otherwise, the access to the data fails.

Zhou et al. [27] proposed a decentralized multi-authority CP-ABE access control scheme, which is more practical for supporting user withdrawal. In addition, this solution can protect data privacy and access policy privacy through policies hidden in the cloud storage system. An access strategy implemented using a linear secret sharing scheme.

Ning et al. [28] proposed an auditable σ time outsourcing CP-ABE, which transfers the expensive pairing operations generated by decryption to the cloud, and at the same time, the correctness of the operations can be effectively audited. In addition, this concept provides fine-grained access control at σ time. The cloud service provider may restrict a specific group of users from enjoying access rights at most σ times within a specified time period. As an independent benefit, the concept also captures key leakage resistance. The leakage of the user's decryption key will not help a malicious third party to decrypt the ciphertext belonging to the user. XUE et al. [29] proposed a novel heterogeneous framework to eliminate single-point performance bottlenecks and provide a more effective access control scheme with an audit mechanism. The framework uses multiple attribute authorities to share the burden of user legality verification. At the same time, a central authority was introduced to generate keys for users verified by legality. Each permission in the scheme manages the entire attribute set individually. The audit mechanism is responsible for detecting which attribute is authorized to perform the legality verification process incorrectly or maliciously.ABE is suitable for cloud computing architecture and can completely realize the access control of data on the cloud platform, but there are problems such as more fine-grained access control, user attribute revocation and multi-factors in encrypted data access, and further research is still needed. Fan et al. [30] proposed an access control system (PS-ACS) with separation of permissions based on privacy protection. In the PS-ACS scheme, users are logically divided into private domain (PRD) and public domain (PUD). In PRD, in order to obtain read access and write access, key aggregation encryption (KAE) and improved attribute-based signature (IABS) are used respectively. In PUD, a new attribute-based encryption (CP-ABE) scheme based on multi-ciphertext strategy with efficient decryption function is constructed to avoid single point of failure and complicated key distribution problems.

3.3 Access Control Based on Risk Perception and Trust Mechanism

Compared with other access control technologies, the research on risk perception and trust mechanism started later. In order to solve the dynamic authorization problem in the cloud computing environment, researchers introduced risk perception technology and trust mechanism into the access control model.

Brucker et al. proposed risk-based access control in response to multinational organizations facing various policies and regulations [31]. Nadav et al. proposed a method of access control based on resource trust to solve the problem of trust access between cloud users and cloud resources. This method introduces trust into the attribute access control model in cloud environment, and proposes an optimization technology of attribute access control based on trust evaluation in cloud computing environment. By introducing the evaluation credibility, entity familiarity and evaluation similarity, the trust degree is calculated through this method, and the comprehensive trust degree of users or resources is achieved through direct trust, indirect trust and recommendation trust, so as to achieve the purpose of improving the security of attribute access control. [32]. The TRAAC proposed by Burnett et al. [32] is a trust and risk-aware access control that provides policy coverage, dynamic access control decisions, and appropriate risk denial and delegation of authority. They claim that their system can be perfectly adapted to the healthcare field, although it can be extended to other fields. First, they defined a regional policy model in which the data owner has complete control over the data privileges that he can share with other users, so they are included in the domain. Trust is defined in terms of shared trust and obligation trust, which allows to verify user whether the requestor has complied with the obligations assigned to him. They use a probability calculation trust model called subjective logic to formulate trust assessments. Chen et al. [33] proposed a risk-based dynamic access control model (DRAC), which emphasizes risk measurement as an auxiliary decision-making index. Moreover, the dynamic threshold of risk is derived from historical records, and the final comprehensive decision will be affected by strategy, risk measurement and dynamic threshold. In order to improve performance, a sliding window calculation method based on data flow is adopted.

Younis A et al. [34] proposed a method that combines risk identification and role-based and task models, as shown in Fig. 4:

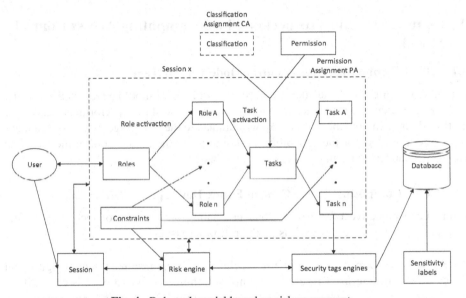

Fig. 4. Role task model based on risk assessment

In the model (R_TRBAC), users are classified according to their actual work. Therefore, the user is in a security domain related to his role. Each role in the model will be assigned a set of tasks that are most relevant and needed to practice that role. Each task has a security classification for accessing data or assets, and the exact permissions required to complete this task. The risk engine is used to handle the user's dynamic and random behavior; it calculates the risk value based on the user's visit. The security label engine is used to publish security labels in semi-or untrusted environments and processes. The model controls access to data or assets by using security labels to tag data or assets. Any application to access the data must ensure that the security label of the target data is classified, and the model uses the security label according to the trust and security level used in the environment.

LIN Guoyuan et al. [35] proposed an access control model MTBAC based on multiple trusts. Unlike the traditional access control mechanism, MTBAC also considers the trust of users' behavior and the trust of cloud service nodes. MTBAC adapts to the characteristics of uncertainty, dynamics and distribution in cloud computing. In the user trust model, the user's behavior is divided into three types, and each attribute has a certain weight. The user's trust level will be quantified through the trust of the user's behavior. The trust model of cloud service nodes is based on ant colony optimization algorithm. Finally, based on the mutual trust between users and cloud service nodes, access control is implemented in the cloud computing environment, and the security of users and cloud servers is effectively protected.

In short, the current research on risk identification and trust mechanism mainly focuses on the combination with cloud computing access control model, so as to solve the problems of dynamic authorization and prevent malicious user access.

4 Comparison and Prospect of Cloud Computing Access Control Model

4.1 Cloud Computing Access Control Model Comparison

In practical applications, the qualified access control model should be selected according to different actual application situations. According to the ability, performance and other metrics defined in documents [34, 36], we summarize the advantages and disadvantages of different models for the capability requirements of the access control model in the cloud computing environment, as shown in Table 2.

4.2 Cloud Computing Access Control Future Development Direction

From the perspective of existing cloud computing access control technologies and research, future research will focus on the following issues:

1. **Standardization.** Cloud computing technology integrates many technologies, and cloud computing itself rarely has a unified technical standard. In this case, different enterprises and cloud service providers adopt different standards, resulting in the inability of the enterprise applications and cloud applications, and the cloud applications provided by different cloud service providers mutual integration.
2. **Fine-grained access control.** The existing cloud access control is a coarse-grained access control based on user identity, and there are hidden security risks in a multi-tenant cloud environment.
3. **Trust relationship.** There is no trust relationship between the data providers, cloud platforms, and users in the cloud computing system. At the same time, they must use a trusted third-party organization to perform the exchange and access control of related keys and data, without high security and manageability.
4. **Cross-cloud authorization.** In order to implement cloud services, the system usually needs to access applications and data from multiple clouds. Since users have different permissions in different clouds and different cloud access control mechanisms, access policies in multiple clouds may conflict. This leads to complex cross-cloud authorization and hidden dangers.

Table 2. Performance comparison among different types of access control models

	RBAC	TBAC	ABAC	ABE	R_TRBAC	MTBAC
Security				✓	✓	✓
Confidentiality				✓		
Flexibility of authorization	✓				✓	✓
Minimum privilege	✓	✓			✓	✓
Separation of duties	✓	✓			✓	✓
Fine-grained control			✓	✓	✓	
Cloud environment attribute		✓	✓			
Constraints description	✓				✓	✓
Compatibility			✓			
Expansibility			✓			
Authentication					✓	✓
Passive and active workflows		✓			✓	
Delegation of capabilities					✓	
Operational and situational awareness					✓	

5. **Risk perception.** The emergence of a cloud platform integrates different computing resources and also contains all the hidden security risks of computing resources, such as processors, memory, and operating systems. These factors will have a huge impact on the performance of the entire system.
6. **Data security and privacy protection.** In cloud computing, the types of nodes participating in cloud computing are diverse, the locations are sparsely distributed, and users often cannot effectively control them. In addition, cloud service providers have the risk of leaking privacy during transmission, processing, and storage.

5 Conclusion

Access control is an important information security technology that is indispensable for companies to protect data and resources in information systems. After years of development, the research on the access control model has made significant progress. Cloud computing is a new paradigm, making access control essential to provide effective protection for cloud computing resources. This makes access control in cloud computing one of the most important issues in current cloud security research. Therefore, it has aroused great concern in academia and industry.

This article studies the common access control techniques used to address security issues in cloud environments. From the three aspects of the improvement based on the traditional access control model, the access control based on the ABE cryptosystem and the risk perception and trust mechanism, the access control technology in the current cloud computing environment is comprehensively reviewed, and the future direction is prospected.

Acknowledgments. This work is supported by the China Aviation Science Foundation (NO. 20101952021), the Fundamental Research Funds for the Central Universities (NO. NZ2013306) and the Key Project supported by Medical Science and technology development foundation, Nanjing Department of Health (NO. YKK18165).

References

1. Singh, S., Jeong, Y.S., Park, J.H.: A survey on cloud computing security: issues, threats, and solutions. J. Netw. Comput. Appl. **75**, 200–222 (2016)
2. Basu, S., Bardhan, A., Gupta, K., et al.: Cloud computing security challenges & solutions-a survey. In: 2018 IEEE 8th Annual Computing and Communication Workshop and Conference (CCWC), pp. 347–356. IEEE (2018)
3. Zhang, Y., Wang, X., Liu, X., et al.: Security overview of cloud computing environment. J. Softw. (6), 1328–1348 (2016)
4. Curry, S., et al.: Infrastructure security: getting to the bottom of compliance in the cloud. In: The Security Division of EMC (2010)
5. Kaur, P.J., Kaushal, S.: Security concerns in cloud computing. In: Mantri, A., Nandi, S., Kumar, G., Kumar, S. (eds.) HPAGC 2011. CCIS, vol. 169, pp. 103–112. Springer, Heidelberg (2011). https://doi.org/10.1007/978-3-642-22577-2_14
6. Shen, H.B., Hong, F.: Review of access control model. Appl. Res. Comput. **22**(6), 9–11 (2005)
7. Bell, D., LaPadula, L.: Secure computer systems: mathematical foundations. Bedford, MA. Accessed 04 Feb 2013
8. Sandhu, R., Bhamidipati, V., Munawer, Q.: The ARBAC97 model for role-based administration of roles. ACM Trans. Inf. Syst. Secur. (TISSEC) **2**(1), 105–135 (1999)
9. Sandhu, R., Coyne, E.J., Feinstein, H.L., Youman, C.E.: Role-based access control models. IEEE Comput. **29**(2), 38–47 (1996)
10. Suhendra, V.: A survey on access control deployment. In: Kim, T., Adeli, H., Fang, W., Villalba, J.G., Arnett, K.P., Khan, M.K. (eds.) SecTech 2011. CCIS, vol. 259, pp. 11–20. Springer, Heidelberg (2011). https://doi.org/10.1007/978-3-642-27189-2_2
11. Luo, Y., Wu, Z.H.: A new method of access control policy descriptive language and its authorization. J. Compute. 1–18 (2017)
12. Cantor, S., Moreh, J., Philpott, R., Maler, E.: Metadata for the OASIS Security Assertion Markup Language (SAML) V2.0. OASIS Open (2005)
13. Gary, C., Sun, M.: OASIS Service Provisioning Markup Language (SPML) Versions 2.0. OASIS Open (2006)
14. Erik, R., Axiomatics, A.B.: OASIS eXtensible Access Control Markup Language (XACML) Versions 3.0. OASIS Open (2013)
15. Thomas, R.K., Sandhu, R.S.: Task-based authorization controls (TBAC): a family of models for active and enterprise-oriented authorization management. In: Lin, T.Y., Qian, S. (eds.) Database Security XI, pp. 166–181. Springer, Boston (1998). https://doi.org/10.1007/978-0-387-35285-5_10
16. Wang, X.W., Zhao, Y.M.: A task-role-based access control model for cloud computing. Comput. Eng. **38**(24), 9–13 (2012)
17. Huang, Y., Li, K.L.: Model of cloud computing oriented T-RBAC. Appl. Res. Comput. **30**(12), 3735–3737 (2013)

18. Pandey, S., Dwivedi, A., Pant, J., et al.: Security enforcement using TRBAC in cloud computing. In: 2016 International Conference on Computing, Communication and Automation (ICCCA). IEEE (2017)
19. Al-Kahtani, M.A., Sandhu, R.: A model for attribute-based user-role assignment. In: 18th Annual Computer Security Applications Conference, 2002. Proceedings, pp. pp. 353e62. IEEE Computuer Society (2002). https://doi.org/10.1109/CSAC.2002.1176307.
20. Karp, A., Haury, H., Davis, M.: From ABAC to ZBAC: the evolution of access control models. HP Laboratories-2009–30 (2009)
21. Li, X.F., Feng, D.G., Chen, Z.W., Fang, Z.H.: Model for attribute based access control. J. Commun. **29**(4), 90–98 (2008)
22. Al-Amri, S.: IaaS-cloud security enhancement: an intelligent attribute-based access control model and implementation. Loughborough University (2017)
23. Bouchami, A., Goettelmann, E., Perrin, O., Godart, C.: Enhancing access control with risk metrics for collaboration on social cloud-platforms. IEEE Trustcom/bigdata/SE/ISPA **1**, 864–871 (2015)
24. Ed-Daibouni, M., Lebbat, A., Tallal, S., et al.: A formal specification approach of Privacy-aware Attribute Based Access Control (Pa-ABAC) model for cloud computing. In: International Conference on Systems of Collaboration. IEEE (2016)
25. Sahai, A., Waters, B.: Fuzzy identity-based encryption. In: Cramer, R. (ed.) Advances in Cryptology – EUROCRYPT 2005. Lecture Notes in Computer Science, vol. 3494, pp. 457–473. Springer, Heidelberg (2005)
26. Vipul, G., Amit, S., Omkant, P., Brent, W.: Attribute-Based encryption for fine-grained access control of encrypted data. In: Proceedings of the ACM Conference on Computer and Communications Security, pp. 89–98 (2006)
27. Zhong, H., Zhu, W., Yan, X.: Multi-authority attribute-based encryption access control scheme with policy hidden for cloud storage. Soft. Comput. **22**(1), 1–9 (2016)
28. Ning, J., Cao, Z., Dong, X., Liang, K., Ma, H., Wei, L.: Auditable σ -time outsourced attribute-based encryption for access control in cloud computing. IEEE Trans. Inf. Forensics Secur. **13**(1), 94–105 (2018). https://doi.org/10.1109/TIFS.2017.2738601
29. Xue, K., Xue, Y., Hong, J., et al.: RAAC: robust and auditable access control with multiple attribute authorities for public cloud storage. IEEE Trans. Inf. Forensics Secur. **12**, 953–967 (2017)
30. Fan, K., Tian, Q., Wang, J., Li, H., Yang, Y.: Privacy protection based access control scheme in cloud-based services. China Commun. **14**(1), 61–71 (2017). https://doi.org/10.1109/CC.2017.7839758
31. Nie, J., Zhang, D.: Research on resource trust access control based on cloud computing environment. In: Li, K., Li, W., Chen, Z., Liu, Y. (eds.) Computational Intelligence and Intelligent Systems, ISICA 2017, Communications in Computer and Information Science, vol. 873, pp. 394–404. Springer, Heidelberg (2018). https://doi.org/10.1007/978-981-13-1648-7_34
32. Burnett, C., Chen, L., Edwards, P., Norman, T.J.: TRAAC: trust and risk aware access control. In: 2014 12th Annual International Conference on Privacy, Security and Trust (PST), pp. 371–378., IEEE (2014)
33. Chen, A., Xing, H., She, K., et al.: A dynamic risk-based access control model for cloud computing. In: IEEE International Conferences on Big Data & Cloud Computing. IEEE (2016)

34. Younis, Y.A., Kifayat, K., Merabti, M.: An access control model for cloud computing. J. Inf. Secur. Appl. **19**(1), 45–60 (2014)
35. Lin, G., Wang, D., Bie, Y., et al.: MTBAC: a mutual trust based access control model in cloud computing. China Commun. **11**(4), 154–162 (2014)
36. Wang, Y.D., Yang, J.H., Xu, C., et al.: Survey on access control technologies for cloud computing. J. Softw. **26**(5), 1129–1150 (2015)

Research and Development of Privacy Protection of WSN Routing Protocol

Panfei Liu[1(✉)], Feng Xu[1,2(✉)], and Ying Zhu[1(✉)]

[1] Nanjing University of Aeronautics and Astronautics, Nanjing 211106, China
panfeil@nuaa.edu.cn, nuaaos@163.com, 294971070@qq.com
[2] Collaborative Innovation Center of Novel Software Technology and Industrialization,
Nanjing 211106, China

Abstract. WSN has developed rapidly in the past few decades based on its low-cost, short-distance and easy-deployment features. However, due to the openness of wireless communication channels, privacy protection in WSN routing protocol has become a hot topic nowadays. Researchers have proposed a variety of different technologies to improve privacy. Whereas, these technologies are numerous and complex, targeting at different scenarios. Based on the application scenarios and protection technology objectives of the routing protocol, this paper analyzes and compares the advantages and disadvantages of various typical privacy protection methods of the routing protocol, and then puts forward some views on the future research direction.

Keywords: Wireless sensor networks · Routing protocols · Privacy protection · Application scenarios and objectives

1 Introduction

Wireless Sensor networks are a distributed sensor network [1], composed of a large number of stationary or moving sensors in a self-organizing and multi-hop manner. These sensors cooperatively sense, collect, process and transmit the information of the perceived objects in the geographical area covered by the network, and finally send the information to the owner of the network. Wireless network sensors are closely related to social development, and have been widely used in industry, military, medical, agriculture, architectural design and other fields, and have aroused social attention. Many technical researchers have strengthened the research on wireless sensor technology and its applications to give full play to the role of wireless sensor networks in life. Exploring the application of wireless sensor networks in various fields can not only optimize the application of wireless sensor networks, but also has profound significance for the development of social modernization. This paper will analyze the privacy protection of WSN routing protocol from four application scenarios: military, environment, medical, and transportation.

The rest of this paper will be arranged as follows: Section 2 briefly introduces the classification and strategy of privacy protection in WSN routing protocol. Section 3

© Springer Nature Switzerland AG 2021
G. Wang et al. (Eds.): SpaCCS 2020, LNCS 12382, pp. 159–172, 2021.
https://doi.org/10.1007/978-3-030-68851-6_11

specifically explains the privacy protection methods in each application scenario, and selects representative methods in related papers for explanation. Section 4 compares the performance of several privacy protection methods. Finally, Sect. 5 summarizes the conclusion and the future prospects.

2 Classification and Strategy of Privacy Protection in WSN Routing Protocol

WSN routing privacy protection technology is mainly divided into two categories: content privacy protection and location privacy protection. Content privacy protection mainly adopts privacy protection technologies such as encryption, packet injection and aggregation, and completes tasks such as data collection, query and access control without revealing private information, which is very different from location privacy protection technology. For example, in medical field, we usually need to transfer medical data to a remote hospital or doctor's computer and these data involve the user's sensitive information. If an attacker obtains or modifies these data by some means, the user's privacy will be greatly compromised. Location privacy protection can be divided into source node location privacy and sink node location privacy. The former includes fixed location privacy and mobile location privacy, while the latter includes local privacy attacks and global privacy attacks, as shown in Fig. 1.

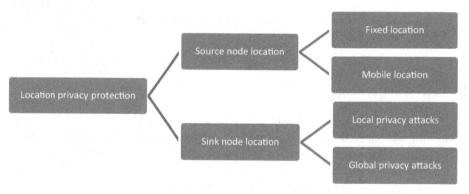

Fig. 1. Classification of WSN location privacy protection

Location privacy protection technology often adopts protection strategies such as disguising real source nodes or base stations, probabilistic flood routing, phantom routing, and random delay forwarding. In event-driven WSN application scenarios, sensor nodes are randomly placed on the battlefield to obtain enemy military information or deployed in natural environmental protection zones to monitor precious wild animals. The node closest to the monitoring target becomes the source node and the collected data is sent to the base station in a multi-hop manner. Therefore, even if the data has been encrypted, the attacker does not need to crack the content of the message, and it is very easy to obtain the source of the message based on the propagation characteristics of the electromagnetic signal. In an attack mode with strong concealment and destructive capabilities, an attacker can unconsciously control certain nodes or even compromise the encryption system, and then reprogram some nodes to pretend to be normal nodes. It can be seen that effectively responding to the leakage of data content and location privacy is critical to the success of wireless sensor applications, especially for mission-critical applications that work in unattended or harsh environments.

3   Typical Privacy Protection Methods in WSN Routing Protocol

Wireless sensor network is composed of a number of small sensor node devices with information transmission and detection capabilities and mainly formed by wireless connection. Moreover, WSN can effectively obtain information, strengthen the real-time control of various factors in the detection area, and transmit the collected information to the gateway node of the system, thereby achieving remote monitoring and target detection. The routing protocol methods are mainly used for content privacy protection and node location privacy protection in WSN. The transmission methods and self-organization of WSN make the privacy protection of content and location particularly important. Since the main resource consumption in WSN lies in the communication module, the routing protocol protection methods need to send a large amount of additional communication to achieve privacy protection. Therefore, these methods have high communication overhead, high energy consumption, and long communication delay. And the current routing protocol research mainly focuses on resisting external attacks, while the research on global attacks, internal attacks and mobile node location protection is relatively small, and the degree of privacy protection is not high. In this section, we will classify and explain privacy protections in WSN routing protocol of various scenarios from military, environment, medical, and transportation scenarios.

3.1   Military Field

WSN applies effectively in the military field, with the advantages of high positioning accuracy, real-time performance and rapid deployment. Real-time monitoring, targets positioning and environment observing can be further completed through the rational arrangement of sensor nodes in harsh battlefields. Therefore, researchers can better grasp the battlefield situation in combination with the information selected and transferred in WSN. A large number of sensor nodes can be arranged in the area to be monitored by means of aircraft. After data collecting and integrating, information is transmitted to the command center, and the commander will make relevant decisions based on the information. After the continuous development of wireless sensor networks, it has become an important application technology in military field, improving national strength. The objective of privacy protection in military is reflected in real-time, concealment and low energy consumption.

3.1.1   Content Privacy Protection

Encryption. This is one of the most commonly used methods in military field of information security and can provide data confidentiality. Applying encryption to privacy protection not only ensures data confidentiality, but also achieves the purpose of privacy protection by adopting the password mechanism to gain the invisibility and lossless of private data. Kakelli [2] proposes NSRP secure multipath routing protocol for secure data transmission. NSRP uses elliptic curve cryptography (ECC) to discover trusted neighbor nodes and establish secure multiple routes to reliably transfer data in Military Heterogeneous Wireless Sensor Network. This protocol has an effective key management mechanism which can provide better security and improve network performance. Compared with existing key management solutions, NSRP achieves lower communication overhead, memory requirements, and energy consumption. However, NSRP only performs well within 200 to 1000 sensor nodes, and still performs poorly for large-scale nodes, such as the range of 1000 to 5000. M. Sliti [3] proposes an authentication framework for heterogeneous wireless sensor networks. In order to prevent the effects of false alarms issued by malicious sensor nodes, a novel concept called k-security is introduced, which relies on elliptic curve cryptography and threshold signature. The main novelty of this method is that the intermediate verification of the alert message allows discarding spoofed messages when forwarding, which saves important processing resources and energy, thereby extending the life of the network. Currently, radio fingerprint technology is under development, and combining them is an improvement direction.

Due to its extremely low computational complexity, packet injection can be widely used in various wireless sensor networks. Data packet injection protects the privacy of sensitive information and facilitates the further fusion of private data by adding disguised data to the original sensor data, at the cost of some network and computing resources. Since these are the constrained aspects of WSN, the focus of this method is how to maximize the lifetime of the network while applying this technology. Furthermore, the key point is to properly inject messages to avoid real events from being tracked. Therefore, Wang [4] proposes a new method based on FPIS (Pseudo Packet Injection Scheme). On the one hand, each real data packet is routed along a random path at a special stage, which confuses adversaries who use packet tracking. On the other hand, forged data packets are injected to some extent to resist traffic analysis attacks. W. Tan [5] involves an opportunistic method, inserting fake packets only when the event occurs.

Aggregation. The privacy preserving of data fusion process belongs to data-oriented privacy preserving. In the basic data fusion process, the data is transferred and fused upward along the constructed data fusion tree layer by layer, and finally the QS (Query Server) obtains the required fusion data. Under the circumstance that the nodes need to fuse the data, the trusted parent node in the network can get the data of its child nodes. If an attacker cracks the wireless link or captures the parent node, the private data will be exposed. However, the basic data fusion technology does not provide a data privacy protection mechanism. It is necessary to study a privacy protection scheme for the data fusion process. On the premise of ensuring the correct data fusion result, even if the collected data is captured externally, decrypted or captured internally by other trusted nodes during transmission and fusion processing, the private data can also be prevented from being obtained [6]. Kim et al. [7] propose a data fusion privacy protection scheme HDA. The first step of the scheme uses a flooding mechanism to perform topology discovery, establishing the topological relationship between nodes. The second step transforms the original data by introducing the seed data of the nodes which can exchange among nodes and form related relationships. Finally, the intermediate node performs the fusion operation without knowing the original data by means of the correlation of the seed data after receiving all the data of the child nodes, and passes it to the next hop after encryption.

3.1.2 Location Privacy Protection

The characteristics of wireless transmission mode and self-organizing mode of WSN make the privacy protection of sensor nodes' locations particularly important. The earliest privacy protection method for the routing protocol is the phantom routing protocol proposed in [8], as shown in Fig. 2 of this paper. Literature [9] proposes a location angle phantom routing named PRLA. This method introduces the inclination angle for direct random walk, avoiding the damage of the path selection to the privacy of the source path, with better security than the single-path phantom routing. The literature [10] propose directed random phantom routing. Unlike the flooded phantom routing, the packets are randomly directed to the base station in the second phase, which has longer security period and lower loss. Chen Juan et al. propose a source location privacy protection protocol PUSBRF protocol based on the limited flooding of source nodes [11]. This protocol can generate phantom source nodes that are far from the real source node and have diverse geographic locations. Compared with single-path phantom routing, the number of random directional paths increases at least 33.33%, which effectively improves the privacy security and average security time of the source location.

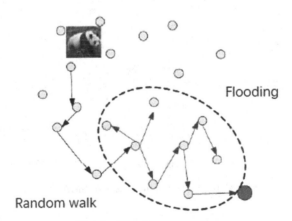

Fig. 2. The phantom routing

3.2 Environment Field

Environmental protection has always been the focus of Chinese attention. It is necessary to use advanced technical means to monitor environmental indicators in real time in order to solve environmental problems in a timely manner and ensure the real-time and effectiveness of environmental monitoring, which is of great significance to the realization of environmental protection goals. In the past, environmental monitoring mainly faced the problem of difficulty in obtaining environmental data, especially in deep sea or complex terrain environments. Whereas, adopting wireless sensor nodes to collect environmental data can avoid the damage caused by human operations to the natural ecological environment, and it can also accurately monitor the environment and provide information support for the development of environmental protection. When actually carrying out environmental monitoring, the main purpose is to comprehensively collect and analyze the data generated by soil analysis, animal migration, crop irrigation, surface monitoring, ocean monitoring and so on, ensuring that the collected information can reflect the actual situation of the regional environment. For example, WSN is applied to the grape growing environment for real-time monitoring, which further guarantees the healthy growth of grapes. The objective of privacy protection in environmental monitoring is reflected in real-time and effectiveness of environmental monitoring.

3.2.1 Content Privacy Protection

Aggregation. He and others first propose the data slicing and reorganization algorithm SMART for data fusion privacy protection in [12]. The algorithm mainly includes data slicing algorithm (Slicing), slicing data mixing algorithm (Mixing) and fusion algorithm (Aggregating), the process is shown in Fig. 3 [12]. Firstly, the node slices the privacy data it perceives, the number of slices is less than the number of adjacent points; then, these slices are sent to neighbor nodes randomly; finally, these slices are transmitted along the existing data fusion tree structure layer by layer, and intermediate node performs data fusion.

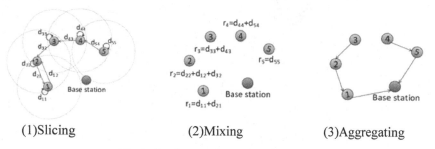

(1)Slicing   (2)Mixing   (3)Aggregating

Fig. 3. Implementation process of SMART

Similar to SMART, Li et al. [13] propose a data slicing technique EEHA for balancing energy consumption and fusion accuracy. Reference [14] introduces a random number sharding technique to reduce the number of shards, and solves the reduction of fusion accuracy caused by the sharding mechanism by adding a data query mechanism. In environmental monitoring, encryption technology is relatively rarely used.

3.2.2   Location Privacy Protection

G. Han [15] proposes a location privacy (KCLP) protection scheme based on k-means clustering for IOT. In order to protect the source location, a forged source node is used to simulate the function of the real source. Then, a fake receiver node and a specific transmission mode are utilized in order to protect the privacy of the receiver location. K-means clustering is applied to create clusters and forged packets that must pass through the area to shorten the security time. However, the radius of k-means and the parameters of the routing mode in this paper still need to be optimized. If the radius can be optimized by combining the network topology and the transmission distance threshold, energy consumption may be further reduced. For the phantom routing algorithm in Literature [16], the phantom source node is concentrated near the real source node, while for the angle-based phantom routing algorithm, the phantom source node focuses on certain areas, and the existing source location privacy protection algorithms have shorter security periods. A location privacy protection algorithm for wireless sensor networks based on angle and network division is proposed. The algorithm selects the next hop according to the angular relationship between neighbors, and ensures that the phantom source node is far away from the real source node, geographical division provides with diversity. Simulation results show that, compared with the existing source location privacy protection algorithms, this algorithm can induce attackers to deviate from the real path and increase the security period.

3.3   Medical Field

In the context of the continuous development of network technology, indoor networks have been relatively common, and WSN technology has shown great development potential in the field of medical and health, which is conducive to improving our nation's overall level of health care. The use of this technology in health care mainly includes remote health management, pathological data collection and patient monitoring. It can not only reduce the work intensity of medical staff, but also improve the efficiency of medical assistance, which is of great significance to social development. The staff can connect the sensor nodes to the hospital's internal network with the help of wireless communication, and then achieve the efficient sharing of relevant information with the support of the network carrier, ensuring the effective development of medical work and help promote the development of the medical field. In healthcare, the goal of privacy protection is the concealment and integrity of medical data.

3.3.1   Content Privacy Protection

Encryption. C. Ma [17] uses a novel cryptographic algorithm, Signcryption, which combines encryption and signature to achieve confidentiality and authenticity simultaneously. It is used to sign and encrypt for query messages sent by network users during the access control process. Because the query messages are no longer sent in clear text, the data type of the accessing user will not be exposed to other users. In this way, we can protect users' privacy during the access control process. In addition, network users can use proxy key pairs (PKP) to sign and encrypt query messages with proxy signatures. The access point (sensor) can verify whether the query message is signed and encrypted by a trusted third party (TTP) proxy, but cannot identify the user. Users can retain the privacy of their access behavior by retaining identity information. This Signcryption method is the basis of the proposed privacy retention access control scheme for WSN. It contains three algorithms, including settings, signcryption, and decryption. The specific process is to run the setting algorithm to initialize system parameters, including key pairs and two powerful one-way hash functions. The signcryptor encrypts the message and sends it to the decryptor and then the decryptor confirms the session key and accepts the decrypted message. Compared with previous WSN privacy protection solutions, this solution can effectively protect user privacy without significantly increasing network overhead and sensor energy consumption.

Aggregation. Girao and Westhoff and others first propose a series of algorithms named CDA for data fusion privacy protection that can achieve end-to-end data encapsulation [18, 19]. The principles of this series of algorithms are basically the same, mainly including the following main implementation steps: firstly, the data collected by the sensor node is randomly divided into several parts; then the sensor node homomorphically encrypts each part and uploads it to the fusion node; In the third step, the encrypted data is directly fused on the fusion node without decryption; finally, the base station decrypts to obtain the fusion result. The main problem of this algorithm is that each sensor node and the base station share the same key. If a malicious node captures one of these nodes, it is easy to cause the privacy of the remaining data to be illegally obtained.

3.3.2 Location Privacy Protection

Li Yun and Jian Ren et al. propose a scheme to protect the privacy of local and global source locations [20]. The scheme consists of two methods, routing to randomly selected intermediate nodes (RRIN) and network hybrid ring (NMR). RRIN protects the privacy of local source locations and uses a two-step routing strategy to transfer information from the actual source node to the sink node. By the means of selecting one or more intermediate nodes randomly, the attacker cannot track the source node through hop-by-hop routing analysis. NMR routes in a network's mixed ring, protecting network-level (global) source location privacy. G. Han [21] proposes a protection scheme named CASLP for IOT in response to a major security issue, SLP. In order to increase the range of the transmission path, the source starts to walk randomly in a given direction. Then, in order to maintain CASLP convergence, the node only selects its next relay node within a certain range. Finally, in order to further improve SLP, the arcs of multiple rings around the base station are connected to form a new closed loop. Compared with ring-based routing schemes, CASLP can reduce latency and energy consumption. Nidhi Sharma [22] uses the principles of multipath routing, secret sharing and hashing to propose a privacy protection scheme for WSN-based medical applications. Healthcare data collected from WSN is divided into multiple parts. In addition, the hash value is calculated for each component by means of well-known hashing techniques. Changes in the hash value are used to detect changes in the message and then, these components are transferred to the server with the help of multipath routing. Nidhi Sharma provides extensive simulations to verify the new method and the results show that secret splitting and multi-path routing help to achieve privacy protection in WSN-based healthcare systems.

3.4 Transportation Field

The application of WSN in the transportation field has the advantages of low data transmission rate, low power consumption, low cost, large network capacity, short delay, high security and flexible working frequency band, which can effectively improve the efficiency of information acquisition in the transportation field and promote the development of transportation automation. In the transportation field, privacy protection focuses on delay, energy consumption and safety.

3.4.1 Content Privacy Protection

Encryption. Elhoseny [23] proposes a new encryption method to protect the data transmission in WSN with dynamic sensor clusters. This method uses an elliptic curve cryptographic algorithm to generate a binary string for each sensor and combines it with the node ID, the distance to the cluster head and the index of the transmission round to form a unique 176-bit encryption key. Using XOR operations and replacement operations can effectively achieve encryption and decryption. Compared with the most advanced methods, the simulation results show that the proposed method has a longer network life and reduces energy consumption evenly in all sensor nodes. More importantly, it overcomes many security attacks, including brute force attacks, HELLO Flood attacks, selective forwarding attacks and damaged cluster head attacks. In literature [24], Steffen et al. propose five public key homomorphic encryption mechanisms which includes EC-NS, OU, EC-OC, EC-P and EC-EG based on elliptic curves, and it further analyzes the performance in the fields of encryption, decryption, addition operations and bandwidth in detail. Bahi J M [25] also proposes an encryption algorithm based on elliptic curves, which guarantees data security by performing n addition operations and 1 multiplication operation on the cipher-text.

Aggregation. Yang G [26] conducts a more in-depth study on the accuracy of data fusion. From the perspective of reducing SMART's fragmentation collision rate and the loss due to collision, optimization factors such as small data factors, positive factors and negative factors, compensation factors, random fragmentation factors and local factors are introduced respectively. Analysis and experimental results show that the introduction of these factors can play a significant role in reducing traffic, lowering energy consumption and improving fusion accuracy.

3.4.2 Location Privacy Protection

The anonymization method protects privacy by obfuscating sensitive information, that is, modifying or hiding local or global sensitive data of the original information. This method can be used for both data privacy protection and location privacy protection, such as mobile node location privacy protection and LBS location protection in wireless sensor networks. Anonymization research mainly focuses on designing better anonymization principles, common anonymization principles include k-anonymity, l-diversity anonymity, and t-Closeness anonymity. [27] Qijun Gu et al. propose an anonymous method to protect the location of the sink node, which is related to the k-anonymity mode in the field of data privacy protection, and proposes a Φ anonymous model for protecting the location of the sink node. Unlike the k-anonymity model, this method does not generate a fixed number of nodes to disguise real sink node, however, it finds a continuous area Φ and uses fictional sink node to blur the position of sink node, and sink node can be hidden anywhere in the area Φ.

Guangjie Han [28] proposes a source location protection protocol based on dynamic routing to solve the source location privacy problem. Guangjie Han introduces a dynamic routing scheme designed to maximize the data transmission path. The proposed scheme first randomly selects an initial node from the network boundary. Each packet goes through a greedy route and subsequent directional route before reaching the receiver. Theoretical and experimental results show that the scheme can protect the privacy of the source location and resist various privacy disclosure attacks (eavesdropping attacks, hop-by-hop backtracking attacks and directional attacks) without affecting the life of the network.

4   Analysis and Comparison of Privacy Protection Scheme in WSN Routing Protocol

This section compares and analyzes the performance of the privacy protection algorithms of the main routing protocols introduced in the article. The performance indicators include privacy protection capabilities, data accuracy, transmission delay, integrity detection capabilities, energy consumption, and computational complexity. The specific comparison results are shown in the following table. Table 1 is the comparison of content privacy protection schemes, and Table 2 is the comparison of location privacy protection schemes.

Table 1. Comparison of content privacy protection schemes

	Privacy	Accuracy	Delay time	Integrality	Energy consumption	Complexity
DAAC	High	High	Medium	Yes	Low	Medium
NSRP	High	High	Low	Yes	Low	Low
EC-EG	High	High	High	No	Low	Low
SLPP	High	High	Low	No	Medium	Medium
IHDA	High	High	Low	Yes	Medium	Medium
CDA	Medium	High	Low	No	Low	Low
SMART	High	High	Medium	No	Medium	Medium
EEHA	High	High	Medium	No	Low	Medium

First, it can be found that the performance of different types of privacy protection schemes varies greatly through analysis. As for content privacy protection, encryption-based schemes have high computational overhead and relatively high latency due to the decryption-fusion-re-encryption calculation process. Packet-injection-based schemes

Table 2. Comparison of location privacy protection schemes

	Privacy	Accuracy	Delay time	Integrality	Energy consumption	Complexity
PRLA	Medium	High	Medium	No	Medium	Medium
PUSBRF	Medium	High	Medium	No	Medium	Medium
CASLP	Medium	High	Low	No	Low	Medium
KCLP	High	High	Medium	No	Medium	Medium
KA	Low	Low	Low	No	Low	Low

have extremely low computational complexity at the cost of some network resources. Aggregation-based schemes such as data privacy protection schemes based on data slicing for the need of slices transmission and reorganization at intermediate nodes, the communication overhead and operation overhead are significantly higher than other schemes. State-of-the-art encryption can directly integrate the encrypted data without hop-by-hop decryption, costing low computing overhead. As for location privacy protection, because the main resource consumption lies in the communication module, and these protection methods need to send a large amount of additional traffic to achieve privacy protection. Therefore, these methods have large communication overhead, high energy consumption, and long communication delay. Current researches on routing technology are mainly focuses on resisting external attacks, especially local attacks in external attacks. There are relatively few studies on global attacks, internal attacks and mobile node location protection, and the degree of privacy protection is not high. When anonymity-based solutions are used for location privacy protection, such as in LBS, due to the need to trust anonymous third parties, the security is not enough, thereby reducing the degree of privacy protection. However, it has the advantages such as simple calculation, short delay and lower resource consumption.

5 Summary and Outlook

Although the researches on the privacy protection technology of WSN routing protocol have made some progress, researchers have also proposed different privacy protection solutions for this aspect, but they are limited in their own scope of application in common, and leave some practical problems to be solved. In addition, with the continuous development of the Internet of Things, the application environment and requirements for sensor networks have changed. In summary, the problems of the researches on privacy protection of the routing protocol are mainly reflected in:

1. The need of reducing additional communications to achieve a balance between traffic and privacy protection. Because sensor nodes in WSN always have limited resources, including limited energy levels, storage space, and computing power. The location privacy protection protocol designed for WSN must be light-weighted and energy-efficient. However, most existing protocols require high energy consumption and long transmission delays. Some technologies, such as encryption and authentication, can provide better protection strength, but requires higher computational complexity.

2. Most of the existing works focus on the location privacy protection of the source node, while less works focuses on the issues related to the receiver. In addition, there are few studies that consider both source and sink protection. Source node and sink node are both key nodes in the network, and attackers can find them around the attack area. Therefore, it is necessary to effectively protect the location privacy of the source node and the sink node at the same time.

3. From the point of view of resisting attacks, many current technologies can only effectively resist local, passive and external attacks, failing to resist global, active, internal attacks and more powerful collusive opponents. Therefore, there is a need to have a more powerful global view, high computing power, sufficient energy and memory attack models and related solutions.

4. In most existing studies, the performance evaluation of privacy protection is based on different evaluation parameters and standards proposed in different protocol, lacking a universal evaluation standard. With the increasing research on privacy protection, there is an urgent need to formulate a unified evaluation standard.

5. Different technologies provide different protections for the location privacy of source and sink nodes. It is difficult to develop a unified and effective technology for all opponents and it is impossible to design a new location privacy protection method to simultaneously ensure a long security period, low energy consumption, short communication delay and high packet transmission rate. However, making appropriate trade-offs between metrics: privacy, power consumption, communication delay, and transmission rate may become one of the solutions.

6. Most existing algorithms are only designed for location privacy protection, without considering data-oriented privacy. However, WSN is a data-centric network, it is vital to protect both location privacy and data privacy in practical applications. Whereas, in the existing solutions, only a few can protect data privacy and location privacy at the same time.

In view of the above, it is necessary to proceed from the practical application requirements of wireless sensor networks and condense the scientific methods and research contents for the problems that need to be further solved in the current privacy protection research of the routing protocol. The design and development of universal privacy protection strategy for sensor networks based on the routing protocol privacy protection provide theoretical basis and application support for the further promotion of wireless sensor networks.

Acknowledgments. This work is supported by the China Aviation Science Foundation (No. 20101952021), the Fundamental Research Funds for the Central Universities (No. NZ2013306) and the Key Project supported by Medical Science and technology development foundation, Nanjing Department of Health (No. YKK18165).

References

1. Liu, Q., Huang, X.H., Leng, S.P.: Deployment strategy of wireless sensor networks for internet of things. China Commun. **8**(8), 111–120 (2011)

2. Kakelli, A.K., Addepalli, V.N.K., Chatrapati, K.S.: New secure routing protocol with elliptic curve cryptography for military heterogeneous wireless sensor networks. J. Inf. Optim. Sci. **38**(2), 341–365 (2017)
3. Sliti, M., Hamdi, M., Boudriga, N.: An elliptic threshold signature framework for k-security in wireless sensor networks. In: 2008 15th IEEE International Conference on Electronics, Circuits and Systems, St. Julien's, pp. 226–229 (2008)
4. Wang, J., Wang, F., Cao, Z., Lin, F., Wu, J.: Sink location privacy protection under direction attack in wireless sensor networks. Wireless Netw. **23**(2), 579–591 (2017)
5. Tan, W., Xu, K., Wang, D.: An anti-tracking source-location privacy protection protocol in WSNs based on path extension. IEEE Internet Things J. **1**(5), 461–471 (2014)
6. Bista, R., Chang, J.W.: Privacy-preserving data aggregation protocols for wireless sensor networks: a survey. Sensors **10**(5), 4577–4601 (2010)
7. Kim, Y.K., Lee, H., Yoon, M., Chang, J.: Hilbert-curve based data aggregation scheme to enforce data privacy and data integrity for wireless sensor networks. Int. J. Distrib. Sensor Networks, Article ID 217876 (2013). 14 p.
8. Kamat, P., Zhang, Y., Trappe, W., et al.: Enhancing source-location privacy in sensor network routing. In: 25th IEEE International Conference on Distributed Computing Systems, pp. 599–608 (2005)
9. Wang, W.P., Chen, L., Wang, J.: A source-location privacy protocol in WSN based on locational angle. In: IEEE International Conference on Communications, pp. 19–23 (2008)
10. Jianbo, Y., Guangjun, W.: Location privacy protection routing for wireless sensor networks. Comput. Appl. **28**(6), 1379–1381 (2008)
11. Juan, C., Binxing, F., Lihua, Y., et al.: Source location privacy protection protocol based on limited source node flooding in sensor networks. Chin. J. Comput. **33**(9), 1736–1746 (2010)
12. He, W., Liu, X., Nguyen, H.V., et al.: PDA: privacy-preserving data aggregation for information collection. ACM Trans. Sensor Networks (TOSN) **8**(1), 6 (2011)
13. Li, H., Lin, K., Li, K.: Energy-efficient and high-accuracy secure data aggregation in wireless sensor networks. Comput. Commun. **34**(4), 591–597 (2011)
14. Liu, C.X., Liu, Y., Zhang, Z.J., et al.: High energy-efficient and privacy-preserving secure data aggregation for wireless sensor networks. Int. J. Commun Syst **26**(3), 380–394 (2013)
15. Han, G., Wang, H., Guizani, M., Chan, S., Zhang, W.: KCLP: A k-means cluster-based location privacy protection scheme in WSNs for IoT. IEEE Wirel. Commun. **25**(6), 84–90 (2018)
16. Bai, L., Li, G.: Location privacy protection of WSN based on network partition and angle. In: 2018 14th International Conference on Natural Computation, Fuzzy Systems and Knowledge Discovery (ICNC-FSKD), Huangshan, China, pp. 1254–1260 (2018)
17. Ma, C., Xue, K., Hong, P.: Distributed access control with adaptive privacy preserving property for wireless sensor networks. Secur. Commun. Networks **7**(4), 759–773 (2014)
18. Girao, J., Westhoff, D., Schneider, M.: CDA: Concealed data aggregation for reverse multicast traffic in wireless sensor networks. In: Proceeding of IEEE International Conference on Communications, pp. 3044–3049 (2005)
19. Westhoff, D., Girao, J., Acharya, M.: Concealed data aggregation for reverse multicast traffic in sensor networks: encryption, key distribution, and routing adaptation. IEEE Trans. Mob. Comput. **5**(10), 1417–1431 (2006)
20. Ren, J., Li, Y., Li, T.: Routing-based source-location privacy in wireless sensor networks. In: IEEE International Conference on Communications, pp. 1–5 (2009)
21. Han, G., Wang, H., Jiang, J., Zhang, W., Chan, S.: CASLP: a confused arc-based source location privacy protection scheme in WSNs for IoT. IEEE Commun. Mag. **56**(9), 42–47 (2018)
22. Sharma, N., Bhatt, R.: Privacy preservation in WSN for healthcare application. Procedia Comput. Sci. (132), 1243–1252 (2018)

23. Elhoseny, M., Yuan, X., El-Minir, H.K., Riad, A.M.: An energy efficient encryption method for secure dynamic WSN. Secur. Comm. Networks **9**, 2024–2031 (2016)
24. Peter, S., Westhoff, D., Castelluccia, C.: A survey on the encryption of converge cast traffic with in-network processing. IEEE Trans. Dependable Secure Comput. **7**(1), 21–34 (2010)
25. Bahi, J.M., Guyeux, C., Makhoul, A.: Efficient and robust secure aggregation of encrypted data in sensor networks. In: Proceedings of the 4th International Conference on Sensor Technologies and Applications (SENSORCOMM), pp. 472–477 (2010)
26. Yang, G., Li, S., Xu, X., et al.: Precision-enhanced and encryption-mixed privacy-preserving data aggregation in wireless sensor networks. Int. J. Distrib. Sens. Netw. **2013**, 333–351 (2013)
27. Gu, Q., Chen, X., Jiang, Z., et al.: Sink-Anonymity Mobility Control in Wireless Sensor Networks IEEE International Conference on Wireless and Mobile Computing, NETWORKING and Communications. IEEE Computer Society, pp. 36–41 (2009)
28. Han, G., Zhou, L., Wang, H., Zhang, W., Chan, S.: A source location protection protocol based on dynamic routing in WSNs for the Social Internet of Things. Future Gener. Comput. Syst. **82**, 689–697 (2018)

Apply Quantum Search to the Safety Check for Mono Operational Attribute Based Protection Systems

Vincent C. Hu[✉]

Computer Security Division, National Institute of Standards and Technology,
Gaithersburg 20899, USA
vhu@nist.gov

Abstract. Interrelated computing device's system such as IoT, RFID, or edge device's systems are pervasively equipped for today's information application and service systems, protecting them from unauthorized access i.e. safety is critical, because a breach from the device may cause cascading effects resulting to data lost or even crash of the whole information system. However, to determine a protection system's safety is proven to be undecidable unless the system has limited management capabilities. And even with such limitation, it is too expensive to perform a safety test in term of computation time when a device has more than hundreds of subjects which is not uncommon for interrelated computing devices. Nevertheless, the required exponential computing time for safety test can be significantly reduced to its square root if computed by quantum algorithm. In this paper we demonstrate an application of quantum search algorithm to reduce the computation time for safety test for limited (i.e. mono operational) protection systems which are based on attribute-based access control model. The improvement of the performance allows the safety test for interrelated computing device's system to be much less expensive to compute.

Keywords: Access control · Protection system · Quantum algorithm · Security model · Quantum search

1 Introduction

Interrelated computing device's systems (ICDSs) [1] such as IoT, RFID, edge device's or similar systems are pervasively equipped for today's information applications and services [2], protecting these systems from unauthorized access i.e. safety is critical, because a breach from an ICDS may cause cascading effects leading to data lost or even crash of the whole system [3]. Further, as Attributed-Based Access Control (ABAC) [4] model is getting more applied for access control [5], an ICDS may apply ABAC for its access control mechanism. We call such protecting system the **Attribute Based Protection System** (ABPS), which also includes its access control **policy management functions**.

© Springer Nature Switzerland AG 2021
G. Wang et al. (Eds.): SpaCCS 2020, LNCS 12382, pp. 173–187, 2021.
https://doi.org/10.1007/978-3-030-68851-6_12

The **safety** for an ABPS is to ensure that it is impossible to leak access **privilege** (perform actions to objects) from authorized subjects to unauthorized subjects through any changes of access state. And **safety test** is to verify if the safety of the system is maintained after any order of access control policy changes. To test that in worst case obviously requires checking access control policy updates evoked by all possible sequences of policy management functions. By HRU[1] [6] theory, such test is proven to be undecidable unless the ABPS is limited to be **mono operational**, which is restricted to have only one primitive commend for each policy management function.

An ICDS's ABPS can be mono operational, because its access control requires limited management capability. But even that, the exponential computation time (NP-Complete) for safety test is still too expensive [7], because subjects, objects, and actions as exponential variables of computing time for most ICDSs can easily reach to hundreds if not thousands. Nevertheless, it can be significantly improved by applying quantum search algorithm, which reduces the computation time to the square root of the time required by classical algorithm, thus, allows the safety test for ICDS's ABPS to be minimum computable.

This paper is divided into six sections, Sect. 1 is the introduction, Sect. 2 describes the ABPS, Sect. 3 explains the safety test algorithm that applied to mono operational ABPS, Sect. 4 introduces quantum algorithm modified from quantum search algorithm for the privilege leak detect process of safety test algorithm. Section 5 demonstrates the performance comparison between quantum and classical algorithms in terms of computation time, and Sect. 6 is the conclusion.

2   Attribute Based Protection System

Attribute Based Access Control (ABAC) is an access control method where subject requests to perform actions on objects are granted or denied based on assigned attributes of the subject and objects, environment conditions, and a set of rules specified by those attributes and conditions [4] called ABAC **policy**, which given the values of the attributes of the subject, object, and environment conditions and their relations make it possible to determine if a requested access should be authorized.

ABPS applies ABAC where a **subject** s_i represents a combination of **subject attributes** $sa_1,\ldots sa_i,\ldots sa_k$ the subject is associated with, and an **object** o_i represents a combination of **object attributes** $oa_1,\ldots oa_j,\ldots oa_l$ that apply to the object. And the access control policy is managed by the policy management functions. The ABPS's access state can be presented by the **HRU access matrix** (Fig. 1) such that the access control policy rules are mapped to rows and columns with intersected cells. A cell contains actions that are permitted to perform the accesses from the subject to the object corresponding to the row and the column, as example in Fig. 1, shows that subject s_j is permitted to perform actions r and w accesses to object o_i, The cell intersected by both row and column of subjects is used for creating or deleting a subject by another subject. ABPS's ABAC policy rules are mapped to the access matrix by adding permitted access actions into cells and removing denied accesses actions from cells if the actions existed.

---

[1] We denote the term HRU to be general references to the systems and theories presented in [5].

Subject\Object	s_1	...	s_n	$o_1 = (....)$	...	$o_i = (oa_1,...oa_j,...oa_l)$	...	$o_m = (....)$
$s_1 = (....)$								
.....								
$s_j = (sa_1,..sa_i,..sa_k)$						r, w		
.....								
$s_n = (....)$								

Fig. 1. ABPS access matrix state.

An ABPS's policy management mechanism, which in general is a set of policy management functions for creating, updating the ABAC policy rules. The function is intrinsically equal to access **matrix update function** such that *assign rule* function: "*assign action a to object o_j to subject s_k*" is equal to: "*add a to the intersect cell of row s_k and column o_j*" add function, and *delete rule* function: "*delete action a to object o_j of subject s_k*" is equal to: "*remove a in the intersect cell of the row s_k and column o_j*" delete function. Figure 2 shows an example ABAC rule: "*users with attribute p or q can read device x*" maps to HRU access matrix. Therefore, an ABPS access state is an instance of an HRU access matrix state, and ABAC policy rules can be configured to rows and columns of an HRU access matrix.

Users/Device	.....	device x	
....			
Attribute p		*read*	
....			
Attribute q		*read*	

Fig. 2. ABPS access matrix state

There are six **primitive commands** for ABPS's policy management functions, and their counter parts for access matrix operations are shown in Table 1:

Access state changes after executing sequences of access state change functions can be presented formally by: $Q_1 \vdash fn_1 Q_2 \vdash ..... Fn_i Q_i \vdash ..... Fn_m Q_m$, ($\vdash$ means complete the function) where Q_i is an access state, and function fn_i makes access state change from Q_i to $Q_i + 1$. The pseudo fn_i for ABPS policy management function is:

Table 1. ABPS'S and HRU primitive commands mapping.

ABPS primitive commands	HRU primitive commands
assign action $(a, s_i = (sa_1.....sa_k), o_i = (oa_1.....oa_j))$	*enter action a into* (s_i, o_i)
delete action $(a, s_i = (sa_1.....sa_k), o_i = (oa_1.....oa_k))$	*delete action a into* (s_i, o_i)
add subject $(s_i = (sa_1.....sa_k))$	*create subject si*
add object $(o_i = (oa_1.....oa_k))$	*create object oi*
remove subject $(s_i = (sa_1.....sa_k))$	*destroy subject si*
remove object $(o_i = (oa_1.....oa_k))$	*destroy object oi*

ABPS_fn$_i$ (subjects, actions, objects){//* *subjects* or *objects* are optional if the functions are *create/destroy* subjects or objects *//

    if no conflict with current ABAC access control policy

    then { execute primitive commands *pc$_1$*;

    execute primitive commands *pc$_2$*;

    ....

    execute primitive commands *pc$_n$*,

    that apply to the *subjects, actions,* and *objects*

    }//*primitive commands update ABAC policy *//

    current access control policy $P_i = P_{i+1}$

}

    And the corresponding *fn$_i$* for HRU access matrix update function is:

HRU_fn$_i$ (subjects, actions, objects) { //* *subjects* or *objects* are optional if the functions are *create/destroy* subjects or objects *//

    if conditions $c_1, c_2....c_k$ then {

    execute primitive commands *pc$_1$*;,

    execute primitive commands *pc$_2$*;,

    ....

    execute primitive commands *pc$_n$*,

    that apply to the *subjects, actions,* and *objects*

    } //*primitive commands update access matrix *//

    curent access matrix $H_i = H_{i+1}$

}

The steps for checking the conflict of access control policy in *ABPS_fn$_i$* are not semantically different from HRU_*fn$_i$*'s *if* condition checks, because satisfying the current ABPS policy is the same as satisfying the state of HRU matrix, which can be translated from the ABPS's policy rules.

3   ABPS Safety Check

HRU defines that:

"given a protection system, we say command c leaks generic action a from the access state if c, when run on the access state, can execute a primitive operation which enter a into a cell of access matrix which did not previously contain a".

From the definition, the **safety** of ABPS is to ensure unintended subjects cannot perform protected actions on objects through executing any sequence of policy management functions ($ABPS\_fn_i$s described in Sect. 2), such that the permitted accesses for the action by the original access control policy remains the same during the system's life cycle. Thus, the **safety test** is to verify that if the system remains safe after all possible sequence of policy management functions being executed. Figure 3 shows the components and relations of an ABPS and its safety test system.

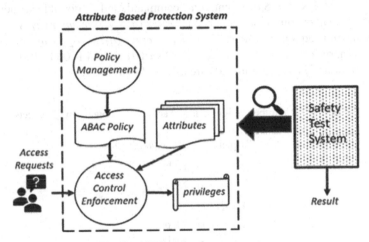

Fig. 3. ABPS and safety test system

According to HRU, safety test for general protection systems including ABPSs is undecidable in term of computation complexity, because to test the safety of a protection system in worst case obviously requires checking all possible sequences of access matrix changes evoked by access matrix update functions with all possible parameters including subjects, actions, and objects, plus that the function may contain unlimited *if* condition checks and arbitrary numbers of primitive commands (Table 1). The undecidability can be proved by configuring the protection system to simulate the behavior of an arbitrary Turing machine, with a safety leakage state corresponding to the Turing machine entering a final state [6].

In addition to general protection systems, from HRU's theory, a restricted type of protection system called **mono operational protection system**, which limits each matrix update function to contain only one primitive command. HRU shows that determining safety for mono operational protection system is decidable in NP-Complete, which is proved by reducing a K-clique problem to a safety decision problem that translating the system's initial access matrix to an **adjacency matrix** for a graph, then test to see if it forms a k-clique before entering an action a to the access matrix causing safety leak. HRU also shows that only the primitive command *enter* can change the access state. To simulates the HRU's algorithm for mono operational ABPS safety test, Fig. 4 illustrates the algorithm *Safety_Test* for an action a. Since a policy management function of a mono operational protection system contains only one primitive command, and only the *enter* primitive command can change the access state, the algorithm needs to tests every possible sequences of *enter* commands for all actions, in other words, try all possible sequences of primitive *enter* commands, (optional starting with a *create* subject command) of length up the $|A| \times |S| \times |O|$ for each sequence, where $|A|$ is the number of all actions, $|S|$ is the number of all subjects, and $|O|$ is the number of all objects. The parameters of an *enter* command are an action-subject-object triplet corresponding to a command sequence, which is identified by a binary number, for example, if there are two subjects s_1 and s_2, two objects o_1 and o_2, and two actions a_1 and a_2 in the ABPS then there are $2 \times 2 \times 2 = 8$ different *enter* command, and 2^8 possible sequences, for instance, the 5th *enter* command sequence is $\{enter\ (a_1, s_1, o_1);\ enter\ (a_1, s_2, o_1)\}$, and the 24th command sequence is $\{enter\ (a_1, s_1, o_1);\ enter\ (a_1, s_2, o_2);\ enter\ (a_2, s_1, o_1)\}$, because the binary form of the sequence 5 is 00000101 and 24 is 00011001, where the bits representations of *enter* commands are assigned in Table 2.

Table 2. Example bit number assignment of 2 actions, 2 subjects and 2 objects pairs.

Triplet	Assigned bit
(a_1, s_1, o_1)	1st bit
(a_1, s_1, o_2)	2nd bit
(a_1, s_2, o_1)	3rd bit
(a_1, s_2, o_2)	4th bit
(a_2, s_1, o_1)	5th bit
(a_2, s_1, o_2)	6th bit
(a_2, s_2, o_1)	7th bit
(a_2, s_2, o_2)	8th bit

The *Bitmap* function translates the action-subject-object triplet of the *enter* command to a binary number to match the current sequence number passed to the function as examples showed in Table 2.

The *State_Compare* function compares cells in original access matrix H_1 to the new access matrix Hi that might be updated after a sequence of *enter* commands were executed, it checks if a privilege leak by action a is found, and the result is returned to the *Safety_Test*. Note that the algorithm only checks the safety against one action a, it is capable of checking multiple actions leaks, and to do that we need to replace (s_i, o_j) with (s_i, a_m, o_j), $\{S \times O\}$ with $\{S \times A \times O\}$, $2^{|S| \times |O|}$ with $2^{|S| \times |A| \times |O|}$, and (a, s_i, o_j) with (a_m, s_i, o_j) and add a For loop for each a_m check in the function.

Safety_Test (P_1, a) {   (1)
    $H_1 = Initial\ P_1$; //* map accesses permitted by the ABPS access control policy to
    the HRU access matrix *//
    (2)
    Privilege_leak = 0 ;   (3)
    $i = 1$;   (4)
    For $k = 0$ to $2^{|G|\times|S|\times|O|} - 1$ //* $|G|$ is the number of actions, $|S|$ is the number of
    subjects, $|O|$ is the number of objects
    *//{   (5)
        For all (a_x, s_i, o_j) //*(a_x, s_i, o_j) $\in \{A\times S \times O\}$; A is the set of actions, S is the
        set of subjects, O is the set of objects *//
        {   (6)
          If Bitmap $(a_x, s_i, o_j, k) = 1$ //*match s_i-o_j pair to binary number k*//
          (7)
            enter (a_x, s_i, o_j) (8)
      {
      }
      $H_i = H_{i+1}$;   (9)
      If State_Compare (H_i, H_1, a) //*check if access state is changed*//   (10)
      Then {   (11)
      privilege_leak = 1;   (12)
      end Safety_Test;   (13)
      }
      else privilege_leak = 0;   (14)
    }
}
Bitmap (a_x, s_i, o_j, k) {
    $i = Numer\_map(a_x, s_i, o_j)$ //* translate s_i-o_j pair to binary number*//
    For $j = 1$ to i
    If the jth bit of Binary(k) == 1 //*check the match of bits*//
      return 1
}
State_Compare (H_i, H_1, a) {
    For each row of s_i {
      For each column of o_i {
        If (((a in the cell of (s_i, o_i)) of H_i) == ((a in the cell of (s_i, o_i)) of H_1))
        Then return leak = 0
        else return leak = 1; //*privilege_leak state is passed to Safety_Test*//
      }
    }
}

Fig. 4. ABPS Safety Test algorithm

For later discussion of quantum algorithm, we call the *For* loop from line 5 to 14 in Fig. 4 the *Leak_Detect* process collectively. Hence, the *Safety_Test* would require $2^{|A|\times|S|\times|O|} \times O(Leak\_Detect)$ computation time (steps) for detecting an access privilege leak, where $O(Leak\_Detect)$ is the time needed for *Leak_Detect* process, which is equal to O(*Bitmap*) × |A| × |S| × |O| + O(*State_Compare*) = 2 × |A| × |S| × |O|, because O(*Bitmap*) take constant and O(*State_Compare*) takes number of steps equals to the size of access matrix: |S| × |O| times |A| to compute.

Some low power ICDSs' (e.g. IoT, RFID, or edge computing devices or similar systems) access control are managed by ABPS, where access control policies are either embed or deployed by central management system rather than managed by the device themselves [8]. For instance, RFID devices include independent storage access control rules, only when the rule needs to be updated, do reading devices need to communicate with the server, and access control rules can be updated by the multicast method. In the same security zone, multiple reading devices can distribute access control rules at the same time, thereby improving the efficiency of rule updates [9]. In addition, some access control mechanisms allow smart objects take the authorization decisions based on current context of the processes in use [10]. For those systems with limited access control management capabilities, the protection systems can be implemented by mono operational ABPS. And these ICDSs usually accessed by a large number of users risking safety leak [11], plus, due to frequently adding new and updating old devices, their safety need to be efficiently verified to satisfy their security and performance requirements of services, thus, need an efficient safety test method that classical algorithms cannot offer.

4   Quantum Search Algorithm for ABPS Safety Check

Even the ABPS safety test is decidable but in NP-Complete as described in the last section, it is still an issue to be efficiently computable for systems having large number of subjects, objects and actions such might sum up to hundreds if not thousands of users, because, for example, an ICDS is used by just 10 subjects (classified by users' attributes) with only two objects (classified by devices' attributes) and 3 actions, the safety will take $2^{10 \times 2 \times 3} \times (2 \times 10 \times 2 \times 3)$ computation time. Thus, it is desirable to improve the exponential computation time (steps) to be feasible to compute. To reduce the computation time, we propose to adopt the Grover Quantum search algorithm [12, 13], which performs the transformation $L|x\rangle|q\rangle = |x\rangle|q \otimes f(x)$ to a black box oracle f to speed up $f(x)$ for multiple x inputs, where $|q\rangle$ is an ancilla qubit for quantum unitary computation. The algorithm finds with high probability the unique input to the black box oracle function that produces a particular output value, using just $\sqrt{N}$ evaluations of the function, where N is the size of the function's domain.

Schema in Fig. 5 shows the application of quantum search algorithm for safety test called *Safety_Test***quantum algorithm**, which uses $n + 1$ qubit register as input (the ancilla 1 qubit is for quantum unitary operation), where $N = 2^n = 2^{|A| \times |S| \times |O|}$ is the number of all possible sequences of *enter* commands, |A| is the number of actions, |S| is the number of subjects, and |O| is the number of objects of the ABPS. The output of the algorithm is a number x_{leak} representing a sequence of *enter* commands that causes privilege leak by the action a. Notice that instead of a leak command sequence, the classical *Safe_Test* algorithm (Fig. 4) only returns a result indicating whether a leak exist. In contrast, the quantum algorithm returns one of the leak sequence numbers (there could be more than one command sequence that cause leakages). The black box oracle function f is hence the *Leak_Detect* process (from line 5 to 14 of the classical *Safety_Test* algorithm in Fig. 4).

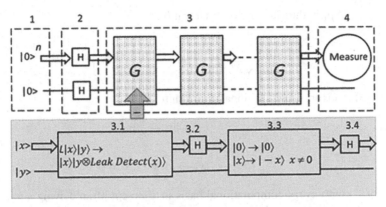

Fig. 5. Quantum Safety Check schema

Safety_Test quantum algorithm requires repeating applications of the Grover quantum search subroutine shown as the **Grover iteration** G in Fig. 5, where each iteration move $1/\sqrt{N}$ amplitude towards solutions, thus $\sqrt{N}$ iterations should suffice to render a x_{leak}. The algorithm is divided into four steps as below.

1) Begins with the initial state, $n + 1$ qubits in the state $|0\rangle : |0\rangle^{\otimes n}|0\rangle$, the extra $|0\rangle$ is for the quantum unitary operation.
2) The Hadamard transform is applied to establish equal superposition state $|\Psi\rangle$ of all possible numbers of *enter* command sequences that

$$|\Psi\rangle = \frac{1}{\sqrt{2^n}} \sum_{x=0}^{2^n-1} |x\rangle \left[\frac{|0\rangle - |1\rangle}{\sqrt{2}} \right]$$

Where $0 \leq x \leq 2^{|A| \times |S| \times |O|}$.

3) Apply the Grover G iteration $K = \lceil \sqrt{N/M} \rceil$ times: where M is the number of sequences of *enter* command sequences (i.e. x_{leak}s) that cause privilege leaks. This step can be subdivided into the following three steps:

3.1) Apply the quantum oracle L

$$L|x\rangle|y\rangle = |x\rangle|y \otimes Leak\ Detect(x)\rangle$$

resulting

$$|x\rangle \to (-1)^{Leak\ Detect(x)}|x\rangle$$

Note that each x is a number representing an enter commands sequence, for example the number 5 represent the sequence; {*enter* (g_2, s_1, o_2); *enter* (g_1, s_2, o_1)}} as shown in Sect. 3. *Leak_Detect* $(x) = 0$ for all $0 \leq x \leq 2^n$ except the x_{leak} for which *Leak_Detect*$(x) = 1$ indicating the *enter* command sequence leaks privilege for action a in the current access control state.

3.2) Apply the Hadamard transform $H^{\otimes n}$

$$|\Psi\rangle \frac{1}{\sqrt{2^n}} \sum_{x=0}^{2^n-1} (-1)^{Leak\,Dectect(x)}|x\rangle \left[\frac{|0\rangle - |1\rangle}{\sqrt{2}}\right]$$

3.3) Performs a conditional phase shift i.e.

$$|0\rangle \rightarrow |0\rangle$$

$$|x\rangle \rightarrow |1 - x\rangle, x \neq 0$$

with every computational basis state except $|0\rangle$, receiving a phase shift of -1, i.e. the leakin g $enter$ command sequence $x = x_{leak} \neq 0$. The conditional phase shift can be calculated by applying the matrix operation of

$$2|0\rangle\langle 0| - I$$

where I is the identity matrix.

3.4) Apply the Hadamard transform $H^{\otimes n}$

4) Measure the first n qubits of $|\phi\rangle$ gets one of the possible leak sequence x_{leak}.

The quantum algorithm requires $H^{\otimes n} \times$ O($Leak\_Detect$) [14] of computation time, where M is the number of $enter$ command sequences that cause leaks, in other words, there could be multiple leaking xs, so, M implies that there is at least one leak sequence exist. After the Grover iterations (calls to oracle $Leak\_Detect$) were performed, one of the M sequences will be measured out with higher probability than the sequences that may or may not causing leak. The algorithm is a quadratic improvement over the $N/M \times$ O($Leak\_Detect$) calls performed by classical computer.

Since measuring from step (4) will render only one result, however, there could be cases that has no or multiple leak sequences exist, hence the result could be a random sequence i.e. mistakenly identified as a leaking sequence. To correct this inaccuracy, three methods can be applied:

a) A planned fake leak sequence x_f: $enter$ (a_f, s_f, o_f) is assigned in between line 9 and 10 of $Leak\_Detect$ process in the $Safet\_Test$ algorithm such that the x_f will be detected as a leak command sequence in $\sqrt{N}$ time with high probability close to 100%, because it is the only leak sequence can be detected that makes $M = 1$. And if after several runs of the algorithm, the results repeatedly measured to be the same x_f, we can confidently determine that there are no other leak sequences besides the planned x_f.

b) To more precisely determine the number of leak command sequences, combine the Grover iteration G with **quantum counting** algorithm [14]. The method is to estimate the number of leak command sequences by quantum counting, which is an application of the phase estimation procedure to estimate the eigenvaluses $e^{i\theta}$ of

Grover iteration G, which in turn enables determining an approximate number of leak command sequences M. The method allows us to decide whether a leak sequence even exists depending on the result number. The phase estimation circuit used for quantum counting is shown in Fig. 6. The function of the circuit is to estimate θ to an accuracy approximate to 2^{-m} (note[2]).

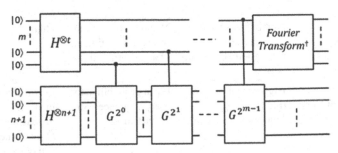

Fig. 6. Approximate quantum counting circuit for G

c) Requires no additional process, but repeatedly running the algorithm enough times, then analyze the measured results. If there is no command sequence causing leak, any random sequence number will be measured with the same probabilities of all other sequence numbers. Such result indicates that there is no concentrate output of one particular leak sequence number meaning that the possibility of having a true leak sequence is low, however, this method is reliable only when the total number of actions, subjects and objects is large enough for the odd that getting a random result, which is true leak sequence is low. Table 3 compares the three methods.

Table 3 shows that the more difficult in implementing the method (as ordered by methods b, a, and c) the more accurate result it will generate, unless depending on the number of possible sequences in method c, which if applied to a large number of total sequences (say no less than hundreds) then the accuracy might equal or better than method a and b, however, repeating the process of c method is not as efficient as the other methods. The detail algorithms and comparison of the three methods is interesting that worth to be discussed by their own topics, due to the limited space and to keep the discussion on focus, we only briefly introduce them in this paper.

---

[2] More accurate, m should be $m + \lceil (2 + 1/2\epsilon) \rceil \log$ qubits.

Table 3. Comparison of testing methods for checking the existence of true leak sequences.

Checking methods	If true leak sequences exist	It no true leak sequence exist	Accuracy
(a) Plan fake leak sequence access x_f	Equal probabilities of getting true leak sequences x_{leak} and x_f	Fake leak sequence x_f has highest possibility being measured	Median
(b) Quantum counting by applying phase estimation	Number of solutions from phase estimation algorithm > 0	Number of solutions from phase estimation of algorithm ≈ 0	Hight
(c) No extra step required but run the algorithm enough times	High probability of a true leak x_{leak} sequence is measured	Equal probability for every sequence will be measured	Low (reliability increased by increasing the number of input (i.e. subjects and objects) sequences)

5 Performance of Safety Check Quantum Algorithm

We can now summarize the performance improvement of safety test for a mono operational ABPS by comparing quantum to the classical algorithms. Assuming there is at least one leak sequence exist, by the quantum safety test algorithm, it will take $\sqrt{N} \times$ O (*Leak Detect*) while classical safety test algorithm requires $N \times$ O (*Leak_Detect*) (for simplicity of demonstration, let's assume $M = 1$). The difference is in the order of $\sqrt{N}$ compared to $N = 2^{|A| \times |S| \times |O|}$, which is the 2's power of the number of actions |A| times the number of subjects |S| times the number of objects |O| managed by the ABPS system. For ICDSs or applications accessed by large number of subjects (users classified by attributes) to multiple number objects (devices classified by attributes), the quadratic difference is significant as shown in comparison listed in Table 4. Note that for the purpose of comparison, the O (*Leak_Detect*) is not counted, because both algorithms take the same polynomial time which does not affect the exponential difference.

The growth of computation time from 5 to 50 (number of subjects times objects) is about 3.5×10^{13} time for classical algorithm, and about 6×10^6 time for quantum algorithm, obviously, the improvement of quadratic reduction by quantum algorithm allows the safety test to be reasonably performed.

An ICDS's device in general is accessed by only one public user class (subject with *public* attribute) plus one administrator (subject with *administrator* attribute) and limited actions available to manage the device, so, at minimum, two subjects can read and write (most common actions) to the object, thus, only require $2^{2 \times 2 \times 1} \times$ O (*Leak_Detect*) computation steps by classical algorithm for safety test. However, some ICDSs may have more than one device to be managed, so the access control policy is deployed from central service to individual device as described in Sect. 3. In such cases, the ICDS's ABPS may apply one-size-fits-all access control policy to its devices, thus even with

Table 4. Computation time comparison of classical and quantum algorithms for ABPS safety test

Number of subjects times objects	Classical algorithm × O (*Leak_Detect*)	Quantum algorithm × O (*Leak_Detect*)
5	32	$5.6568542494492 \approx 6$
10	1024	32
15	32768	$181.0193359838 \approx 181$
20	1048576	1024
25	33554432	$5792.61875148 \approx 5793$
30	1.073741824×10^9	32768
35	$3.4359738368 \times 10^{10}$	$185363.8000474 \approx 185364$
40	$1.099511627776 \times 10^{12}$	1048576
45	$3.518437208883 \times 10^{13}$	$5931641.601516 \approx 5931642$
50	$1.125899906843 \times 10^{15}$	33554432

limited allowed actions, but has multiple number of administration subjects and device objects. Further even with a single device (object), it is not uncommon that an ICDS has more than tens even hundreds of subjects and objects. So the computation time for safety test is not practical by classical algorithm for these systems, but if instead use quantum algorithm, the difference is enormous even for small number of actions, subjects and objects as shown in Fig. 7, the growth is measured in 1000 computation time per unit for up to 20 in comparison of classical and quantum algorithm. It shows that there is not much benefit using quantum algorithms if the number is less than 10, however, the difference is obvious when the number is greater. Note that the comparison is for detecting leak for only one action, if there are multiple actions involved, the computation time will increase even exponentially greater by |A|, which is the number of the actions under test as a factor of exponent.

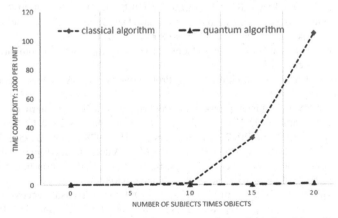

Fig. 7. Computation time comparison of quantum and classical algorithms for safety test

6   Conclusion

To determine the safety of a protection system is to find if there are privilege leaks from protected actions to unauthorized subjects of the system. HRU shows that for mono operational protection system, the computation time for the safety test is decidable, however take NP complete computation time, which is too expensive to perform for a system with large number of subjects and objects such as ICDS (e.g. IoT, RFID systems etc.) that applies attribute based access control (ABAC) model.

We demonstrate that an ABPS (protection system that applies ABAC model) such as ICDS can be simulated by an HRU access matrix and its matrix management functions. And adapted from Grover quantum search algorithm, we propose a quantum safety test algorithm, which determines the safety by returning a command sequence that will cause access leak for a mono operational ABPS. We conclude that if N equals to $2^{|A| \times |S| \times |O|}$ where $|A|$ is the number of actions, $|S|$ is the number of subjects, and $|O|$ is the number of objects, and each of subject, object represent a set of attributes associate to them, the quantum algorithm for a mono operational ABPS requires computation steps $\sqrt{N}$ times the time required for classical leak detection process, compared to N times the time required for classical leak detection process, the quantum algorithm reduces the computation time quadratically. The saving is significant for ICDS or similar systems that its devices usually are accessed by large number of subjects with limited available actions. In addition to the quantum algorithm, three methods are explained to ensure that the test result are genuine instead of some random command sequence that does not but mistakenly rendered as a command sequence that causes access privilege leak.

References

1. Rouse, M.: Internet of Things (IOT), IoT Agenda, Tech Target (2019). https://internetofthing sagenda.techtarget.com/definition/Internet-of-Things-IoT
2. Voas, J., Kuhn, R., Laplante, P., Applebaum, S.: Internet of Things (IoT) Trust Concerns. NIST Cybersecurity White Paper (2018)
3. Siboni, S., Glezer, C., Shabtai, A., Elovici, Y.: A weighted risk score model for IoT devices. In: Wang, G., Feng, J., Bhuiyan, M.Z.A., Lu, R. (eds.) SpaCCS 2019. LNCS, vol. 11637, pp. 20–34. Springer, Cham (2019). https://doi.org/10.1007/978-3-030-24900-7_2
4. Hu, V., et al.: Guide to Attribute Based Access Control Definition and Considerations, National Institute Standards and Technology NIST SP 800-162 (2014)
5. AXIOMATIC: Attribute Based Access Control (ABAC). https://www.axiomatics.com/attrib ute-based-access-control/
6. Harrison, M.A., Ruzzo, W.L., Ullman, J.K.: Protection in operating system. Commun. ACM Mag. **19**(8), 461–471 (1976)
7. Xu, Z., Li, X.: Secure transfer protocol between app and device of Internet of Things. In: Wang, G., Atiquzzaman, M., Yan, Z., Choo, K.-K. (eds.) SpaCCS 2017. LNCS, vol. 10658, pp. 25–34. Springer, Cham (2017). https://doi.org/10.1007/978-3-319-72395-2_3
8. Skarmeta, A.F., Hernández-Ramos, J.L., Moreno, M.V.: A decentralized approach for security and privacy challenges in Internet of Things. In: IEEE World Forum on Internet of Things (2014). https://ieeexplore.ieee.org/abstract/document/6803122
9. Dhillon, P., Singh, M.: Internet of Things attacks and countermeasure access control techniques: a review. Int. J. Appl. Eng. Res. **14**(7), 1689–1698 (2019). ISSN 0973-4562. https://www.ripublication.co

10. Mali, A., Darade, S.: Security and Privacy in Web-based Access Control in Internet of Things, Academia. https://www.academia.edu/28002646/Security_and_Privacy_in_Web-based_Access_Control_in_Internet_of_Things
11. Maddison, J.: The Importance of Access Control for IoT Devices, SECURITYWEEK (2018). https://www.securityweek.com/importance-access-control-iot-devices
12. Grover, L.: A fast quantum mechanical algorithm for database search. In: Annual ACM Symposium on the Theory of Computation, pp. 212–219. ACM Press, New York (1996)
13. Grover, L. K.: Quantum mechanics helps in searching for a needle in a haystack. Phys. Rev. Lett. **79**(2), 325 (1997). arXive e-print quant-ph/9706033
14. Nielsen, M., Chuang, I.L.: Quantum Computation and Quantum Information. Cambridge University Press, Cambridge (2000)

A Semi-supervised Intrusion Detection Algorithm Based on Auto-encoder

Xiangtong Du[1], Yongzhong Li[1(✉)], and Zunlei Feng[2]

[1] Jiangsu University of Science and Technology, Zhenjiang 212100, China
liyongzhong61@163.com
[2] Zhejiang University, Hangzhou 310058, China

Abstract. In network intrusion detection, the recognition and detection rate of intrusion detection may be reduced due to the lack of sample attributes or insufficient labels. In order to overcome this problem, this paper proposes a semi-supervised intrusion detection algorithm based on auto-encoder. The auto-encoder is adopted to extract features from all samples. For the labeled samples, cross-entropy is adopted for classification. For the unlabeled samples, first, initialize K (number of categories) category centers in the feature space based on the characteristics of partially labeled samples. Constrain the representation of unlabeled samples at the center of a certain category, and then place the restricted representation into the classifier for classification. By combining data from labeled samples and unlabeled samples, and simultaneously updating network parameters and category centers, semi-supervised intrusion detection is achieved. The proposed algorithm is verified on NSL-KDD and KDD CUP99 datasets. Experimental results show that the method can not only effectively reduce the dependence on labeled samples, but also improve the accuracy of intrusion detection to a certain extent.

Keyword: Intrusion detection · Semi-supervised learning · Auto-encoder · Cross-entropy · Feature extraction

1 Introduction

Security is the most significant issue in concerns of protecting information or data breaches, and how to identify network attacks is a key problem [1]. Intrusion detection technology is one of the key technologies of network security, which has aroused the widespread concern around the world [2]. Due to the intelligence and complexity of today's networks, it is difficult to apply traditional intrusion detection techniques to new network intrusions.

Intrusion detection technology based on traditional machine learning and deep learning has been widely used, and has greatly improved the efficiency of intrusion detection. However, most traditional machine learning based methods need to construct features manually, and deep learning based methods require a large amount of data and the detection effect is poor if the unlabeled samples is insufficient.

© Springer Nature Switzerland AG 2021
G. Wang et al. (Eds.): SpaCCS 2020, LNCS 12382, pp. 188–199, 2021.
https://doi.org/10.1007/978-3-030-68851-6_13

To solve these problems, a semi-supervised intrusion detection algorithm based on auto-encoder is proposed in this paper. The semi-supervised intrusion detection is composed of the following two parts. For some labeled samples, the frequently-used cross-entropy is adopted for classification. For the remaining unlabeled samples, K category centers are firstly initialized based on the representation of the partially labeled samples in the feature space. The hyper parameter K is the data category number. Then, after extracting the representation of the unlabeled sample with the encoder, the representation is constrained to be close to one of the K category centers and far away from other category centers, which is devised for minimizing the intra-class distance and maximizing the inter-class distance. Finally, the semi-supervised intrusion detection algorithm combines labeled and unlabeled samples to update network parameters and category centers simultaneously. The proposed approach was verified on the NSL-KDD and KDD CUP99 datasets. Exhaustive experiments demonstrate that the proposed algorithm can achieve better performance than existing methods.

There are three main contributions in this paper. First, we proposed semi-supervised intrusion detection algorithm based on the auto-encoder. Then, the semi-supervised framework can effectively reduce the dependence on labeled samples and improve the efficiency of intrusion detection. Moreover, the proposed method achieves state-of-the-art performance on par with existing methods.

The rest of the paper is organized as follows. In Sect. 2, we introduce the related work about the development of intrusion detection technology. We then introduce the semi-supervised intrusion detection algorithm based on auto-encoder in Sect. 3. Furthermore, the experimental results and analysis are reported as well as the related analysis in Sect. 4. Finally, we conclude this paper in Sect. 5.

2 Related Work

Machine learning is considered as a potential solution for promoting the performance of malware detection [3]. With the traditional machine learning based intrusion detection technology, there have been a large number of applications in intrusion detection.

Common traditional machine learning algorithms include support vector machine SVM, K nearest neighbor algorithm KNN and random forest algorithm RFC. On the aspect of the traditional machine learning algorithms, Hamid et al. [4] proposed a network intrusion detection method based on non-linear SNE and SVM. Aburomman et al. [5] proposed a novel SVM-KNN-PSO ensemble method for intrusion detection system. Masarat et al. [6] used forests to improve the intrusion detection system. Li et al. [7] proposed an effective two-step intrusion detection method based on binary classification and KNN. The above traditional machine learning based intrusion detection methods have improved the performance of intrusion to a certain extent. However, the traditional machine learning based algorithms cannot learn features autonomously, and need to manually construct features. To solve above drawbacks, some deep learning based intrusion detection methods have been widely developed.

Based on deep neural networks and deep belief networks, Potluri et al. [8] proposed an accelerated deep neural networks for enhanced intrusion detection system, Zhao et al. [9] proposed an intrusion detection model using deep belief networks and probabilistic neural networks. Based on recurrent neural networks, Chuan-Long Y et al. [10] proposed an intrusion detection algorithm using recurrent neural networks. Based on AI framework combines monitoring agent and AI-based reaction agent, Bagaa et al. [11] proposed a machine learning security framework for IoT systems. However, existing methods based on deep learning require a large amount of data, and the performance is not satisfactory when there is too much unlabeled data.

3 Semi-supervised Intrusion Detection Algorithm Based on Auto-encoder

In practice, supervised learning based intrusion detection is often impossible due to excessive cost or limited labeling staff level. This paper proposes an intrusion detection algorithm based on self-encoder and semi-supervised learning, which can effectively solve the problems of dependence of intrusion detection algorithm on large amount of data annotation and poor classification effect when there are large amount of unlabeled samples by training the labeled samples and unlabeled samples respectively.

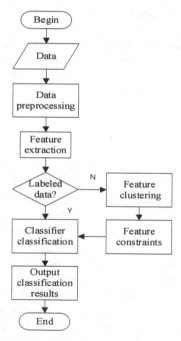

Fig. 1. Flow diagram of AE-SSL

3.1   Intrusion Algorithm Structure Design

In this section, we construct a semi-supervised intrusion detection network structure based on auto-encoder (AE-SSL), which is shown in Fig. 1. The proposed intrusion detection algorithm contains four parts: data preprocessing, feature extraction, sample classification, output results.

3.2   Algorithm Description

After preprocessing the data, data input is performed, and the data classification is divided into two parts at the same time. First, feature extraction is conducted on some labeled samples, and a preliminary classification is performed using a classifier. For the remaining unlabeled samples, K(number of categories) category centers is firstly initialized based on the representation of the labeled samples in the feature space. Then, after extracting the representation of the unlabeled sample using the encoder, the representation is constrained to be close to one of the K category centers and far away from the other category centers. Finally, the softmax classifier is used to achieve five categories classifications of the data, which corresponds to DoS, U2R, R2L, Probe and Normal, respectively.

Feature Extraction Based on Auto-encoder. The labeled and unlabeled samples are simultaneously input into the auto-encoder. The auto-encoder is trained with the combination loss of feature reconstruction and classification. Algorithm 1shows the details of feature reconstruction steps on the labeled samples, the algorithm is shown below.

Input: Dataset (X, Y), Number of iterations T
Output: The low dimension of the dataset X represents X'
Step1:   Initialize the weight W and the bias b.
Step2:   From t=1to T
   Assuming that the function to be optimized is $J(W, b)$, calculate $\nabla_{b_{(l)}} J(W, b)$ and $\nabla_{W_{(l)}} J(W, b, X)$.
   1) $\Delta b^{(l)} = \Delta b^{(l)} + \nabla_{b_{(l)}} J(W, b)$,
   2) $\Delta W^{(l)} = \Delta W^{(l)} + \nabla_{W_{(l)}} J(W, b, X)$.
Step3:   Update weight parameters
   $W^{(l)} = W^{(l)} - \alpha \left[\left(\frac{1}{T} \Delta W^{(l)} \right) + \lambda W^{(l)} \right], b^{(l)} = b^{(l)} - \alpha \left[\frac{1}{T} \Delta b^{(l)} \right],$
Step4:   Set the auto-encoder loss function as
$$L_1(\theta) = \|X' - X\|^2,$$
Step5: after minimizing the loss, the reconstructed features are obtained.

Labeled Sample Classification. After the feature is reconstructed by the auto-encoder, the feature is directly input into the softmax classifier and the loss function of the softmax classifier is defined as follows.

$$L_2(\theta) = -\frac{1}{n}\left[\sum_{i=1}^{n}\sum_{j=1}^{k} 1\{y^i = j\}log\left(\frac{e^{\theta_j^T x^i}}{\sum_{l=1}^{k} e^{\theta_j^T x^i}}\right)\right]. \tag{1}$$

where k denotes the classification label, θ_j^T denotes the weight vector, and $1\{y^i = j\}$ denotes that if $y^i = j$, the equation is equal to 1, otherwise 0. Algorithm 2 shows the details of classification steps on the labeled samples, the algorithm is shown as follows.

Input: Dataset (X, Y) .
Output: Classification results.
Step1: Initialization weight W, deviation b, number of cycle layers i=1, set number of cycle layers I, number of cycles T.
Step2: Set the loss function $L_2(\theta)$ and calculate the error of layer i.
Step3: Deriving for $L_2(\theta)$, $\nabla_{JI}L_2(\theta) = \frac{\partial L_2(\theta)}{\theta_{JI}}$.
Step4: Updating the weight vector, $\theta_j^T = \theta_{JI} - \lambda\nabla_{JI}L_2(\theta)$.
Step5: Determine if there is an i+1 layer, if so, return step2.
Step6: After minimizing the loss, the classifier classification results are output to classify the data into five categories which are DoS, U2R, R2L, Probe and Normal, as the final output.

Unlabeled Sample Classification. After labeled data classification, K (number of categories) category centers are firstly initialized in the feature space based on the characterization of the tagging samples center. Then, after extracting the representation of the unlabeled sample using the encoder, the representation is constrained to be similar to only one of the K category centers and far from other category centers. Algorithm 3 shows the details of classification steps on the unlabeled samples, the algorithm is shown as follows.

Input: Unlabeled sample X.

Output: Classification results.

Step1: Given training tuple $(X, \{Y_i^x\}, \{Y_j^x\})$,

where X is the training element of the unlabeled sample, $\{Y_i^x\}$ is a potentially positive value set (matching cluster centers), $\{Y_j^x\}$ is the negative value set (non-matching cluster centers).

Step2: This set of potential positive value sets contains at least one positive value item that should match the training element, and find the most matching potential positive value item Y_{i*}^x:

$$Y_{i*}^x = \text{argmin}_{Y_i^x}\, d_\theta(X, Y_j^x), \tag{2}$$

Step3: The query in all negative value sets makes the distance $d_\theta(X, Y_{i*}^x)$ between the training element X and the best matching positive value Y_{i*}^x smaller than the distance between the queries (X, Y_j^x).

$$(X, Y_{i*}^x) < d_\theta(X, Y_j^x), \quad \forall j, \tag{3}$$

Step4: Set the data classification loss after the unlabeled samples are characterized and constrained:

$$L_3(\theta) = \sum_j l\left(min_i\, d_\theta^2(X, Y_i^x) + m - d_\theta^2(X, Y_j^x)\right). \tag{4}$$

where l is the hinge loss $l(x)= \max(x,\ 0)$, and m is the constant parameter giving the margin. For each negative value, if the distance between the query and the negative value set is greater than the distance between the query and the best matching positive value, the loss is zero. Conversely, if the margin to the distance between the negative value and the best matching positive value is violated, the

loss is proportional to the amount violated.

Step5: After minimizing the loss, it means that the feature is constrained to a certain cluster center, and the cluster center is minimized within the cluster center and maximized with other cluster centers, and the classification result is output to classify the data into five categories: DoS, U2R, R2L, Probe, and Normal, as the final output.

Intrusion Detection Loss Summary. The total loss of intrusion detection model contains three parts:

A. The loss function of the auto-encoder:

$$L_1(\theta) = \left\| X' - X^2 \right\|,$$

B. Loss function of softmax classifier:

$$L_2(\theta) = -\frac{1}{n}\left[\sum_{i=1}^n \sum_{j=1}^k 1\{y^i = j\}log\left(\frac{e^{\theta_j^T x^i}}{\sum_{l=1}^k e^{\theta_j^T x^i}}\right)\right],$$

C. Clustering constraint loss function:

$$L_3(\theta) = \sum_j l\left(\min_i d_\theta^2(X, Y_i^x) + m - d_\theta^2(X, Y_j^x)\right).$$

Consequently, the total loss $L(\theta)$ is defined as following $L(\theta) = L_1(\theta) + \alpha L_2(\theta) + \beta L_3(\theta)$, where α and β are the balance parameters. In the experiment, the α and β are set as 1 and 5, which can achieves best performance. By combining the labeled and unlabeled samples, the network parameters and category centers are trained and updated simultaneously.

4   Experimental Results and Analysis

4.1   Data Set

The datasets used in the experiments contain KDD CUP99 [12] and NSL-KDD. The number and category distribution of the datasets are shown in Table 1. The KDD CUP99 dataset consisted of nine weeks of network connection data collected from a simulated USAF LAN, divided into identified training data and unidentified test data. The test data and the training data have different probability distribution, and the test data contains some attack types that do not appear in the training data, which makes the intrusion detection more realistic. The NSL-KDD is a classic intrusion detection dataset, the data in it are all 42-dimensional, the first 41 are feature attributes and the last one are decision attributes. Feature attributes are used for intrusion detection algorithms, and decision attributes are used to detect algorithm effects. The attack behavior of the two datasets can be divided into four categories, namely DoS, U2R, R2L, Probing.

Table 1. Dataset category distribution

Data	Normal	Dos	U2R	R2L	Probing
CUP99	22440	15856	256	1057	8180
NSL-KDD	43574	32386	298	1325	12585

4.2   Data Processing

The KDD CUP99 and NSL-KDD datasets are pre-processed, and the numeric character data is converted into character data. Standardize the training set and test set by using standardized methods. Use Min-Max standardization for processing:

$$v' = \frac{v - min_i}{max_i - min_i}. \tag{5}$$

where v is a value of the i attribute column, min_i is the minimum value of the i-th attribute column, and max_i is the maximum value of the i-th attribute column. In the process of classification using the model mentioned in this article, five-category classification is adopted. The five-category classification can also be converted into five two-category classifications through setting one as positive and the remaining categories as negative.

4.3   The Process of Experimental Results and Analysis

Due to the unbalanced distribution of the data set, it is not appropriate to judge the advantages and disadvantages of the algorithm solely based on accuracy. In the field of intrusion detection, there are two important evaluation indicators, one is false alarm rate, the other is missing alarm rate, and missing alarm rate $= 1 -$ detection rate. The accuracy rate reflects how much of the network behavior predicted as abnormal is actually abnormal, F1 score is an important indicator of the quality of the reaction algorithm, considering the calculation results of model precision and recall. Therefore, in this paper, Accuracy (ACC), False positive rate (FPR), Detection rate (DR), Precision rate (PR) and F1 score (F1-Score) are selected as evaluation indexes. The calculation formula of evaluation index is as follows.

$$ACC = \frac{TP + TN}{TP + FP + TN + FN}, \tag{6}$$

$$DR = \frac{TP}{TP + FN}, \tag{7}$$

$$PR = \frac{TP}{TP + FP}, \tag{8}$$

$$FPR = \frac{FP}{TN + FP}, \tag{9}$$

$$F1 = \frac{TP}{TP + \frac{FN + FP}{2}}. \tag{10}$$

where TP and TN indicate that the attack record and normal record have been correctly classified, FP represents the normal record that was mistaken for the attack, FN represents the attack record that was incorrectly classified as a normal record.

The selected comparison models include intrusion detection model ICA-DNN [13], independent component analysis ICA based deep neural network DNN, model SFID [14], intrusion detection method based on stacked asymmetric deep auto-encoder SNADE [15] and an intrusion detection algorithm based on semi-supervised learning (SSL) [16].

Experiment on Cup99 Dataset. In this section, we give the experiment results on the Cup99 dataset. The labeled dataset used in this experiment accounts for 1/5, 1/5, 3/5, 4/5 of the total dataset. The intrusion detection experiments were conducted on various models with accuracy as the evaluation index. The experimental comparison results of each algorithm on the Cup99 dataset are shown in Table 2.

From the experimental results, it can be observed that in the case of large amount of unlabeled sample data, the unlabeled sample classification algorithm presented in this paper is not good at training the representational constraints, but still has better classification effect compared with other algorithms. With the increase of the number of labeled samples, the detection efficiency of this algorithm is gradually improved after more comprehensive training through the combination of labeled data and unlabeled data.

Table 2. Classification comparison of different methods

	AE-SSL	SSL	SFID	ICA-DNN	SNADE
Data1	**0.897**	0.889	0.858	0.822	0.781
Data2	**0.936**	0.916	0.904	0.856	0.828
Data3	**0.948**	0.931	0.916	0.903	0.886
Data4	**0.962**	0.945	0.924	0.922	0.913

Table 3. Comparison of evaluation indexes of various algorithms on KDD CUP99 dataset

	ACC	DR	FPR	PR	F1
AE-SSL	**0.968**	**0.905**	0.009	0.952	**0.933**
SFID	0.927	0.826	0.014	0.898	0.849
ICA-DNN	0.920	0.846	**0.008**	0.918	0.879
SNADE	0.915	0.857	0.011	0.933	0.861
SSL	0.945	0.868	0.010	**0.964**	0.921

The comparison results of different methods on the CUP99 dataset are shown in Table 3, where we can see that the proposed method in this paper has higher ACC, DR and F1 scores than other algorithms, which achieves the best performance on par with other algorithms.

Experiment on NSL-KDD Dataset. The model in this paper is compared with the ICA-DNN, SFID, SNADE and semi-supervised learning model on the NSL-KDD dataset. The results are shown in Table 4.

Table 4. Comparison of evaluation indexes of various algorithms on NSL-KDD dataset

	ACC	DR	FPR	PR	F1
AE-SSL	**0.972**	**0.916**	0.008	**0.961**	**0.935**
SFID	0.907	0.842	0.012	0.902	0.856
ICA-DNN	0.931	0.862	**0.006**	0.921	0.898
SNADE	0.921	0.887	0.013	0.953	0.889
SSL	0.956	0.902	0.011	0.952	0.926

It can be seen from Table 4, after adjusting the parameters of the model, the experimental efficiency of the model is higher. Compared with other algorithms, the performance of the AE-SSL model is superior to other algorithms. At the same time, the detection results of various types of data are shown in Table 5.

Table 5. Test results of various types of data

	ACC	DR	FPR	PR	F1
DoS	0.975	0.923	0.010	0.967	0.943
Probe	0.960	0.836	0.008	0.907	0.902
R2L	0.926	0.725	0.012	0859	0.886
U2R	0.987	0.786	0003	0.873	0.851
Normal	0.945	0.907	0.007	0.982	0.962

It can be seen from Table 5 that the algorithm in this paper has a good detection effect for each type of data after training, which indicates that the algorithm in this paper has a good universality.

The ROC curves of several methods are shown in Fig. 2. The ROC curve uses the true positive rate (TPR) as the ordinate and the false positive rate (FPR) as the abscissa. It can be used to judge the quality of the classifier.

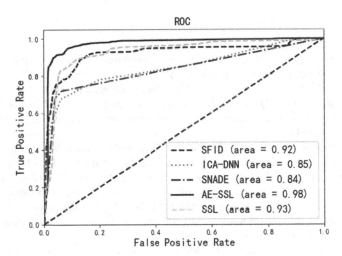

Fig. 2. ROC curves of various algorithms

As can be seen from the Fig. 2, the curve of the proposed AE-SSL method is closer to 1, and the AE-SSL curve completely covers the ROC curve generated by other methods, which demonstrates that the AE -SSL is better than other methods.

5   Conclusion

In this paper, we proposed a semi-supervised intrusion detection method based on the auto-encoder. The auto-encoder is adopted to extract features from the training samples. The proposed method is devised for classifying the intrusion category with some labeled samples and vast unlabeled samples. For labeled samples, we adopt the cross-entropy for classification, which can guide the classification of unlabeled samples. For the unlabeled samples, K category centers are firstly initialized. Then the clustering constraint is adopted to constrain the extracted representation of the unlabeled sample is close to one of the K category centers and far away from other category centers, which can minimize the intra-class distance and maximize the inter-class distance. With some labeled samples and vast unlabeled samples, the network parameters and K category centers are trained and updated together. Exhaustive experiments show that the proposed semi-supervised method can reduce the dependence of labeled samples, improves the accuracy of intrusion detection, and reduces the false alarm rate. In the future, we will focus on the semi-supervised intrusion detection method with only a few labeled samples as guidance.

Acknowledgments. This work was supported in part by the National Nature Science Foundation of China (Grant No. 61471182), the Postgraduate Research & Practice Innovation Program of Jiangsu Province (Grant No. KYCX20_2993), and the Natural Science Foundation of the Jiangsu Higher Education Institutions of China (Grant No. 15KJD52004).

References

1. Alrowaily, M., Alenezi, F., Lu, Z.: Effectiveness of machine learning based intrusion detection systems. In: Wang, G., Feng, J., Bhuiyan, M.Z.A., Lu, R. (eds.) SpaCCS 2019. LNCS, vol. 11611, pp. 277–288. Springer, Cham (2019). https://doi.org/10.1007/978-3-030-24907-6_21
2. Gao, N., Gao, L., Gao, Q., Wang, H.: An intrusion detection model based on deep belief networks. In: 2014 Second International Conference on Advanced Cloud and Big Data, pp. 247–252 (2014)
3. Song, Y., Chen, Y., Lang, B., Liu, H., Chen, S.: Topic model based android malware detection. In: Wang, G., Feng, J., Bhuiyan, M.Z.A., Lu, R. (eds.) SpaCCS 2019. LNCS, vol. 11611, pp. 384–396. Springer, Cham (2019). https://doi.org/10.1007/978-3-030-24907-6_29
4. Hamid, Y., Journaux, L., Lee, J.A., Sugumaran, M.: A novel method for network intrusion detection based on nonlinear SNE and SVM. Int. J. Artif. Intell. Soft Comput. 6(4), 265 (2018)
5. Aburomman, A., Reaz, M.: A novel SVM-kNN-PSO ensemble method for intrusion detection system. Appl. Soft Comput. 38(C), 360–372 (2016)
6. Masarat, S., Sharifian, S., Taheri, H.: Modified parallel random forest for intrusion detection systems. J. Supercomput. 72(6), 2235–2258 (2016). https://doi.org/10.1007/s11227-016-1727-6
7. Li, L., Yu, Y., Bai, S., Hou, Y., Chen, X.: An effective two-step intrusion detection approach based on binary classification and k-NN. IEEE Access 6, 12060–12073 (2018)
8. Potluri, S., Diedrich, C.: Accelerated deep neural networks for enhanced Intrusion Detection System. In: IEEE 21st International Conference on Emerging Technologies and Factory Automation (ETFA), Berlin, 2016, pp. 1–8 (2016)
9. Zhao, G., Zhang, C., Zheng, L.: Intrusion detection using deep belief network and probabilistic neural network. In: IEEE International Conference on Computational Science and Engineering (CSE) and IEEE International Conference on Embedded and Ubiquitous Computing (EUC), pp. 639–642 (2017)
10. Yin, C., Zhu, Y., Fei, J., He, X.: A deep learning approach for intrusion detection using recurrent neural networks. IEEE Access 5, 21954–21961 (2017)

11. Bagaa, M., Taleb, T., Bernabe, J.B., Skarmeta, A.: A machine learning security framework for iot systems. IEEE Access **8**, 114066–114077 (2020)
12. Hasan, M.A.M., Nasser, M., Pal, B., Ahmad, S.: Support vector machine and random forest modeling for intrusion detection system (IDS). J. Intell. Learn. Syst. Appl. **6**(1), 45–52 (2014)
13. Liu, J.H., Mao, S.P., Fu, X.M.: Intrusion detection model based on ICA algorithm and deep neural network. Netinfo Secur. **19**(3), 1–10 (2019)
14. Feng, W.Y., Guo, X.B., He, Y.Y.: Intrusion detection model based on feedforward neural network. Netinfo Secur. **19**(9), 101–105 (2019)
15. Shone, N., Ngoc, T.N., Phai, V., Shi, Q.: A deep learning approach to network intrusion detection. IEEE Trans. Emerg. Top. Comput. Intell. **2**(1), 41–50 (2018)
16. Kumari, V.V., Varma, P.R.K.: A semi-supervised intrusion detection system using active learning SVM and fuzzy c-means clustering. In: International Conference on I-SMAC (IoT in Social, Mobile, Analytics and Cloud) (I-SMAC), pp. 481–485 (2017)

Research on Arm TrustZone and Understanding the Security Vulnerability in Its Cache Architecture

Pengfei Guo(✉), Yingjian Yan, Chunsheng Zhu, and Junjie Wang

School of Cryptographic Engineering, Strategic Support Force Information Engineering University, Zhengzhou 450001, China
guoyifei322@gmail.com

Abstract. Arm TrustZone technology is the most widely used system-level security framework, which provides a trusted execution environment (TEE) for embedded system SoC. This paper introduces the technical principle of TrustZone in detail, explains how to extend the security features from CPU to the whole system through various security components, and briefly introduces the secure boot, the application of TrustZone in mobile devices and the variant technology based on TrustZone. At the same time, there are many attacks on TrustZone. According to the cache architecture of TrustZone, each cache line uses a NS bit to indicate whether the line belongs to secure world or normal world. The purpose is to avoid refreshing when switching the two worlds, thus reducing the performance loss. However, it supports cache lines in the two worlds to compete and evict each other, this provides an opportunity for cache attacks, and this article details this security Vulnerability.

Keywords: Secure isolation · Arm TrustZone · TEE · Cache architecture · Cache attacks

1 Introduction

With the development of electronic information technology, mobile devices (such as mobile phones, BYOD) have reached the computing power and network bandwidth comparable to traditional PCs, and have now become an important tool for people to handle daily life and work affairs. The distribution of apps is mostly based on app stores, and there are many untrusted third-party apps. At the same time, even officially certified apps may have the risk of stealing user privacy, because people often perform mobile payment, fingerprint recognition, digital rights management and other data processing involving key sensitive information on mobile devices [1]. In our daily life, we may all have the impression that you have just used search engines (such as Google, Baidu) to search for a book, and when you open a shopping app, the book is automatically recommended to you, indicating that "it" monitors your behavior in the background.

At present, the two most commonly used means to solve information security problems are encryption and isolation [2]. Encryption is a very effective traditional means,

G. Wang et al. (Eds.): SpaCCS 2020, LNCS 12382, pp. 200–213, 2021.
https://doi.org/10.1007/978-3-030-68851-6_14

but in some scenarios, encryption needs the effective cooperation of isolation to give full play to its real power. The core idea of isolation is not to completely identify or completely remove malware or vulnerabilities, but only to provide a trusted execution environment for critical data or services, which can greatly reduce the attack interface. The goal of isolation is to protect sensitive code from attack and destruction in a complex environment where system vulnerabilities cannot be completely avoided.

TrustZone proposed by Arm is a typical representative of system-level isolation scheme, and has been widely recognized and applied. We all know that there is no absolute security in the world, and inevitably, TrustZone has its vulnerabilities. At present, many studies have proven that TrustZone can be successfully cracked [3], and cache attacks are a representative one.

In this article, we mainly focus on two parts, one is the system principle of Trust-Zone, introduced in Sect. 3, and the other is how to exploit the vulnerability in the TrustZone cache architecture to implement cache attacks, introduced in Sect. 4. The Sect. 2introduces several commonly used security isolation techniques, and the last section, Sect. 5, is about the conclusion.

2 Security Isolation Technology

There are three common isolation mechanisms: hardware isolation, software isolation and system-level isolation.

Hardware isolation mechanisms are usually reflected in the form of external encryption modules, such as the early IBM4758 encryption coprocessor, which is mainly used to verify authorization services, banking and financial systems and industrial control fields. Mobile phone SIM card and set-top box IC card, which are closely related to our daily life, can also be regarded as a kind of hardware isolation module, but it is lightweight application. This kind of card form module is mainly used for identity authentication, secure storage, financial services and so on. The external hardware security module can protect the sensitive data in a relatively secure physical peripheral, and can adopt more advanced technology and physical security protection technology according to the security requirements, but its disadvantage is that it increases the cost of the design, increases the power consumption of the system, and the scope of the external security hardware module is also limited. The limited communication bandwidth between the two domains will also reduce the performance of the system.

Now the popular TPM (Trusted Platform Module) developed and advocated by TCG (Trusted Computing Group) can also be regarded as an external hardware security module, its main task is to establish a hardware-based trust root, from the infrastructure to provide the necessary mechanism for trusted computing environment [4]. With reference to the TPM1.2 architecture, China has launched a self-developed Trusted Cryptography Module (TCM) specification, which changed the module from passive invocation to active control, and also supports national secret algorithms SM1, SM2, SM3, SM4.

Software isolation technology is mainly to use virtualization technology to achieve the purpose of isolation, such as the use of MMU to achieve the isolation of the address space, the use of privilege management mechanism to achieve the separation of the operating system kernel mode and user mode. In addition, there are software isolation technologies such as containers, sandboxes, and honeypots. Software isolation technology usually uses the entire core as a trusted computing base (TCB), which has a large attack interface and many vulnerabilities. At the same time, it lacks the root of trust of the hardware, and its own security is difficult to be guaranteed. In addition, DMA and GPU with bus master interface function IP can bypass some software security isolation mechanisms and bring additional security risks.

Both hardware and software isolation mechanisms have their own problems and defects, so many researchers focus on how to enhance the security of the system kernel and applications through the dual-domain execution environment provided by the architecture, and propose a system-level security isolation. The mechanism can also be called the isolation protection mechanism of software and hardware cooperation. Trust-Zone technology is a typical representative among them. This system-level isolation mechanism can provide considerable isolation and flexibility.

The ultimate goal of the above three isolation mechanisms is to build a trusted execution environment. For ease of comparison, the corresponding execution environment that can provide rich functions is generally called REE. TEE is a trusted environment for secure executing applications. TEE itself does not require that it must be implemented based on hardware. However, in practice, it is found that TEE without hardware support is difficult to ensure its security, therefore, the researchers classify the hardware-based TEE schemes into the following three types, as shown in Fig. 1.

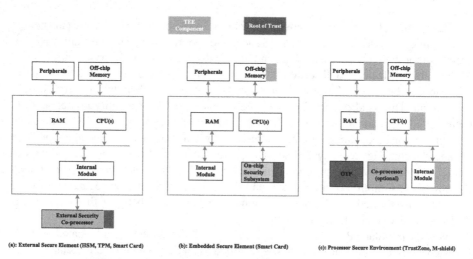

(a): External Secure Element (HSM, TPM, Smart Card)   (b): Embedded Secure Element (Smart Card)   (c): Processor Secure Environment (TrustZone, M-shield)

Fig. 1. Implementation scheme of TEE based on hardware.

From left to right, the first scheme is the external security module mentioned above, and the second scheme is the built-in security module, but this scheme does not have the ability to extend the security domain to the whole system, and the third scheme is the system-level solution. In comparison, the third scheme takes into account both flexibility and security, and is mainstream in both industry and academia.

3   Detailed Explanation of TrustZone Technology

3.1   Overview

Arm proposed the TrustZone technology as early as 2004 [5]. This technology realizes the isolation between security environment and normal environment through hardware without affecting the power consumption, performance and area of the system as far as possible. The software provides basic security service interface, and the system security is constructed by the combination of software and hardware. The TrustZone architecture extends the secure isolation mechanism to the entire system instead of a single module [6]. The overall hardware architecture is shown in Fig. 2 [7].

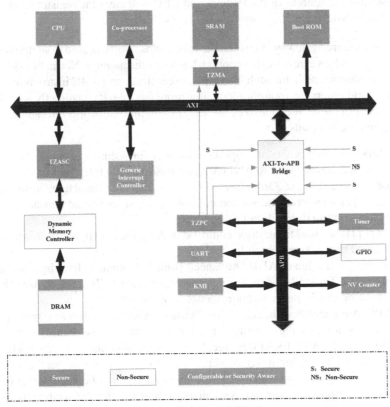

Fig. 2. An example of the overall hardware architecture of TrustZone.

In the early days when this technology was proposed, TrustZone did not get widespread attention and application, maybe people's security awareness is not strong enough, or it is limited by the cost of security design. Fortunately, in the past 10 years, the design concept of TrustZone has been widely recognized and applied on a large scale. To some extent, TrustZone has become a de facto TEE standard reference, especially in the field of embedded systems.

3.2 Security Extension of TrustZone Architecture [8, 9]

CPU. TrustZone technology virtualizes a single physical CPU into two virtual CPU, one is called secure processor core, the other is called normal processor core, the running environment of secure processor is called secure world or security domain, and the running environment of normal processor core is called normal world or normal domain. The two worlds run in a time-sharing manner, and to some extent, the two worlds can be regarded as two big processes. The security extension of CPU is realized through hardware, and the security state of the processor is characterized by the NS bit of SCR registers. NS bits can only be configured in the secure world. At the same time, NS bit can also be extended to each IP through the system-on-chip bus. Therefore, the normal world cannot access the resources unique to the secure world, while the secure world can access all the resources of the system, and CPU will clear the register status of the previous world when switching between the two worlds.

There is a secure "gateway" between the two worlds, which is used to switch between the two worlds and save (restore) the context, known as the monitor. Normal world, which can fall into monitor mode through interrupts, exceptions, and SMC instructions. When the secure world enters the monitor mode, it is more flexible. It can directly write CPSR registers, and of course, it can also be switched to the normal world through interrupts and exception mechanisms.

On-chip Bus. On-chip bus is an important support for secure extension. Two secure extension bits are introduced into AXI (Advanced eXtensible Interface) bus. These two bits can be equivalent to the 33rd address line for read/write transactions, respectively.

AWPROT [1]: bus write transaction control signal, secure write transaction is low level, non-secure write transaction is high level.

ARPROT [1]: bus read transaction control signal, secure read transaction is low level, non-secure read transaction is high level.

The security extension of AHB (Advanced High-Performance Bus) bus can be realized through AXI-To-AHB bridge, in implementation, two AHB buses are usually used to separate secure components and non-secure components.

The APB (Advanced Peripheral Bus) bus is usually used to connect low-speed peripherals, but it does not have the security extension attribute, and the security extension is responsible for by the AXI-To-APB bridge. Each peripheral connected to the bridge has a separate TZPCDECPROT input signal, which is used to determine whether the peripheral is configured as secure or non-secure. These input signals can be fixed and connected during design synthesis, or can be dynamically controlled by the security peripheral TrustZone protection controller (TZPC), so that the security state can be dynamically switched during operation. TZPC itself is also a peripheral on APB, but TZPC is fixed as a security peripheral. In Fig. 1, TZPC, Timer and Non-Volatile Counter are fixed with "0" when designing synthesis, indicating that it is always secure, while GPIO is fixed with "1" when designing synthesis, indicating that it is always non-secure state. The security state of UART and KMI (Keyboard and Mouse Interface) is configurable, and the control signals is given by TZPC.

MMU, TLB and Cache. The processors provide an MMU for each of the two worlds, each corresponding to a virtual processor, which ensures that there is a separate page table structure in the two worlds. Arm does not provide a mandatory isolation standard for TLB, but it is recommended that vendors add a bit to the TLB descriptor according to their specific needs to identify whether the content in the TLB belongs to the normal world or the secure world, so as to avoid refreshing the TLB each time the world is switched. There is also a bit added in the CPU cache to indicate the current security status of the cache accessed by the CPU, so that the caches of the normal world and the secure world can coexist to avoid refreshing the cache during switching. When a cache replacement occurs, the replacement policy does not consider whether the cache line is in a secure state or not, a secure cache line may evict a non-secure cache line, and a non-secure cache line may evict a secure cache line. This provides an opportunity for cache side-channel attacks.

Interrupts and Exceptions. The mode recommended by Arm is to use IRQ as the interrupt source for the normal world and FIQ as the interrupt source for the secure world. If a corresponding interruption occurs in the current world, there is no need to switch the world, otherwise, the world needs to be switched to handle the current interruption. For example, if an IRQ interrupt occurs in the normal world, there is no need to switch the world, if an FIQ interrupt occurs, you need to switch to the secure world to handle the FIQ interrupt.

TZMA (TrustZone Memory Adapter). TZMA divides the on-chip ROM or RAM into security domains. Compared with providing separate memory for the secure world and the normal world, it saves cost and area. TZMA can support a maximum of 2MB memory area division, where the low address area is the security domain, the high address area is a non-secure domain, and the division of the secure domain and the non-secure domain is aligned with 4KB bytes. The size of the security domain is determined by the input signal R0SIZE. This signal can be fixed during design synthesis or can be given by TZPC and can be dynamically configured.

TZASC (TrustZone Address Space Controller). TZASC is usually mounted on the AXI bus, which can divide multiple storage areas of the address space of the AXI bus from the device. The typical application is to place TZASC between the AXI bus and the dynamic memory controller DMC (Dynamic Memory Controller) to divide the DRAM security domain. It is important to note that TZASC can only be used for partition memory mapping devices, not for partition block devices such as NandFlash.

Thus, through the above security components, the security attributes will be extended from CPU to the entire system, which is why TrustZone is called the system-level isolation architecture.

3.3 Secure Boot

Secure boot is the cornerstone of system security. If the security at startup cannot be guaranteed, then system security is a castle in the air. Secure boot depends on two technologies, one is hardware-based trusted root technology, and the other is trust chain transfer mechanism.

ROM is non-rewritable and has strong resistance to hardware attacks, so the first stage bootloader (FSBL) is usually solidified in ROM as the trusted root of the whole system, and the rest of the code is stored in the on-chip eFlash. If the code is large, the code of the normal world such as the operating system can be stored in mass memory such as NandFlash.

When secure booting, except for the FSBL stored in ROM by default, other program components need to be verified for integrity and authenticity before running. The method is to calculate the hash value of the program code first, and use the Public Key (PuK) of the trusted manufacturer stored in the chip in advance to check the signature attached to the program, compare the two hash values, and pass if consistent, otherwise, stop booting. The transmission of trust chain can use chain transmission or star transmission, or a combination of both.

Secure boot also faces some risks. The traditional method is to store the PuK in ROM. Because all devices use the same PuK, when the Private Key (PrK) is cracked or reversed, it is vulnerable to class-break attacks. To defend against this attack, the system can use OTP (One-Time-Programmable) ROM to store PuK. This enables different devices to have different PuK, to increase the ability to resist class-break attacks. At present, some scholars use PUF technology to build trusted roots [10]. PUF is the abbreviation of Physical Unclonable Functions, also known as chip fingerprint.

3.4 Application of TrustZone Technology in Mobile Terminal

Instead of providing a fixed one-size-fits-all solution, TrustZone provides an overall framework that allows SoC designers to choose, tailor, or add from a range of components that can implement specific functions in a secure environment. At present, TrustZone technology has been widely used, and the typical application on the mobile side are Apple's Secure Enclave, Qualcomm's QSEE (Qualcomm Secure Execution Environment), Samsung's Knox, Huawei's TrustedCore [8]. This technology is mainly used in face recognition, fingerprint recognition and password protection in mobile phones.

3.5 Variants of TrustZone Technology

Dual-Core Architecture. In the dual-core architecture, one physical CPU is replaced by two physical CPU, one CPU is fixed secure and one CPU is fixed non-secure. This architecture can reduce the switching between the two worlds, and does not require CPU to have TrustZone extension properties, which significantly broadens the application field of TrustZone technology.

Multicore Architecture. In the multi-core architecture, whether it is heterogeneous multi-core or homogeneous multi-core, each core can be configured as a secure core or a normal core, or support the switching between the secure world and the normal world at the same time. In practical applications, considering the complexity of the software, usually only one CPU core has the ability to run the secure world, while other CPU can run in the normal world. Sometimes, in order to improve the utilization of multiple cores as much as possible, normal cores and secure cores can also be switched dynamically, but this scheme will obviously increase the complexity of the software.

Multi-domain Architecture. Ferdinand Brasser et al. [11] proposed a multi-domain architecture called SANCTUARY. The innovation of this architecture is that the isolation zone is placed in the user's normal world instead of the security world. Multiple isolation zones called SANCTUARY can be instantiated. SANCTUARY can achieve two-way isolation from the normal world and the secure world, the architecture effectively reduces the trusted computing base TCB, and can tolerate malicious SA (SANCTUARY APP). SA is a program that runs in the SANCTUARY zone, which reduces the security risk of malicious TA to the system, and facilitates the secondary development of TrustZone by third parties. But the architecture needs to rely on Arm's latest TZC-400 memory controller and is only applicable to multi-core SoCs.

TrustZone for ARMv8-M. With the evolution of the Cortex-A series instruction set, Arm has also brought TrustZone to the Cortex-M series to build a trusted execution environment on the MCU. The TEE here has the low power consumption of the MCU, and the switching speed of the secure world and the normal world is faster than that of the A series CPU. The introduction of TrustZone on Cortex-M is mainly used for secure boot, firmware security, creating a root of trust, and at the same time can control secure peripherals, such as independent secure storage, random number generator, secure clock, etc. [8]. Although the isolated security world is introduced on the M series, it will not reduce the real-time performance of the service (compared to the deterministic delay of MCUs without TEE). Currently, some manufacturers have produced TrustZone M series chips, such as MicroChip's SAML10 and L11 (based on CortexM23).

4   The Security Vulnerability in TrustZone Cache Architecture

4.1   Memory Hierarchy of TrustZone

The memory hierarchy of TrustZone is shown in Fig. 3. Each cache line extends the NS bit, which specifies the security state of the cache line. The original intention of this design is to use the NS bit to distinguish between the cache line of the normal world and the cache line of the secure world, thereby reducing the system overhead of refreshing the cache during world switching. Any cache line can be evicted to make room for new data regardless of its security status. In other words, secure cache line filling can evict non-secure cache lines, and vice versa. This design is a key factor in launching cache side-channel attack on TrustZone.

4.2   Introduction to Cache Side-Channel Attack

In the field of cryptanalysis, the method of using the side channel information leaked during the implementation of the cryptographic algorithm to attack the key is called the side channel attack. The side information usually refers to power consumption, electromagnetism, sound, fault, photon, time, cache and so on [13].

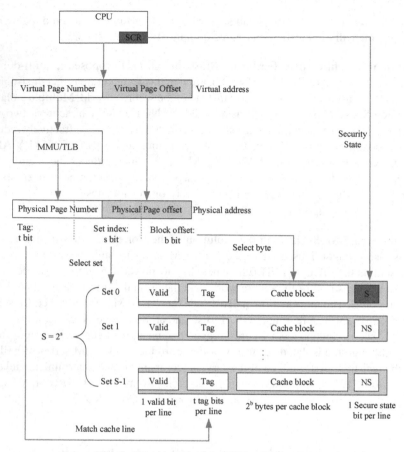

Fig. 3. Memory hierarchy of TrustZone [12].

Cache is designed to solve the mismatch between computing speed and memory speed of CPU, and it is an important means of processor design optimization at present. Table 1 [14] enumerates the access latency at all levels of memory in modern computer systems.

4.3 Cache Basics [15]

Cache Organization. There are three mapping modes between cache and main memory, namely, associative mapping, direct mapping, set-associative mapping. Direct mapping can be regarded as 1-way set-associative mapping, associative mapping can be regarded as a set-associative mapping with only one set, set-associative mapping combines the advantages of direct mapping and associative mapping. Modern caches are usually organized with N-way associative.

Table 1. The ubiquity of caching in modern computer systems.

Type	What cached	Where cached	Latency (cycles)	Managed by
CPU registers	4-byte or 8-byte words	On-chip CPU registers	0	Compiler
TLB	Address translations	On-chip TLB	0	Hardware MMU
L1 cache	64-byte blocks	On-chip L1 cache	4	Hardware
L2 cache	64-byte blocks	On-chip L2 cache	10	Hardware
L3 cache	64-byte blocks	On-chip L3 cache	50	Hardware
Virtual memory	4-KB pages	Main memory	200	Hardware + OS
Disk cache	Disk sectors	Disk controller	100,000	Controller firmware

Cache Replacement Strategy. There are three common replacement strategies for cache, namely least-recently used (LRU), pseudo-random replacement strategy and first-in first-out replacement strategy. Intel processors often use LRU replacement strategies, while Arm processors usually use pseudo-random replacement strategies in order to reduce power consumption and complexity. It is worth noting that the pseudo-random replacement strategy will bring additional difficulty to cache side channel attacks [16].

Addressing Modes. Both the index and tag in the cache address field can use physical addresses or virtual addresses, and there are four addressing modes by arrangement. They are virtually-indexed virtually-tagged (VIVT), Physically-indexed physically-tagged (PIPT), physically-indexed virtually-tagged (PIVT), and virtually-indexed physically-tagged (VIPT). The specific mode is related to the processor.

Inclusiveness. There are three types of inclusiveness in multi-level cache, namely Inclusive cache, Exclusive cache, and Non-inclusive cache. Take two-level cache as an example, Inclusive cache refers to L1 cache is a subset of L2 cache, exclusive cache refers to the data in memory can only exist in a certain level of cache, and cannot exist in multi-level cache at the same time, Non-inclusive cache refers to the above two properties not satisfied. It is worth mentioning that cross-core attacks require an inclusive multi-level cache architecture.

4.4 Cache-Attack Technology

The underlying principle of cache attacks is simple, which is to use the difference in access time caused by whether the data is in the cache. To implement cache attacks, the following conditions need to be met:

- The attacker and the victim share the cache, or at least share a part of the cache.
- The attacker and the victim will have a competitive use of the cache, that is, they can evict each other's cache line.
- After the attacker competes with the victim to use cache, the state of cache can be retained, in other words, the state of cache cannot be refreshed.
- Different states of cache line will lead to differences in execution time, and this time difference can be accurately distinguished by timing means.

The three most common attack techniques are described below [15].

Evict + Time. Osvik et al. [17] put forward the attack method of Evict + Time, which indirectly measures the total execution time of the victim to observe the total number of cache hits and misses. This method is relatively simple to implement, but the signal-to-noise ratio is very low and its practicability is not strong, so it is seldom used at present.

Prime + Probe. Prime + Probe is also proposed by Osvik et al. [17], which is more efficient than Evict + Time, and this method does not require the attacker process and the victim process to share memory. The attack flow is shown in Fig. 4. This method is mainly used in cache attacks on TrustZone.

Flush + Reload. Flush + Reload [18] is a more efficient method of attack, but there are two prerequisites, one is that the CPU needs to have cache refresh instructions, such as the cflush instruction of the Intel processor, and the other is that the attacker process and the victim process share memory. If there is no flush instruction, you can use Evict + Reload instead. Because the two worlds of TrustZone are isolated and it is impossible to share memory, this approach is not suitable for attacks on TrustZone.

The common timing method is to use precise Performance Interface, such as x86 processor's rdtsc instruction and Arm's performance monitor register, but the use of these performance interfaces may require kernel permissions. In addition, you can also use unprivileged system call, POSIX function, dedicated thread timer and other methods to implement timing [15].

4.5 Cases of Cache Attacks on TrustZone

Zhang Ning et al. [12] proposed an attack called TruSpy, the first study of timing-based cache side-channel information leakage of TrustZone. TruSpy used Prime + Probe cache attacks technology to successfully implement the attack in the user mode of the normal world and the kernel mode of the normal world. The difference is that in the user mode, the attacker cannot access virtual-to-physical address translation and high precision timers, which will cause great trouble for cache attacks. TruSpy devise a novel method that uses the expected channel statistics to allocate memory for cache probing, and shows how to implement timing with less accurate performance time interfaces. The attack model is described as follows [12]: Running OpenSSL in the secure world as a security service, fast software-based AES implementation in the OpenSSL 1.0.1f, T-Tables uses precomputed look-up tables. In the OS-based attack, the attacker has full control of the

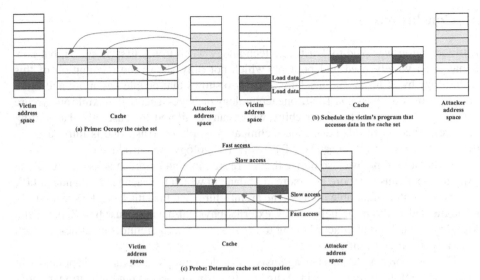

Fig. 4. Illustration of the Prime + Probe attack by means of a 4-way (columns) cache with 6 sets (rows).

normal world, in the app-based attack, the attacker has only user privileges. The goal is to obtain the AES key. To successfully carry out an attack, two conditions need to be met. First, the attack process must be able to fill the cache lines of each cache set, which will cause cache contention with the victim process. Second, the attacker must be able to detect changes in the cache state [19].

TruSpy focuses on the last round of the AES, the last round key can be recovered by taking the XOR of the T-table entry and the cipher text value. There are certain differences in the access time between cache hit and miss. The Prime + Probe attack technology can be used to get which cache line (set) is accessed by the victim, further, we can figure out which entry of the T-Tables the victim accessed (provided that it is known the mapping between the T-table and cache), according to the fast software-based AES algorithm implementation, If we know which entry of T-Tables is accessed, we know the result of $k_i \oplus P$i, in the case of known-plaintext attack, Ki can be determined, and the original key can be deduced from the last round key [20].

MoritzLipp et al. [21] use prime + probe technology to distinguish whether the provided key is valid based on Alcatel One TouchPop2 (with QSEE platform running on it). The key master trustlet on the Alcatel One Touch Pop 2 provides an interface to generate hardware backed RSA keys. In addition, it can be used for the signature creation and verification of data inside the TrustZone.

Ben Lapid et al. [22] only need 1 min to recover the AES-256 key using laptop GPUs for parallel optimization analysis. The attack platform is Samsung's Galaxy S6, which deployed TrustZone framework.

5 Conclusions

Little attention was paid to TrustZone technology when it was first proposed, but now it has been widely used and popular, which not only shows the recognition of this technology by industry and academia, but also shows that people pay more and more attention to security issues. TrustZone technology provides a general, flexible and secure framework for embedded system chips, which can be tailored and customized according to specific needs. In this paper, the technical principle of TrustZone is introduced in detail, and some variants based on TrustZone technology are introduced.

At the same time, we also notice that there are more and more attacks on TrustZone [3], and the means are more and more abundant, in which the cache side channel attack makes use of the vulnerable in the cache architecture, and the attack can be successfully implemented without the help of any external physical devices. Just like Spectre and Meltdown, this kind of attacks belong to the scope of micro-architecture attacks, which have a wide range of influence.

The common countermeasure against cache side channel attacks are still applicable in TrustZone architecture, mainly including cache partition, access randomization, removing high resolution timers, runtime attack detection, cache flushing, cache prefetching [15], but these countermeasures will more or less affect the performance of the system, which requires users to make tradeoffs.

References

1. Enck, W., Ongtang, M., McDaniel, P.: Understanding android security. IEEE Secur. Priv. Mag. **7**, 50–57 (2009)
2. Ravi, S., Raghunathan, A., Kocher, P.C., Hattangady, S.: Security in embedded systems: design challenges. ACM Trans. Embed. Comput. Syst. **3**, 461–491 (2004)
3. Cerdeira, D., Santos, N., Fonseca, P., Pinto, S.: SoK: understanding the prevailing security vulnerabilities in TrustZone-assisted TEE systems. In: IEEE Symposium on Security and Privacy (SP), pp. 1416–1432 (2020)
4. Feng, W., Feng, D., Wei, G., Qin, Y., Zhang, Q., Chang, D.: TEEM: a user-oriented trusted mobile device for multi-platform security applications. In: International Conference on Trust and Trustworthy Computing (TRUST), pp. 133–141(2013)
5. Alves, T.: TrustZone: integrated hardware and software security. Inf. Q. **3**, 18–24 (2004)
6. Ngabonziza, B., Martin, D., Bailey, A., Cho, H., Martin, S.: TrustZone explained: architectural features and use cases. In: International Conference on Collaboration and Internet Computing (CIC), pp. 445–451 (2016)
7. Jang, J., et al.: PrivateZone: providing a private execution environment using ARM TrustZone. IEEE Trans. Dependable Secure Comput. **15**, 797–810 (2018)
8. Pinto, S., Santos, N.: Demystifying ARM TrustZone. ACM Comput. Surv. **51**, 1–36 (2019)
9. Mukhtar, M.A., Bhatti, M., Gogniat, G.: Architectures for security: a comparative analysis of hardware security features in intel SGX and ARM TrustZone. In: International Conference on Communication, Computing and Digital systems (C-CODE), pp. 299–304 (2019)
10. Zhao, S., Zhang, Q., Hu, G., Qin, Y., Feng, D.: Providing root of trust for ARM TrustZone using on-chip SRAM. In: Proceedings of the 4th International Workshop on Trustworthy Embedded Devices (TrustED 2014), pp. 25–36 (2014)

11. Brasser, F., Gens, D., Jauernig, P., Sadeghi, A., Stapf, E.: SANCTUARY: ARMing TrustZone with user-space enclaves. In: Network and Distributed Systems Security Symposium (NDSS), p. 15 (2019)
12. Zhang, N., Sun, K., Shands, D., Lou, W., Hou, Y.T.: TruSpy: cache side-channel information leakage from the secure world on ARM devices. Cryptol. ePrint Arch. **2016**, 980 (2016)
13. Zhou, Y., Feng, D.: Side-channel attacks: ten years after its publication and the impacts on cryptographic module security testing. Cryptol. ePrint Arch. **2005**, 388 (2005)
14. Bryant, R.E., O'Hallaron, D.R.: Computer Systems: A Programmer's Perspective. 3rd edn. 650 (2016)
15. Lyu, Y., Mishra, P.: A survey of side-channel attacks on caches and countermeasures. J. Hardware Syst. Secur. **2**, 33–50 (2018)
16. Zhang, L., Tang, B.: A cost-effective cloud storage caching strategy utilizing local desktop-based storage. In: International Conference on Security, Privacy and Anonymity in Computation, Communication and Storage (SpaCCS) Workshops, pp. 382–390 (2016)
17. Osvik, D.A., Shamir, A., Tromer, E.: Cache attacks and countermeasures: the case of AES. Cryptol. ePrint Arch. **2005**, 271 (2005)
18. Yarom, Y., Falkner, K.: FLUSH+RELOAD: a high resolution, low noise, L3 cache side-channel attack. In: USENIX Security Symposium, pp. 719–732 (2014)
19. Zhang, N., Sun, K., Shands, D., Lou, W., Hou, Y.T.: TruSense: information leakage from TrustZone. In: IEEE Conference on Computer Communications (INFOCOM), pp. 1097–1105 (2018)
20. Apecechea, G.I., Inci, M.S., Eisenbarth, T., Sunar, B.: Wait a minute! A fast, cross-VM attack on AES. In: International Symposium on Research in Attacks, Intrusions and Defenses (RAID), pp. 299–319 (2014)
21. Lipp, M., Gruss, D., Spreitzer, R., Maurice, C., Mangard, S.: ARMageddon: cache attacks on mobile devices. In: USENIX Security Symposium, pp. 549–564 (2016)
22. Lapid, B., Wool, A.: Cache-attacks on the ARM TrustZone implementations of AES-256 and AES-256-GCM via GPU-based analysis. Cryptol. ePrint Arch. **2018**, 621 (2018)

Scrutinizing Trust and Transparency in Cash on Delivery Systems

Xuan Son Ha[1], Trieu Hai Le[2], Tan Tai Phan[3], Hung Huy Duc Nguyen[1], Hong Khanh Vo[1], and Nghia Duong-Trung[1(✉)]

[1] FPT University, Can Tho 94000, Vietnam
sha@uninsubria.it, ndhhung1011@gmail.com, khanhvh@fe.edu.vn,
duong-trung@ismll.de
[2] Can Tho University of Technology, Can Tho 94000, Vietnam
lhtrieu.0127@gmail.com
[3] National Chiao Tung University, Hsinchu 30010, Taiwan
phantantai.dv@gmail.com

Abstract. Most of the current decentralized blockchain approaches have disadvantages that need to be improved to have efficiency and completion. First, there is no motivation for any participants to take action honestly. Seller, buyer, and shipper do not trust each other completely. Second, the delivery depends on a trusted third party or arbitrator to act as a deposit and keep all the money from the start of the sales process until the end. Only a trusted third party who keeps money could be a focal point of failure and also costly. Moreover, there is no dispute settlement mechanism if it occurs. Therefore, there will be a loss for the seller, buyer, or both sides for any acts of dishonesty. In this article, we review technology deployment and develop distribution solutions using blockchain technology. We use Hyperledger Composer in our system to protect the rights of merchants and smart contracts to remove any third party or arbitrator.

Keywords: Cash on delivery · Trust · Transparency · Hyperledger composer · Smart contracts · Blockchain

1 Introduction

In recent years, shopping online has become trendy on the global market, so that the consumers are easy to access product information from the seller which is a wide range of the products on the market, thus saving consumers time. Thereby, the delivery of goods to the consumer is to highly put concern on. Currently, Cash on Delivery (COD) is a prominent model which uses to make the transaction between the shop seller and buyer, neither online shopping nor offline shopping. The pros of COD is to make sure the transparency of the transaction and the convenience of the payment methods that is the reason why COD becomes well-known on the global trade. However, there is another advantage of this model

G. Wang et al. (Eds.): SpaCCS 2020, LNCS 12382, pp. 214–227, 2021.
https://doi.org/10.1007/978-3-030-68851-6_15

is that the consumers might check the parcel before receiving it, and they also can immediately cancel the transaction if they receive unexpected order.

In fact, everything has two sides of the coin, COD still possesses some short-comings such as it does not guarantee the rights of the participants involved, and the system might dependent with the third party which might be express delivery provider or the arbitrator who impacts cost management and ensures that parcels are unchanged. Our proposed solution is distributed system based on blockchain. Blockchain utilizes ordered logs and event to generate traceability and auditability functions which utilize to ensure the needed transparency. First, accountability means the participants must possess the responsibility for their execution or action in the system. It is likely to avoid the participants ignore their own action which has already done by themselves. Second the system must ensure the reward mechanism for the party to perform well. Otherwise, the penalty is given to the party that has poorly performance. Auditability is a tracking events and actions mechanism which is well-known as a way to increase the security and reliability. Integrity, there is a recording specification time and event mechanism to avoid anti-counterfeiting. Authentication and authorization are to ensure that events or actions are performed by appropriate authorized people [12–16]. Timebound utilizes to ensure that the orders are delivered from the seller to the buyer within in the certain of time. Off-chain arbitration means there is an arbitrator will resolve all the disputes that arbitrator assigned to have the right to access the resources necessary for handling this dispute.

In this paper, we have proposed a solution based on Blockchain to solve the trust between every participant on the COD system such as seller, buyer and delivery. The solution is to encourage the issue of trust, the necessity for third parties and bring transparent benefits to the parties involved. The main contributions of this paper is to propose a process to protect the interests of sellers and buyers in the COD model. The contribution of this paper is three-fold: (i) providing a mechanism to protect all members' right on e-commerce system; (ii) incentivizing all the participants to act honestly and fulfill their obligations without resorting to a trusted third party; and (iii) implementing the proof of concept by using the smart contract in Hyperledger Composer.

2   Background

2.1   Smart Contract Based on Blockchain

Blockchain is a decentralized database which used to store the information in a block associated together by coding and extending over time. It is designed to prevent data from being changed: Once the network has accepted the data, there is no way to change it. The initialization time is stored in the block information and associated with the previous block, along with the time code and transaction data. It is guaranteed by using a decentralized computing system with high byzantine fault tolerance. Thanks to these potential functions, the system helps to eliminate significant consequences when data is altered in the context of global trade. The critical point of blockchain technology is distributed and decentralized. Distributed data networks leverage the power of the participating computer networks to optimize the tasks which used a huge of resources under the operation of intermediaries, or the governing party has become faster, more economical, and more democratic [7]. With the launching of the Blockchain Ethereum platform [4], it is expected to explore a hundred of the application that depends on the intermediary unit such as healthcare [6], delivery services [11]. A smart contract is a digital contract that is written on the Blockchain platform. It allows automatable operation, and the participant exchanges the virtual properties, services, stocks in a transparent manner without intermediaries. Because of this reason, we have applied smart contracts to ensure benefits for participants.

2.2 Ethereum and Hyperledger

Ethereum is developed as same as a permissionless public Blockchain, which the developers utilize Solidity as a programing language to write the smart contracts and decentralized applications [5,10]. The development of Ethereum has been developed independently of any particular application. Any existing programing language is utilized to build the application which interacts with the Ethereum Blockchain. In Ethereum, all of the participants possess the right to contribute the approval of a transaction or data states regardless of who is the owner, the subject or object of the transaction. The data states or the data order of the transaction will be stored permanently and might not be changed once it is recorded. Due to blockchain Ethereum network is generated of members anonymously untrusted therefore needs a mechanism to combat fraud mechanisms known as consensus [3]. Unlike Ethereum, Hyperledger Fabric utilizes different consensus mechanisms, and it does not base on proof of work derivatives. Hyperledger provides an open-source, and the module is utilized in different cases, and it is generated independently of any particular application. Fabric mechanism covers a wide range and entire transaction flow. Moreover, it is an assumption that node play in different roles and task in the consensus process. It means that it is opposite with Ethereum when the roles and task of the nodes in consensus are the same each other. Hyperledger Fabric allows controlling the consensus in detail and restricted access to the transaction so that it might enhance the scalability, the performance, and the privacy of the network. It is the reason we have utilized Fabric in the previous work.

2.3 Hyperledger Composer

As we have known, Hyperledger Composer is a high-level set with APIs and Tools for modeling, building, integrating, and deployment of the blockchain network, and it might pack and execute on Hyperledger Fabric. For more detail, Hyperledger Composer is a set of collaboration tools to build blockchain business networks, which helps the business owner and the developer to simply generate smart contracts and blockchain applications to solve the business issues. Composer is built by JavaScript, Node.js, NPM, CLI to provide business-focused abstractions as well as applications to test design processes to generated robust blockchain solutions. Composer is a creation pattern tool, user-driven, which runs on the top of Hyperledger Fabric. It allows easy management of assets (data stored on the blockchain), participant (identity management or member services), transaction (Chaincode, aka Smart Contracts), operate on Assets on behalf of participants. The application might be exported as a package (a BNA file), which executes on a Hyperledger, with the support of a Node.js app (based on Loopback application) and provide the REST interface for the party application.

2.4 Hyperledger Caliper

Hyperledger Caliper is a blockchain standard tool, and it is a Hyperledger project hosted by the Linux Foundation. It is used to measure the performance of the specific blockchain implementation with a predefined set of use cases. The performance reports, transaction latency, resource usage are generated by the Hyperledger Caliper so that the other project of Hyperledger might leverage these resources. Hyperledger Caliper is an open-source contributed by Huawei, Hyperchain, Oracle, Bitwise, IBM, and Budapest University of Technology and Economics.

2.5 Hyperledger Composer and Ethereum

Currently, Hyperledger Ecosystem and Ethereum are the two most popular blockchain platforms, depending on transaction needs and system existed to have a selection criteria. This paper used Hyperledger Composer to implement the cash on delivery theory model.

Based on supported features such as privacy, transaction validation, programming language diversity and no-fees transaction, this paper uses the Hyperledger Composer platform to build smart contracts for cash on delivery mechanismSmart contract. Smart contract is a core application that defines the transactional functions between organizations. Application will invokes the functions defined within the smart contract to initiate transactions, which will then be stored at the ledger.

3 Related Work

The Authors[1] have utilized Hash code and key. Then, the shipper delivers the package, which includes the key. The key is entered to authenticate and receive the package by the buyer when the shipper delivers the destination. Once the hash code from the buyer is matched with the hash code on the smart contract, the seller will receive the money from the buyer. This solution is easy to implement because it only depends on one key. However, this method is inadequate in that delivered the package to complete without further action with a key before arriving, and it does not guarantee benefits for the seller also take in an account.

---

[1] https://dappsforbeginners.wordpress.com/tutorials/two-party-contracts/.

There is another solution which is utilized blockchain technology to create a distributed trade market peer-to-peer. LocalEthereum[2] utilized a third party as a escrow. The buyer and seller agree with the trusted third party that they must to mortgage money and trust until the end of the transaction. This solution requires that the participant must trust in the third party, and the cost is higher due to demanding mortgage money. On the other hand, the seller must mortgage money with the third party, and the buyer provides direct payment to the seller. The mortgage is returned to the buyer when the transaction is finished. However, if a dispute occurs, the participants may allow the localEthereum to act as an arbitrator. This solution is costly because it uses a third party, and it also requires trust and honesty but offers convenience in the dispute.

Similar to LocalEthereum is OpenBazaar. It based on a sponsored deposit and an agreement by the seller and the buyer or the trader, which is known as a Multisignature escrow[3]. The sponsored deposit also acts as an operator when the dispute occurs. So, three participants are joining the transaction, such as the seller, the buyer, and the trader. The buyer mortgaged the Bitcoin into the sponsored deposit account. Payments will only be issued to the destination under the agreement based on the votes of the participants. Two over three of the votes determine the destination of the payment transfer. This method is not related to the shipper in the entire transaction. The shipper is trusted without any incentive to take goods from the seller and deliver it to the buyer out of the chain. Therefore, shipping is not tracked on the chain.

Hasan and Salah [8] have introduced a delivery process consists of the buyer, seller, and shipper. If the delivery company would like to deliver the goods, they must mortgage an amount of money which equals the second time of the valuation of the products, once the goods successfully deliver, the money immediately return to the participants. If there is a failure, the system resolves disputes base on the delivery time, so that the system will make decisions without human intervention. Doubling the mortgage money of products not only increases transaction costs but also prevents fraudulent frauds from avoiding losing money.

The researchers [1] have proposed a mechanism based on Ethereum Blockchain, which is related to deliver the goods between the buyer and seller. As their solutions, the shipper plays an essential role in the system. The delivery process based on two steps: (i) A key and goods are delivered to the buyer, and (ii) the buyer enters the key to receive the smart contract. [9] Ethe is placed in the account of the buyer if the key is entered by the buyer, which matches the key in the smart contract, and the Ether immediately transfers to the seller after successfully connecting. This solution quickly implements since it depends on the seller. However, it leads up to the dependence on the trust of the shipper that they will not leverage the key before handing to the buyer. Therefore, this solution is not recommended on the COD mechanism.

Krishnamachari et al. [2] proposed the mechanism to make trades with any asset using digital keys, and these processes do not need a reliable third party.

---

[2] https://blog.localcryptos.com/how-our-escrow-smart-contract-works/.
[3] https://www.openbazaar.org/features/.

Also, the authors describe a double deposit transaction method for the payment transactions against fraud and delivery between two parties where the trader can use digital signatures for verification. The seller and the buyer (client) use a pair of symmetric keys to verify the goods. They use smart contracts to decide and process the seller and buyer by raising the deposit. But this article has not analyzed on a shipping issue. If it is a physical product and the sender does not comply with the commitment, then the system is not resolved.

4 System Architecture

4.1 General Design

Figure 1 illustrates the generic model. Buyer orders item (1). The package data is generated, such as the detail information of the order and hash code for authorization in the next step (2). The data will be transmitted to the seller (3). After receiving the order information, the seller establishes bond time with the delivery enterprise (4). The parcel will be confirmed with the seller by the first-shipper (5). If the authentication process is successful, the first-shipper will confirm with the delivery group so that the delivery group deposits an amount of money as same as the valuation of the order (6). In the next step, the delivery process will be initiated from the first-shipper to the next-shippers. When the package is handed over to the next-shipper, they must confirm with the first-shipper and similarly works sequentially to last-shipper (7). Finally, the last-shipper confirms the parcel with the buyer to guarantee that the parcel is matched with the original order (8) and make the payment (9).

4.2 Scenarios

When the shipper receives the parcel from the seller, if the hash code which the seller hashes the product does not match with the shipper that is queried by the ID, then the seller will be responsible for not being delivered. Consequently, the penalty of the seller will not sell the product. If the hash code which is returned by the system does not match, the product is not being delivered, and the order is canceled.

Next is the case of matching hash code, and the order is delivered. While the order is being delivered, the next shipper will query the hash code based on the previous ID. The next shipper will not accept the package from the previous shipper if the system returns failed status. The aforementioned delivery group is responsible for the shipper who will possess the responsibility to compensate mortgage money for the seller as same as the penalty of the delivery group when the order status is changed to cancel.

Finally, the last shipper delivers the parcel to the buyer. It could be opened when the shipper and buyer are simultaneously there. The shipper will hash the product which is already retrieved again, if the hash matches with the hash from the buyer, there are the rewards for all of the group of participants because of

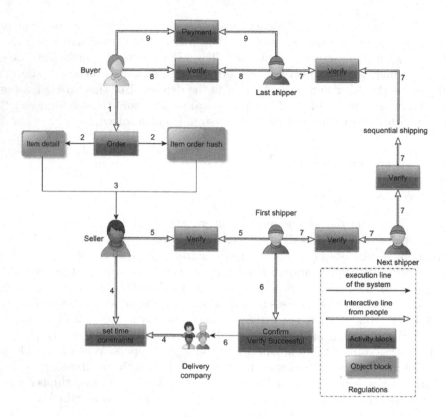

Fig. 1. General design of our proposed Cash on Delivery Systems.

achieving the intention. The rewards of each participant, such as the seller, sold their products, the buyer completely buys their desirable item, and the delivery group delivers the order successfully so that the mortgage money is returned to the delivery group. On the other hand, the buyer will not accept the parcel if the hash does not match, and the seller reserves the right to withdraw money from the mortgage account as compensation if the delivery time exceeds the binding.

4.3   Procedures

Figure 2A illustrates the operating process of the system when the buyer orders goods. The smart-contract will generate the detail and Hash code of the products (2) when the buyer orders goods. Besides, the ID of the order is decoded by the system.

Figure 2B illustrates the settings of the seller before starting the delivery process. The seller initializes the order (1), time delivery constraint is established between seller and shipper (2). The seller will create a virtual account, which is the balance equal to zero for a mortgage.

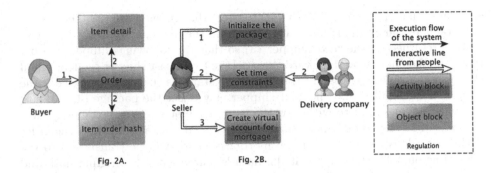

Fig. 2A.   Fig. 2B.

Fig. 2. Figure 2A presents procedure 1: a buyer places an order. Figure 2B illustrates procedure 2: a seller establishes a package before shipping.

Figure 3 describes the process of receiving the order of the first shipper from the seller. First, the order is decoded by the seller (1) and forward the hash of the order to the shipper (2). Second, shipper utilizes the ID to query the original hash from the system (3), the system will compare hash from the seller with the unique hash, the result will be returned to the shipper (4). After the comparison process, the delivery company which manages the shipper will transfer the mortgage money to the virtual account, and this amount of money will be locked if the two Hashes match each other (5), the shipper will receive the package and begin the delivery process immediately. In contrast, the status of the order will be changed to cancel if the two Hashes do not match each other, and the shipper may reject the order (5.1).

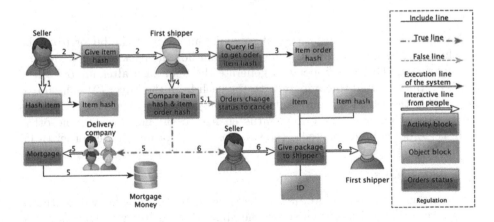

Fig. 3. Procedure 3: the first shipper receives a package from a seller.

Figure 4 Illustrates the transition process in the multi-shipping model. In this model, the current shipper will provide the ID, order's hash (1) to the next shipper so that they can utilize this ID to query the original hash (2). The system will compare the original Hash with Hash from the previous shipper. The result will be returned to the next shipper (3) so that the following shipper whether receiving the package and forward this package to the last shipper sequentially if the system notifies successful (4) or the order status is turned to canceled if the system notifies failed and the next shipper may reject the package (4.1). Thus, the seller has the right to withdraw the mortgage money (5) if the delivery time is longer than the commitment time so that they decide either cancel the order if the hash does not match, or the mortgage money will be transferred to the virtual account by the shipper if the hash is paired with the original hash and the money will be locked.

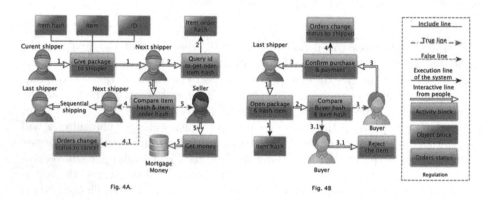

Fig. 4. Fig. 4A presents procedure 4: multi-shipping model. Figure 4B shows procedure 5: the last shipper deliveries goods to a buyer.

Figure 4 illustrates the process of receiving an order of the buyer from the last shipper. The last shipper has the right to un-box the package when meeting the buyer, and the last-shipper will generate the final hash after unboxing the package, which is used to compare with the hash from the buyer (2). The buyer then makes the payment and confirm finishing transaction if the two hashes match each other, and the order status change to shipped (4). On the other hand, the order will be rejected if the two Hashes do not match each other (3.1).

4.4   Algorithms

In Algorithm 1, for each product ordered by a buyer, a seller will initialize and package the package, then select the appropriate delivery to transport the package. Next, a shipper of delivery will confirm the shipment with the seller if the authentication process is successful. Shipper receives the package and delivers the order; otherwise, if the verification process fails, the shipper refuses to receive the package. In the process of transporting packages, the shipper carries out authentication with each other. If the authentication process is successful, the shipper will continue to transport packages if the shipper fails to accept the package. In Algorithm 2, with each product selected by the buyer, the system encrypts the information and displays the product's hash code.

In Algorithm 3, for each product in the package, the system will compare the hash string of the package ID with the ID provided by the previous shipper. The next shipper will continue to transport the package if the two hash chains match; otherwise, the next shipper refuses to receive the package. In Algorithm 4, for each product delivered to the buyer, the shipper will eventually encrypt the product information again and display the product's hash string. Then the buyer will compare the generated hash string with the hash string that he/she hold. If the two hash chains are the same, the buyer receives the goods and makes payment to the shipper. The seller and shipper get profit. In case the hash string does not match, the buyer will refuse to receive the package, the order is canceled, and the seller can take the mortgage on the system.

Algorithm 1: Cash on delivery workflow.

```
 1: for Asset chosen by a buyer do
 2:    Seller creates a package and chooses a delivery
 3:    Seller verifies shipper
 4:    if Verification of the shipper is successful then
 5:       Transport package
 6:       if Verification of the buyer is successful then
 7:          Buyer gets the asset
 8:          Seller gets money
 9:       end if
10:    else
11:       Refuse to give package
12:       Cancel delivery
13:       Seller gets mortgage money
14:    end if
15: end for
```

Algorithm 2: Data encryption of asset.

```
1: for Asset to be encrypted do
2:    Get asset's properties
3:    Encrypt asset's properties
4: end for
5: return Encrypted hash
```
---

5   Experiments

The experiments have been conducted in a standard laptop with the following specifications: Ubuntu 19.10, CPU Intel Core i5 M540 2.53 GHz, 8 GB of RAM. Table 1 presents the performance and capacity of our proposed smart contract model. We assess it through 10 rounds, where the number of the transaction starts from 1000 to 10000. Figure 5, e.g., the left sub-figure, shows the delay in making smart contract transactions. The number of transactions, in turn, increased from 1,000 to 10,000. The max latency and avg latency ratios are proportional to the number of transactions but remain low compared to the number of transactions performed. The min latency is always maintained at around 2s. The throughput quantity is stable at 40 to 50 tps. Figure 5, e.g., the right sub-figure, shows the system's ability to execute transactions. The transactions sent above 90 tps, but the current system's processing capability is just below 51 tps. The ability to handle transactions is still limited because of the system's specifications.

Table 2 describes the number of resources that the system uses, with 10,000 transactions to be executed. The amount of memory used remains low, with a maximum of 145.5MB. Besides, the average performance of the CPU only ranges

---

Algorithm 3: Verification of shipper-shipper.

1: **for** Asset in package **do**
2:     **if** Package information matches its ID **then**
3:         Verify successfully
4:         Transport the package
5:     **else**
6:         Verify failed
7:         Cancel package
8:         Seller gets mortgage money
9:     **end if**
10: **end for**

Algorithm 4: Verification of shipper-buyer.

1: **for** Asset **do**
2:     Generate hash string from the asset's data
3:     **if** Hash string does not match **then**
4:         Buyer refuses asset
5:         Cancel package
6:         Seller gets mortgage money
7:     **else**
8:         Buyer gets package
9:         Seller and shipper get profit
10:         Shipper gets mortgage money
11:     **end if**
12: **end for**

Table 1. Performance metrics.

Round	# Transaction	Send rate (tps)	Max latency (s)	Min latency (s)	Avg latency (s)	Throughput (tps)
0	1000	93.2	14.31	2.56	12.14	42.6
1	2000	99.1	23.07	2.47	19.42	50.9
2	3000	99.1	32.58	2.47	28.97	50.7
3	4000	98.4	45.88	2.48	41.56	48.0
4	5000	99.2	52.98	2.38	47.60	49.3
5	6000	99.7	62.19	2.67	57.42	50.1
6	7000	99.7	70.58	2.57	64.78	50.2
7	8000	98.1	84.95	2.4	77.56	48.9
8	9000	90.8	117.05	2.40	93.10	45.9
9	10000	99.2	107.59	2.53	94.10	48.3

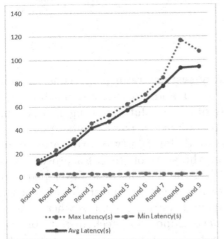 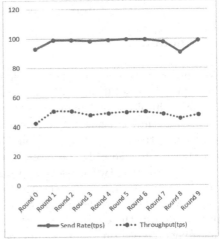

Fig. 5. Performance metrics: latency (sub-figure on the left), and transaction per second (sub-figure on the right).

from 9% to 12%. In general, the max and min memory indicators increase with time of operation. Traffic in and traffic out increase slightly as the number of transactions increases. Disc write increases with the system's storage capacity, but disc read remains low, up to 1.5MB for 10,000 transactions. CPU usage is at a low level, maximum from 18.19% to 31.6%, with average CPU processing speed, ranges from 9% to 11%.

The authors provide the sources codes, instruction of installation, and a YouTube tutorial on how to install and run experiments. Interesting readers might refer to our GitHub repository[4].

---

[4] https://github.com/Masquerade0127/luan_van_CoD.

Table 2. Resource consumption.

Round	# Transaction	Max memory (MB)	Avg. memory (MB)	Max CPU load (%)	Avg. CPU load (%)	Traffic in (MB)	Traffic out (MB)	Disc read (MB)	Disc Write (MB)
0	1000	42.7	40.6	18.19	9.91	2.6	2.1	0.06	5.1
1	2000	47.5	45.4	19.41	11.07	5.1	4.3	0.01	10.2
2	3000	54.9	50.9	18.74	11.17	7.8	6.5	0	15
3	4000	63.5	59.1	19.95	10.24	10.3	8.6	0.06	20.2
4	5000	74.8	68.6	19.23	10.57	13.0	11.1	0.03	27.1
5	6000	86.2	80.8	21.66	11.38	15.4	12.9	0.03	30.6
6	7000	98.7	92.4	23.05	11.06	18.1	15.1	0	41.1
7	8000	108.7	102.5	19.37	10.35	20.8	17.6	0.3	40.5
8	9000	125.9	117.8	31.60	10.22	23.1	19.2	1.5	53.5
9	10000	145.5	134.7	22.09	9.69	25.9	21.8	1.5	60.2

6   Conclusion

Trust and transparency in cash on delivery systems raise many concerns and require practical solutions. We have reviewed and summarized much-related work for technology deployment and distribution solutions using Blockchain. We point out that trust is not completed committed by participants. As a result of miss-trust, the systems depend on a trusted third party or arbitrator to act as a deposit and keep all the money from the start of the sales process until the end. To address two un-solved problems, the authors have developed cash on the delivery mechanism to scrutinize transparency and trust throughout the process. We have described how it works in multi-parties scenarios where several shippers can join the chain. The authors have proposed a mechanism to protect all members' rights on the e-commerce system. The participants act honestly and fulfill their obligations without resorting to a trusted third party. Furthermore, we have implemented the proof of concept by using the smart contract in Hyperledger Composer. Due to its implementation in permitted Blockchain, the system provides a better decentralization and access control and transparency mechanism, as well as scrutinizes the trust of the participants. The well-designed experiments prove that the proposed solution is applicable.

References

1. Antonopoulos, A.M., Wood, G.: Mastering Ethereum: Building Smart Contracts and Dapps. O'reilly Media, Newton (2018)
2. Asgaonkar, A., Krishnamachari, B.: Solving the buyer and seller's dilemma: a dual-deposit escrow smart contract for provably cheat-proof delivery and payment for a digital good without a trusted mediator. In: 2019 IEEE International Conference on Blockchain and Cryptocurrency (ICBC), pp. 262–267. IEEE (2019)
3. Baliga, A.: Understanding blockchain consensus models. Persistent **4**, 1–14 (2017)
4. Dannen, C.: Introducing Ethereum and Solidity, vol. 1. Springer, Heidelberg (2017). https://doi.org/10.1007/978-1-4842-2535-6

5. Duong-Trung, N., et al.: Multi-sessions mechanism for decentralized cash on delivery system. In: Editorial Preface From the Desk of Managing Editor..., vol. 10, no. 9 (2019)
6. Duong-Trung, N., Son, H.X., Le, H.T., Phan, T.T.: On components of a patient-centered healthcare system using smart contract. In: Proceedings of the 2020 4th International Conference on Cryptography, Security and Privacy, pp. 31–35 (2020)
7. Duong-Trung, N., Son, H.X., Le, H.T., Phan, T.T.: Smart care: integrating blockchain technology into the design of patient-centered healthcare systems. In: Proceedings of the 2020 4th International Conference on Cryptography, Security and Privacy, pp. 105–109 (2020)
8. Hasan, H.R., Salah, K.: Blockchain-based solution for proof of delivery of physical assets. In: Chen, S., Wang, H., Zhang, L.-J. (eds.) ICBC 2018. LNCS, vol. 10974, pp. 139–152. Springer, Cham (2018). https://doi.org/10.1007/978-3-319-94478-4_10
9. Hileman, G., Rauchs, M.: Global cryptocurrency benchmarking study. Camb. Centre Altern. Financ. **33**, 33–113 (2017)
10. Le, H.T., Le, N.T.T., Phien, N.N., Duong-Trung, N.: Introducing multi shippers mechanism for decentralized cash on delivery system. Money **10**(6), 590–597 (2019)
11. Le, N.T.T., et al.: Assuring non-fraudulent transactions in cash on delivery by introducing double smart contracts. Int. J. Adv. Comput. Sci. Appl. **10**(5), 677–684 (2019)
12. Son, H.X., Chen, E.: Towards a fine-grained access control mechanism for privacy protection and policy conflict resolution. Int. J. Adv. Comput. Sci. Appl. **10**(2), 507–516 (2019)
13. Son, H.X., Dang, T.K., Massacci, F.: REW-SMT: a new approach for rewriting XACML request with dynamic big data security policies. In: Wang, G., Atiquzzaman, M., Yan, Z., Choo, K.-K.R. (eds.) SpaCCS 2017. LNCS, vol. 10656, pp. 501–515. Springer, Cham (2017). https://doi.org/10.1007/978-3-319-72389-1_40
14. Son, H.X., Hoang, N.M.: A novel attribute-based access control system for fine-grained privacy protection. In: Proceedings of the 3rd International Conference on Cryptography, Security and Privacy, pp. 76–80 (2019)
15. Son, H.X., Nguyen, M.H., Vo, H.K., Nguyen, T.P.: Toward an privacy protection based on access control model in hybrid cloud for healthcare systems. In: Martínez Álvarez, F., Troncoso Lora, A., Sáez Muñoz, J.A., Quintián, H., Corchado, E. (eds.) CISIS/ICEUTE -2019. AISC, vol. 951, pp. 77–86. Springer, Cham (2020). https://doi.org/10.1007/978-3-030-20005-3_8
16. Xuan, S.H., Tran, L.K., Dang, T.K., Pham, Y.N.: Rew-xac: an approach to rewriting request for elastic abac enforcement with dynamic policies. In: 2016 International Conference on Advanced Computing and Applications (ACOMP), pp. 25–31. IEEE (2016)

Expansion Adaptation of Attack-Aware Controller-Link-Switch Cost Minimization Placement in Software-Defined Networking

Cheng Chi Qin[1], Tan Saw Chin[1(✉)], Lee Ching Kwang[2], Zulfadzli Yusoff[2], and Rizaluddin Kaspin[3]

[1] Faculty of Computing and Informatics, Multimedia University, Cyberjaya, Malaysia
sctan1@mmu.edu.my
[2] Faculty of Engineering, Multimedia University, Cyberjaya, Malaysia
[3] Telekom Malaysia Research & Development Sdn Bhd, Cyberjaya, Selangor, Malaysia

Abstract. As a network expands over time, the initial attack recovery and prevention measure may suffer from hiccup where Software-Defined Networking (SDN) controller supply is overwhelmed by traffic demand. The amount of SDN controller increases as demand increases, yet, the recovery planning is lacking behind. As such, network recovery reconstruction is advised as it is impractical to remodel the whole network. Conventional attack-aware placement scheme placed a number of backup controller (BC) dedicated to a controller at node. This will cause the network planning cost to surge drastically over time. Heretofore, centralized placement of a pool of backup controller is rarely observed in SDN field. Thus, we would like to introduce an Attack-Aware Recovery and Expansion controller-link-switch Cost minimization placement in software defined network (ARE_C) with the aim of reducing network planning cost while producing a backup controller pool placement for existing SDN. ARE_C is extended from a prior work, attack-aware recovery controller-switch link cost minimization placement algorithm (ARC) by revolutionizing the technique of selecting and placing backup controller in a SDN. We suggest the employment of BC concentrated as a pool at an unused node. The BC pool is readily used as a replacement or to reduce network traffic load in the event where controller malfunction occur due to attack and failure. Compared to ARC, the ARE_C proved to reduce cost of network planning in BC and link cost while tackling demand issue due to network expansion.

Keywords: Software-defined network · Controller placement · Recovery · Expansion · Attack-aware algorithm

1 Introduction

Software Defined Network (SDN) redefined the backbone network architecture of data center and telco network integrating a unified and centralized control across multiple network components. SDN design minimizes the cost for the network planning and operation when compared to conventional IP network architecture [1, 2]. It is also worth

G. Wang et al. (Eds.): SpaCCS 2020, LNCS 12382, pp. 228–240, 2021.
https://doi.org/10.1007/978-3-030-68851-6_16

notice that SDN is highly scalable to support expansion of network over time as user demand increases.

In spite of that, SDN architecture faces a lethal security threat that will possibly cause the network to shutdown partially and eventually escalate to incapacitate whole network when under DDoS attack [3]. Network forwarding function is the core feature of a network to allow transmission of data. A single fault or error at the control layer will soon impact the data layer in directing the flow of the network forwarding which leads to buffer overflow scenario known as single point failure [4]. Researcher in [4] outlined several techniques to counter single point failure in SDN, such as mitigation, detection and prevention. Detection method usually works in pair with mitigation technique. Detection methods start off by identifying possible attack and type of attack in prior and utilize the information to devise an attack mitigation plan. Mitigation method is responsible to dynamically rerouting network flow to avoid buffer overflow and reducing the load of controller under attack. Prevention requires planning ahead of attack or failure and planning for recovery which is conventionally done by placing additional backup controller. A prior work, Attack-aware Recovery Controller-switch link cost minimization placement algorithm, ARC, was proposed to perform recovery placement in SDN [5]. It places one or more backup controller at each node with high frequency of attack or failure. Network expansion problem is excluded from the model and the placement yielded by ARC is not versatile to adapt to changes in network requirement. Thus, in this article, a new algorithm, Attack-Aware Recovery and Expansion controller-link-switch Cost minimization placement in software defined network (ARE_C) is proposed to reduce the cost of network planning while tackling demand issue due to network expansion.

In Sect. 2, the related work of SDN controller placement is described. Section 3 illustrates the proposed algorithm of ARE_C. Performance evaluation and results comparison of ARE-C is presented in Sect. 4. Summary is given in Sect. 5.

2 Related Works

In this section, the related work from the top of the SDN controller placement to down of the defense mechanism will all be discussed. Algorithm in [6] provides defense mechanism using real-time monitoring and generates switch placement for SDN. Similar to [6, 7] is capable of detecting potential DoS attack on the fly and placing Intrusion Detection System (IDS) into a network. While both [6] and [7] focused on mitigation method to counter potential attack, backup controller placement and SDN expansion issue is excluded from consideration in both model. Meanwhile, [8] pointed out the issue of network expansion and suggested a technique to overcome the issue by introducing new network components into existing SDN with concern of cost reduction. Nonetheless, the technique does not consider possibility of controller failure and attack. Researcher in [9] proposed a solution for electric power or data communication network expansion problem by utilizing SDN architecture and a centralized controller for dynamic rerouting and network restoration. Network component placement, however, is excluded from the solution proposed.

With the above shortcoming, it is our objective to introduce an attack-aware recovery and expansion backup controller placement method (ARE_C) to provide BC placement and selection with the intention of minimizing cost of network planning. Moreover, ARE_C is modeled to ameliorate recovery placement problem caused by network expansion. ARE_C uses a pool approach to generate array of distinct BC, BC Pool. BC Pool is placed into network at an unused state that is centralized among nodes that is prone to attack or failure. This is to remedy an existing SDN with anticipation of attack and failure by reducing the load of controller which is under attack.

3 Attack-Aware Recovery and Expansion Backup Controller Cost Minimization Placement Algorithm (ARE_C)

3.1 Description

ARE_C deals with selection and placement problem of BC in SDN. It yields pseudo-random selections of backup controller and group them in a pool. The fitness of each BC to be chosen is computed by determining the significance of metrics in each BC over the aggregated score of all metrics. The list of available BC is then sorted to produce a negative binomial distribution order of arrangement such that the most suitable BC is placed somewhere in the list that is near to the head of the list to increase the chance of being selected. The average of 100 and above pseudo-random generated (seeding with date time) numbers is acquired to identify the BC to be selected into pool. ARE_C then proceeds to place the pool of backup controller(s) at an unused node that is relatively close to nodes with controller that is exposed to potential attack or failure by employing Adelson-Velsky and Landis (AVL) binary tree.

There are several inputs required to operate this method.

- Controllers of different type with specification on the number of port, processing power, quantity and cost.
- Switches of varying type with specification on the number of packet and quantity.
- BC of different type with specification on the number of port, processing power, quantity and cost.
- Individual network node with its ascending identification number start from one.
- Frequency of attack at each node based on application type. The method will generates more backup controllers in the following scenario:

  i) network operations which requires high availability such as military, health, banking and data centre or/and
  ii) those nodes which experiencing higher frequency of attack or/and
  iii) the changes in demand of processing power caused by expansion of network over time.

- Link of various types with bandwidth and cost.
- Existing network components placement matrix of controllers, switches, links, and BC.

3.2 Notation

- *Sets:*

  1. $C = \{c_1, c_2, \ldots\}$, set of controllers of type $c \in C$ that is available to be selected.

     - j^c, the number of port of a controller of type $c \in C$.
     - k^c, processing power of a controller of type $c \in C$.
     - v^c, cost of a controller of type $c \in C$.
     - t^c, controller quantity of type $c \in C$.

  2. $R = \{c_1, c_2, \ldots\}$, combination of controllers of type $r \in R$ that is selected from C to be installed in the SDN with the following property

     - j^r, the number of port of a controller of type $r \in R$.
     - k^r, processing power of a controller of type $r \in R$.
     - v^r, cost of a controller of type $r \in R$.
     - t^r, controller quantity of type $r \in R$.

  3. $S = \{s_1, s_2, \ldots\}$, set of switches to be placed.

     - p^s, the number of packet of a switch of type $s \in S$.

  4. $B = \{b_1, b_2, \ldots\}$, set of backup controllers that is available to be installed.

     - j^b, the number of port of a controller of type $b \in B$.
     - k^b, processing power of a controller of type $b \in B$.
     - v^b, cost of a controller of type $b \in B$.
     - t^b, controller quantity of type $b \in B$.

  5. $L = \{l_1, l_2, \ldots\}$, set of link types that can be used to connect controller to controller, backup controller to controller, and switches to controller.

     - v^l, cost of a link of type $l \in L$.
     - b^l, bandwidth Mbps of a link of type $l \in L$.

  6. $N = \{1, 2, \ldots\}$, set of network nodes that can be installed with a controller.

     - i, index of a node where $i \in N$.
     - f^i, frequency of attack or failure at node i where $i \in N$ according to application requirement.

  7. M, set of end nodes that mirror the set of nodes N and can be connected to a connector node in N to form a matrix of connection.

- *Constant:*

  1. D_{ab} = Range between two points 'a' to 'b'. It's the distance between either two controllers D_{NM}, switch to controller D_{SC} or backup controller to controller D_{BC}.

- *Decision variables:*

  1. $T_{ci} = 1$, if a controller of type c $\in$ C is installed to node i $\in$ N, else 0.
  2. $T_{bi} = 1$, if a backup controller of type b $\in$ B is installed to node i $\in$ N, else 0.
  3. $Z_{si}^l = 1$, if a link of type l $\in$ L is connected between switches of type s $\in$ S and controller installed at node i $\in$ N, else 0.
  4. $R_{bi}^l = 1$, if a link of type l $\in$ L is connected between backup controller of type b $\in$ B and controller installed at node i $\in$ N, else 0.
  5. $R_{ih}^l = 1$, if a controller location i $\in$ N is connected to controller location h $\in$ M where h $\neq$ i with a link of type l $\in$ L, else 0.

3.3 Formulation of ARE_C

Cost of network planning is denoted as objective function f_v. The objective function f_v is defined by summation of the cost of selected controller, f_C, backup controller, f_B, link for connection of controller to switch, f_{LS}, link for connection of backup controller to controller, f_{LB}, and link for connection of controller to controller at different nodes, f_{LC}.

- Cost of all controller placed into network.

$$f_C = \sum_{c=1}^{|C|} v^c \times T_{ci} \quad \forall i \in N \tag{1}$$

- Cost of all BC placed into network.

$$f_B = \sum_{b=1}^{|B|} v^b \times T_{bi} \quad \forall i \in N \tag{2}$$

- Cost of link used for connection of controller to switch.

$$f_{LS} = \sum_{l=1}^{|L|} v^l \times Z_{si}^l \times D_{SC} \quad \forall i \in N, \forall s \in S \tag{3}$$

- Cost of link used for connection of BC to controller.

$$f_{LB} = \sum_{l=1}^{|L|} v^l \times R_{bi}^l \times D_{BC} \quad \forall i \in N, \forall b \in B \tag{4}$$

- Cost of link used for connection of controller to controller at different nodes.

$$f_{LC} = \sum_{l=1}^{|L|} v^l \times R_{ih}^l \times D_{NM} \quad \forall i \in N, \quad \forall h \in M \tag{5}$$

- Existing network components placement matrix of controllers, switches, links, and BC.

$$minimize\ f_v = f_C + f_B + f_{LS} + f_{LB} + f_{LC} \qquad (6)$$

The objective of ARE_C is to minimize the objective function value and subject to the following constraints:

- Ensure that the number of controller placed is n.

$$\sum_{c=1}^{|C|}\sum_{i=1}^{|N|} T_{ci} = n \qquad (7)$$

where $T_{ci} \in \{0, 1\}$, 1 when there is a controller placed in node i, and otherwise 0.
- Ensure that each switch is only connected to one and only one controller.

$$\sum_{i=1}^{|N|} Z_{si}^l \leq 1 \quad \forall s \in S, \forall l \in L. \qquad (8)$$

where $Z_{SN}^L \in \{0, 1\}$, 1 if there is a switch connected to a controller in node i for switch s, and otherwise 0.
- Ensure that each switch is connected to a node that has a controller installed in it.

$$\sum_{i=1}^{|N|} Z_{si}^l \leq T_{ci}$$

$$\forall s \in S, \forall l \in L, \forall c \in C. \qquad (9)$$

- Ensure that the total processing power of all BC in pool equals to larger than or equal to the sum of processing power of controller at nodes that has frequency of attack $f^i > 0$.

$$\sum_{b=1}^{|B|} T_{bi} * k^b \geq \sum_{c=1}^{|C|} T_{ci} * k^c \quad \forall i \in N \qquad (10)$$

where $T_{bi} \in \{0, 1, 3, ..., n\}$, $n > 0$ when there is a backup controller pool placed in node i, and otherwise 0.
- Ensure only one link is used for each connection.

$$\sum_{l=1}^{|L|}\sum_{s=1}^{|S|}\sum_{i=1}^{|N|} Z_{si}^l = |S| \qquad (11)$$

$$\sum_{l=1}^{|L|}\sum_{i=1}^{|N|}\sum_{b=1}^{|B|} R_{bi}^l = \sum_{i=1}^{|N|}\sum_{b=1}^{|B|} T_{bi} \qquad (12)$$

$$\sum_{l=1}^{|L|}\sum_{i=1}^{|N|}\sum_{h=1}^{|N|} R_{ih}^l = \sum_{i=1}^{n}(n-i) \tag{13}$$

where $Z_{si}^l \in \{0, 1\}$, 1 if there is a switch connected to a controller in node i for switch s, and otherwise 0. $R_{bi}^l \in \{0, 1\}$, 1 if there is a backup controller connected to a node with controller in node i, and otherwise 0. $R_{ih}^L \in \{0, 1\}$, 1 if there is a node with controller connected to another node with controller in node i and j, and otherwise 0.

3.4 Algorithm

Processing power and the number of port required by all controllers at node that is prone to attack or failure is calculated in Step 1 as shown in Fig. 1. Step 2 to 9 is a generalization of multiple-objectives genetic algorithm. Sum of fitness score of BC is generated in Step 2. Step 3 calculates the fitness score of each available BC using weighted sum fitness function. BC list is sorted in Step 4 in apropos to the positively skewed Negative Binomial Distribution (NBD) where the fittest backup controller is distributed at right end of BC list till left end region which is close to center of BC list. Next, Step 5 to 9 is a loop to iteratively use the mean of 100 pseudo-random generated number which value is lesser but close to 0.5 to select BC based on their fitness score into a pool. In Step 10, all available nodes in the network is appended into an AVL binary tree. In step 11 shown in Fig. 1, the occupied and used nodes are removed from the AVL binary tree iteratively. The root node of the AVL binary tree is selected as the node to host the BC pool. AVL binary tree is utilized to identify a node that is unused and centralized between all nodes that are prone to attack or failure. As such, the BC pool is placed at the selected node and connected to all affected nodes. It is worth notice that the connections between all affected nodes are removed and replaced by direct linking to BC pool. This technique will reduce number of link used as the size of network increases. Link with sufficient bandwidth and cost is selected to connect the backup controller pool node to controller at the affected node.

Finally, matrices of controller-to-node connection, T_{ci}, backup controller-to-node connection, T_{bi}, switch-to-node connection, Z_{si}^l, link used for backup controller-to-node connection, R_{bi}^l, link used for node-to-node connection, R_{ih}^l, and the cost of all network components, f_v are produced as an output from the algorithm. Active connection is indicated as positive (1) in the matrices, otherwise negative (0).

A case of single BC placement is pictured in Fig. 2 while normal BC pool placement case is demonstrated in Fig. 3.

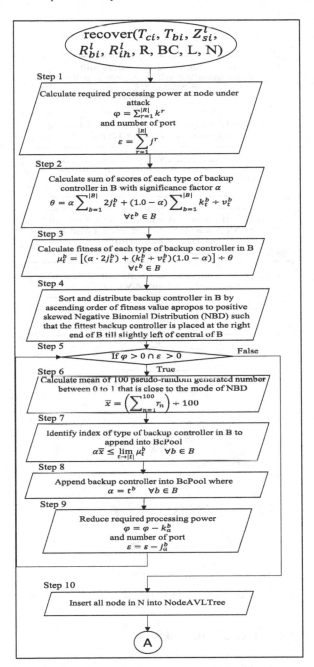

Fig. 1. ARE_C algorithm

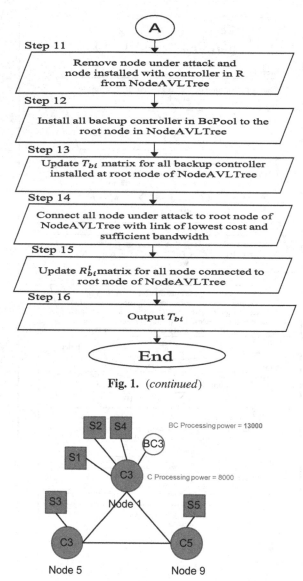

Fig. 1. (*continued*)

Fig. 2. Single BC placement case from ARE_C method

4   Simulation Result and Analysis

Multiple tests were conducted but only five most representative test cases of different characteristics are selected to demonstrate the effectiveness of the proposed scheme on a computer with Intel Core i7-4720HQ CPU at 2.60 GHz and 16 GB RAM running Windows 10 operating system. Table 1 tabulated all the summarized information of test cases. Test case 1 and 2 are SDN outputted from ARC method [5] in prior work. The remaining is derived from real world scenario.

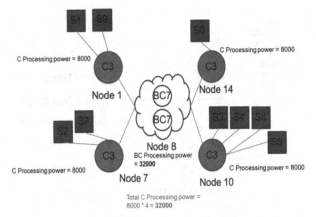

Fig. 3. BC pool placement from ARE_C method

Table 1. Difference among input

Difference	Test case				
	1	*2*	*3*	*4*	*5*
|B|	190	75	190	190	280
Objective function value, f_v	64451.75	43350.75	43452.75	18850.75	324507.75
Network grid, $g - \|N\| \times \|N\|$	9×9	9×9	15×15	15×15	100×100
Cost of backup controller	20500.00	9200.00	24400.00	4600.00	162200.00
Total processing power of controller at node affected by attack or failure	47000	8000	32000	16000	99000
Total processing power of backup controller	85000	18500	54500	8000	360000
Total cost of link	1451.75	1650.75	1052.75	750.75	16307.75

Statistics from Fig. 4 demonstrated the consistency of ARE_C method to yield recovery placement with lowest cost (with slight deviation) in all test cases with test size of 1000 without compromising on metrics such as processing power and number of port.

For complexity analysis of ARE_C, the runtime analysis provided in Fig. 5, ARE_C logically has the best case of O(n) and is bounded to worst case of O(n log n) due to the employment of AVL binary tree data type. The test is conducted using test case 1 from Table 1 and repeated it for a number of times, n to observe the performance of ARE_C.

The simulation result of ARE_C on the five test cases is outlined in Table 2. Total processing power of controller at node affected by attack or failure is a constant variable as ARE_C does not meddle with the placement of controllers and switches in a network.

Test case 5 peaked the rank with 100 by 100 network grid which increases the complexity of ARE_C by introducing more choices. Test case 1, 2, 3, and 5 have their total processing power of BC exceeded the total processing power of controllers at nodes

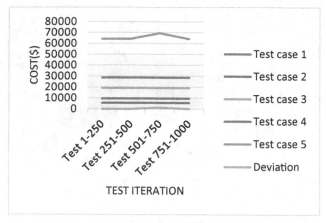

Fig. 4. Deviation test of ARE_C method.

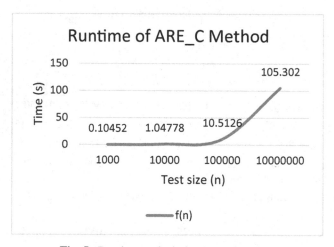

Fig. 5. Runtime analysis for ARE_C method

affected. As a result, wastage in processing power and cost is presented. Contrariwise, test case 4 supply is insufficient to support the demand Test Case 1 and 5 have higher demand and, therefore, require more BC in general. Thus, the BC selection will consumes longer time.

Table 2 portrayed the potency of ARE_C with enhancement of placing a pool of backup controller to a SDN based on the frequency of attack or failure at node according to application requirement. ARE_C is fed with unenhanced SDN to generate an enhanced version of SDN.

Meanwhile, comparison of original network and enhanced network using ARE_C for all test cases is portrayed in Fig. 6. The results between original SDN and ARE_C enhanced SDN is compared with metrics such as objective function value, total cost of backup controller, average total processing power of backup controller, and average total

Table 2. ARE_C simulation result

Difference	Test case				
	1	*2*	*3*	*4*	*5*
Objective function value, f_v	71851	39650	37451	23650	223502
Cost of backup controller	28500	5500	19000	9500	64000
Total processing power of controller at node affected by attack or failure	47000	8000	32000	16000	99000
Total processing power of backup controller	48000	9000	32000	16000	112000
Total cost of link	851.00	1650.00	451	650	13502

cost of link. It is obvious that ARE_C enhanced SDN has lower cost for dedicated for link, and in some cases, lower objective function value. Another important improvement is the overall difference between total processing power of controller at node affected by attack or failure and total processing power of backup controller is lesser after enhanced by ARE_C. This shows that the processing power of backup controller pool is just enough to handle the load of affected node without too much of wastage.

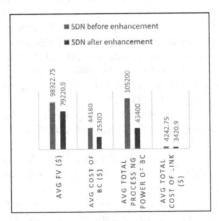

Fig. 6. Comparison of original SDN and ARE_C enhanced SDN

5 Conclusion

In this article, an attack-aware recovery placement scheme with objective of minimizing cost named as ARE_C is proposed to address recovery placement under network expansion for existing SDN. The proposed scheme is tested in five different test cases ranging from simple to very complex network configurations. The result demonstrates that the proposed ARE_C scheme achieved cost reduction while tackling with recovery placement problem introduced by network expansion in existing SDN. In conclusion,

ARE_C is characterized by its agile and generic nature for being capable to solve problem of different sizes and inputs. In conclusion, ARE_C can be deemed as a noteworthy preventive approach for cost reduction and recovery placement for existing SDN on the run.

Acknowledgment. This research is supported by grants from TM R&D. This research work is fully supported by Telekom Malaysia (TM) R&D and Multimedia University (MMU), Cyberjaya, Malaysia. We are very thankful to the team of TM R&D for providing the support to our research studies.

References

1. Karakus, M., Durresi, A.: Economic viability of software defined networking (SDN). Comput. Netw. **135**, 81–95 (2018)
2. Guodong, W., Yanxiao, Z., Jun, H., Wei, W.: The controller placement problem in software defined networking: a survey. IEEE Netw. **31**(5), 21–27 (2017)
3. Scott-Hayward, S., O'Callaghan, G., Sezer, S.: SDN security: a survey. In: IEEE SDN for Future Networks and Services (SDN4FNS), pp. 1–7 (2013)
4. Fonseca, P., Bennesby, R., Mota, E., Passito, A.: A replication component for resilient OpenFlow-based networking. In: Network Operations and Management Symposium (NOMS), pp. 933–939. IEEE (2012)
5. Qin, C., Chin, T., Kwang, L., Yusoff, Z., Kaspin, R.: Attack-aware recovery controller-switch-link cost minimization placement algorithm in software-defined networking. In: Wang, G., Feng, J., Bhuiyan, M., Lu, R. (eds.) SpaCCS 2019. LNCS, vol. 11611, pp. 297–308. Springer, Cham (2019). https://doi.org/10.1007/978-3-030-24907-6_23
6. Collaborative theory-based DDoS (Distributed Denial of Service Attack) defence system and method. CN Patent CN106921666A, July 4 (2017)
7. Dridi, L., Zhani, M.: A holistic approach to mitigating DoS attacks in SDN networks: a holistic approach to mitigating DoS attacks in SDN networks. Int. J. Netw. Manag. **28**(1), e1996 (2018). https://doi.org/10.1002/nem.1996
8. Sallahi, A., St-Hilaire, M.: Expansion model for the controller placement problem in software defined networks. IEEE Commun. Lett. **21**(2), 274–277 (2017). https://doi.org/10.1109/LCOMM.2016.2621746
9. Zhang, X., Wei, K., Guo, L., Hou, W., Wu, J.: SDN-based resilience solutions for smart grids. In: 2016 International Conference Software Networking (ICSN), pp. 1–5. IEEE, May 2016

A Weighted Federated Averaging Framework to Reduce the Negative Influence from the Dishonest Users

Fengpan Zhao[1], Yan Huang[2(✉)], Saide Zhu[1], Venkata Malladi[2], and Yubao Wu[1]

[1] Department of Computer Science, Georgia State University,
Atlanta, GA 30303, USA
{fzhao6,szhu5}@student.gsu.edu, ywu28@gsu.edu
[2] Department of Software Engineering and Game Development,
Kennesaw State University, Kennesaw, GA 30144, USA
yhuang24@kennesaw.edu, vmalladi@students.kennesaw.edu

Abstract. Federated learning becomes popular for it can train an excellent performance global model without exposing clients' privacy. However, most FL applications failed to consider there exists fake local trained models returned from attackers or dishonest users. Not only would the fake parameters be harmful to the convergence of the global model but also be wasting of other users' computational resources. In this paper, we propose a framework to grade the users' credit score based on the performances of the returned local models on the testing dataset. We also consider historical data using the exponential moving average to give a relatively higher weight for the most recent testing results. The experiments show that our system can efficiently and effectively find out the fake local models and then speed up the convergence of the global model.

Keywords: Federated learning · Fake model · Exponential moving average · Weighted federated averaging

1 Introduction

Recently, wild-distributed machine learning applications convenience people's daily life in plenty of aspects. However, most of these applications require collecting users' data from multiple kinds of IoT devices into the data center [1], which inevitably increases the chance to touch clients' private data [2]. Collecting users' data to the central server will cause a privacy leak. There's no denying that a large number of researches provide plenty of algorithms to protect users' privacy in a variety of aspects. It's generally recognized that clients' privacy is a significant problem since the data privacy-related laws are published or preparing [3]. For instance, the European data protection rules, designed by EU data Protection Regulation, begun to take effect on May 25, 2018 [4]. On the other

© Springer Nature Switzerland AG 2021
G. Wang et al. (Eds.): SpaCCS 2020, LNCS 12382, pp. 241–250, 2021.
https://doi.org/10.1007/978-3-030-68851-6_17

hand, people now have the right to decline the related data-usage statistic agreement directly when they are using the associated applications. These restrictions and changes, in turn, require the traditional machine learning to find out a novel training process to obtain a well-trained model. Nothing is more important than the fact that keep the data under users' supervision [5].

In 2016, Federated Learning (FL) [6] provided an innovative way to train the model by distributing the model to the clients' devices and avoid the server directly collecting data into the data center. Federated Averaging (FedAvg) is one popular tool in FL [6]. The Fig. 1 shows the structure of FedAvg. Mainly, a server randomly picks up several participants from available devices and shares a global model with them. Those selected devices locally train the received model and then return it to the server. The server then aggregates the returned local models together. Then it will iterates the procedure many times till the shared model becomes convergence.

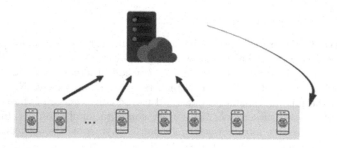

Fig. 1. FedAvg structure.

Most FL applications assume that the selected devices are honest and aggregate the returned models without detecting the attackers or dishonest clients. However, in some FL applications, the fake local model has brought much harm in aggregating the demand of the shared model. First, it slows down the convergence of the global model, which wastes a large number of computing resources and communication time. Second, it acts as noisy that reduce the accuracy of the global model.

To deal with this problem, we design a system to evaluate each user's credit to detect the attackers or dishonest devices. The difficulty lies in how to effectively pick up those give the noisy to our model without treat the honest to the bad one. In this paper, we prepare a test dataset to verify every returned local model, give a weight based on the testing accuracy and then apply a time series averaging method to give weight to each user to merge into the global model. The natural idea comes from finding out the poor performance returned local models through a testing procedure. Although it seems add extra steps and in turn cost extra time, the whole procedure will definitely boost the convergence of the global model due to the high demand of the communication cost. Our experiments show the difference in details. It can be said with certainty that out method can not only speedup the convergence of the model but also reduce the affect from the attackers or dishonest devices. Our main contribution are as follows:

- We design a evaluation system to compute user's credit to detect the dishonest devices. The dishonest devices with poor performance will not participate the aggregation of the global model.
- We designed a new strategy that consider the historical performances from each round as time series and use Exponential Moving Averages (EMA) to calculate devices' weights.
- We can also detect normal users but with special events happened such as offline suddenly, device power off, etc. The strategy can skip these users at current stage but re-consider them after several rounds if they turn into normal condition.

2   Related Work

The privacy preservation is more important than ever before because of the massive data generated from Social Networks [7], IoT [8], Smart City [9], Industry 4.0 [10], etc. To preserve privacy in AI training, the concept of FL was first introduced in [6]. It can train the global model without leak the users' privacy. The server selects users as participants to distribute the shared model to the IoT devices. The participants use their raw data to train the model and return the model to the server. The users' raw data keep on their own devices. The server will aggregate the returned models, and then the server repeats the procedure many times until the model become stable. This strategy gives research organizations and industries a novel solution to train a model without touching users' raw data, which in turn protects users' privacy.

There are some sophisticated federated learning methods published recently. In [11], Zhu and Jin provide a multi-objective evolutionary algorithm to reduce the communication time. Meanwhile, the global model can be trained efficiently, especially in a scalable environment, by encoding the network connectivity. The methods from reinforcement learning under federated learning also offered effective solutions under federated settings [12,13]. In [14], Smith et al. provide a multi-task based federated learning method. The theory deals with high communication cost and fault tolerance under federated settings. In [15], Kang et al. give reliable federated learning on mobile networks. They use consortium blockchain techniques to manage the users' reputation. The simulations show that their method can improve the reliability of the global model [15]. However, we consider that the users' resources are valuable and we prefer to consume more energy from the server instead of users', we provide a credit score grading framework to distribute the weights to users then further reduce the negative influence from the dishonest users.

3   Algorithm Design

In this section, we first present a quick review of the Federated Averaging (FedAvg) [6], then give details of our framework.

3.1 Background: Federated Averaging

In FedAvg settings, there is a center server that selects u_a devices in each stage from u devices [6]. At each stage, the server distributes the shared model w_t to those selected devices. Every device trains the received global model separately with the same parameter settings, such as the same local epochs, the same learning rate *eta* [6]. Once the local model training is completed, it sends back the model to the server at once.

The server aggregates the local models when it receives all selected devices' return as follows [6]:

$$w_{t+1} = \sum_{i=1}^{U_a} p_i w_{t+1}^i,$$ (1)

where p_i is [6]:

$$p_i = \frac{N_i}{N},$$ (2)

N_i represents the data sizes in *ith* device, N is samples size and $\sum_i p_i = 1$ [16].
The objective of FedAvg is [6] :

$$min_w f_{(w)} = \sum_{i=1}^{U} p_i F_i(w),$$ (3)

where F_i is average loss of the prediction on *ith* device and is calculated by [6]

$$F_i(w) = \frac{1}{N_i} \sum_{j \in N_i} \ell(j; w),$$ (4)

where the $\ell(j; w)$ is the loss of the prediction on the sample j with parameters w.

3.2 Overview: Self-weighted Federated Averaging

We design a credit score grading system to evaluate users' reliability and then give different weights to users. Instead of randomly choosing devices in each round and then treating them equally without checking out the negative influences from some unusual users, we evaluate the returned models at each round and then give the weights based on the performance.

Figure 2 shows the structure of our framework. We first select users from the available users with equal opportunity and send the global model. After all, devices have finished the training, before averaging the returned gradients, we run the local models on a test dataset and use the testing accuracy to evaluate the models' performance. Moreover, we use the exponential moving average [17] method to compute the score for users. The global model can then be aggregated and updated according to the credit score. The procedure repeats many times until the global model's performance is stable. Our objective is minimizing the summation of prediction losses from all devices with corresponding weight:

$$min_w f_{(w)} = \sum_{i=1}^{U} W_i p_i F_i(w),$$ (5)

where W_i stands for the computed credit score ith device.

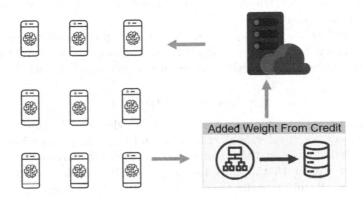

Fig. 2. Algorithm framework

3.3   The Grading System Designing

We design this grading system to calculate the weights for each client by evaluating their overall performance. The system considers the current users' testing accuracy and uses a time series method to obtain a relatively balanced weight for every user. Mainly, there are two stages to compute the score for each selected client in our proposed grading system. The first part tests the returned local model's performance on the testing dataset, and the second part is maintaining and updating a global matrix to grading the credit score to each user.

Testing Accuracy as Grading Factor. Every round, a specific number of devices will be randomly selected to participate in training and then return the locally trained model to the server. Before sending the local model to the server for aggregating demand, we first apply the returned models to a testing dataset. The performance is evaluated by the testing accuracy directly. Generally, those returned fake models cannot achieve satisfying testing results.

Historical Scores as Round Series Data. However, directly using the current testing results as the weight to mark a user as dishonest is not accurate since some normal users may return a 'fake' model occasionally due to the bad connection, the complex communication condition. To avoid this, we consider the historical testing results from previous rounds to grade the credit score.

We maintain a grading matrix G storing the testing results. Each row stores each users' performance, and each column indicates each round. The element in this matrix is g_{it}, which is the testing accuracy tested by the local model trained on ith device at rth round. After we get the latest testing accuracy, we calculate an overall credit score for each client with it along with their historical data by using the exponential moving average (EMA) [17]. It is worth pointing out that our data is round series, which can be considered as time series if we mark each round as a time point.

Exponential Moving Average is one of the most popular techniques to deal with time-series data. Unlike moving average treat every data point equally, the EMA method gives a higher weight to recent observations than the older one. It is computed by [17]:

$$W_{it} = \alpha g_{it} + (1 - \alpha)W_{i(t-1)}, \tag{6}$$

where W_{it} means the computed weight of ith device at rth round, g_{it} is the testing accuracy for ith device at rth round and the W_{it-1} is previous round's weight. By default, we set the $alpha$ to 0.9 to reach the purpose of giving relatively higher weight to the most recent points. W_{i0} could be initialized by computing g_{i0}. We mitigate the recent older results from exponential computing and give relatively more weight to last weights. This formula gives us a flexible solution to detect unusual users. The regular users with special events happened may be marked as dishonest at the current stage, but they can be re-participate the training when they have a reasonable performance again. In other words, the past data are not that important for the latest weight. For dishonest users, they are still be blocked if recent performances are still weak. The most recent data is more heavily weighted. The pseudo-code is shown in Algorithm 1.

4   Experiments

In this section, we present the details of the federated settings and the experiment results. The experiments are completed in Python 3.7, and deployed on a server with Intel I9-9820× 3.30 GHZ 64 GB CPU, GeForce RTX 2080 Ti GPU, 32G memory, and Ubuntu 18.04 OS.

4.1   Data Source

We select two ground-truth datasets, MNIST and CIFAR-10, to evaluate the difference between the FedAvg and our proposed framework. The MNIST dataset [18] is a handwritten digits dataset where images are classified into 10 classes. The dataset consists of 60,000 training images and 10,000 test images [18]. The last image dataset, CIFAR-10, contains a smaller size than the previous two, with 50,000 images for training and 10,000 images for testing. The images are in 32×32 pixel intensities [19].

Algorithm 1. Grading Score Algorithm

    Input: w_{t+d}, H, N
    Output: to do

1: **Server executes:**
2: $t \leftarrow 0$;
3: initialize w_0, G;
4: **for** $t = 0,..,T$ -1
5:     $S_t \leftarrow$ (indices of u_a randomly selected clients from n)
6:     server send w_t to r selected clients;
7:     **for** i in S_t
8:         $w_{t+1}^i \leftarrow$ (client locally train w_t);
9:         $g_{ie} \leftarrow$ (testing accuracy from the w_{t+1}^i);
10:         Update G;
11:         $W_{it} \leftarrow \alpha g_{it} + (1 - \alpha)W_{it-1}$
12:     $w_{t+1} \leftarrow \sum_i^{S_t} W_{it} \frac{n_i}{n} w_{t+1}^i$;

4.2 Experiments Setup

We compare our framework with FedAvg in a particular environment that there are dishonest users. For the simulation, we have two kinds of users. The first type of user is the regular user, and the second one is the dishonest user. We select five dishonest among a total of 100 users as fraudulent users. All dishonest users have a 5 percent opportunity to be selected each round in our experiments.

According to [6], we set similar parameters of the Convolutional neural network (CNN) in our federated settings. We set the total round E to 100, the ϵ to 0.5. We distribute the images to 100 users, and we randomly select ten users as a dishonest user. At each round, we intentionally choose one untrustworthy user who will return the fake model to the server.

4.3 Experiments Results

To illustrate our experiments' results, we first evaluate the effectiveness of our framework and then show its efficiency compared to FedAvg in a particular simulation environment.

Effectiveness. In Fig. 3, we show the detected dishonest users for the MNIST. The x-axis is the IDs of returned local models, and the y-axis is the testing accuracy of the corresponding local model before aggregation. The commons users are marked as green dots, and the detected unusual user is red 'x'. It verifies our assumption that the unusual user can be effectively detected based on the testing results.

Following the procedures introduced in the previous section, different weights will be given to the returned models, and then be merged and calculated with

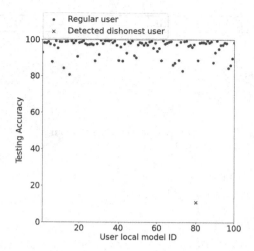

Fig. 3. MNIST testing accuracy at round 100 (Color figure online)

historical weights together. The global model then is aggregated based on the latest moving averages rank. Table 1 shows the final global model testing accuracies. The higher accuracy is in bold. We can see that our framework has higher final accuracies at round 100 than the FedAvg's under our simulation that there is one dishonest user per round.

Table 1. The final global model testing accuracies at around 100.

Data set	Testing accuracy	
	FedAvg	Credit-based FedAvg
MNIST	0.91	**0.95**
CIFAR-10	0.19	**0.49**

Efficiency. The Fig. 4 shows the training loss from the two benchmarks. The x-axis indicates which round and the y-axis is the corresponding training loss. For all two datasets, we can see that our credit-based FedAvg curves become stabilized earlier than FedAvg, and the training loss are higher than the FedAvg curve. For dataset MNIST, compared with FedAvg, our credit-based FedAvg curve stops fluctuating around round 58, and for CIFAR-10, it is around 73. However, for all two datasets, the FedAvg curves are all still fluctuating. Thus, the figures lead us to the conclusion that our framework efficiently trains the global model.

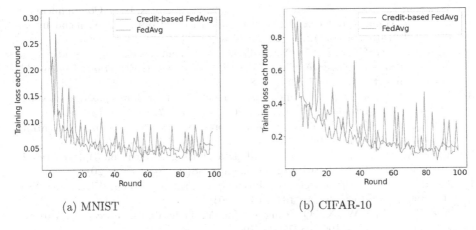

(a) MNIST   (b) CIFAR-10

Fig. 4. Training loss with $E = 100$

5 Conclusion

The global model's performance could be affected by dishonest users or attackers who returned the fake local trained models to the server. We design and implement a credit score grading system to give users dynamic weights to mitigate the influences from the fake local models before the server aggregates the global model. We test the returned local models on the testing dataset and then use the exponential moving average method to calculate the latest users' weight. The simulations on two ground truth datasets, MNIST and Cifar-10, show that our new system can effectively detect the dishonest user. The global model trained in our framework can achieve convergence effectively and efficiently.

Acknowledgments. This research is supported, in part, by the SunTrust Fellowship Grant (ST20-07).

References

1. Li, K., Lu, G., Luo, G., Cai, Z.: Seed-free graph de-anonymiztiation with adversarial learning. In: Proceedings of the 29th ACM International Conference on Information & Knowledge Management, pp. 745–754 (2020)
2. Liang, Y., Cai, Z., Yu, J., Han, Q., Li, Y.: Deep learning based inference of private information using embedded sensors in smart devices. IEEE Netw. **32**(4), 8–14 (2018)
3. Liu, Y., et al.: Federated forest. IEEE Trans. Big Data (2020)
4. De Hert, P., Papakonstantinou, V., Malgieri, G., Beslay, L., Sanchez, I.: The right to data portability in the GDPR: towards user-centric interoperability of digital services. Comput. Law Secur. Rev. **34**(2), 193–203 (2018)
5. Zheng, X., Cai, Z., Li, Y.: Data linkage in smart internet of things systems: a consideration from a privacy perspective. IEEE Commun. Mag. **56**(9), 55–61 (2018)

6. McMahan, B., Moore, E., Ramage, D., Hampson, S., Arcas, B.A.: Communication-efficient learning of deep networks from decentralized data. In: Artificial Intelligence and Statistics, pp. 1273–1282. PMLR (2017)
7. Cai, Z., He, Z., Guan, X., Li, Y.: Collective data-sanitization for preventing sensitive information inference attacks in social networks. IEEE Trans. Dependable Secure Comput. 15(4), 577–590 (2018)
8. Cai, Z., Zheng, X.: A private and efficient mechanism for data uploading in smart cyber-physical systems. IEEE Trans. Netw. Sci. Eng. 7(2), 766–775 (2020)
9. He, Z., Cai, Z., Yu, J.: Latent-data privacy preserving with customized data utility for social network data. IEEE Trans. Veh. Technol. 67(1), 665–673 (2018)
10. Zheng, X., Cai, Z.: Privacy-preserved data sharing towards multiple parties in industrial IoTs. IEEE J. Sel. Areas Commun. 38(5), 968–979 (2020)
11. Zhu, H., Jin, Y.: Multi-objective evolutionary federated learning. IEEE trans. Neural Netw. Learn. Syst. 31(4), 1310–1322 (2019)
12. Zhuo, H.H., Feng, W., Xu, Q., Yang, Q., Lin, Y.: Federated reinforcement learning. arXiv preprint arXiv:1901.08277 (2019)
13. Pang, J., Huang, Y., Xie, Z., Han, Q., Cai, Z.: Realizing the heterogeneity: a self-organized federated learning framework for IoT. IEEE Internet Things J. (2020)
14. Smith, V., Chiang, C.-K., Sanjabi, M., Talwalkar, A.S.: Federated multi-task learning. In: Advances in Neural Information Processing Systems, pp. 4424–4434 (2017)
15. Kang, J., Xiong, Z., Niyato, D., Zou, Y., Zhang, Y., Guizani, M.: Reliable federated learning for mobile networks. IEEE Wirel. Commun. 27(2), 72–80 (2020)
16. Li, T., Sanjabi, M., Smith, V.: Fair resource allocation in federated learning. ArXiv abs/1905.10497 (2020)
17. Klinker, F.: Exponential moving average versus moving exponential average. Mathematische Semesterberichte 58(1), 97–107 (2011)
18. LeCun, Y., Bottou, L., Bengio, Y., Haffner, P.: Gradient-based learning applied to document recognition. Proc. IEEE 86(11), 2278–2324 (1998)
19. Krizhevsky, A., Sutskever, I., Hinton, G.E.: Imagenet classification with deep convolutional neural networks. Commun. ACM 60(6), 84–90 (2017)

I Can Think Like You! Towards Reaction Spoofing Attack on Brainwave-Based Authentication

Wei-Yang Chiu[1], Weizhi Meng[1,3(✉)], and Wenjuan Li[2,3]

[1] Department of Applied Mathematics and Computer Science,
Technical University of Denmark, Lyngby, Denmark
weme@dtu.dk
[2] Department of Computing, Hong Kong Polytechnic University, Kowloon, China
[3] Institute of Artificial Intelligence and Blockchain, Guangzhou University,
Guangzhou, China

Abstract. In the coming period of Internet of Things (IoT), user authentication is one important and essential security mechanism to protect assets from unauthorized access. Textual passwords are the most widely adopted authentication method, but have well-known limitations in the aspects of both security and usability. As an alternative, biometric authentication has attracted much attention, which can verify users based on their biometric features. With the fast development of EEG (electro-encephalography) sensors in current headsets and personal devices, user authentication based on brainwaves becomes feasible. Due to its potential adoption, there is an increasing need to secure such emerging authentication method. In this work, we focus on a brainwave-based computer screen unlock mechanism, which can validate users based on their brainwave signals when seeing different images. Then, we analyze the security of such brainwave-based scheme and identify a kind of reaction spoofing attack where an attacker can try to imitate the mental reaction (either familiar or unfamiliar) of a legitimate user. In the user study, we show the feasibility and viability of such attack.

Keywords: EEG · Biometric authentication · Brainwave-based unlock · Biometric security · Reaction spoofing attack

1 Introduction

The Internet of Things (IoT) is developing speedily and steadily, which allows various Internet-enabled devices and equipment to be connected with each other [30]. The Gartner report [9] predicted that the market of enterprise and automotive IoT will grow by around 21% and reach 5.8 billion endpoints by the end of 2020, compared with 2019. With so many endpoint devices, user authentication becomes a necessary and important security mechanism to protect assets from unauthorized access.

The traditional user authentication scheme is mainly based on either textual passwords or hardware tokens (e.g., smart cards, keys), which requires

© Springer Nature Switzerland AG 2021
G. Wang et al. (Eds.): SpaCCS 2020, LNCS 12382, pp. 251–265, 2021.
https://doi.org/10.1007/978-3-030-68851-6_18

interrupting users to obtain their credentials. The system permits their access by successfully verifying their credentials. Password-based systems are still popular and widely used nowadays due to the simplicity and efficiency. However, such kind of authentication scheme may not be considered as user-friendly and secure enough in practice [7]. For example, a password-based system relies heavily on the complexity of the password. That is, the more complex or longer the password, the more secure the system. While due to both the long-term memory limitation [39] and the multiple password interference issue [24], users are often difficult to remember such complex (or random) strings. In this case, users may choose simple passwords instead, which greatly degrade the system security.

To complement the traditional password-based authentication, biometric authentication receives much more attention, which relies on the uniqueness of human's biological characteristics for authentication [21], such as face, hand, retina, fingerprint and so on. As compared with the traditional authentication scheme, the early adoption rate of biometric authentication is not high mainly due to the limitation of sensor accuracy and cost. With the recent advancement of technologies, sensors have become smaller, more accurate and more affordable. Biometrics as an authentication token are being considered in the market, i.e., many operating systems and platforms provide native support. For example, Microsoft introduces Windows Hello, an authentication method that allows users to take their fingerprints or face images as their credentials, and log into the system [11]. Google's Android platform provides the support for developers to combine their scheme with biometric authentication [12], and Apple's iOS platform also provides a similar library to support this [13].

More specifically, biometric authentication can be typically classified as either physiological authentication or behavioral authentication [21]. The former is based on the physical features for user authentication, like face, fingerprint, iris, palmprint, but the main limitation is that these features are constrained resources and cannot be changed. Table 1 shows some popular physiological features. If we considered each characteristic as a single set of passwords, we have a set of non-renewable passwords no greater than the number of 15.

Table 1. Utilizable sets of token of popular physiological authentication.

Biometrics method	Attributes Counts
Face	1
Fingerprints	10
Iris	2
Palmprints	2

With the advancement in bio-sensor technologies, brainwave research based on EEG (electro-encephalography) becomes very popular in recent years. Brainwave, a kind of complicated signal of the active brain, represents every single action or intent humans make. It gives a possibility to investigate the connection between specific brainwaves and actions. The Brain-Computer Interfaces (BCI) have been applied in some certain domains like healthcare [38] and security [8]. For brainwave-based authentication, EEG sensors can capture the brainwave signals and the system can verify the signal patterns for user authentication. For instance, Marcel and Millan [20] focused on user identification using brainwaves and introduced a statistical framework based on Gaussian mixture models and a posteriori model adaptation. Chuang et al. [6] studied the brainwave authentication and achieved an error rate of around 1% by setting a threshold for each user when they complete custom tasks.

Contributions. In practical usage, brainwave-based authentication also suffers from some challenges. One is that the authentication accuracy may be fluctuant due to high signal similarity of users [20]. While this issue can be mitigated when users perform a particular task. Then Becker et al. [2] tried to identify security issues of brainwave-based authentication by designing a comprehensive framework, but their work did not introduce any findings. With the increasing popularity of brainwave-based authentication, its security receives more attention. Motivated by this issue, the purpose of our work is to investigate the security of a particular brainwave-based authentication method, namely brainwave-based screen unlock. The contributions can be summarized as below.

- We advocate that the accuracy of brainwave-based authentication can be enhanced by giving users a particular task, and introduce a brainwave-based computer-screen unlock mechanism that can validate users based on their mental reaction to the displayed image.
- We then analyze such brainwave-based mechanism and introduce a kind of attack called *reaction spoofing attack*, where an attacker is able to unlock the screen by imitating the reaction of a legitimate user.
- In our user study with 37 participants, the results demonstrate the feasibility and viability of *reaction spoofing attack*.

The remaining parts of this paper are organized as follows. In Sect. 2, we review some related research studies about brainwave-based user authentication and screen unlock schemes. Section 3 describes the brainwave-based screen unlock mechanism and introduces our identified attack. Section 4 describes our experimental settings, analyzes the study results and discusses some challenges. We conclude our work in Sect. 5.

2   Related Work

2.1   Brainwave and User Authentication

The human brain is the complex and central organ of the human nervous system, which contains billions of nerve cells (namely neurons). Emotions and behaviours are the communication between neurons in the brain. Generally, the brain can include three major parts: the cerebrum, the brainstem and the cerebellum. The cerebrum is the largest part of the human brain, which connects the brainstem and the spinal cord.

Brainwaves are believed to be generated through synchronised electrical pulses from neurons. Our brainwaves can change according to our activities and feelings. People would feel tired when slower brainwaves are dominant, while the higher brainwaves would make people wired. Currently, we can capture brainwave signals using various headset-like devices. For instance, users can mount brainwave-sensing headset like Neurosky [32] and meditation made headband like Muse [29]. Some studies have shown that a computer system was able to identify a person's "brainprint" with nearly 100% accuracy [36]. Motivated by this trend, many research studies started focusing on applying brainwaves for user authentication.

As we know, traditional authentication schemes like password-based authentication often require interrupting or prompting the user to manually input or provide credentials, which may require more external equipment hooked on the device. Instead, the use of brainwaves does not need any physical interactions that can provide a transparent authentication process. As compared with some biometrics like fingerprint, brainwave signals are believed to be more difficult to copy and replay [2]. Moreover, brainwaves can be changed and revoked based on the authentication methods. For example, a person's brainwave signals can be different under particular tasks [41].

In addition, the traditional authentication scheme only checks the legitimacy of a user at the moment of user login. After that, the system would not require further authentication. Hence the scheme can only protect the system at the moment of login, but cannot secure the system during the whole session. Similar to some other biometrics like keystroke dynamics [26] and touch dynamics [25], brainwaves can provide a continuous authentication process as well. The system can keep checking the brainwave signals during the whole session.

2.2 Brainwave-Based Authentication

Similar to other biometrics, machine learning is an important tool for classifying brainwave signals. Many algorithms have been studied in EEG classification like kNN [40], Neural Network [4] and SVM [35]. For instance, Liew et al. [17] focused on EEG signals and explored the use of Fuzzy-Rough Nearest Neighbour (FRNN) classifier for EEG authentication. They extracted visual evoked potentials (VEPs) brainwaves data from the lateral and midline electrodes to elicit training and testing datasets. Based on the features like mean, cross-correlation and coherence, their algorithm could achieve an authentication rate of around 90%. To handle the issue of limited training data, they further introduced an Incremental Fuzzy-Rough Nearest Neighbour (IncFRNN) algorithm to reform the personalized knowledge granules via insertion and deletion of a participating object [18]. The algorithm of IncFRNN could reach an accuracy rate of around 96%, based on the similarity measures and predefined window size.

Marcel and Millan [20] used a statistical framework for personal EEG authentication based on Gaussian mixture models. By considering participants' reactions towards imagination movements and words consideration, their method could achieve an authentication rate of 93%. Tran et al. [35] focused on EEG data and introduced an SVM binary classification method to improve the performance of the minority class in imbalanced datasets. By exploring participants' reactions towards the motor imagery of hand, foot and tongue, their improved SVM could reach an accuracy rate of 96.10%. Chiu et al. [5] also focused on studying the link between experienced events and brainwave reaction, and established an authentication system based on such reactions. With an SVM classifier and 20 participants, their system could achieve an accuracy rate of almost 100%, which validated the results in [36].

Zhou et al. [41] explored the feasibility of extracting long-term memory ability from users' brainwaves and identified the bio-features in the brainwaves. In their settings, their SVM classifier could reach an authentication rate of 90%. Pham et al [33] advocated that EEG could enhance the existing authentication mechanisms, and introduced an approach of using EEG to authenticate users in a multilevel security systems. Users need to conduct motor imagery tasks while their EEG signals would be tested for authentication. Based on the Graz datasets 2008, their method could provide an accuracy rate of around 90%. They further introduced an algorithm of The Small Sphere Two Large Margins Support Vector Data Description (SS2LM-SVDD), in order to build an optimal hyper-sphere in feature space [34]. They then designed an improved multilevel security system by combining mental tasks, age and gender information, which could reach an accuracy rate of around 97%.

Altahat et al. [1] tried to identify the factors that may affect the robustness of EEG-based authentication. They explored some factors such as the enhancement threshold value, EEG frequency rhythms, mental task and the person identity on the selected EEG channels. Their results demonstrated that the idle mental task may provide the highest accuracy rates as compared with other mental tasks in the settings. They also showed that the combined frequency rhythms could provide better authentication performance than using a single rhythm. Wang et al. [37] then proposed a multi-modal biometrics system that can continuously verify the identity of current user by considering both face images and Electroencephalography (EEG) signals. For authentication, their system fused the matching scores from these two modalities, and an overall accuracy rate of 90% could be achieved. Abo-Zahhad et al. [28] introduced a multi-level biometric authentication by using Electro-Encephalo-Gram (EEG) signals and eye blinking Electro-Oculo-Gram (EOG) signals. They applied density based and canonical correlation analysis strategies, and used the autoregressive model for EEG signals during relaxation or visual stimulation. With 31 participants and Neursky Mindwave headset, their results showed an authentication rate of 99%.

The results from the above studies indicate the feasibility of building EEG-based user authentication, but also show that classifier performance is not stable based on concrete datasets. For instance, Lotte et al. [19] found that many classifiers like FRNN and Probabilistic Neural Network could be effective in classifying EEG signals from stimulation and reaction, but are not suitable for classifying all EEG signals. Some more related studies can refer to recent studies [10, 14, 27, 31] and a survey [3].

2.3   Screen Unlock Mechanism

To against unauthorized access on devices, designing unlocking schemes are a basic and efficient solution. Currently, Android unlock patterns [22,23] are the most widely implemented unlock scheme on mobile devices, which requires users to input a correct pattern in a 3 × 3 grid.

There are many different unlock schemes in the research community. Izuta et al. [15] introduced a screen unlocking system based on an accelerometer and pressure sensor arrays mounted on a mobile phone. When a user takes the phone from the pocket, the system could authenticate the user's behavior. Their system could achieve a false acceptance rate of 0.43. Li et al. [16] proposed a method of verifying swiping behavior and designed SwipeVlock, a supervised unlocking mechanism on smartphones, which can authenticate users based on their way of swiping the phone screen with a background image. With 150 participants, their results showed that participants could perform well with a success rate of 98% during login and retention. However, unlock mechanisms would be compromised when the pattern is leaked. Hence there is a developing trend of combining unlock schemes with biometrics.

3   Brainwave-Based Unlock Mechanism and Our Identified Attack

In this section, we introduce the brainwave-based unlock scheme and the identified reaction spoofing attack.

3.1   Brainwave-Based Unlock Scheme

As discussed above, due to the unstable performance given by learning classifiers, we notice that brainwave-based authentication is often used to help control legitimate access to assets. In this work, we focus on brainwave-based authentication and its application in designing a screen unlock mechanism on common computers, based on previous work [5,41].

Figure 1 shows the design of such screen unlock mechanism, which can verify users based on their mental reaction (either familiar or unfamiliar) towards the images shown on the screen. The image pool contains various images that are pre-defined by the system. An image example is depicted in Fig. 1, which shows the desktop of a user's computer with an ordinary word processor running, a taskbar, a wallpaper, and several application icons. If the user presents a correct brainwave pattern, then the authentication is successful.

In practice, the system can display different images and check users' mental reactions (familiar or not) as compared with the recorded EEG pattern. In the literature, most studies follow such idea to design different authentication schemes. For instance, Chuang et al. [6] showed that the error rate could reach 1% when given a particular custom task to users, which is similar to the unlock scheme in this work.

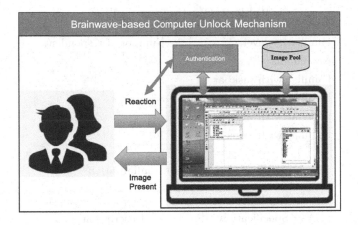

Fig. 1. The design of brainwave-based screen unlock mechanism

3.2   Our Identified Attack

In practical usage, we notice that many things may create a feeling of familiarity among different users, such as an iconic logo of a brand, an iconic design, and an iconic appearance of people. It is a phenomenon that would usually not cause any trouble, but it may bring a security concern to the brainwave-based authentication. This is because the mental reactions rely heavily on the experience and familiarities of a person. Then a question comes to the above brainwave-based screen unlock mechanism: what if the displayed image(s) is/are not only familiar to the legitimate user? For instance, different people may have the same feeling of familiarity regarding a smartphone with the same brand and model.

Survey. To investigate this issue, we perform a survey via Facebook platform with a total of 88 respondents regarding their familiarity level toward the image as shown in Fig. 1. The responses are classified into five categories as below.

    I am not familiar with the image.
- I feel familiar because of the taskbar and titlebar.
- I feel familiar because of the wallpaper.
- I feel familiar because of the application icon.
- I feel familiar because of the word processor.

    The survey result is summarized in Table 2. It is found that only four respondents were not familiar with the image, whereas up to 95.5% respondents were shown familiar with part(s) of the image. It is worth noting that some respondents can choose to be familiar with several parts of the image, like both wallpaper and application icon. The results validate that the screen unlock mechanism based on familiarity level may be vulnerable to some attacks.

Reaction Spoofing Attack. Motivated by the above observation, we figure out that an imposter has a good chance to imitate the mental reactions (either familiar or unfamiliar) of a legitimate user toward the displayed image(s), called

Table 2. Questionnaire result.

Familiarity level	Number of respondents
Not familiar	4
Familiar with taskbar	37
Familiar with wallpaper	35
Familiar with word processor	8
Familiar with icons	16

Table 3. Environment configuration

Hardware Software	Attributes	
	Specification	Description
Notebook	Acer TravelMate 4750	Collect Brainwave and Displaying Pictures to the participants
Desktop	Asus BM6AF	Receive the data from notebook and perform data classification
Brainwave Headset	BRI BR8-801	The brainwave headsets for participants.
Operating System	Microsoft Windows 10	
Program Platfom	Oracle Java 11	The program platform for displaying pictures, sending marks to the brainwave collector program
Brainwave Collector	BRI Brainwave Collector	The collector extracts the Brainwave headset's signal, and receives marks from our custom program
Classifier	libSVM	The main classifier for the experiment

reaction spoofing attack. The attack effectiveness is due to that classifiers cannot differentiate the people if they all show the same mental reactions toward the displayed image.

4   Evaluation

To explore the feasibility and performance of our identified attack, we perform a user study with a total number of 37 participants. The recruitment was performed via Emails and colleague recommendation.

4.1 Environmental Settings

All the participants are students from the same campus, who have an interest in our study. Before the experiment, we explained the study goal and how we collect and store the data. Table 3 summarizes the environmental settings. As a study, our brainwave-based screen unlock mechanism adopts support vector machine (SVM) as the classifier to verify users based on their familiarity level toward the displayed image(s). The selection is due to its popularity and the capability of handling high-dimensional data.

To ensure that all participants can generate the brainwave signals with a familiar feeling, we selected the iconic images from the university campus, such as library surroundings, department building, and administration building. The participants should wear the BRI brainwave headset (refer to Fig. 2), which can capture their brainwave signals when they see the displayed images on the computer screen.

Fig. 2. The participant should wear headset while seeing the image(s)

In addition, with the purpose of collecting good-quality brainwave signals without the potential influence by image display, we adopted the following steps to display images, based on the previous studies [5,41].

- A 15 s blank screen to attract participants and make them calm down.
- To display the images from the iconic building within the campus. Each image was displayed for 3 s, and there is a 3s blank between any two images to prevent fatigue.
- To display the images with cold topics captured from the Internet, with the above same steps.

To preclude the potential influence caused by the screen display, we collected the brainwave signals by playing the image in the fullscreen mode. For data collection, the BRI headset stores the data in CSV format, with a special mark placed at the end of data records. These special marks are created based on the front image, whenever there is an event occurred. Figure 3 shows an example, in our program, we send an ASCII character 'G' to the BRI Brainwave Collector if the program starts to display an image. When the program is about to close the display, we send an ASCII character 'C'. The practice of sending marks is important, which enables us to extract the accurate duration of image display with participants' brainwave signals. As the image is displayed in a fixed order, there is no need to send extra information to identify images.

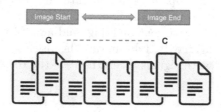

Fig. 3. An example of marks

As all the existing brainwave headsets are non-invasive, the environmental issues can affect the process of data collection, such as participant's skin conductivity, electric cords in the wall, and appliances nearby. The BRI Brainwave Collector provides the built-in filter for alternating the current nearby electric cords. However, to minimize the unwanted effect like group shifting, instead of directly using the brainwave raw data, we retrieve only the delta value between records as the input data, based on the following equation [5].

$$\Delta_R = R_i - R_{i-1} \tag{1}$$

where R_i means the brainwave raw data at record i.

4.2   Study Results

To analyze the data and train the SVM classifier, we used 70% of the data for training and the rest for testing (with ten-fold cross validation).

With four Participants. We first investigate the initial performance with four participants (namely CYU, RYC, WYN and YZW) as shown in Figure 4. It is found that SVM classifier has the tendency by classifying all participants as just one participant (e.g., YZW).

To abstain any potential issues caused by the classifier itself, we also collected the participants' brainwave signals regarding unfamiliarity. Figure 5 shows that the SVM classifier has the capability of distinguishing both familiarity and unfamiliarity for each participant. Thus, the results indicate that our identified reaction spoofing attack is feasible, i.e., YZW can impersonate as the other three participants and unlock the screen.

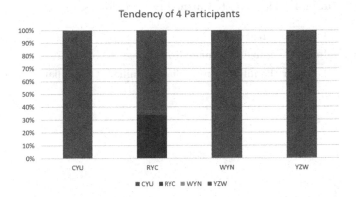

Fig. 4. User classification based on familiarity with 4 participants

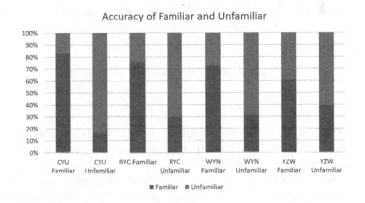

Fig. 5. Classification between familiarity and unfamiliarity by SVM

With 37 Participants. We then investigate the performance of our identified attack with the data from all participants. Table 4 summarizes the expected mental reaction for each image, with either familiarity or unfamiliarity.

When all participants show the same feeling of either familiarity or unfamiliarity, Figure 6 depicts the classification result given by SVM. It is found that CBH has a possibility of above 50% to impersonate as others and then successfully unlock the computer screen. The observation indicates the practicability of our identified reaction spoofing attack in a real-world scenario.

4.3 Discussion

In the study, our results indicate that the SVM classifier is able to tell the familiarity and unfamiliarity, but cannot tell the difference between individuals if they have the same feeling of either familiar or unfamiliar, even if they show the same feeling according to a different thing (or image). Hence the brainwave-

Table 4. The expected mental reaction for each image.

Image and reaction				
Image 1	Image 2	Image 3	Image 4	Image 5
Familiar	Familiar	Unfamiliar	Familiar	Unfamiliar

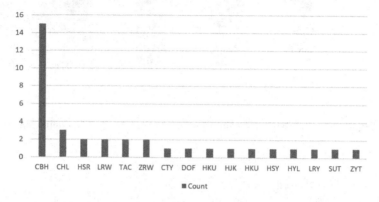

Fig. 6. Classification result with 37 participants

based screen unlock mechanism based on familiarity and unfamiliarity is not secure in practice, i.e., it would be vulnerable to our identified reaction spoofing attack, and some additional security mechanisms should be considered.

Due to the privacy concerns and the time consumption of collecting brainwave signals, most existing research studies often adopted around 20 or fewer participants. For example, there are 9 participants in [20], 15 participants in [6] and 18 participants (two datasets) in [35]. By contrast, in this work, we involved a total of 37 participants, which we considered is a good number. Indeed, how to involve more participants is an open challenge in the research of brainwave-based authentication. In our future work, we plan to involve more participants to validate our results.

5   Conclusion

With the rapid growth of IoT devices, brainwave-based authentication has received much attention, aiming to provide an enhanced user experience and protect assets from unauthorized access. However, we notice that such brainwave-based authentication may be vulnerable in practical usage. In this work, we focus on the brainwave-based computer-screen unlock mechanism and identify a kind of reaction spoofing attack, in which an imposter is able to unlock the screen by imitating the mental reaction (either familiar or unfamiliar) of a legitimate user. In the user study with 37 participants, our results demonstrate the feasibility and viability of such attack. Our work attempts to complement existing studies and stimulate more research on designing more secure brainwave-based authentication.

Acknowledgments. This work was partially supported by National Natural Science Foundation of China (No. 61802077).

References

1. Altahat, S., Chetty, G., Tran, D., Ma, W.: Analysing the robust EEG channel set for person authentication. In: Arik, S., Huang, T., Lai, W.K., Liu, Q. (eds.) ICONIP 2015. LNCS, vol. 9492, pp. 162–173. Springer, Cham (2015). https://doi.org/10.1007/978-3-319-26561-2_20
2. Becker, K., Arias-Cabarcos, P., Habrich, T., Becker, C.: Poster: towards a Framework for assessing vulnerabilities of brainwave authentication systems. In: Proceedings of CCS, pp. 2577–2579 (2019)
3. Bidgoly, A.J., Bidgoly, H.J., Arezoumand, Z.: A survey on methods and challenges in EEG based authentication. Comput. Secur. **93**, 101788 (2020)
4. Chen, C.H., Chen, C.Y.: Optimal fusion of multimodal biometric authentication using wavelet probabilistic neural network. In: Proceedings of ISCE, pp. 55–56 (2013)
5. Chiu, W., Yeh, K.-H., Nakamura, A.: Seeing is believing: authenticating users with what they see and remember. In: Su, C., Kikuchi, H. (eds.) ISPEC 2018. LNCS, vol. 11125, pp. 391–403. Springer, Cham (2018). https://doi.org/10.1007/978-3-319-99807-7_24
6. Chuang, J., Nguyen, H., Wang, C., Johnson, B.: I think, therefore i am: usability and security of authentication using brainwaves. In: Adams, A.A., Brenner, M., Smith, M. (eds.) FC 2013. LNCS, vol. 7862, pp. 1–16. Springer, Heidelberg (2013). https://doi.org/10.1007/978-3-642-41320-9_1
7. Crawford, H.: Understanding user perceptions of transparent authentication on a mobile device. J. Trust Manag. **1**(1), 7 (2014)
8. Damasevicius, R., Maskeliunas, R., Kazanavicius, E., Wozniak, M.: Combining cryptography with EEG biometrics. Comput. Intell. Neurosci. **1867548**, 1–11 (2018)
9. Gartner Says 5.8 Billion Enterprise and Automotive IoT Endpoints Will Be in Use in 2020. https://www.gartner.com/en/newsroom/press-releases/2019-08-29-gartner-says-5-8-billion-enterprise-and-automotive-io. Accessed 12 Apr 2020
10. Gupta, E., Agarwal, M., Sivakumar, R.: Blink to get. In: Biometric Authentication for Mobile Devices using EEG Signals. ICC 2020, pp. 1–6 (2020)
11. Biometric Facial Recognition - Windows Hello. Microsoft. https://www.microsoft.com/en-us/windows/windows-hello. Accessed 21 Apr 2020
12. Biometrics—Android Open Source Project. Google. https://source.android.com/security/biometric. Accessed 24 Apr 2020
13. Human Interface Guidelines - Apple Developer: Authentication - User Interaction - iOS - Apple Developer. Apple. https://developer.apple.com/design/human-interface-guidelines/ios/user-interaction/authentication/. Accessed 24 Apr 2020
14. Huang, H., Hu, L., Xiao, F., Du, A., Ye, N., He, F.: An EEG-based identity authentication system with audiovisual paradigm in IoT. Sensors **19**(7), 1664 (2019)
15. Izuta, R., Murao, K., Terada, T., Iso, T., Inamura, H., Tsukamoto, M.: Screen unlocking method using behavioral characteristics when taking mobile phone from pocket. In: MoMM 2016, pp. 110-114 (2016)
16. Li, W., Tan, J., Meng, W., Wang, Y.: A swipe-based unlocking mechanism with supervised learning on smartphones: design and evaluation. J. Netw. Comput. Appl. **165**, 102687 (2020)

17. Liew, S.H., Choo, Y.H. and Low, Y.F.: Fuzzy-rough nearest neighbour classifier for person authentication using EEG signals. In: Proceedings of iFUZZY, pp. 316–321 (2013)
18. Liew, S.H., Choo, Y.H., Yusoh, Z.I.M., Low, Y.F.: Incrementing FRNN model with simple heuristic update for brainwaves person authentication. In: Proceedings of IECBES, pp. 115–120 (2016)
19. Lotte, F., et al.: A review of classification algorithms for EEG-based brain-computer interfaces: a 10 year update. J. Neural Eng. **15**, 031005 (2018)
20. Marcel, S., Millan, J.R.: Person authentication using brainwaves (EEG) and maximum a posteriori model adaptation. IEEE Trans. Pattern Anal. Mach. Intell. **29**(4), 743–752 (2007)
21. Meng, W., Wong, D.S., Furnell, S., Zhou, J.: Surveying the development of biometric user authentication on mobile phones. IEEE Commun. Surv. Tutor. **17**(3), 1268–1293 (2015)
22. Meng, W.: Evaluating the effect of multi-touch behaviours on android unlock patterns. Inf. Comput. Secur. **24**(3), 277–287 (2016)
23. Meng, W., Li, W., Wong, D.S., Zhou, J.: TMGuard: a touch movement-based security mechanism for screen unlock patterns on smartphones. In: Manulis, M., Sadeghi, A.-R., Schneider, S. (eds.) ACNS 2016. LNCS, vol. 9696, pp. 629–647. Springer, Cham (2016). https://doi.org/10.1007/978-3-319-39555-5_34
24. Meng, W., Li, W., Lee, W.H., Jiang, L., Zhou, J.: A pilot study of multiple password interference between text and map-based passwords. In: Gollmann, D., Miyaji, A., Kikuchi, H. (eds.) ACNS 2017. LNCS, vol. 10355, pp. 145–162. Springer, Cham (2017). https://doi.org/10.1007/978-3-319-61204-1_8
25. Meng, W., Wang, Y., Wong, D.S., Wen, S., Xiang, Y.: TouchWB: touch behavioral user authentication based on web browsing on smartphones. J. Netw. Comput. Appl. **117**, 1–9 (2018)
26. Monrose, F., Rubin, A.D.: Keystroke dynamics as a biometric for authentication. Future Gener. Comput. Syst. **16**(4), 351–359 (2000)
27. Moctezuma, L.A., Molinas, M.: Event-related potential from EEG for a two-step identity authentication system. In: INDIN, pp. 392–399 (2019)
28. Abo-Zahhad, M., Ahmed, S.M., Abbas, S.N.: A new multi-level approach to EEG based human authentication using eye blinking. Pattern Recognit. Lett. **82**, 216–225 (2016)
29. Muse™ - Meditation Made Easy with the Muse Headband. Muse. https://choosemuse.com/. Accessed 24 Apr 2020
30. Noor, M.B.M., Hassan, W.H.: Current research on Internet of Things (IoT) security: a survey. Comput. Netw. **148**, 283–294 (2019)
31. Nakamura, T., Goverdovsky, V., Mandic, D.P.: In-Ear EEG biometrics for feasible and readily collectable real-world person authentication. IEEE Trans. Inf. Forensics Secur. **13**(3), 648–661 (2018)
32. EEG-ECG-Biosensors. NeuroSky. http://neurosky.com/. Accessed 24 Apr 2020
33. Pham, T., Ma, W., Tran, D., Nguyen, P., Phung, D.: EEG-based user authentication in multilevel security systems. In: Motoda, H., Wu, Z., Cao, L., Zaiane, O., Yao, M., Wang, W. (eds.) ADMA 2013. LNCS (LNAI), vol. 8347, pp. 513–523. Springer, Heidelberg (2013). https://doi.org/10.1007/978-3-642-53917-6_46
34. Pham, T., Ma, W., Tran, D., Nguyen, P., Phung, D.Q.: Multi-factor EEG-based user authentication. In: IJCNN 2014, pp. 4029–4034 (2014)

35. Tran, N., Tran, D., Liu, S., Trinh, L., Pham, T.: Improving SVM classification on imbalanced datasets for EEG-based person authentication. In: Martínez Álvarez, F., Troncoso Lora, A., Sáez Muñoz, J.A., Quintián, H., Corchado, E. (eds.) CISIS/ICEUTE -2019. AISC, vol. 951, pp. 57–66. Springer, Cham (2020). https://doi.org/10.1007/978-3-030-20005-3_6
36. Researchers can identify you by your brain waves with 100 percent accuracy. https://www.sciencedaily.com/releases/2016/04/160418120608.htm
37. Wang, M., Abbass, H.A., Hu, J.: Continuous authentication using EEG and face images for trusted autonomous systems. In: PST 2016, pp. 368–375 (2016)
38. Wolpaw, J., Wolpaw, E.W.: Brain-Computer Interfaces: Principles and Practice. Oxford University Press, Oxford (2012)
39. Yan, J., Blackwell, A.F., Anderson, R.J., Grant, A.: Password memorability and security: empirical results. IEEE Secur. Priv. 2(5), 25–31 (2004)
40. Yiu, M.L., Lo, E., Yung, D.: Authentication of moving kNN queries. In: Proceedings of ICDE, pp. 565–576 (2011)
41. Zhou, L., Su, C., Chiu, W., Yeh, K.H.: You think, therefore you are: transparent authentication system with brainwave-oriented bio-features for IoT Networks. IEEE Trans. Emerg. Topics Comput. 8(2), 303–312 (2020)

Cubic Permutation Polynomials-Based Block RLNC Algorithm in Wireless Networks

Hongwei Luo[1], Wanyi Feng[1], Baolin Sun[2(✉)], and Ying Song[2]

[1] School of Information and Industrial Technology, Wuhan International Trade University, Wuhan 430205, China
whicu@189.cn

[2] School of Information and Communications Engineering, Hubei University of Economics, Wuhan 430205, China
blsun@163.com, prisong@163.com

Abstract. Cubic permutation polynomials provide excellent coding performance and parallel access. Random linear network coding (RLNC) is an improved coding scheme for wireless channel communication and video data flow, which can improve the network throughput and network lifetime of wireless networks (WN). This paper study the characteristics of cubic permutation polynomials (CPP) and RLNC by increasing the amount of available data to the users through the encode nodes. The paper proposes a cubic permutation polynomials-based block RLNC algorithm in WNs (CPP-RLNC). CPP-RLNC algorithm can better control the decoding complexity of each received packet and restore the original data. The performance of the CPP-RLNC algorithm is studied using NS2 and evaluated in terms of the encoding overhead, decoding delay, packet loss probability and throughput when a packet is transmitted. The simulations result shows that the CPP-RLNC algorithm with our proposition can significantly improve the network throughput and encoding efficiency.

Keywords: Wireless networks · Network coding · Cubic permutation polynomials · Packet block

1 Introduction

Network coding (NC) is a new approach for sending information and has been recently proposed as an alternative for routing [1–5]. Routing is a method of finding the best possible path between the sender and receiver to send data via routing. In the routing algorithm, the intermediate node can only receive data packets from the input and send them to the corresponding output. In the network coding approach, the intermediate node is allowed to recode data packets. This allows each node to re-packet inputs and sends them to its output [1–5].

Random linear network coding (RLNC) [3] algorithm is an effective coding algorithm for data transmission in mobile, complex environment or lost communication network. RLNC creates coding information by combining source packets linearly on

© Springer Nature Switzerland AG 2021
G. Wang et al. (Eds.): SpaCCS 2020, LNCS 12382, pp. 266–275, 2021.
https://doi.org/10.1007/978-3-030-68851-6_19

binary Galois field GF(2). Block-based RLNC [3–5] divides a large message or long packet stream into blocks, each consisting of g consecutive source symbols. The block based RLNC encoder and decoder operate only on the symbols within a given block at a time. In addition, block-based RLNC strategy can reduce the delay caused by coding processing and quickly recover discarded symbols by allocating coding information between source symbols [4], thus generating higher transmission capacity of source symbols. Chatzigeorgiou *et al.* [5] proposed an encoding algorithm based on source data packet, which can be used for encoding and packet transmission by erasing broadcast channels. Douik *et al.* [6] reviewed classifies, evaluates and discusses various algorithms proposed in typical literatures, and summarizes the advantages of RLNC algorithm and block-based RLNC algorithm.

In our previous study, we proposed a network coding-based maximum lifetime algorithm for sliding window in wireless sensor network (NC-MLSW) [7] which improves the throughput and network lifetime wireless sensor network. Literature [8] introduces energy consumption control into network coding, proposed a sliding window-based energy consumption network coding algorithm, and conducted performance analysis and research to improve the performance of network coding.

This paper proposes cubic permutation polynomials (CPP)-based block RLNC algorithm in WNs (CPP-RLNC). Our contributions towards packet block, low-complexity, RLNC are in the following.

Firstly, the paper provides a complete description of the CPP. The size of the block is determined according to the CPP, and the packet within the block is coded by the RLNC algorithm. CPP-RLNC realizes the control of coding and decoding complexity.

Secondly, the performance of the CPP-RLNC algorithm is studied using NS2 and experimentation to assess the encoding efficiency, the decoding complexity of CPP-RLNC enabled wireless node.

The rest of the paper is organized as follows. Section 2 discusses some related work. Section 3 describes models of quadratic permutation polynomials. Section 4 designs a packet encoding block mechanism. Some simulating results are provided in Sect. 5. Finally, the paper concludes in Sect. 6.

2 Related Works

Using more processors for parallel network coding is an important issue to speed up the processing at the receiver of a communication system. The encoder is the key component of coding operation. The algebraic interleave device based on permutation polynomial has the advantages of analysis and design, outstanding performance, simplicity, practicality, high speed, low power consumption and small memory requirements. Trifina *et al.* [9] proposed parallel decoding of turbo codes with any degree permutation polynomial (PP) encoder and almost regular permutation (ARP) encoder can be performed using butterfly networks to improve the encoding performance of the networks. Nieminen *et al.* [10] studied the control bits of quadratic permutation polynomial (QPP) encoder in butterfly networks and obtained a simple method to determine the control bits of this special encoder. Wang *et al.* [11] proposed a structure based on butterfly network, which can match four types of turbo decoder parallelization, and reduce the complexity of coding better.

Its main advantage is to provide a large number of new parallel structures for high speed turbo decoders to support QPP on sets. Guan *et al.* [12] proposed a different irregular Block-LDPC code based on QPP to replace the identity matrix. This scheme has better error performance and lower complexity. Fu *et al.* [13] designed an all-optical linear block code encoder based on micro-resonators for the optical network integrated on the chip, which improved the reliable communication of optical network. Lucian *et al.* [14] determine the number of different packets of cubic permutation polynomial (CPPs) and QPPs algorithm. The sufficient and necessary conditions of QPPs and CPPs based on quadratic polynomial coefficient and cubic polynomial coefficient are analysis, respectively, and on the Chinese remainder theorem. This algorithm has better coding performance, lower complexity and coding error rate. Trifina *et al.* [15] studied and generalized the performance of cubic permutation polynomial (CPP) in encoder, and the results showed that the performance of CPP in encoder was significantly higher than that of QPP encoder.

In order to reduce the time complexity of optimization, Ostovari *et al.* [16] presented a distributed approach to optimally utilize the helpers, which adapts to the changes in the requested videos and the joining or departure of the nodes. Wunderlich *et al.* [17] studied and evaluated efficient RLNC computing strategies for the Internet of things architectures, including emerging heterogeneous networks and coding algorithms. Through single instruction optimization and multi instruction optimization of matrix block, an optimization method of RLNC matrix operation is proposed. Yu *et al.* [18] purposed a throughput-optimal linear network coded (LNC) techniques, including RLNC, decodable network coding techniques. Hu *et al.* [19] proposed a dynamic adaptive approach based on Round Trip Time to optimal the size of Encoding Blocks in real-time network conditions and achieve the purpose of reducing throughput burst.

3   Quadratic Permutation Polynomials

3.1   Permutation Polynomial (PP)

Given an integer $N \geq 2$, an integer set Z_N, a polynomial function $p(x) = a_k x^k + \ldots + a_1 x + a_0 \pmod{N}$ for all x in Z_N, where a_i are nonnegative integer coefficients, k is an integer, is said to be a PP over Z_N when $p(x)$ starts in the set $\{0, 1, 2, \ldots, N-1\}$.

Theorem 1: Let $p(x) = a_k x^k + \ldots + a_1 x + a_0 \pmod{N}$ be a polynomial function with integer coefficients. $p(x)$ is a PP over the integer ring N, if and only if:

1)   If N is a prime factor, all prime numbers are $p(x) = a_k x^k + \ldots + a_1 x + a0 \pmod{N}$ is PP;
2)   Let n be the largest prime number, satisfy $p^n | N$.

3.2   Cubic Permutation Polynomial (CPP)

For the PP function $p(x)$, when $k = 2$, we call $p(x)$ the quadratic permutation polynomial (QPP); when $k = 3$, we call $p(x)$ the cubic permutation polynomial (CPP), It can also be represented as $p(x) = a_3x^3 + a_2x^2 + a_1x + a_0$ $(a_0, a_1, a_2, a_3 \in Z_N)$. Since the coefficient a_0 only plays a shift role in encoding and does not affect the performance of encoding/decoding, it is usually omitted to make $a_0 = 0$. The quadratic polynomial function $p(x)$, defined function by $p(x) = a_3x^3 + a_2x^2 + a_1x \pmod{N}$ with a_1, a_2, a_3 are positive integer coefficients.

Obviously, four integers a_1, a_2, a_3, and N $(a_1, a_2, a_3, N \in Z_N)$ have to satisfy a specific set of integer Z_N requirements. If function $p(x)$ is a PP function on Z_N, then the three integers number a, b, and N must satisfy certain conditions, and each integer number can be expressed as a product of a prime power. The prime divisor factorization of integers number is always greater than or equal to 1.

Theorem 2 [15] : If and only if PP function $p(x) = a_3x^3 + a_2x^2 + a_1x \pmod{N}$ on Z_N to be a CPP $p(x)$ are to satisfy the following three-step algorithm:

$$N = \prod_{p \in P} p^{n_{N,p}}$$

1) For each p and the corresponding $n_{N,p}$ exponent, judge whether the conditions in Table 1 are satisfied with the p in the previous step.
2) $p(x)$ is a CPP if and only if all the judgments in the steps are satisfied.
3) We determine the number of CPP for each type of prime factor. The prime factor 2 is considered the first one, the prime set $P = \{2, 3, 5, \ldots\}$. For example: $p(x) = 10x^3 + x \pmod{40}$ is a CPP over Z_{40}. $N = 40 = 2^3 \times 5$, for $p = 5$, since $n_{40,p} = 1$, the conditions of $3 \nmid p - 1 (p > 3)$ and $n = 1$ are satisfied. Therefore, the coefficients of a CPP over Z_{40} have to satisfy the conditions of $a_2^2 = 3a_1a_3, a_3 \neq 0 \pmod{p}$, as given in Table 1 [15].

The expanded search results for wireless channels are shown in Table 2. Different polynomials can be obtained for CPP of length 112, 136, 160, 184, and so on.

Table 1. A simple coefficient judge for CPP

$p = 2$	$n = 1$	$(a_1 + a_2 + a_3)$ is odd
	$n > 1$	a_1 is odd, a_2, is even, a_3 is even
$p = 3$	$n = 1$	$a_1 + a_3 \neq 0, a_2 = 0 \pmod{3}$
	$n > 1$	$a_1 \neq 0, a_1 + a_3 \neq 0, a_2 = 0 \pmod{3}$
$3 \nmid p - 1$	$n = 1$	$a_1 \neq 0, a_2 = 0, a_3 = 0 \pmod{p}$
	$n > 1$	$a_1 \neq 0, a_2 = 0, a_3 = 0 \pmod{p}$
$3 \nmid p - 1$	$n = 1$	$a_2^2 = 3a_1a_3, a_3 \neq 0 \pmod{p}$
$(p > 3)$	$n > 1$	$a_1 \neq 0, a_2 = 0, a_3 = 0 \pmod{p}$

Figure 1 shows that when $N = 112$, the degree of parallel access is 7 and the length of the packet block is 16. The number in each cell represents the serial number of packets e_i for $i = 0, 1, 2, \ldots, 111, 112$.

Table 2. CPP encoder with the best parameters

N	p(x)	Maximum value D	No. pol.
112	$28x^3 + 41x$	14	8
136	$34x^3 + 19x$	10	8
160	$40x^3 + 40x^2 + 19x$	16	8
184	$46x^2 + 25x$	14	8
...	...	...	...

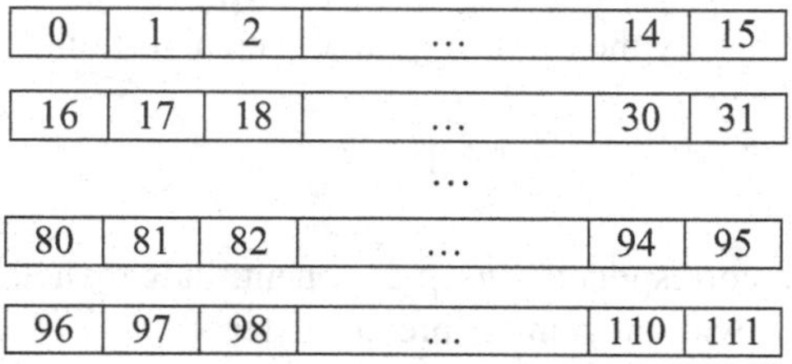

0	1	2	...	14	15
16	17	18	...	30	31

...

80	81	82	...	94	95
96	97	98	...	110	111

Fig. 1. The length of packet block is 16 and $N = 112$.

4   Packet Encoding/Decoding Block Mechanism

4.1   Packet Block Mechanism

WN undirected graph can be expressed as $G = (V, E)$, where V represents the node set in the G and E represents the undirected wireless link set. Each link $e = (i, j) \in E$ means that node i can transmit to node j. Let's assume that the linkage is symmetric, that $(i, j) = (j, i) \in E$.

This paper focus on the network stream, with the source packet serial number i, $i = 0, 1, 2, \ldots$, are to be sequentially from a single source to one or more destinations. For the transmission of block P ($p_0, p_1, \ldots, p_i, \ldots, p_{P/M}$, block P can be divided into small block with block size M. The source selects the blocks $(x_{i+0}, x_{i+1}, \ldots, x_{i+M-1})$ and coding vector $(c_{i+0}, c_{i+1}, \ldots, c_{i+M-1})$ to combine with in a packet encoding block of size $1 \leq p_i \leq P/M$, The elements of the encoding vector that do not belong to the encoding packet block are equal to zero. We define f_i and e_i the leading edge and the trailing edge of the i-th packet encoding block $p_i = e_i - f_i + 1$. A packet encoding block of size p_i is a sequence of blocks $(x_f, \ldots, x_e)$ where $f \leq e$. Figure 1 shows the encoding vector for a generation of size $M = 16$.

4.2 Block RLNC Encoding Mechanism

The RLNC [3] algorithm is an encoding mechanism such that coding vector $c_i = (c_{i0}, c_{i1}, ..., c_{iM-1})$ is given, and input packet $X = (x_0, x_1, ..., x_{M-1})$ is converted into output packet block p_i by the following expression.

$$p_i = \sum_{j=0}^{M-1} c_{ij}x_j \tag{1}$$

$$\mathbf{P} = \mathbf{C} \bullet \mathbf{X} \tag{2}$$

Then, the elements c_i of the encoding vector g are set to one with probability $p = 1/2$ for $i \in [f_i, e_i]$, with probability $p = 0$ otherwise. The destination node can decode input packets block because the coding vector $c_i = (c_{i0}, c_{i1}, ..., c_{iM-1})$ and output packet block data $P = (p_0, p_1, ..., p_{P/M})$ are obtained from the received packets, and an inverse matrix exists in C.

4.3 Block RLNC Decoding Approach

In general, decoding operation is the inverse operation of encoding. For the block-based RLNC algorithm, the receiver will collect M linearly independent coding coefficient vectors and the matrix corresponding to the received symbol $\overline{\mathbf{P}}$ into the receiver coding coefficient matrix C. The source grouping information can be recalculated by Gaussian elimination method to calculate the inverse matrix and multiplication of the coefficient matrix:

$$\mathbf{X} = \mathbf{C}^{-1} \bullet \mathbf{P} \tag{3}$$

with computational complexity $O(M^3)$. After a block finishes decoding or receives the next block's packet information, the matrices C and $\overline{P}$ are cleared and reused in the cache to decode the next packet block.

5 Simulation Experiments

5.1 Simulation Scenario

In this section, we present various simulation results for the proposed a cubic permutation polynomials-based block RLNC algorithm in WNs (CPP-RLNC). We evaluated the CPP-RLNC algorithm in a free-viewpoint video streaming scenario, where one source node sends video streaming data to multiple cooperating receiving nodes. Nodes are randomly and uniformly distributed in a 1000 m × 1000 m area, and the transmission radius of nodes is 250 m [20]. Node movement follows the random path point model and is set to 10 m/s. Wireless link packet loss probability is independent and uniform distribution, the average loss rate is 10^{-4}. The video stream is subdivided by the source node into packet block sequences with the same play time C_t. The other parameters are shown in Table 3.

Table 3. For example optimal QPP $p(x)$ and $p^{-1}(x)$.

Name	Parameter
Number of mobile nodes	100
Network area	1000 m × 1000 m
Node's transmission radius	250 m
Simulation time	600 s
Beacon period	100 ms
Mobile transmission model	Constant Bit Rate (CBR)
Message size (b_{msg})	512 bytes/packet
Examined routing protocol	Block-LDPC [12], DIST [16]

5.2 Simulation Resultss

In this section, the paper present computer simulation results in order to demonstrate the efficiency of the proposed a cubic permutation polynomials-based block RLNC algorithm in WNs (CPP-RLNC). The CPP-RLNC algorithm was compared with Block-LDPC algorithm [12] and video streaming with helper nodes using random linear network coding (DIST) [16] in WN environment. The results of the simulation are positive with respect to performance. The paper uses the NS-2 simulator [21] to evaluate the CPP-RLNC algorithm.

Firstly, the paper tests the CPP-RLNC algorithm performance in encoding overhead. In Fig. 2, the paper compare the coding overhead of the three algorithms when number of nodes changes. The packet overhead increases as the packets transmission increases because the number of nodes increases. As can be seen from Fig. 2, the coding overhead of CPP-RLNC algorithm depends on the coding block ($M = 16$), and CPP-RLNC algorithm is lower than Block-LDPC algorithm and DIST algorithm in terms of coding overhead.

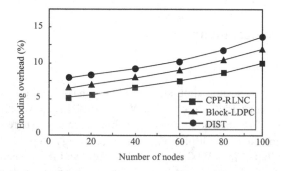

Fig. 2. Encoding overhead with different number of nodes.

Then, the paper compares the decoding delay of CPP-RLNC algorithm with that of Block-LDPC and DIST algorithm after receiving data packets. It can also be seen from Fig. 3 that the decoding delay of CPP-RLNC algorithm is minimal. This is because the CPP-RLNC algorithm uses the QPP mechanism of the block, which provides the optimal number of encoding/decoding blocks in the packet block.

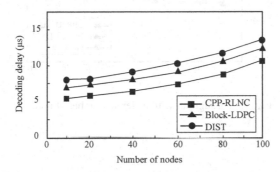

Fig. 3. Decoding delay with different number of nodes.

The paper analyzes the performance of CPP-RLNC algorithm, Block-LDPC algorithm and DIST algorithm from the perspective of packet loss probability. Figure 4 shows a comparison of the actual packet loss probability due to packet decoding reported as a function of block size. As can be seen from Fig. 4, CPP-RLNC can increase number of network nodes load by adjusting packet block size M ($M = 16$), and QPP provides the optimal block size.

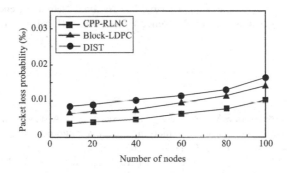

Fig. 4. Packet loss probability with different number of nodes.

The performance of CPP-RLNC algorithm is analyzed from the view of throughput. Figure 5 shows the throughput comparison of the three algorithms when the number of network nodes increases. As can be seen from Fig. 5, when the number of network nodes increases, the throughput of the three algorithms also increases, but the throughput of CPP-RLNC algorithm is higher than that of the Block-LDPC algorithm and DIST algorithm. This is because CPP-RLNC algorithm uses QPP to obtain the optimal encoding/decoding block.

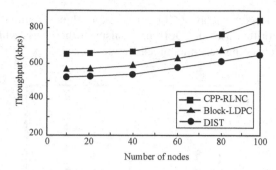

Fig. 5. Throughput with different number of nodes.

6   Conclusion

This paper proposes a cubic permutation polynomials-based block RLNC algorithm (CPP-RLNC). Firstly, the paper introduces cubic permutation polynomials, packet block, and RLNC that preserves the packet degree distribution through the recombination at the coding nodes. Secondly, the performance of the CPP-RLNC algorithm is studied using NS2 and experimentation to assess the encoding efficiency, the decoding complexity of CPP-RLNC algorithm enabled mobile node. The simulation result shows that CPP-RLNC algorithm produces encoding overhead, decoding delay, packet loss probability and throughput. This technique can guarantee the same reliability while consuming the least energy.

Acknowledgments. This work is supported by The National Natural Science Foundation of China (No. 61572012), The Key Natural Science Foundation of Hubei Province of China (No. 2018CFB661).

References

1. Farooqi, M.Z., Tabassum, S.M., Rehmani, M.H., Saleem, Y.: A survey on network coding: from traditional wireless networks to emerging cognitive radio networks. J. Netw. Comput. Appl. **46**, 166–181 (2014). https://doi.org/10.1016/j.jnca.2014.09.002
2. Song, Y., Luo, H.W., Pi, S.C., Gui, C., Sun, B.L.: Graph kernel based clustering algorithm in MANETs. IEEE Access **8**(1), 107650–107660 (2020). https://doi.org/10.1109/ACCESS.2020.3001137
3. Ho, T., Médard, M., Koetter, R., Karger, D.R., Effros, M., Shi, J.: A random linear network coding approach to multicast. IEEE Trans. Inf. Theory **52**(10), 4413–4430 (2006). https://doi.org/10.1109/TIT.2006.881746
4. Huang, C.L., Sun, B.L., Song, Y., Gui, C.: A quadratic permutation polynomials enhancement of a RLNC approach in MANETs. In: The 2019 6th International Conference on Systems and Informatics (ICSAI 2019), Shanghai, China, 2–4 November 2019, pp. 683–687 (2019). https://doi.org/10.1109/ICSAI48974.2019.9010353
5. Chatzigeorgiou, I., Tassi, A.: Decoding delay performance of random linear network coding for broadcast. IEEE Trans. Veh. Technol. **66**(8), 7050–7060 (2017). https://doi.org/10.1109/TVT.2017.2670178

6. Douik, A., Sorour, S., Al-Naffouri, T.Y., Alouini, M.-S.: Instantly decodable network coding: from centralized to device-to-device communications. IEEE Commun. Surv. Tutorials 19(2), 1201–1224 (2017). https://doi.org/10.1109/COMST.2017.2665587
7. Sun, B.L., Gui, C., Song, Y., Chen, H.: Network coding-based maximum lifetime algorithm for sliding window in WSNs. KSII Trans. Internet Inf. Syst. 13(3), 1298–1310 (2019). https://doi.org/10.3837/tiis.2019.03.010
8. Feng, W.Y., Luo, H.W., Sun, B.L., Gui, C.: Performance analysis of sliding window network coding for energy efficient in MANETs. In: 7th IEEE International Conference on Electronics Information and Emergency Communication (ICEIEC 2017), Macau, China, July 21–23 2017, pp. 219–222 (2017). https://doi.org/10.1109/ICEIEC.2017.8076548
9. Trifina, L., Tarniceriu, D.: Parallel access by butterfly networks for any degree permutation polynomial and ARP interleavers. J. Franklin Inst. 356, 3139–3168 (2019). https://doi.org/10.1016/j.jfranklin.2018.12.018
10. Nieminen, E.: On quadratic permutation polynomials, turbo codes, and butterfly networks. IEEE Trans. Inf. Theory 63(9), 5793–5801 (2017). https://doi.org/10.1109/TIT.2017.2717579
11. Wang, J., Zhang, K., Kröll, H., Wei, J.: Design of QPP interleavers for the parallel turbo decoding architecture. IEEE Trans. Circuits Syst. I Regul. Pap. 63(2), 288–299 (2016). https://doi.org/10.1109/TCSI.2015.2512715
12. Wu, G., Liang, L.P.: Construction of Block-LDPC codes based on quadratic permutation polynomials. J. Commun. Netw. 17(2), 157–161 (2015). https://doi.org/10.1109/JCN.2015.000029
13. Fu, L.X., Xie, Y.Y., Song, T.T., Su, Y., Chai, J.X., Ye, Y.C., Li, L.L.: Exploring reliable communication in optical networks-on-chip based on all-optical linear block codes encoder. J. Lightwave Technol. 37(16), 3963–3971 (2019). https://doi.org/10.1109/JLT.2019.2917210
14. Trifina, L., Tarniceriu, D.: A simple method to determine the number of true different quadratic and cubic permutation polynomial based interleavers for turbo codes. Telecommun. Syst. 64(1), 147–171 (2016). https://doi.org/10.1007/s11235-016-0166-2
15. Trifina, L., Tarniceriu, D.: On the Equivalence of cubic permutation polynomial and ARP interleavers for turbo codes. IEEE Trans. Commun. 65(2), 473–485 (2017). https://doi.org/10.1109/TCOMM.2016.2628744
16. Ostovari, P., Wu, J., Khreishah, A., Shroff, N.B.: Scalable video streaming with helper nodes using random linear network coding. IEEE/ACM Trans. Networking 24(3), 1574–1587 (2016). https://doi.org/10.1109/TNET.2015.2427161
17. Wunderlich, S., Cabrera, J.A., Fitzek, F.H.P., Reisslein, M.: Network coding in heterogeneous multicore IoT nodes with DAG scheduling of parallel matrix block operations. IEEE Internet Things J. 4(4), 917–933 (2017). https://doi.org/10.1109/JIOT.2017.2703813
18. Yu, M., Sadeghi, P.: Approximating throughput and packet decoding delay in linear network coded wireless broadcast. In: 2018 IEEE Information Theory Workshop (ITW 2018), Guangzhou, China, 25–29 November (2018). https://doi.org/10.1109/ITW.2018.8613407
19. Hu, H.F., Liu, M.Y., Yuan, D.M., Ran, J.: A block based encoding approach for improving sliding window network coding in wireless networks. In: 3rd IEEE International Conference on Computer and Communications (ICCC 2017), Chengdu, China, 13–16 December, pp. 300–304 (2017). https://doi.org/10.1109/CompComm.2017.8322560
20. Waxman, B.: Routing of multipoint connections. IEEE J. Sel. Areas Commun. 6(9), 1617–1622 (1988). https://doi.org/10.1109/49.12889
21. The Network Simulator - NS-2. https://www.isi.edu/nsnam/ns/

A Lightweight Blockchain-Based Trust Model for Smart Vehicles in VANETs

Seyedvalyallah Ayobi[1(✉)], Yongli Wang[1], Mahdi Rabbani[1], Ali Dorri[2],
Hamed Jelodar[1], Hucheng Huang[3], and Siamak Yarmohammadi[1]

[1] School of Computer Science and Technology, Nanjing University of Science
and Technology, Nanjing 210094, China
s.valyallahayobi@njust.edu.cn
[2] School of Computer Science, Queensland University of Technology,
Brisbane, Australia
[3] School of Computer, Jiangsu University of Science and Technology,
Zhenjiang 212003, China
schuang6@126.com

Abstract. Nowadays, vehicular networks can play a pivotal role in providing an efficient and safe traffic transportation by bringing a reliable platform for transmitting messages among participants. However, we are facing an integral challenge in trusting received messages. In this paper, we propose a lightweight blockchain-based decentralized trust model for preserving the privacy in vehicular ad hoc network (VANET). So, smart vehicles use reputation score of senders and the distance between sender and the location of reported event to evaluate the reliability of each received message. Thus, they are able to make an appropriate decision about the correctness of received messages by using Dempster-Shafer theory. Afterwards, nodes generate a trust value for each received message from the source vehicle and Roadside Units (RSUs) aggregate uploaded trust values from vehicles to accomplish trustful reported events. Eventually, RSUs store the verified and reliable messages into the cloud servers and add the hash of the data into blockchain to assure that our data will not be manipulated. An algorithm is proposed to punish or reward smart vehicles based on their historical experience to restrain the dissemination of false messages in the network. The experimental analyses reveal that the proposed trust model can set up a trust model to deal with imprecise data in vehicular networks.

Keywords: Cyber-physical systems · Blockchain · IoV · VANET · Trust model

1 Introduction

At this moment in time, intelligent transportation systems (ITSs) which are being used to provide a safe and efficient environment in transportation have made a big step. The main purpose of ITSs is to enhance the safety of roads

© Springer Nature Switzerland AG 2021
G. Wang et al. (Eds.): SpaCCS 2020, LNCS 12382, pp. 276–289, 2021.
https://doi.org/10.1007/978-3-030-68851-6_20

and driving conditions. The VANET is a subclass of MANET (mobile ad hoc network) establishing a connection between vehicles and infrastructures to provide a secure and efficient transportation. The general communications model between the participants in VANET consist of two groups: i) Peer-to-Peer communication between vehicles (V2V) and ii) communication between vehicle and infrastructure (V2I) [9]. As illustrated in Fig. 1, in V2V communication model, vehicles exchange the data of detected events in their vicinity with neighboring vehicles and in V2I communication model they communicate with roadside units (RSUs) directly [2]. The aim of trust management in the network is recognized as empowering vehicles to evaluate the trustworthiness of the received messages and ensuring that only trustworthy vehicles are able to disseminate messages. Malicious participants may generate unreal information to have a negative effect on the decision-making of other vehicles about incidents, e.g., broadcasting unreal messages about a traffic jam.

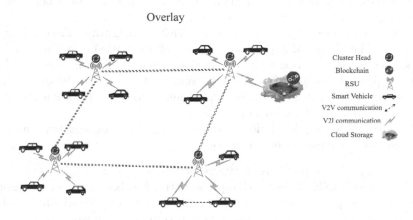

Fig. 1. An overview of Overlay network and Vehicular ad hoc network system model.

This, in turn, calls attention to the demand of establishing trust among the vehicles in the network. In addition, the safety of participants in the network can be compromised by attackers due to their high stage of connectivity and different range of devices in which installed. For instance, authors in [7] mentioned to a key problem in centralized approach in which Tesla exploits a VPN to conduct software updates in a centralized security architecture that does not meet the privacy requirements. The large number of sensors and devices which are installed in the vehicles accumulate privacy sensitive data about the participants, e.g., their location, while in turn highlight the privacy challenges in VANET. In addition, due to the high mobility of vehicles in the network, they need to make decisions in a short time to take appropriate actions.

The mobility characteristic of the smart vehicles brings a challenge into evaluating trust as the participants constantly change their position as well as the neighboring nodes are changing. Also, RSUs are located distributively outside and they are susceptible to faults and violations. Based on the aforementioned challenges, VANET needs a decentralized trust management model that can handle the high degree of mobility of the nodes. Blockchain technology is recognized as a permanent digital distributed ledger providing a secure structure to ease the process of storing transactions and tracking the assets in a network by establishing trust among untrusted nodes. With this in mind, assets are categorized as tangible which namely are cash, house, cell phone- or intangible such as copyrights, patents, etc. The contributions of this paper is summarized as follows:

- We proposed a novel blockchain-based trust model among untrusted entities in VANETs in which nodes evaluate the received information based on set of defined features and share the results with RSUs. RSUs aggregate uploaded trust values from vehicles to accomplish trustful reported events. Eventually, RSUs store the verified and reliable messages into the cloud servers and add the hash of the data into blockchain to assure that our data is not manipulated.
- We designed a mechanism to avert broadcasting untruthful messages in the network. The historical experience of each vehicle is used to evaluate a reputation score which is a part of the trustworthiness check of messages and can play an pivotal role as an incentive for vehicles to relay trustful driving data in the network constantly. All evaluated and updated reputation scores are stored in a persistent blockchain.
- We perform a set of simulations to reveal that our proposed trust model is efficient for vehicular ad hoc networks.

The remainder of this paper is organized as follows: In Sect. 2, we survey the related works in VANETs. Section 3 represents the drawbacks and security issues. Section 4, our proposed trust model is described in detail. Performance analysis of our work is given in Sect. 5. Finally, Sect. 6 concludes the work.

2   Related Work

In this section, we provide a state-of-the-art discussion of trust model in VANETs. Authors in [1] proposed a protocol (EDRP: Efficient Decentralized Revocation Protocol) for authorizing the vehicles and revoking the digital certificate of vehicles. The process of revocation lies on the aggregated voting results which are evaluated by trusted vehicles. Furthermore, the revoked digital certificates will be disseminated to the neighboring vehicles quickly to inform them about the malicious vehicle. A Bayesian Network is proposed in [10] to develop a trust management model which is based on Guassian distribution in order to boost its functionality by combining the direct and the indirect trust values into a final trust value and using the recommendation of the third-party. Malik, et al. [18] proposed a trust model in VANET including the phase of securing the message transmission and the phase of predicting the trustworthiness of nodes which the trustworthiness of a node is evaluated by the "two-level evaluation process". A blockchain is considered as a sequence chained of blocks where each block comprises certain numbers of transactions (TXs) in distributed networks that hold a complete and perpetual database among all entities. These historical transactions are created by peers, who have made a trade, and are disseminated throughout the decentralized network. All blocks are chained together by a hash value of their previous block. Therefore, any modifications in data of a specific block will result in the faulty integrity of hole the network. In 2008, Satoshi Nakamato proposed the conceptual architecture of distributed blockchain, which is the backbone of the well-known digital currency, i.e., the bitcoin. The major advantage of blockchain technology, which discriminates it from the other, is decentralization. It supports peer to peer transactions and all entities equally cooperate and collaborate in a network without requiring trust to other entities [19]. Several methods such as data encryption, time stamping, distributed consensus, and economic point of storing have been used by blockchain to solve the common problems of centralized frameworks that namely are high costs of data storing and processing, inefficiency, and unsafe data storage [15]. Several consensus algorithms have been proposed, namely proof-of-work, proof-of-stake, and a lightweight consensus algorithm which is called DTC (Distributed time-based Consensus) [8] to elect a miner for broadcasting the block to others. In addition, blockchain employs cryptography to keep data secure and irreversible. Thus, due to the aforementioned features of blockchain, it has the potential to serve as a solution.

In [23], authors proposed a decentralized ridesharing model which integrates a blockchain to maintain data privacy and give an assurance to the main factors of a marketplace in a decentralized manner. Authors in [4] proposed an encrypted decentralized storage approach based on blockchain technology, which can support trustworthy and private keyword search operations, to control dishonest behaviors of entities. In this construction, blockchain is responsible for holding important information such as the digests, metadata of integrity checking and tokens, which offers unbiased judgments for storage and services. Besides, in [17] a framework based on blockchain has been proposed to make the distributed key management more simple in heterogeneous vehicular communication systems (VCS). blockchain enables this system to transmit a key securely among decentralized security manager (SM) network. Authors in [6] combined blockchain with proxy re-encryption to ensure the integrity and confidentiality of files. Thus, this approach provides a scalable key management method for multiple access. Authors in [15] analyzed the potentiality of blockchain technology for deploying it into the application of vehicle networking. They have presented how entities on the internet of vehicle (IoV) can collaborate in the blockchain. In [20], author have proposed a blockchain-based anonymous protocol for solving the computation overhead problem of blockchain and preserving its privacy. Blockchain-based trust models for vehicular ad hoc networks are generally a subset of combined trust models because these trust models concentrate on trustworthy of both entity and data. The reason we devoted a specific section is to emphasize on these models and make a contrast from others.

3   Drawbacks and Security Issues

Participants and devices on which installed in VANET are at risk against malicious attackers, which may pose a danger to the traffic safety of nodes by interfering in the function of trust management such as tampering or overhearing messages to accumulate information etc. [5]. Authors in [14] categorized malicious attacks into four groups: 1- those attacks which can weaken the security of wireless interface, 2- those attacks which can put both hardware and software parts of system in danger, 3- those attacks which can trigger the safety of sensors input in the smart vehicle, 4- those attacks which are able to compromise infrastructure. In this paper, we categorize attackers into compromised RSU and untrusted smart vehicles.

1. *Compromised RSU:* All RSUs are distributed along the roads and their security may be compromised by attackers sporadically. Once an attacker takes the control of RSU in which they can add, delete, and tamper data. Whereas, due to the limited capability of attackers, it is roughly impossible to compromise the majority of RSUs in the network for a long time and also the network engineers check RSUs periodically. Thus, they are only able to tamper the minor portion of data.

2. *Untrusted Vehicles:* malicious vehicles are able to disrupt the normal operation of the network according to their own motives. These type of misbehavior can seriously pose a threat to traffic safety or capability of well-behaved vehicles. In below we briefly explain some of the important malicious behaviors.

   – *Denial of Service (DoS) attack:*
     In this attack, the attacker floods the target with a large number of packets which takes all the resources of the target an thus make it inaccessible to honest nodes in the network. A group of nodes may collaborate to flood the target at a specific time which is known as Distributed DOS (DDoS) [11].
   – *Sybil attack:*
     In this attack, a malicious node pretends to be multiple nodes by creating fake identities. The aim of the attacker is to flood the network with packets or inject false information [13].
   – *Message Spoofing attack:*
     A vehicle starts to forge its identity or use the stolen passwords to enter the network as an authorized node to broadcast false messages for its own advantages [16]. For instance, an attacker pretends to be an ambulance to clear the road for itself.
   – *Message Suppression/Alteration/Fabrication attack:*
     The attacker drops or alters some packets of transmitting messages. Also in *Fabrication Attack* a new message is generated [21].
   – *Bad Mouthing and Ballot Stuffing attack:*
     Malicious vehicle generates and uploads negative ratings (*Bad Mouthing*) for trustful messages or positive ratings (*Ballot Stuffing*) for bogus messages.

We studied the attacks mentioned above based on which communication mode and security services they hit.

4 Our Proposed Trust Model

Our model includes four parts which namely are Nodes, Smart contract, cloud Storage and overlay network.

- **Nodes:** Nodes, smart vehicles and RSUs gather all the perceived and received such information as traffic jam, or accident to name but two, from the vicinity to make right decisions about the events according to the evaluated data and share their valid results with the other nodes. In the proposed framework, we exploit blockchain to maintain the hash of verified data to keep data in vehicular ad hoc network securely. Blockchain uses a digital signature to protect data. Thus, each vehicle holds a pair of the private key and public key that the private key is solely held by the vehicle to sign hashed messages or verify the sender of messages. In this work, we use the elliptic curve digital signature algorithm (ECDSA), due to its fast process in signing and verifying messages.
- **Smart Contracts:** Smart contracts let the agreements to be created in any smart vehicle which are executed when required conditions are met. Consider we set the condition for accident events, once the event is verified then a message will be sent to the related emergency service divisions for decreasing the possibility of further damages and keeping passengers safe.
- **Cloud Storage:** In this work, we exploit cloud storage servers to save our data despite of using blockchain. In the cloud storage, all date are grouped into similar blocks which are related to an exclusive block number. These clouds are connected to RSUs, once the data is saved in a block, the hash of the data block will be sent to the RSU by the cloud server.
- **Overlay Network:** An overlay is defined as a P2P network which is based on a distributed structure. In this network, nodes–smart vehicles and RSUs–are clustered and a cluster head (CH) is designated to manage the blockchain and execute its main function (Fig. 1). In our system, we consider RSUs as CHs. Thus, all evaluated messages are sent to and validated by CHs to exclude the demand for a centralized intermediary. To decrease the latency in case of distancing a smart vehicle from its correlated CH, the smart vehicle will automatically connect to the closest CH and leave the previous network. Once the smart vehicle is connected to the new CH, it updates the K_{List}, which is a key list in the CH, with its public and private key pairs to let other nodes to broadcast messages to this smart vehicle. In addition, CH adds the reputation score of the newly joined smart vehicle into Rep_{List} and updates K_{List} and Rep_{List} to send to the members of cluster periodically.

4.1 Phase 1: *Trust Evaluation*

All historical experiences of nodes are evaluated by other members of cluster and recorded in the cloud servers. Thus, a reputation score is devoted to each node for evaluating data efficiently. In addition, we defined a threshold for reputation score where lets the system to estimate the trustworthy of messages from the potential trusted smart vehicles. Once a smart vehicle joins a network in the range of a CH, it requests K_{List} and Rep_{List}. If the sender's reputation score of the received message is lower than the threshold then $RepS = 0$, otherwise $RepS = 1$. In following we explain how vehicles exploit data from received messages to evaluate the trustworthy of them and their senders. Thus, our trust evaluation framework is based on evaluating the distance between the sender and the location of the reported event. To acquire the distance of the sender and event, we calculate the distance of the receiver to event and to sender. In our framework, messages in V2V communication contain $Loc_E = (X_E, Y_E)$ and $Loc_s = (X_s, Y_s)$, which are global positioning signal (GPS) coordinates of the event occurred and sender respectively. Once vehicle V_i receives the message from vehicle V_s, it obtains the distance between itself and the event according to Eq. 1,

$$D_{GPS}^{i-E} = \sqrt{(|X_i - X_E|^2) + (|Y_i - Y_E|^2)} \tag{1}$$

where, D_{GPS}^{i-E} indicates distance between receiver vehicle V_i and the reported event by vehicle V_s based on GPS coordinates, which (X_i, Y_i) is coordinate of the receiver vehicle V_i. In addition, V_i calculates D_{GPS}^{i-s} with use of Eq. 1 and transceivers' GPS coordinates. In the other hand, we exploit received signal strength indicator $(RSSI)$ [3] to compute the distance between V_i and V_s to verify the sender's location as,

$$D_{RSSI}^{i-s} = 10^{\frac{TX_{Power} - RSSI}{10\eta}} \tag{2}$$

where η represents as the path loss exponent, TX_{Power} is the received power signal 1 m from the receiver. Eventually, with the use of Eq. 3, we calculate the credibility of the message as follows,

$$Credit_{Msg}^s = e^{-\delta.D_{diff}.D_{GPS}^{s-E}} + c \tag{3}$$

where $Credit_{Msg}^s$ implies the credibility of the received message from vehicle V_s, $D_{diff} = \sqrt{|D_{GPS}^{i-s} - D_{RSSI}^{i-s}|}$, $D_{GPS}^{s-E} = |D_{GPS}^{i-E} - D_{GPS}^{i-s}|$, δ and c are predefined parameters for controlling the lower bound and change the range of message credibility, respectively.

After calculating $Credit_{Msg}^s$, receiver vehicle computes a reliability index with use of Eq. 4 to calculate the reliability value of received messages.

$$r = RepS.e^{(Credit_{Msg} - \gamma)} \tag{4}$$

where r indicates the evaluated reliability value for the received message.

Trust Value Computation: Vehicle V_r calculates $Credit_{Msg}$ of Msg_{V2V}^i $i \in (0, s)$ to generate trust values $T_{value} \in (0 \quad 1)$, which indicates the trustworthy score given by V_r, for the message sent by V_i. V_r groups reliability values (based on the event that is reporting) into related event $E = \{e^1, e^2, ...\}$, which $R_i =$

$\{r_1, r_2, ...\}$ is reliability set for e^i. we exploit Dempster-Shafer theory to evaluate trustworthiness of events based on received messages [22]. Dempster-shafer is a method to aggregate opinions about an evidence and generate a belief value for it. In addition, the difference with Bayesian theory is the value of belief in an event and its repudiation need not sum to 1 [12]. In this work, as computed in Eq. 5 the belief value $bel_k(e^i)$ refers to an event $e^i \in E$ and the vehicle v_k reported it.

$$bel_k(e^i) = \sum_{j:e^j \subset e^i} m_k(e^j) \qquad (5)$$

where set of e^j are all basic events that form event e^i and m_k is the mass function that in this study $m_k(e^i) = r_k$, which r_k is the evaluated reliability value of vehicle V_k for event e^i and the total belief for e^i will be calculated by Eq. 6

$$bel^T(E) = \bigoplus_{k=1}^{K} r_k \qquad (6)$$

where,

$$bel^T(E) \in [0, 1].$$

Once $bel^T(E)$ exceeds the predefined threshold Th_{event}, the system will consider the event as true and generate a $T_{value} \in [-1; 1]$ for the message which reported this event as,

$$T_{value}^k = \begin{cases} r_k, & \text{Event is accepted} \\ -r_k, & \text{Otherwise} \end{cases} \qquad (7)$$

where represents the system after it assured the event is true or false, it compares each reliability values with the Th_{event} for generating T_{value}. Eventually, the smart vehicle aggregates all evaluated messages into the message M (which its structure is given as below) and sends the signed M to CH.

$$M = \begin{bmatrix} Pub_{Key}^{S_j} & Msg_{S_j} & Time_j & T_{value}^j \\ \cdot & & & \cdot \\ \cdot & & & \cdot \\ \cdot & & & \cdot \\ Pub_{Key}^{S_\beta} & Msg_{S_\beta} & Time_\beta & T_{value}^\beta \end{bmatrix}_{Q \times 4}$$

where $Q \in [1, \beta]$.

4.2   Phase 2: *Decision Engine*

CH sums up all related T_{value}s of each received messages based on the corresponding event as,

$$T_{value}^{Ag}(E) = \frac{\sum_{k=0}^{K} T_{value}^k}{K},$$

where $T_{value}^{Ag}(E)$ is the aggregated trust value for $e^i \in E$ and K indicates the number of reports. If $T_{value}^{Ag}(E)$ is bigger than the defined threshold, then the CH considers the event E valid. In addition, we proposed a reputation update algorithm (as shown in Fig. 2) to reward honest and punish malicious vehicles to motivate smart vehicles to broadcast trustful data in the network. Thus, Events can be considered valid or invalid by the RSUs. Therefore, we calculate and update the reputation score of each participated smart vehicles in the network. Thus, CH will record this information into the cloud servers and store the signed hash of the data in the blockchain.

We assumed that the computation capacity of all RSUs is equal. We exploit **proof-of-stake (PoS)** to choose miners. In this system, the CH with more evaluated Events will be elected to store the transactions into blockchain. In addition, after CH sent its block, a distributed consensus system is used to check the credibility of the nonce and prevent the system from forking situation, in terms of receiving blocks at the same time by CH.

Algorithm 1: Reward/Punishment

---

if $T_{value}^{Ag} >= Th$ **then**

    if *The vehicle reported the Event correctly* **then**

        $Rep_k+ = EXP(\log(1 - T_{value}^{Ag-k}(E)))$**else**

        | $Rep_k- = EXP(\log(1 - T_{value}^{Ag-k}(E)))$**end**

    else

        if *The vehicle reported the Event* **then**

            $Rep_k- = EXP(\log(1 - T_{value}^{Ag-k}(E)))$**else**

            | *continue;*

        end

    end

Fig. 2. Reward/punishment algorithm.

5   Evaluations and Discussions

In this section, our proposed framework is evaluated in two points of view. Thus, to validate the robustness and plausibility of this work, we implement it in the python environment to simulate vehicular and blockchain platform. The main parameters are described in Table 1 which Rep_{th} is experience based parameter for reputation threshold.

Table 1. Key parameters

Parameters	Defined Values
Vehicular number	100
Distance between transceivers	Constant distribution between 10 to 200
γ	3
δ	0.014
Rep_{th}	20
Hash algorithm	SHA-256

5.1   Discussion

In following we discuss about robustness of our approach against five important security attacks to which VANETs are susceptible.

1. *Denial of Service (DoS) attack:* Majority of both DoS and DDoS attacks, briefly described in Section III, target centralized manners. Our proposed methodology exploits blockchain that is intrinsically based on distributed ledger to secure the hash chain of disseminated data in the network. This type of attacks mostly aim individual participants in decentralized manner which cannot fully compromise the network. In addition, for compromising the whole network, known attacks should take the control over the majority of the nodes which is roughly possible because of the topology of network in VANET which is changing sporadically. Furthermore, malicious nodes are whether vehicles or compromised RSUs. With this in mind, malicious peers will be exposed by the benign vehicles and their reputation values degrades continuously to below the defined threshold. Thus, other smart vehicles discard their messages. In addition, it is less possible to take the control over the majority of RSUs in VANETs, due to the checking and maintenance of RSUs regularly.
2. *Sybil attack:* Using PoW consensus algorithm protects our model against Sybil attacks. This approach makes it unfeasible to the malicious nodes to launch Sybil attacks because the capability of creating a block ought to be proportional to the total computing power of PoW.
3. *Message Spoofing attack:* All communications are encrypted and only the nodes that knows the private key corresponding to a public key is able to read messages.
4. *Message Suppression/ Alteration/ Fabrication attack:* All messages are signed by the senders and any alteration or manipulation on the content of messages can be recognized by receivers immediately.
4. *Bad Mouthing and Ballot Stuffing attack:* Malicious nodes may allocate trust values to the trustful messages unfairly. However, In our framework, only RSUs have the authority to update the reputation scores. So, they estimate the score of the smart vehicles based on the evaluation of records from different senders.

5.2   Performance Analysis

The main performance evaluations of our proposed method are as follows, Fig. 3 plots the correlation between bogus messages from malicious vehicles and evaluated unfair $bel(E)$ for reported event E. Consider three scenarios for malicious entities, who broadcast untruthful messages intentionally.

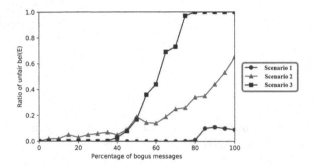

Fig. 3. Correlation between percentage of bogus messages and ratio of unfair $bel(E)$.

Scenario 1: In this scenario, we assumed that the reliability values of malicious vehicles, which are generated by the benign vehicle, are Low ($r_k \in [0, 0.45], k =$ number of malicious vehicles). Therefore, they cannot puzzle the benign vehicle by their fake messages.

Scenario 2: In this scenario, we assumed that the reliability values of malicious vehicles are Medium ($r_k \in [0.35, 0.6], k =$ number of malicious vehicles). It means they may have an average distance to the event. Thus, they can mislead the benign vehicle by their fake messages when they are in the majority (more than 75%).

Scenario 3: In this scenario, we assumed that the reliability values of malicious vehicles are High ($r_k \in [0.55, 1], k =$ number of malicious vehicles). Thus, they can deceive the benign vehicle by their fake messages when they are more than 40% of the vehicles, who reported about a specific event. This is because of the Dempster-Shafer theory that can find the truth based on uncertain reports from other vehicles. However, it is less possible these vehicles become the majority to delude the system. Dempster-Shafer theory is conducted to aggregate all evaluated reliability values to generate T_{value} for each vehicle. Therefore, the system can conclude a belief value on uncertain messages and allocate trust values to senders.

Reputation Evaluation Analysis. To examine our proposed algorithm, we regard a scenario, which includes two vehicles with different behaviors in 100 h. According to Fig. 4, vehicle A and B started to disseminate messages with other participants. From the beginning to t_1 both vehicles broadcast trustful messages with others and their reputation score increased gradually. At the time

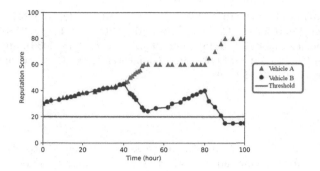

Fig. 4. Reputation score of two vehicles with different behaviors

interval, t_1 to t_2, vehicle B starts to send forged messages which are exposed by the others and its reputation decreased quickly. On the contrary, vehicle A broadcasts trustful messages and earned more reputation score. During t_2 to t_3 vehicle B broadcasts honest messages and its reputation scores increased. Eventually, at t_3 to t_4 vehicle A starts to relay true messages and its reputation score increased. On the other hand, vehicle B at this time interval starts to send bogus messages where after exposing by the others its reputation score shrinks to below the defined threshold for the reputation score. Thus, other smart vehicles did not evaluate their messages due to their low reputation score.

6 Conclusion

In this study, we use blockchain technology to preserve privacy in vehicular ad hoc networks (VANETs). First, vehicles evaluate received messages by using the sender's reputation score and the distance between the sender and the location of the event. And with use of Dempster-Shafer theory generate a trust value $\in [-1; 1]$ for each message to indicate trustworthy of the message, which 1 indicates highest positive T_{Value} for trustful message, while -1 represents the highest negative T_{Value} for dishonest one. Afterward, each vehicle starts to broadcast all evaluated T_{Value}s to the nearby RSU, which groups messages into different categories according to the event they have reported. Each RSU aggregates received reliability values (r), which are related to a specific event, to generate an aggregated trust value for the corresponding events. Thus, if the aggregated trust value is bigger than the threshold then RSU considers the evaluated events valid. Furthermore, RSU calculates reputation scores for vehicles by the designed algorithm and update the reputation score of smart vehicles in the cloud server. We implemented our methodology in the Python and Matlab environments for simulation, and our proposed system successfully detected 95.8% of malicious behaviors and 96.1% trustful events.

Acknowledgment. The authors would like to appreciate the anonymous reviewers for their advantageous comments. This article has been awarded by the National Natural

Science Foundation of China (61170035, 61272420, 81674099, 61502233), the Fundamental Research Fund for the Central Universities (30918015103, 30918012204), Nanjing Science and Technology Development Plan Project (201805036), and "13th Five-Year" equipment field fund (61403120501), China Academy of Engineering Consulting Research Project(2019-ZD-1-02-02).

References

1. Asghar, M., Pan, L., Doss, R.R.M.: An efficient voting based decentralized revocation protocol for vehicular ad hoc networks. Digit. Commun. Netw. **6**, 1–18 (2020)
2. Azees, M., Vijayakumar, P., Deborah, L.J.: Comprehensive survey on security services in vehicular ad-hoc networks. IET Intell. Transp. Syst. **10**(6), 379–388 (2016)
3. Benkic, K., Malajner, M., Planinsic, P., Cucej, Z.: Using RSSI value for distance estimation in wireless sensor networks based on ZigBee. In: 2008 15th International Conference on Systems, Signals and Image Processing, pp. 303–306. IEEE (2008)
4. Cai, C., Yuan, X., Wang, C.: Towards trustworthy and private keyword search in encrypted decentralized storage. In: 2017 IEEE International Conference on Communications (ICC), pp. 1–7. IEEE (2017)
5. Nirbhay Kumar Chaubey: Security analysis of vehicular ad hoc networks (VANETs): a comprehensive study. Int. J. Secur. Appl. **10**(5), 261–274 (2016)
6. Cui, S., Asghar, M.R., Russello, G.: Towards blockchain-based scalable and trustworthy file sharing. In: 2018 27th International Conference on Computer Communication and Networks (ICCCN), pp. 1–2. IEEE (2018)
7. Dorri, A., Steger, M., Kanhere, S.S., Jurdak, R.: Blockchain: a distributed solution to automotive security and privacy. IEEE Commun. Mag. **55**(12), 119–125 (2017)
8. Dorri, A., Kanhere, S.S., Jurdak, R., Gauravaram, P.: LSB: a lightweight scalable blockchain for IoT security and privacy. arXiv preprint arXiv:1712.02969 (2017)
9. Dua, A., Kumar, N., Bawa, S.: A systematic review on routing protocols for vehicular ad hoc networks. Veh. Commun. **1**(1), 33–52 (2014)
10. Fang, W., Zhang, W., Liu, Y., Yang, W., Gao, Z.: BTDS: Bayesian-based trust decision scheme for intelligent connected vehicles in VANETs. Trans. Emerg. Telecommun. Technol. e3879 (2020)
11. Feng, Y., Hori, Y., Sakurai, K.: A detection system for distributed DoS attacks based on automatic extraction of normal mode and its performance evaluation. In: International Conference on Security, Privacy and Anonymity in Computation, Communication and Storage, pp. 461–473. Springer, Heidelberg (2017)
12. Gordon, J., Shortliffe, E.H.: The Dempster-Shafer theory of evidence. Rule-Based Expert Systems: The MYCIN Experiments of the Stanford Heuristic Programming Project **3**, 832–838 (1984)
13. Grover, J., Laxmi, V., Gaur, M.S.: Sybil attack detection in VANET using neighbouring vehicles. Int. J. Secur. Netw. **9**(4), 222–233 (2014)
14. Hasrouny, H., Samhat, A.E., Bassil, C., Laouiti, A.: VANET security challenges and solutions: a survey. Veh. Commun. **7**, 7–20 (2017)
15. Jiang, T., Fang, H., Wang, H.: Blockchain-based internet of vehicles: distributed network architecture and performance analysis. IEEE Internet Things J. (2018)
16. Kahtani, M.S.A.: Survey on security attacks in vehicular ad hoc networks (VANETs). In: 2012 6th International Conference on Signal Processing and Communication Systems, pp. 1–9. IEEE (2012)

17. Lei, A., Cruickshank, H., Cao, Y., Asuquo, P., Ogah, C.P.A., Sun, Z.: Blockchain-based dynamic key management for heterogeneous intelligent transportation systems. IEEE Internet Things J. **4**(6), 1832–1843 (2017)
18. Malik, N., Nanda, P., He, X., Liu, R.P.: Vehicular networks with security and trust management solutions: proposed secured message exchange via blockchain technology. Wirel. Netw. 1–20 (2020)
19. Nakamoto, S., et al.: Bitcoin: a peer-to-peer electronic cash system (2008)
20. Ra, G.-J., Seo, D., Bhuiyan, M.Z.A., Lee, I.-Y.: An anonymous protocol for member privacy in a consortium blockchain. In: International Conference on Security, Privacy and Anonymity in Computation, Communication and Storage, pp. 456–464. Springer (2019)
21. Rawat, A., Sharma, S., Sushil, R.: VANET: security attacks and its possible solutions. J. Inf. Oper. Manag. **3**(1), 301 (2012)
22. Raya, M., Papadimitratos, P., Gligor, V.D., Hubaux, J.-P.: On data-centric trust establishment in ephemeral ad hoc networks. In: IEEE INFOCOM 2008-The 27th Conference on Computer Communications, pp. 1238–1246. IEEE (2008)
23. Semenko, Y., Saucez, D.: Distributed privacy preserving platform for ridesharing services. In: Wang, G., Feng, J., Bhuiyan, M., Lu, R. (eds.) International Conference on Security, Privacy and Anonymity in Computation, Communication and Storage, pp. 1–14. Springer, Heidelberg (2019). https://doi.org/10.1007/978-3-030-24907-6_1

Light Intensity Based IoT Device Positioning for Indoor Monitoring

Gaofei Sun[1,2], Xiaoshuang Xing[1(✉)], Zhenjiang Qian[1], Zhiguo Wang[1], and Saide Zhu[2]

[1] School of Computer Science and Engineering, Changshu Institute of Technology, Suzhou 215500, China
{gfsun,xing,qian,zhwang}@cslg.edu.cn
[2] Department of Computer Science, Georgia State University, 30303 Atlanta, Georgia
szhu5@student.gsu.edu

Abstract. With the prosperous deployment of IoT devices in recent years, more data are collected by ubiquitous sensors. Hence, there are two main challenges needed to be solved. Firstly, how to accommodate the communication links among these devices and collect their data effectively? Secondly, how to track or localize these devices and well organize the IoT network? The common way to track these devices is achieved by registering locations of these devices manually or RSSI measurement. However, these measures suffer from high complexity and inaccuracy, and cause boring reconfiguration process with shift of devices. In this framework, we proposed a novel and low cost IoT monitoring system with self-location awareness. The collected data by sensors, such as the light intensity, can be used for device localizations. By using the proposed algorithm, we derived the critical parameters for light curves, and interpolated for the predicted light intensity inside the whole room. The experiment results indicated the proposed algorithm is useful for inferring device location with low cost, which are suitable for device management without privacy information.

Keywords: IoT network · Light intensity · Device positioning · Indoor monitoring · Feature extractions

1 Introduction

Inspiring by advances in powerful 5G mobile network and other communication technologies, the deployments of Internet of Things (IoT) are boosting rapidly all around the world [1]. A multitude of sensors and devices are deployed across the globe, up to exceed 50 billion in 2022, which revealed by Juniper Research. Hence, plenty of data would be gathered from anywhere to form a data pool, called as big data, which facilitated further processing, such as statistical analysis, machine learning [2], and eventually lead to data driven based artificial intelligence [3]. Finally, the flourishing vision of IoT network between devices can be realized, without any inter-operations with human.

© Springer Nature Switzerland AG 2021
G. Wang et al. (Eds.): SpaCCS 2020, LNCS 12382, pp. 290–300, 2021.
https://doi.org/10.1007/978-3-030-68851-6_21

However, there are several obstacles needs to be solved. Firstly, the quantity of IoT devices are greatly larger than cellular phones and other network devices ever before, which caused a heavy spectrum access demands for current network infrastructures. Fortunately, facilitated by 5G technology, and newly designed protocols or mechanisms, such as NB-IoT, eMTC, which tailored for IoT devices, capable for more than 100K one-hop connections per section of base stations and more than 99% outdoor and indoor coverage [4]. Besides, along with the cable network, WiFi coverage, IoT devices can easily merge into network for data uploading and reverse controls. Secondly, the uploading data of IoT devices facing high risks when uploading or sharing [5] to cloud servers, the data privacy can hardly be guaranteed [6]. By inspecting the traffic characteristics, useful information can be derived refer to the uploading data[7–10]. Fortunately, by incorporating edge computing [11] and fog computing [12] with data uploading networks [13], most of data processing can be done with nearby end devices and thus minimize the data flow and decrease the possibility of data privacy leakage [14–16]. Thirdly, due to the huge amount of IoT devices deployed almost everywhere, it is a hard task to maintain these devices with their status, such as locations, CPU states, energy consumptions. Moreover, some devices may change their deployments occasionally or unintentionally. As for device positioning, received signal strength (RSS) based measures are widely used, such as GPS, base station [17] or WiFi fingerprinting [18], UWB-based technology. However, GPS and cellular downlink based positioning methods suffering from inaccurate in indoor scenario, and fingerprinting may induce additional cost for offline training in each rooms which deployed devices, UWB-based is power-hungry. Besides, other approaches are also introduced for indoor position determination, such as light-based technology.

Noteworthy, the light-based positioning for indoor IoT devices is a promising approach. In [19], the authors designed a visible light communication based system PIXEL, which can achieve the indoor localization with sub-meter accuracy. Basically, this system is used for wearable devices, and a novel color-based modulation scheme is induced. Hence, additional component are needed for decoding, and also extra light is indispensable. In [20], the authors designed a prototype implementation for both 2D and 3D localization, with several infrared LED lamps. The experiments indicated that the proposed scheme produces a median location accuracy less than 3.8 cm. However, the light sensor equipped by devices must have the ability of decoding these light signals. In [21], the authors proposed a visible light enabled localization system, called Foglight, by adding simple off-the-shelf light sensors. By decoding the gray-coded binary images, the average accuracy of location is 1.7 mm with refresh rate 84 Hz. The main features of Foglight is computation efficient and high accuracy. However, a DLP projector is needed in each room where IoT devices deployed. Although these studies already achieved a good balance between localization accuracy and system complexities, their applications still limited in several conditions: Firstly, the cost may become unacceptable with huge number of deployed devices, for that extra devices which provide encoded light signal are needed in each room; Secondly, when devices are deployed by consumers in a commercial way, it is an impossible task to install extra devices for positioning of IoT devices, due to personal privacy issues.

The pervasive idea is that we collect the sensing data from devices, including light, temperature, pressure, etc., and infer the relative positions between devices without extra components, at the expense of lower positioning accuracy. Hence, we proposed a natural light based IoT device positioning and monitoring system, which aims at maintaining devices easily. In our framework, several backbone IoT devices are deployed in a building, and also multi-layer servers architecture with WiFi access point as main wireless connections are provided. The light based location determination for IoT devices is provided, and the main contributions are listed as follows:

- We constructed an indoor IoT system for environment monitoring, which are low cost and can be easily expanded to extensive applications;
- A light intensity based location determination process is proposed. By comparing its sensing data with the predicted light intensity, the location of devices can be inferred.

The rest of this work is organized as follows. In Sect. 2, we describe the system architecture and introduce the functions of each unit. In Sect. 3, we focus on algorithms for positioning of IoT devices. In Sect. 4, the data of experiments are provided. Finally, we conclude this work in Sect. 5.

2 The Architecture of Proposed Monitoring System

Facilitating by access point deployed inside the building, we build the IoT monitoring system by accessing the existed WiFi network seamlessly. Moreover, by incorporating the cellular network terminals with IoT devices, this system can spread into outdoor or other environment, such as other buildings. The main features of proposed system lies as follows:

- Multi-layer Network Architecture: to accommodate large number of devices in the bottom layer with more than 10 devices deployed inside a room, a central device is proposed as access point for other devices. Meanwhile, the cost for devices may decrease, such as Bluetooth, Zigbee, low cost transmission module can be used for data uploading to cloud severs via central device.
- Edge Computing Sever Assisted: By utilizing a central layer device as an access point, also it may act as an edge computing server. Inside a room, plenty of sensing data can be processed in edge sever, thus decrease the volume of data that uploads to cloud servers. For device positioning determination inside a room, it is better to proceed in edge sever.
- Capable Cloud Severs: At the top layer, there are several powerful central servers, which are used for data storage and processing data among different rooms. Besides, in order to aware of newly access or transfer devices, and also provide a useful reference to the environment conditions inside the target buildings, further processing of data analysis can be conducted in cloud severs, such as the environment evaluations for each room.

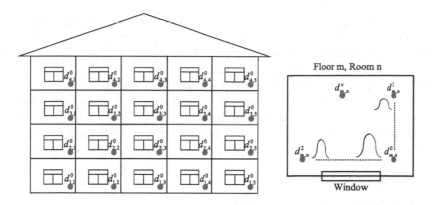

Fig. 1. The architecture of proposed IoT monitoring system and device deployments.

As we described above, Fig. 1 is plotted as the architecture of proposed IoT monitoring system inside a building, and also the device deployments inside a room. For IoT devices, the sensors are selected according to the functions of devices. Based on SCM or ARM platform, the sensors are reconfigurable, thus easy to add or reduce sensors. Basically, these sensors can be sorted into three categories:

- Multifunction sensors: such as light density sensor, Atmospheric pressure sensor. These sensors are capable of environmental monitoring, and also for determining the location of devices. Besides, by using the WiFi module, the RSSI values can also used for verify the accuracy of locations.
- Essential sensors: such as temperature sensor, humidity sensor, which are the basic sensors to monitor the living environment, facilitating the users to better control applicants, sustaining a comfort surroundings and decrease the energy consumptions.
- Specialized sensors: these sensors contains the carbon dioxide sensor, PM2.5 sensor, TVOC sensor, gas sensor, etc.

The monitoring system can be operated separately as a unidirectional information acquisition, and also can be a part of an integral IoT network, which contains the information gathering and reverse control over devices. Overall, the whole system is constructed and operated in following steps: Firstly, the sensor device is constructed by aimed monitored variables. As the purpose is given, then select the proper sensors and build the device with single chip machine (SCM) or Advanced RISC Machine (ARM) based chip and communication module. The basic function for devices are two fold: acquire the data from sensors and send the data to servers periodically. In order to compare the data derived from different locations, time alignment is important. For simplicity, the current time can be acquired from the server in middle layer once the device is power-on or reset after a given period, perhaps 24 h. Secondly, the middle layer server is acted as a relay node for devices in bottom layer, and undertaken three functions: the data storage, the access point for nearby devices, and also an edge computing server. For minimizing the cost of devices, the data acquired from sensor send directly to middle layer server by using TCP protocol, without storage locally. The middle layer server then records and labels the data with timestamps and tags for distinguishing from different devices. Moreover, as the number of devices increases, the spectrum access management and data flow control are needed to avoid transmission failures among multiple devices. Finally, there are several high computing empowered servers in the upper layer, with their functions as, data processing and storage for all devices, and also data analysis to display in charts or web pages.

3   Light Intensity Localization

In section above, we introduce the main function of proposed system, and illustrate the operation flow for devices and servers. Then, we will focus on the data of light intensity sensor, and omit other parts of system.

First of all, we establish a uniform data format for devices, and thus facilitate the data processing. For example, after the central layer device $d_{m,n}^0$ received the uploading data from device $d_{m,n}^1$ in room n of floor m, the data should be uploaded in format as {'Received date', '2020-01-01'; 'Received time', '15:00:05'; 'Device tag', '$d_{m,n}^1$'; 'Sent date', '2020-01-01'; 'Sent time', '15:00:02'; 'Sensor 1', '15.0'; 'Sensor 2', '25.0'}. Here, Received date and time are added by device $d_{m,n}^0$ when the uploading data received successfully, Sent data and time are added by device $d_{m,n}^1$ who performed the data transmission. Besides, the sent time of devices may different due to the limited ports and spectrum bands in central layer device $d_{m,n}^0$, but the sensing data can be derived at the identical time, thus we can make sure that these data are producing sensing data simultaneously.

Next, the collected uploading data need to be cleaned for further usage. The data can be polluted due to several factors: the sensing platform doesn't work well with wrong time or no response from sensors, the data uploading is failure due to network conflict, etc. Therefore, the data from different devices need for alignment, otherwise the data comparisons become useless. After the data cleaning, the starting time and ending time of uploading data are identical, and '-1' is added as a tag whenever no sensing data is uploaded. Hence, we focus on the light intensity data, and thus the data gathered by device $d_{m,n}^0$ denoted as $L_{N_d, K_{m,n}+1} = \{T_d, l_1, \cdots, l_{m,n}\}$. Here, $T_d = \{t_0, \cdots, t_i, \cdots, t_j, t_d\}$ denotes the time sequence, the time interval is predefined, such as 10 min, l_k denotes the light intensity of device $d_{m,n}^k$. For data collected by 3 devices, the cleaning data is plotted in Fig. 2.

3.1   Feature Extractions

As we analyzed in the section above, there exist multiple methods for determining device locations, such as GPS receiver, RSSI based fingerprint. However, GPS is not suitable for indoor environment, and RSSI based fingerprint bring

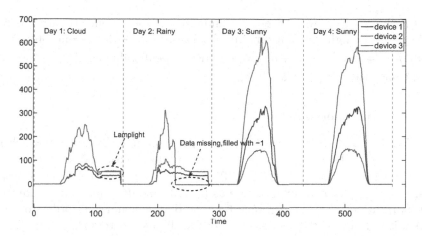

Fig. 2. The light intensity data of 3 devices after cleaning.

large complexity. In Fig. 4, we plotted light intensity data of 4 days from these devices. There are several features: Firstly, the weather condition is vital to the light intensity, sunny day is much larger than cloudy or rainy. Especially, the movement of cloud or other shadows also cause influences on curves. Secondly, the influence of lamp is not ignored in night or cloudy, rainy days.

Hence, we summarize the possible metrics which can be used for device location determination, listed as follows:

- The peak value $p_{m,n}^k$: which is an obvious metric to measure the light intensity and thus provide the relative distance between devices. With larger maximal light intensity, the device may be more close to the windows than others.
- The opening size $\gamma_{m,n}^k$: which indicates the light change rate between the sunrise and the sunset. With larger opening size, it means that the light is changed slowly comparing to those devices with small opening size.

For device $d_{m,n}^k$, we denote the light intensity over 24 h as $l_{m,n}^k = [l_1, \cdots, l_{144}]$. However, the actual data is affected by human activities and cloud movements. Thus, we take two steps to minimize these interference. Firstly, we select the "good" data, which means a day with less cloud and human activities interference. Secondly, we omit the data before the sunrise and after the sunset, to avoid the lamp influence. After these processing, the remaining data $\hat{l}_{m,n}^k$ could better reflect the light intensity which only rely on sun light.

Next, in order to derive peak value $p_{m,n}^k$ and opening size $\gamma_{m,n}^k$ for device $d_{m,n}^k$, we need to incorporate the curve fitting refer to $\hat{l}_{m,n}^k$. The polynomial function denoted as $f(x) = a_1 x^m + a_2 x^{m-1} + \cdots + a_0, x = 1, \cdots, 144$, we need to find the optimal solution for

$$\min_{a_0, a_1, \cdots} |\hat{l}_{m,n}^k - f(x)|^2 \tag{1}$$

By derived $a_0, a_1, \cdots$, we can better minimize the interference by other factors and focus on the light intensity mainly from sunshine. As for second-order polynomial $f(x) = a_1 x^2 + a_2 x + a_0$, we can derive peak value as $p_{m,n}^k = a_0 - \frac{a_2^2}{4a_1}$, and opening size as $\gamma_{m,n}^k = a_1$.

3.2   Data Interpolation

As in Fig. 1, we already place 3 devices inside room m in floor n, which are $d_{m,n}^0, d_{m,n}^1, d_{m,n}^2$. These devices are with known locations, and already derived $p_{m,n}^k, k = 0, 1, 2$ and $\gamma_{m,n}^k, k = 0, 1, 2$. Taking device $d_{m,n}^0$ as the origin of coordinates, thus $d_{m,n}^1$ has coordinate value as $(d_{0,1}, 0)$ and $d_{m,n}^2$ has coordinate value as $(0, d_{0,2})$, here $d_{k,l}$ is the distance between device k and l. In order to derive the location of device $d_{m,n}^x$, we need to derive the parameters $p_{m,n}^k$ and $\gamma_{m,n}^k$ for every point and comparing with the data collected by device $d_{m,n}^x$. As we know, the light intensity vary among the room according to distance changes. As for peak value $p_{m,n}^k$, we suppose that it is vary with distance in two directions, that is $p_{m,n}^x = b_1(\bar{d}_x - d_x)^{\alpha_1} + b_2(\bar{d}_y - d_y)^{\alpha_2}$. Here, b_1, b_2 are weights for different directions, and α_1, α_2 are the light attenuations refer to distances, and $\bar{d}_x, \bar{d}_y$ are the upper bound constraint by the room size. By using the parameters of three devices, we need to solve the following problem as

$$\min_{b_1, b_2, \alpha_1, \alpha_2} \sum_{k=0,1,2} |p_{m,n}^k - b_1(\bar{d}_x - d_x)^{\alpha_1} - b_2(\bar{d}_y - d_y)^{\alpha_2}|^2 \tag{2}$$

Similarly, we define $\gamma_{m,n}^x = c_1(\bar{d}_x - d_x)^{\beta_1} + c_2(\bar{d}_y - d_y)^{\beta_2}$ and solve by

$$\min_{c_1, c_2, \beta_1, \beta_2} \sum_{k=0,1,2} |\gamma_{m,n}^k - c_1(\bar{d}_x - d_x)^{\beta_1} - c_2(\bar{d}_y - d_y)^{\beta_2}|^2 \tag{3}$$

After these two problems are solved, we can derive the predicted values as $\hat{p}_{m,n}^k, \hat{\gamma}_{m,n}^k$ for devices inside this room.

3.3   Device Localization

As we constructed the peak value $\hat{p}_{m,n}^k$ and opening size $\hat{\gamma}_{m,n}^k$ for this room. Next, by comparing with the data of device $d_{m,n}^x$, we would derive the position of the device. Hence, the problem is listed as follows:

$$\min_{d_x, d_y} |\gamma_{m,n}^x - \hat{\gamma}_{m,n}^k|^2 \leq \eta_1 \cup \min_{d_x, d_y} |p_{m,n}^x - \hat{p}_{m,n}^k|^2 \leq \eta_2, \tag{4}$$

here η_1, η_2 are upper bounds.

4 Experiment Verifications

In this section, we conduct the data processing which collected from several deployed devices inside a campus building. These sensors collected light intensity, temperature, humidity, etc., from December 2019 to July 2020. Specifically, we select 3 devices inside a room which deployed in typical locations, as plotted in Fig. 1. These devices is conducted with an Esp8266 Wifi Module and several sensors, with the whole cost no more than 25 RMB per device.

Firstly, we selected the sensing data which are less affected by human activities and weather changes. As in Fig. 3, these 3 curves are selected from more than 200 days, and also the dotted line are curve fitting by second order polynomial. It is observed that the curve of polynomial well coincided with the light intensity collected by light sensors, and also eliminated other interferences.

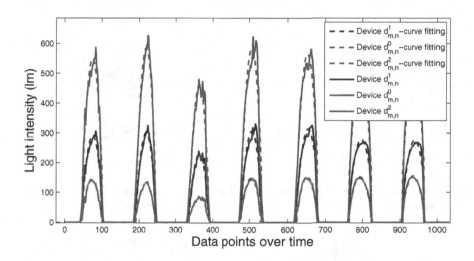

Fig. 3. The selected and curve fitting light intensity of 3 devices.

As in Fig. 4, 5, we derived the parameters refer to the curve-fitting second order polynomials. Device B has the largest peak value among these devices, and also the smallest a_0 for rapid light variations, for that its location is near the window.

Next, we constructed the predicted light intensity among the whole room by using the data of these 3 devices. After the interpolation in an area of 4 m × 4 m, with the interval between points are 0.1 m, thus we derived the parameter a_0 and peak value p of predicted light intensity inside room (m, n) as in Fig. 6 and 7.

Finally, by using the predicted light intensity, we verify if the position of devices can be well inferred by its light intensity data. Therefore, we take 2 devices named as x_1 and x_2, with their coordinates $(0.55, 4)$ and $(4, 1.95)$. We

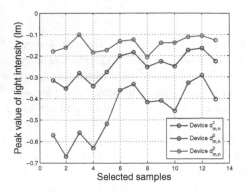

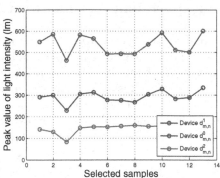

Fig. 4. The a_0 for selected light intensity of 3 devices.

Fig. 5. The peak value for selected light intensity of 3 devices.

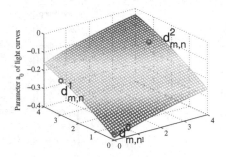

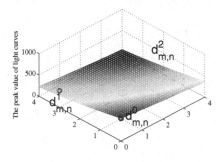

Fig. 6. The predicted a_0 of light intensity in room (m, n).

Fig. 7. The predicted $p_{m,n}^x$ of light intensity in room (m, n).

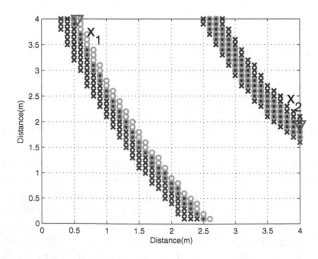

Fig. 8. The possible locations for devices x_1 and x_2. (Color figure online)

deployed these two devices for 1 months, and derived their parameter a_0 and $p_{m,n}^x$ as $(-0.23, 338.5)$ and $(-0.11, 141.2)$. As in Fig. 8, the red area is predicted by using parameter a_0, and blue area is predicted by using parameter $p_{m,n}^x$. Hence, the most possible locations are in their overlapping area. The largest width of the overlapping area is less than 0.4 m, and the largest length of this area is over several meters. It is not a realistic results for location predictions by using the light intensity only. However, considering the structure and placements of furnitures, we cannot put these devices anywhere we want to, mostly near the walls or tables. Thus, the possible area can be reduced to 2–3 positions.

5   Conclusion

In this paper, we proposed a novel and low cost IoT monitoring system with self-location awareness. The collected data by sensors, such as the light intensity, can be used for device localizations. By using proposed algorithm, we derived the critical parameters for light curves, and interpolated for the predicted light intensity inside the whole room. The experiments shows that the location of devices can be inferred by its sensing data. However, by using light sensor only, it cannot give an accurate position as other positioning methods. Therefore, for our future work, we will incorporate other sensors for better location accuracy.

Acknowledgments. The authors would like to thank the support from the Natural Science Foundation of China (No. 61702056); the Natural Science Foundation of Jiangsu Province in China under grant No. BK20191475; the Qing Lan Project of Jiangsu Province in China under grant No. 2019; Key Areas Common Technology Tendering Project of Jiangsu Province in 2017 (Research on Information Security Common Technology of Industrial Control System); Science and Technology Project of State Grid Corporation in 2019 (Research on Lightweight Active Immune Technology for Power Monitoring System).

References

1. Palattella, M.R., et al.: Internet of Things in the 5G era: enablers, architecture, and business models. IEEE J. Sel. Areas Commun. **34**(3), 510–527 (2016)
2. Mohammadi, M., Al-Fuqaha, A., Sorour, S., Guizani, M.: Deep learning for IoT big data and streaming analytics: a survey. IEEE Commun. Surv. Tutor. **20**, 2923–2960 (2018)
3. Javaid, N., Sher, A., Nasir, H., Guizani, N.: Intelligence in IoT-based 5G networks: opportunities and challenges. IEEE Commun. Mag. **56**, 94–100 (2018)
4. Vejlgaard, B., Lauridsen, M., Nguyen, H., Kovacs, I.Z., Mogensen, P., Sorensen, M.: Coverage and capacity analysis of Sigfox, LoRa, GPRS, and NB-IoT. In: IEEE 85th Vehicular Technology Conference (VTC Spring), pp. 1–5 (2017)
5. Zheng, X., Cai, Z.: Privacy-preserved data sharing towards multiple parties in industrial IoTs. IEEE J. Sel. Areas Commun. (JSAC) **38**(5), 968–979 (2020)
6. Li, C., Palanisamy, B.: Privacy in Internet of Things: from principles to technologies. IEEE Internet Things J. **6**, 488–505 (2019)

7. Sivanathan, A., Gharakheili, H.H., Loi, F., Radford, A., Wijenayake, C., Vishwanath, A., et al.: Classifying IoT devices in smart environments using network traffic characteristics. IEEE Trans. Mob. Comput. **18**, 1745–1759 (2019)
8. Cai, Z., He, Z.: Trading private range counting over big IoT data. In: 39th IEEE International Conference on Distributed Computing Systems (ICDCS 2019) (2019)
9. Cai, Z., He, Z., Guan, X., Li, Y.: Collective data-sanitization for preventing sensitive information inference attacks in social networks. IEEE Trans. Dependable Secur. Comput. **15**(4), 577–590 (2018)
10. Cai, Z., Zheng, X., Yu, J.: A differential-private framework for urban traffic flows estimation via taxi companies. IEEE Trans. Ind. Inform. (TII) **15**(12), 6492–6499 (2019)
11. Pan, J., McElhannon, J.: Future edge cloud and edge computing for Internet of Things applications. IEEE Internet Things J. **5**, 439–449 (2018)
12. Alazeb, A., Panda, B.: Ensuring data integrity in fog computing based health-care systems. In: Wang, G., Feng, J., Bhuiyan, M.Z.A., Lu, R. (eds.) SpaCCS 2019. LNCS, vol. 11611, pp. 63–77. Springer, Cham (2019). https://doi.org/10.1007/978-3-030-24907-6_6
13. Cai, Z., Zheng, X.: A private and efficient mechanism for data uploading in smart cyber-physical systems. IEEE Trans. Netw. Sci. Eng. (TNSE) **7**(2), 766–775 (2020)
14. Zheng, X., Cai, Z., Li, J., Gao, H.: Location-privacy-aware review publication mechanism for local business service systems. In: 36th Annual IEEE International Conference on Computer Communications (INFOCOM 2017) (2017)
15. Zheng, X., Cai, Z., Li, Y.: Data linkage in smart IoT systems: a consideration from privacy perspective. IEEE Commun. Mag. **56**(9), 55–61 (2018)
16. He, Z., Cai, Z., Yu, J.: Latent-data privacy preserving with customized data utility for social network data. IEEE Trans. Veh. Technol. **67**(1), 665–673 (2018)
17. Lin, X., Bergman, J., Gunnarsson, F., Liberg, O., Razavi, S.M., Razaghi, H.S., et al.: Positioning for the Internet of Things: a 3GPP perspective. IEEE Commun. Mag. **55**, 179–185 (2017)
18. Fonseka, P., Sandrasegaran, K.: Indoor localization for IoT applications using fingerprinting. In: 2018 IEEE 4th World Forum on Internet of Things (WF-IoT), pp. 736–741 (2018)
19. Yang, Z., Wang, Z., Zhang, J., Huang, C., Zhang, Q.: Wearables can afford: lightweight indoor positioning with visible light. In: Proceedings of the 13th Annual International Conference on Mobile Systems, Applications, and Services, pp. 317–330 (2015)
20. Xie, B., Tan, G., He, T.: Spinlight: a high accuracy and robust light positioning system for indoor applications. In: Proceedings of the 13th ACM Conference on Embedded Networked Sensor Systems, pp. 211–223 (2015)
21. Ma, S., Liu, Q., Sheu, P.C.: Foglight: visible light-enabled indoor localization system for low-power IoT devices. IEEE Internet Things J. **5**, 175–185 (2018)

A Blockchain-Based Reconstruction Framework for UAV Network

Gongzhe Qiao🆔 and Yi Zhuang$^{(\boxtimes)}$ 🆔

College of Computer Science and Technology, Nanjing University of Aeronautics
and Astronautics, Nanjing 211100, China
{qgz,zy16}@nuaa.edu.cn

Abstract. With the popularity of unmanned aerial vehicles (UAVs) and the development of the network technology, the UAV network has become a new research hotspot. However, due to various factors such as terrain, transmission distance, and hacker attacks, UAV network needs to reconstruct the network architecture and restore data according to the actual situation. The blockchain technology can be applied to the UAV network for its high reliability and distributed characteristics. Therefore, this paper proposes a blockchain-based adaptive reconstruction technology framework for UAV networks. Also, to solve possible data damage or missing problems in UAV networks, a data recovery and update approach as well as the corresponding algorithms are given. Furthermore, this paper uses the blockchain to record the behavior of the UAV nodes in the UAV network, and proposes an algorithm to check whether the UAV is malicious or malfunctioning. So that the ground control station (GCS) can reconstruct the UAV network communication link.

Keywords: Blockchain · UAV network · Adaptive reconstruction · Data recovery · Security

1 Introduction

Nowadays, UAVs appear in people's lives more and more frequently, and are widely used in military and civilian applications [1]. In some celebrations, we can also see drone formation flight demonstrations. UAVs have gradually developed from independent tasks to networking, enabling independent UAVs to communicate with each other and improving UAV work efficiency. However, while the UAV network brings all kinds of convenient and fast services to people, it also has to face threats such as cyber-attacks and wireless interference [2]. Under these threats, UAV nodes are likely to be hijacked and sensitive data may leakage via inadvertent or side channel, unsecured sensitive data storage, data transmission, and many others [3]. When an UAV is attacked, it may also lose some important information which is helpful to complete the mission, which may lead to mission failure or even crash itself. Therefore, how to ensure that important information can be safely distributed among UAV nodes, and how to safely and reliably restore the information lost by the UAV nodes have become important issues.

© Springer Nature Switzerland AG 2021
G. Wang et al. (Eds.): SpaCCS 2020, LNCS 12382, pp. 301–311, 2021.
https://doi.org/10.1007/978-3-030-68851-6_22

The most commonly used data recovery technology is triple modular redundancy (TMR). While, UAVs have the characteristics of miniaturization, light weight, low power consumption. On the one hand, TMR technique will increase the storage cost. On the other hand, TMR cannot guarantee that the data stored locally is correct after being attacked. Another traditional method of data recovery is to recover data through data center or ground control station (GCS). Compared with nearby UAVs, the distance between the attacked UAV and GCS is longer, which will bring higher time delay. Blockchain [4] is a term of the field of information technology, proposed by Satoshi Nakamoto in 2008. At present, the blockchain has developed well and new platforms are emerging, such as Ethereum [5] and Hyperledger Fabric [6] based on consortium chain. Blockchain technology has laid a solid foundation of trust and created a reliable cooperation mechanism. Moreover, the high reliability and distributed characteristics of blockchain technology are compatible with the UAV network, and the communication information and requests between UAV nodes will be recorded by the blockchain. Therefore, while recording the behavior of UAVs, the entire UAV network can also check the maliciousness of UAV nodes. At the same time, UAV Nodes that have lost data can recover lost messages through other UAV nodes in the blockchain network and prevent false messages.

Although some scholars have conducted a lot of research on the combination of blockchain and UAVs, these network models rarely consider the problem of UAV network reconstruction. During the execution of the task, there are various problems such as data loss and disconnection of UAVs due to various factors such as environment, weather, and human interference. Therefore, this paper proposes an adaptive reconstruction framework of UAV network based on blockchain. The organizational structure of this paper is as follows: Sect. 2 describes the related research works; Sect. 3 proposes a blockchain-based UAV network adaptive reconstruction technical framework; Sect. 4 describes a data recovery and update method in the self-reconfiguration of the UAV network; Sect. 5 gives a communication link reconstruction method in the UAV network; Sect. 6 summarizes the research work of this paper.

2   Related Work

Due to the unreliable wireless channel and high-dynamic topology of unmanned aerial vehicle ad hoc networks (UAANETs), the situation that a node is missing broadcast messages occurs frequently. To address this problem, Liu Donggang *et al.* [7] proposed the concept of mutual-healing. Instead of waiting for the next broadcast, this method can get assistance from its neighbors to recover that lost keys instantly. Zuojie Deng *et al.* [8] proposed provable multi-copy data possession scheme with data dynamics, and the performance show that the scheme has strong security and good performance. Subsequently, Tian *et al.* [9] proposed a specific mutual-healing scheme based on bilinear pairing in wireless sensor networks. In this method, a node with missed data can broadcast a request message to its one-hop neighbors to restore data. While in Tian's scheme, the location information of both request and cooperative nodes will be exposed to the adversary. Then Xinghua Li *et al.* [10] present a mutual-healing data distribution scheme based on the blockchain. While this scheme does not consider the problem of damaged data recovery.

To secure communications during data acquisition and transmission, as well as diminish the probability of attacking by malicious manipulated UAVs, Ge Chunpeng, et al. [11] propose a distributed UAVs scheme harnessing blockchain technology whose network has similar topology to Internet of things (IoT) along with cloud server. With the network following a hierarchical layout, even the near-user site evaluations can be impacted by the overheads associated with maintaining a perpetual connection and other factors. Vishal, et al. [12] present a novel neural-blockchain-based drone-caching approach, focus on the ultrareliable communication and use drones as on-demand nodes for efficient caching. The communication between UAVs is subject to potential cyber threats. Anik Islam et al. [13] represents a blockchain based data acquisition process in which information is gathered from IoT using UAV and the integrity of the data can be maintained after storing into local storage. Caching mechanism of UAANETs brings a new security challenge that poisoned content can contaminate the cache on the routers and isolate valid content from the network, leading to performance degradation or denial of service. Lei Kai, et al. [14] proposes a systematic framework that integrates interest-key-content binding and introduce a lightweight permissioned blockchain system over NDN and develop a scalable adaptive delegate consensus algorithm. These methods do not take into account the aspects of safe recovery of damaged data and network reconstruction when the UAV formation performs tasks in coordination. Anik Islam et al. [15] presents a blockchain enabled secure data acquisition scheme utilizing an unmanned aerial vehicle (UAV) swarm where data are collected from the Internet of Things (IoT) devices and subsequently. Before adding data in blockchain, consent from all validators is required. Then the data are stored in blockchain with the approval of validators. The decentralized database in blockchain emphasizes data security and privacy, and Machine Learning involves the rational amount of data to make precise decisions. Hence, Sudeep Tanwar et al. [16] present a detailed study on Machine Learning adoption for making blockchain-based smart applications more resilient against attacks. Data sharing and content offloading among vehicles is an imperative part of the Internet of Vehicles. So, Hassija Vikas et al. [17] propose a Directed Acyclic Graph enabled IoV framework and make use of a tangle data structure where each node acts as a miner and eventually the network achieves consensus among the nodes.

Also, there are some studies on data recovery and connectivity reliability. Chi Yang et al. [18] propose an approach, which is based on the prediction of a recovery replacement data by making multiple data sources based approximation, to achieve fast error recovery in a scalable manner on cloud. Songyun Wang et al. [19] investigate the data recovery problem for QoS guarantee and system robustness, and propose a rarity-aware data recovery algorithm, which is to establish the rarity indicator to evaluate the replica distribution and service requirement comprehensively. Hyungsoo Jung et al. [20] propose a data recovery service framework on cloud infrastructure, a parity cloud service, which provides privacy-protected personal data recovery service while requiring a small storage space in the cloud. Reliability evaluation of interconnection network is important to the design and maintenance of multiprocessor systems. Hence, Weihua Yang et al. [21] explore the extra connectivity and the extra edge-connectivity of blockchain networks, and discuss the structure of blockchain networks with many faults. Also, considering the hypercubes, Mobius cubes, crossed cubes, and twisted cubes of the blockchain networks, Qiang Zhu *et al.* [22] prove that the h-extra connectivity of an n-dimensional BC network, by exploring the boundary problem of the blockchain networks.

3   Blockchain-Based Adaptive Reconstruction Framework

At present, the technique of UAV network is developing rapidly. It's common for hundreds or even thousands of UAVs working together. In the process of collaboration, UAVs are easily affected by attacks and wireless interference, causing data loss or damage. The blockchain-based adaptive reconstruction approach for UAV network proposed in this paper can recover the data lost by UAV nodes without hardware damage. The proposed framework is shown in Fig. 1.

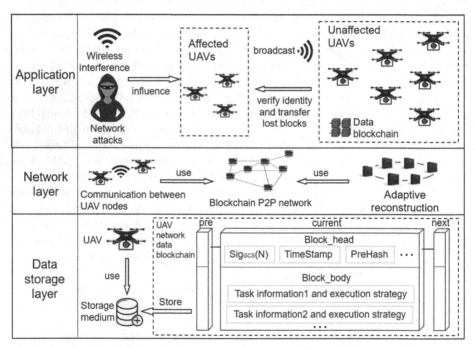

Fig. 1. Blockchain-based adaptive reconstruction framework

The framework proposed in this paper consists of three layers: data storage layer, network layer and application layer. In the data storage layer, after UAV nodes join the UAV network, they use local storage media to store and maintain the UAV network data blockchain. The UAV network data blockchain proposed in this paper saves the mission information of the UAV network and the corresponding execution strategies. We denote the *i-th* block as *Blocki = {Block_head, Block_body}*, where *Block_body* represents the block body, which is a list containing task information and corresponding execution strategies, which can be expressed as *Block_body = [Task information, Execution strategy]*. *Block_head* represents the block header, which is a 5-tuple as (1).

$$Block\_head = \{Sig_{GCS}(N), TimeStamp, PreHash, N, CHash\} \tag{1}$$

In Eq. (1), N represents the random number generated by the ground control station (GCS); $Sig_{GCS}(N)$ represents the signature of the random number by the GCS; *TimeStamp* is the timestamp of the block generated by the GCS; *PreHash* is the hash value of the previous block; *CHash* represents the hash value of the current block.

In the network layer, P2P communication mechanism is used for UAV node communication and adaptive reconstruction. In the application layer, we assume that when the UAV is attacked by hackers, the UAV's mission data and corresponding execution strategy will be damaged or changed. When the UAV finds data damage, it will broadcast the damaged data block number to its neighbors to request data recovery. After the UAVs filter illegal requests and check the identity of the requesting UAV, they will transmit the lost or damaged block to the requesting UAV to complete the UAV recovery.

4   Data Recovery and Update Approach in UAV Network

In the UAV network, there are many UAV nodes. The mission information and execution strategy information stored in the UAV are relatively large. The problems are how to find data damage and locate the location of the damaged data quickly, and how to ensure that the data obtained is authentic and credible. In this paper, the UAV nodes are represented by the set $U = \{U1, U2,..., Un\}$. Similar to the wallet address, each UAV node has a unique identification (ID), which is provided by GCS when the UAV is registered. At the same time, the GCS uses an asymmetric key method to generate key pairs (PK_{GCS}, SK_{GCS}), where PK_{GCS} represents the public key generated by the GCS and is issued to the UAV. SK_{GCS} represents the private key generated by the GCS and is stored by the GCS for signature verification. At the same time, we define the signature function $Sign(SK_{GCS}, N)$ and the verification function $Ver(PK_{GCS}, Sign(SK_{GCS}, N))$. If and only if the UAV node holds the correct public key of the GCS, and the block is signed by the GCS, the UAV node can get the correct message N and pass the verification.

In the UAV network, the UAV node is equivalent to the service provider, and the GCS is equivalent to the manager of the UAV node. The task information and execution strategy of the UAV nodes are provided by the GCS. We assume that the GCS is safe and reliable, and all the blocks are generated by the GCS, which solves the problem of data chain bifurcation caused by the large number of UAVs. The data recovery process in the self-reconstruction of the UAV network proposed in this paper is shown in Fig. 2.

The UAV node in the UAV network performs hash verification on the important data stored in the data chain each time interval, and compares it with the *CHash* value in the block header to check whether the data is damaged. If the data is damaged, the UAV node Uq updates the list of connectable nodes $List\_nb_{Uq}$ by broadcasting, and sends a data recovery request $Req\_Uq = \{ID_{Uq}, cn, CHash_{cn-1}, cn', CHash_{cn'}\}$ according to the address in the list. ID_{Uq} is the address of the UAV node making the request and cn represents the block number of data loss. $CHash_{cn-1}$ represents the hash value of

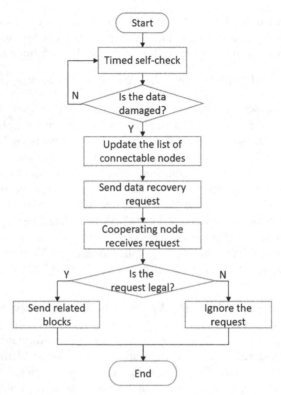

Fig. 2. Data recovery process in the self-reconstruction of the UAV network

the previous block of the block where the data is lost. UAV nodes may lose data in consecutive blocks. Therefore, we use cn' to represent the value of the next block in the data loss block sequence. $CHash_{cn'}$ represents the hash value of the next block of the data loss block sequence. The self-check request algorithm of UAV node is given in Table 1.

After receiving the data recovery request, every UAV node in the list of connectable nodes $List\_nb_{Uq}$ checks the hash value of the forward block of the block numbered cn in the local data chain, $CHash_{cn-1}*$ and the hash value of the backward block $CHash_{cn'}*$, and compare with the $CHash_{cn-1}$ and $CHash_{cn'}$ in the request Req_Uq. After the verification is passed, the UAV node Ui checks the connectivity of Uq and then gives a response $Res\_Ui = \{ID_{Uq}, Block_{cn}\}$. The UAV node response algorithm is shown in Table 2.

The UAV node Uq sends a request to the UAV nodes in the list $List\_nb_{Uq}$. Therefore, the UAV node Uq will receive multiple response messages $Res\_Set = \{Res\_Uj \mid \forall Uj \in List\_nb_{Uq}\}$ from the UAV nodes in the list $List\_nb_{Uq}$. The UAV node Uq verifies the authenticity of the received block through the verification function $Ver(PK_{GCS}, Sign(SK_{GCS}, N))$, and adopts the great majority principles to choose the most trusted block for data recovery.

Table 1. UAV node self-checking and request algorithm

Algorithm 1: UAV node self-checking and Request algorithm

Input: Self information
Output: Data recovery request Req_Uq
1. Initialize int variable cn_lost = 0
2. Initialize int list variable block_lost = []
3. while (true)
4.   for (Blocki in Block)
5.   If (hash(Blocki) != Blocki.CHash)
6.   cn_lost = Blocki.cn
7.   block_lost.append(cn_lost)
8.   end if
9.   end for
10. sleep(t) // Set time interval t
11. end while
12. Initialize int variable i = 0
13. while (true)
14. cni = block_lost[i]
15. get (Block$_{cni-1}$.CHash) -> Req_Uq.CHashcn-1 // Obtain the hash value of the forward block and submit it to the request. If the block is the first block, GCS authentication recovery is required to ensure security.
16. while (cni + 1 in block_lost)
17.   cnl += 1 and i +=1
18. end while
19. get (Block$_{cni+1}$.CHash) -> Req_Uq.CHashcn' // Obtain the hash value of the next block of the data loss block sequence and submit it to the request
20. If (i+1 <= block_lost.length)
21.   i += 1
22. else break
23. end if
24. end while

Table 2. UAV node response algorithm

Algorithm 2: UAV node Response algorithm

Input: Data recovery request Req_Uq
Output: Data recovery response Res_Ui
1. while (true)
2.   keep listening()
3.   If (receive request Req_Uq from Uq)
4.   get(Req_Uq.cn, Req_Uq.CHashcn-1, Req_Uq.cn', Req_Uq.CHashcn')
5.   check(Ui.Block)
6.   If((CHashcn-1 = CHashcn-1*) & (CHashcn' = CHashcn'*))
7.   Send Res_Ui -> Uq
8.   end if
9.   end if
10. end while

Every UAV node stores the public key and verification algorithm of the GCS. Therefore, when the GCS performs important data updates, it can be packaged into a block *Blockm* to pass the block to the nearest UAVs. When the UAV node receives the message, it will verify the message through the public key stored in the GCS and the verification function *Ver (PK$_{GCS}$, Sign (SK$_{GCS}$, N))*. If the confirmation is correct, the UAV node will forward the received block *Blockm* to the neighbor nodes through the blockchain network, and the UAVs which receive the message verifies, saves, and continues to forward the block until all the nodes in the UAV network receive the update information.

5 Reconstruction Approach of Communication Link in UAV Network Based on Blockchain

Since the UAV nodes are registered in the GCS, the GCS can use asymmetric cryptography or certificates to prove the identity of the UAV node. At the same time, in the UAV network, all the actions of the UAV will be recorded and passed to the GCS. Therefore, we use a reputation-based method to check whether a node is a malicious node or whether there is a fault, so that the GCS can reconstruct the communication link in the UAV network. We give the following definitions used in our approach:

1) The normal event is to receive a message, verify the authenticity of the message, and forward the message when the message is true;
2) Malicious events are not forwarding when receiving correct messages, or transmitting false messages to interfere with normal UAVs;
3) The suspicious event is a declaration of data damage and request for data recovery.

If multiple neighbor UAVs receive the same encrypted information from the GCS and pass the verification, the information can be considered authentic. For suspicious events, we set a time window K. Multiple submissions of suspicious events within the time window K will be considered as malicious events. In order to track UAVs that report or forward false messages, UAVs in the network will keep a list of IDs of UAVs that forward messages. The trust degree of each UAV is calculated by (2).

$$t = \begin{cases} 1, & if \ (S+C) < m \\ (kc*c)/(ks*s+kc*c) & other \end{cases} \tag{1}$$

In Eq. (2), s is the number of malicious events generated by the UAV, c is the number of normal events generated by the UAV, ks is the coefficient of the number of malicious events generated by the UAV, and kc is the coefficient of the number of normal events generated by the UAV. And m is the minimum number of events that can be judged malicious. In this way, we can judge whether the node is a malicious node. Also, when the UAV network is in a trusted environment, we can predict whether the node is faulty.

In this way, the UAVs in network can detect malicious UAV or other problems, and the network can also restructure. The UAV network self-reconfiguration process is shown in Fig. 3.

For each communication and forwarding event, the UAV network records it on the blockchain. After a period of time, UAVs in the network send UAVs behavior event

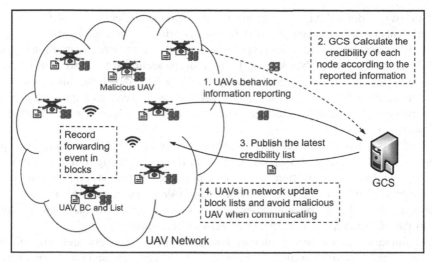

Fig. 3. The UAV network self-reconfiguration process

blockchain to GCS. The GCS receiving the information will calculate the latest credibility of each UAV node through the great majority principles and Eq. (2). Then, the ground control center releases the latest UAV node credibility list to the UAVs network. UAVs in the network update the list, and can re-plan the communication links in the network according to the list.

6 Analysis and Conclusion

Above all, we make the assumption that GCSs are generally deployed in secure environments and attackers cannot deduce the private key from the public key, as mentioned in Sect. 4. For each UAV has verification function $Ver(*)$ to verify the authenticity of the block. In our proposed framework, it is difficult for attackers to forge false block information. Hence, it can guarantee the authenticity of block information.

When the UAV that is attacked or loses data needs to recover information, it will get the necessary information from the neighbor UAV nodes. Compared with nearby UAVs, the distance between the attacked UAV and GCS is longer, which will bring higher time delay. Hence, the proposed framework has high data recovery efficiency.

Also, due to the large number of UAVs in the network, it is difficult for attackers to attack or hijack most of them at the same time. Even if the UAV has lost important data, such as the verification function $Ver(*)$, it can request data from neighboring UAVs, and use the great majority principles to recover data. Hence, the UAV network has invulnerability to some extent.

Another advantage of our proposal is that UAVs and UAV network can observe problems timely and reliably. By using blockchain technique, the behavior of UAVs in the network is recorded on the blockchain and the data on the blockchain is open and transparent to UAVs and GCS in the network. Hence, the malicious behavior or faulty

UAV is easy to detect. Also, according to Algorithm 1 in Sect. 4, each UAV in the network will check itself regularly to detect missing data as soon as possible.

As discussed above, this paper proposes a novel self-adaptive reconstruction method of UAV network based on blockchain. In terms of the technical framework of the self-adaptive reconstruction of the UAV network based on the blockchain, this article gives a specific description from the data storage layer, network layer and application layer, and improves the block data structure to make it satisfy the needs of network adaptive reconstruction.

To address the problems of data damage or missing in the UAV network, this paper proposes a data recovery and update method in the self-reconfiguration of the UAV network, and gives a description of the corresponding algorithms. Finally, this article uses the blockchain to record the behavior of the UAV nodes in the UAV network, and proposes an algorithm to check whether the UAV is malicious or whether there is a fault. So that the GCS can reconstruct the UAV network communication link.

For future work, we will go deeper into the message recovery and safe delivery mechanism, the adaptive routing planning of the UAV network, and the reconstruction when the hardware equipment is damaged in the UAV network.

Acknowledgments. This work was supported by the National Natural Science Foundation of China (General Program) under Grant No. 61572253. This work is also supported by Jiangsu Collaborative Innovation Center of Novel Software Technology and Industrialization.

References

1. Sanchez-Garcia, J., Garcia-Campo, J.M., Arzamendia, M., et al.: A survey on unmanned aerial and aquatic vehicle multi-hop networks: wireless communications, evaluation tools and applications. Comput. Commun. **119**(2018), 43–65 (2018)
2. Mehta, P., Gupta, R., Tanwar, S.: Blockchain envisioned UAV networks: challenges, solutions, and comparisons. Comput. Commun. **151**(2020), 518–538 (2020)
3. Shahriar, H., et al.: Data protection labware for mobile security. In: Wang, G., Feng, J., Bhuiyan, M., Lu, R. (eds.) Security, Privacy, and Anonymity in Computation, Communication, and Storage. SpaCCS 2019. Lecture Notes in Computer Science, vol. 11611. Springer, Cham (2019). https://doi.org/10.1007/978-3-030-24907-6_15
4. Kosba, A., Miller, A., Shi, E., et al.: Hawk: the blockchain model of cryptography and privacy-preserving smart contracts. In: IEEE Symposium on Security and Privacy (SP 2016), San Jose, CA, pp. 839–858 (May 2016)
5. Gavin, W.: Ethereum: a secure decentralised generalised transaction ledger. Ethereum Proj. Yellow Pap. **151**(2014), 1–32 (2014)
6. Androulaki, E., Barger, A., et al.: Hyperledger fabric: a distributed operating system for permissioned blockchains. In: Proceedings of the Thirteenth EuroSys Conference (EuroSys 2018), Porto, Portugal, p. 15 (April 2018). Article No.: 30
7. Liu, D., Ning, P., Sun, K.: Efficient self-healing group key distribution with revocation capability. In: Proceedings of the 10th ACM Conference on Computer and Communications Security (CCS 2003), Washington D.C., USA, pp. 231–240 (October 2003)

8. Deng, Z., Chen, S., Tan, X., Song, D., Wu, F.: An efficient provable multi-copy data possession scheme with data dynamics. In: Wang, G., Chen, J., Yang, L. (eds.) Security, Privacy, and Anonymity in Computation, Communication, and Storage. SpaCCS 2018. Lecture Notes in Computer Science, vol. 11342. Springer, Cham (2018). https://doi.org/10.1007/978-3-030-05345-1_34

9. Tian, B., Han, S., Jiankun, H., Dillon, T.: A mutual-healing key distribution scheme in wireless sensor networks. J. Netw. Comput. Appl. **34**(1), 80–88 (2011)

10. Li, X., Wang, Y., Vijayakumar, P., et al.: Blockchain-based mutual-healing group key distribution scheme in unmanned aerial vehicles ad-hoc network. IEEE Trans. Veh. Technol. **68**(11), 11309–11322 (2019)

11. Ge, C., Ma, X., Liu, Z., et al.: A semi-autonomous distributed blockchain-based framework for UAVs system. J. Syst. Archit. **107**, 101728 (2020)

12. Sharma, V., You, I., Nalin, D., et al.: Neural-blockchain-based ultrareliable caching for edge-enabled UAV networks. IEEE Trans. Ind. Inf. **15**(10), 5723–5736 (2019)

13. Islam, A.A., Shin, S.Y.: BUAV: a blockchain based secure UAV-assisted data acquisition scheme in Internet of Things. J. Commun. Netw. **21**(5), 491–502 (2019)

14. Lei, K., Zhang, Q., Lou, J., et al.: Securing ICN-based UAV ad hoc networks with blockchain. IEEE Commun. Mag. **57**(6), 26–32 (2019)

15. Islam, A.A., Shin, S.Y.: Bus: a blockchain-enabled data acquisition scheme with the assistance of UAV swarm in Internet of Things. IEEE Access **7**, 103231–103249 (2019)

16. Tanwar, S., Bhatia, Q., Patel, P., et al.: Machine learning adoption in blockchain-based smart applications: the challenges, and a way forward. IEEE Access **8**, 474–488 (2019)

17. Hassija, V., Chamola, V., Han, G., et al.: DAGIoV: a framework for vehicle to vehicle communication using directed acyclic graph and game theory. IEEE Trans. Veh. Technol. **69**(4), 4182–4191 (2020)

18. Yang Chi, X., Xianghua, R.K., et al.: A scalable multi-data sources based recursive approximation approach for fast error recovery in big sensing data on cloud. IEEE Trans. Knowl. Data Eng. **32**(5), 841–854 (2019)

19. Wang, S., Yuan, J., Li, X., et al.: Active data replica recovery for quality-assurance big data analysis in IC-IoT. IEEE Access **7**, 106997–107005 (2019)

20. Jung, H., Park, Y., Song, C.-W., et al.: PCS: a parity-based personal data recovery service in cloud. Clust. Comput. **20**(3), 1–4 (2017)

21. Weihua, Y., Lin, H.: Reliability evaluation of BC networks in terms of the extra vertex and edge-connectivity. IEEE Trans. Comput. **63**(10), 2540–2548 (2013)

22. Qiang, Z., Wang, X., Cheng, G.: Reliability evaluation of BC networks. IEEE Trans. Comput. **62**(11), 2337–2340 (2012)

A New Certificateless Aggregate Signature Scheme for Wireless Sensor Networks

Yihong Wen[1], Yi Yang[2(✉)], Shicheng Wang[1], Li Li[2], and Min Luo[2(✉)]

[1] The 54th Research Institute of China Electronics Technology Group Corporation, Shijiazhuang, China
yihwen@139.com, wang.shicheng@163.com
[2] School of Cyber Science and Engineering, Wuhan University, Wuhan, China
yangyi.ip@qq.com, lli@whu.edu.cn, mluo@whu.edu.cn

Abstract. Nowadays, the Internet of Things (IoT) has been rised. As an important branch, the Healthcare Wireless Medical Sensor Networks (HWMSNs) also have a huge developing prospect. The security, privacy and effiency in HWMSNs also have become the hot topics because of HWMSNs' vulnerability in an open wireless channel. In such a scenario, various aggregate signature schemes for HWMSNs have been proposed. Nevertheless, the certificate-based aggregate signature schemes face with a common issue (i.e. complicated certificate management). While Identity-based (ID-based) aggregate signature schemes can mitigate this issue, they cannot resist varied attacks (e.g. the modification attack, the impersonation attack etc.). On the other hand, they usually use complicated computations (e.g. bilinear pairing), being intractable for lightweight devices of HWMSNs. After analyzing proposed aggregate signature schemes, we improve Gayathri et al.'s scheme [1] which is the most efficient in current schemes and propose a certificateless aggregate signature scheme with enhanced security and efficiency (CLAS) scheme. At the same time, the security analysis and performance analysis provided by this paper indicate our scheme can provide privacy preserving, resist current known attacks and has the utility for HWMSNs.

Keywords: IoT · HWMSNs · CLAS · Security · Privacy · Effiency

1 Introduction

The IoT [2], having promoted the third wave of global information industrialization, is an intelligent network to connect objects through the Radio Frequency Identification (RFID) devices, Global Positioning System (GPS) and Wireless Sensor Networks (WSN) [3,4]. It can do intelligent information exchange to realize the intelligent and customized monitoring, tracking, location, identification and management [5].

As a bellwether of the IoT, HWMSNs [6–8], having a huge developing prospect, make full use of wireless network to realize the tracking and service of

G. Wang et al. (Eds.): SpaCCS 2020, LNCS 12382, pp. 312–330, 2021.
https://doi.org/10.1007/978-3-030-68851-6_23

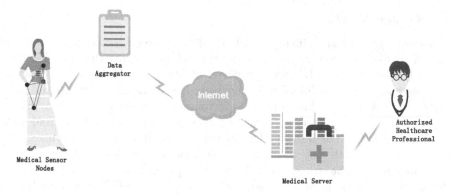

Fig. 1. HWMSNs

health care. The HWSNs can have human physiological data by integrating multidisciplinary knowledge of biosensors, medical electronics, multi-sensor analysis and data fusion, artificial intelligence, pervasive sensing, wireless communications and other innovative applications, being very helpful for studying human diseases [9]. In addition, they also have unique application in medicine management, research and development of new medicine, blood management and many other aspects. And the most prominent advantage of HWMSNs is that it can provide universal health care for human in a sensible, cost effective way. Figure 1 shows the structure of HWMSNs [10]. It has four entities (Authorized Healthcare Professional (AHP), Medical Server (MS), Data aggregator (DA), Medical Sensor Nodes (MSNs)) in HWMSNs. The HWMSNs are on or in the patients' body which have ability to collect health data (eg. blood pressure, heart rate, body temperature) and send these data to DA. The DA can aggregate these messages and send them to remote MS through Internet. The AHP always is a medical establishment which can generate healthcare proposals by analyzing information from MS.

Although HWMSNs have unique advantage in the construction of medical monitoring system, many problems of practical application in HWMSNs still need to be addressed [11]. With the further study of HWMSNs, researchers find that verifying the MSN validity and message integrity are urgent because of suffering many kinds of attacks in HWMSNs communicating. In a real HWMSNs, it is also important to achieve the privacy preserving for every patient. In addition, the MSNs and DA have limited storage and computing power which cause an imperative need to use a lightweight signature scheme for HWMSNs. In such a scenario, various aggregate signature schemes which have the ability of privacy preserving for HWMSNs have been proposed. But most of these schemes can not balance between the security and performance. After analyzing current aggregate signature schemes, we propose a certificateless aggregate signature scheme with enhanced security and efficiency for HWMSNs.

1.1   Related Works

The security, privacy and efficiency in IoT [12–20] have been researched in recent years. A certificate-based aggregate signature scheme having the modified Public Key Infrastructure (PKI) was proposed by Raya and Hubaux [21]. For one sensor node, there are a lot of public/private key pairs and corresponding certificates in this scheme. The sensor node randomly chooses one public/private key pair when it generating a signature. This structure can hide its real identity. The real IoT needs lightweight algorithms and storage. But in this CPPA scheme, public/private key pairs and corresponding certificates for every legal sensor node need to be stored and CA also be required to store these information of legal sensor nodes. In order to solve these problem, an ECPP scheme having temporary anonymous certificates was proposed by Lu et al. [22]. When a sensor node tends to generate a signature, it will have a request to nearby server device for getting a new anonymous certificate in this scheme. This algorithm is un-efficient in real IoT. Then a signature aggregate scheme having Hash Message Authentication Code (HMAC) was proposed by Zhang et al. [23]. It had improved the efficiency. However, all these certificate-based aggregate signature schemes have a weakness on certificates managing.

In such a scenario, an ID-based aggregate signature scheme was proposed by Zhang et al. [23]. It took sensor node's identity as its public key and add conditional privacy preserving for IoT. This scheme needs small storage space because of no need storing certificates and has lower verification and communication. Then Lee and Lai [24] figured out that the scheme proposed by Zhang et al. [23] can not withstand the replay attack by detail security analysis. In order to improve the ID-based signature schemes, Shim [25] proposed a CPAS scheme which is suitable for real HWMSNs. But it can not resist the modification attack by Liu et al.'s research [26]'s research. Then an efficient ID-based aggregate signature scheme was proposed by HE et al. [27]. Even if the ID-based signature schemes are being improved all the time, these schemes have a weakness on key escrow problem.

With the progress of the HWMSNs, a branch of the IoT, many certificateless aggregate signature schemes which is able to deal with the above weaknesses for HWMSNs [28–30] had been proposed recently. But most of them have weaknesses on security or efficiency. In order to make the certificateless aggregate signature scheme being better suitable for HWMSNs, Gayathri et al. [1] proposed a certificateless aggregate signature scheme using ECC instead of bilinear pairing and having a full aggregate signature to reducing the computation cost. However, there are some problems of security and performance in Gayathri et al.'s scheme [1]. They are described and analyzed as follows.

– **the signature generation phase** in N.B. Gayathri et al.'s scheme [1]: the sensor node, having the private key (x_i, d_i) and public key $(X_i = x_iP, R_i)$, randomly chooses $y_{1i}, y_{2i} \in Z_q^*$ and computes:
$Y_{1i} = y_{1i}P$,
$Y_{2i} = ((y_{2i}x_i + h_{2i}d_i) \bmod q)P_{pub} = (u_i, v_i)$,
$w_i = (u_i(y_{1i} + h_{3i}x_i) + h_{4i}d_i) \bmod q$,

$$h_{2i} = H_2(m_i, PID_i, Y_{1i}),$$
$$h_{3i} = H_3(m_i, PID_i, PK_i, T_i),$$
$$h_{4i} = H_4(m_i, PID_i, PK_i, T_i).$$

- **Security:** Firstly, there is no timestamp T_i in the inputs of hash functions H_2 making this scheme can not resist the reply attack. Secondly, the hash functions H_3, H_4 are only related to m_i, PID_i, PK_i, T_i, not to the random integers y_{1i}, y_{2i} in this scheme. Basing on above analysis, we can forger a signature $\sigma_i^* = (Y_{1i}, u_i^*, w_i^*)$:

   (i) We get a valid signature $\sigma_i = (Y_{1i}, u_i, w_i)$ and responding parameters $(X_i, R_i, h_{2i}, h_{3i}, h_{4i})$.

   (ii) Accoring to the equation $w_i P - u_i(Y_{1i} + h_{3i}X) = h_4(R + H_{1i}P_{pub})$, we choose a different random integer y_{2i}^* to get different parameters (u_i^*, w_i^*), the same parameters $(Y_{1i}, R_i, X_i, R_i, h_{1i}, h_{2i}, h_{3i}, h_{4i})$. The purpose of this operation make the equation $w_i^* P - u_i^*(Y_{1i} + h_{3i}X) = h_4(R + H_{1i}P_{pub})$ holds.

   Then we can get a forgery signature $\sigma_i^* = (Y_{1i}, u_i^*, w_i^*)$.

- **Performance:** Firstly, there are redundant hash functions H_3, H_4, mapping to point, adding computation cost in the signature generation phase. Secondly, the v_i, a part of Y_{2i}, is not used in the scheme and it is unecessary to choose the random integer y_{2i} to compute $Y_{2i} = [(y_{2i}x_i + h_{2i}d_i mod q)]P_{pub}$. Using the random integer y_{1i} correctly can ensure the security of the signature. Finally, sending the signature $\sigma_i = (Y_{1i}, u_i, w_i)$ needs high communication cost.

1.2 Our Research Contribution

Facing the security, privacy and performance challenges, we propose a scheme. The main contributions in this paper are summarized as bellows.

(i) Aiming at address the disadvantages of N.B. Gayathri et al.'s scheme [1], We propose a Certificateless Aggregate Signature Scheme with enhanced security and efficiency for HWMSNs.

(ii) The security analysis indicates that the CLAS scheme is Existential Unforgeability against chosen-message attacks (EU-CMA) and can resist many kinds of attacks.

(iii) It shows that shows that the communicating and computing efficiency of our CLAS scheme have been significantly improved in performance analysis.

1.3 Organization of the Article

The rest organization of this article is presented as bellows. Section 2 shows the modified network model and corresponding security model in HWMSNs. Section 3 presents the scheme's detailed algorithms. Section 4 describes the security analysis for the CLAS scheme. Section 5 depicts performance analysis of our CLAS scheme.

2   Background

2.1   Network Model

The HWMSNs in our scheme have four entities, namely, Authorized Healthcare Professional (AHP), Medical Server (MS), Data aggregator (DA), Medical Sensor Nodes (MSNs). For improving the security and performance in HWMSNs, HRSUs are added in our scheme.

- **AHP:** The AHP can provide individualized treatment plans for patients basing on the information from the MS.
- **MS:** The MS, having big storage space and strong computing power, can receive the aggregate information from the DA and sending addressed information to the AHP. In our CLAS scheme, it is also a trusted third party (TA). After successful interacting between MS (TA) and MSN, the MSN can get a full secret key, pseudo identity, full public key from the MS (TA).
- **DA:** A certain amount of MSNs will have a corresponding DA to collecting and aggregating signatures by these MSNs. Compared with MSN, the DA has more computing power.
- **MSNs:** The MSNs are in patient's body and collecting corresponding patient's information (eg. heart rate, blood pressure, temperature, respirations) and their storage space and computing power are limited (Fig. 2).

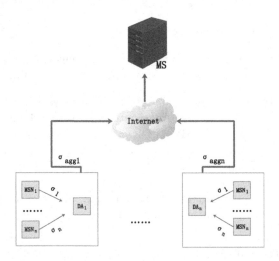

Fig. 2.   Network framework

2.2   Elliptic Curve Discrete Logarithm Problem (ECDLP)

Giving $P, Q \in G$, finding an integer $x \in Z_q^*$ and making this equation $Q = xP$ holding is the ECDLP.

2.3   Security Model

We consider various security parameters (e.g. message integrity, authority distribution, privacy preservation, traceability, un-linkability, resistance against attacks) in HWMSNs. Two types adversaries are considered by us baing on the potential adversary behavior. The key replacement attack can be done by *Type I Adversary*. This adversary can compromise the vehicle secret value or replace the vehicle public key. But it can not get the master secret key. The malicious TA attack can be done by the *Type II Adversary*. This adversary can get master secret key of TA. But it can not replace any public key.

We define the Existential Unforgeability under a Chosen Message Attack (EU-CMA) by considering the following two games against the two types adversaries.

Game I: This game has a challenger ξ and an adversary ADV_1. The executing process is shown as follows.

- *Initialization Phase:* The System Initialization is run by the challenger ξ for getting system parameters which will be given to the adversary ADV_1 and master secret key which will be kept in a secure way.
- *Queries Phase:* The adversary ADV_1 makes queries on the random oracle.
  (i) *Reveal Partial Secret Key Oracle:* The ADV_1 makes a query to the ξ. According to the input ID, the ξ computes d_{ID} and sends it to the ADV_1.
  (ii) *Reveal Secret Value Oracle:* The ADV_1 makes a query to the ξ. According to the input ID, the ξ returns x_{ID} to the ADV_1.
  (iii) *Reveal Public Key Oracle:* The ADV_1 makes a query to the ξ. According to the input ID, the ξ computes PK_{ID} and sends it to the ADV_1.
  (iv) *Replace Public Key Oracle:* Giving a ID, the ADV_1 replaces the public key PK_{ID}.
  (v) *Signing Oracle:* The ADV_1 makes a query. input $M \in \{0,1\}^*$, sign oracle returns a valid signature σ of the user ID.
- *Forgery Phase:* According to the message M_i^*, the ADV outputs σ^* as a forger signature of the identity ID_i^* with the public key $PK_{ID_i}^*$. It will win the game if the following conditions are matched.
  (i) The signature σ^* is valid.
  (ii) The ID^* has not been queried in reveal partial secret key oracle and reveal secret key oracle.
  (iii) The signature σ^* has not been queried in the query phase.

Game II: This game has a challenger ξ and an adversary ADV_2. The executing phase is shown as follows.

- *Initialization Phase:* The System Initialization is run by the challenger ξ for getting system parameters which will be given to the adversary ADV_2 and master secret key which will be kept in a secure way.
- *Queries Phase:* The adversary ADV_2 makes queries on the random oracle.

(i) *Reveal Public Key Oracle:* The ADV_2 makes a query to the ξ. According to the input ID, the ξ computes PK_{ID} and sends it to the ADV_2.

(ii) *Reveal Secret Value Oracle:* The ADV_2 makes a query to the ξ. According to the input ID, the ξ returns x_{ID} to the ADV_2.

(iii) *Signing Oracle:* The ADV_2 makes a query. input $M \in \{0,1\}^*$, sign oracle returns a valid signature σ of the user ID.

- *Forgery Phase:* According to the message M_i^*, the ADV outputs σ^* as a forger signature of the identity ID_i^* with the public key $PK_{ID_i}^*$. It will win the game if the following conditions are matched.

  (i) The signature σ^* is valid.

  (ii) The ID^* has not been queried in reveal secret key oracle.

  (iii) The signature σ^* has not been queried in the query phase.

3   The Proposed Scheme

In this section, we propose a Certificateless Aggregate Signature Scheme with enhanced security and efficiency which is able to protect privacy and construct efficient aggregate signatures for secure communication in HWMSNs. The notations throughout the scheme are described as below.

Notations

p, q: two large prime numbers.

E: an elliptic curve $y^2 = x^3 + ax + b \bmod p$,
   defined over the prime field F_p.

G: an additive group with the order q,
   and all points on the elliptic curve E make up the G.

P: a random non-zero base point in E.

H: hash functions, $H_0: G \times \{0,1\}^* \to Z_q^*$.
   $\qquad H_1: G \times G \times \{0,1\}^* \to Z_q^*$.
   $\qquad H_2: G \times G \times G \times \{0,1\} \times \{0,1\}^* \to Z_q^*$
   $\qquad H_3: G \times G \times \{0,1\} \times \{0,1\} \times \{0,1\}^* \to Z_q^*$
   $\qquad H_4: G \to Z_q^*$

s: the master secret key.

P_{pub}: the master public key.

M_i: the i-th message.

RID_i: the i-th real vehicle identity.

PID_i: the i-th pseudo vehicle identity.

C_i: the ciphertext of the PID_i.

sk_i: the private key of the i-th vehicle.

PK_i: the public key of the i-th vehicle.

RID_j: the j-th real RSU identity.

sk_j: the private key of the j-th RSU.

PK_j: the public key of the j-th RSU.

σ_i: the signature of the M_i.

3.1 The Proposed CLAS Scheme

There are seven phases in CLAS scheme: System Initialization, Public/Secret Key Pair Generation, Signing, MSN to DA Verification, Aggregate signature and DA to MS Verification.

1) System Initialization

In the System Initialization, the MS generates system parameters which are pre-loaded into tamper-proof device of every MSN. The specific steps are described as follows.

- The MS selects a group G of prime order q, a generator P of G. Then it chooses a random number $s \in z_q^*$ as its master secret key and sets $P_{pub} = sP$ as its master public key.
- The MS selects four hash functions $H_0: G \times \{0,1\}^* \to Z_q^*$, $H_1: G \times G \times \{0,1\}^* \to Z_q^*$, $H_2: G \times G \times G \times \{0,1\} \times \{0,1\}^* \to Z_q^*$, $H_3: G \times G \times \{0,1\} \times \{0,1\} \times \{0,1\}^* \to Z_q^*$. After that, the MS publishes the system parameters as $params = \{q, G, P, P_{pub}, H_0, H_1, H_2, H_3\}$ and keeps the master secret key secure.

2) Public/Secret Key pair Generation

The MSN public/secret Key pair generation phase is as below.

- The MSN sets a password PWD_i and sends $\{PWD_i, RID_i\}$ to the MS. The RID_i is the real identity of this MSN.
- After receiving $\{PWD_i, PID_i\}$, the MS chooses a random number $r_i \in Z_q^*$ and computes:

$$R_i = r_i P,$$
$$PID_i = RID_i \oplus H_0(r_i P_{pub}, T_i),$$
$$h_{1i} = H_1(PID_i, R_i, P_{pub}),$$
$$d_i = r_i + s h_{1i} \mod q.$$

Then the MS sets $D_i = (d_i, R_i)$ and sends $\{PID_i, D_i, d_i\}$ to this MSN in a secure channel.

- When getting $\{PID_i, D_i, d_i\}$, the MSN verifies the equation $d_i P = R_i + h_{1i} P_{pub}$. If it is false, this MSN will fail to register. Otherwise, this vehicle chooses a random number $x_i \in Z_q^*$ and computes $X_i = x_i P$.

The public key of this MSN is $PK_i = (X_i, R_i)$ and the private key of this MSN is $sk_i = (d_i, x_i)$.

3) Signing

In the signing phase, the MSN uses its private key sk_i to sign a message M_i.

- The MSN chooses a random number $y_i \in Z_q^*$ and computes:

$$Y_i = y_i P,$$
$$h_{2i} = H_2(M_i, PID_i, PK_i, Y_i, T_i),$$
$$h_{3i} = H_3(M_i, PID_i, PK_i, h_{2i}, T_i),$$
$$w_i = y_i - h_{2i} x_i - h_{3i} d_i \mod q,$$
$$\sigma_i = (h_{2i}, w_i).$$

The σ_i is the signature of the M_i. When these two steps have been completed, the MSN sends $\{\sigma_i, M_i, PK_i, E_i, C_i, T_i\}$ to the corresponding DA.

4) **MSN to DA Verification**

In the MSN to DA Verification, the DA verifies the valid of MSN. If the identity is valid, the DA computes:

$$Y_i' = w_i P + h_{2i} X_i + h_{3i}(R_i + h_{1i} P_{pub}),$$
$$h_{2i}' = H_2(M_i, PID_i, PK_i, Y_i', T_i).$$

Then the DA verifies the equation $h_{2i}' = h_{2i}$. If it false, the DA will reject this message. Otherwise, the DA accepts the signature and sets $\sigma_i' = (Y_i', w_i)$.

5) **Aggregate Signature**

In the aggregate signature, the DA aggregates n messages $\{M_i, \sigma_i', PK_i, PID_i, T_i\}$ and sends them to the MS. The specific steps are described as follows.

- The DA sets $\widehat{T} = \emptyset$, $\widehat{PK} = \emptyset$, $w = 0$, $Y = \mathcal{O}$.
- For $i = 1$ to n, The DA computes:

$$\widehat{T} = \widehat{T} \bigcup \{M_i\},$$
$$\widehat{PK} = \widehat{PK} \bigcup \{PK_i\},$$
$$w = w + w_i \mod q,$$
$$Y = Y + Y_i' \mod q,$$

Then the DA sends $\{\widehat{T}, \widehat{PK}, w, Y\}$ to the corresponding MS through the wired network.

6) **DA to MS Verification**

In the DA to MS Verification, the MS verifies the aggregate signature. It checks the equation $|\widehat{T}| = |\widehat{PK}|$. If it is false, the MS will reject this aggregate signature. Otherwise, for $i = 1$ to n, the MS computes:

$$Q_i = h_{3i}(R_i + h_{1i} P_{pub}),$$
$$S_i = h_{2i} X_i.$$

Then it verifies the equation $wP - Y + \sum_{i=1}^{n}(S_i + Q_i) = \infty$. If it is false, the MS will rejects this aggregate signature. Otherwise, it will accept these messages.

3.2   Correctness of the CLAS Scheme

The description of correctness in the proposed CLAS scheme is divided into two parts: the correctness of the signing phase, the correctness of the aggregate signature.

Correctness of signing:

$$Y_i' = w_i P + h_{2i} X_i + h_{3i}(R_i + h_{1i} P_{pub})$$
$$= (y_i - h_{2i} x_i - h_{3i} d_i) P + + h_{2i} X_i + h_{3i} R_i + h_{3i} h_{1i} P_{pub}$$
$$= y_i P - h_{3i}(r_i + s h_{1i}) P + h_{3i} r_i P + h_{3i} h_{1i} s P$$
$$= Y_i$$

Therefore, $h_{2i}' = H_2(M_i, PID_i, PK_i, Y_i', T_i) = h_{2i}$. It shows that the signing phase is correct.

Correctness of aggregate signature: We have the equations $Q_i = h_{3i}(R_i + h_{1i} P_{pub})$ and $S_i = h_{2i} X_i$. The reason why aggregate signature is correct is described as follows.

$$w P - Y + \sum_{i=1}^{n}(S_i + Q_i)$$
$$= (\sum_{i=1}^{n}(y_i - h_{2i} x_i - h_{3i} d_i)) P - Y + \sum_{i=1}^{n}(S_i + Q_i)$$
$$= \sum_{i=1}^{n}(Y_i - h_{2i} X_i - h_{3i} R_i - h_{1i} h_{3i} P_{pub}) - Y + \sum_{i=1}^{n}(S_i + Q_i)$$
$$= \infty$$

4   Security Analysis

In this section, we prove the security of the proposed CLAS scheme in the random oracle model and analyze its security requirements.

4.1   Security Proof

Basing on the Sect. 3(C), we have a detail description on the security proof of the proposed CLAS scheme in this section.

Theorem: The proposed CLAS scheme is EU-CMA under the assumption that the ECDLP is hard in the random oracle model.

This proof of the *Theorem* is depending on the next *Lemma* 1, *Lemma* 2, *Lemma* 3 and *Lemma* 4.

Lemma 1: *There is a Type I Adversary who can forge a valid signature of the CLAS scheme in an attack model by the Game I in the random oracle model. Then the challenger can use the ability of the adversary to solve the ECDLP.*

Proof: According to the section of the security model, the ξ is an ECDLP challenger and the ADV_1 is an adversary who can forge a valid signature of the proposed CLAS scheme in the *Game I*. The ξ can use the ability of ADV_1 to solve the ECDLP. Giving the $\{P, P_1 = aP\}$ as a ECDLP random instance to the challenger ξ. The goal for the ξ is to find a after the interaction with ADV_1. And the ID^* is the target identity for the ξ. The corresponding message is M^*.

- *Initialization Phase:* The ξ publish system parameter:

$$\{G, P, P_{pub}, H_0, H_1, H_2, H_3\}$$

to the ADV_1 and keeps the s secretly. The ξ sets $P_{pub} = P_1$.
- *Queries Phase:* The ADV_1 queries and the ξ which has initially empty lists

$$L_1, L_2, L_3, L_{PSK}, L_{SV}, L_{PK}.$$

(i) *Queries on oracle H_1:* The ξ has a list $L_1 : (ID_i, R_i, P_{pub}, h_{1i})$. The ADV_1 takes a query on H_1. If $(ID_i, R_i, P_{pub}, h_{1i})$ has existed in the list L_1, the ξ returns corresponding h_{1i}. Otherwise, the ξ randomly selects a $h_{1i} \in Z_q^*$ and inserts it into the L_1. Then the ξ sends h_{1i} to the ADV_1.

(ii) *Queries on oracle H_2:* The ξ has a list $L_2 : (M_i, ID_i, PK_i, Y_i, T_i, h_{2i})$. The ADV_1 takes a query onH_2. If the $(M_i, ID_i, PK_i, Y_i, T_i, h_{2i})$ has existed in the list L_2, the ξ returns corresponding h_{2i}. Otherwise, the ξ randomly selects a $h_{2i} \in Z_q^*$ and inserts it into the L_2. Then the ξ sends h_{2i} to the ADV_1.

(iii) *Queries on oracle(H_3):* The ξ has a list $L_3: (M_i, ID_i, PK_i, h_{2i}, T_i, h_{3i})$. The ADV_1 takes a query on H_3. If the $(M_i, ID_i, PK_i, h_{2i}, T_i, h_{3i})$ has existed in the list L_3, the ξ returns corresponding h_{3i}. Otherwise, the ξ randomly selects a $h_{3i} \in Z_q^*$ and inserts it into the L_3. Then the ξ sends h_{3i} to the ADV_1.

(iv) *Reveal Partial Secret Key Oracle ($PSK(ID_i)$):* The ξ has a list $PSK(ID_i): (ID_i, r_i, d_i)$. The ADV_1 takes a query on $PSK(ID_i)$. If the (ID_i, r_i, d_i) has existed in the list L_{PSK}, the ξ returns corresponding d_i. Otherwise, the ξ randomly selects a $r_i \in Z_q^*$, searches h_{1i} from the list L_1 and makes $d_i = r_i + ah_{1i}$ if $ID_i \neq ID^*$. Then the ξ inserts (ID_i, r_i, d_i) into the L_{PSK}. At last, the ξ sends d_i to the ADV_1. If $ID_i = ID^*$, abort.

(v) *Reveal Secret Value Oracle($SV(ID_i)$):* The ξ has a list $SV(ID_i): (ID_i, x_i)$. The ADV_1 takes a query on $SK(ID_i)$. If $ID_i \neq ID^*$, the ξ searches the (ID_i, x_i) in the L_{SV}. If the ID_i is existing, the ξ returns x_i to the ADV_1. If the ID_i is not existing, the ξ randomly selects a $x_i \in Z_q^*$ and inserts the produced (ID_i, x_i) into L_{SV}. Then the ξ returns the x_i to the ADV_1. If $ID_i = ID^*$, abort.

(vi) *Reveal Public Key Oracle($PK(ID_i)$):* The ξ has a list $L_{PK}: (ID_i, pk_i)$. The ADV_1 takes a query on $PK(ID_i)$. If the (ID_i, pk_i) has existed in the list L_{PK}, the ξ returns corresponding pk_i. Otherwise, the ξ searches the L_{SV} to get the x_i, computes $X_i = x_i P$ and sets $pk_i = (R_i, X_i)$. At last, the ξ inserts (ID_i, pk_i) into the L_{PK} and sends pk_i to the ADV_1.

(vii) *Replace Public Key Oracle($RPK(ID_i)$):* The ADV_1 inputs (ID_i, pk_i) for querying on $RPK(ID_i)$. The ξ replaces $PK_i = PK_i'$.

(viii) *Signing Oracle*: The ADV_1 takes a query on (ID_i, M_i, T_i). If $ID_i = ID^*$, abort. Otherwise, the ξ gets:

$(ID_i, R_i, P_{pub}, h_{1i})$ from the L_1,

$(M_i, ID_i, PK_i, Y_i, T_i, h_{2i})$ from the L_2,

$(M_i, ID_i, PK_i, h_{2i}, T_i, h_{3i})$ from the L_3,
(ID_i, r_i, d_i) from the L_{PSK},
(ID_i, x_i) from the L_{SV}.
Then the ξ randomly chooses $y_i \in Z_q^*$ and sets $w_i = y_i - h_{2i}x_i - h_{3i}d_i$.
According to the signature definition and simulation, we have :
$$Y_i' = w_iP + h_{2i}X_i + h_{3i}(R_i + h_{1i}P_{pub})$$
$$= (y_i - h_{2i}x_i - h_{3i}d_i)P + h_{2i}X_i + h_{3i}(R_i + h_{1i}P_{pub})$$
$$= y_iP - h_{2i}X_i - h_{3i}R_i - h_{3i}h_{1i}P_{pub} + h_{2i}X_i + h_{3i}(R_i + h_{1i}P_{pub})$$
$$= Y_i.$$
Therefore, the signature $\sigma_{M_i} = (h_{2i}, w_i)$ is valid.

- *Forgery Phase:* The ADV_1 forges a valid signature. The following operations is shown as below.

(i) If the $ID_i \neq ID^*$, abort.
(ii) If $ID_i = ID^*$ and $M_i = M^*$, the ADV_1 can output a valid signature $\sigma_i = (h_{2i}, w_i)$. The ξ computes $Y_i' = w_iP + h_{2i}X_i + h_{3i}(R_i + h_{1i}P_{pub})$, $h_{2i}' = H_2(M_i, PID_i, PK_i, Y_i', T_i)$ and verifies the equation $h_{2i} = h_{2i}'$. Basing on Forking Lemma [31], the ADV_1 can output another valid signature $\sigma_i^* = (h_{2i}, w_i^*)$. Using same $(y_i, x_i, r_i, h_{2i}, h_{3i})$ and get different hash values h_{1i}, it has the equation $Y_i' = w_i^*P + h_{2i}X_i + h_{3i}(R_i + h_{1i}^*P_{pub})$.
There is the derivation:
$$Y_i' - Y_i' = w_i^*P - w_iP + h_{2i}X_i - h_{2i}X_i + h_{3i}(R_i + h_{1i}^*P_{pub}) - h_{3i}(R_i + h_{1i}P_{pub});$$
$$(w_i^* - w_i)P = h_{3i}(h_{1i} - h_{1i}^*)aP.$$
Then the ADV_1 can output s by computing $a = (w_i^* - w_i)(h_{3i}(h_{1i} - h_{1i}^*))^{-1}$.
Since it contradicts the ECDLP, the proposed CLAS scheme can resist the attack of *Type I Adversary.*

Lemma 2: *There is a Type I Adversary who can forge a valid aggregate signature of the CLAS scheme in an attack model by the Game I in the random oracle model. Then the challenger can use the ability of the adversary to solve the ECDLP.*

Proof: Excepting the *Forgery Phase*, the proof of *Lemma 2* is identical to the *Lemma 1*. The ADV_1 forges a valid aggregate signature and the ξ can use the ability of ADV_1 to solve the ECDLP.

Forgery: The ADV_1 outputs a valid aggregate signature (w, Y). The ξ verifies the correctness of $wP - Y + \sum_{i=1}^{n}(S_i + Q_i) = \infty$. If it is false, abort. Otherwise, basing on Forking Lemma [31], the ADV_1 can outputs another valid aggregate signature (w^*, Y). Choosing different h_{1i}, the ADV_1 can get $w^*P - Y + \sum_{i=1}^{n}(S_i + Q_i^*) = \infty$.
Then it has $(w^* - w)P = \sum_{i=1}^{n}(h_{3i}(R_i + h_{1i}^*aP))$. Thus, the ξ can get $a = (w^* - w)\sum_{i=1}^{n}(h_{3i}(h_{1i} - h_{1i}^*))^{-1}$. Since it contradicts the ECDLP, the proposed CLAS scheme can resist the attack of *Type I Adversary.*

Lemma 3: *There is a Type II Adversary who can forge a valid signature of the CLAS scheme in an attack model by the Game II in the random oracle model. Then the challenger can use the ability of the adversary to solve the ECDLP.*

Proof: According to the section of the security model, the ξ is an ECDLP challenger and the ADV_2 is an adversary who can forge a valid signature of the proposed CLAS scheme in the *Game II*. The ξ can use the ability of ADV_2 to solve the ECDLP. Giving the $\{P, P_1 = aP\}$ as a ECDLP random instance to the challenger ξ. The goal for the ξ is to find a after the interaction with ADV_2. And the ID^* is the target identity for the ξ. The corresponding message is M^*.

- *Initialization Phase:* The ξ publish system parameters:

$$\{G, P, P_{pub}, H_0, H_1, H_2, H_3\}$$

  and master secret key s to the ADV_1.

- *Queries Phase:* The ADV_1 queries and the ξ which has initially empty lists $L_1, L_2, L_3, L_{SV}, L_{PK}$ answers.

  (i) *Queries on oracle H_1:* The ξ has a list $L_1 : (ID_i, R_i, P_{pub}, h_{1i})$. The ADV_2 takes a query on H_1. If $(ID_i, R_i, P_{pub}, h_{1i})$ has existed in the list L_1, the ξ returns corresponding h_{1i}. Otherwise, the ξ randomly selects a $h_{1i} \in Z_q^*$ and inserts it into the L_1. Then the ξ sends h_{1i} to the ADV_2.

  (ii) *Queries on oracle H_2:* The ξ has a list $L_2 : (M_i, ID_i, PK_i, Y_i, T_i, h_{2i})$. The ADV_2 takes a query on H_2. If the $(M_i, ID_i, PK_i, Y_i, T_i, h_{2i})$ has existed in the list L_2, the ξ returns corresponding h_{2i}. Otherwise, the ξ randomly selects a $h_{2i} \in Z_q^*$ and inserts it into the L_2. Then the ξ sends h_{2i} to the ADV_2.

  (iii) *Queries on oracle(H_3):* The ξ has a list $L_3 : (M_i, ID_i, PK_i, h_{2i}, T_i, h_{3i})$. The ADV_2 takes a query on H_3. If the $(M_i, ID_i, PK_i, h_{2i}, T_i, h_{3i})$ has existed in the list L_3, the ξ returns corresponding h_{3i}. Otherwise, the ξ randomly selects a $h_{3i} \in Z_q^*$ and inserts it into the L_3. Then the ξ sends h_{3i} to the ADV_2.

  (iv) *Reveal Secret Value Oracle($SV(ID_i)$):* The ξ has a list $SV(ID_i)$: (ID_i, x_i). The ADV_2 takes a query on $SK(ID_i)$. If $ID_i \neq ID^*$, the ξ searches the (ID_i, x_i) in the L_{SV}. If the ID_i is existing, the ξ returns x_i to the ADV_2. If the ID_i is not existing, the ξ randomly selects a $x_i \in Z_q^*$ and inserts the produced (ID_i, x_i) into L_{SV}. Then the ξ returns the x_i to the ADV_2. If $ID_i = ID^*$, abort.

  (v) *Reveal Public Key Oracle($PK(ID_i)$):* The ξ has a list $L_{PK}: (ID_i, pk_i)$. The ADV_2 takes a query on $PK(ID_i)$. If the (ID_i, pk_i) has existed in the list L_{PK}, the ξ returns corresponding pk_i. Otherwise, if $ID = ID^*$, the ξ sets $P_i = P_1$. If $ID_i \neq ID^*$, the ξ searches the L_{SV} to get the x_i, computes $P_i = x_i P$ and sets $pk_i = (R_i, P_i)$. At last, the ξ inserts (ID_i, pk_i) into the L_{PK} and sends pk_i to the ADV_2.

  (vi) *Signing Oracle:* The ADV_2 takes a query on (ID_i, M_i, T_i). If $ID_i = ID^*$, abort. Otherwise, the ξ gets:

$(ID_i, R_i, P_{pub}, h_{1i})$ from the L_1,
$(M_i, ID_i, PK_i, Y_i, T_i, h_{2i})$ from the L_2,
$(M_i, ID_i, PK_i, h_{2i}, T_i, h_{3i})$ from the L_3,
(ID_i, x_i) from the L_{SV}.

Then the ξ randomly chooses $y_i \in Z_q^*$ and sets $w_i = y_i - h_{2i}x_i - h_{3i}d_i$. According to the signature definition and simulation, we have :

$$\begin{aligned}
Y_i' &= w_i P + h_{2i} X_i + h_{3i}(R_i + h_{1i}P_{pub}) \\
&= (y_i - h_{2i}x_i - h_{3i}d_i)P + h_{2i}X_i + h_{3i}(R_i + h_{1i}P_{pub}) \\
&= y_i P - h_{2i}X_i - h_{3i}R_i - h_{3i}h_{1i}P_{pub} + h_{2i}X_i + h_{3i}(R_i + h_{1i}P_{pub}) \\
&= Y_i.
\end{aligned}$$

Therefore, the signature $\sigma_{M_i} = (h_{2i}, w_i)$ is valid.

- *Forgery Phase:* The ADV_1 forges a valid signature. The following operations is shown as below.

(i) If the $ID_i \neq ID^*$, abort.

(ii) If $ID_i = ID^*$ and $M_i = M^*$, the ADV_1 can output a valid signature $\sigma_i = (h_{2i}, w_i)$. The ξ computes $Y_i' = w_i P + h_{2i}X_i + h_{3i}(R_i + h_{1i}P_{pub})$, $h_{2i}' = H_2(M_i, PID_i, PK_i, Y_i', T_i)$ and verifies the equation $h_{2i} = h_{2i}'$. Basing on Forking Lemma [31], the ADV_1 can output another valid signature $\sigma_i^* = (h_{2i}, w_i^*)$. Using same $(y_i, x_i, r_i, h_{1i}, h_{3i})$ and get different hash values h_{2i}, it has the equation $Y_i' = w_i^* P + h_{2i}X_i + h_{3i}(R_i + h_{1i}^* P_{pub})$. There is the derivation:

$$\begin{aligned}
Y_i' - Y_i' &= w_i^* P - w_i P + h_{2i}^* X_i - h_{2i}X_i + h_{3i}(R_i + h_{1i}P_{pub}) - h_{3i}(R_i + h_{1i}P_{pub}); \\
(w_i^* - w_i)P &= (h_{2i} - h_{2i}^*)aP.
\end{aligned}$$

Then the ADV_2 can output s by computing $u = (w_i^* - w_i)(h_{2i} - h_{2i}^*)^{-1}$. Since it contradicts the ECDLP, the proposed CLAS scheme can resist the attack of *Type II Adversary.*

Lemma 4: *There is a Type II Adversary who can forge a valid aggregate signature of the CLAS scheme in an attack model by the Game II in the random oracle model. Then the challenger can use the ability of the adversary to solve the ECDLP.*

Proof: Excepting the *Forgery Phase*, the proof of *Lemma 4* is identical to the *Lemma 3*. The ADV_2 forges a valid aggregate signature and the ξ can use the ability of ADV_2 to solve the ECDLP.

Forgery: The ADV_2 outputs a valid aggregate signature (w, Y). The ξ verifies the correctness of $wP - Y + \sum_{i=1}^n (S_i + Q_i) = \infty$. If it is false, abort. Otherwise, basing on Forking Lemma [31], the ADV_2 can outputs another valid aggregate signature (w^*, Y). Choosing different h_{2i}, the ADV_2 can get $w^* P - Y + \sum_{i=1}^n (S_i^* + Q_i) = \infty$.

Then it has $(w^* - w)P = \sum_{i=1}^n (h_{2i} - h_{2i}^*)aP)$. Thus, the ξ can get $a = (w^* - w)\sum_{i=1}^n (h_{2i} - h_{2i}^*)^{-1}$. Since it contradicts the ECDLP, the proposed CLAS scheme can resist the attack of *Type II Adversary.*

4.2 Other Security Requirements

The CLAS scheme we proposed has achieved the following security requirements for HWMSNs. They have five aspects: message authentication, privacy preservation, traceability, un-linkability and resistant against various types of attacks.

(i) **Message Authentication.** According to the *Lemma* 1, *Lemma* 2, *Lemma* 3 and *Lemma* 4, the CLAS scheme achieves the message authentication requirement.

(ii) **Privacy Preservation.** Each MSN uses it's pseudo identity $PID_i = RID_i \oplus H_0(r_i P_{pub}, T_i)$ in the communication with a DA. Thus, the malicious attacker can not get the real identity of MSN. It shows that our proposed scheme achieves the privacy preservation requirement.

(iii) **Traceability.** The MS (TA) computes the pseudo identity $PID_i = RID_i \oplus H_0(r_i P_{pub}, T_i)$. If a vehicle has malicious behavior, the MS (TA) can easily find it. Hence, the CLAS scheme achieves the traceability requirement.

(iv) **Un-linkability.** When a MSN tends to generate a signature, it will chooses a random number $y_i \in Z_q^*$ and y_i is a parameter for signing. So it is difficult to link two signatures from the same MSN. It shows that the CLAS scheme achieves the un-linkability requirement.

(v) **Resistant Against Various Types of Attacks.** Basing on the security proof, the CLAS scheme can resist the impersonation attack, the modification attack, the replay attack and the man-in-the-middle attack.

5 Performance Analysis

In this section, we analyze the communication cost and computation cost of our CLAS scheme. The communication cost and computation cost are the most important factors to decide whether the aggregate signature scheme is suitable for HWMSNs.

Table 1. Communication cost

References	Sending a signature	Sending n signatures
Liu et al.'s scheme [28]	$2\|G_1\| = 2048$ bits	$3\|G_1\| = 3072$ bits
Wu et al.'s scheme [29]	$2\|G_1\| = 2048$ bits	$(n+1)\|G_1\| = (n+1)1024$ bits
Gayathri et al.'s scheme [1]	$\|G_2\| + 2\|Z_q^*\| = 640$ bits	$2\|G_2\| + \|Z_q^*\| = 800$ bits
Our work	$2\|Z_q^*\| = 320$ bits	$\|G_2\| + \|Z_q^*\| = 480$ bits

First, we compare the communication cost of our CLAS scheme with Liu et al.'s scheme [28], Wu et al.'s scheme [29] and Gayathri et al.'s scheme [1]. On account of using bilinear paring in Liu et al.'s scheme [28] and Wu et al.'s scheme [29], for achieving the same security, we take the bilinear paring on super singular elliptic curve having point G_1 which q is 512 bits and the elliptic curve on Koblitz elliptic curve having point G_2 which q is 160 bits. As shown in the Table 1, sending a signature by a MSN in our CLAS scheme is $2|Z_q^*| = 320$ bits and sending n signatures by a MSN is $|G_2| + |Z_q^*| = 480$ bits which are the lowest cost in all schemes.

Table 2. Computation Cost

References	Single sign.	Single Verif.	Agg. Sign.	Agg. Verif.
Liu et al. [28]	$2T_{BPSM}$ $+T_{BPPA}$ $-1902T_{ECPA}$	$2T_{BP}$ $+T_{MTPH}$ $+T_{BPSM}$ $+T_{BPPA}$ $=8079T_{ECPA}$	nT_{BPSM} $+(3n-1)T_{BPPA}$ $=(961n-4)T_{ECPA}$	$2T_{BP}$ $+T_{BPPA}$ $=2343T_{ECPA}$
Wu et al. [29]	$4T_{BPSM}$ $+2T_{BPPA}$ $+T_{MTPH}$ $=6252T_{ECPA}$	$3T_{BP}$ $+2T_{MTPH}$ $+2T_{BPSM}$ $+1T_{BPPA}$ $=13815T_{ECPA}$	$(n-1)T_{BPPA}$ $=4(n-1)T_{ECPA}$	$3T_{BP}$ $+(n+1)T_{MTPH}$ $+2nT_{BPSM}$ $+(3n-2)T_{BPPA}$ $=(4368n+9457)T_{ECPA}$
Gayathri et al. [1]	$2T_{ECSM}$ $+3T_{MTPH}$ $=492T_{ECPA}$	$5T_{ECSM}$ $+3T_{ECPA}$ $=1231T_{ECPA}$	$2nT_{ECSM}$ $+2(n-1)T_{ECPA}$ $=(494n-2)T_{ECPA}$	$(2n+1)T_{ECSM}$ $+(2n+1)T_{ECPA}$ $=(494n+2)T_{ECPA}$
Our work	T_{ECSM} $=246T_{ECPA}$	$4T_{ECSM}$ $+3T_{ECPA}$ $=985T_{ECPA}$	nT_{ECPA}	$2nT_{ECSM}$ $+(n+1)T_{ECPA}$ $=(493n+1)T_{ECPA}$

Then, we compare the computation cost of our CLAS scheme with Liu et al.'s scheme [28], Wu et al.'s scheme [29] and Gayathri et al.'s scheme [1]. From the [1], we can get the execution time of different cryptographic operations. The execution of elliptic curve point addition is $T_{ECPA} = 0.0018$ ms. The execution of elliptic curve multiplication is $T_{ECSM} = 0.4420$ ms $= 246T_{ECPA}$. The execution of map to point hash function is $T_{MTPH} = 4.4060$ ms $= 2448T_{ECPA}$. The execution of bilinear pairing point addition is $T_{BPPA} = 0.0071$ ms $= 4T_{ECPA}$. The execution of bilinear pairing multiplication is $T_{BPSM} = 1.7090$ ms $= 949T_{ECPA}$. The execution of bilinear pairing is $T_{BP} = 4.2110$ ms $= 2339T_{ECPA}$. The Table 2 shows the single signature and verification cost, aggregate signature and verification cost and the total cost in these 4 schemes.

When the number of signatures is increasing, we compare the total computation cost of our scheme with Liu et al.'s scheme [28], Wu et al.'s scheme [29] and Gayathri et al.'s scheme [1] in Fig. 3. It indicates that our CLAS scheme have high efficiency when verifying multiple messages. Basing on all above tables and figures, the proposed CLAS scheme have advantages on computation and communication in real HWMSNs.

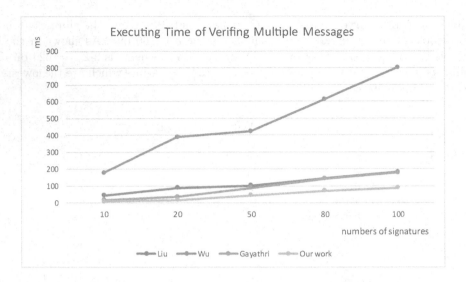

Fig. 3. Executing time of verifying multiple messages

6   Conclusion

In recent years, many signature aggregate scheme for the HWMSNs have been proposed. They have made great contributions to improving computing and communicating efficiency. But most of them can not strike a good balance between the efficiency and security. To overcome it, we proposed a certificateless aggregate signature scheme with enhanced security and efficiency for HWMSNs. The security analysis indicates that our CLAS scheme can achieve message authentication requirement, privacy preservation requirement, traceability requirement, un-linkability requirement and resist against various types of attacks. The performance analysis shows that our CLAS scheme has high performance. They all indicate that our CLAS scheme is more suitable for HWMSNs.

Acknowledgments. This work is partially supported by the National Key Research and Development Program of China (No. 2018YFC1315404), the National Natural Science Foundation of China (Nos. 61972294, 61932016), the Opening Project of Guangdong Provincial Key Laboratory of Data Security and Privacy Protection (No. 2017B030301004-11) and the Science and Technology planning project of ShenZhen (No. JCYJ20170818112550194).

References

1. Gayathri, N.B., et al.: Efficient and secure pairing-free certificateless aggregate signature scheme for healthcare wireless medical sensor networks. IEEE Internet Things J. **6**(5), 9064–9075 (2019)

2. Gubbi, J., Buyya, R., Marusic, S., Palaniswami, M.: Internet of things (IoT): a vision, architectural elements, and future directions. Future Gener. Comput. Syst. **29**(7), 1645–1660 (2013)
3. Bellavista, P., Cardone, G., Corradi, A., Foschini, L.: Convergence of manet and WSN in IoT urban scenarios. IEEE Sens. J. **13**(10), 3558–3567 (2013)
4. Alazeb, A., Panda, B.: Ensuring data integrity in fog computing based health-care systems. In: Wang, G., Feng, J., Bhuiyan, M.Z.A., Lu, R. (eds.) SpaCCS 2019. LNCS, vol. 11611, pp. 63 77. Springer, Cham (2019). https://doi.org/10.1007/978-3-030-24907-6_6
5. Zhang, Z.K., Cho, M.C.Y., Wang, C.W., Hsu, C.W., Chen, C.K., Shieh, S.: IoT security: ongoing challenges and research opportunities. In: 2014 IEEE 7th International Conference on Service-Oriented Computing and Applications (SOCA) (2014)
6. Kumar, P., Lee, H.J.: Security issues in healthcare applications using wireless medical sensor networks: a survey. Sensors **12**(1), 55–91 (2012)
7. Sghaier, N., et al.: Wireless sensor networks for medical care services. In: Proceedings of the 7th International Wireless Communications and Mobile Computing Conference, IWCMC 2011, Istanbul, Turkey, 4–8 July 2011 (2011)
8. Othman, S.B., Bahattab, A.A., Trad, A., Youssef, H.: Secure data transmission protocol for medical wireless sensor networks. In: IEEE International Conference on Advanced Information Networking & Applications (2014)
9. Semenko, Y., Saucez, D.: Distributed privacy preserving platform for ridesharing services. In: Wang, G., Feng, J., Bhuiyan, M.Z.A., Lu, R. (eds.) SpaCCS 2019. LNCS, vol. 11611, pp. 1–14. Springer, Cham (2019). https://doi.org/10.1007/978-3-030-24907-6_1
10. Hao, Y., Foster, R.: Wireless body sensor networks for health-monitoring applications. Physiol. Meas. **29**(11), R27–R56 (2008)
11. Baker, C.R., et al.: Wireless sensor networks for home health care. Int. J. Theoret. Phys. **34**(8), 1697–1710 (2007)
12. Sedjelmaci, H., Senouci, S.M., Al-Bahri, M.: A lightweight anomaly detection technique for low-resource IoT devices: a game-theoretic methodology. In: 2016 IEEE International Conference on Communications (ICC), pp. 1–6. IEEE (2016)
13. Stergiou, C., Psannis, K.E., Gupta, B.B., Ishibashi, Y.: Security, privacy & efficiency of sustainable cloud computing for big data & IoT. Sustain. Comput.: Inf. Syst. **19**, 174–184 (2018)
14. Sicari, S., Rizzardi, A., Grieco, L.A., Coen-Porisini, A.: Security, privacy and trust in internet of things: the road ahead. Comput. Netw. **76**, 146–164 (2015)
15. Zhou, J., Cao, Z., Dong, X., Vasilakos, A.V.: Security and privacy for cloud-based IoT: challenges. IEEE Commun. Mag. **55**(1), 26–33 (2017)
16. Kumar, J.S., Patel, D.R.: A survey on internet of things: security and privacy issues. Int. J. Comput. Appl. **90**(11), 20–26 (2014)
17. Challa, S., et al.: Secure signature-based authenticated key establishment scheme for future IoT applications. IEEE Access **5**, 3028–3043 (2017)
18. Zhang, Y., Deng, R.H., Zheng, D., Li, J., Wu, P., Cao, J.: Efficient and robust certificateless signature for data crowdsensing in cloud-assisted industrial IoT. IEEE Trans. Ind. Inform. **15**(9), 5099–5108 (2019)
19. Feng, Q., He, D., Zeadally, S., Khan, M.K., Kumar, N.: A survey on privacy protection in blockchain system. J. Netw. Comput. Appl. **126**, 45–58 (2019)
20. Yang, Y., He, D., Wang, H., Zhou, L.: An efficient blockchain-based batch verification scheme for vehicular ad hoc networks. Trans. Emerg. Telecommun. Technol. (2019)

21. Raya, M., Hubaux, J.-P.: Securing vehicular ad hoc networks. J. Comput. Secur. **15**(1), 39–68 (2007)
22. Lu, R., Lin, X., Zhu, H., Ho, P.H., Shen, X.: ECPP: efficient conditional privacy preservation protocol for secure vehicular communications. In: IEEE INFOCOM 2008-The 27th Conference on Computer Communications, pp. 1229–1237. IEEE (2008)
23. Zhang, C., Lin, X., Lu, R., Ho, P.H., RAISE: An efficient RSU-aided message authentication scheme in vehicular communication networks. In: 2008 IEEE International Conference on Communications, pp. 1451–1457. IEEE (2008)
24. Lee, C.-C., Lai, Y.-M.: Toward a secure batch verification with group testing for VANET. Wirel. Netw. **19**(6), 1441–1449 (2013). https://doi.org/10.1007/s11276-013-0543-7
25. Shim, K.-A.: CPAS: an efficient conditional privacy-preserving authentication scheme for vehicular sensor networks. IEEE Trans. Veh. Technol. **61**(4), 1874–1883 (2012)
26. Liu, J.K., Yuen, T.H., Au, M.H., Susilo, W.: Improvements on an authentication scheme for vehicular sensor networks. Expert Syst. Appl. **41**(5), 2559–2564 (2014)
27. He, D., Zeadally, S., Baowen, X., Huang, X.: An efficient identity-based conditional privacy-preserving authentication scheme for vehicular ad hoc networks. IEEE Trans. Inf. Forensics Secur. **10**(12), 2681–2691 (2015)
28. Liu, J., Cao, H., Li, Q., Cai, F., Du, X., Guizani, M.: A large-scale concurrent data anonymous batch verification scheme for mobile healthcare crowd sensing. IEEE Internet Things J. **PP**(99), 1 (2018)
29. Libing, W., Zhiyan, X., He, D., Wang, X.: New certificateless aggregate signature scheme for healthcare multimedia social network on cloud environment. Secur. Commun. Netw. **1–13**, 2018 (2018)
30. Xie, Y., Li, X., Zhang, S., Li, Y.: ICLAS: an improved certificateless aggregate signature scheme for healthcare wireless sensor networks. IEEE Access **7**, 15170–15182 (2019)
31. Pointcheval, D., Stern, J.: Security arguments for digital signatures and blind signatures. J. Cryptol. **13**(3), 361–396 (2000). https://doi.org/10.1007/s001450010003

Blockchain and IoT Based Textile Manufacturing Traceability System in Industry 4.0

Muhammad Shakeel Faridi[1], Saqib Ali[1,3](✉), Guihua Duan[2], and Guojun Wang[3](✉)

[1] Department of Computer Science, University of Agriculture, Faisalabad 38000, Pakistan
{2007ag51,saqib}@uaf.edu.pk
[2] School of Computer Science and Engineering, Central South University, Changsha 410083, China
duangh@csu.edu.cn
[3] School of Computer Science and Cyber Engineering, Guangzhou University, Guangzhou 510006, China
{saqibali,csgjwang}@gzhu.edu.cn

Abstract. Growth towards Industry 4.0 has a significant impact on the textile manufacturing industry. In this emerging technology the business and engineering processes are interconnected. The product traceability system is playing a vital role in each sector. Unfortunately, the traditional systems in textile manufacturing industries faced a lot of challenges due to in-house process and supply chain complexity. These systems do not provide a means for reliable and rapid response to backtrack data throughout the textile process of the product. Blockchain and Internet of Things (IoT) based processes have the capacity to overcome these challenges while deploying over the traditional product traceability system. The blockchain and IoT based system provides many benefits such as communication between product process flow to improve the performance and reduce risk, improve quality, continuous involvement of worker, product fault traceability, increase supply chain visibility, and customer's reliability and trust-ability. In this paper, we proposed Blockchain and IoT based product traceability system. This system facilitates all stakeholders like Raw Material Suppliers, Yarn Manufacturers, Customers, and Consumers to track, monitor, and quality of the product and efficient tracking of the supply chain. This proposed solution will help textile manufacturers to improve the efficiency and quality of each product. The customer's reliability and trust-ability will boost the manufacturer due to automated data insertion through the IoT technology, decentralized, immutable, auditable, and fault tolerance blockchain technology and traceability features.

Keywords: IoT · Blockchain · Supply chain · Industry 4.0 · Traceability

© Springer Nature Switzerland AG 2021
G. Wang et al. (Eds.): SpaCCS 2020, LNCS 12382, pp. 331–344, 2021.
https://doi.org/10.1007/978-3-030-68851-6_24

1   Introduction

Traceability and reliability are two main problematic areas in textile manufacturing. The result of traceability and reliability is that actual demand and actual production, do not match the planned phase of time that have been developed by some ideal model or simple planning logic. Many techniques are used to overcome the effects of traceability and reliability to reconcile real production with the planned production. These include forecasting at various levels, performance measurement, simulation, regular decision-making and re-planning. Traceability means that a unique electronic product code (EPC) which is a sign to develop a product. It helps to retrace and verify the steps that have taken place throughout the product development processes. Traceability allows us to track material makes up a part and which component are in development process. It is important to keep track of the details of every production process in the textile processing, production, warehousing and transportation.

IoT is a centralized architecture where all things/objects connected through internet, interact with users, and collect sensitive business information. The business systems can receive and analyze that data for insights and act on the data, by discrete decisions. It is an automated way that is triggered by a specific set of conditions [1]. Blockchain is decentralized architecture where every node is considered equal to every other node [9]. With the rise and popularity of Bitcoin, decentralized architecture and blockchain distributed ledger technology have attracted the attention of many industrial sectors, including the non-financial and IoT sectors [12,24]. The [4] proposed the purpose and goals of Facebook's Libra cryptocurrency, as it is not well defined as compared to Bitcoin and other public defined blockchain cryptocurrency. They also tried to explore the Facebook's Libra challenges, security and privacy features relating to three billion social media ecosystem users. A secure communication can be made by utilizing PUF operation. This protocol provides faster responsive time by using less computation cost on top level security [19].

The blockchain and IoT based traceability system has become very popular. It is a decentralized and prevention of data tampering and provide solutions to the shortcomings of traditional systems. However, the transfer of trust to a blockchain-based traceability system may also face some new technical difficulties, such as information explosions [17]. [15] developed a blockchain-based digital content distributed system in 2015 to record and identify information of supply chain processes. Another RFID system was developed by [21] in 2016 for traceability of agriculture product in supply chain. This system collect information automatically through RFID and blockchain technology. Another great achievement in year 2016 when IBM launched blockchain Hyper-Ledger supply chain management system for Walmart with the collaboration of Tsinghua University and Walmart. They used the blockchain framework and designed Wal-Mart food supply chain system for tracking the food quality and origin [13]. A decentralized storage framework for PingER introduced by [3] to control/remove its dependencies on a centralized storage. In 2018 an AgriBlock IoT based solution was proposed by [8]. This system was integrated with IoT and blockchain by using

Ethereum platform and Hyper-ledger technology for food traceability system. This system provide traceability, immutability, transparency and auditability for Agri-Food system.

The traditional product traceability system in textile manufacturing industries faced lot of challenges due to its in-house process complexity. These systems do not provide a means for reliable and rapid response to backtrack data throughout the textile process of product. The available data may also be difficult to analyze for onward decision-making. It is also difficult to understand that what attributes required to track and where these attributes will be available in system. Moreover, it is also difficult to understand the flow of data that is required for tracking the product and how that data will fulfill the requirement. Industry 4.0 has a significant impact on the textile manufacturing industry. The use of emerging technologies in such a way that business and engineering processes are interconnected, consistently high quality and low cost with production, flexibility of work and efficiently work in progress.

The blockchain and IoT based system provides many benefits such as communication between product process flows to improve the performance and reduce risk. It also helps to improve quality, product fault traceability, increase supply chain visibility and customer's reliability and trust-ability. Our objective in this paper is to propose a Blockchain and IoT based product traceability system. This system facilitates all stakeholders to track and monitor floor management at each production stage, product fault traceability, increase supply chain visibility and customer's reliability and trust-ability. This proposed solution will help textile manufacturers to get customer's satisfaction against each quality product. The customer's reliability and trust-ability will boost towards the manufacturer due to automated data insertion through IoT, decentralized, immutable, auditable, fault tolerance blockchain technology and traceability features.

This paper comprises the following sections. Section 2 contains a review of literature in terms of Industry 4.0, Traceability, Blockchain, and IoT. In Sect. 3, we proposed a traceability system for textile industry. Finally, the Sect. 4 concludes the paper.

2   Review of Literature

In this section, we discuss the requirements of industry 4.0 in textile manufacturing, usage of IoT and blockchain features and the usage in textile manufacturing industries.

2.1   Industry 4.0

Industry 4.0 is a big word flying around the world and the next era of industrial revolution Fig. 1 and modernization. Its 4th industry revolution we have seen transform of technologies that have changed industry. The main idea of Industry 4.0 is to use emerging technologies in which business and engineering processes are interconnected [23]. It consists of smart factories, products and services that

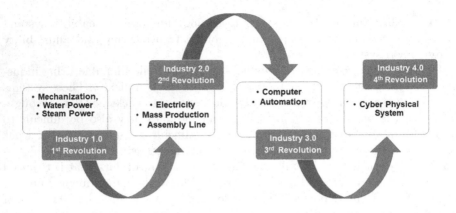

Fig. 1. Illustration of industrial revolution

are part of the IoT and services also known as industrial interns [18]. In industry 4.0, these smart machines and sensors are connected to networks and talk to each others so they can diagnose their problems and alerts someone going wrong with this machines during production process. These computerized machines having big data connectivity capability because all of the machine have generating huge volume of data. This data can be used for analysis, artificial intelligence, and machine learning to make sense of the data. This will help us to predict of maintenance of machine on assembly line and will tells us that might be break down in coming days. Therefore, we can fix the things before it happen. We now have interconnected supply chain where ships are talking to warehouses, warehouses talking to trucks. It also enables us robots that are more intelligent. We can now ship deliveries through robots and make our production line more smooth and flexible.

2.2 Traceability

According to [7] traceability is measured as quality key in textile manufacturing industry. Storing information and handling of sensitive case data becomes mandatory worldwide for tracking in the textile manufacturing industry. Regulations have been endorsed to enable the detection and identification of all materialized items that uses in production line as claimed by [10]. Traceability is the ability of a system to identify the current or historical status of an activity. Traceability is a term that is used in quality system and has gained recent popularity through its use in the ISO 9001/BS 5750 standard procedure. Traceability in these cases specifically refers to the ability to take action and verify that certain events have occurred on specific product.

Technologies like IoT are playing vital role in traceability management system. IoT based applications provide live goods production information as well as defective information to the management. IoT enabled applications pointed out technical problems, production status, constraints and redesign/optimal production inline status, as stated by [25].

The existing system in textile manufacturing industries does not provide a means for reliable and rapid response to backtrack data throughout the textile process of product. The available data may also be difficult to analyze for onward decision-making. It is also difficult to understand that what attributes are required to track, where these attributes will be available in system. It is also difficult to understand the flow of data that is required for tracking the product and how that data will fulfill the requirement. The IoT integrated blockchain system provides many benefits such as communication between product process flows to improve the performance, continuous involvement of worker, product fault traceability during production process and after sale product traceability by the customer. This proposed system will help the all stakeholders to track and monitor floor management at each production stage, as well as quality and efficient tracking of the supply chain.

IoT-enabled applications and related technologies such as radio frequency identification (RFID) revolutionize the industry by digitizing information so that real-time examinations and controls can take place. All these technologies are making remarkable changes in textile manufacturing business, reshaping the business processes and operational procedures, and the current business analysis model as shown in Fig. 2.

Fig. 2. IoT enabled business processes

2.3   Blockchain and IoT

In current research, several textile manufacturers are moving towards IoT and blockchain enabled solutions to capture the stakeholder's satisfactions. Survey articles have pursued to examine these proposed solutions in varying scenario and scope [20]. Blockchain enabled IoT integration architecture discussed in many surveys. The purpose of IoT devices are communication over the internet to collect complete business information and provide comprehensive automation service with a minimal human interaction. To accomplish this task, these IoT devices connected with a centralized server hosted by third party. These third parties provided services like system authorization, coordination among devices and data communication. This methodology requires a high-end server machines that proves the objects are connected and freely exchange data without human interference. In the centralized communication model, central servers allow objects to communicate with each other, so the increasing number of devices communicating with each other permanently over the Internet [5]. The [16] proposed a key sharing and key derivation security approach by using blockchain technology. This approach confirms and proves that by adding extra security layer, we can reduce latency, more packet loss and improve link stability. IoT based device registration and identification ensure device integrity and smart contracts through blockchain Advances in Cloud and IoT Networks. Hence, comprehensive provenance of data smart contract in the blockchain to secure the provenance towards the data stored in the cloud [2]. [11] describe the smart contract solution to facilitate the end-user for securely connect and interact with IoT devices. This technology is based on Ethereum smart contracts that helps to make it secure and realistic.

Blockchain technology recognizes and offer opportunities like the process of transaction initiation, authorization, processed and recorded data for the IoT. The developers and researchers have initiated to start decentralized application development for textile manufacturing industries. These IoT blockchain enabled applications may help to change in textile business processes and models. It also supports back-office financial transactions, reporting and government revenues likes taxes etc. The inherent blockchain features like decentralizations, immutability, auditability and fault tolerance makes it reliable and helps developers to develop a secure distributed application for IoT and cloud computing.

Recent developments provide a meaningful solution using blockchain technology to ensure the traceability for textile manufacturing industries and eliminate the need for reliable central options [14]. Due to immutable transactions and transparency, blockchain has gain popularity in supply chain and logistics sectors. It boosts the customer's reliability and trust-ability towards the manufacturer due to strong features like decentralization, immutability, auditability, better security and increased capacity.

3   Proposed Traceability System for Textile Industry

Over the past few years, integration of blockchain technology with supply chain system has become a new trend. Blockchain inherited features like decentralization and immutability made it more popular among manufacturing industries. Mainly the research focused on two directions. One is to redesign the whole blockchain and IoT based manufacturing system to meet the business requirement. The second one is to optimize the existing manufacturing application and enabling the IoT and blockchain features for better stakeholder's satisfactions and trust-ability.

In this section, we are going to propose our research work that will work through RFID and smart contracts by using Blockchain for product traceability, performance monitoring and resolve real time quality assurance issues. This proposed solution will help textile manufacturers to improve efficiency and quality of each product. This research work will also help to gain the customer's reliability and trust-ability towards the manufacturer due to automated data insertion through IoT technology, decentralized, immutable, auditable, and traceability features of Blockchain.

3.1 Structure and Processes of Textile Manufacturing Industry

Three level conceptual model of textile manufacturing industry consist of strategic planning, planning and design of product and product development level as shown in Fig. 3. These models already proposed by [22] and [6]. These conceptual models are integrated in our proposed Blockchain and IoT based product traceability system.

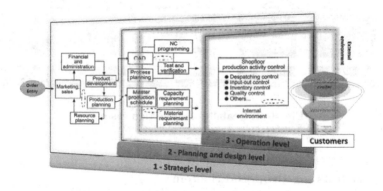

Fig. 3. Structure of textile manufacturing industry

Smart Contracts have the ability to protect against the mutual understanding between the manufacturer and customers. It helps to provides quality of the products to the customers. Our proposed work ensures the transaction made through smart contracts that are executed on private blockchain platform. The transaction occurs against smart contracts on the entire network and all mining nodes/blocks agree the result of executed transaction. The data and results of these transactions synchronized with all blocks and stored information in a ledger. In this way, all blocks have the replica of all transactions in every block. This makes information reliability, worker data regarding their productivity, quality and efficiency. Our proposed solution will focus on textile product manufacturing specially garments manufacturing industry. Figure 4. demonstrate key business processes of textile manufacturing traceability information system. These key business processes are raw material (cotton, accessories, etc.), yarn, knitting, and dyeing process for garments, retailers, and consumers. In blockchain transaction, every stakeholder will have a unique identity through blockchain address account. This Address Account will assign stakeholders private key, which will use for digitally sign in, validation and integration of data within the system.

Each business process like raw material, yarn suppliers, garments production, customers and consumers interact with the system by using his unique identity and cryptographically assigned digital private key. These business processes Fig. 4 has association, assigned roles and interaction with the system as per smart contracts.

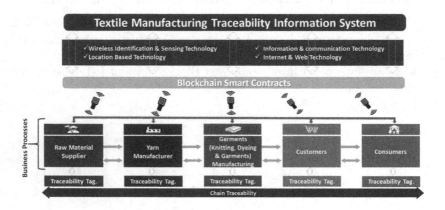

Fig. 4. Traceability information system

3.2 Algorithms for Proposed System

Smart contracts are an important part of the blockchain and IoT based product tracking system for the textile product. The whole system needs to understand the business logic through smart agreement. A smart contract is a decentralized, immutable and auditable digital protocol. In smart contracts, an event is triggered automatically on specific conditions. This help to monitor business protocols on blockchain networks.

In this section, we will describe the proposed algorithms that define the business process of our blockchain and IoT based traceability system. As we discussed earlier that the manufacturer and customers create smart contracts against the manufacturing products. The manufacturer and customers start communication to develop a garments article and to build a business relationship as per mutual communication. Electronic Product Code (EPC) is designed as a universal identifier that provides a unique identity for every physical object anywhere in the world, all the time. This EP code is stored on a RFID tag to trace the product. In our proposed system, every business process will have the product tag and this tag will help to trace the product at any stage. This technology will help textile manufacturer to get real time production activity and item tracking. Algorithm 1 describes the steps of product development traceability.

Algorithm 1. Product Fault Traceability

Input: EPC {Electronic Product Code}
Input: Fault_Code {Product Fault Code}
1: **if** $(Fault\_Code = \text{Dedected})$ **then**
2:     Machine Operator stop operation
3:     SmartContractCondition modifies to ProductChangeRequest
4:     ProductionInLineCondition modifies to ProductFaultTrace
5:     Final Inspector will stop the production.
6:     Final inspector puts a kanban card and scan EPC and fault code
7:     Ring the buzzer to call the supervisor and show him the fault
8:     Supervisor verifies and track the product from raw material to stitching
9:     Supervisor will trace the operator who made this product through system
10:     Supervisor will send the product to the operator for correctness.
11:     **if** $(Fault\_Correction = \text{success})$ **then**
12:         Operator will hand over the product to the supervisor
13:         Supervisor will hand over the product back to the final inspector for verification
14:         **if** $(verification = \text{success})$ **then**
15:             Scans EPC to clear fault
16:             SmartContractCondition modifies to ProductRequestSucceeded
17:             ProductionInLineCondition modifies to ProductFaultClear
18:         **else**
19:             SmartContractCondition changed to ProductChangeRequest
20:             ProductionInLineCondition modifies to ProductFaultTrace
21:             Final inspector reports back
22:         **end if**
23:     **else**
24:         SmartContractCondition modifies to ProductRequestSucceeded
25:         ProductionInLineCondition modifies to ProductFaultClear
26:         Return notification message "Product is okay"
27:     **end if**
28: **else**
29:     SmartContractCondition modifies to ProductRequestSucceeded
30:     ProductionInLineCondition modifies to ProductFaultClear
31:     Product forward to next department
32: **end if**

For smooth production line and workers efficiency, each bundle will have a unique tracking identification. This unique tracking number will help to track the textile product at every business process. Blockchain will facilitate the manufacturer to use product data exchange from manufacturing to store. Production data copied to RFID chips. The RFID chips will feed into the bundling area. RFID will contain information such as employee code, size, quantity of cut parts and color etc. In every production line, each worker performs a specific task on garments. Each worker has a smart tracker to track and record the process information. They input each task by using the IoT – blockchain enabled RFID chip all the way through production line. The management can also track worker's productivity has slowed or is in progress. Each process of production is integrated with this technology. This tracking system is following jidoka and kanban system to improve product quality on the shop floor. Jidoka and Kanban is a system where the manufacturers can control and monitor the wastage of the product. It detects the problem and enables the machine operators to stop production. When, any fault detected by the final inspector, he/she put a kanban card to the product then he/she scans his/her RFID card to add the fault code.

The system has capability to display the live fault traceability. He/she put a buzzer to call her immediate supervisor and show him/her the fault on product. Supervisor verifies the fault and track the operator who made this product through this technology. The supervisor explains the fault to the operator, the operator makes correction, verifies the fault and return the product to the quality supervisor. Quality supervisor hands over that faulty product to the final inspector, he/she verifies and place that product to good production pieces. When the final inspector receives the faulty product, he/she scan his/her RFID Card to clear the fault and place the product in good production pieces.

This RFID technology helps real time production activity and item tracking. It is a real time shop floor data tracking management system that keeps the management updated what is happening on the production floor. Through this technology, the management can extract each worker data regarding their productivity, quality and efficiency. With the help of this technology, workers can also report back on Quality Assurance issues in real time for corrective action. By this way, the management can easily monitor each worker activity and system accuracy.

In product tracking system, the manufacturers can reduce the wastage through considering the overproduction, waiting (man or machine), transportation and work in process. This technology provides management a live dashboard view to monitor the productivity statistics and information as shown in Fig. 5.

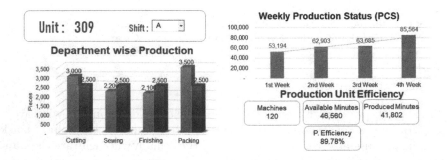

Fig. 5. Management dashboard

This propose system will help the company's initiative towards innovative technology. Every worker's performance and efficiency could be monitor for accountability and rewards. This technology will help textile manufacturers to improve efficiency and quality of each product. The customer's reliability and trust-ability will boost towards the manufacturer due to automated data insertion through IoT network, decentralized, immutable, auditable, and fault tolerance blockchain technology. In addition, because of the flexibility of the system, we can reduce the cost by using traceability systems for small and medium-sized textile manufacturing businesses.

Algorithm 2. Product Tracking by Manufacturer or Customer

Input: EPC {Electronic Product Code}
Input: BlockchainAddress (BA) of Manufacturer
Input: BlockchainAddress (BA) of Customer
 1: Customer state is CustomerTrackingProduct
 2: Manufacturer state is ManufacturerTrackingProduct
 3: Access Restriction only to Customer and Manufacturer
 4: **if** (EPC = succeeded) **then**
 5:    SmartContract update to ProductTracebyCustomer
 6:    Generate and store information of ProductTrackingID and TrackingDate
 7:    System will display the history of product
 8: **else**
 9:    SmartContract update ProductTraceRefused
10:    Return notification message "Electronic Product Code is not Correct"
11: **end if**

Finally, the finished goods traceability Algorithm 2 works. By using this algorithm, manufacturer and customer can track the finished goods product. The manufacturer or customer will enter the unique Electronic Product Code (EPC) of each product. The IoT-blockchain enabled system will show them the history of product from yarn, knitting, fabric processing, cutting, stitching operations and inspections to packing and shipment. The main parameters considered to track the product are unique EPC, blockchain address of customer and blockchain address of manufacturer. The manufacturer or customer state will change as ManufacturerTrackingProdcut or the customer state will change CustomerTrackingProduct. Here the smart contracts will restrict the access to only customers and manufacturers. Upon successfully enter the EPC, system will generate and store a ProductTrackingID, TrackingDate. This will help the manufacturer to see the log status of each product. The system will display record query purchase order number, size, color, cutting information like Cutting Lot No, Fabric Quality, Fabric Type, Color, Stitching Information like, Stitching Date, Unit No. Operator Code, Machine Type and process completed by the operator against each EPC Fig. 6. The manufacturer and customers can also track fabric composition by using lot no. It will show the fabric composition from cotton purchase to finished fabric including raw material consumed. It will also help to identify the final inspector information, who made the product good for packing and shipping.

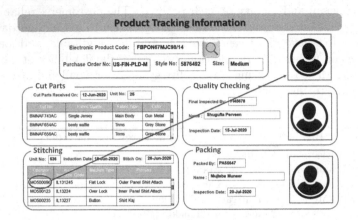

Fig. 6. Product tracking board

4 Conclusion

In this paper, we proposed IoT blockchain based product traceability system to help the manufacturer and customer to track the product during production process and after that. This proposed system will help the textile manufacturers to initiative towards innovative technology. Every worker's performance and efficiency could be monitored for accountability and rewards. This technology will help textile manufacturers to improve efficiency and quality of each product. In this system every business process will have the Electronic Product Code (EPC) and this code will help to trace the product at any process stage. This proposed system will also facilitate to track the finished goods product. The manufacturer and customer can track the finished goods product by enter the unique EPC of each product. The blockchain and IoT based system will show the history of product from cotton to packing and shipment. This unique feature will boost the customer's reliability and trust-ability towards the manufacturer. In addition, because of the flexibility of the system, we can reduce the cost by using traceability systems for small and medium-sized textile manufacturing businesses. We will try to implement this proposed system into textile manufacturing industry and optimize as per requirement of the industry in our future work.

Acknowledgments. This work was supported in part by the National Natural Science Foundation of China under Grant 61632009, in part by the Guangdong Provincial Natural Science Foundation under Grant 2017A030308006, in part by the High- Level Talents Program of Higher Education in Guangdong Province under Grant 2016ZJ01.

References

1. Ali, M.S., Vecchio, M., Pincheira, M., Dolui, K., Antonelli, F., Rehmani, M.H.: Applications of blockchains in the Internet of Things: a comprehensive survey. IEEE Commun. Surv. Tutor. 21(2), 1676–1717 (2019). https://doi.org/10.1109/COMST.2018.2886932
2. Ali, S., Wang, G., Bhuiyan, M.Z.A., Jiang, H.: Secure data provenance in cloud-centric internet of things via blockchain smart contracts. In: 2018 IEEE SmartWorld, Ubiquitous Intelligence & Computing, Advanced & Trusted Computing, Scalable Computing & Communications, Cloud & Big Data Computing, Internet of People and Smart City Innovation (SmartWorld/SCALCOM/UIC/ATC/CBDCom/IOP/SCI), pp. 991–998. IEEE (2018). https://doi.org/10.1109/SmartWorld.2018.00175
3. Ali, S., Wang, G., White, B., Cottrell, R.L.: A blockchain-based decentralized data storage and access framework for pinger. In: 2018 17th IEEE International Conference on Trust, Security and Privacy in Computing and Communications/12th IEEE International Conference on Big Data Science and Engineering (TrustCom/BigDataSE), pp. 1303–1308. IEEE (2018). https://doi.org/10.1109/TrustCom/BigDataSE.2018.00179
4. Ali, S., Wang, G., White, B., Fatima, K.: Libra critique towards global decentralized financial system. In: Wang, G., El Saddik, A., Lai, X., Martinez Perez, G., Choo, K.-K.R. (eds.) iSCI 2019. CCIS, vol. 1122, pp. 661–672. Springer, Singapore (2019). https://doi.org/10.1007/978-981-15-1301-5_52
5. Ammar, M., Russello, G., Crispo, B.: Internet of Things: a survey on the security of IoT frameworks. J. Inf. Secur. Appl. 38, 8–27 (2018). https://doi.org/10.1016/j.jisa.2017.11.002
6. Bilberg, A., Alting, L.: When simulation takes control. J. Manuf. Syst. 10(3), 179–193 (1991). https://doi.org/10.1016/0278-6125(91)90032-W
7. Bosona, T., Gebresenbet, G.: Food traceability as an integral part of logistics management in food and agricultural supply chain. Food control 33(1), 32–48 (2013). https://doi.org/10.1016/j.foodcont.2013.02.004
8. Caro, M.P., Ali, M.S., Vecchio, M., Giaffreda, R.: Blockchain-based traceability in agri-food supply chain management: a practical implementation. In: 2018 IoT Vertical and Topical Summit on Agriculture-Tuscany (IOT Tuscany), pp. 1–4. IEEE (2018). https://doi.org/10.1109/IOT-TUSCANY.2018.8373021
9. Christidis, K., Member, G.S.: Blockchains and smart contracts for the Internet of Things. IEEE Access 4, 2292–2303 (2016). https://doi.org/10.1109/ACCESS.2016.2566339
10. Dabbene, F., Gay, P., Tortia, C.: Traceability issues in food supply chain management: a review. Biosyst. Eng. 120, 65–80 (2014). https://doi.org/10.1016/j.biosystemseng.2013.09.006
11. Fotiou, N., Siris, V.A., Polyzos, G.C.: Interacting with the Internet of Things using smart contracts and blockchain technologies. In: Wang, G., Chen, J., Yang, L.T. (eds.) SpaCCS 2018. LNCS, vol. 11342, pp. 443–452. Springer, Cham (2018). https://doi.org/10.1007/978-3-030-05345-1_38
12. Fujimura, S., Watanabe, H., Nakadaira, A., Yamada, T., Akutsu, A., Kishigami, J.J.: BRIGHT: a concept for a decentralized rights management system based on blockchain. In: 2015 IEEE 5th International Conference on Consumer Electronics-Berlin (ICCE-Berlin), pp. 345–346. IEEE (2015). https://doi.org/10.1109/COMST.2018.2886932

13. Kamath, R.: Food traceability on blockchain: Walmart's pork and mango pilots with IBM. J. Br. Blockchain Assoc. **1**(1), 3712 (2018). https://doi.org/10.31585/jbba-1-1-(10)2018

14. Khan, M.A., Salah, K.: IoT security: review, blockchain solutions, and open challenges. Future Gener. Comput. Syst. **82**, 395–411 (2018). https://doi.org/10.1016/j.future.2017.11.022

15. Kishigami, J., Fujimura, S., Watanabe, H., Nakadaira, A., Akutsu, A.: The blockchain-based digital content distribution system. In: 2015 IEEE Fifth International Conference on Big Data and Cloud Computing, pp. 187–190. IEEE (2015). https://doi.org/10.1109/BDCloud.2015.60

16. Lee, H., Ma, M.: Blockchain-based mobility management for LTE and beyond. In: Wang, G., Feng, J., Bhuiyan, M.Z.A., Lu, R. (eds.) SpaCCS 2019. LNCS, vol. 11611, pp. 36–49. Springer, Cham (2019). https://doi.org/10.1007/978-3-030-24907-6_4

17. Lin, Q., Wang, H., Pei, X., Wang, J.: Food safety traceability system based on blockchain and EPCIS. IEEE Access **7**, 20698–20707 (2019). https://doi.org/10.1109/ACCESS.2019.2897792

18. Machado, C.G., Winroth, M.P., Ribeiro da Silva, E.H.D.: Sustainable manufacturing in Industry 4.0: an emerging research agenda. Int. J. Prod. Res. **58**(5), 1462–1484 (2020). https://doi.org/10.1080/00207543.2019.1652777

19. Mall, P., Bhuiyan, M.Z.A., Amin, R.: A lightweight secure communication protocol for IoT devices using physically unclonable function. In: Wang, G., Feng, J., Bhuiyan, M.Z.A., Lu, R. (eds.) SpaCCS 2019. LNCS, vol. 11611, pp. 26–35. Springer, Cham (2019). https://doi.org/10.1007/978-3-030-24907-6_3

20. Panarello, A., Tapas, N., Merlino, G., Longo, F., Puliafito, A.: Blockchain and IoT integration: a systematic survey. Sensors **18**(8), 2575 (2018). https://doi.org/10.3390/s18082575

21. Tian, F.: An information system for food safety monitoring in supply chains based on HACCP, blockchain and internet of things. Ph.D. thesis, WU Vienna University of Economics and Business (2018)

22. Vollmann, T.E., Berry, W.L., Whybark, D.C.: Manufacturing planning and control systems, homewood, IL: Dow Jones-Irwin, 1988. In: Plossl, G.W. (ed.) Production and Inventory Control: Principles and Techniques, 2nd edn., pp. 88–93. Prentice-Hall, Englewood Cliffs (1985)

23. Wang, S., Wan, J., Li, D., Zhang, C.: Implementing smart factory of industrie 4. 0: an outlook. Int. J. Distrib. Sens. Netw. (2016). https://doi.org/10.1155/2016/3159805

24. Wu, J., Luo, S., Wang, S., Wang, H.: NLES: a novel lifetime extension scheme for safety-critical cyber-physical systems using SDN and NFV. IEEE Internet Things J. **PP**(c), 1 (2018). https://doi.org/10.1109/JIOT.2018.2870294

25. Zhu, Z., Chu, F., Dolgui, A., Chu, C., Zhou, W., Piramuthu, S.: Recent advances and opportunities in sustainable food supply chain: a model-oriented review. Int. J. Prod. Res. **56**(17), 5700–5722 (2018). https://doi.org/10.1080/00207543.2018.1425014

A Network Security Situational Awareness Framework Based on Situation Fusion

Sai Lu and Yi Zhuang$^{(\boxtimes)}$

School of Computer Science and Technology, Nanjing University of Aeronautics
and Astronautics, Nanjing 211106, China
zy16@nuaa.edu.cn

Abstract. With the rapid development of the Internet, security issues in
cyberspace have received more and more attention, and network security situation awareness has become a research focus. This paper proposes a network
security situation awareness framework based on situation fusion, which decomposes the network security situation into two parts: the host security situation and
the network attack situation. First, the host asset information and network topology
information are used to calculate the weight vector of all hosts to make the weight
setting more reasonable. Then using CVSS to evaluate the host security situation
value. Meanwhile, security events are extracted from the alarm information of the
intrusion detection system, and we designed threat downgrading rules and escalation rules based on system environment matching and the attacker's willingness,
so as to calculate the threat of network attacks, and ultimately integrated into the
overall network security situation value. The results of the case analysis show that
the framework proposed in this paper can quantify the security situation better.

Keywords: Network security · Host security · Weight optimization · Situation
awareness · Situation fusion

1 Introduction

With the rapid development of computer technology and the growing scale of the network, the Internet has been integrated into people's daily life. However, at the same time,
the security problems in cyberspace have become increasingly prominent, and security
incidents emerge one after another. However, the complexity and changeability of cyber
environment severely hinder the understanding of the current situation by security teams
[1]. In this environment, traditional defense methods, such as firewall technology, intrusion detection system, virtual private network and so on, resist network attacks to a
certain extent, but these technologies cannot guarantee absolute security. At the same
time, with the increasing expansion of the scale of the network, they cannot directly
quantify the security status of the system, for example, continuously running intrusion
detection systems often produce massive alarm data, but a large number of data are
usually irrelevant alarms. Therefore, in the face of a large amount of data, managers are
still unable to have a comprehensive understanding of the security threats of the system,
resulting in the inability to better manage the system or take defensive measures.

© Springer Nature Switzerland AG 2021
G. Wang et al. (Eds.): SpaCCS 2020, LNCS 12382, pp. 345–355, 2021.
https://doi.org/10.1007/978-3-030-68851-6_25

Endsley [2] first proposed the concept of situational awareness, which is described as the perception of environmental elements in a certain time and space, the understanding of their meaning, and the prediction of the state in the near future. Bass [3] proposed the concept of network security situational awareness in 1999 and applied it to the data fusion analysis of multiple NIDS detection results [4], and believed that multi-sensor data fusion technology provides an important functional framework for the next generation of intrusion detection systems and network situational awareness. It can integrate multi-source heterogeneous IDS data to identify the identity of the intruder, attack frequency and threat level, etc. Currently, network security situational awareness has become a research hotspot.

Common situational awareness models are usually divided into three levels [5]. The first layer is mainly to extract indicators related to security assessment, such as massive alarm data of intrusion detection system. The second layer understands and evaluates the data collected by the first layer, and generates the relevant information about the current network security situation macroscopically. The third layer realizes the situation prediction based on the existing situation information, which is used to perceive the evolution process of the security situation in the future. We mainly focus on the index extraction and situation assessment in the three-tier model in this study.

Our main work is as follows:

1. We designed a network security situation awareness framework and proposed a network security situation calculation process.
2. A host weight calculation method is proposed, which considers the comprehensive calculation weight of host asset information and network topology information, which not only reflects the inherent importance of the host, but also considers the host's network status in the overall system topology environment.
3. We divide the network security situation into the host security situation and the network attack situation, and give a method to calculate them, which will merge into the network security situation value.

2 Related Works

A large number of research results have appeared in the field of network security situational awareness. Wang [6] et al. proposed a network security situation assessment model and quantitative method based on analytic hierarchy process, and used D-S evidence theory to fuse the fuzzy results of multi-source equipment to solve the problem of single information source and large accuracy deviation. Research [7] proposed a quantitative evaluation method for network security based on attack graphs, quantified the importance of nodes and the maximum reachability probability of nodes, and constructed a security evaluation function to calculate the security risk score. Hu [8] used dynamic Bayesian attack graphs to realize attack prediction, and then proposed a security situation quantification algorithm based on attack prediction. This method can realize situation quantification in a timely and flexible manner and help administrators take defensive measures. Pu [9] also used dynamic Bayesian network to comprehensively evaluate the attack effect of network nodes, and proposed a complex scientific network attack method to realize the attack. Literature [10] conducted an in-depth analysis of the association between attack intent and network configuration information. Then from the attacker's point of view, a network security situation assessment method based on the identification of attack intentions is proposed. The situation value obtained can more accurately reflect the actual information of the attack. Liu [11] et al. started from the vulnerability information, combined with the risk assessment method to calculate the risk level, and presented the security situation in a qualitative way. Although this method can help manage network risks that may occur in the near future, it does not consider real-time traffic information and therefore lacks real-time performance.

With the development of machine learning, there have been related studies on how to apply machine learning methods to situational awareness. For example, Li [12] used a neural network structure based on LSTM to establish the time correlation between situational data, and improved LSTM through cross-entropy functions, rectified linear units and appropriate layer stacking, which have good results. Literature [13] proposed a situation assessment method based on cuckoo search optimization back-propagation neural network, which can achieve faster convergence speed and higher prediction accuracy. Wang [14] et al. used the Levenberg-Marquard algorithm to optimize the BP neural network, which also achieved better evaluation results.

Based on the above research, we propose a new network security situation awareness framework, which decomposes the network security situation into host security situation and network attack situation. Combine information such as host assets, vulnerabilities, and real-time network traffic to comprehensively calculate the situation value.

3   Proposed Network Security Situational Awareness Framework

The proposed network security situational awareness framework is shown in Fig. 1. Our framework is divided into three steps: initialization step, weight calculation step and network security situation calculation step.

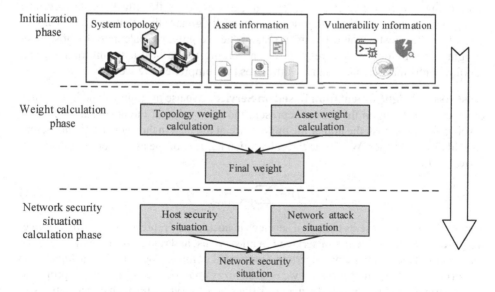

Fig. 1. Network security situation awareness framework

Initialization phase: The initialization phase mainly constructs the basic data used in the situational awareness process, including three types of data: topology, assets, and vulnerabilities. Topology information describes the connection relationship between hosts in the system, and is used to calculate the topological weight of the host; the asset information in this article refers to the service information provided by the host, and is used to calculate the asset weight of the host; the vulnerability information records the known vulnerability information of the host, this information It reflects the vulnerability of the host and is mainly used to calculate the security threat value of the host.

Weight calculation phase: This phase calculates the weight information of all hosts in the system. We respectively calculate the host topology weight and host asset weight to obtain the comprehensive weight of the host. The weight is used to reflect the importance of different hosts in the calculation process of the situation value. It should be noted that the weight of the host is not static. When the network topology in the system changes or the asset information of the host changes, the weight calculation process needs to be re-executed to obtain the latest weight information.

Network security situation calculation phase: This phase calculates the network security situation value. The network security situation in this paper is divided into host security situation and network attack situation. The host security situation describes the security threats caused by the unfixed vulnerabilities in the host. This value is updated only when the manager adopts a defense strategy and the vulnerability information changes. The network attack situation extracts security events from IDS, and calculates the security situation value caused by the network attack.

3.1 Host Weight Calculation

Different hosts in the network have different levels of damage to the entire network after being attacked. For example, the damage caused by the attack on the key host that provide data services to other hosts is obviously greater than that of ordinary hosts. Therefore, the hosts should be given reasonable weights. we calculate the host asset weight and topology weight respectively according to the host asset information and topology information, and finally synthesizes the comprehensive weight.

Host Asset Weight Calculation Based on Service. We use the number and importance of services running on the host to represent the asset value of the host. The higher the asset value of the host, the higher the importance of the host in the network, so the weight should also be higher. We define the calculation method of the asset weight of host i as shown in Eq. 1.

$$w_a(i) = \sum_{j \in Service_i} w_s(j) \tag{1}$$

Where $Service_i$ represents the list of services in host i, and j represents a specific service. $w_s(j)$ Represents the weight of service j in all services, and represents the importance of the service. Due to the many uncertain factors and complex logical relationships in the importance evaluation of services, we use the fuzzy analytic hierarchy process proposed in the research [15] to obtain the weight values of all services through expert ratings.

Host Topology Weight Calculation Based on PageRank Algorithm. PageRank algorithm is a web page sorting algorithm in directed network proposed by Brin S and Page L [16]. It is based on quantity and quality assumptions: (1) the more links a page is, the more important it is; (2) the more important pages will transfer more weights to other pages through directed edges. The algorithm uses PR value to describe the im-portance of web pages. The higher the PR value is, the higher the importance of web pages is.

We find that the connection relationship of nodes in the network can form a directed graph, and it also satisfies the quantity hypothesis and quality hypothesis, that is, (1) the more nodes in a network are connected, the more important the node is. For example, the server that provides web service in the system can be connected by all the client nodes in the system. Obviously, the loss caused by the attack of this node is much greater than that caused by the breach of the ordinary client node. (2) the higher the importance of other network nodes connected to the network node, the higher the importance of the node. For example, when the web server provides services, it may connect to the file server or database server to request data, if they are in an insecure state, then through the web server will still cause greater malicious impact. Therefore, we think that the PageRank algorithm can theoretically migrate to the calculation process of host importance in network security situational awareness. In this paper, the PageRank algorithm is introduced to sort the host nodes in the network, and the PR value is used to calculate the host topology weight.

Let the set of hosts in the network be $host = \{1, 2 \cdots, N\}$, N denote the total number of hosts, $outdeg(i)$ denotes the number of degrees of host i, B_i denotes the set of hosts with links to host i, then the weight of I in the t iteration is given by formula (2). Where α is the damping factor, usually $\alpha = 0.85$. After iterative convergence, the final result is the topological weight of host i. Brin S and Page L have proved theoretically that the algorithm can converge no matter how the initial value is selected.

$$w_t(i) = \alpha \sum_{j \in B_i} \frac{w_{t-1}(j)}{outdeg(j)} + \frac{1 - \alpha}{N} \tag{2}$$

According to formula (1) and formula (2), we use formula (3) to get the comprehensive weight $w(i)$ of host i. It is important to note that $w(i)$, $w_a(i)$, and $w_t(i)$ all need to be normalized.

$$w(i) = w_a(i) + w_t(i) \tag{3}$$

3.2 Host Security Situation

We use CVSS (Universal vulnerability scoring system) [17] to measure the host security situation caused by the host containing vulnerabilities. CVSS is an industry open standard proposed by NIAC and maintained by FIRST. It is designed to assess the severity of the vulnerability and to help users determine the urgency and importance of the response required by the vulnerability.

CVSS contains three metric groups: basic group, temporary group and environment group, each of which contains the relevant attributes needed for evaluation. Take CVSS

2.0 as an example, the basic group evaluation process is shown in formula (4) to formula (7).

$$BaseScore = ((0.6 \times Imp) + (0.4 \times Exploitability) - 1.5) \times f(Imp) \qquad (4)$$

$$Imp = 10.41 \times (1 - (1 - ConfImp) \times (1 - IntegImp) \times (1 - AvailImp)) \qquad (5)$$

$$Exploitability = 20 \times AccessVector \times AccessComplexity \times Authentication \qquad (6)$$

$$f(Imp) = \begin{cases} 0, & Imp = 0 \\ 1.176, & otherwise \end{cases} \qquad (7)$$

The final evaluation score can be obtained by adding temporary assessment index impact factors and environmental assessment index impact factors on the basis of *BaseScore*. The value range of the score is [0,10], in which the detailed value range and classification are shown in Table 1.

Table 1. Range of vulnerability score

Heading level	Example
0–3.9	Low risk vulnerabilities
4–6.9	Medium risk vulnerability
7–10	High risk vulnerability

Suppose the set of vulnerabilities contained in host i is V, and we accumulate the CVSS score of all vulnerabilities to get the host security situation R_i as shown in Formula (8). Where $v \in V$ represents a vulnerability, $S(v)$ represents the score of vulnerability v.

$$R_i = \sum_{v \in V} S(v) \qquad (8)$$

It should be noted that because we have combined the host assets in the weight calculation process of Sect. 3.1, the importance of the host assets is not repeatedly reflected in the host security situation calculation process.

3.3   Network Attack Situation

We use the alarm log of intrusion detection system as the data source of network attack situation calculation. We refer to the Snort user manual to classify network attack threat levels into high, medium and low levels. Some attack types and levels are shown in Table 2.

Table 2. Attack type and threat level

Heading level	Example	Font size and style
Attempted-Admin	Attempt to gain administrator privilege	High
Attempted-User	Attempt to gain ordinary user privilege	High
Attempted-Dos	Attempt to denial of service	Medium

Chen [18] degrades the threat of security events according to the specific conditions on which the attack event depends and the vulnerability information set of the target system. We have made improvements and defined threat degradation and escalation rules respectively, as shown in Formula (9) and (10).

$$\{A, \ (A_{DIP} = i_{ip} \in host) \ \cap \ (A_{DS} \neq i_s) \ \cup \ (A_{DP} \notin i_P) \ \cup \ (A_V \neq i_V)\} \Rightarrow A_{pri} = low \tag{9}$$

$$\{A, (A_{SIP} = sip) \ \cap \ sum(sip, \ \Delta t) \geq m\} \Rightarrow A_{pri} = high \tag{10}$$

In formula (9), i represents host i, $host$ is a legitimate collection of hosts, and A_{DIP}, A_{DS}, A_{DP} and A_V represent the destination address, required operating system, port number and vulnerability of security events, respectively. i_{ip}, i_s, i_P and i_V represent the address, operating system, open port, and vulnerability information of host i, respectively. The rule shows that as long as the conditions of the security event are not fully met, which means that the attack is not successful, the threat level is adjusted to a low level.

In formula (10), A_{SIP} represents the source address, $sum(sip, \Delta t)$ indicates the number of security events caused by sip in Δt time period, and m represents the tolerable number threshold, which is set by the manager. We use the number of attacks to describe the attacker's willingness to attack. if it is found that an attack event that exceeds the threshold has been launched from the same source address within Δt time, it will show that the attacker is constantly trying to attack and has a strong intention to attack. Then it is very likely that the system will be breached at some point, which requires the attention of the administrator, so the threat level will be adjusted to a high level.

3.4 Network Security Situation

Let $NSSA_t$ denote the network security situation quantization value of the period t, then the $NSSA_t$ is given by the formula (11). Where $w(i)$ represents the weight value of host i, and $\sum_{i=1}^{N} w(i) = 1$. R_{net}^t represents the threat of a network attack at period t. The higher the value of $NSSA_t$, the more dangerous the network situation.

$$NSSA_t = \sum_{i=1}^{N} w(i)R_i + R_{net}^t \tag{11}$$

4 Case Analysis

4.1 Data Set

In order to measure the effectiveness of the framework proposed in this paper, we select the November data from the HoneyNet dataset as the experimental data. The HoneyNet dataset [19] is used to "analyze the past and predict the future", which reflects the behavior pattern characteristics of hackers and helps to find security trends and rules. Because the dataset does not provide network topology data and host details, we give the network topology through analysis in reference [19], as shown in Fig. 2. The key information of the equipment is also given in the reference [19], which will not be repeated here.

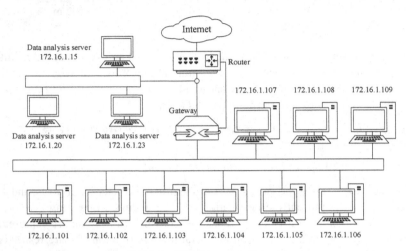

Fig. 2. HoneyNet data network topology

There is no access connection relationship between hosts in Fig. 2. In order to measure the effectiveness of the PageRank algorithm, we will combine the host information to abstract the key hosts into the directed graph shown in Fig. 3, and the arrows represent the access connection relationship. It is important to note that Fig. 3 is only used as experimental data and does not fully represent the real connection relationship of the HoneyNet dataset.

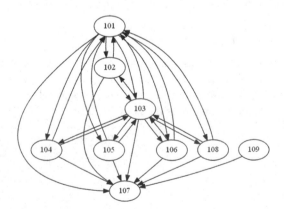

Fig. 3. Directed graph of key hosts

4.2 Experimental Results and Analysis

Table 3 shows the calculation results of the comprehensive weight of the host. It can be seen that 101, 103 and 107 are more important, 102, 104, 105, 106 and 108 have the same importance, and 109 is the least important.

Table 3. Host weight.

Host	101	102	103	104	105	106	107	108	109
Weight	0.15	0.09	0.15	0.09	0.09	0.09	0.22	0.09	0.05

Figure 4 shows the iterative process of topology weight calculation, and the algorithm achieves convergence after 14 iterations, so the extra overhead caused by introducing PageRank algorithm to calculate topology weight is within the affordable range.

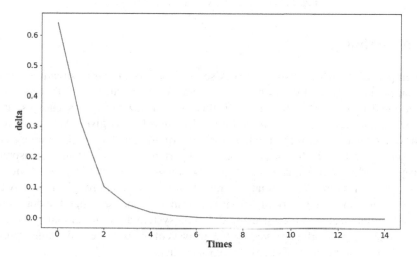

Fig. 4. Iterative process of PageRank algorithm

Let the sampling period t be 1 day, and the changing trend of the network security situation of the whole system within one month is shown in Fig. 5.

It can be seen that both methods can depict the overall trend of the situation, but some details need to be paid attention to. In the analytic hierarchy process [18], there is no alarm information in some time, so the situation value is 0, but this paper thinks that because there are still a large number of loopholes in each host in the system, so the situation value is not 0. The reason why the value of this paper is larger than that of the analytic hierarchy process on the 25th is that the attack launched by the same attacker occurred in a very short time interval that day, triggering the rules described in formula (10), so the situation value is higher.

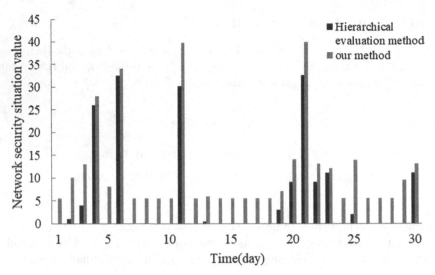

Fig. 5. Trends in network security situation

5 Conclusion

As an important means to ensure network security, network security situational awareness can intuitively depict the trend of the overall security situation of the system and provide rapid guidance for managers. In this work, a new network security situation awareness framework is proposed, and the calculation flow is given. We calculate the weight of the host according to the host asset information and network topology information respectively, which can describe the importance of the host more reasonably. We propose to decompose the network security situation into host security situation and network attack situation. We evaluate the host security situation through the widely used CVSS standard. In the network attack situation calculation, we design the degradation rules and upgrade rules of the intrusion detection system alarm log. Finally, the effectiveness of our framework is proved by the analysis of an example. Our future research work will focus on network security situation prediction.

Acknowledgments. This work was supported by the National Natural Science Foundation of China (General Program) under Grant No. 61572253 and Jiangsu Province Software New Technology and Industrialization Collaborative Innovation Center.

References

1. Komárková, J., et al.: CRUSOE: data model for cyber situational awareness. In: Proceedings of the 13th International Conference on Availability, Reliability and Security, ARES. ACM (2018)
2. Endsley, M.: Design and evaluation for situation awareness enhancement. Proc. Hum. Factors Ergon. Soc. Ann. Meet. **32**(2), 97–101 (1988)

3. Tim, B., Gruber, D.: A glimpse into the future of id. Mag. USENIX SAGE **24**(3), 40–49 (1999)
4. Tim, B.: Intrusion detection systems and multisensor data fusion. Commun. ACM **43**(4), 99–105 (2000)
5. Xi, R., et al.: Research survey of network security situation awareness. J. Comput. Appl. **32**(1), 1–4 (2012)
6. Wang, H., et al.: Research on network security situation assessment and quantification method based on analytic hierarchy process. Wirel. Pers. Commun. **102**(2), 1401–1420 (2018). https://doi.org/10.1007/s11277-017-5202-3
7. Zheng, Y., Lv, K., Hu, C.: A quantitative method for evaluating network security based on attack graph. In: Yan, Z., Molva, R., Mazurczyk, W., Kantola, R. (eds.) NSS 2017. LNCS, vol. 10394, pp. 349–358. Springer, Cham (2017). https://doi.org/10.1007/978-3-319-64701-2_25
8. Hao, H., et al.: Quantitative method for network security situation based on attack prediction. Secur. Commun. Netw. **38**(10), 1–9 (2017)
9. Zaiyi, P.: Network security situation analysis based on a dynamic Bayesian network and phase space reconstruction. J. Supercomput. **76**(2), 1342–1357 (2018). https://doi.org/10.1007/s11227-018-2575-3
10. Guang, K., et al.: A network security situation assessment method based on attack intention perception. In: 2016 2nd IEEE International Conference on Computer and Communications, ICCC, pp. 1138–1142. IEEE (2016)
11. Liu, Y., Mu, D.: A network security situation awareness model based on risk assessment. In: Krömer, P., Zhang, H., Liang, Y., Pan, J.S. (eds.) ECC 2018. AISC, vol. 891, pp. 17–24. Springer, Cham (2018). https://doi.org/10.1007/978-3-030-03766-6_3
12. Li, S., Zhao, D.: A LSTM-based method for comprehension and evaluation of network security situation. In: 2019 18th IEEE International Conference on Trust, Security and Privacy in Computing and Communications/13th IEEE International Conference on Big Data Science and Engineering, TrustCom/BigDataSE, pp. 723–728. IEEE (2019)
13. Xie, L., Wang, Z.: Network security situation assessment method based on cuckoo search optimized back propagation neural network. J. Comput. Appl. **7**, 1926–1930 (2017)
14. Wang, D., et al.: Research on computer network security evaluation method based on Levenberg-Marquardt algorithms. In: 2019 International Conference on Communications, Information System and Computer Engineering, CISCE, pp. 399–402. IEEE (2019)
15. Zhang, J.: Fuzzy analytic hierarchy process (FAHP). Fuzzy Syst. Math. **14**(2), 80–88 (2000)
16. Sergey, B., Page, L.: The anatomy of a large-scale hypertextual web search engine. Comput. Netw. ISDN Syst. **30**, 107–117 (1998)
17. Peter, M., Scarfone, K., Romanosky, S.: Common vulnerability scoring system. IEEE Secur. Priv. **4**(6), 85–89 (2006)
18. Chen, X., et al.: Hierarchical quantitative assessment method of cyber security threat situation. J. Softw. **17**(4), 885–897 (2006)
19. Xi, R., Yun, X., Zhang, Y.: Quantitative assessment method of cyber threat situation based on environmental attributes. J. Softw. **26**(7), 1638–1649 (2015)

Intelligent Medical Security Framework of Body Area Network Based on Fog Computing

Songpeng Zhang, Yi Zhuang$^{(\boxtimes)}$, and Zining Cao

School of Software Engineering,
Nanjing University of Aeronautics and Astronautics, Nanjing 211106, China
zy16@nuaa.edu.cn

Abstract. Aiming at the main problems of terminal data storage, long service delay and transmission security of (WBAN) in wireless body area network, combined with fog computing distributed computing model, this paper proposes an intelligent medical service framework in wireless body area network, which is divided into intelligent medical terminal layer, fog computing central layer and cloud computing data storage layer, and proposes a real-time encrypted transmission scheme for data transmission between each layer. Security analysis shows that the framework and scheme can reduce the cost and delay, while ensuring the security and dispersion of data transmission between layers.

Keywords: Wireless body area network · Intelligent health care · Fog computing · Encrypted transmission · Bilinear mapping

1 Introduction

In recent years, with the rapid development of wireless communication technology and the innovative integration of ubiquitous sensing and pervasive computing, the Internet of things has a broad prospect in the medical field. Intelligent medical service is a kind of integration networking, cloud computing and other technologies, with user data as the center of medical service model. Wireless human body local area network ((WBAN)) is a collection of intelligent medical sensors in or around patients for real-time health care monitoring and support. The sensor is a portable and small-size interworking device, which can be worn or implanted into the individual to observe the life symptoms of patients, combine treatment and prevention, and effectively control the disease. In the intelligent medical service, the personal health information (PHI) is collected by the wireless human body local area network (WBAN), and the data is transmitted to the cloud computing center for storage and processing. Then, the feedback results are sent to users and medical staff and appropriate clinical diagnosis is provided. Recently, some schemes have been designed to solve the security and privacy problems in wireless domain networks [2–7]. However, most of them bear high computing costs and do not have certain security requirements, such as perfect forward confidentiality and untraceability. In addition, they will not resist some malicious technologies, such as key disclosure simulation attacks. The storage and computing capacity of wireless body area

© Springer Nature Switzerland AG 2021
G. Wang et al. (Eds.): SpaCCS 2020, LNCS 12382, pp. 356–366, 2021.
https://doi.org/10.1007/978-3-030-68851-6_26

network terminal equipment is limited, so processing massive data locally will bring processing delay that can not be ignored. On the other hand, transferring massive data to the CVM for processing can reduce the processing delay with the help of powerful cloud computing capabilities, but the transmission process will bring a delay of more than 100 ms, resulting in a substantial increase in the overall delay, which is difficult to meet the real-time requirements of a large number of tasks (such as hazard early warning, diagnostic updates, etc.) in the body domain network. Therefore, ensuring the real-time performance of information transmission and data processing in the body area network is an important prerequisite for the safe and effective work of the body area network.

In order to reduce the data transmission delay in the body domain network, the data must be processed at the edge of the network. One of the feasible methods is fog computing, which reduces the transmission delay by shortening the data transmission distance. At the same time, in order to reduce the data processing delay in the body domain network, fog computing can also be used to help intelligent medical terminal nodes with insufficient computing power to carry out data processing through the cooperation of multiple fog nodes at the edge of the network. Reduce the high processing delay of a single node [8, 9].

Fog computing refers to the deployment of the computing power of the network at the edge of the network, is a multi-level computing architecture from the cloud to the physical end, with the distribution of computing, communication, storage, control, networking and other functions. The processing, storage and application of the data generated by the network terminal by using the computing power of the fog node at the edge of the network can greatly reduce the delay of task transmission and processing. Fog computing provides a new way for the intelligence and information of body area network, which can process the tasks requested by users nearby and distributed in the network, and effectively reduce the transmission and processing delay of tasks. In addition to real-time, the body area network in intelligent medicine also has high requirements for the security of user data. At present, cloud computing, which is widely used, uploads all the data to the cloud server, and the data is uniformly processed in the cloud server to return the results to the user. The CVM used by users is a public cloud, and cloud administrators can obtain all user data. Therefore, under the architecture of unified and centralized management of resources on CVM, data security is faced with great challenges. Compared with cloud computing, the fog node of fog computing belongs to the local edge node, and the fog computing of intelligent medical terminal is isolated from the rest of the network when calculating and sharing resources, that is, a black box processing mechanism. The data is only processed in the black box node and is not visible to the outside world, so the processing of information by users and other nodes is unknown, and a task may be processed by multiple nodes. Send back user node summary with high security [10]. Fog computing as the current research hotspot, many scholars have conducted in-depth research on the application of fog computing in intelligent medical services, and achieved some research results. For example, He S and others proposed the CEP architecture of fog computing-based personalized medical service [11], and optimized it through clustering and other methods, which can solve the problems of response time delay and resource waste in the case of increased complexity. Chakraborty S et al. proposed a fog-based cloud model [12, 13] for time-sensitive medical applications, which can solve the problem of time delay and ensure data accuracy and consistency. Cerina L et al. proposed a multi-level architecture based on fog computing [14]. In this paper, an edge node based on field programmable gate array ((FPGA)) technology is proposed to minimize the delay. Sood S K et al. designed a medical and health department based on fog-aided computing [15], which classifies the types of user infection through the decision tree and generates diagnostic alarms at the fog layer to diagnose and prevent the outbreak of Chikungunya virus. Hamid H An et al. proposed a health care privacy data protection scheme based on fog computing [16] and designed a three-party authentication key agreement protocol to solve the problem of user privacy data theft. These research results show that fog computing will have a wide application prospect in intelligent medical services in the future.

Based on the characteristics of high real-time requirements for information transmission and processing, high security requirements for data storage and use, and high flexibility and inclusiveness of network architecture in intelligent medical services, this paper proposes a body area network intelligent medical security framework based on fog computing, which integrates fog computing distributed computing model into intelligent medical services in wireless body area network. An optimized scheme is found for the data transmission and storage between the intelligent medical terminal and the cloud computing center, which can effectively reduce the cost and delay, while ensuring the security and dispersion of data transmission between each layer.

The main work of this paper is as follows:

(1) combining the concept of wireless body area network with intelligent medical treatment, through a variety of intelligent medical terminals to collect and real-time monitor the health status of users, treatment and prevention can be combined to effectively control diseases.

(2) the architecture of fog computing is introduced between the intelligent medical terminal of body area network and the cloud computing center, and a security framework of intelligent medical treatment of body area network based on fog computing is proposed, which effectively solves the problem of excessive transmission delay and storage overhead.

(3) A real-time encrypted transmission scheme is proposed for the data transmission between intelligent medical terminal, fog computing center and cloud computing center, and the attack model is simulated to verify its security and feasibility.

2   Intelligent Medical Service Framework of Wireless Body Area Network

Aiming at the security and real-time problems of intelligent medical service in body area network, this paper proposes a fog computing security framework for intelligent medical service in wireless body area network. On the one hand, the framework can monitor intelligent medical devices to detect whether there are malicious attacks, and feedback the detection results to users; on the other hand, the framework processes users' personal health data in fog computing center and encrypts and decrypts the transmission process to ensure the security and dispersion of the data.

2.1 Body Area Network Intelligent Medical Terminal

In the wireless body area network, the intelligent medical terminal (sensor) is responsible for collecting and sending the health status information of the user. Figure 1 is a diagram of all kinds of commonly used intelligent medical terminals. Intelligent medical terminals are divided into three categories: (1) portable small medical terminals, or micro intelligent chips that can be embedded in the human body. Such as: smart bracelet, intelligent pacemaker and so on. The smart bracelet can monitor the heart rate and body temperature in real time. Once the value exceeds the normal range, the bracelet will maximum prompt the user and nearby people. At the same time, the bracelet is embedded with GPS and emergency contact function. When the user's physical signs are abnormal, it will send a distress signal and location to the nearest medical institution at the first time of reminding, so as to provide the user with the instantly rescue. (2) small family nursing terminal. Such as: smart medicine box and so on. (3) the Intelligent medical terminal used by the hospital. Such as: Intelligent infusion pump, Intelligent dispensing machine and so on.

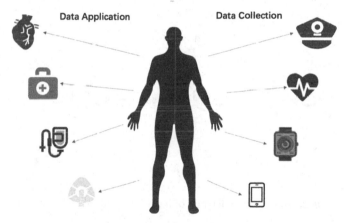

Fig. 1. Schematic diagram of commonly used intelligent medical terminals

The intelligent medical terminal is divided into two parts:

In the part of data perception and collection, the intelligent medical terminal can collect health data through all kinds of sensors on the users, and upload it to the health care monitoring and management center, so as to monitor the user's health status for 24 h. The data involved in the section is shown in Fig. 1. ECG: monitor heart rate and other information. Blood pressure: the user's blood pressure can be recorded. Blood: through the smart bracelet to monitor red blood cells, white blood cells and blood oxygen concentration and other information. Brain waves: monitor brain biological signals through smart helmets. Bioelectric signals: through the analysis of bioelectric signals produced by human movement, to judge the state of muscles and so on.

In the data application part, the collected data will be sent to the fog computing center for analysis, and then get the most suitable problem solution for users, so as to achieve medical plan customization. For example, the intelligent medicine box can remind the user of the medication time and dose, etc.; the intelligent infusion pump can adjust the infusion rate by observing the changes of human blood pressure and other information; and the intelligent dispensing machine can accurately configure user-customized drugs through user information. More oriented and adaptable.

2.2 Security Framework Based on Fog Computing

The fog computing Center is a highly virtualized platform that provides computing, storage and networking services between end devices and traditional cloud computing data centers. Fog computing is closer to users, it has less bandwidth and network strain, can reduce costs and reduce latency. Such computing not only expands the capabilities of the cloud, but also provides adequate data processing and storage support.

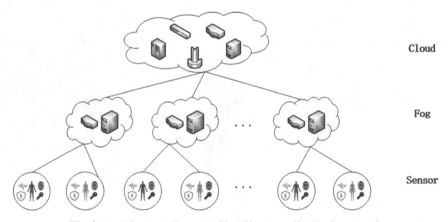

Fig. 2. Architecture diagram of intelligent medical body network

The architecture diagram of the designed intelligent medical body network is shown in Fig. 2. It is composed of cloud computing center, fog computing center and intelligent medical terminal equipment. The logical architecture diagram of the intelligent medical body network is shown in Fig. 3. The cloud computing center is mainly responsible for data storage management, computing, information processing and so on. That is, when the fog computing center needs to exceed its own computing power, or beyond its storage capacity, the cloud computing center will provide computing and storage resources. Important information can also be stored in the cloud computing center as a redundant backup, and users' personal files can be generated. The fog computing center can also be called the management side. It is mainly composed of middleware that provides a certain degree of distributed transparency, provides computing and storage resources for the lower layer, provides transmission function to make the information exchange between the upper and lower layers, carries on data analysis and management, and has the function of security protection. Intelligent medical terminal devices include intelligent bracelets, intelligent sphygmomanometers, intelligent pacemakers, intelligent medicine boxes, intelligent dispensing machines and other medical devices, which are mainly responsible for perceiving and collecting health information and performing simple information processing, and send the information to the fog computing Center for processing.

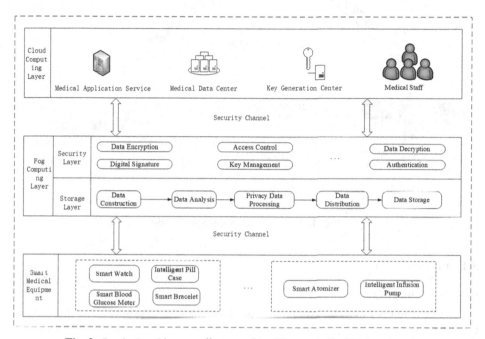

Fig. 3. Logical architecture diagram of intelligent medical body network

3   Encrypted Transmission Scheme Between Layers

In this section, the proposed encrypted transmission scheme is described in detail, as shown in Fig. 4 below, which is mainly divided into three stages: initialization phase, transmission phase and verification processing phase.

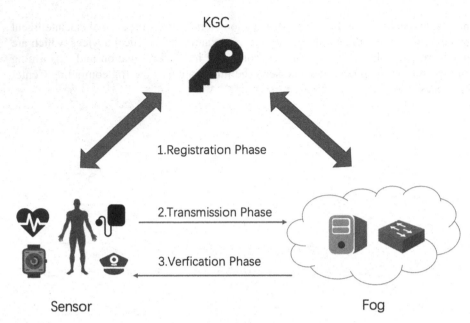

KGC

1.Registration Phase

2.Transmission Phase

3.Verfication Phase

Sensor

Fog

Fig. 4. Encrypted transmission scheme

3.1 Preliminaries

- Bilinear mapping

Let G1 and G2 be cyclic groups of order p [17], and p be prime. If the mapping e: $G_1 \times G_1 \rightarrow G_2$

satisfies the following properties:

1) Bilinear:

For any a, b $\in Z_p$ and R, S $\in G_1$, there is $e(R^a, S^b) = e(R, S)^{ab}$; which can be described in the following way: for any P, Q, R $\in G_1$, there is $e(P + Q, R) = e(P, R) e (Q, R)$.

2) non-degenerative:

There exists R, S $\in G_2$ such that $e(R, S) \neq 1_{G2}$. Here 1_{G2} represents the unit of G_2 group.

3) calculability:

There is an effective algorithm to calculate the value of e (R, S) for any R, S $\in G_1$. Then e is called a bilinear mapping.

- Key Generation Center (KGC)

The cloud computing center is mainly responsible for data storage management, computing and information processing, but it is also equipped with a key generation center to ensure secure transmission. Its main role is to generate the corresponding private key for verification according to the user identity information when the intelligent medical service terminal and fog computing center carry out the private data transmission of users.

3.2 Encrypted Transmission Scheme

Initialization Phase

During initialization, before the user uses the intelligent medical service of the body area network, the KGC of the cloud computing center will send an identity key t to the intelligent medical service terminal (sensor) used by the user to communicate with the fog computing Center. The health data of a user (data collected by the sensor) is used as a terminal node n, and the node ID number is ID_n. The data transmission process is shown in Fig. 4. The public key P_{pub} and identity parameter q_n: are calculated by formula (1) and hash function (2).

$$P_{pub} = tP, \tag{1}$$

$$H_1 : q_n = H_1(ID_n), \tag{2}$$

The private key s of node n is obtained by formula (3):

$$s = tq_n, \tag{3}$$

Transmission Phase

The transmission phase actually refers to the process that the health information collected by the user through the intelligent medical service terminal is compiled into a file and encrypted and transmitted to the central node of fog computing.

The user selects an arbitrary positive integer r as a random number, and the random parameter R is calculated by formula (4). Then the parameter w is calculated in formula (5) using the previously defined bilinear mapping (where q_1 is the user identity parameter obtained by formula (2) above):

$$R = rP, \tag{4}$$

$$w = e(P, P)^{rq_1}, \tag{5}$$

Then the user privacy data collected by the intelligent medical terminal is compiled into a file m, and the encryption result M and authentication parameter V are obtained by hashing and XOR operation (6) and (7) calculation:

$$M = m \oplus H_2(w), \tag{6}$$

$$V = \frac{q_2 s_1 R}{s_1 + r}, \tag{7}$$

Finally, the user data is sent to the fog computing Center by a set of encryption result M, random parameter R, and authentication parameter $V(M, R, V.$

Verification Processing Phase
It refers to the process that the fog computing central node receives the health information sent by the user for verification and performs the relevant calculation and storage operation.

When the fog computing center receives the result, it first calculates the auxiliary parameter A using formula (8) (where s_2 is the sensor private key obtained by formula (3)):

$$A = \frac{q_1 P_{pub} + R}{s_2}, \tag{8}$$

After the parameter w' prime is obtained in formula (9), the decrypted user privacy data file m is obtained by hashing and XOR operation (10):

$$w' = e(A, V), \tag{9}$$

$$m = M \oplus H_2(w'), \tag{10}$$

When we get the verified privacy data file m, fog computing Center will store and process the file information, and send the calculated feedback results back to users as soon as possible, so that users can get safe and reliable suggestions. At the same time, the data will be sent from the fog node to the cloud computing storage center in the same encrypted transmission mode as a backup, and the user's personal profile will be generated to prevent data loss.

4   Safety Analysis

In this section, we first verify the correctness of the scheme, and then analyze the security from two aspects: forged sender data and MITM attacks.

4.1   Correctness Verification

The correctness of the encrypted transmission scheme means that the intelligent medical terminal and fog computing center can encrypt and decrypt the transmitted health data through our method. Here, we record the new intermediate parameter calculated by the fog computing Center as w', w' can be calculated by the following formula:

$$
\begin{aligned}
w' = e(A, V) &= e\left(\frac{q_1 P_{pub} + R}{s_2}, \frac{q_2 s_1 R}{r + s_1}\right) \\
&= e\left(\frac{q_1 tP + rP}{tq_2}, \frac{tq_1 q_2 rP}{r + tq_1}\right) \\
&= e\left(\frac{r + q_1 t}{tq_2} P, \frac{tq_1 q_2 r}{r + tq_1} P\right) = e(P, q_1 rP)
\end{aligned}
$$

$$= e(P, P)^{rq_1} = w$$

From the consistency test of the above results, it is not difficult to see that the scheme we designed is correct.

4.2 Forged Sender

One is that malicious attackers may destroy or invade some intelligent terminals to send some false early warning messages; the other is that the identity information of this intelligent terminal is stolen. In our scheme, the attacker can forge the private key of a terminal to replace s_1, but he does not know the identity key t issued by the cloud computing center, so he cannot match it with his forged private key $s_1 = tH_1(ID_1)$, which means that the forged sender cannot send a verifiable random parameter R.

4.3 MITM Attacks

A MITM attack refers to an attacker trying to tamper with the contents of the data by intercepting the data we send. Suppose the attacker can intercept the message of our scheme (M, R, V). First of all, if he wants to capture a specific message, he needs to decrypt the encrypted M, because every time he sends and transmits the data, he needs to generate a random number r that the attacker does not know about, so he cannot decrypt it. Second, the attacker cannot know the transmission private key s_2 of any fog computing center. In addition, if the attacker wants to tamper with the message, we can see from the analysis in the previous section that this will not work. Finally, assuming that the attacker can constantly collect the encrypted message ciphertext M and the original message m sent by the intelligent terminal to infer the encryption method, the transmissible data will generate a different random number r each time, which makes it impossible for the attacker to crack the encrypted information.

5 Conclusion

In view of the rapid development of the Internet of things, this paper fully combines the wireless body area network and intelligent medical care to make medical services more intelligent and information -based. In order to meet the high requirements of real-time and security of data transmission in body area network, a body area network intelligent medical security framework based on fog computing is proposed, and a real-time encrypted transmission scheme for data communication between layers is proposed. Its security and feasibility are verified and analyzed by simulated attack model.

Acknowledgments. This work was supported in part by the Aviation Science Foundation of China under Grant NO.20185152035 and Grant NO.20150652008, in part by the National Natural Science Foundation of China under Grant NO.61572253, in part by the Fundamental Research Funds for the Central Universities (NJ2019010, NJ20170007, NJ2020022), and also supported by Jiangsu Province Software New Technology and Industrialization Collaborative Innovation Center.

References

1. He, D., Zeadally, S., Wu, L.: Certificateless public auditing scheme for cloud-assisted wireless body area networks. IEEE Syst. J. **12**(1), 64–67 (2018)
2. Gope, P., Prosanta, T., Wang, H.: A realistic lightweight anonymous authentication protocol for securing real-time application data access in wireless sensor networks. IEEE Trans. Industr. Electron. **63**(11), 7124–7132 (2016)
3. Kumari, S., et al.: A user-friendly mutual authentication and key agreement scheme for wireless sensor networks using chaotic maps. Future Gener. Comput. Syst. **63**, 56–75 (2016)
4. Srinivas, J., Mishra, D., Mukhopadhyay, S.: A mutual authentication framework for wireless medical sensor networks. J. Med. Syst. **41**(5), 1–9 (2017). https://doi.org/10.1007/s10916-017-0720-9
5. He, D., et al.: Anonymous authentication for wireless body area networks with provable security. IEEE Syst. J. **11**(4), 2590–2601 (2017)
6. Wei, F., et al.: A provably secure password-based anonymous authentication scheme for wireless body area networks. Comput. Electr. Eng. **65**, 322–331 (2017)
7. Wazid, M., Das, A.K., Vasilakos. A.V.: Authenticated key management protocol for cloud-assisted body area sensor networks. J. Netw. Comput. Appl. **123**, 112–126 (2018)
8. Pande, V., Marlecha, C., Kayte, S.: A review-fog computing and its role in the Internet of Things. Int. J. Eng. Res. Appl. **6**(10), 2248–96227 (2016)
9. Puliafito, C., et al.: Fog computing for the Internet of Things: a survey. ACM Trans. Internet Technol. **19**(2), 18 (2019)
10. Ni, J., et al.: Security, privacy, and fairness in fog-based vehicular crowdsensing. IEEE Commun. Mag. **55**(6), 146–152 (2017)
11. He, S., et al.: Proactive personalized services in large-scale IoT-based healthcare application. In: IEEE International Conference on Web Services (ICWS)IEEE (2017)
12. Chakraborty, S., et al.: Fog networks in healthcare application. In: IEEE 13th International Conference on Mobile Ad Hoc and Sensor Systems (MASS) IEEE (2017)
13. Sood, S.K., Mahajan, I.G.: A Fog Based Healthcare Framework for Chikungunya. IEEE Internet Things J. **5**(2), 794–801 (2017)
14. Hamid, H., Abdulaziz, A., et al.: A security model for preserving the privacy of medical big data in a healthcare cloud using a fog computing facility with pairing-based cryptography. IEEE Access. **5**, 22313–22328 (2017)
15. Cerina, L., et al.: A fog-computing architecture for preventive healthcare and assisted living in smart ambients. In: IEEE International Forum on Research & Technologies for Society & Industry (RTSI). IEEE (2017)
16. Gibler, C., Crussell, J., Erickson, J., Chen, H.: AndroidLeaks: automatically detecting potential privacy leaks in android applications on a large scale. In: Katzenbeisser, S., Weippl, E., Camp, L.J., Volkamer, M., Reiter, M., Zhang, X. (eds.) Trust 2012. LNCS, vol. 7344, pp. 291–307. Springer, Heidelberg (2012). https://doi.org/10.1007/978-3-642-30921-2_17
17. Kiendl, H., Adamy, J.: Vector norms as Lyapunov functions for linear systems. IEEE Trans. Autom. Control **37**(6), 839–842 (1992)

Secure and Traceable Attribute-Based Sequential Aggregate Signature

Ruili Yang, Jiageng Chen$^{(\boxtimes)}$, and Shangle Li

School of Computer,
Central China Normal University, Wuhan 430070, China
youngruili@163.com, chinkako@gmail.com, shangle.lee@mails.ccnu.edu.cn

Abstract. Attribute-based signatures allow a signer with a set of attributes to anonymously sign a message about some signature policy. However, in the environments that require accountability and preventing abuse, the anonymity revocation function is vital important and necessary. In order to meet the requirements that multiple different authorized participants can sequentially aggregate and sign the same message while maintain the accountability of the signers, we propose a secure and traceable attribute-based sequential aggregate signature scheme with multiple attribute authorities. It is based on the flexible threshold access structure, and it also supports extension to any linear secret sharing scheme access structures. Our scheme can be proved secure under the CDH assumption and subgroup decision assumption in the selective model without random oracle. The security analysis shows that our attribute-based sequential aggregate signatures scheme can realize existential unforgeability, traceablity and unlinkability. It is believed that it can also be widely used in e-commerce and e-government related applications.

Keywords: Attribute-based signature · Sequential aggregate signature · Multiple attribute authorities · Traceability · Unlinkability

1 Introduction

In attribute-based cryptography systems, only users who have the attributes satisfying the policy in question can execute decryption or signature operation. The first proposals of attribute-based cryptosystems were: an encryption scheme by Goyal et al. [6] which was inspired by fuzzy identity-based encryption [18], and a signature scheme by Maji et al. [13]. In the attribute-based signature (ABS) scheme, the receiver is convinced that someone who has a set of attributes that satisfy the signature predicate has indeed verified the message without needing to know identity of the signer or how the predicate is satisfied. For the purpose of both authentication and privacy, many applications have adopted ABS schemes, such as electronic personal health record systems, e.g. [8] and [12]. The ABS scheme is anonymous and can hide the identity of signer, but the signer

G. Wang et al. (Eds.): SpaCCS 2020, LNCS 12382, pp. 367–381, 2021.
https://doi.org/10.1007/978-3-030-68851-6_27

can use this feature to abuse the signature. Liu et al. proposed attribute-based sequential aggregate signature [11] and attribute-based multi-signature scheme [10], which both were not traceable and with a single attribute authority. The traceable ABS scheme can prevent the signer from abusing the signature. Given a valid signature, the private key generation center can use the tracking key to recover the identity of signer; but for other verifiers who do not know the tracking key, it is impossible to confirm whether multiple signatures using the same signing strategy were signed by the same signer. The traceable ABS was first introduced by Escala et al. [5], which extends the standard ABS by adding an anonymous revocation mechanism that allows a tracking authority to restore the identity of signer. Although it might seem intuitive that the traceable ABS is similar to group signatures [1,3,4], which allow members of the group to sign on behalf of the group, and only the group administrator can reveal the identity of signers in the group. The difference is that ABS does not indicate a group and does not need to establish a group, but declares that the set of attributes they possess meets a certain signature policy, thus hiding the identity of signer. Zhang et al. [20] proposed an identity traceable ABS scheme, which is not suitable for signing long messages. Considering the following facts: the attributes of different users may come from different authorities and single authority may cause a computing bottleneck, some multi-attributes authority schemes [15,19] have been proposed. Okamoto et al. [16] proposed decentralized ABS. Inspired by [5] and [16], Kaafarani et al. proposed decentralized traceable ABS, which uses twice non-interactive zero-knowledge (NIZK) proofs and its construction is extremely complex.

Therefore, in order to achieve convenient and efficient management for multi-stakeholder systems, we introduce attribute-based sequential aggregate signature with multiple attribute authorities management. Each attribute authority independently assigns attributes and signature private keys to its users. In the signature process, the identity of the signer can be bound to both the signature and secret key through a commitment scheme, similar to the technology proposed in [14], which the user's identity is bound to generated secret key. We use flexible threshold access to construct our ABS. Moreover, using the method in [6], it is easy to extend the threshold traceable ABS scheme to an access structure that can be expressed by any linear secret sharing scheme. In this paper, we store the results of the aggregate signature on cloud servers. For data security, one can adaptively encrypt the signature results. This paper does not discuss this. Our solution can also be deployed on the blockchain platform, combining with the un-tamperability of blockchain technology, and promote deep mutual trust among the participants. In many fields such as e-commerce and e-government, etc., our scheme is also applicable.

Our Contributions. In this paper, in order to meet the requirement of that multiple people sign the same file in sequence and data traceability in many fields such as e-commerce and e-government and so on, we construct a powerful attribute-based sequential aggregate signature scheme with multiple attribute authorities. The aggregate signature in our scheme is anonymous, unlinkability, and traceable if needed. Compared with [9], in our scheme if an attribute authority wants to add or revoke, it does not affect any other attribute authorities. Compared with [11], our scheme can trace the identity of signers and sign long messages.

2 Preliminaries

In this section, we introduce the notions related to bilinear maps, complexity assumptions, Boneh-Goh-Nissim commitment scheme and a NIZK proof of bit encryption, which are used in our scheme.

2.1 Bilinear Maps

We will construct our system in composite order bilinear groups, which were introduced in [2]. Let $\mathbb{G}$ and $\mathbb{G}_T$ be two (multiplicative) cyclic groups of finite order N, which $N = pq$ is a product of two distinct primes. Let g be a generator of $\mathbb{G}$ and $e : \mathbb{G} \times \mathbb{G} \to \mathbb{G}_T$ be a bilinear map. The map has the following properties:

- Bilinearity: For any $u, v \in \mathbb{G}$ and $a, b \in \mathbb{Z}_N$, we have $e(u^a, v^b) = e(u, v)^{ab}$.
- Non-degeneracy: There exists $g \in \mathbb{G}$ such that $e(g, g)$ has order N in $\mathbb{G}_T$.

Here the map e is symmetric since $e(u^a, v^b) = e(u^b, v^a) = e(u, v)^{ab}$. Assuming that group operations in $\mathbb{G}$ and $\mathbb{G}_T$ as well as the bilinear map e can be efficiently computed in polynomial time, and the group descriptions of $\mathbb{G}$ and $\mathbb{G}_T$ both include a generator of each group. The subgroups $\mathbb{G}_p$ and $\mathbb{G}_q$ of $\mathbb{G}$ are mutually "orthogonal" under the bilinear map e: if $u \in \mathbb{G}_p$ and $v \in \mathbb{G}_q$, then $e(u, v) = 1$.

2.2 Complexity Assumption

We shall make use of two complexity assumptions: the first is Computational Diffie-Hellman assumption in the prime order subgroup $\mathbb{G}_p$, the second is Subgroup Decision assumption in the full group $\mathbb{G}$.

CDH Assumption: Let $a, b \in \mathbb{Z}_p$ at random and given a triple $(g, g^a, g^b) \in \mathbb{G}_p^3$. The CDH assumption is to compute $g^{ab} \in \mathbb{G}_p$ with non-negligible probability for probabilistic polynomial time (PPT) adversary. We shall require the CDH assumption in $\mathbb{G}_p$ to remain true when the factorization of N is known [3].

Subgroup Decision Assumption: [2] Let $\lambda \in \mathbb{Z}^+$ and $(N, \mathbb{G}, \mathbb{G}_T, e)$ be a tuple produced by an algorithm $\mathcal{G}(\lambda)$, where $N = pq$. Given $(N, \mathbb{G}, \mathbb{G}_T, e)$ and an element $x \in \mathbb{G}$, output 1 if the order of x is p and output 0 otherwise i.e. the subgroup decision problem is without knowing the factorization of the group order N, decide if an element x is in a subgroup of $\mathbb{G}$. An algorithm $\mathcal{A}$ has advantage in solving the subgroup decision problem $SDadv_{\mathcal{A}}(\lambda)$ is defined as:

$$SDadv_{\mathcal{A}}(\lambda) = |Pr[\mathcal{A}(N, \mathbb{G}, \mathbb{G}_T, e, x) = 1] - Pr[\mathcal{A}(N, \mathbb{G}, \mathbb{G}_T, e, x^q) = 1]|.$$

Definition 1. *The subgroup decision assumption holds if for any PPT algorithm $\mathcal{A}$ we have that $SDadv_{\mathcal{A}}(\lambda)$ is a negligible function in λ.*

2.3 Boneh-Goh-Nissim Commitment Scheme

Boneh-Goh-Nissim commitment scheme [2] bases on the Subgroup Decision Assumption. The scheme consist of three algorithms as follows:

KeyGen: The algorithm runs the group generator algorithm $\mathcal{G}(1^\lambda)$ and outputs a tuple $(p, q, g, \mathbb{G}, \mathbb{G}_T, e)$ where $\mathbb{G}, \mathbb{G}_T$ are groups of order $N = pq$, $e : \mathbb{G} \times \mathbb{G} \to \mathbb{G}_T$ is a bilinear map and g is a random generator of $\mathbb{G}$. And, it picks a random generator h from $\mathbb{G}_q$. Then, it sets $(\mathbb{G}, \mathbb{G}_T, e, g, N, h)$ as the public parameters pk and q as the perfectly binding key sk.

Commitment: The algorithm takes as input the public parameters pk and the message m. To commit to the message m, the algorithm chooses a random value $r \in \mathbb{Z}_N$ and computes $com(m, r) = c = g^m h^r$. It then outputs the commitment c.

DeCommit: The algorithm takes as input the perfectly binding key sk and a commitment c. The algorithm computes $c^q = (g^m h^r)^q = (g^q)^m$, and exhaustively searches for m. Then it outputs the message m.

    Note that in [2], the commitment scheme described above is homomorphic. Specifically, for any message m and randomizers we have $com(m_1 + m_2, r_1 + r_2) = g^{m_1 + m_2} h^{r_1 + r_2} = g^{m_1} h^{r_1} g^{m_2} h^{r_2} = com(m_1, r_1) com(m_2, r_2)$. And decommitment in this scheme takes polynomial time in the size of message space. Therefore, this scheme can only be used to commit short messages. One can speed-up decryption by precomputing a (polynomial-size) table of powers of g^q so that decryption can occur in constant time.

2.4 NIZK Proof of Bit Encryption

Groth et al. [7] used the Boneh-Goh-Nissim cryptosystem [2] to construct an effective statistical zero-knowledge proof system for any NP language. In this paper, we use the non-interactive witness indistinguishable (NIWI) proof of bit encryption. The scheme consist of four algorithms as follows:

Common Reference String: The algorithm runs the group generator algorithm $\mathcal{G}(1^\lambda)$ and outputs a tuple $(p, q, g, \mathbb{G}, \mathbb{G}_T, e)$ where $\mathbb{G}, \mathbb{G}_T$ are groups of order $N = pq$, $e : \mathbb{G} \times \mathbb{G} \to \mathbb{G}_T$ is a bilinear map and g is a random generator of $\mathbb{G}$. And, it picks a generator h randomly from $\mathbb{G}_q$. Then, it sets $CRS = (\mathbb{G}, \mathbb{G}_T, e, g, N, h)$ as the public parameters pk and q as the perfectly binding key sk.

Statement: The algorithm takes as input the public parameters pk and a message $m \in \{0, 1\}$. To commit the message m, the algorithm chooses a random value $r \in \mathbb{Z}_N$ and computes $com(m, r) = c = g^m h^r$. The statement is c.

Proof: It inputs (CRS, c, m, r). For the statement $c = g^m h^r$, its NIWI witness is $\pi = \left(g^{2m-1} h^r \right)^r$.

Verify: It inputs (CRS, c, π) and check $e(c, c/g) = e(h, \pi)$. It returns 1 if the check pass, else return 0.

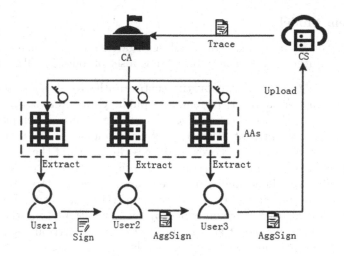

Fig. 1. System model.

3 Definition and Security Models

3.1 Participants

Our secure and traceable attribute-based sequential aggregate signature scheme with multiple attribute authorities involves three types of entities: a central authority, multiple attribute authorities, and the cloud server. (see Fig. 1. Suppose there are three attribute authorities).

- **The Central Authority (CA):** The central authority is the administrator of the entire system and assumed to be fully trusted. The central authority is responsible for all attribute authorities to generate authority secret key. It can also track and reveal the relevant responsible persons according to the last aggregate signature of the documents from the cloud servers.
- **The Attribute Authorities (AAs):** There are multiple attribute authorities, which are a finite number of distributed authorities. We assume that each attribute authority can be compromised. The attribute authorities are responsible for users to generate identity, attributes and private key. Each authority has its own users, assuming each user will not belong to two or more attribute authorities at the same time. When a subtask is completed, users with attributes that meet a specific attribute policy will sign the message and aggregate the signature in sequence. Finally, the last signer in the system uploads the final aggregate signature to the cloud storage server.
- **The Cloud Server (CS):** The cloud server provides a public platform for storing and sharing data. In order to protect the security of data stored on the cloud, they can be adaptively encrypted, this paper will not discuss.

3.2   System Model

Our traceable attribute-based sequential aggregate signature scheme with multiple attribute authorities can be described as a set of following algorithms:

- **Setup:** The algorithm is run by the central authority. Firstly, it takes the security parameter as input. It generates public parameters *params* and the traceable key *tsk*. It keeps *tsk* to itself. Then, it generates different authority secret keys α_k for different attribute authority and sends the secret keys to them by secret channel. Moreover, it defines the length of the user ID as n_u. It specifies the scope of each attribute authority assigned to its user ID.
- **AuthoritySetup:** This algorithm is executed by each attribute authority AA_k. Every attribute authority AA_k sets user ID for its internal users.
- **Extract:** This algorithm is controlled by each the attribute authority AA_k. It takes the authority secret key α_k, user ID u and an attribute set Ω of user as input. Then, it generates a sign private key for the user.
- **Sign:** The user u performs this algorithm to sign a message M under certain predicate $\Upsilon_{\kappa,\Phi}(\cdot)$ with the input of a sign private key, its ID and *params*. Then, the algorithm outputs the signature σ.
- **Verify:** This algorithm allows user to verify the normal signature by giving a signature σ, a message M, an attribute set and *params*. It outputs *accept* if a valid signature on M for the attribute set; else, it outputs *reject*.
- **AggSign:** This algorithm allows multiple different users to sign on same message and sequential aggregates into single signature. It inputs the private key of the current user, message M and its current user's signature σ which is needed to be aggregated and aggregate-so-far $a\sigma'$ on message M. It generates a new sequential aggregate signature $a\sigma$ on message M.
- **AggVerify:** The user who received aggregate-so-far signatures checks the aggregate signature to proof the message involved in aggregate signature is not modified by malicious users. It inputs an aggregate signature $a\sigma$ on message M, *params* and attribute sets. If $a\sigma$ is a valid aggregate signature, the algorithm outputs *accept* or it outputs *reject* otherwise.
- **Trace:** The central authority takes as input the last sequential aggregate signature $a\sigma$, *params* and *tsk*. It first runs *AggVerify* and verifies whether $a\sigma$ is valid or not so as to determine whether $a\sigma$ is tampered. Then, if it's true, it extracts the signers' ID from the commitment which is inserted in the $a\sigma$. It then outputs a set of correct ID of users.

3.3   Existential Unforgeability of the Scheme

Under the selective signature policy and message attack model, the existential unforgeability of ABS scheme means that if the private key of the signer is not known and the signer has not been asked to sign the message M^* about the signature predicate $\Upsilon^*_{\kappa,\Phi^*}(\cdot)$. Then the adversary cannot forge the message signature pair (M^*, σ^*) about the predicate $\Upsilon^*_{\kappa,\Phi^*}(\cdot)$. For this security model, the user u is adaptive. Then, this security model between a challenger and an adversary is as follows:

Init: The adversary declares to the challenger a challenge signature predicate $\Upsilon^*_{\kappa,\Phi^*}(\cdot)$.

Setup: The challenger generates the public parameter *params*, the attribute authority secret key α, and the tracking key *tsk*, and sends *params* to the adversary.

Queries: The adversary can adaptively make a polynomial bounded number of queries: *Extract query*, *Sign query*, *AggSign query*, and *Trace query*, where attribute set Ω does not satisfy the signature predicate $\Upsilon^*_{\kappa,\Phi^*}(\cdot)$ for user u in *Extract query*.

Forge: The adversary outputs the forged signature σ^* of user u, message M^*, and signature predicate $\Upsilon^*_{\kappa,\Phi^*}(\cdot)$. Moreover, the adversary has not made *Extract query* of u, and the adversary has not asked the user u about the signature of the message M^* and the signature predicate $\Upsilon^*_{\kappa,\Phi^*}(\cdot)$. If the signature is valid, the adversary wins.

Definition 2. *The attribute-based signature scheme is existence unforgeable if no PPT adversary can win the above game with non-negligible advantage.*

3.4 Unlinkability of the Scheme

Similar to [7,20], unlinkability refers that given two valid signatures used the same signature predicate without knowing the tracking key, even if the adversary knows the private key of the signer, the adversary cannot tell whether the two signatures are signed by the same signer. The attack game between a challenger and an adversary is as follows: *Init, Setup, Phase 1* are the same as *Init, Setup, Queries* in the previous section, respectively.

Challenge: The adversary selects the user u_0 (its attribute set is Ω_0). There is an attribute set $\omega \in \Omega_0$ satisfying $\Upsilon^*_{\kappa,\Phi^*}(\cdot)$. Then, it also selects $u_1(\neq u_0)$ and $\Upsilon^*_{\kappa,\Phi^*}(\Omega_1) = 1$. The adversary makes *Extract query* for (u_0, Ω_0), (u_1, Ω_1). The challenger chooses $b \in \{0,1\}$ to generate signature σ^* about (u_b, Ω_b), message M^*, $\Upsilon^*_{\kappa,\Phi^*}(\cdot)$ and sends σ^*, (u_0, Ω_0), (u_1, Ω_1) to the adversary.

Phase 2: It is almost same as *Phase 1*, except that the adversary cannot inquiry *Trace σ^**.

Guess: The adversary outputs a guess of b'. If $b' = b$, the adversary wins.

Definition 3. *The ABS scheme is unlinkability under the selective signature predicate and selective message attack model, if and only if there is no PPT adversary to have a non-negligible advantage in the above game.*

4 Our Construction

Let g is a random generator of $\mathbb{G}$, and $e : \mathbb{G} \times \mathbb{G} \to \mathbb{G}_T$ is a bilinear map. In addition, Let the Lagrange coefficient $\Delta_{j,S}$ for $j \in \mathbb{Z}_N$ and a set S of elements in

$\mathbb{Z}_N$ define as: $\Delta_{j,S}(i) = \prod_{\eta \in S, \eta \neq j} \frac{i-\eta}{j-\eta}$. The scheme consists the following eight algorithms. The details are present as follows.

Setup: The central authority first runs the group algorithm $\mathcal{G}(1^\lambda)$ and outputs a tuple $(p, q, g, \mathbb{G}, \mathbb{G}_T, e)$ where $\mathbb{G}, \mathbb{G}_T$ are group of composite order $N = pq$ and $p \neq q$. $\mathbb{G}_p, \mathbb{G}_q$ are subgroups of $\mathbb{G}$ with order p, q, respectively. Next, the algorithm chooses random element $\tau \in \mathbb{G}$. It picks a random generator $h \in \mathbb{G}_q$. Let $\mathcal{N}$ be the set $\{1, \cdots, n+1\}$ and t_j is a random generator of $\mathbb{G}$ for $j \in \mathcal{N}$. We define a function T as $T(x) = \tau^{x^n} \prod_{j=1}^{n+1} t_j^{\Delta_{j,\mathcal{N}}(x)}$. The central authority chooses a hash function $H : \{0,1\}^* \to \mathbb{G}$. It selects a random element $u' \in \mathbb{G}$, defines the length of user identity as n_u, and defines a vector $U = \{u_i\}$ of length n_u, where $u_i \in \mathbb{G}$. It also specifies the scope to which each attribute authority assigns its users' ID, just like dividing a subnet. The central authority assigns different attribute authority secret key $\alpha_k \in \mathbb{Z}_N^*$ for each attribute authority and sends the secret keys to them by secret channel. Compute $g_k = g^{\alpha_k}$ and $Z_k = e(g_k, \tau)$.

Finally, it sets $(\mathbb{G}, \mathbb{G}_T, N, e, g, \tau, h, u', U, H, Z_k, d, t_1, \cdots, t_{n+1})$ as the public parameters $params$ and q as the traceable secret key tsk. Meanwhile, $params$ are public and tsk keeps to itself.

AuthoritySetup: The attribute authority defines $d - 1$ default attribute sets $\mathbb{U} = \{\mathbb{U}_1, \cdots, \mathbb{U}_{d-1}\}$ as the element in $\mathbb{Z}_N^*$. Each of them is in charge of the issue of attribute set A_k. And for each of attribute authorities internal users, it sets a unique user identity u which is represented by a binary string of length n_u, let $u[i]$ denote the i-th bit of u. Define $W(u) = u' \prod_{i=1}^{n_u} u_i^{u[i]} = u' \prod_{i \in U} \mu_i$. The secret key of attribute authority AA_k is α_k.

Extract: The attribute authority AA_k generates a sign private key for a user u with an attribute set Ω. The algorithm takes the following steps:

- Firstly, it choose a $d - 1$ degree polynomial at random with $q(0) = \alpha_k$. It selects a random value s from $\mathbb{Z}_N^*$ and sets $d_{u,0} = g^s, d_{u,1} = h^s$.
- For each $i \in \Omega$, chooses ν_i and computes $d_{ki,0} = \tau^{q(i)} \cdot T(i)^{\nu_i} \cdot W(u)^s$ and $d_{ki,1} = g^{\nu_i}$.
- Finally, it outputs the sign private key as

$$D_{ki} = (d_{u,0}, d_{u,1}, \{(d_{ki,0}, d_{ki,1})_{i \in \Omega}\}).$$

Sign: The user u inputs private keys D_{ki} of the attribute set Ω, message M and predicate $\Upsilon_{\kappa,\Phi}(\cdot)$. To sign message M with predicate $\Upsilon_{\kappa,\Phi}(\cdot)$. Namely, to prove a subset $\omega \subseteq \Omega \cap \Phi$ with $1 \leq \kappa \leq |\Phi|$, and define $\omega' = \Phi/\omega$. It runs as follows:

- Firstly, for every bit $u[i] (i = 1, \cdots, n_u)$ of user u, the algorithm chooses $\theta_i \in \mathbb{Z}_N$ randomly. It computes $c_i = u_i^{u[i]} \cdot h^{\theta_i}, \pi_i = \left(u_i^{2u[i]-1} \cdot h^{\theta_i}\right)^{\theta_i}$, where c_i is the commitment of $u[i]$, π_i is the witness of c_i. The user calculates $\theta = \sum_{i=1}^{n_u} \theta_i$, $c = u' \prod_{i=1}^{n_u} c_i = \left(u' \prod_{i=1}^{n_u} u_i^{u[i]}\right) \cdot h^\theta = \left(u' \prod_{i \in U} \mu_i\right) \cdot h^\theta = W(u) \cdot h^\theta$.

- Then, the user u selects a random value $\beta \in \mathbb{Z}_N$. After, it picks a default attribute subset $\mathbb{U}' \subseteq \mathbb{U}$ with $|\mathbb{U}'| = d - \kappa$ and picks $\zeta_i \in \mathbb{Z}_N$ randomly for $i \in \Phi \cup \mathbb{U}'$. The algorithm computes

$$\sigma_0 = [\prod_{i \in \omega \cup \mathbb{U}'} d_{ki,0}^{\Delta_{i,\omega}(0)}][\prod_{i \in \Phi \cup \mathbb{U}'} T(i)^{\zeta_i}] d_{u,1}^\theta H(M)^\beta;$$

$$\{\sigma_{1,i} = d_{ki,1}^{\Delta_{i,\omega}(0)} g^{\zeta_i}\}_{i \in \omega \cup \mathbb{U}'}, \{\sigma_{1,i} = g^{\zeta_i}\}_{i \in \omega'};$$

$$\sigma_2 = g^\beta; \sigma_3 = d_{u,0} = g^s.$$

- Finally, it outputs the signature:

$$\sigma = (\sigma_0, \{\sigma_{1,i}\}_{i \subset \Phi \cup \mathbb{U}'}, \sigma_2, \sigma_3, c_1, \cdots, c_{n_u}, \pi_1, \cdots, \pi_{n_u}).$$

Verify: The algorithm inputs σ on M with threshold κ for attributes set $\Phi \cup \mathbb{U}'$, and *params*. The verifier first computes $c = u' \prod_{i=1}^{n_u} c_i$ and verifies the correctness of the equation $e(c_i, u_i^{-1} c_i) = e(h, \pi_i)$, for $i = 1, \cdots, n_u$. In order to achieve fast verification and reduce computational overhead, we can use the method of [3]. Specifically, it uses randomization to batch the n_u equation into one multi-pairing. The verifier selects $r_1, \cdots, r_{n_u} \in \mathbb{Z}_N$, and checks the equation $\prod_{i=1}^{n_u} (e(c_i^{r_i}, u_i^{-1} c_i) \cdot e(h^{-r_i}, \pi_i)) = 1$. If this is true, then it is proved that for all $u[i](i = 1, \cdots, n_u)$, the equation $c_i = u_i^{u[i]} \cdot h^{\theta_i}$ holds. Therefore, the c calculated by the verifier has the correct format. Then, the verifier tests the following equation whether holds:

$$\frac{e(g, \sigma_0)}{[\prod_{i \in \Phi \cup \mathbb{U}'} e(T(i), \sigma_{1,i})] e(H(M), \sigma_2) e(c, \sigma_3)} = Z_k. \tag{1}$$

If the equation holds, it indicates that the signature is indeed from the user u with at least κ attributes among Φ. Otherwise, it denotes the signature is invalid.

AggSign: The another user u takes a private key for his attribute set Ω_2, signature σ' on M which is to aggregate, the aggregation so-far $a\sigma'$ on M under *params* as input. To verify that the aggregate-so-far $a\sigma'$ by running the *AggVerify* algorithm. If the aggregate signature is not pass the verification equation, it directly outputs fail and halt. Otherwise, it makes the following steps:

- Firstly, the algorithm initial the component of the aggregate signature $a\sigma_0$, $a\sigma_{1,i}$, $a\sigma_2$, $a\sigma_3$ such that $a\sigma_0 = 1, a\sigma_{1,i} = 1, a\sigma_2 = 1, a\sigma_3 = 1, \omega \cup \mathbb{U}' = \emptyset$ and $\omega' = \emptyset$. Then, the algorithm iteratively calculates $a\sigma_0 = a\sigma_0' \cdot \sigma_0', a\sigma_2 = a\sigma_2' \cdot \sigma_2'$.
- After that, for every $i \in \omega_2 \cup \mathbb{U}_2'$, if i does not exist in $\omega \cup \mathbb{U}'$, it adds attribute i to the attribute set $\omega \cup \mathbb{U}'$ and sets $a\sigma_{1,i} = \sigma_{1,i}' = d_{ki,1}^{\Delta_{i,\omega}(0)} g^{\zeta_i}$; if i exists in $\omega \cup \mathbb{U}'$, it generates $a\sigma_{1,i} = a\sigma_{1,i}' \cdot \sigma_{1,i}' = a\sigma_{1,i}' \cdot d_{ki,1}^{\Delta_{i,\omega}(0)} g^{\zeta_i}$. For every $i \in \omega_2'$, if i does not exist in ω', it adds attribute i to the attribute set ω' and sets $a\sigma_{1,i} = \sigma_{1,i}' = g^{\zeta_i}$; if i exists in ω', it generates $a\sigma_{1,i} = a\sigma_{1,i}' \cdot \sigma_{1,i}' = a\sigma_{1,i}' \cdot g^{\zeta_i}$.

– The fourth part of aggregate signature, the commitment and witness of signers' identities are handled in an additional way. So, $a\sigma_3$ is $\sigma_3^{(1)}, \cdots, \sigma_3^{(j)}$. The signers' ID commitment and witness are $\{c_1, \cdots, c_{n_u}, \pi_1, \cdots, \pi_{n_u}\}^{(1)}, \cdots, \{c_1, \cdots, c_{n_u}, \pi_1, \cdots, \pi_{n_u}\}^{(j)}$, where j is the number of aggregations.

The user outputs the aggregate signature as:

$$a\sigma = (a\sigma_0, \{a\sigma_{1,i}\}_{i \in \Phi \cup \mathbb{U}'}, a\sigma_2, \sigma_3^{(1)}, \cdots, \sigma_3^{(j)}, \{c_1, \cdots, c_{n_u}, \pi_1, \cdots, \pi_{n_u}\}^{(1)}, \cdots,$$
$$\{c_1, \cdots, c_{n_u}, \pi_1, \cdots, \pi_{n_u}\}^{(j)}).$$

AggVerify: The verifier takes the aggregate so-far $a\sigma$ on message M under *params* as input. The verifier first computes $c = u' \prod_{i=1}^{n_u} c_i$. Then, the verifier selects $r_1, \cdots, r_{n_u} \in \mathbb{Z}_N$, and checks equation $\prod_{i=1}^{n_u} \left(e\left(c_i^{r_i}, u_i^{-1} c_i\right) \cdot e\left(h^{-r_i}, \pi_i\right)\right) = 1$ for each commitment and witness tuple. If these are all true, then it is proved that for all $u[i](i = 1, \cdots, n_u)$ of aggregate signers $1, \cdots, j$, the equation $c_i = u_i^{u[i]} \cdot h^{\theta_i}$ holds. Therefore, the c calculated by the verifier has the correct format. Then, the algorithm would test whether the following equation is hold or not.

$$\frac{e(g, a\sigma_0)}{[\prod_{i \in \Phi \cup \mathbb{U}'} e(T(i), a\sigma_{1,i})]e(H(M), a\sigma_2) \prod_{k=1}^{j} e(c^{(k)}, \sigma_3^{(k)})} = \prod_{k=1}^{j} Z_k. \qquad (2)$$

If the equation holds, it outputs *valid*; if not, outputs *invalid*.

Trace: The central authority inputs the message M, the last sequential aggregate signature $a\sigma$ and the traceable private key tsk and outputs ID of j signers. Firstly, it executes the algorithm *AggVerify*$(a\sigma, M)$. If it is halt, the central authority output *invalid*. Otherwise, the last aggregate signature $a\sigma$ is valid. Then, it will use the traceable key tsk to extract signers' ID from the commitment $\{c_1, \cdots, c_{n_u}\}^{(1)}, \cdots, \{c_1, \cdots, c_{n_u}\}^{(j)}$ in $a\sigma$ as follows:

For the k-th tuple $\{c_1, \cdots, c_{n_u}\}^{(k)}$ and $1 \le k \le j$, the central authority computes $(c_i)^q$, if $(c_i)^q = \left(u_i^{u[i]} \cdot h^{\theta_i}\right)^q = g^0$, then $u[i] = 0$; if $(c_i)^q = \left(u_i^{u[i]} \cdot h^{\theta_i}\right)^q = u_i^q$, then $u[i] = 1$. In this way, it gets the k-th signer's ID. Thus, all of j signers' ID can be recovered.

4.1 Correctness

For a constant function $f(\cdot)$, there is $f(0) = \sum_{i\in\omega}(f(i)\cdot\Delta_{i,\omega}(0)) = \sum_{i\in\omega}\Delta_{i,\omega}(0) = 1$. The correctness of Eq. (1) is verified as follows:

$$\sigma_0 = [\prod_{i\in\omega\cup U'} d_{ki,0}^{\Delta_{i,\omega}(0)}][\prod_{i\in\Phi\cup U'} T(i)^{\zeta_i}]d_{u,1}^\theta H(M)^\beta$$

$$= [\prod_{i\in\omega\cup U'}(\tau^{q(i)}\cdot T(i)^{\nu_i}W(u)^s)^{\Delta_{i,\omega}(0)}][\prod_{i\in\Phi\cup U'} T(i)^{\zeta_i}]h^{s\theta}H(M)^\beta$$

$$= \tau^{\alpha_k}[\prod_{i\in\omega\cup U'} T(i)^{\nu_i\Delta_{i,\omega}(0)+\zeta_i}]W(u)^s[\prod_{i\in\omega'} T(i)^{\zeta_i}]h^{s\theta}H(M)^\beta$$

$$= \tau^{\alpha_k}[\prod_{i\in\omega\cup U'} T(i)^{\nu_i\Delta_{i,\omega}(0)+\zeta_i}][\prod_{i\in\omega'} T(i)^{\zeta_i}]c^s H(M)^\beta$$

$$\frac{e(g,\sigma_0)}{[\prod_{i\in\Phi\cup U'} e(T(i),\sigma_{1,i})]e(H(M),\sigma_2)e(c,\sigma_3)}$$

$$= \frac{e(g,\tau^{\alpha_k}[\prod_{i\in\omega\cup U'} T(i)^{\nu_i\Delta_{i,\omega}(0)+\zeta_i}][\prod_{i\in\omega'} T(i)^{\zeta_i}]c^s H(M)^\beta)}{[\prod_{i\in\omega\cup U'} e(T(i),d_{ki,1}^{\Delta_{i,\omega}(0)}g^{\zeta_i})][\prod_{i\in\omega'} e(T(i),g^{\zeta_i})]e(H(M),g^\beta)e(c,g^s)}$$

$$= \frac{e(g,\tau^{\alpha_k}[\prod_{i\in\omega\cup U'} T(i)^{\nu_i\Delta_{i,\omega}(0)+\zeta_i}][\prod_{i\in\omega'} T(i)^{\zeta_i}]c^s H(M)^\beta)}{[\prod_{i\in\omega\cup U'} e(T(i),g^{\nu_i\Delta_{i,\omega}(0)}g^{\zeta_i})][\prod_{i\in\omega'} e(T(i),g^{\zeta_i})]e(H(M),g^\beta)e(c,g^s)}$$

$$= e(g,\tau^{\alpha_k}) = Z_k.$$

Similarly, we can verify the correctness of Eq. (2).

4.2 Security Proof

We give the security analysis of the traceable attribute-based sequential aggregate signature scheme with multiple attribute authorities.

Theorem 1. *If the CDH assumption holds, the ABS of our proposed scheme is existential unforgeable.*

Proof Idea: Suppose that p, q are two different large primes and $N = pq$. $\mathbb{G}, \mathbb{G}_T$ are multiplicative cyclic groups of composite order N, and $e : \mathbb{G} \times \mathbb{G} \to \mathbb{G}_T$ is a bilinear map. $\mathbb{G}_p, \mathbb{G}_q$ are subgroups of $\mathbb{G}$ with order p, q; $\mathbb{G}_{Tp}, \mathbb{G}_{Tq}$ are subgroups of $\mathbb{G}_T$ with order p, q, respectively. h is a random generator of $\mathbb{G}_q$. Suppose that there is an adversary $\mathcal{A}$ having advantage ϵ in attacking our attribute-based aggregate signature scheme in the selective model. We will construct an adversary $\mathcal{B}$ that break the CDH assumption with probability at least ϵ'. The algorithm $\mathcal{B}$ will be given the group $\mathbb{G}_q$, a generator g of $\mathbb{G}_q$ and the elements g^a and g^b. In order to utilize $\mathcal{A}$ to compute the g^{ab}, $\mathcal{B}$ must simulate a challenger for $\mathcal{A}$. If the game does not abort, such simulation is complete. The proof idea is taken from [3,17,20]. The detailed proof can refer to the full version of this paper.

Theorem 2. *If the subgroup decision assumption holds for cyclic group $\mathbb{G}$, the ABS of our scheme is unlinkable.*

Proof Idea: For $\sigma = (\sigma_0, \{\sigma_{1,i}\}_{i \in \Phi \cup \mathbb{U}'}, \sigma_2, \sigma_3, c_1, \cdots, c_{n_u}, \pi_1, \cdots, \pi_{n_u})$, where $\sigma_2 = g^\beta$ and $\sigma_3 = g^s$ are random. For $\{\sigma_{1,i}\}_{i \in \Phi \cup \mathbb{U}'}$, each $\sigma_{1,i}$ is randomized by ζ_i. Therefore, $\sigma_{1,i}$ is also random. And, $s, \zeta_i, \beta, \theta$ are all random values in σ_0, then σ_0 is indistinguishable from random numbers for the adversary.

It can be seen from [20] and NIWI proof of bit encryption [7] that based on the subgroup decision assumption, for all $i = 1, \cdots, n_u$ of user u, c_i is the commitment of $u[i] \in \{0, 1\}$, π_i is the NIWI of c_i. Therefore, the pairs (c_i, π_i) will not reveal any information of $u[i] \in \{0, 1\}$. Interested readers can find a more detailed proof of this process in [7]. In summary, our ABS scheme satisfies unlinkability. Obviously, unlinkability implies anonymity.

5   Comparison and Discussion

A thorough comparison of our scheme with several related schemes is shown in Table 1 on traceability, unlinkability, aggregate, multi-authority and some computational overhead. The ABS scheme of our proposed has traceability, unlinkability, aggregate and multi-authority properties. Compared with [9], each attribute authority of our scheme is independent of each other. Thus, if a certain attribute authority wants to add or revoke, it does not affect any other attribute authorities. Therefore, there is no need to regenerate relevant public parameters. In terms of parameter size and computational overhead, our unaggregated signature scheme does not add much computation and storage overhead while achieving traceability and multi-authority. In our ABS scheme, the size of signatures are linearly related to the number of attributes in the policy. The size of aggregated signatures are linearly related to both the number of attributes in the policy and the number of aggregations. Therefore, this scheme is suitable for multiple units to sign the same file, but not for too many times aggregation. And, compared with [9,11], our scheme can also sign long messages.

Our solution can not only be applied to the fields of e-commerce and e-government, but also can be introduced to other multi-stakeholder participation scenarios. For example, with the vigorous development of the construction industry, safety accidents occur frequently in construction. Thus, we can instantiate our solution into the engineering quality control system. The central authority can initiate data tracing when the building accident occurs (such as a security incident, a dispute over interests, etc.). In this way, corruption and abuse by privileged parties can be effectively avoided.

Table 1. Comparison with related works.

Property	Scheme			
	Boyen et al. [3]	Li et al. [9]	Liu et al. [11]	Ours
Traceability	$\checkmark$	$\times$	$\times$	$\checkmark$
Unlinkability	$\checkmark$	$\times$	$\times$	$\checkmark$
Multi-authority	$\times$	$\checkmark$	$\times$	$\checkmark$
Aggregate	$\times$	$\times$	$\checkmark$	$\checkmark$
Private key size	$2|\mathbb{G}| + |\mathbb{G}_q|$	$2n|\mathbb{G}_q|$	$2n|\mathbb{G}_q|$	$(2n+1)|\mathbb{G}| + |\mathbb{G}_q|$
Signature size	$(2n_u + 3)|\mathbb{G}|$	$(n+2)|\mathbb{G}_q|$	$(n+2)|\mathbb{G}_q|$	$(n + 2n_u + 3)|\mathbb{G}|$
Sign overhead	$(5n_u + 3)e + 2i$	$(3n + n_m + 2)e$	$(3n + n_m + 2)e$	$(3n + 5n_u + 4)e$
Verify overhead	$2n_u + 3$	$(n+2)p + n_m e + i$	$(n+2)p + n_m e + i$	$(n + 2n_u + 3)p + i$

[1] e, p, i respectively denote exponent operation, pairing operation and modular inverse. n_m and n_u represent the length of message and identity. And, n is the maximum number of attributes in the attribute set.

6 Conclusion

In this paper, we present a secure and traceable attribute-based sequential aggregate signature scheme with multiple attribute authorities. Our schemes can be proved secure under the CDH assumption and Subgroup Decision assumption in the selective model without random oracle. Moreover, the scheme could also be used for different scenarios of providing secure and controllable service for multi-stakeholder participation. Our next step is to optimize the size of the signature to make the scheme more efficient.

Acknowledgment. This work has been partly supported by the National Natural Science Foundation of China under Grant No. 61702212 and the research funds of CCNU from colleges basic research and operation of MOE under Grand No. CCNU16A05040.

References

1. Bellare, M., Micciancio, D., Warinschi, B.: Foundations of group signatures: formal definitions, simplified requirements, and a construction based on general assumptions. In: Proceedings of the Advances in Cryptology - EUROCRYPT 2003, International Conference on the Theory and Applications of Cryptographic Techniques, Warsaw, Poland, 4–8 May 2003, pp. 614–629 (2003). https://doi.org/10.1007/3-540-39200-9_38

2. Boneh, D., Goh, E., Nissim, K.: Evaluating 2-DNF formulas on ciphertexts. In: Proceedings of the Theory of Cryptography, Second Theory of Cryptography Conference, TCC 2005, Cambridge, MA, USA, 10–12 February 2005, pp. 325–341 (2005). https://doi.org/10.1007/978-3-540-30576-7_18

3. Boyen, X., Waters, B.: Compact group signatures without random oracles. In: Proceedings of the Advances in Cryptology - EUROCRYPT 2006, 25th Annual International Conference on the Theory and Applications of Cryptographic Techniques, St. Petersburg, Russia, 28 May–1 June 2006, pp. 427–444 (2006). https://doi.org/10.1007/11761679_26

4. Chaum, D., van Heyst, E.: Group signatures. In: Davies, D.W. (ed.) EUROCRYPT 1991. LNCS, vol. 547, pp. 257–265. Springer, Heidelberg (1991). https://doi.org/10.1007/3-540-46416-6_22

5. Escala, A., Herranz, J., Morillo, P.: Revocable attribute-based signatures with adaptive security in the standard model. In: Nitaj, A., Pointcheval, D. (eds.) AFRICACRYPT 2011. LNCS, vol. 6737, pp. 224–241. Springer, Heidelberg (2011). https://doi.org/10.1007/978-3-642-21969-6_14
6. Goyal, V., Pandey, O., Sahai, A., Waters, B.: Attribute-based encryption for fine-grained access control of encrypted data. In: Proceedings of the 13th ACM Conference on Computer and Communications Security, CCS 2006, Alexandria, VA, USA, 30 October–3 November 2006, pp. 89–98 (2006). https://doi.org/10.1145/1180405.1180418
7. Groth, J., Ostrovsky, R., Sahai, A.: Perfect non-interactive zero knowledge for NP. In: Vaudenay, S. (ed.) EUROCRYPT 2006. LNCS, vol. 4004, pp. 339–358. Springer, Heidelberg (2006). https://doi.org/10.1007/11761679_21
8. Guo, R., Shi, H., Zhao, Q., Zheng, D.: Secure attribute-based signature scheme with multiple authorities for blockchain in electronic health records systems. IEEE Access 6, 11676–11686 (2018). https://doi.org/10.1109/ACCESS.2018.2801266
9. Li, J., Au, M.H., Susilo, W., Xie, D., Ren, K.: Attribute-based signature and its applications. In: Proceedings of the 5th ACM Symposium on Information, Computer and Communications Security, ASIACCS 2010, Beijing, China, 13–16 April 2010, pp. 60–69 (2010). https://doi.org/10.1145/1755688.1755697
10. Liu, X., Ma, J., Li, Q., Xiong, J., Huang, F.: Attribute based multi-signature scheme in the standard model. In: Ninth International Conference on Computational Intelligence and Security, CIS 2013, Emei Mountain, Sichuan Province, China, 14–15 December 2013, pp. 738–742 (2013). https://doi.org/10.1109/CIS.2013.161
11. Liu, X., Zhu, H., Ma, J., Li, Q., Xiong, J.: Efficient attribute based sequential aggregate signature for wireless sensor networks. IJSNet 16(3), 172–184 (2014). https://doi.org/10.1504/IJSNET.2014.066808
12. Liu, Z., Liu, Y., Fan, Y.: Searchable attribute-based signcryption scheme for electronic personal health record. IEEE Access 6, 76381–76394 (2018). https://doi.org/10.1109/ACCESS.2018.2878527
13. Maji, H.K., Prabhakaran, M., Rosulek, M.: Attribute-based signatures: achieving attribute-privacy and collusion-resistance. IACR Cryptology ePrint Archive 2008, 328 (2008). http://eprint.iacr.org/2008/328
14. Ning, J., Cao, Z., Dong, X., Wei, L.: White-box traceable CP-ABE for cloud storage service: how to catch people leaking their access credentials effectively. IEEE Trans. Depend. Secure Comput. 15(5), 883–897 (2018). https://doi.org/10.1109/TDSC.2016.2608343
15. Okamoto, T., Takashima, K.: Efficient attribute-based signatures for non-monotone predicates in the standard model. In: Catalano, D., Fazio, N., Gennaro, R., Nicolosi, A. (eds.) PKC 2011. LNCS, vol. 6571, pp. 35–52. Springer, Heidelberg (2011). https://doi.org/10.1007/978-3-642-19379-8_3
16. Okamoto, T., Takashima, K.: Decentralized attribute-based signatures. In: Kurosawa, K., Hanaoka, G. (eds.) PKC 2013. LNCS, vol. 7778, pp. 125–142. Springer, Heidelberg (2013). https://doi.org/10.1007/978-3-642-36362-7_9
17. Paterson, K.G., Schuldt, J.C.N.: Efficient identity-based signatures secure in the standard model. In: Batten, L.M., Safavi-Naini, R. (eds.) ACISP 2006. LNCS, vol. 4058, pp. 207–222. Springer, Heidelberg (2006). https://doi.org/10.1007/11780656_18
18. Sahai, A., Waters, B.: Fuzzy identity-based encryption. In: Cramer, R. (ed.) EUROCRYPT 2005. LNCS, vol. 3494, pp. 457–473. Springer, Heidelberg (2005). https://doi.org/10.1007/11426639_27

19. Xue, K., et al.: RAAC: robust and auditable access control with multiple attribute authorities for public cloud storage. IEEE Trans. Inf. Forensics Secur. **12**(4), 953–967 (2017). https://doi.org/10.1109/TIFS.2016.2647222
20. Zhang, Q., Xu, Z., Ye, D.: Identity traceable attribute-based signature scheme. J. Softw. **23**(9), 2449–2464 (2012). https://doi.org/10.3724/SP.J.1001.2012.04172

Social Spammer Detection Based on PSO-CatBoost

Shupeng Li[1], F. Jiang[1(✉)], Yunbai Qin[1(✉)], and Kunkun Zheng[2]

[1] College of Electronics and Engineering, Guangxi Normal University, Guilin 541004, China
Jiangvic2021@163.com, 1053778575@qq.com
[2] Guangdong Aohong Technology Co., LTD., Zhongshan 528437, China

Abstract. With the rapid development of social networks, more and more organizations or individuals use social media to communicate with each other, passing on information and getting information, etc. However, while bringing convenience to people, social media has also become the main target of malicious attackers who try to take advantage of the system vulnerability and cause harm to other normal users, they obtain benefits mainly through sending false information, advertising links, phishing, etc. In this paper, firstly, we collect the features of spammers from the four views (profile, behavior, relationship, and interaction) for a more comprehensive analysis of spammers, secondly, we creatively combine the features of Particle Swarm Optimization (PSO) and CatBoost algorithm, and finally, we propose a novel PSO-CatBoost model based on the CatBoost model for detecting spammers. In order to validate the effectiveness of our proposed model, some ensemble learning algorithms are compared, and the experimental results show that our model outperforms other models.

Keywords: Social media · Spammer detection · PSO · CatBoost

1 Introduction

One of the defining phenomena reshaping the present time of the world is the worldwide accessibility to the Internet. Social networks, as a popular people interactive platform of the Internet era, such as Twitter, Facebook, Weibo, and so on, have become a closely integral part of people's lives, since it can provide convenient, efficient, and diverse services for all aspects for people's life, work, study, and entertainment.

The power of social networks lies in the fact that by 2023, the number of global users is expected to reach about 3.43 billion active social media users per month, which is about one-third of the total population of the planet [1]. Unfortunately, social media spammers use these social platforms to spread phishing, scams, post malicious content and links, and promote product information [2–4]. According to a Nexgate research [5], social media spam increased by more than 355% during the first half of 2013, which equates to an average of 1 in 200 social postings, and 15% of all spam contains links to high-risk websites. Spammers are so secretive and sophisticated that they change their posting strategies from time to time to disguise themselves as normal users and collude with

© Springer Nature Switzerland AG 2021
G. Wang et al. (Eds.): SpaCCS 2020, LNCS 12382, pp. 382–395, 2021.
https://doi.org/10.1007/978-3-030-68851-6_28

each other to build criminal communities [6]. The malicious behavior of spammers not only hinders the development of social media [7], but also threatens the security of social network information and personal privacy [8]. Therefore, the need to innovate spammer detection techniques for social networks as attackers change their attack methods has been a technical challenge in the field of information security research.

Social media networks provide different types of methods to users, such as following, tweeting, mentioning, liking, etc. and spammers escape detection by frequently changing interaction methods. Traditional detection methods are limited to detecting spammers by extracting content features such as URL rate, tag rate, and similarity of tweets sent by users in combination with machine learning [9], and because spammers follow a large number of users to spread malicious messages, resulting in a large follow ratio, we detection spammers by extracting these relational features of users and combining them with machine learning SVM [10]. However, this single-perspective information cannot fully detect spammers, so we propose a classification method that combines the multi-views (profile, behavior, relationship, interaction) features of users and ensemble learning to detect spammers, which is the trend of machine learning and performs more stable and excellent than a single model. RandomForest model, one of the ensemble learning models, performs better than other machine learning methods in most cases, especially in classification problems. The CatBoost model proposed by the Russian company Yandex [11, 12] in 2018 uses the oblivious tree structure and introduces target statistics and Orderboosting to solve the prediction shift problem, thus improving the efficiency of the algorithm and providing exceptional performance in classification problems. CatBoost model has been widely used in industry and medicine [13–15]. However, in machine learning systems, the parameters of the model largely determine the performance of the model. There are more parameters in the CatBoost model, and the complexity of the work increases if the parameters are set only by human experience. The swarm intelligence algorithm optimizes targets based on the behavior of the population. It is centered on the collaboration between individuals to achieve complex functions, and PSO is one of the most widely used swarm intelligence algorithms.

In this paper, a PSO-CatBoost model that combines swarm intelligence optimization with machine learning algorithms is proposed. In the hybrid model, the parameters of the CatBoost model are optimized by using the excellent search capability of PSO. The main contributions of the work are as follows:

(1) We develop a novel PSO-CatBoost model based on the CatBoost model and use PSO to adaptively optimize its parameters. This can effectively improve the performance and accuracy of spammer detection.
(2) To evaluate the performance of the PSO-CatBoost model, we measure the overall metrics of the model and compare it with other ensemble learning models (e.g., RandomForest, Xgboost, and Lightgbm).

The rest of this paper is organized as follows. Section 2 reviews the relevant work in the field. Section 3 describes the basic theory of the models and the construction of the PSO-CatBoost model. Section 4 presents the comparative experiments and performance evaluations that demonstrate the effectiveness of the proposed model. Section 5 concludes the work.

2 Related Work

Spammers post harmful information in different forms, such as malicious information propagation, publishing false news, commercial links, and harmful content, which seriously endangers the rights and interests of normal and legitimate users. With the development of social networks and people's reliance on it, it is increasingly important to protect users' rights and privacy security.

Currently, the methods for detecting spammers mainly use classification algorithms based on machine learning environments combined with users' features. Cao et al. [16] analyzed and investigated various behaviors of users. These behavioral features can be used to detect anomalous URLs in social networks. Soiraya et al. [17] used the decision tree J48 model to detect Facebook spammers, using features including keywords, the average number of words, text length, and the number of links. McCord and Chuah [18] extracted two types of features of users, namely user-based features and content-based features, and use traditional classifiers (e.g., SVM and Naïve Bayes) to detect social media spammers in Twitter, where user-based features include the number of follows and followers and reputation score, and content-based features include the number of URLs, keywords, and topic tags in the messages posted by users. Lee et al. [19] proposed a method based on social honeypot classification, where the authors collect anomalous information profiles from social networks such as Twitter based on social honeypots and statistically analyze the attributes of the profiles to create spammer classifiers, which ultimately achieve high accuracy and low false positive rates. Chen et al. [20] proposed a malicious link-based anomalous information detection method that analyzes the click-through rate of various users on social media platforms for anomalous information links. Yang et al. [21] analyzed and designed an LDA-based algorithm in the Sina network environment to detect spammers who post malicious messages, and they also used the linked structure in the graph approach to detect Sybil nodes and unwanted links that spread malicious content in different social network platforms. Hu et al. [22] proposed to detect spammers based on the textual content of their tweets and explored to use the resources of email, SMS, and web anomaly spam to help train the classifier, however, social media spammers constantly change their behavior and attributes to pretend to be normal users, they may post the normal tweets besides the anomalous tweets, these strategies may reduce the accuracy of the classifier. Dingguo Yu et al. [23] present a novel semi-supervised social media spammer detection approach (CNMF), making full use of the message content and user behavior as well as the social relation information. Sohrabi et al. [24] proposed a filtering system based on clustering techniques using unsupervised learning methods called DB index and SVM for higher precision and decision tree method for better time management to detect spammers in social network platforms. Aslan et al. [25] proposed an auto-detection system for users related to cybersecurity on the microblogging platform to detect malicious content by analyzing various features with the ML algorithms. Agarwal et al. [26] first performed feature reduction methods for anomalous information and then compared seven different classifier methods, including Nave Baysian, AdaBoost, RandomForest, Support Vector Machine, J48, Bagging, and JRip. Mussa et al. [27] proposed the use of the Xgboost algorithm for dealing with the SMS spam detection problem and obtained higher accuracy. And in most cases, the combination of optimization algorithms can effectively improve model performance. Particle Swarm Optimization (PSO) and its variants are widely used for anomaly detection in social networks. Frank et al. [28] propose a discrete binary HPSOWM which operates on binary-based problem space, and termed as "Binary Hybrid Particle Swarm Optimization with Wavelet Mutation". Zhang et al. [29] used the PSO algorithm in combination with the decision tree (C4.5) for detecting spammers, and the error rate of misclassifying nonspam as spams was only 1%, which was better than the traditional method.

3 Spammer Detection Based on PSO-Catboost

3.1 CatBoost Model

The CatBoost algorithm is based on GBDT [30]. The GBDT algorithm, which is a combination of gradient boosting and decision tree, uses the forward distribution and the approximation of the steepest descent to fit the base learner by calculating the negative gradient of the loss function. The key of the algorithm is the forward distribution, which is the idea of front-to-back, learning a base function and its coefficients at each step, and eventually gradually approximating the optimization objective function. In BDT (Boosting Decision Tree), the ensemble learning method with the decision tree as the base learner is represented as follows.

$$f_0(x) = 0 \tag{1}$$

$$f_m = \sum_{m=1}^{M} T(x, \theta_m) \tag{2}$$

The $f_0(x)$ in (1) means that the initial decision tree is 0, the f_m in (2) means that it is iterated m times and contains the value of the first m decision trees, and $T(x, \theta_m)$ means the value of the mth decision tree.

Whereas at the mth step of the forward distribution algorithm, given the current model $f_{m-1}(x)$, the $f_m(x)$ and the current loss function can be expressed in Eqs. (3) and (4) as follows.

$$f_m(x) = f_{m-1} + T(x, \theta_m) \tag{3}$$

$$\min\left(\sum_{i=1}^{N} L(y_i, f_{m-1}(x) + T(x, \theta_m)) \right) \tag{4}$$

$$L(y, f_{m-1}(x) + T(x, \theta_m)) = (y - f_{m-1} - T(x, \theta_m))^2 = (r - T(x, \theta_m))^2 \tag{5}$$

When the squared loss function is used in Eq. (5), where y denotes the true value and $r = y - f_{m-1}$ denotes the residuals of the current model fit to the data, it is only necessary to simply fit the residuals of the current model for the boosting tree.

In the GBDT algorithm, its loss function can be expressed in (6) as

$$L(y_i, F(x_i)) = \frac{1}{2}(y_i - F(x_i))^2 \tag{6}$$

The derivation of its loss function is expressed by Eq. (7).

$$\frac{\partial L(y_i, F(x_i))}{\partial F(x_i)} = F(x_i) - y_i \tag{7}$$

$$r_{t_i} = y_i - F_{t-1}(x) = -\left[\frac{\partial L(y_i, F(x_i))}{\partial F(x_i)}\right]_{F(x)=F_{t-1}(x)} \tag{8}$$

Combining the Eq. (5) and (8), it can be seen that the key is to use the negative gradient of the loss function as an approximation r_{t_i} of the residuals of the boosting tree, and get the final learner.

Compared to GBDT, the advantage of the CatBoost algorithm is that it uses a new and effective method for dealing with categorical features during the learning process and incorporates Orderboosting to resolve prediction shift problem and make the results more accurate, CatBoost has the following principles.

Target Statistics. The CatBoost algorithm was originally designed to better deal with the categorical features in GBDT. If the base number of a categorical feature in the data is small, the one-hot encoding is used to convert the feature to a numeric type, but in the case of the large base number of categorical features, this encoding would create a large number of new features and cause dimensional disasters. CatBoost uses a more efficient strategy which reduces overfitting and allows to use the whole dataset for training. Namely, we perform a random permutation of the dataset and for each example, we compute the average label value for the example with the same category value placed before the given one in the permutation. Let $\sigma = (\sigma_1, \ldots, \sigma_n)$ be the permutation, then $x_{i,k}$ is substituted with (9).

$$x_{i,k} = \frac{\sum_{j=1}^{p-1}\left[x_{\sigma_j,k} = x_{\sigma_i,k}\right] * Y_j + a * p}{\sum_{j=1}^{p-1}\left[x_{\sigma_j,k} = x_{\sigma_i,k}\right] + a} \tag{9}$$

The [P] denotes Iverson Brackets, and it can be expressed as (10), p is the added prior term, and a is a weighting coefficient greater than 0. The practice of adding an a priori term is that can help to reduce the noise obtained from low-frequency categories.

$$[P] = \begin{cases} 1 \; If \; P \; is \; true \\ 0 \; Otherwise \end{cases} \tag{10}$$

Feature Combinations. The CatBoost algorithm considers combinations in a greedy way when constructing new split points for the current tree. The first segmentation in the tree does not consider combinations. For the next segmentation, CatBoost combines all combinations and categorical features in the current tree with all categorical features in the dataset. And the new combined categorical features are dynamically converted to numeric features.

Oblivious Trees. The CatBoost algorithm uses it as the base learner, and its structure allows it to have fewer parameters, faster training and testing, and higher accuracy, using this method to calculate leaf node values can avoid the overfitting problem that occurs with direct calculations in multiple dataset arrangement.

Ordered Boosting. In order to overcome the prediction shift created by the gradient bias caused by using the same dataset for the loss function, CatBoost replaces the traditional gradient estimation with ordered boosting to reduce the bias of the gradient estimation and improve the generalization ability of the model.

A randomly generated training sample $[1, n]$ of the arrangement σ.

Support n different models $M_1, \ldots, M_n$ such that M_i learns with only the first i samples in the arrangement.

For each iteration step, we get the jth sample residual through modeling M_{j-1}.

3.2 Particle Swarm Optimization

Particle swarm optimization(PSO) was proposed by Wang et al. [31]. The idea comes from the study of the foraging behavior of bird swarms, and particles are the simulation for birds. Each particle has two main properties: velocity v_i and position x_i, Each particle individually searches for the optimal value in the search space and records it as the current individual optimal value, shares the individual optimal value with other particles in the whole particle swarm, finds the optimal extreme value as the current global optimal value, and all particles in the particle swarm adjust their velocity and position according to their current individual optimal value and the global optimal value in the particle swarm The expressions for the updated velocity (11) and position (12) of each particle are as follows.

$$v_{id} = \omega * v_{id} + c_1 * rand() * (pbest_{id} - x_{id}) + c_2 * rand() * (gbest_d - x_{id}) \quad (11)$$

$$x_{id} = x_{id} + v_{id} \quad (12)$$

The c_1 and c_2 represent individual and global learning factors, $pbest_{id}$ represents the individual optimal value of the d-dimension of the ith particle, $gbest_d$ represents the current global optimal value of the d-dimension, and ω is the inertia factor, which satisfied the linear decreasing weighting strategy and can better find the optimal value, and its expression is (13).

$$\omega^t = \frac{(\omega_{ini} - \omega_{end})(G_k - g)}{G_k} + \omega_{end} \quad (13)$$

The ω_{ini} and ω_{end} denote the inertial weights at the initializations and the maximum number of iterations, respectively, the G_k and g denote the maximum number of iterations and the current number of iterations, respectively.

3.3 PSO-CatBoost Model

For different parameters of the CatBoost model, five parameters are selected which have a great influence on the model: iteration(ite), learing_rate(rate), L2_leaf_value(L2), depth, random subspace method(rsm). Parameter information is presented in Table 1.

Table 1. Parameter information of the CatBoost model

Parameters	Default	Range	Explanations
iteration	1000	$[0, \infty]$	Number of iterations, maximum number of trees built in the learning process
learing_rate	0.03	$[0, 1]$	Learning rate and for gradient step reduction
L2_leaf_value	3	$[0, \infty]$	L2 regular parameters, related to the cost function
depth	6	$[0, 16]$	The depth of the tree, the larger of the value the more accurate the model learning
rsm	1	$(0, 1]$	Random subspace methods, When selecting features randomly, the percentage of selected features in each split

The pipeline of the PSO-CatBoost model is shown in Fig. 1, and the steps of the PSO-CatBoost model are as follows.

(1) Initialize the parameters of the PSO model, the parameters include the number of particles, the maximum number of iterations, the individual and global learning factors, the inertia factor, and the particle dimension. Parameter information is presented in Table 2.

Table 2. The parameters settings of PSO

Parameters	Value
The number of particles	100
The maximum number of iterations	80
Individual learning factor	2
Global learning factor	2
Decreasing range of inertia factor	(0.4,0.9)
Particle dimensions	5

(2) Initially set the position and velocity of the particle according to the important parameters of the CatBoost model, and determine the position and velocity of the particle as a 5-dimensional vector, each dimension corresponds to different parameters of the CatBoost model with a different search range, so the position

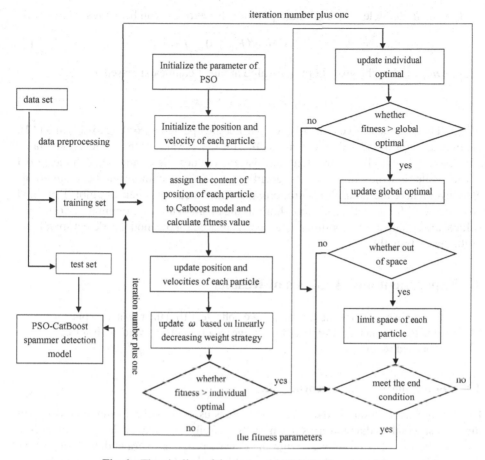

Fig. 1. The pipeline of the proposed PSO-CatBoost model

(14) and velocity (15) of the t th iteration of the *ith* particle can be represented as follows.

$$P_{i(t)} = \left[P_{i(t)}^{ite}, P_{i(t)}^{rate}, P_{i(t)}^{L2}, P_{i(t)}^{depth}, P_{i(t)}^{rsm} \right] \qquad (14)$$

$$V_{i(t)} = \left[V_{i(t)}^{ite}, V_{i(t)}^{rate}, V_{i(t)}^{L2}, V_{i(t)}^{depth}, V_{i(t)}^{rsm} \right] \qquad (15)$$

The position vector is assigned to the corresponding parameter of the model, and the average of the performance values of the 5 cross-validations on the training set is used as a fitness value to evaluate the overall performance. Then the fitness value of the *ith* particle at the t th iteration is expressed as

$$F_{i(t)} = \frac{P\left(CatBoost|_{trainingset}\right)}{5} \Big|_{param=P_{i(t)}, Fold=5} \qquad (16)$$

For the *ith* particle, its individual optimal value at time t can be expressed as

$$pbest_{i(t)} = \max(F_{i(j)}), 0 \leq j \leq t \tag{17}$$

For m particles, the global optimal value at time t can be expressed as

$$gbest_{(t)} = pbest_{k(t)}, 1 \leq k \leq m \tag{18}$$

(3) The position and velocity of each particle are updated according to (11) and (12), the inertia factor is updated according to (14), the fitness value of the model is calculated after each update, and compared with the historical value to determine whether the global optimal value is achieved. When the algorithm reaches the maximum number of iterations or convergence, the algorithm iterations are terminated, and then the global optimal position, i.e., the model's corresponding optimal parameters and optimal performance values, are output, and the optimal parameters are used for the model to detect spammers in the test set finally.

4   Experiment and Analysis of Results

In this section, we first present the dataset we collected from the real social platform Sina Weibo, and then we perform some comparative experiments to evaluate the effectiveness of our proposed method.

4.1   Data Collection and Preprocessing

Due to the lack of a public dataset of anomalous users in social media, and as one of the largest social media platforms in China, Sina Weibo provides APIs for developers to process the data. Therefore, we design the crawler program to crawl data through Sina Weibo APIs, and the program crawls the relevant data from four views: user profile, behavior, relationship, and interaction. The crawler program collected data from 10,325 users from December 2018 to May 2019.

In order to ensure the authenticity and validity of the user data labels collected by the crawler, we adopt a manual label approach, where multiple Judges integrated their intuition, background knowledge, historical experience and information from real-world data to give a firm conclusion. Each individual Judges were asked to identify clues from the user's profile, behavior, relationship, interaction and message contexts but not only from the content of the messages to give the final conclusion. The labeling processes of judges were considered dependable if they have high consistency. Finally, we selected the more reliable category labels. A total of 5,023 user data were labeled manually, of which 3,652 are normal users and 1,371 are spammers.

The data obtained by the crawler was mixed with numeric content, categorical content, raw content and Chinese character content, so data pre-processing is necessary. We take the next two steps to preprocess these data. Firstly, we perform data cleaning to remove extra or unidentifiable data. Secondly, we compute statistical values, including URLs, hashtags, mentions, followers and follow ratio, posting time, daytime and nighttime posting variance for each user. We extract features from the preprocessed data according to their definitions. Feature categories are shown in Table 3. According to the extracted features and labels, we could clearly identify the characteristics such as spammers having lower levels than normal users, posting more tweets, having a larger ratio of followers to followees, etc. Because of the CatBoost model's unique target statistical approach for the categorical features, it is the most efficient way to handle categorical features with minimal information loss, and not necessary to process categorical features in the data preprocessing stage.

Table 3. Feature Categories

View	Feature	Description
Profile	class	Class of user
	post_num	Num of post messages
	figure_#_num	Num of messages with hashtags
	figure_url_num	Num of messages with URLS
Behavior	active_day_ratio	Ratio of daily activity
	day_interval_variance	Variance of night activity
	day_in_variance	Variance of day activity
	late_night_times	Raito of night-time activity
	is_regular	Regularity of posting
Relationship	follower_num	Num of follower
	followee_num	Num of followee
	follow_ratio	Ratio of follower number to followee number
Interaction	average_repost	Average number of reposts per messages
	average_comments	Average number of comments per messages
	figure_@_num	Num of messages with mentions

4.2 Comparative Experiments and Results

The experiment environment of this paper is based on Python 3.7.3. First of all, we conducted two sets of experiments for PSO-CatBoost and CatBoost with the default parameters. The PSO-CatBoost algorithm iterates and terminates when it meets the maximum number of iterations or convergence. Then it outputs the optimal fitness value and the corresponding optimal position. We compared three sets of experimental parameter settings (Shown in Table 4), where the first set represents the optimal parameter settings and the corresponding fitness value of the PSO-CatBoost model, the second set represents a random particle of parameter settings and the corresponding fitness value of the PSO-CatBoost model during the experiment, and the third set represents the default parameters and the corresponding fitness value of the CatBoost model, which shows that the final performance of the model with optimal parameters is much higher than the CatBoost model with the default parameters.

Table 4. Three sets of optimal parameters and the corresponding fitness values

Parameters	1	2	3
iteration	600	200	1000
learing_rate	0.31	0.76	0.03
L2_leaf_value	2	5	3
depth	7	6	6
rsm	0.7	0.8	1
F(t)	0.942	0.913	0.904

In order to demonstrate the effectivity of the experiment, we compared the PSO-CatBoost model with other ensemble learning algorithm models, such as RandomForest, Xgboost, and Lightgbm. The final parameters of PSO-CatBoost appear in an irregular form and are not artificially specified in advance by grid search method, and the Random-Forest, Xgboost, and Lightgbm algorithm models all set default parameters without tuning any hyperparameters manually. Experiments used Precision, Recall, and F1-measure as the final metrics. The final results of the experiment are shown in Table 5, we can see that the ensemble learning algorithm has better advantages for spammer detection, especially Xgboost and Lightgbm have higher scores for spammer detection in terms of Precision, Recall, and F1-measure metrics. However, our proposed PSO-CatBoost model combines the target statistics of the dataset and the use of Orderboosting to solve the final prediction shift problem, and finally achieves the best results in Precision, Recall, and F1-measure metrics for spammer, and the final experimental results verify the validity and feasibility of this model in the spammer detection problems in social media network.

Table 5. Compared experiment results

Classifier	Precision	Recall	F1-measure
RandomForest	0.847	0.812	0.882
Xgboost	0.876	0.935	0.904
Lightgbm	0.847	0.938	0.890
PSO-CatBoost	0.904	0.968	0.934

5   Conclusion

In this paper, the datasets are from the Sina Weibo platform and we extract features from four user views (profile, behavior, relationship, and interaction) and manually label the dataset. Then we propose the PSO-CatBoost algorithm to detect spammers, and develop the compared experiment with the other ensemble learning algorithm to demonstrate the effectivity of the model we proposed, and the experimental results show that our method is better than the other methods. However, we cannot collect completed social information that we needed ideally from the sites because of privacy. For example, we can only get as most as ninety followers for a user in Sina Weibo. We plan to extend our work in the following directions. We will employ more information for our social spammer detection approach, such as external media information and sentiment information to extend our dataset size. Since we use the PSO-CatBoost model, which is the supervised learning method, for the experimental data preprocessing stage, labeling data consumes a lot of labor and resources, so our next step is to use semi-supervised learning or unsupervised learning method, which only requires less labeled data to achieve better classification performance.

Acknowledgments. This work was supported by National Natural Science Foundation of China (61762018), the Guangxi 100 Youth Talent Program (F-KA16016) and the Colleges and Universities Key Laboratory of Intelligent Integrated Automation, Guilin University of Electronic Technology, China (GXZDSY2016-03),the research funding of Guangxi Key Lab of Multi-source Information Mining & Security (18-A-02-02), Natural Science Foundation of Guangxi (2018GXNS-FAA281310), the Guangxi Key Research and Development Funding (2019AB35004). This work was supported in part by the Innovation special project of Zhongshan Science and Technology Bureau under Grant 2019AG001.

References

1. Inuwa-Dutse, I., Liptrott, M., Korkontzelos, I.: Detection of spam-posting accounts on Twitter. Neurocomputing **315**, 496–511 (2018)
2. Fakhraei, S., Foulds, J., Shashanka, M., Getoor, L.: Collective spammer detection in evolving multi-relational social networks. In: Proceedings of the 21th ACM SIGKDD International Conference on Knowledge Discovery and Data Mining (KDD), pp. 1769–1778 (2015)
3. Zheng, X., Zeng, Z., Chen, Z., Yu, Y., Rong, C.: Detecting spammers on social networks. Neurocomputing **159**, 27–34 (2015)
4. Li, Z., Zhang, X., Shen, H., Liang, W., He, Z.: A Semi-supervised framework for social spammer detection. In: Cao, T., Lim, E.-P., Zhou, Z.-H., Ho, T.-B., Cheung, D., Motoda, H. (eds.) PAKDD 2015. LNCS (LNAI), vol. 9078, pp. 177–188. Springer, Cham (2015). https://doi.org/10.1007/978-3-319-18032-8_14
5. NexGate: State of Social Media Spam Research Report. Nexgate (2013)
6. Liu, D., Mei, B., Chen, J., Lu, Z., Du, X.: Community based spammer detection in social networks. In: Dong, X.L., Yu, X., Li, J., Sun, Y. (eds.) WAIM 2015. LNCS, vol. 9098, pp. 554–558. Springer, Cham (2015). https://doi.org/10.1007/978-3-319-21042-1_61
7. Ng, C.K., Jiang, F., Zhang, L.Y., Zhou, W.: Static malware clustering using enhanced deep embedding method. Concurrency Comput. Pract. Exp. **31**(19), e5234 (2019)

8. Wu, F., Shu, J., Huang, Y., Yuan, Z.: Co-detecting social spammers and spam messages in microblogging via exploiting social contexts. Neurocomputing **201**, 51–65 (2016)
9. Jiang, F., Dong, D., Cao, L., Frater, M.R.: Agent-based self-adaptable context-aware network vulnerability assessment. IEEE Trans. Netw. Serv. Manag. **10**(3), 255–270 (2013)
10. Wang, J., Li, H., Zhao, J.: Micro-blog spammer detection based on characteristics of social behaviors. In: 2017 8th IEEE International Conference on Software Engineering and Service Science (ICSESS), pp. 358–362 (2017)
11. Dorogush, A.V., Ershov, V., Gulin, A.: CatBoost: gradient boosting with categorical features support. arXiv preprint arXiv:1810.11363 (2018)
12. Prokhorenkova, L., Gusev, G., Vorobev, A., Dorogush, A.V., Gulin, A.: CatBoost: unbiased boosting with categorical features. In: Advances in Neural Information Processing Systems (NIPS), pp. 6638–6648 (2018)
13. Massaoudi, M., Refaat, S.S., Abu-Rub, H., Chihi, I., Wesleti, F.S.: A hybrid bayesian ridge regression-CWT-Catboost model for PV power forecasting. In: 2020 IEEE Kansas Power and Energy Conference (KPEC), pp. 1–5 (2020)
14. Diao, L., Niu, D., Zang, Z., Chen, C.: Short-term weather forecast based on wavelet denoising and Catboost. In: 2019 Chinese Control Conference (CCC), pp. 3760–3764 (2019)
15. Postnikov, E.B., Esmedljaeva, D.A., Lavrova, A.I.: A CatBoost machine learning for prognosis of pathogen's drug resistance in pulmonary tuberculosis. In: 2020 IEEE 2nd Global Conference on Life Sciences and Technologies (LifeTech), pp. 86–87 (2020)
16. Cao, C., Caverlee, J.: Detecting Spam URLs in Social media via behavioral analysis. In: Hanbury, A., Kazai, G., Rauber, A., Fuhr, N. (eds.) ECIR 2015. LNCS, vol. 9022, pp. 703–714. Springer, Cham (2015). https://doi.org/10.1007/978-3-319-16354-3_77
17. Soiraya, M., Thanalerdmongkol, S., Chantrapornchai, C.: Using a data mining approach: spam detection on Facebook. Int. J. Comput. Appl. **58**(13) (2012)
18. McCord, M., Chuah, M.: Spam detection on Twitter using traditional classifiers. In: Calero, J.M.A., Yang, L.T., Mármol, F.G., García Villalba, L.J., Li, A.X., Wang, Y. (eds.) ATC 2011. LNCS, vol. 6906, pp. 175–186. Springer, Heidelberg (2011). https://doi.org/10.1007/978-3-642-23496-5_13
19. Lee, K., Caverlee, J., Webb, S.: Uncovering social spammers: social honeypots+ machine learning. In: Proceedings of the 33rd International ACM SIGIR Conference on Research and Development in Information Retrieval, pp. 435–442 (2010)
20. Chen, C., Wen, S., Zhang, J., Xiang, Y., Oliver, J.: Investigating the deceptive information in Twitter spam. Future Gener. Comput. Syst. **72**, 319–326 (2017)
21. Yang, X., Yang, Q., Wilson, C.: Penny for your thoughts: searching for the 50 cent party on Sina Weibo. In: The 9th International AAAI Conference on Web and Social Media (ICWSM), pp. 694–697 (2015)
22. Hu, X., Tang, J., Liu, H.: Leveraging knowledge across media for spammer detection in microblogging. In: Proceedings of the 37th International ACM SIGIR Conference on Research & Development in Information Retrieval, pp. 547–556 (2014)
23. Yu, D., Chen, N., Jiang, F., Fu, B., Qin, A.: Constrained NMF-based semi-supervised learning for social media spammer detection. Knowl.-Based Syst. **125**, 64–73 (2017)
24. Sohrabi, M.K., Karimi, F.: A feature selection approach to detect spam in the Facebook social network. Arab. J. Sci. Eng. **43**(2), 949–958 (2018)
25. Aslan, Ç.B., Sağlam, R.B., Li, S.: Automatic detection of cyber security related accounts on online social networks: Twitter as an example. In: Proceedings of the 9th International Conference on Social Media and Society (SMSociety 2018), pp. 236–240 (2018)

26. Agarwal, B., Mittal, N.: Comparative study of feature reduction and machine learning methods for spam detection. In: Babu, B.V., Nagar, A., Deep, K., Pant, M., Bansal, J.C., Ray, K., Gupta, U. (eds.) Proceedings of the Second International Conference on Soft Computing for Problem Solving (SocProS 2012), December 28-30, 2012. AISC, vol. 236, pp. 761–769. Springer, New Delhi (2014). https://doi.org/10.1007/978-81-322-1602-5_81
27. Mussa, D.J., Jameel, N.G.M.: Relevant SMS spam feature selection using wrapper approach and XGBoost algorithm. Kurdistan J. Appl. Res. **4**(2), 110–120 (2019)
28. Jiang, F., Xia, H., Tran, Q.A., Ha, Q.M., Tran, N.Q., Hu, J.: A new binary hybrid particle swarm optimization with wavelet mutation. Knowl.-Based Syst. **130**, 90–101 (2017)
29. Zhang, Y., Wang, S., Wu, L.: Spam detection via feature selection and decision tree. Adv. Sci. Lett. **5**(2), 726–730 (2012)
30. Al Daoud, E.: Comparison between XGBoost, LightGBM and CatBoost using a home credit dataset. Int. J. Comput. Inf. Eng. **13**(1), 6–10 (2019)
31. Wang, D., Tan, D., Liu, L.: Particle swarm optimization algorithm: an overview. Soft. Comput. **22**(2), 387–408 (2017). https://doi.org/10.1007/s00500-016-2474-6

Software Developer Recommendation in Terms of Reducing Bug Tossing Length

Muhammad Zubair Baloch[1], Shahid Hussain[2](✉), Humaira Afzal[3],
Muhammad Rafiq Mufti[4], and Bashir Ahmad[5]

[1] Department of Computer Science, COMSATS University, Islamabad 44000, Pakistan
zubair.baloch5510@gmail.com
[2] Department of Computer and Information Science, University of Oregon,
Eugene, OR 97401, USA
shussain@uoregon.edu
[3] Department of Computer Science, Bahadin Zakeria University, Multan 60800, Pakistan
humairaafzal@bzu.edu.pk
[4] Department of Computer Science, COMSATS University, Vehari 61200, Pakistan
rafiq_mufti@ciitvehari.edu.pk
[5] Department of Computer Science, Qurtuba University, Dera Ismail Khan 90250, Pakistan
bashahmad@gmail.com

Abstract. In close software development, it is easy for the project manager to recommend the right developer to resolve a bug that is reported by an end-user. However, in the case of open-source software developments, where most developers are engaged on different project either on the same or different repositories. Due to their agile involvement on repositories, bug triaging might be slow and increases the Bug Tossing Length (BTL) which is encounter as the time between reporting and resolving bugs. In open-source software repositories like GitHub, numerous developers are involved with well-known projects to resolve the issue reported by end-users. The assignment of the reported bug to an appropriate developer may lead to a reduced BTL time. Though, several metrics based and Machine Learning (ML) based approaches have been introduced to recommend the appropriate developer on the bases of several parameters. However, few studies are related to the recommendation of developers on the bases of their historical information regarding their attempts to reduce the BTL. To address this issue, we have proposed a new approach to recommend a developer for bug triaging on the bases of their involvement in reducing the BTL. In the proposed study, the model is trained once and new bug reports are automatically assigned to relevant developers. In this regard, we exploit the proposed methodology through using the XGBoost, Support Vector Machine, Random Forest, Decision Tree, KNearest Neighbor, and Naïve Bayes for the recommendation of the developer for a reported bug. We used widely-known two datasets namely Eclipse, and Mozilla. The experimental result indicate the effectiveness of proposed methodology in terms of developer recommendation for a new reported bug.

Keywords: Recommendation · Open source software · Github · Bugs report · Machine learning

© Springer Nature Switzerland AG 2021
G. Wang et al. (Eds.): SpaCCS 2020, LNCS 12382, pp. 396–407, 2021.
https://doi.org/10.1007/978-3-030-68851-6_29

1 Introduction

Software bugs are inevitable and are necessary tasks yet it is a costly and time-consuming phase during software development. The National Institute of Standards and Technology reported in a survey that software bug annual cost is $59.5 billion. Software maintenance study [1] shows that 50% is software bug handling and maintenance cost while in some cases software maintenance cost is more than 90% of the total cost of a software product [2]. The term Bug Tossing (BT) refers to the reassignment of bug, while Bug Tossing Length (BTL) refers to the time consume in reassignment from developers to developers to resolve an issue from the start date of its reporting. BTL can be reduced when the project manager assigns bugs to an appropriate developer. However, due to the involvement of agile developers, an issue cannot be resolved at an appropriate time. To improve the efficiency and reduce the Bug Tossing Length (BTL), there is a need to assign the bug report to the right developer. The assignment of bugs reports to the developer is called bug triaging. Usually, the bug report is not assigned to the correct developer which can lead to an increase in BTL. The assignment of bug reports to the correct developer may aid to decrease the BTL and improve the probability of bug fixes. The layout of the Bug Tossing process is shown in Fig. 1.

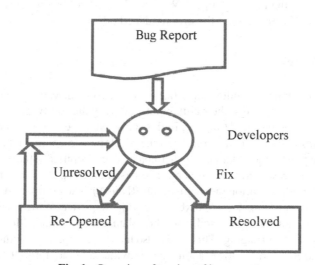

Fig. 1. Overview of tossing of bug report

In a recent empirical study, authors present that in the Eclipse project, almost take 40 days average time is required to assign the bug to the first developer, while more than 100 days average time is required to assign the bug to a second developer. The information about open source software bugs is stored in a distributed and searchable database called Issue Tracking System or Bug Repositories. Apart from the bug report, the bug repository also contains the requests for enhancement of features from users which is invalid for bug assignments. Usually, supervised learning techniques are used to classify the issue report either as valid or invalid bug reports [3]. Each day numerous bugs are reported but only valid and unique bugs' reports are triaged. In such a scenario, a bug fixer is overloaded due to a large number of bug report submissions. Consequently, the reassignment of the bug report is a serious problem. To address this issue, few empirical studies using metrics and ML-based approaches have been performed to rank the developers and assign a new bug report to the correct developer. However, these techniques are limited to the developer's involvement in terms of resolving the bug report and reducing the BTL. However, the information about the severity level of bugs report (already resolved) and the developer's involvement in reducing BTL at these levels could aid to recommend the correct developer more effectively. To proof this assumption, we conduct an empirical study and present a three-stage method to aid the project manager to assign a bug report to correct developers. In the first stage, the information about the developer's participation in terms of reducing the BTL is mined to construct the developer's profile. Subsequently, in the second stage, the widely used supervised learning algorithm namely Support Vector Machine (SVM), KNearest Neighbor (KNN), Decision Tree (DT), Logistic Regression (LR), Random Forest (RF), and XGBoost are used train the model on the constructed developer's profile (i.e. the output of stage 1). Finally, in the third stage, the information of a new bug report is used and a developer is recommended using the train models. The effectiveness of the proposed method is evaluated in terms of selecting the correct developers concerning the severity level of the new bug report. We formulate the following research questions to investigate the effectiveness of the proposed method.

2 Related Work

Though, several empirical studies have been performed to investigate the developer's involvement in resolving bugs, their collaboration during the resolving process, and the developer's recommendation. However, in this study, we have summarized the existing efforts which are conducted in the context of the developer's recommendation to resolve the bugs in adequate time. Mani et al. [4] conduct an empirical study and present a novel bug report representation approach that is based on Deep Bidirectional Recurrent Neural Network with Attention mechanism (DBRNN-A): The proposed deep algorithm is capable of remembering the context over a long sequence of words. The description and summary attributes are used from three datasets chromium, Mozilla Core, and Mozilla Firefox for bug triaging. This study also made a comparison with BOW Model Naïve Bayes and Support Vector Machine and provides a higher rank-10 average accuracy. Jsuri et al. [5] introduce a metric based approach to recommend the developer by reducing the BTL. The proposed method is functional in two stages. The stage I is an offline process for detecting the developers based on developer expertise score (DES) that computes the score using versatility, priority average fix time for his contribution. Stage II is the online process that simply ranks the developers. The DES accuracy is calculated in reassignment and hit ration. This metric-based approach was compared to a Machine learning-based bug triaging approach using three types of classifiers: C4.5, Support Vector Machine, and Naive Bayes. Shikai et al. [6] presented a new approach for assignment of the bug report to an appropriate developer that is based on convolution neural network and developer activities (CNN-DA). Word2Vec approach is used to perform the word to the vector representation of text data and then used the CNN model with batch normalization, pooling, and the fully connected layer is used to conduct supervised learning of bug reports represented by word vectors. Three datasets from Eclipse, Mozilla, and NetBeans are used to validate the process. This approach is also compared with the Support Vector Machine and Naïve Bayes Model and shows Top-10 accuracy better than supervised machine learning models. In this study [7], the author presented a new approach to deal lightweight attribute bug report assignment. The IDF and Topic modeling approach are combined and then used Support Vector Machine and Back Propagation Neural Network for bug report assignment. The datasets are Bugzilla, Eclipse, Baidu Input dataset, and Mooctest dataset to evaluate the effectiveness of the proposed approach. The average Accuracy of the proposed technique improves about 5% over the traditional classification model that proves the effectiveness of our proposed framework. The author in this study [8] used the n-gram representation for the string on summary and description attributes and performed approximate string matching with a flexible similarity threshold parameter on Bugzilla and Jira dataset. The four similarity measuring techniques are used are Cosine, Jaccard, Dice, and Overlap coefficients. In this study [9], the author focuses on the bug fixing method and formulate two methods to find whether a fix resolves a bug: coverage and disruption. The author also presented distance bounded the weakest prediction for the developer practical that helps to find out disruption of a fixed bug and coverage. The Huzefaet al. [10] proposed a technique to recommend a ranked list of expert developers to aid in the implementation of software change requests (e.g., feature request and bug report). An Information Retrieval based concept location technique is proposed to handle a specific report and recommend the appropriate developer. In this study, three benchmark open-source datasets are used from bug tracking repositories that are ArgoUML, Eclipse, and KOffice. The overall accuracies for developer recommendation are achieved in this paper is 47 to 96% while for feature request overall accuracies are 43 to 60%. In this study [11], the author used the KNN algorithm and REPtopic for bug severity prediction and bug assignment. KNN is used to classify the bug report and REPtopic is used to measure the similarity of bug reports on five open-source dataset repositories, including GNU Compiler Collection, (GCC), Mozilla, Eclipse, Open Office, NetBeans, and Mozilla. In this study [12], a hybrid bug triaging algorithm is proposed that combined probability and experienced model to rank all candidate developers for bug triaging. Smooth Unigram model is used instead of the Vector Space Model. In the probability model, social network analysis is used for analyzing the probability of fixing a new bug. In the experience model, then the number of fixed bugs and fixing the cost of all candidate developers is adopted as an estimated factor. The experimental study is conducted two datasets JBoss and Eclipse. The drawback of the proposed approach in business projects, each product feature is a specific group. Bug reports are assigned to that particular based on the product attribute. The Tian et al. [13] proposed the state of the art technique for bug recommendations. The proposed technique is unified learning to rank approach the get data from developer activities and bug location to capture 16 attributes showing developers' appropriateness for fixing the bug report. The experimental study is conducting 11,000 bugs reports from three open source repositories. The assignee recommendation attributes are divided into parts: activity-based attributes and location-based attributes. The combination of both attributes in unified learning to rank approach that produced eleven most suitable developers for bug assignment. This approach is evaluated on activity-based and location-based features to recommend the appropriate developers. The Kevick et al. [14] used a collaborative recommendation approach that combines information of bug reports from changeset. Changeset provides the list of qualified developers and this approach focused on an interactive user interface for the Microsoft Surface Table (MST). The study is divided into four parts, i) Producing the vector space for bug report ii) Finding similar bug reports iii) Determine the expert developers iv) Providing information to decide on a collaborative approach. In this study [15], the author proposed used the topic modeling approach Discriminative Probability Latent Semantic Analysis (DPLSA) model and Jansen Shannon divergence (DPLSA-JS). The proposed approach initialize the word distribution for various topics. In the training step, the post assigned bug report with the same components is considered. The experimental analysis is carried out on five projects GCC, Platform, Bugzilla, Mylyn, and Firefox. The Gondaliya et al. [16] used the Long short term memory model (LSTM) to handle the unstructured text data of bug reports and assign the bug to the appropriate developer. He proposed that the bug of word approach does not preserve the order of words and duplication of the same words occur. The LSTM model fits over the preprocessed the textual feature of bug of Eclipse and Firefox and recommend the appropriate developers. In this paper [17], the author presents a novel approach to recommend the appropriate developer for bug report assignment by combining the topic model and developer relations (e.g. assignee and bug reporter) to judge the developer the interest and expertise on particular bug reports. The experimental study is conducted on three open-source projects Eclipse, Mozilla Firefox, and Netbeans. The LDA model is used to extract the historical information of the bug report and map with new bug reports to verify the similarity.

The bug repository contains a bug report submitted daily that is necessary to recommend the correct developer. The correct developer is not available and assigned to other developers that may cause an increase of BTL time. The reassignment of the bug report is a problem that causes delays and costly in software maintenance [18]. Kim et al. [19] used the Machine Learning Algorithm Naïve Bayes for classification of labels and each report used the training model. An Ngoc Lam et al. [20] used a neural network model with a vector space model as an information retrieval approach. VSM is used for finding the textual similarity of bug reports and then used DNN to get the information from Bug reports. Ye et al. [21] source files of bug reports have leverage features. The source file of the bug report is computed based on bug API description and bug history. Rocha et al. [22] suggest a similarity bug report recommendation system that is called Next Bug. Yang et al. [23] used the TF_IDF model to recommend similar bugs that use the word embedding technique with an information retrieval approach. Researchers are using the neural network to the software domains like bug report identification and bug report assignment [24]. Chen et al. [25] used word embedding techniques in Q & A discussion on the summary attribute of a bug report and assign the bug to the relevant developer. Murphy et al. [26] Presentation was the first one who used a text classification method to automate the bug report assignment. Title and description contain keywords that are used to find the appropriate developer by using the Naïve Bayes classifier. The author in the empirical study [27] used Naïve Bayes, K-near neighbors (KNN), Linear

Discriminate Analysis (LDA), Support Vector Machine (SVM) with different Kernels, Random Forest (RF) and Decision Tree for automatic classification of software bugs. Limsetho et al. [28] used unsupervised machine learning techniques to group bug reports automatically based on their textual similar representation. In et al. [29] used a machine learning approach for bug assignment on a proprietary project, SoftPM. The bug report consists of 2576 for experiment and an average prediction accuracy of 77.64%. Bettenburg et al. [30] described that duplicate bug reports are useful for high prediction accuracy of classifiers by including the training set of bug reports. Matter et al. [31] develop a model based on the source code that contains developer expertise information and recommends the potential developer for new bug reports [32, 33].

3 Proposed Methodology

The goal of the proposed study is to recommend appropriate developers for a new bug report on the bases of historical information of the developer's contribution in terms of reducing BTL and resolving the reported bugs. The proposed methodology (Shown in Fig. 2) is functional in three stages namely Developer's profiling, trained the model and Developer's Recommendation based on the pre-trained model. The experimental work is conducted on two open-source projects Eclipse and Mozilla. The detailed description of bug report datasets are given Table 1.

Table 1. Target dataset and number of bug reports

Dataset	No. of bug reports
Eclipse	342
Mozilla	331

The datasets from the bug repository are mined into two forms based on the variables of nature. One is about the bug report and the other one is about the developer profile attributes. The bug report contains the following three attributes Bug_type, priority, and Severity while the developer attributes consist of Assignee and component. The datasets do not contain any missing values. These datasets that contain categorical values are converted into numeric form by using the label encoding technique.

The datasets attribute are joined together with five attributes in which the assignee attribute is the class label. Standard Scalar technique is used to normalize the values of dataset variables. The proposed methodology consists of three phases to recommend the developer. At phase 1, the datasets bug repositories are mined to form the bug report attributes and developer profile attributes. In phase 2, supervised machine learning algorithms are used to train on the different types of bug reports and automatically assign the unseen bug type to the assignee. In phase 3, as the model is trained on different types of bug reports, new bug reports are automatically assigned to relevant developers. The dataset is split into a 70% and 30% ratio with 10 fold cross-validation. The experienced developers are considered in the proposed study as they have experience and version history of dealing with different types of bug reports.

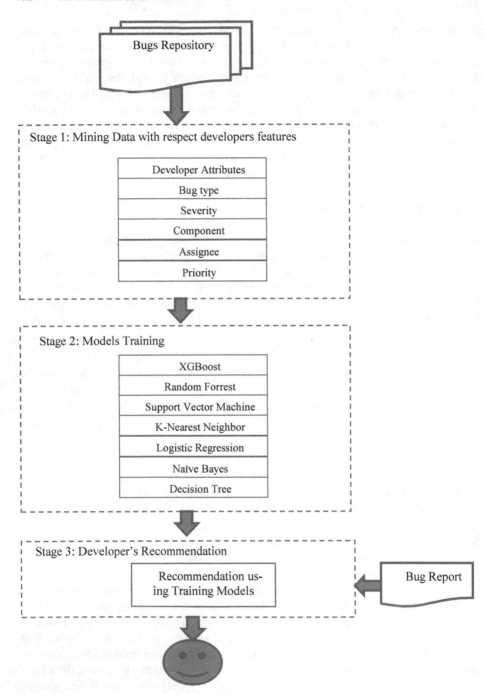

Fig. 2. Overview of proposed methodology

4   Results and Discussion

We evaluated the quality proposed approach by using the three most commonly used evaluation metrics in recommendation systems that are precision, recall, and F-Measure measures. Equation 2 shows the precision measures that reclaim that relevant bug type reports are recommended in response to the target class assignee developer.

$$precision = \frac{\sum(Relevant\ Bug - Type) \cap \sum(Retrieved\ Developers)}{\sum(Retrieved\ Developers)} \qquad (1)$$

The Eq. 2 of recall measures the capability of the used machine learning models to reclaim some irrelevant software developers in the response of target assignee class developers.

$$Recall = \frac{\sum(Relevant\ Bug - Type) \cap \sum(Retreived\ Developers)}{\sum(Relevant\ Bug - Type)} \qquad (2)$$

Further, the F-measure given by Eq. 3 represents the harmonic mean between precision and recall.

$$F - measure = \frac{2 \times precision \times recall}{precision + recall} \qquad (3)$$

The Naïve Bayes Algorithm outperforms on the benchmark datasets. Naïve Bayes machine learning algorithm achieves the highest accuracy on the Eclipse dataset and Mozilla dataset that are 0.988 and 0.979 respectively. The K-nearest neighbor has the poor result on both datasets as it does perform well in case of multi-classification.

Table 2. Performance evaluation of leverage classifiers on Eclipse dataset

Classifier	Accuracy	Precision	F-Measure	Recall
SVM	0.978	0.931	0.933	0.932
KNN	0.933	0.924	0.945	0.951
NB	0.988	0.951	0.944	0.940
DT	0.960	0.924	0.945	0.944
LR	0.953	0.914	0.945	0.954
RF	0.979	0.951	0.962	0.964
XGBoost	0.972	0.964	0.957	0.956

All the proposed models show very good precision, recall, and F-Score measures and recommend the appropriate developers. The higher precision rate value represents that classifiers are correctly recommendation the right developers. The high fractional recall value represents that a large number of developers are correctly recommended over the

Table 3. Performance evaluation of leverage classifiers on Mozilla dataset

Classifier	Accuracy	Precision	F-Measure	Recall
SVM	0.968	0.963	0.956	0.948
KNN	0.907	0.901	0.916	0.911
NB	0.979	0.971	0.967	0.957
DT	0.935	0.924	0.915	0.913
LR	0.928	0.918	0.924	0.918
RF	0.971	0.966	0.962	0.963
XGBoost	0.954	0.944	0.952	0.913

total number of developers. The result of eclipse and Mozilla dataset are shown Table 2 and Table 3 respectively. The F-measure analysis of the machine learning algorithms on the Mozilla and Eclipse dataset shows that the Naive Baye Algorithm has the highest value on the Mozilla dataset while the random forest shows the highest value on the Eclipse dataset.

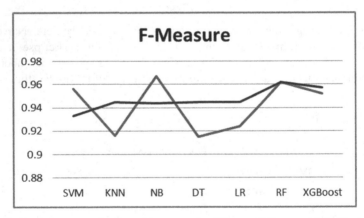

Fig. 3. Performance evaluation of leverage classifiers on Eclipse and Mozilla dataset

The Naive Bayes Algorithm has the highest precision score on the Mozilla dataset while XGboost has the highest precision score on the Eclipse dataset (Shown in Fig. 3). The KNN algorithm has the lowest precision value on the Mozilla dataset and logistic regression shows the lowest value on the Eclipse dataset. Most of the work for the recommendation of bug developers is based on textual features like description and summary. Texture features consist of unstructured data and needs to much pre-processing task. TFIDF techniques are used to convert the text data into numeric form. However, text data some time contain unnecessary information that causes the problem of misleading to the wrong assignment of the report to the appropriate developers. Some researchers are also using the metrics based technique to recommend the developers. In the proposed study, the developer is automatically assigned based on the pertained model. The model is trained on seven different machine learning models. We compare our approach with the metric-based approach used in the study [5]. The pertained recommendation model shows an improvement of up to 20% in respect of mean accuracy score, precision, recall, and F-measure.

5   Thread to Validity

In this study, we observe some threats. Firstly, in this paper is the assignee attribute in which only highly professional experienced developers are considered. The naïve developers have no good experience so during designing of developers profile in stage 1, and the only limited numbers of experienced developers are included. Secondly, in this paper, we also do not use text-based attributes like summary and description.

6   Conclusion

In this paper, we propose a methodology by leveraging the capabilities of classical machine learning techniques and collaborative filtering approach with available non-text based attributes to leverage the advantages in recommending a set of appropriate developers to a specific bug type. This pre-trained trained recommendation model help us to deal with similar kind of bug dealing and automatically assigning bug report to experienced developers. The proposed pre-trained model aims to reduces the BTL time 10% more as compared to textual based techniques. We used two datasets to assess the efficacy of classifiers. We used widely used performance measure namely precision, recall, and F-measure to present the effectiveness of classifiers and benchmark their performance. We observe Naïve Bayes classifier as outperformed as compared to other classifiers used in the proposed methodology. In future work, we will benchmark the efficacy of proposed methodology by considering more data sets and will leverage the implication of deep learning for the recommendation of the appropriate developers and automate the process of bug triaging.

References

1. Seacord, C., Plakosh, D., Lewis, A.: Modernizing Legacy Systems, Software Technologies, Engineering Process and Business Practices. Addison-Wesley, Boston (2003).ISBN.0321118847
2. Sommerville, I.: Software Engineering, 7th edn. Pearson Addison Wesley, Boston (2004).ISBN.0321210263
3. Sebastiani, F.: Machine learning in automated text categorization. ACM Comput. Surv. 34(1), 1–47 (2002)
4. Mani, S., Sankaran, A., Aralikatte, R.: Exploring the effectiveness of deep learning for bug triaging. IBM Research, pp. 7–18 (2018)
5. Asmita, Y., Sandeep, S., Jasjit, S.: Ranking of Software Developers Based on Expertise Score for Bug Triaging. Elsevier, Amsterdam (2019)

6. Shikai, G., Xinyi, Z., Rong, C.: Developer activity motivated bug triaging: via convolutional neural network. Neural Process. Lett. **51**, 2589–2606 (2020)
7. Yuan, Z., Tieke, H., Zhenyu, C.: A unified framework for bug report assignment. Int. J. Softw. Eng. Knowl. Eng. **29**(4), 607–628 (2019)
8. Hussain, S., et al.: Mining version history to predict the class instability. PLOS One **14**, e0221780 (2019)
9. Zhongixian, G., Earl, B., David, H.: Has the bug really been fixed? In: International Congress on Software Engineering, pp. 55–64 (2010)
10. Huzefa, K., Malcom, G., Denys, P., Maen, H.: Assigning change requests to software developers. J. Softw. Evol. Process **24**, 3–33 (2011)
11. Tao, Z., Jiachi, C., Geunseok, Y., Byungjeong, L., Xiapu, L.: Towards more accurate severity prediction and fixer recommendation of software bugs. J. Syst. Softw. **117**, 166–184 (2016)
12. Tao, Z., Byungjeong, L.: A hybrid bug triage algorithm for developer recommendation. In: Proceedings of the ACM Symposium on Applied Computing (2013)
13. Tian, Y., Wijedasa, D., Lo, V., Goues, C.: Learning to rank for bug report assignee recommendation. In: 2016 IEEE 24th International Conference on Program Comprehension (ICPC), p. 10 (2016)
14. Kevic, K., Müller, S., Fritz, T., Gall, H.: Collaborative bug triaging using textual similarities and changeset analysis. In: 6th International Workshop on Cooperative and Human Aspects of Software Engineering (CHASE), San Francisco, CA, pp. 17–24 (2013)
15. Yang, M., Zhang, X., Yang, D.: A component recommender for bug reports using discriminative probability latent semantic analysis. Inf. Softw. Technol. **73**, 37–51 (2016)
16. Gondaliya, K., Peters, J., Rueckert, E.: Learning to categorize bug reports with LSTM networks. In: International Conference on Advances in System Testing and Validation Lifecycle (2018)
17. Zhang, T., Yang, G., Lee, B., Lua, E.: A novel developer ranking algorithm for automatic bug triage using topic model and developer relations. In: 21st Asia-Pacific Software Engineering Conference, Jeju, pp. 223–230 (2014)
18. Chen, R., Guo, S., Wang, X., Zhang, T.: Fusion of multi-RSMOTE with fuzzy integral to classify bug reports with an imbalanced distribution. IEEE Trans. Fuzzy Syst. **27**, 2406–2420 (2019)
19. Kim, D., Zeller, A., Tao, Y., Kim, S.: Where should we fix this bug?: a two-phase recommendation model. IEEE Trans. Softw. Eng. **99**(I), I (2013)
20. Lam, A., Nguyen, A., Nguyen, H., Nguyen, T.: Combining deep learning with information retrieval to localize buggy files for bug reports. In: ASE, pp. 476–481 (2015)
21. Ye, X., Bunescu, R., Liu, C.: Learning to rank relevant files for bug reports using domain knowledge. In: FS, pp. 689–699. ACM (2014)
22. Yang, X., Lo, D., Xia, X., Bao, I., Sun, J.: Combining word embedding with information retrieval to recommend similar bug reports. In: ISSRE, pp. 127–137. IEEE (2016)
23. Rocha, H., Valente, T., Marques-Neto, H., Murphy, G.: An empirical study on recommendations of similar bugs. In: SANER, vol. 1, pp. 46–56. IEEE (2016)
24. Dongyang, H., et al.: Recommending similar bug reports: a novel approach using document embedding model. In: APSEC. IEEE (2018)
25. Hussain, S.: Threshold analysis of design metrics to detect design flaws. In: ACM Symposium on Applied Computing (SRC), pp. 4–8 (2016)
26. Hussain, S.: A methodology to predict the instable classes. In: 32nd ACM Symposium on Applied Computing (SAC), Morocco (2017)
27. Nitish, P., Debarshi, K., Abir, H.: Automated classification of software issue reports using machine learning techniques. IEEE (2017)

28. Limsetho, N., Hata, H., Monden, A., Mastsumoto, K.: Automatic unsupervised bug report categorization. In: IEEE/ACIS International Conference on Software Engineering in Practice, pp. 7–12 (2014)
29. Lin, Z., Shu, F., Yang, Y., Hu, C., Wang, Q.: An empirical study on bug assignment automation using Chinese bug data. In: ESEM (2009)
30. Bettenburg, N., Premraj, R., Zimmermann, T., Kim, S.: Duplicate bug reports considered harmful... really? In: ICSM (2008)
31. Matter, D., Kuhn, A., Nierstrasz, O.: Assigning bug reports using a vocabulary-based expertise model of developers. ACM (2009)
32. Hussain, S., et al.: Automated framework for classification and selection of software design patterns. Appl. Soft Comput. **75**, 1–20 (2019). ISSN 1568-4946
33. Hussain, S., Keung, J., Khan, A.A.: Software design patterns classification and selection using text categorization approach. Appl. Soft Comput. **58**, 225–244 (2017). ISSN 1568-4946

A Methodology to Automate the Security Patterns Selection

Khudema Zahra[1], Shahid Hussain[2(✉)], Humaira Afzal[3], Muhammad Rafiq Mufti[4], Dost Muhammad Khan[5], and Muhammad Khalid Sohail[6]

[1] Department of Computer Science, COMSATS University, Islamabad 44000, Pakistan
khudemaa@gmail.com
[2] Department of Computer Science, University of Oregon, Eugene, OR 97401, USA
shussain@uoregon.edu
[3] Department of Computer Science, Bahaudin Zakeria University, Multan 60800, Pakistan
humairaafzal@bzu.edu.pk
[4] Department of Computer Science, COMSATS University, Vehari 61200, Pakistan
rafiq_mufti@ciitvehari.edu.pk
[5] Department of Computer Science, The Islamia University of Bahawalpur,
Bahwalpur 61300, Pakistan
khan.dostkhan@iub.edu.pk
[6] Department of Management Science, Bahria University, Islamabad 44000, Pakistan
ksohail.buic@bahria.edu.pk

Abstract. Security has become an important issue for software systems. The numbers of threats are advancing day by day making it more challengeable to cope with it. During the software development life cycle (especially security oriented applications) it is difficult for the novice users to adopt the security measures correctly. A lot of security patterns are available but the question is how to choose the right pattern from the set of given patterns. For this reason we proposed a three step methodology which will help in automating the security pattern selection process. We exploit the proposed methodology by leveraging the capabilities of Fuzzy c-mean and Text categorization approach. We used a sample of security patterns along with a set of 3 security problems to assess the efficacy of proposed methodology. The experimental results are promising in terms of organization and selection of security design patterns for given design problems at hand.

Keywords: Security patterns · Software design pattern · Text mining · Fuzzy c-means · Classification · Selection

1 Introduction

In software development lifecycle of security oriented applications, recently security has become one of the important topic. Due to the increase in number of various distributed and open source platforms, security concerns must be taken into account during all the phases of development. It is difficult to do so because most of the developers had no idea of security specifications. Usually, security is considered in the later stages of the system

© Springer Nature Switzerland AG 2021
G. Wang et al. (Eds.): SpaCCS 2020, LNCS 12382, pp. 408–419, 2021.
https://doi.org/10.1007/978-3-030-68851-6_30

development. The system created without considering security specifications is vulnerable and less trust worthy for any organization. Patterns are reusable solutions encapsulated with expert knowledge and opinion. These patterns contain proven knowledge to deal with problems like that. Over many years, software developers are considering and suggesting design patterns for satisfying design problems [1]. The experience and knowledge gain from these developers is captured in the form of these patterns which can be considered by anyone. Similarly, we have security patterns which can help the developers and novice users to solve their security related issues.

The question arises here is how these patterns can be adopted and utilized by the novice designer for real security problem at hand. Selection of an appropriate pattern is still remains the issue. To address this problem [3, 4] several techniques are available in the literature with similar problems. Some of them have addressed the design pattern selection and others help in integration of the design patterns. The proposed solution are based on Ontology, UML based solutions, Case-Based Reasoning and text categorization approach [5]. Almost all of them are related to help the designers to choose an appropriate pattern but there are two main issues related to the selection of a right pattern. First, there is a variety of patterns available online and in the form of books and catalogs some of them are overlapping due to variety of descriptions; secondly these are not easily assessable as most of them are just present in the books and not on the internet. From last two decades a number new security threats and problems were reported which are not categorized correctly and it can create difficulties for a novice user in choosing a right security pattern towards a specific problem. In order to address this issue we proposed a methodology shown in Fig. 1, to systematize pattern selection process in three steps. Selection of security related patterns based on the feature similarity gathered from a catalog of correlated patterns. The features gather are based on the security problem description and problem definition of security patterns collection. Our proposed methodology includes text preprocessing on the data and use of the unsupervised learner namely Fuzzy c-mean and Cosine Similarity (CS) measure on processed data for the selection of appropriate security design pattern.

2 Related Work

We shortened the techniques already presented in the literature into 2 groups that is Problem and solution based groups [11–13]. Moreover, UML [15–17] and text categorization based techniques [1, 2] have been reported. The UML based approaches suggest to select a software design problem by knowing the solution domain only. Literature shows that new classification techniques for grouping of design patterns are used on the bases of their experience and interest in the domain, such as software quality research is mainly targeted on the improvements in the fault tolerance of the product. It is mostly focused on the user's ease. The user can perform their tasks easily on the system. In that context, research society groups and security patterns developers choose a pattern and match their needs in terms of solving the problem or any other security issue. A developer cannot ensure the right design pattern on its own. Hussain et al. [1] employed text categorization and unsupervised learning techniques to classify the software design patterns and perform selection of design patterns through the specification of problem group.

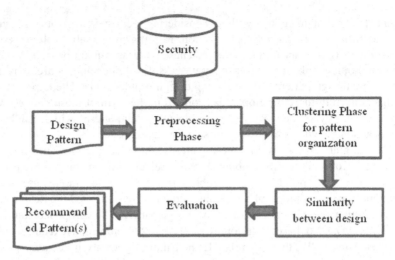

Fig. 1. Overview of proposed methodology

Moreover, in the subsequent study [2] Hussain et al. thoroughly investigated the proposed methodology [1] and reported its implications in terms of organization and selection of software design patterns. According to the study conducted by Singh and Bala [3], to break down the development of life cycle requirements into two main classes of functional and non-functional requirements. Their study aimed to analyze the non-functional requirements of a system [6, 7]. The results of their study had recommended that if the security problems are adopted from the start of the development process then they cannot become an issue in later stages.

Root Cause Analysis (RCA) and Orthogonal Defect Classification (ODC) are built to provide structure in the fault tracing process [6–9]. This analysis helps to identify and classify the root causes of the errors. These analyzing and classification techniques can also help to identify the triggers which caused these problems. It helps to deal with a problem and saves a lot of work and time of tracing the origin of the problem. A concept maximize originates from dependencies between different activities [10–13]. Developers and Software Engineers are working together as a squad on a project. Due to these dependencies on each other, some of the errors and vulnerabilities can arise naturally within the system. Developers may have a lack of coordination and understanding among each other which can lead them to adopt different design patterns to resolve the security problems. In [14–17] it is observed that errors in the software can be system-specific which means once an error has occurred it can be observed on individual bases to improve the overall system [18–21].

3   Analysis of Security Patterns

In order to understand the concept of security patterns we must know its language. Patterns are usually divided into two Sections namely Problem Domain and Solution Domain. The problem domain defines the problem context of the pattern and the solution domain gives us the reasoning to apply that pattern. Like [1, 2], we consider the problem domain section of security design patterns to automated the selection process. The pattern shown below is a general format of how a pattern is usually presented as follow and which could not be the only possible way of the representation:

- Context: Situation in which we may use that pattern.
- Problem: Discussion of the problem a pattern addressing to solve.
- Structure: Details about the specification, this section also includes the structural aspects of the problem.
- Dynamic: Scenarios to describe the running behavior of pattern.
- Implementation: Guidelines for the implementations of the pattern.
- Example: Similar cases or discussions
- Known Uses: If the pattern is ever used before.
- Consequences: Possible outcomes of the pattern in use

This pattern language act as a guide for the users to understand the meaning behind the available patterns. We also include a pattern taken from a reputable security patter repository for the users to have a better understanding of a security pattern [22–25].

4 Proposed Methodology

The main purpose of this study is to automate the process of classification and retrieval for security patterns. To do so, we uses widely known unsupervised learner namely Fuzzy c-mean and Tex categorization approach as the base process. It will help us in learning the classification on the sample of security pattern collection, to suggest a right pattern for a novice user in security domain.

4.1 Preprocessing

The initial step in our proposed methodology is preprocessing. In general, text classification is a machine learning technique. Text cannot be directly used by the classifiers either supervised or unsupervised. Therefore, this step is necessary to be performed on the text documents (i.e. description of problem domain of security patterns and design problems). This phase is comprised of few steps as shown in Fig. 2. Firstly, we performed remove stop words (conjunction, articles, prepositions etc.) and word stemming activities. These two preprocessing activities will help us to remove extra words from the documents. Plurals and from nouns and 'ing' from the verbs is also removed (Table 1).

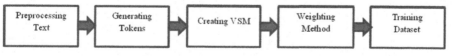

Fig. 2. Preprocessing steps

Table 1. Template of a security pattern

Problem domain	
Intent	"There are many security-relevant attributes which may be associated with a subject; that is, an entity (human or program). Attributes may include properties of, and assertions about, the subject, as well as security-related possessions such as encryption keys. Control of access by the subject to different resources may depend on various attributes of the subject. Some attributes may themselves embody sensitive information requiring controlled access. Subject Descriptor provides access to subject attributes and facilitates management and protection of those attributes, as well as providing a convenient abstraction for conveying attributes between subsystems. For example, an authentication subsystem could establish subject attributes including an assertion of a user's identity which could then be consumed and used by a separate authorization subsystem."
Motivation	"A subsystem responsible for checking subject attributes (for example, rights or credentials) is independent of the Subsystem which establishes those attributes. Several subsystems establish attributes applying to the same subject. Different types or sets of subject attributes may be used in different contexts. Selective control of access to particular subject attributes is required. Multiple subject identities need to be manipulated in a single operation."
Solution domain	"Encapsulate the attributes for a subject in a Subject Descriptor, and support operations to provide access to the complete current set of attributes, or a filtered subset of those attributes."
Participants	
Consequences	"Encapsulates subject attributes Subject Descriptor allows a collection of attributes to be handled as a single object. New types of attributes can be added without modifying the Subject Descriptor or code which uses it. Provides a point of access control Subject Descriptor allows construction of Attribute Lists including access control functionality to ensure that unauthorized callers will not have access to confidential attributes (such as authentication tokens)."

(continued)

Table 1. (*continued*)

Problem domain	
Uses	"Principals and public credentials may be retrieved by any caller which has a reference to the Subject object. Private credentials require a permission to be granted in order to access them, which may be specified down to the granularity of a particular credential object class within Subjects having a particular Principal class with a particular name. The JAAS Subject class includes a method to set a read-only flag which specifies that the Sets of Principals returned will be read-only (that is, the add ()and remove ()methods will fail). This is useful where a privileged caller gets a reference to a Subject object which it then wishes to pass on to an untrusted recipient. Increases system cost per unit of functionality."

Subsequently, we performed indexing activity to describe the model for text representation. For example, Vector Space Model (VSM) is the most common indexing method used for construction of model. This model helps us to determine the frequency of the terms in the document of target repository. To improve the performance of the proposed methodology, noises must be removed from the document. In this regard, terms are weighted. With weights we can reveal the importance of a term/word in a specific collection of documents. There are several weighting techniques such as Document Frequency (DF), Term Frequency (TF), Term Frequency Inverse Document Frequency (TFIDF) and so on. Each feature vector gives N features as top weighting words. In this study, we applied TFIDF weighting method to rank the features and remove the unnecessary features.

4.2 Security Pattern Classification and Class Determination

In this phase of proposed methodology, we consider the process to determine 1) Security pattern classification and 2) Class determination of a given security pattern. For this purpose, we used unsupervised learner to explore data and find hidden patterns for clustering or grouping of data. There is a huge number of unsupervised learners present in the literature such as Hierarchical clustering, Self-organizing maps, K-Means clustering and so on. In this study, we used Fuzzy c-mean as our basic function of learning from security design patterns and grouping them in to their respective classes. Fuzzy c-mean assigns class value to each object and then group them accordingly [1].

The input for this unsupervised learner is the security design pattern collection which has been processed and the output will be the classification of these security patterns into their specific groups and determining the right class for a given problem. Moreover, we considered a well reputed security pattern repository with cluster size c = 3 as the input of our unsupervised learner. The cluster size 3 is adjusted because security patterns of target collection are divided into three base classes known as architectural, design and implementation patterns. To judge the quality of the clusters in terms of classification the patterns Silhouette Coefficient measure is used.

4.3 Security Pattern Selection

After grouping the patterns on the bases of their similarity and determination of a pattern class for each design problem, next step is to select the appropriate pattern for each class. Usually, similarity measure is used for determining objects which are describes in vector or generic forms. Further, there are a number of similarity measures available but we will be using Cosine Similarity (CS) measure due to widely usage and importance in the context of text mining. The Eq. 1 is used to describe the CS measure as follow

$$CS_i = \sum_{j=1}^{N} w(P_i, t_j) \times w(Problem, t_j) \tag{1}$$

The subscript i and j present the pattern indexing and word indexing j for each pattern. After determining the CS value of each pattern with a given security problem, we used Eq. 2 to recommend an appropriate pattern with highest CS value as follow.

$$k = \arg \max CS_i \tag{2}$$

The pattern i with highest CS value is recommended as appropriate pattern for the given design problem.

5   Evaluation Criteria

5.1   Performance Measures

Firstly, we used fuzzy silhouette coefficient to determine the cluster quality though Fuzzy c-mean with respect to expert opinion. Table 2 presents the meaning of the Coefficients and their description.

Table 2. Description of Silhouette coefficient

Silhouette coefficient	Description
1	Clusters are clear
0	Distance between clusters is not significant
−1	Clusters assigned wrongly

The highest positive value Silhouette Coefficient refers to appropriate grouping of security patterns with respect to expert opinion. Besides, we used the ARI (Adjusted

Random Index) measure to assess the effectiveness of proposed methodology to determine the appropriate pattern for the given problem. The Eq. 3 and 4 are used to describe ARI as follows.

$$RI = \frac{P_a + P_b}{Cl_2^N} \tag{3}$$

$$ARI = \frac{RI - E[RI]}{\max(RI) - E[RI]} \tag{4}$$

Where CL refer to class labels at ground truth level. Pa and Pb refer to pairs of agreement and disagreements respectively.

5.2 Security Design Pattern Collection

To assess the efficacy of proposed methodology, we consider a pattern collection consist of 46 security patterns which are grouped in to 3 categories namely Architectural, Design and Implementation.

5.3 Design Problems

We consider a set of three real security problems and analyze the effectiveness of proposed methodology for the selection of appropriate patterns.

Security Problem 1 (SP-1): "The intent of the PrivSep pattern is to reduce the amount of code that runs with special privilege without affecting or limiting the functionality of the program. The PrivSep pattern is a more specific instance of the Distrustful Decomposition pattern."

Security Problem 2 (SP-2): "The intent of the Secure Chain of Responsibility pattern is to decouple the logic that determines user/environment-trust dependent functionality from the portion of the application requesting the functionality, simplify the logic that determines user/environment-trust dependent functionality, and make it relatively easy to dynamically change the user/environment-trust dependent functionality."

Security Problem 3 (SP-3): "It is possible that sensitive information stored in a reusable resource may be accessed by an unauthorized user or adversary if the sensitive information is not cleared before freeing the reusable resource. The use of this pattern ensures that sensitive information is cleared from reusable resources before the resource may be reused."

6 Results and Discussion

We have performed several experiments to organize security design, to determine the pattern categories for the security problems and to select the correct pattern for each problem. Firstly, we observe the Silhouette Coefficient (i.e. 0.58) to describe the efficacy of proposed methodology for the organization of design patterns according to opinion of experts. Secondly, we observe the Silhouette Coefficient value for each problem by including them part of target security pattern collection and to determine the pattern category for each security problems such as in case of SP-1, Silhouette Coefficient (i.e. 0.55) indicate that Fuzzy c-mean is effective to group the security pattern with respect to SP-1 and to determine appropriate pattern class for SP-1. Similarly, we observe Silhouette Coefficient value for SP-2 (i.e. 0.59) and SP-3 (i.e. 0.52). The actual and predicted pattern classes for security problems are as follow (Table 3);

Table 3. Pattern classes for security problems

Security problems	Actual pattern class	Predicted pattern class
SP-1	Design	Design
SP-2	Implementation	Implementation
SP-3	Implementation	Implementation

In case of recommendation of correct pattern for the SP-1, the list of patterns of its candidate with cosine values is shown in Table 4.

Table 4. Recommended patterns for SP-1

Pattern	CS value
Distrustful decomposition	0.16
Privilege separation	**0.68**
Defer to kernel	0.29

The "Privilege Separation" pattern with highest CS value (i.e. 0.68) is recommended as correct pattern for SP-1. Similarly, in case of recommendation of correct pattern for the SP-2, the list of patterns of its candidate with cosine values is shown in Table 5.

Table 5. Recommended patterns for SP-2

Pattern	CS value
Secure factory	0.25
Secure builder factory	0.18
Secure chain of responsibility	**0.73**
Secure state machine	0.32
Secure visitor	0.08

The "Secure Chain of Responsibility" pattern with highest CS value (i.e. 0.73) is recommended as correct pattern for SP-2. Finally, in case of recommendation of correct

Table 6. Recommended patterns for SP-3

Pattern	CS value
Secure logger	0.51
Clear sensitive information	**0.72**
Secure directory	0.43
Pathname canonicalization	0.17
Input validation	0.25
Resource acquisition is initialization	0.34

pattern for the SP-3, the list of patterns of its candidate with cosine values is shown in Table 6.

The "Clear Sensitive Information" pattern with highest CS value (i.e. 0.72) is recommended as correct pattern for SP-3. Finally, we observed the average ARI value (i.e. 0.76) indicate the effectiveness of proposed methodology for the recommendation of appropriate patterns list for determining the correct pattern effectively.

7 Conclusion and Future Work

In this paper, we have introduce a new methodology by leveraging the capabilities of Text categorization approach and Fuzzy c-mean to organize security patterns and recommendation of correct pattern for the real security design problems. Moreover, we used widely used performance measure to assess the performance of proposed methodology. We consider a security design pattern collection and set of three design problems. The average Silhouette Coefficient value (i.e. 0.57) indicate the performance of proposed methodology for the organization of security design patterns and recommendation of appropriate candidate class for the given design problems. We observe the ARI value (i.e. 0.76) which indicate the highest agreement between pattern list of actual and predicted category, which can aid in effective pattern selection process. In future we want to assess the performance of proposed methodology by considering more security pattern collection and list of more design problems.

References

1. Hussain, S., Keung, J., Sohail, M.K., Khan, A.A., Ilahi, M.: Automated framework for classification and selection of software design patterns. Appl. Soft Comput. **75**, 1–20 (2019). ISSN 1568-4946
2. Hussain, S., Keung, J., Khan, A.A.: Software design patterns classification and selection using text categorization approach. Appl. Soft Comput. **58**, 225–244 (2017). ISSN 1568-4946
3. Singh, C., Bala, A.: A transform-based fast fuzzy C-means approach for high brain MRI segmentation accuracy. Appl. Soft Comput. **76**, 156–173 (2018)
4. Fernandez, E.B., Washizaki, H., Yoshioka, N., Kubo, A., Fukazawa, Y.: Classifying security patterns. In: Zhang, Y., Yu, G., Bertino, E., Xu, G. (eds.) APWeb 2008. LNCS, vol. 4976, pp. 342–347. Springer, Heidelberg (2008). https://doi.org/10.1007/978-3-540-78849-2_35

5. Dangler, J.Y.: Categorization of Security Design Patterns. Electronic Theses and Dissertations. Paper 1119 (2013)
6. Laverdiere, M.A., Mourad, A., Hanna, A., Debbabi, M.: Security design patterns: survey and evaluation conference. In: Proceedings: Canadian Conference on Electrical and Computer Engineering. IEEE, May 2006
7. Hasheminejad, S.M.H., Jalili, S.: Design patterns selection: an automatic two-phase method. J. Syst. Softw. **85**, 408–424 (2012)
8. Hotho, A., Nurnberger, A., Paab, G.: A brief survey of text mining. J. Comput. Linguist. Lang. Technol. **20**, 19–62 (2005)
9. Hussain, S., et al.: Mining version history to predict the class instability. PLoS ONE **14**, e0221780 (2019)
10. Douglass, B.P.: Real-Time Design Patterns: Robust Scalable Architecture for Real-Time Systems. Addison-Wesley/Longman Publishing Co., Inc., Boston (2002)
11. Silberschatz, A., Galvin, P.B., Gagne, G.: Operating System Concepts, 6th edn. (2002)
12. Tichy, W.F.: A catalogue of general-Purpose software design patterns. In: Proceedings of Technology of Object-Oriented Languages and Systems, pp. 330–339 (1997)
13. Sung, E., Kelley, T.R.: Identifying design process patterns: a sequential analysis study of design thinking. Int. J. Technol. Des. Educ. **29**(2), 283–302 (2018). https://doi.org/10.1007/s10798-018-9448-1
14. Dwivedi, A.K., Tirkey, A., Rath, S.K.: Applying learning-based methods for recognizing design patterns. Innovations Syst. Softw. Eng. **15**(2), 87–100 (2019). https://doi.org/10.1007/s11334-019-00329-3
15. Klotins, E., Unterkalmsteiner, M., Gorschek, T.: Software engineering in start-up companies: an analysis of 88 experience reports. Empir. Softw. Eng. **24**(1), 68–102 (2018). https://doi.org/10.1007/s10664-018-9620-y
16. Jha, Shambhu Kr., Mishra, R.K.: Predicting and accessing security features into component-based software development: a critical survey. In: Hoda, M.N., Chauhan, N., Quadri, S.M.K., Srivastava, P.R. (eds.) Software Engineering. AISC, vol. 731, pp. 287–294. Springer, Singapore (2019). https://doi.org/10.1007/978-981-10-8848-3_28
17. Peng, J., Zhao, S., Dong, J., Liu, Y., Meersmans, J., Li, H., Wu, J.: Applying ant colony algorithm to identify ecological security patterns in megacities. Environ. Model Softw. **117**, 214–222 (2019)
18. Asif, M., Ali, I., Malik, M.S.A., Chaudary, M.H., Tayyaba, S., Mahmood, M.T.: Annotation of software requirements specification (srs), extractions of nonfunctional requirements, and measurement of their tradeoff. IEEE Access **7**, 36164–36176 (2019)
19. van Niekerk, J., Futcher, L.: The use of software design patterns to teach secure software design: an integrated approach. In: Bishop, M., Miloslavskaya, N., Theocharidou, M. (eds.) WISE 2015. IAICT, vol. 453, pp. 75–83. Springer, Cham (2015). https://doi.org/10.1007/978-3-319-18500-2_7
20. Hamdy, A., Elsayed, M.: Automatic recommendation of software design patterns: text retrieval approach. J. Softw. **13**(4), 260–268 (2018)
21. Hussain, S.: Threshold analysis of design metrics to detect design flaws. In: ACM Symposium on Applied Computing (SRC), pp. 4–8, April 2016
22. Hussain, S.: A methodology to predict the instable classes. In: 32nd ACM Symposium on Applied Computing (SAC), Morocco, April 2017
23. Nahar, N., Sakib, K.: ACDPR: a recommendation system for the creational design patterns using anti-patterns. In: Proceedings of the IEEE 23rd International Conference on Software Analysis, Evolution, and Reengineering (2016)

24. Suresh, S., Naidu, M., Kiran, S.A., Tathawade, P.: Design pattern recommendation system: a methodology, data model and algorithms. In: Proceedings of the International Conference on Computational Techniques and Artificial Intelligence (2011)
25. Smith, S., Plante, D.R.: Dynamically recommending design patterns. In: Proceedings of the 24th International Conference on Software Engineering and Knowledge Engineering (2012)

Author Index

Printed in the United States
By Bookmasters